Green Management

Theory and Applications

Green Management

Theory and Applications

Dr. M. Karpagam
Associate Professor
Department of Economics
Meenakshi College for Women
Chennai-24

and

Dr. Geetha Jaikumar
Associate Professor
Department of Commerce
Meenakshi College for Women
Chennai-24

Ane Books Pvt. Ltd.

New Delhi ♦ Chennai

Green Management : Theory and Applications
Dr. M. Karpagam and Dr. Geetha Jaikumar

Pages: xviii + 410= 428 (PB)
Size : (7.25" × 9.50")
Paper Quality (GSM) : 70

Published by

Ane Books Pvt. Ltd.

4821, Parwana Bhawan, 1st Floor, 24 Ansari Road, Darya Ganj,
New Delhi - 110 002, Tel.: +91(011) 23276843-44, Fax: +91(011) 23276863
e-mail: kapoor@anebooks.com, Website: www.anebooks.com

Branch Office:

- Avantika Niwas, 1st Floor, 19 Doraiswamy Road, T. Nagar,
  Chennai - 600 017, Tel.: +91(044) 28141554, 28141209
  e-mail: anebookschennai@gmail.com, rathinam@anebooks.com

ISBN : 978-93-8061-814-2

Printed at : Sagar Colorscan, New Delhi.

Foreword

The Corporate sector is keen to project a "green" image to their stakeholders. The general public has also become discerning about the environment and would like to see industries do more to decrease pollution and use natural resources in a sustainable manner. There is growing interest in corporate social responsibility including environmental management in the corporate sector.

Dr. M. Karpagam and Dr. Geetha Jaikumar, Meenakshi College for Women, Chennai have put together a comprehensive volume covering a vast canvas consisting of theoretical topics such as environmental ethics, environmental economics and polices such as environmental ethics, environmental economics and policy, as well as applied areas such as environmental management systems, environmental auditing and accounting and environmental certification. The book will be invaluable not only for practitioners but also for researchers, teachers and anyone interested in environmental management. The volume has been painstakingly put together from many different sources and includes exercises at the end of each chapter for students. This book will be particularly useful for courses in corporate environmental management and corporate social responsibility which are increasingly taught in management schools throughout country.

Paul P. Appasamy
Vice Chancellor
Karunya University

Preface

Environmental Economics and Sustainable Management Practices have been taught in Indian universities since the early 1990s for both undergraduate and postgraduate students. A number of books have been published on Environmental Economics and on Business and Sustainable Development as well. Yet there is no single text that covers both business theory / practices for sustainable development with the economics of environment. This book is one such attempt to integrate economic theory with business theory and practices for sustainable development.

This book is meant for the undergraduate and postgraduate students in Commerce, Business Economics, as well as for the students of the MBA programmes. The book uses basic economic tools and concepts from Environmental Economics to facilitate better understanding of policy to promote corporate environmental practices. This integration has been attempted in a mutually complementary way.

A multi-disciplinary approach has been adopted to present a holistic view of the economic, managerial and environmental perspectives to development and industrialization. Further, the book also includes environmental ethics and the fundamentals of ecology and environmental pollution to facilitate a better understanding of the concepts and models included.

Another feature that would distinguish this book from the other books is the case study methodology attempted throughout the book. Wherever possible, data from empirical case studies at the global and national level have been provided to authenticate and augment the theory.

Importance of the Book and its Relevance Today

- No business can afford to ignore the environmental impact of its operations, except at its peril.
- As global warming, the energy crisis, and environmental concerns become more and more important to consumers, businesses are seeing this as an opportunity to go green.
- There are few text books available in the Indian market today, on environmental ethics and management practices in India which address the needs of the academic community.

- This book therefore, would be extremely relevant for students (undergraduate and postgraduate, as also students pursuing management degrees) to study the concept of sustainable development and green business practices and the strategies that should be adopted by all forward looking and environmentally conscious companies.

To test the understanding of the students, exercises are given at the end of each chapter. Web links and additional resources on the topics covered are also provided, besides the reference list. The book comprises 28 chapters.

Dr. M. Karpagam
Dr. Geetha Jaikumar

Acknowledgments

In our quest for knowledge and information about all things connected with the environment, we have been inspired by a number of articles, working papers and books authored by renowned scholars, economists, management experts and environmental activists.

This book would not have been written without the help of many people.

We are grateful to Dr. N. Ramagopal, Associate Professor, Department of Economics, Annamalai University, for going through the manuscript and for the constructive feedback provided by him.

Our grateful thanks to Dr. Paul P Appasamy, Vice Chancellor, Karunya University, Coimbatore, for taking time off from a very busy schedule, to pen the foreword for the book, at very short notice.

The continuous support and encouragement that we have received from our family members at every stage of the book needs to be specially acknowledged.

We thank the staff at Ane Books Pvt. Ltd., for their hard work, patience and encouragement in our endeavour.

Contents

Foreword v

Preface vii

1. Environmental Philosophies and Environmental Ethics **1**

1.1 Environmental Ethics – A Brief History 1

1.2 Understanding the Meaning of Value 2

1.3 Environmental Philosophies 4

1.4 Conclusion 8

Questions 9

Exercises 9

2. Basics of Ecology and Environment **11**

2.1 Ecosystem – Definition 11

2.2 Forest Ecosystem 16

2.3 Biodiversity 18

2.4 Environmental Pollution 23

2.5 Air Pollution 23

2.6 Air Pollution and Climate Change 27

2.7 Air Pollution Industrial Accidents 31

2.8 Water Pollution 33

2.9 Pollution of the River Ganga and the Ganga Action Plan 37

2.10 Land Pollution – Pollution by Solid Wastes 40

2.11 Pollution by Hazardous Wastes 42

2.12 Conclusion 44

Questions 45

Exercises 45

3. Environmental Movement **47**

3.1 Evolution of the Environmental Movement – Before the Publication of *Silent Spring* in 1962 49

3.2 Environmental Movement from 1962 to 1992 51

3.3 Environmental Movement since the 1980s to the Present Day 59

3.4 Conclusion 70

Questions 70

Exercises 71

4. Business Ethics and Its Relevance Today **73**

4.1 What is Business Ethics? 73

4.2 Conflicting Interests 74

4.3 What is Ethical Behaviour? 74

4.4 Management and Business Ethics 75
4.5 Corporate Ethics Policies 75
4.6 Other Factors Impacting Organizational Ethics 76
4.7 Overview of Issues in Business Ethics 76
4.8 Certification for Socially and Environmentally Responsible Business Practices – Some Examples 80
4.9 Conclusion 83
Questions 84
Exercises 84
Case Studies 84

5. Economics-Environment Interlinkages **87**
5.1 Economic Functions of the Environment 87
5.2 Law of Thermodynamics and the Environment – Economics Inter-Linkages 88
5.3 Boulding's Spaceship Earth View 91
5.4 Greening of National Income 91
5.5 Conclusion 93
Question 93
Exercises 93

6. Economic Development and Environmental Degradation **95**
6.1 Environmental Impact 95
6.2 Some Facts on Environmental Degradation 96
6.3 The Environmental Threats to Health 98
6.4 Ecological Footprint 98
6.5 Limits to Growth 99
6.6 Environmental Kuznet's Curve 100
6.7 Need for Sustainable Development 102
6.8 Conclusion 103
Questions 104
Exercises 104

7. Economics of Pollution **107**
7.1 Pollution as an Externality 108
7.2 Impact of Pollution under Perfect Competition 109
7.3 Solutions to the Problem of Externality 111
7.4 Conclusion 112
Question 113
Exercises 113

8. Sustainable Development **115**
8.1 Sustainable Development and Environmental Protection Compared 117
8.2 The Components of Sustainable Development 117
8.3 Weak and Strong Sustainable Development 119
8.4 Components and Goals of Sustainable Development 120
8.5 Conditions for Sustainable Development 121
8.6 The IUCN/UNEP Strategies for Sustainable Development 122
8.7 Policy Measures for achieving Sustainable Development 123
8.8 Conclusion 124
Questions 125
Exercises 125

9. The Rise of Green Consumerism **127**
9.1 Green Consumerism – Definition 127
9.2 The Green Consumer 128
9.3 Can Green Consumerism Stop the Ecological Crisis? 130
9.4 Conclusion 131
Questions 132
Exercises 132

10. The Greening of Company Managements **133**
10.1 Defects of the Market Economy 133
10.2 Corporate Responsibility for Environmental Problems 134
10.3 Pressure for a Greener Business Environment 135
10.4 Why Do Businesses Go Green? 136
10.5 Defining "Greenness" in Companies 137
10.6 Five Stage Model of Corporate Environmental Responsibility 138
10.7 Financial Reasons for Going Green 139
10.8 Conclusion 141
Questions 142
Exercises 142

11. Environmental Management Systems in Industry **143**
11.1 What is EMS? 143
11.2 EMS Models 144
11.3 Total Quality Management 145
11.4 Why do Firms Certify their EMS? 145
11.5 Ten Elements of an Environmental Management System 146
11.6 Can EMS bring about Positive Change? 147
11.7 Can EMS be Proposed as a Total Substitute for Environmental Regulation? 147
11.8 Advantages of EMS over Government Imposed Standards 148
11.9 Benefits of EMS 148
11.10 Impact of EMS on Technological Innovation 150
11.11 EMS and Green Supply Chain Management (GSCM) 151
11.12 Management-Based Strategies and Environmental Management Systems 152
11.13 Barriers to EMS Adoption 154
11.14 Conditions Essential for the Successful Implementation of EMS 155
11.15 Conclusion 156
Questions 156
Exercise (Case Study) 156

12. Stakeholders and Their Relevance Today **159**
12.1 What is a Stake? 159
12.2 Who is a Stakeholder? 160
12.3 Primary and Secondary Stakeholders 161
12.4 Interactive Model of Business-Society Relations 164
12.5 Stakeholder Interests and Power Wielded by Them 165
12.6 Stakeholder Coalitions 166
12.7 Stakeholder Management 167
12.8 Conclusion 171
Questions 171
Exercise (Case Study) 171

13. The Precautionary Principle **173**
13.1 Precautionary Principle – Definition 173
13.2 Application of the Principle 175
13.3 Scientific Uncertainty 176
13.4 Ignorance and Indeterminacy 177
13.5 The Burden of Proof 178
13.6 Criticisms 179
13.7 Conclusion 180
Questions 180
Exercises 180

14. The Polluter Pays Principle **181**
14.1 Definition of PPP 181
14.2 History of the PPP 182
14.3 Defining Pollution in the Context of PPP 182
14.4 Application of PPP 184
14.5 Persistent Questions 184
14.6 Approach of the Indian Judiciary 185
14.7 Some Landmark Cases 186
14.8 Conclusion 187
Questions 188
Exercise 188

15. Sustainable Industrialization **189**
15.1 Evolution of Production Paradigms 189
15.2 Trade, Consumption Patterns, and the Environment 192
15.3 The Concept of Sustainable Industrialization 193
15.4 Sustainable Development: A Business Definition 193
15.5 Principles of Sustainable Industrialization 194
15.6 The Sustainable Development Journey 195
15.7 Steps Required For Managing an Enterprise According to Sustainable Development Principles 198
15.8 Business Charter for Sustainable Development 202
15.9 Conclusion 204
Questions 205
Exercises 205

16. Industrial Ecology **207**
16.1 Industrial Ecology – Meaning and Definition 207
16.2 Origin of the Concept 208
16.3 Goals of Industrial Ecology 209
16.4 Key Concepts of Industrial Ecology 209
16.5 Evolution of Industrial System 210
16.6 Industrial Ecology as a Potential Umbrella for Sustainable Development Strategies 212
16.7 The Industrial Symbiosis at Kalundborg, Denmark 212
16.8 Lessons from the Experience of Kalundborg 215
16.9 Conclusion 215
Questions 216
Exercise 216

17. Economic Theory of Pollution Control – I: Optimum Pollution and Pollution Control Policy Measures **217**
17.1 Optimum Pollution or Zero Pollution 218
17.2 Costs of Pollution 218
17.3 Total Damage Costs and Total Abatement Costs 218
17.4 Marginal Pollution Abatement Cost and Marginal Damage Cost 219
17.5 Optimum Pollution 221
17.6 Conclusion 223
Questions 223
Exercises 223

18. Pollution Control Policy – II: Command and Control **225**
18.1 A General Definition of Command and Control 225
18.2 Command and Control as an Environmental Policy Measure 225
18.3 Command and Control and Standards Fixation 226
18.4 Setting the Standard 227
18.5 Uniform Vs Variable Standards 227
18.6 Merits and Limitations of Command and Control 228
18.7 Conclusion 230
Questions 230
Exercise 230

19. Pollution Control Policy – III: Taxes and Subsidies **231**
19.1 Market – Based Instruments 232
19.2 Evolution of Market Based Solutions 232
19.3 Types of Economic Instruments/Market Based Instruments 233
19.4 Level of Charge 235
19.5 Emission Charges and Incentives to Innovate 236
19.6 Distributional Impact of Pollution Tax 237
19.7 Advantages of a Pollution Tax 238
19.8 Limitations of Pollution Tax 238
19.9 Experiences with Pollution Tax/Charge 239
19.10 Subsidies 240
19.11 Types of Subsidies 241
19.12 Advantages and Limitations of Subsidies 242
19.13 Environmental Subsidies in India 245
19.14 Conclusion 245
Questions 246
Exercises 246

20. Pollution Control Policy – IV: Transferable Discharge Permits and Refundable Deposits **247**
20.1 Permits – Definition 248
20.2 Types of Permits 249
20.3 Working of Permits – A Simple Example 250
20.4 Design and Implementation of Pollution Permits 252
20.5 Requirements of an Effective Permit System 252
20.6 Advantages of Tradable Permits 253

20.7 Problems and Proposed Solutions 254
20.8 Experiences with Permits 254
20.9 Tax Vs Permits 257
20.10 Carbon Emission Trading 258
20.11 Refundable Deposits 260
20.12 Merits and Limitations of Refundable Deposits 261
20.13 Performance Bonds 262
20.14 Conclusion 262
Question 263
Exercises 263

21. Comparison of Pollution Control Policy Instruments **265**
21.1 Comparison of Environmental Policy Instruments 268
21.2 Performance of the Pollution Control Policy Tools 270
21.3 Environmental Regulation in Developing Countries 272
21.4 Conclusion 272
Questions 273
Exercise 273

22. Life Cycle Analysis and Cradle to Cradle Concept of Industrial Design **275**
22.1 Definition of LCA 275
22.2 Goals and Purpose of LCA 277
22.3 Applications of LCA 277
22.4 Advantages of LCA 278
22.5 Four Main Phases 278
22.6 Problems with LCA 280
22.7 Variants of LCA Approach 281
22.8 Cradle-to-Cradle Analysis (C2C) 282
22.9 The Foundations of Cradle-to-Cradle Design 283
22.10 C2C Certification 284
22.11 Some Examples of C2C Design 285
22.12 The Triple Bottom Line - to Triple Top Line 286
22.13 Conclusion 289
Questions 289
Exercises 289

23. Environmental Management Accounting **291**
23.1 Environmental Management Accounting – Definition and Context 291
23.2 Role of Accountants in Environmental Management 292
23.3 Accounting for Sustainability 295
23.4 Types of Information Included under EMA 296
23.5 Uses and Benefits of EMA 297
23.6 Limitations of EMA 298
23.7 Legal Framework for Environmental Accounting in India 301
23.8 Practice of Environmental Accounting in India 302
23.9 Conclusion 302
Questions 303
Exercise 303

24. Environmental Auditing **305**

24.1 Definition 305
24.2 Aims and Objectives of Environmental Audit 306
24.3 Advantages of Environmental Audit 307
24.4 Audit Principles 308
24.5 Incentives to Undertake the Audit 308
24.6 Implementing the Audit 309
24.7 Success Factors 311
24.8 Conclusion 312
Questions 312
Exercise 312

25. Environmental Impact Assessment **313**

25.1 Objectives of an EIA 313
25.2 Evolution of EIA 314
25.3 The EIA Process 314
25.4 Guiding Principles of EIA 317
25.5 EIA Methodology 318
25.6 Benefits of EIA 322
25.7 Limitations of EIA 323
25.8 Requirements for the Introduction of an EIA 324
25.9 EIA in India 326
25.10 Conclusion 328
Questions 328
Exercise 328

26. Environmental Certifications **329**

26.1 The ISO 14000 Family 330
26.2 Components of ISO 14000 331
26.3 Global ISO Certifications 332
26.4 Relevance of ISO 14000 to Businesses 332
26.5 Why Should Environmentalists be Interested? 333
26.6 Related Initiatives 334
26.7 Conclusion 337
Questions 337
Exercise 337

27. Environmental Marketing **339**

27.1 Definitions 339
27.2 Reasons for the Adoption of Green Marketing by Firms 340
27.3 Problems with Green Marketing 341
27.4 Greenwashing Defined 341
27.5 Eco-labelling: A Mark for the Future 342
27.6 Eco Labels Schemes in Various Countries 344
27.7 Some Popular International Eco-Labels 344
27.8 Indian Eco Mark 346
27.9 Conclusion 347
Questions 347
Exercise 347

28. India's Pollution Control Policy **349**

28.1 A Brief Profile of India's Environmental Issues 350
28.2 Control of Industrial Pollution in India 354
28.3 Institutional Structure for Control of Pollution in India 354
28.4 Legislation to Prevent and Control Industrial Water Pollution 358
28.5 The Water (Prevention and Control of Pollution) Act, 1974 (Amended in 1978 and 1988) 359
28.6 The Water (Prevention and Control of Pollution) Cess Act, 1977 (Amended in 1991) 361
28.7 The Air (Prevention and Control of Pollution) Act, 1981 (Amended in 1987) 362
28.8 The Environment Act (1986) 363
28.9 Hazardous Waste (Management and Handling) Rules, (HW Rules) 1989, amended in 2000 364
28.10 Manufacture, Storage and Import of Hazardous Chemical Rules 1989, amended in 2000 367
28.11 The Manufacture, Use, Import, Export and Storage of Hazardous Micro organisms or Cells Rules, 1989 368
28.12 Bt Cotton and Bt Brinjal Cultivation in India - Case Study on GMOs in India 369
28.13 Public Liability Insurance Act, 1991 371
28.14 The Environmental Impact Assessment of Development Projects Notification (1994 and as amended in 1997) 372
28.15 The National Environment Tribunal Act, 1995 372
28.16 The National Environment Appellate Authority Act, 1997 373
28.17 The National Green Tribunal Bill, 2009 373
28.18 Fiscal incentives for Pollution Control 373
28.19 National Environment Policy, 2006 374
28.20 Status of Environmental Compliance by Indian Industries 377
28.21 Multilateral Agreements 378
28.22 Conclusion 380
Questions 381
Exercises 381

Glossary **383**

Bibliography **393**

References Websites **405**

1

Environmental Philosophies and Environmental Ethics

> *We have forgotten how to be good guests,*
> *how to walk lightly on the earth as its other creatures do.*
> **Barbara Ward**

The word environment is open to very wide interpretation. And consequently, environmental ethics is also open to an extremely broad spectrum of meaning and interpretation. While a one-sentence definition of environmental ethics would probably be difficult to provide, we can at best say that environmental ethics deals with how human beings should interact with the non-human world around them.

1.1 ENVIRONMENTAL ETHICS – A BRIEF HISTORY

Historically, the main focus of environmental ethics has been in the area of preservation of the wilderness and the wild creatures inhabiting that wilderness. However, more recently, environmental ethicists have been exploring the human-ethical relationships with less wild aspects of the environment, such as domesticated animals and agricultural and urban landscapes.

The Natural Law Tradition

One of the oldest ways of approaching ethics is known as the natural law tradition which can be traced to the writings of the Greek philosopher, Aristotle and later to the Christian scholar, Thomas Aquinas. Fundamental to this approach is the belief that all things have a built-in potential, and that all things aim to fulfill this potential. An acorn, for instance, would fulfill its potential by growing into an adult oak tree. Aristotle maintained that humans also have this built-in potential, although these go beyond growth and reproduction, to include development of intellectual and moral capacities or virtues. Morality, then, is an expression of human nature, and moral behaviour is the behaviour that expresses or develops moral virtues. Aristotle felt that moral virtues varied among different societies but can be identified as qualities like courage, moderation, prudence and justice.

A Rights and Duties Approach

A Rights and Duties Approach, on the other hand, believes in the existence of fundamental rules that should be respected. Natural rights exist independent of the existence of legal codes; in particular, the right to life. The German philosopher, Emmanuel Kant maintained that humans have one fundamental ethical duty – to treat other human beings as ends in themselves rather than as means to an end. He felt strongly that this principle should never be compromised, whatever the consequences might be. Kant's arguments about ethics have been hugely influential among Western philosophers and been extremely significant in the development of thinking on environmental ethics.

The Consequentialist/Utilitarian Approach

The Consequentialist Approach takes the ethically correct behaviour as one which brings about the best possible consequences. However, this is extremely difficult to put into practice for how does one decide what is the best possible consequence? The most widely known and popular answer to this question is associated with a school of Consequentialist thought known as Utilitarianism. One of the most famous Utilitarian philosophers, John Stuart Mill argued that "actions are right in proportion as they tend to promote happiness, wrong as they tend to promote the reverse of happiness." Here, the best consequences are achieved by creating the greatest amount of happiness. Other Consequentialists have proposed other measures of best consequences – for instance, the satisfaction of the greatest number of human preferences.

Utilitarianism, however, like other approaches to ethics, is not without its difficulties. Firstly, happiness is a rather difficult thing to add up in order to decide how the greatest amounts can be created. Secondly, since Utilitarians recognize no absolute rules (like right to life) it is not difficult to imagine circumstances in which killing someone might produce the greatest happiness – for instance, killing of one person in order that their bodily organs be used to keep alive twenty individuals who would otherwise have died. Such a proposal illustrates how controversial utilitarianism can be in some circumstances.

1.2 UNDERSTANDING THE MEANING OF VALUE

All these approaches to environmental ethics rest on some understanding of value. For those who espouse anthropocentrism (*i.e.,* a human-centered approach to the natural world), human life is of central value. For Utilitarians, like Mill, happiness is the key value. Philosophers have engaged in endless debates and hotly disputed the meaning of value. One helpful distinction is the one commonly drawn between instrumental and non-instrumental value. Instrumental value is the value given to something because of its usefulness to us. Air, for instance, is useful to us because it keeps us alive. We thus value it instrumentally; it is not valuable in itself but only because it helps us to achieve another goal – staying alive. However, when it comes to preserving our lives we do not regard it as a means to an end but as an end in itself. This kind of value can be referred to as non-instrumental or intrinsic value.

The above distinction is of importance, especially in issues involving the natural and living world. For example, take a wildlife sanctuary, such as Periyar, in Kerala, home of the Asian elephant and countless other flora and fauna, widely thought to be a valuable forest. But is it valuable? We might value it as a place to pursue leisure activities such as hiking and bird watching, or a magnificent place to photograph or paint wild creatures. We may value it aesthetically as a stunning, thickly forested, mountain scenery, as a place of retreat from the stresses of modern day living. All of these are instrumental values. But does Periyar have intrinsic value in itself? Is it valuable in the same way that we think of human lives as valuable?

BOX 1.1

The Grounding of the Sea Empress – Ethical Issues

On 10 February 1996, the oil tanker *Sea Empress,* carrying 1,40,000 tons of light crude oil, ran aground off Milford Haven in Wales. Despite several attempts to pull the ship off the rocks, she remained there for nearly a week, leaking over half her cargo into Welsh coastal waters. Within days, oil slicks surrounded the Welsh coastline and coated the beaches of Britain's only two marine nature reserves, Lundy Island and Skomer Island. The spill threatened not only the local marine wildlife, but also the livelihoods of hundreds of local people–the fishermen, the tourism industry, among others

Looking at the incident more closely, will cast some light on the complex characteristics of environmental problems and the ethical issues they raise. At first glance, the cause might seem straightforward: some kind of mechanical failure on the tanker, some sort of human error, stormy weather, or some combination of these factors. This sort of reasoning might suggest that the responsibility lay with the captain and crew of the ship, with the mechanics responsible for maintaining the ship, or with the company that owned the ship for not maintaining it adequately. While this is one way of looking at the incident, it is not the whole story. Just three months earlier, another oil tanker had run aground but there was no oil spill because it had been double hulled, a technical change, which makes tankers more resistant to spillage when they run aground. The *Sea Empress* had no double hull, as the British Government had not made double hulls compulsory for all oil tankers in British waters, despite recommendations to this effect. So was the British Government then, responsible for the accident? This again is only part of the picture, as the oil was being transported as part of the vast global oil industry that is a central part of all industrialized economies. The lifestyles of those industrialized economies float on a sea of oil, essential to industry, transport, and energy production. By creating such a demand, the individuals sanction the continued international transportation of oil at sea, and by demanding oil at the lowest prices, they encourage businesses to cut corners in safe shipping of oil products. If the question is viewed in this way, who is NOT responsible, at least indirectly, for this incident? In a sense, we all seem to be implicated.

The causes for environmental problems are thus, extremely complex and responsibility for them is multilayered.

Source: Palmer, Clare (1997)

The concept of intrinsic value inevitably raises a second question about where such value comes from: is it created by human beings, or is it something that already exists in the world, something that human beings recognize rather than bring into being? Value objectivists think that intrinsic value is not something that human beings create but something that is built into the world around them. They might argue that by placing value on the Periyar Wildlife Sanctuary, they are not creating value but rather recognizing value already present, value that would continue to exist even if there were no human beings left in this world to value it.

1.3 ENVIRONMENTAL PHILOSOPHIES

A number of philosophies dealing with man's relationship with the environment have been put forward over time and have been briefly outlined below:

Anthropocentrism

Anthropocentrism is the world view that considers humans to be the most important factor and value in the universe. Anthropocentrism means human chauvinism–the idea that humans are the crowns of creation, the source of all value and the measure of all things. It considers humans to be the most important life form, and other forms of life to be important only to the extent that they affect humans or can be useful to humans.

Since the time of the classical Greeks, Western thinking has been overwhelmingly anthropocentric or human-centered. As Bertrand Russell (1979) pointed out in his *History of Western Philosophy*, "What is amiss, even in the best philosophy...is an undue emphasis on man as compared with the universe."

Anthropocentrism considers that humans are the centre of the universe. It considers humans to be the most important life form, and other forms of life to be important only to the extent that they affect humans or can be useful to humans. In an anthropocentric ethic, nature has moral consideration because degrading or preserving nature can in turn harm or benefit humans. For example, using this ethic it would be considered wrong to cut down the rainforests because they contain potential cures for human diseases.

Anthropocentricism is basically simple human chauvinism. Supporters of the anthropocentric outlook hold that man is the measure of all things. Sophocles, for example, held that the wonders are many on earth, and the greatest of these is man. Manetti stated "Nothing in the world can be found that is worthy of more admiration than man". Mao proclaimed, "Of all the things in the world, people are most precious". The theory of anthropocentrism, thus says that the world exists for humanity. Believers in this philosophy would say that humans can rightfully try to benefit as much as possible from the environment.

These arguments are obviously objectionable to environmentalists who argue that animals have the right to coexist with humans in nature, and some would also add that nature has inherent value beyond its use to humanity. Many environmental philosophies encompass some degree of anthropocentrism. Even environmentalists often argue in favour of saving the environment for the sake of humanity.

Perhaps, the area where anthropocentrism most commonly occurs is politics. A tradition of disregard for the environment, and the fact that plants and animals do not vote, has led to a primarily human-centered perspective in some decision makers.

Opposition to anthropocentrism is widespread. The simplest argument against it is that animals have feelings too, and action vis-à-vis animals must bear a certain degree of morality.

Anthropocentrism has been posited by some environmentalists, in such books as *Confessions of an Eco-Warrior* by Dave Foreman and *Green Rage* by Christopher Manes, as the underlying if unstated reason why humanity dominates and sees the need to "develop" most of the Earth. Anthropocentrism has been identified by these writers and others as the root cause of the ecological crisis, human overpopulation, and extinction of many non-human species observed today.

Shallow Ecology or Shallow Environmentalism

Shallow ecology is anthropocentric or human-centered. It views humans as above or outside of nature, as the source of all value, and ascribes only instrumental or "use" value to nature.

Arne Naess, a Norwegian philosopher and linguist, coined the term "shallow ecology" in the early 1970s for this human-centered or "anthropocentric" way of viewing the world. Shallow ecology represents anthropocentric conservationism, epitomized by Gifford Pinchot, who saw the earth as a set of natural resources that needed to be managed for present and future generations of humans. With shallow ecology, people start from an assumption, that human beings are the central species in the earth's ecosystem, and that other beings and parts of systems are of less importance or value. Shallow ecology views other beings and features of the earth as resources for human use, and fails to see their intrinsic value or their value to each other.

Naess was of the opinion that the environmental movement was also approaching its efforts to protect the earth from a shallow standpoint, focusing mostly on human health and well-being rather than seeing the environment as a seamless whole with inherent value throughout. Opponents of deep ecology (shallow ecologists) say that the deep ecologists place insufficient value on human life. By placing too much importance on the lives of animals, opponents say that the deep ecologists failed to properly regard the lives of people.

Deep Ecology

The core principle of deep ecology is the claim that, like humanity, the living environment as a whole has the same right to live and flourish. Deep ecology is a holistic approach to the environment that stresses the intrinsic equality of species, including human beings.

Deep ecology describes itself as "deep" because it persists in asking deeper questions concerning "why" and "how" and thus, is concerned with the fundamental philosophical questions about the impact of human life on the ecosphere, rather than with a narrow view of ecology as a branch of biological science, which is concerned with resource management of the environment for human purposes. In recent years, the most concerted attempt to challenge the anthropocentric tradition has come from a loose grouping of philosophers writing under the banner of "deep ecology". Deep ecology was first put forward in 1972 by Arne naess, in his paper, *The Shallow and the Deep, Long-Range Ecology Movement* to express the idea that nature has intrinsic value, namely, value apart from its usefulness to human beings, and that all life forms should be allowed to flourish and fulfill their evolutionary destinies. According to deep ecology, all beings have inherent value, apart from their usefulness or interest to humans, and people do not have the right to kill other creatures wantonly, destroy their habitats or cause pollution of the air, land or water on the presumption that human needs and human wants are more important and powerful than any other creature's right to exist. This view is also called "ecocentric", because it is centered on the entire earth and sees human beings as being within the earth, an integral part, rather than at the centre or on top.

For Arne Naess, ecological science, concerned with facts and logic alone, cannot answer ethical questions about how we should live. For this we need ecological wisdom. Deep ecology seeks to develop this by focusing on deep experience, deep questioning and deep commitment. These constitute an interconnected system. Each gives rise to and supports the other, whilst the entire system is, what Naess calls, an ecosophy: an evolving but consistent philosophy of being, thinking and acting in the world that embodies ecological wisdom and harmony. Naess rejected the idea that beings can be ranked according to their relative value. For example, judgments on whether an animal has an eternal soul, whether it uses reason or whether it has consciousness (or indeed higher consciousness) have all been used to justify the ranking of the human animal as superior to other animals. Naess states that from an ecological point of view "the right of all forms [of life] to live is a universal right which cannot be quantified. No single species of living being has more of this particular right to live and unfold than any other species." This metaphysical idea is elucidated in Warwick Fox's (1990) claim that we and all other beings are "aspects of a single unfolding reality". As such, Deep Ecology would support the view of Aldo Leopold in his book, *A Sand County Almanac* that humans are "plain members of the biotic community". They also would support Leopold's "Land Ethic": "a thing is right when it tends to preserve the integrity, stability and beauty of the biotic community. It is wrong when it tends otherwise."

Deep ecology, however is more than science. It also involves a spiritual approach to life, since respect for all beings entails, at a minimum, recognition of their intrinsic value. A deep approach to ecology also involves an understanding of the connection of all beings with each other and with the Earth, the matrix of all life. The deeper one goes into the awareness of this connection, the more it takes on a spiritual dimension. Many of the ideas of deep ecology are consistent with ancient religious and cultural philosophies. Zen Buddhism, among other religions, taught that humans should respect nature. Gandhi also taught that human beings should respect non-human life and the environment.

Deep ecology can be summarized and said to comprise three main ideas:

The first is the idea of ecocentrism, that is, the idea of adopting an ecology-centered (or an earth-centered) approach. In this view, the non-human world is considered to be valuable *in and of itself* and not simply because of its obvious use-value to humans.

The second basic idea is that of asking deeper questions about the ecological relationships of which we are a part, by addressing the root causes of our interlinked ecological crises rather than simply focusing on their symptoms.

The third idea is that we are all capable of identifying far more widely and deeply with the world around us than is commonly recognized, and that this form of self-development, self-unfolding, or "self-realization", as Naess would say, leads us spontaneously to appreciate and defend the world around us. This third sense of deep ecology can be called "transpersonal ecology", because it clearly points to the realization of a sense of self that extends beyond (or that is *trans*) any narrowly delimited biographical or egoic sense of self. Broadening and deepening our identification - or our sense of felt commonality - with the world around us leads us from a relatively narrow, atomistic, isolated, or particle-like sense of self to a wide, expansive, participatory, or field-like one.

Although all these ideas are interlinked in Naess's thought, they are, in fact, analytically distinct and can be evaluated independently with respect to their novelty, defensibility, and distinctiveness. It can be said that the last of these three ideas is the one that most distinguishes the work of deep ecological writers from that of other ecophilosophical ones.

In a restricted sense, deep ecology is characterized by the following principles:

(*i*) **Holism:** Nature is seen holistically, as an integrated system, rather than as a collection of individual things.

(*ii*) **No Ontological Divide:** Humans are fully a part of nature, and there is no separation between our species and other ones.

(*iii*) **Biocentric Egalitarianism:** Nature has unqualified intrinsic value, with humans having no privileged place in nature's web. Emphasis is placed on value at holistic levels, such as populations, ecosystems, and the earth as a whole, rather than individual entities.

(*iv*) **Intuition:** A sensuous, intuitive communion with the earth is possible, and it gives us needed insight into nature and our relationship to it.

(*v*) **Environmental Devastation:** Nature is undergoing a ruinous degradation, an ecological holocaust, at the hands of human societies.

(*vi*) **Anti-anthropocentrism.** This destructiveness is rooted in anthropocentrism, a view that we are separate from and superior to nature, which exists to serve our needs.

(*vii*) **An Ecocentric Society:** The goal at a social level is a society that is based on an ecocentric view of nature and that lives in harmony with the natural tendencies and the limits of the natural world.

(*viii*) **Self-Realization:** The goal at an individual level is to fully realize one's identification with nature.

(*ix*) **Intuitive Morality:** The moral ideal, then, is a realization of our identification with nature which yields a spontaneous, intuitive tendency to avoid harm and to flourish.

Thus, deep ecology offers a philosophical basis for environmental advocacy which may, in turn, guide human activity against perceived self-destruction. Deep ecology and environmentalism hold that the science of ecology shows that ecosystems can absorb only limited change by humans or other dissonant influences. Further, both hold that the actions of modern civilization threaten global ecological well-being. Ecologists have described change and stability in ecological systems in various ways, including homeostasis, dynamic equilibrium, and "flux of nature". Regardless of which model is most accurate, environmentalists contend that massive human economic activity has pushed the biosphere far from its "natural" state, through reduction of biodiversity, climate change, and other influences. As a consequence, civilization is causing mass extinction. Deep ecologists hope to influence social and political change through their philosophy.

Ecocentrism

A natural follow up of deep ecology is the philosophy of ecocentrism which refers to the idea that all life has intrinsic value. Ecocentrism is a philosophy that recognizes that the ecosphere, rather than any individual organism, is the source and support of all life. It focuses on the biotic community as a whole, and strives to maintain ecosystem composition and ecological processes.

The ecocentric ethic was conceived by Aldo Leopold and recognizes that all species, including humans, are the products of a long evolutionary process and are inter-related in their life processes. Ecocentrism puts the ecosphere first. It recognizes the importance of the environment and the web of life and realizes that no single organism is more important than another. Ecocentrism does not even distinguish between animate life and inanimate matter or process. The entire "sphere" of life is important. This philosophy is also outlined by James Lovelock, in the Gaia Hypothesis, where he stresses the importance of viewing the earth as a living, breathing single organism, working through a vast network of relationships, many unknown to man, to maintain a balance in which all life forms can exist and flourish. (Refer Box 1.2)

BOX 1.2

The Gaia Hypothesis

It was propounded by James Lovelock – Gaia being named after the Greek Goddess of the earth – where he argues that the earth in its entirety, including rocks and atmosphere, is a single living organism, and that the living organisms on earth can control their non-living environment to make it comfortable for life. He emphasized the need for a holistic approach vis-à-vis a reductionist approach to tackle the problems relating to the environment. He feels that if human beings tamper with the planet earth, then they will be eliminated by Gaia, replacing it with what James Lovelock calls more "amenable" species. He says, "It follows that if the world is made unfit by what we do, there is the possibility of a change in regime to one that will be better for life, but not necessarily ourselves."

Source: James Lovelock (1979), *A New Look at Life on Earth*, Oxford University Press.

Thus, in an ecocentric ethic, nature has moral consideration because it has intrinsic value, aside from its usefulness to humans. Using this ethic, for example, one could judge that it would be wrong to cut down the rainforests because it would cause the extinction of many plant and animal species.

1.4 CONCLUSION

Thus we see the evolution of environmental philosophies and ethics over time, from an extremely human centered and materialistic approach to nature and nature's resources, to one that recognizes the imperative of putting the ecosystem at the centre, and working for the benefit of **all** beings –

not just the humans. As Theodore Roszak, so eloquently remarks in his book, *The Voice of the Earth,* "What the modern cultural environment has required of us, is an enormous extroversion of attention and energy for the purpose of reshaping the Earth into a global industrial economy. For two centuries we have been subordinating the planet and our deepest personal needs to that project. This great act of collective alienation, I have suggested, lies at the root of both the environmental crisis and individual neurosis. In some way, at some point, a change of direction, a therapeutic turning inward, had to take place within a culture as maniacally driven as ours has been by the need to achieve and conquer."

QUESTIONS

1. Discuss the environmental philosophies which deal with man's relationship with the environment.
2. What is environmental ethics? Trace its history and evolution over time.
3. Bring out the difference between shallow ecology and deep ecology.
4. Sustainable development is based on the shallow ecology concept. Examine the statement.
5. Why should we adopt a holistic solution to environmental issues? Give examples and explain.
6. Explain the underlying principles behind deep ecology. Also discuss its similarity with the Gaia hypothesis propounded by James Lovelock.

EXERCISES

1. From the internet, collect information on any environmental case study, such as the Love Canal tragedy or the Bhopal Gas tragedy or Minamata tragedy and examine the ethical issues raised by the case study.
2. Assuming that you are working for a chemical firm and you come to know that your company is secretly disposing off the toxic wastes in a most unsafe way. Taking this issue with the management will cost you your job. Not taking any action to stop the same will have serious consequences. How will you react?

❑❑❑

2

Basics of Ecology and Environment

> *To halt the decline of an ecosystem,*
> *it is necessary to think like an ecosystem.*
> **Douglas P. Wheeler**

Human well-being and the progress towards sustainable development are vitally dependent upon the earth's ecosystems. The impact of human activities on the ecosystem adversely affects the supply of ecosystem services, and changes in the availability of ecosystem services, in turn, adversely affect human well-being.

2.1 ECOSYSTEM – DEFINITION

An ecosystem is a dynamic complex of plant, animal and microorganism communities and the non-living environment, interacting as a functional unit. The ecosystem is the basic unit in ecology.

The term "ecosystem" was first coined by Roy Clapham in 1930, but it was the British ecologist, Arthur Tansley, who fully defined the ecosystem concept in 1935, to denote the physical and biological components of an environment considered in relation to each other as a unit. The word ecosystem is an abbreviation of the term, "ecological system". A river, a swamp, a lake, a meadow, and a cave are all examples of ecosystems. Ecosystems embody the concept that living organisms continually interact with each other and with the environment, to produce complex systems with emergent properties, such that "everything is connected".

Components of an Ecosystem

An ecosystem mainly consists of the living, or biotic components and the non-living, or abiotic, components.

Biotic or Living Components

The biotic or living components of an ecosystem are its organisms, like plants, animals, and microbes, which together form the communities of the ecosystem. Living organisms (biotic components) in an ecosystem can be classified as either producers or consumers, depending on how they get their food.

(*a*) **Producers or Autotrophs:** (*i.e.,* self feeders) can make the organic nutrients they need, using simple inorganic compounds in their environment: for instance, the green plants on land and the small algae in aquatic ecosystems produce their food by the process of photosynthesis. The producers convert radiant energy into a chemical form. Hence, they are also called converters or transformers.

(*b*) **Consumers or Heterotrophs:** (*i.e.,* other feeders) are those organisms, which directly or indirectly depend on food provided by producers. The consumers, depending on their food habits, can be further classified into three types:

- **Herbivores** derive their nutrition from plants and hence, feed directly on producers *e.g.,* deer, rabbits, cattle, etc. In a food chain, they are referred to as the **primary consumers**.
- **Carnivores** are meat eaters and they feed on herbivores. They are thus known as **secondary consumers**. They are animal eaters, *e.g.*, lions, tigers.
- **Omnivores** eat both plants and animals, *e.g.*, pigs, rats, and humans. They are also known as tertiary consumers.

A simple example of an autotrophic-heterotrophic relationship is the alfalfa (fodder) – human food chain. Energy captured by photosynthesizing alfalfa serves as the food base for cows/ goats and the latter in turn become food for human beings. In this chain, the alfalfa is the autotroph and the sheep and human beings are heterotrophs. While the sheep is a primary consumer, the human beings are secondary consumers or carnivores.

(*c*) **Decomposers:** The decomposers (primarily bacteria, fungi; nematodes, like tapeworms; mites and certain insects) are organisms that feed by degrading organic matter. They are essential components of all nutrient cycles and food chains. Decomposers break down organic waste and recycle the nutrients present in it. If decomposers are removed from the biosphere, the earth will become a vast dump of dead organisms, as the nutrients for life would be tied up in the dead organisms.

Producers, consumers and decomposers are linked together by the food chain, wherein each category forms a trophic level.

Non-living Components

The non-living (or abiotic) components of an ecosystem include all the physical and chemical factors that influence living organisms, like air, water, soil, rocks etc. It is an assemblage of organic and inorganic substances present in an ecosystem. Inorganic substances are temperature, water, light, humidity, soil pH, etc., which are required for the synthesis of organic substances by the producers. Organic substances are derived from dead plants and animals, as well as from their excreta. Decomposition of such substances release minerals. The various climatic factors that affect the ecosystem functioning are also a part of the abiotic component. The non-living components are essential for the living world. Without sunlight, water, air and minerals, life cannot exist.

Each of the abiotic factors listed in Table 2.1 acts as a limiting factor, determining the types of organisms that exist in the environment. For example, a low annual temperature determines the species of plants that can exist in that area and the amount of dissolved oxygen in a body of water determines the species of fish that can live in it.

Table 2.1 Abiotic Components of an Ecosystem

Sunlight
Temperature
Precipitation
Water or Moisture
Various types of substratum (soil or rock type)
Inorganic substances, such as minerals
Gases, such as oxygen, carbon dioxide and nitrogen
pH

Functioning of an Ecosystem

The two major functions within an ecosystem are the transfer of energy *through*, and the recycling of nutrients *within*, the ecosystem.

Energy Flow in an Ecosystem

Primary producers or autotrophic organisms convert light energy and inorganic substances (carbon dioxide, water and various mineral nutrients) into organic (carbon based) molecules, (carbohydrates) by photosynthesis. Photosynthesis is the process by which light energy from the sun is absorbed by plants to produce new plant cell material, which forms the food source for plant eating animals (herbivores).

In the energy cycle, herbivores such as caterpillars and field mice consume the plant carbohydrates and the chemical energy from autotrophs is transferred to them. When carnivores consume the herbivores, energy is transferred to the next trophic level. Thus, all energy available to organisms originates in plants; **herbivores** obtain their energy by consuming plants or plant products, **carnivores** eat herbivores, and **detritivores** consume the droppings and carcasses of all dead organisms. It is estimated that 90 per cent of the energy is used up at each trophic level and only 10 per cent of it is transferred to the next trophic level. Finally, at the last trophic level, there is no more energy available for recycling. The energy flows from the sun, through producers to consumers, and is unidirectional and non-cyclic. This is illustrated in Figure 2.1.

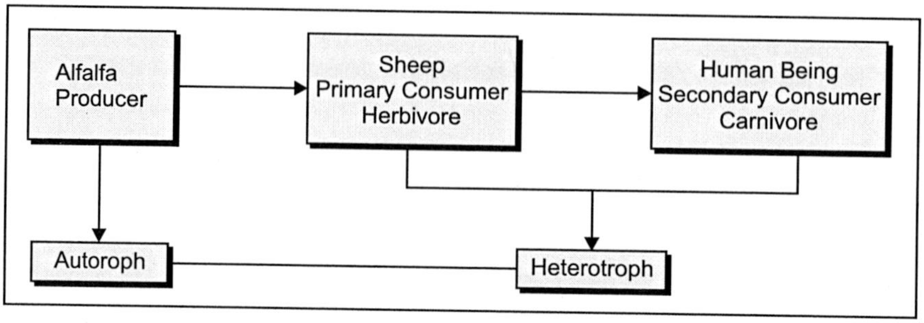

Fig. 2.1 Energy Flow in an Ecosystem.

Nutrient Flow in an Ecosystem

A second major process linking the biotic and abiotic constituents of an ecosystem is the flow of nutrients. Unlike energy, which is not cycled, inorganic nutrients are cycled in ecosystems. Producers obtain nutrients from the inorganic nutrient pool, which is usually the soil or water surrounding the plants or algae. Inorganic nutrients are passed from organism to organism as one organism is consumed by another. Ultimately, all organisms die and become detritus, which serves as the food source for decomposers. At this stage, the inorganic nutrients are returned to the soil or water to be taken up again. While the inorganic nutrients are recycled, the energy is not. The flow of energy and nutrients through the components of an ecosystem is illustrated in Figure 2.2.

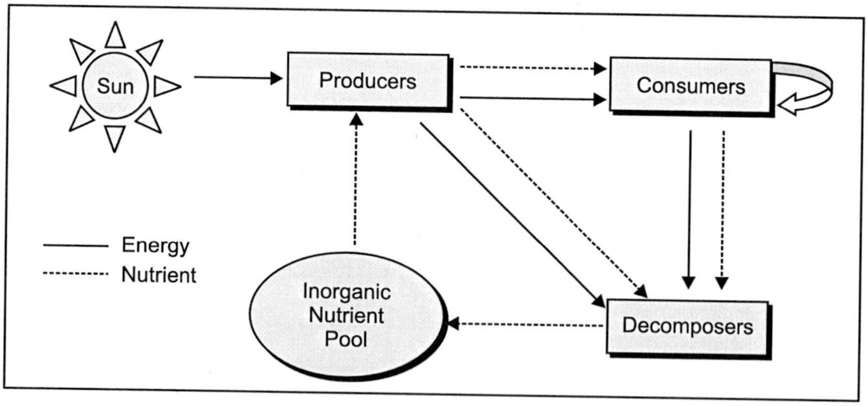

Fig. 2.2 The Energy and Nutrient Movement in an Ecosystem.

BOX 2.1

A Pond Ecosystem

A pond ecosystem is a freshwater ecosystem. There are mainly four habitats in a pond ecosystem, namely shore habitat, surface film habitat, open water habitat and bottom water habitat.

Shore Habitat: The organisms living in this habitat vary depending upon whether the shore is rocky, sandy or muddy. In case of rocky shores, plants might not be able to grow, whereas in muddy or sandy or mixed type, plants like grasses, algae and rushes can be present, along with organisms, such as earthworms, protozoa, snails, insects, small fishes and microorganisms.

Surface Film Habitat: Surface film habitat refers to the surface of the pond. Organisms that are free-floating and those that can walk on the surface of water inhabit the surface habitat. They nourish on the floating plants, dead insects, and sometimes, feed upon each other. Example: insects like water striders and marsh skaters.

Open Water Habitat: Open water habitat is inhabited by fishes and tiny organisms such as algae and zooplankton, insect larvae, rotifers, tiny crustaceans and invertebrates. Fishes feed on plankton.

Bottom Water Habitat: Depending on whether the pond is shallow or deep, the bottom habitat varies. For example, if a pond is shallow and has a sandy bottom, organisms like earthworms, snails and insects inhabit the bottom, whereas, if the pond is deep and has a muddy bottom, microorganisms, flatworm, rat-tailed maggot and nymphs of dragonflies mostly inhabit the bottom habitat.

Food Chain in a Pond Ecosystem: Food chain in a pond ecosystem is divided into three basic trophic levels. The first trophic level is represented by the producer organisms, like phytoplankton and plants. The second trophic level is characterized by the herbivores, such as insects, crustaceans and invertebrates inhabiting the pond. The third trophic level comprises the carnivores, especially the fishes, which can feed on both plants and the herbivores of the first and second trophic levels respectively.

In addition to the three trophic levels, there are the decomposers, which are mostly the bacteria and fungi. All the organic matter from the dead and decayed organisms is converted into nutrients which are used by algae and plants for the production of food to be consumed by the herbivores. Thus, the flow of energy is maintained in a pond ecosystem.

Source: http://www.buzzle.com/articles/pond-ecosystem.html

Services of an Ecosystem

Mankind benefits from a multitude of **ecosystem services,** which include products like clean drinking water and processes such as the decomposition of wastes. The ecosystem services can be subdivided into four main categories:

(*i*) Provisioning services that include products obtained from ecosystems such as, food and fibre, fuel, genetic resources, biochemicals, natural medicines, pharmaceuticals, ornamental resources and fresh water.

(*ii*) Regulating services are the benefits obtained from the regulation of ecosystem processes, and include air quality maintenance, climate regulation, water regulation, erosion control, water purification and waste treatment, regulation of human diseases, biological control, and storm protection.

(*iii*) Supporting services such as nutrient cycles and pollination that are necessary for the functioning of all other ecosystem services.

(*iv*) Cultural services are the non-material benefits that people obtain from ecosystems through spiritual enrichment, cognitive development, reflection, recreation, and aesthetic experiences.

2.2 FOREST ECOSYSTEM

The forest ecosystem covers the flora, fauna and ground conditions within the parameters of a forest. Forests serve many functions. Firstly, forests protect and form other natural resources. Thanks to the processes of photosynthesis, they renew the oxygen stock in the atmosphere. Forests also allow for the existence of many species of plants and animals, thus protecting diversity of nature and its gene stock. Though tropical forests cover only 7 per cent of the Earth's land mass, they are home to more than 50 per cent of the world's 10-50 million plant and animal species. The plants in the forests also provide us with medicines. Forests clean the environment by muffling noises, lowering the wind strength, as well as by stopping dust and gases. They have a regulatory influence on surface water run-off and they moderate high and low temperatures and prevent soil erosion.

The functions of forests can be classified under three main categories:

(*i*) Production Function: Includes supply of timber and other forest products, such as resin, cork, animal fodder, fruits etc. Production of wood and non-wood forest products is the primary function for 34 per cent of the world's forests.

(*ii*) Protective Function: Include the various ecosystem services by forests, such as maintenance of water supply and quality, carbon sequestration and climate maintenance, preventing soil erosion, coastal protection and a host of other benefits derived from biodiversity. The coastal forests, particularly mangroves, reduce shoreline erosion and siltation and the impacts of storm surges and tsunamis. That mangroves play a vital role in protecting the coastal areas against the action of waves, wind, and water currents is well known. (Box 2.2) (*iii*) **Special Functions:** Performed by special-purpose forests, include the following sub-categories:

(*a*) Forests in buffer zones of reservoirs that guarantee adequate water quality of reservoirs

(*b*) Recreational forests for public recreation

(*c*) Forests as game reserves and pheasant enclosures

(*d*) Forests for nature conservation

(*e*) Forests for educational purposes and research.

BOX 2.2

Mangroves and the Asian Tsunami

The term mangrove refers to a diverse group of salt-tolerant trees and other plant species that are found along sheltered tropical and subtropical shores and estuaries. These unique coastal forests provide other important services: conservation of biological diversity and – by trapping sediment from upland erosion – protection of coral reefs, sea-grass beds and shipping lanes against siltation. Mangrove forests store and process huge amounts of organic matter, dissolved nutrients, pesticides and other pollutants that are dumped into them by human activities, and by absorbing excess nitrates and phosphates, they prevent the contamination of coastal waters. In doing so, they play a vital role in protecting coral reefs and sea grasses from siltation and eutrophication.

The mangrove ecosystems also play an important role in preventing and reducing coastal erosion, providing nearby communities with protection against the effect of wind, waves and water current. This was demonstrated during the 2004 tsunami in Asia – in locations in which extensive areas of mangroves existed, coastal villages suffered less damage. All the countries that were hit hardest by the tsunami – Indonesia, Sri Lanka, India and Thailand – have experienced recent net losses of mangrove cover. According to FAO statistics, between 1980 and 2000, the total area of mangroves in these four countries was reduced by 28 per cent.

The reports that emerged after the Tsunami in 2004, from scientists, environmentalists and local people, reported of cases, where mangrove forests had saved lives and property. Mangroves not only broke the impact of the waves, but also trapped debris and prevented people from being washed out to sea, which was a major cause of death. It was reported that in Tamil Nadu, the tsunami did lesser damage to lives and property in the regions of Pichavaram and Muthupet, both of which are shielded by dense mangroves, than in areas where mangroves had been cleared or were absent. The mangrove forest reduced the impact of the tsunami by reducing the velocity of the incoming waves (due to friction created by the dense mangrove forest), and by distributing water among the canals and creeks of the mangroves, thus decreasing the level of inundation. The satellite images taken before and after the tsunami support these claims.

Source: http://www.ejfoundation.org/pdf/tsunami_report.pdf

2.3 BIODIVERSITY

Biological diversity or biodiversity is the combination of life forms and their interactions with one another and with the physical environment that has made earth habitable for humans. The term encompasses the number and variety of species, ecological systems and the genetic variability they contain, together with their relative abundance. Most experts estimate the world's species diversity at 10 to 30 million of which only 1.4 million species have been identified.

Uses of Biodiversity

Biodiversity supports a number of natural ecosystem processes and services. Some ecosystem services that benefit society are air quality, climate (both global CO_2 sequestration and local), water purification, pollination, and prevention of erosion. Plant species provide a variety of products, like food, medicines and raw materials. Some plant extracts are used in the manufacture of glue, soaps, cosmetics, dyes, lubricants and polishes. The plants also provide an important source of renewable energy.

Supply of Food: One of the most fundamental uses of plant biodiversity is in supplying food for humans, domesticated and wild animals and different organisms. Of the estimated 250,000 species of flowering plants at the global level, about 3000 are regarded as food sources and only 200 species out of these have been cultivated.

Supply of Medicines: A significant proportion of drugs are derived, directly or indirectly, from biological sources. At least 50 per cent of the pharmaceutical compounds on the market in the US are derived from natural compounds found in plants, animals, and microorganisms, while about 80 per cent of the world population depends on medicines from nature (used in either modern or traditional medical practice) for primary healthcare. Around 119 pure chemical substances, extracted from some 90 species of higher plants are used in medicines throughout the world. Indian medicine system is largely dependent on such medicinal plants. The local people, particularly the tribal population, relies on indigenous and traditional medicines. The Indian subcontinent is a rich emporia of 2500 plant species used in indigenous treatment. The WHO has listed over 21,000 medicinal plants and most of these are temperate species.

Supply of Industrial Materials: A wide range of industrial materials are derived directly from biological resources. These include building materials, fibers, dyes, resirubber and oil. There is enormous potential for further research into sustainably utilizing materials from a wider diversity of organisms. The loss of biodiversity is increasingly recognized as a significant risk factor in business development and a threat to long term economic sustainability.

Ecosystem Services: Biodiversity plays an important role in regulating the chemistry of our atmosphere and water supply. Biodiversity is directly involved in water purification, recycling of nutrients and in the provision of fertile soils. The stability of ecosystems is also related to biodiversity, with higher biodiversity producing greater stability over time, reducing the chance that ecosystem services will be disrupted as a result of disturbances, such as extreme weather events or human exploitation. As the natural habitat declines, the ecological processes slow down. The rich biodiversity helps in the sustainability/stability required for existence, and risk aversion.

Leisure, Cultural and Aesthetic Values: Many people derive value from biodiversity through leisure activities, such as hiking, bird watching or natural history study. Popular activities such as gardening, caring for aquariums and collecting butterflies are all strongly dependent on biodiversity. A visit to a botanical garden or zoo is as much an aesthetic or cultural experience as an educational one.

State of Biodiversity

According to the Millennium Ecosystem Assessment Report (2005) the changes in important components of biological diversity were more rapid in the past 50 years than at any time in human history. Some of the findings of the report are:

(*i*) Species extinction rates are now 100 to1000 times above the background rate.

(*ii*) The distribution of species on Earth is becoming more homogenous.

(*iii*) Between 10 per cent and 50 per cent of well-studied higher taxonomic groups (mammals, birds, amphibians, conifers, and cycads) are currently threatened with extinction.

(*iv*) Some 12 per cent of bird species, 23 per cent of mammals, and 25 per cent of conifers are currently threatened with extinction. In addition, 32 per cent of amphibians are threatened with extinction.

(*v*) Genetic diversity has declined globally, due to intensification of agricultural systems, coupled with specialization by plant breeders and the harmonizing effects of globalization. Such declines in genetic diversity lower the resilience and adaptability of domesticated species.

Threats to Biodiversity

"The one process ongoing in the 1980s that will take millions of years to correct is the loss of genetic and species diversity by the destruction of natural habitats. This is the folly that our descendents are least likely to forgive us". **— E.O. Wilson, 1985**

Species and ecosystems are threatened with destruction to an extent rarely seen in earth's history. The loss of species and ecosystems is attributed to the accelerating transformation of the earth by a growing human population. There are five specific types of human actions that threaten species and ecosystems:

(*i*) Over hunting

(*ii*) Habitat loss/degradation/fragmentation

(*iii*) Invasion of non-native species

(*iv*) Pollution

(*v*) Climate Change

(*i*) **Over Hunting:** Most extinction over the past several hundred years is mainly due to over-harvesting for food, fashion, and profit. Commercial hunting, both legal and illegal (poaching), is the principal threat. Snowy egret, Passenger pigeon, and the Heath hen are a few examples. Some rhino species are down to only a few thousand individuals, with only a slim hope of survival in the wild, mainly because of the price on their horn that ranges from $40,000 to $100,000 per horn. The pet and decorative plant trade also fall within this commercial hunting category and their annual trade, both due to legal and illegal activities (1/4 to 1/3 of the trade is illegal) is estimated to be worth at least $5 billion.

(ii) **Habitat Loss/Degradation:** Habitat damage, especially the conversion of forested land into agriculture is an important factor causing biodiversity loss. Other factors include population growth, inequitable land and income distribution, development policies that target forests, particularly tropical forests. Tropical forests are so important because they harbour at least 50 per cent, and perhaps more, of the world's biodiversity. The data from direct observations which have been reinforced by satellite data show that the tropical forests are declining. The original extent of tropical rain forests was 15 million km^2. Now there remains about 7.5 to 8 million km^2; so half is already gone. The current rate of loss is estimated at near 2 per cent annually. It is estimated that tropical forests will be reduced to 10 per cent to 25 per cent of their original extent by late 21st Century.

(iii) **Invasion of Non-native Species:** This is an important and often overlooked cause of extinctions. Non-native species, introduced either by humans or through habitat modification, cause extinction of native plants and animals. This phenomenon can be especially detrimental for rare species coming into contact with more abundant ones. The abundant species interbreed with the rarer, swamping the entire gene pool by creating hybrids, thus causing extinction of the entire native stock.

In agriculture and animal husbandry, the green revolution popularized the use of conventional hybridization to increase yield by creating "high-yielding varieties". Local governments and industry have been pushing hybridization which has resulted in several of the indigenous breeds becoming extinct or threatened. Huge gene pools of various wild and indigenous breeds have collapsed, causing widespread genetic erosion and genetic pollution due to uncontrolled intentional and unintentional cross-pollination and cross-breeding. This has resulted in loss of genetic diversity and biodiversity as a whole.

The African Great Lakes—Victoria, Malawi and Tanganyika—are famous for their great diversity of endemic species, termed "species flocks", of cichlid fishes. In Lake Victoria, the purposeful introduction of a single, exotic species, the Nile Perch, for subsistence and sports fishing, has caused the extinction of most of the native species, proving the introduction of the Nile Perch to be a great disaster.

A genetically modified organism (GMO) is an organism whose genetic material has been altered using the genetic engineering techniques. Genetically Modified (GM) crops today have become a common source for genetic pollution, not only of wild varieties, but also of other domesticated varieties derived from relatively natural hybridization. It is reported that genetic erosion, coupled with genetic pollution, may be destroying unique genotypes, thereby posing a severe threat to our food security. The case of Bt Brinjal and Bt Cotton are discussed in Chapter 28.

(iv) **Pollution:** Chemical contaminants pose a serious threat to species and ecosystems, particularly for species whose range is extremely small, and threatened by contamination.

BOX 2.3

Cases of Extinct Species

Case 1

The seeds of the tree *Calvaria major,* now found exclusively on the island of Mauritius, must pass through the abrasive gut of a large animal in order to germinate. Their tough seed coats are a kind of living coffin, for the seed cannot germinate unless abraded. The Dodo, a 25 kg pigeon, hunted to extinction in the late 17th century, ate the fallen fruits of *Calvaria.*

The seeds of *Calvaria* were unable to germinate, without first being abraded and scarified in the gizzard of a Dodo. *Calvaria* pits withstood the crushing forces that were generated by a Dodo's gizzard; the endocarp was progressively abraded until it was thin enough to be crushed.

The fruits of *Calvaria* had become highly specialized through co-evolution with the Dodo. After the Dodo became extinct, no other animal in Mauritius was capable of ingesting the large pits. As a result, *Calvaria major* has apparently been unable to reproduce for 300 years and has nearly become extinct.

Case 2

The black footed ferret was once very abundant in the western prairies. It preyed upon prairie dogs and used their burrows to nest in. Poisoning of prairie dogs has greatly reduced their abundance, and the black footed ferret is now the rarest mammal in North America.

Source: Stanley A. "Temple, Plant-Animal Mutualism: Co-evolution with Dodo Leads to Near Extinction of Plant". http://www.ecologia.unam.mx/laboratorios/comunidades/pdf/pdf%20curso%20posgrado%20Elena/Tema3/mutualismos/Temple1977.pdf

http://www.globalchange.umich.edu/globalchange2/current/lectures/biodiversity/biodiversity.html

(*v*) **Climate Change:** Climate change causes shift in the distribution of species, to which plants and animals are not able to adjust. Reports of ecosystem changes due to the recent global warming have been reported already from many parts of the world. Costa Rica's golden toad is likely to become extinct because of its inability to adapt to climate changes; birds such as the Great Tit in Scotland and the Mexican Jay in Arizona are beginning to breed earlier in the year; butterflies are shifting their ranges northwards throughout Europe; alpine plants are moving to higher altitudes in Austria; and mammals in many parts of the Arctic - including polar bears, walrus and caribou - are beginning to feel the impacts of reduced sea ice and warming tundra habitat. Russia, Canada, Kyrgyzstan, Norway, Sweden, Finland, Latvia, Uruguay, Bhutan and Mongolia are likely to lose 45 per cent or more of their current habitat. Scientists fear that by the end of the next century, perhaps 25 per cent of the existing species will be lost. The rate of global warming may be a critical determinant in the future of global biodiversity.

Policy to Protect Biodiversity

Protecting global biodiversity has emerged in the past three decades as one of the major challenges in international relations. Over ten global biodiversity-related treaties have been negotiated, as well as literally hundreds of regional and bilateral agreements have been signed. Governments have also endorsed dozens of comprehensive action plans, most notably, the Agenda 21, which set forth a blueprint for implementing sustainable development. Some of the measures adopted to protect the world's biodiversity from extinction are:

The Convention on Biological Diversity (CBD) — 1992

The CBD was signed by over 150 governments at the Rio Earth Summit in 1992 and entered into force in 1993. The Convention has three main goals:

(*i*) Conservation of biological diversity

(*ii*) Sustainable use of its components

(*iii*) Fair and equitable sharing of benefits arising from genetic resources.

The convention covers the rapidly expanding field of biotechnology through its Cartagena Protocol on Biosafety, addressing technology development and transfer, benefit-sharing and biosafety issues. Importantly, the Convention is legally binding; countries that are parties to it are obliged to implement its provisions.

Cartagena Protocol on Biosafety (CPB) — 2000

The Conference of the Parties to the Convention on Biological Diversity adopted a supplementary agreement to the Convention, known as the Cartagena Protocol on Biosafety, on 29 January 2000. The Protocol seeks to protect biological diversity from the potential risks posed by living modified organisms resulting from modern biotechnology.

Convention on International Trade in Endangered Species (CITES) — 1975

Known as CITES, the Convention on International Trade in Endangered Species of Wild Fauna and Flora, entered into force on 1 July 1975 and now has a membership of 152 countries. These countries act by banning commercial international trade in an agreed list of endangered species, and by regulating and monitoring trade in others that might become endangered. Roughly, 5,000 species of animals and 28,000 species of plants are protected by CITES against over-exploitation through international trade.

International Convention for the Regulation of Whaling (ICRW) — 1946

The International Convention for the Regulation of Whaling was signed in Washington DC on 2nd December 1946. The purpose of the Convention is to provide for the proper conservation of whale stocks and thus make possible, the orderly development of the whaling industry.

Convention on the Conservation of Migratory Species of Wild Animals — (Bonn Convention) — 1983

Also known as CMS or the Bonn Convention, it aims to conserve terrestrial, marine and avian migratory species throughout their range.

While biodiversity makes important contributions to human well-being, many of the actions needed to promote economic development are likely to reduce biodiversity. What is needed is the identification of nationally and locally tailored combinations of measures for reducing biodiversity loss, using a range of approaches. The challenges before us are great, but the cost of doing nothing is far greater.

2.4 ENVIRONMENTAL POLLUTION

Civilization . . . wrecks the planet from seafloor to stratosphere. **—Richard Bach**

Among the various forms of environmental pollution problems that degrade the environment, we will briefly consider in this section, the pollution of the air and water, generation of solid wastes and hazardous wastes generation.

Pollution is the undesirable change in the physical, chemical and biological characteristics of air, water and soil which directly or indirectly affects human life, property, flora and fauna.

Environmental pollution is the contamination of the physical and biological components of the planet earth to such an extent that normal environmental processes are adversely affected. Pollution is caused when the environment is not able to assimilate the wastes generated from human activities.

Based on the nature of pollutants, pollution may be classified as pollution by decomposable or biodegradable wastes and by non-decomposable or non-biodegradable wastes.

Biodegradable or decomposable wastes are naturally occurring organic compounds which are degraded by biological or microbial agents. Domestic sewage, food residues and remains of dead animals and plants are biodegradable wastes.

Non-biodegradable wastes on the other hand, include metallic wastes, polythene, glass, etc., which do not break down for many years.

On the basis of the component of the environment that is polluted, pollution is classified as air pollution, water pollution and soil pollution.

2.5 AIR POLLUTION

Air pollution is the presence of contaminants in the air, in sufficient quantities and duration, to interfere with the comfort, safety and health of human beings and cause adverse impacts on flora, fauna and properties.

Air pollution is essentially an urban and industrial phenomenon. Air pollution in rural areas is mainly due to smoke from firewood used in domestic cooking and from rural and cottage industries, such as rice mills and brick kilns. In urban areas, air pollution is mainly from vehicles and from industries.

Besides natural sources, such as volcano eruptions, dust storms, forest fires etc., artificial pollution caused by anthropogenic activities are on the increase. These include pollution from industries, burning from agricultural activities, and from automobiles. It is reported that in India, 10 lakh tonnes of carbon dioxide, two lakh tones of hydrogen sulphide and 50 lakh tonnes of suspended particulate matter are released into the air every day (Gautam Gupta, 2001).

Some of the main air pollutants are:

(i) **Gaseous Pollutants:** Such as oxides of sulphur and nitrogen, hydrocarbons, carbon monoxide and ozone.

(ii) **Aerosols:** Such as smoke, fumes, dust and particulates.

Table 2.2 Sources and Health Effects of Major Air Pollutants

Pollutant	Source	Human Health Effects
Particulates	Internal combustion engines (*e.g.,* cars and trucks). Industry (*e.g.,* factories) Burning wood and cigarette smoke.	Long term exposure is linked to: Lung cancer, heart disease, lung disease, asthma attacks.
Nitrogen Oxide-NO_2	Motor Vehicles Other combustion processes.	Lung damage respiratory disease.
Sulphur dioxide-SO_2	Power plants, petroleum refining.	Irritates eyes, nose, throat, Damages lungs when inhaled.
Ozone	Formed by various complex chemical reactions involving the exposure of the oxides of nitrogen and some hydrocarbons.	Lining of lungs Lining of respiratory tracts Eye irritation.
Carbon Monoxide	Motor vehicle exhaust and burning of materials such as coal, oil and wood. It is also released from industrial processes and waste incineration.	Disrupts the supply of oxygen to the body's tissues Affects central nervous system.
Lead	Largely derived from the combustion of lead additives in motor fuels, as well as lead smelting.	Retards learning in children and the development of their nervous system.
Hydro Carbons	Most fuel combustion processes result in the release of hydrocarbons to the environment. The largest fuel sources are natural gas and petrol. They are also a component of the smoke from wood fires.	Exposure can cause headaches or nausea, while some compounds may cause cancer. Some may also damage plants.
Ammonia	Agriculture, livestock.	Lung damage, death.
Air-borne particles/ particulates	Transport, power plants, production processes.	Asthma, lung cancer, cardio-vascular problems.

Source: http://www.epa.vic.gov.au/air/aq4kids/main_pollutants.asp
http://www.tropical-rainforest-animals.com/Air-Pollutants-Summary.html

Besides affecting the health of human beings, air pollution also affects animals, birds and properties. Oxides of sulphur and nitrogen make rain acidic, which affects soil quality and fertility. Acid rain caused by the reaction of sulphur and nitrogen oxides with rain water, causes serious havoc to soil productivity and properties.

Sulphur dioxide and chlorine cause bleaching of leaves. Fluorides cause necrosis on tips and edges of leaves, turning the leaves brown. Air pollutants, such as ozone and sulphur dioxide, cause yellowing of the leaves due to loss of chlorophyll. This is called chlorosis. Some air pollutants have adverse impact on buildings, fabrics and cars. Ozone cracks the tyres of automobiles, while SO_2 damages buildings, fabrics, leather and steel.

BOX 2.4

Acid Rain

Rain is said to be acidic when there is a fall in the pH value of rain water. This is caused by the presence of gases, such as sulphur and nitrogen oxides in the atmosphere, emitted by refineries, burning of fossil fuels and vehicles.

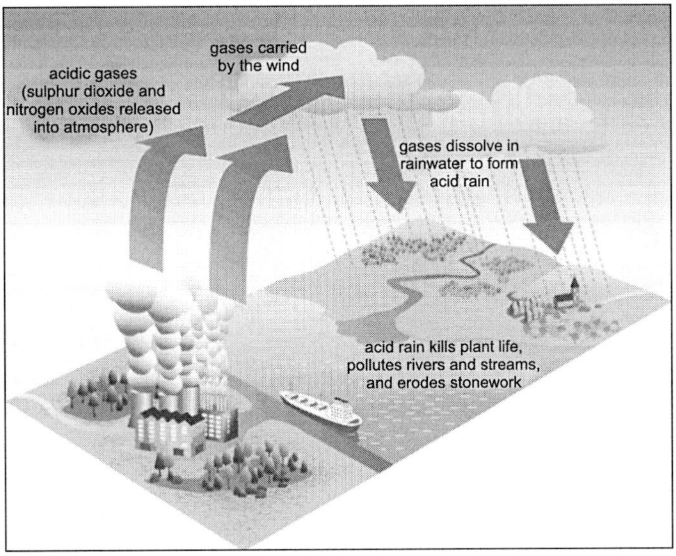

Acidity is measured in terms of pH which refers to potential of hydrogen. It is measured on a scale from 0 to 14, with 7 being the neutral value. Lower the value on the scale, greater the acidity of the substance. Normal rain water has a pH of 5.6. When the pH value of rain water goes below 5.6, it is considered to be acid rain.

When the sea water becomes acidic, with a pH value of less than 4.5, all the sea life and most of the frogs and insects that live in the water will die. A pH of 5.5, kills bacterial decomposers, the absence of which pollutes the water. A pH value of 6.0 is fatal to all fresh water shrimps.

Acid rain harms trees by causing damage to the waxy outer coating of the leaves that protects it. This prevents photosynthesis in plants and eventually causes the death of the plants and trees. Besides, acid rain also damages the soil by removing all the nutrients from the soil.

Acid rain causes havoc on buildings, statues and sculptures by its reaction on rocks, building material and paints.

Source: http://library.thinkquest.org/CR0215471/acid_rain.htm

BOX 2.5

The Taj Trapezium Case

The Taj Mahal, one of the finest garden tombs in the world, stands on the bank of the river Yamuna in India. It was built by the Mughal Emperor, Shah Jahan to enshrine the mortal remains of his Empress, Mumtaz Mahal. Environmental pollution spurred by industry and automobiles has long been observed to be progressively destroying the Taj Mahal's white marble surface. The white marble has yellowed and blackened in places. It is inside the Taj that the decay is more apparent. Yellow pallor pervades the entire monument. In places, the yellow hue is magnified by ugly brown and black spots. Fungal deterioration is worst in the inner chamber where the original graves of Shah Jahan and Mumtaz Mahal lie.

The area was identified as a "pollution intensive zone" by the World Health Organization (WHO). Pollution around the Taj provoked the establishment of the "Taj Trapezium Zone" (TTZ) in 1982 to restrict such activities within an area of approximately 50 km radius around Agra. TTZ is so named since it is located around the Taj Mahal and is shaped like a trapezoid.

Taj Trapezium Zone is a defined area of 10,400 sq kms around the Taj Mahal to protect the monument from pollution. The Supreme Court of India delivered a ruling on December 30, 1996 regarding industries covered under the TTZ, in response to a PIL seeking to protect the Taj Mahal from environmental pollution. "Not even a one per cent chance can be taken when – human life apart – the preservation of a prestigious monument like the Taj is involved", stated the court order. It banned the use of coal/ coke in industries located in the TTZ with a mandate for switching over from coal/ coke to natural gas, and relocating them outside the TTZ or shutting down. Continuous monitoring of sulphur dioxide at Taj Mahal had been initiated since 1981 and a complete ban was imposed on the establishment and expansion of air polluting activities within the trapezium area. The court ordered 292 coal-based industries to switch to natural gas or else to relocate outside the protected zone by April 30, 1997.

Quite a number of factories did nothing about relocating or switching to natural gas. Some claimed that the cost of these operations was prohibitive. In August 1999, the Supreme Court struck again, ordering the closure of 53 iron foundries and 107 other factories in Agra that had not cleaned up their act. However, the industry filed a review petition through the Uttar Pradesh State government and obtained a reprieve on the court order's implementation. Daily electricity black outs in the area have complicated the problem. This has had a negative effect on the functioning of the sensitive pollution monitoring system of the Taj. In April 2002, the Supreme Court ordered the Agra Heritage Fund to set up a solar power plant to meet the energy needs of the Taj Mahal and the surrounding area. Additionally, conventional cars and automobiles are banned within a 500-metre radius of the monument.

While experts agree that some of these measures have helped to improve air around the Taj, pollution levels have not dropped to safer limits as none of the factories have actually been closed down. To date, the Taj trapezium issue is still a battle between politicians who have tended to side with industry and the judiciary which has supported the cause of the Taj.

2.6 AIR POLLUTION AND CLIMATE CHANGE

The global climate is changing due to the emissions in large quantities of greenhouse gases, and is therefore, known as the greenhouse effect.

Greenhouse effect refers to the increase in the mean temperature of the planet earth due to the presence of gases that absorb and emit infrared radiation. Greenhouse gases trap heat within the surface-troposphere system, causing heating at the surface of the planet. The greenhouse effect is enhanced by human activities, which increase greenhouse gases, such as carbon dioxide, methane, water vapour etc. in the atmosphere.

The Greenhouse Effect

The greenhouse effect is a phenomenon whereby greenhouse gases create a condition in the upper atmosphere, causing a trapping of heat and leading to increased surface and lower tropospheric temperatures. When sunlight reaches the Earth's surface, some is absorbed which warms the earth and the rest is radiated back to the atmosphere at a longer wavelength than the sunlight. Some of these longer wavelengths are absorbed by greenhouse gases in the atmosphere before they are lost to space. The absorption of this longwave radiant energy warms the atmosphere.

The major natural greenhouse gases are water vapor, which causes about 36 to 70 per cent of the greenhouse effect on Earth; carbon dioxide, CO_2, which causes 9 to 26 per cent of the green house effect; methane, which causes 4 per cent to 9 per cent, and ozone, which causes 3 to 7 per cent of the greenhouse effect. These gases act like the glass covering a greenhouse, letting sunlight in but blocking some of the infrared radiation from the earth's surface that carries heat back into space. Hence the name "greenhouse effect".

Different greenhouse gases have very different heat-trapping abilities. Some of them can even trap more heat than CO_2. A molecule of methane produces more than 20 times the warming of a molecule of CO_2. Nitrous oxide is 300 times more powerful than CO_2. Other gases, such as chlorofluorocarbons (which have been banned in much of the world because they degrade the ozone layer), have heat-trapping potential that is thousands of times greater than CO_2. But because their concentrations are much lower than CO_2, none of these gases add as much warmth to the atmosphere as CO_2 does.

In 2007, the Intergovernmental Panel on Climate Change (IPCC) reported that CO_2 levels had increased from about 280 ppm before the industrial era to 379 ppm in 2005. During the same time span, atmospheric methane concentrations rose from 715 parts per billion (ppb) to 1,774 ppb and N_2O concentrations increased from 270 ppb to 319 ppb.

Effects of Global Warming

There are two major effects of global warming:

(*a*) Increase of temperature on the earth by about 3°–5°C (5.4–9°F) by the year 2100.

(*b*) Rise of sea levels by at least 25 metres (82 feet) by the year 2100.

(*a*) **Increase in Temperature:** Global surface temperature increased 0.74 ± 0.18 °C (1.33 ± 0.32 °F) between the start and the end of the 20th century. The latest IPCC report projects that the global surface temperature is likely to rise a further 1.1 to 6.4 °C (2.0 to 11.5 °F) during the 21st Century.

Table 2.3 Changes in the CO_2 Emissions between 1992 and 2008 of 20 Countries with the Most (Estimated) 2008 Emissions

Country	Change in Greenhouse Gas Emissions (1992–2008) (%)	2008 Per Capita CO_2 Emissions (MT per person)	Share of Worldwise CO_2 Emissions (%)
China	166.50	5.3	22.2
USA	16.80	18.6	17.8
India	124.10	1.5	5.5
Russia	23.10	11.3	5
Japan	8.50	10.3	4.1
Germany	17	9.4	2.4
Canada	20.50	17	1.8
UK	6.80	8.9	1.7
South Korea	81.80	10.8	1.6
Iran	98.50	7.5	1.5
Italy	5.60	7.9	1.4
Mexico	13.50	4.1	1.4
South Africa	36	9.1	1.4
Saudi Arabia	52.60	15.5	1.4
Brazil	84.10	2.1	1.3
France	4.40	5.9	1.2
Indonesia	78.90	1.5	1.1
Australia	18.80	16.8	1.1
Spain	42.60	8.5	1.1
Poland	2.80	8.6	1
Remaining Countries	45.10	3	23.7
World Total	**41.70**	**4.7**	**100**

Note: The 2008 emission numbers from which the table has been created are not actual published emission numbers, but are instead, preliminary estimates made by CDIAC using some extrapolation methods. The population data used for per-capita calculations is taken from US Census Bureau's International Data Base (IDB).

Source: http://en.wikipedia.org/w/index.php?title=Carbon_credit

(*b*) **Increase in Sea Level:** When the Earth warms, the oceans will warm and expand causing an increase in the level of the sea. This process is thought to be responsible for about a quarter of the sea level rise recorded during the 20th Century. The melting of ice sheets in

Greenland and Antarctica could be another major cause. Current predictions suggest that the sea level may rise by half a metre in the next 100 years. Higher sea levels will threaten the low-lying coastal areas of the world, such as the Netherlands and Bangladesh. Many important fisheries would become threatened and coastal ecosystems would be damaged. Droughts in countries that currently experience them may become more severe. Brazil, South East Asia, China and parts of Africa are likely to be affected the most and many people could suffer from hunger. Low-lying agricultural land is at risk from rising sea levels. South East Asia would be badly affected as most farming takes place on low-lying deltas.

The ecosystems most at risk from global warming include:

- Tropical forests
- Coral reefs
- Deserts
- Polar (ice) regions
- Coastal marshes
- Mountains
- Low lying land

Global warming will increase the risk of forest fires as soils and plants will become drier. Changes in pest populations may also place stress on forests. This rapid change in temperature would be harmful to many ecosystems, and many species of plants and animals. Global warming will lead to lower water levels in lakes and rivers since water evaporation may increase by a greater amount than rainfall. Other expected effects include some adverse health effects from changes in the range of climate-dependent disease vectors, particularly resulting in increases in the prevalence of malaria and dengu fever.

In order to understand the effects of all the gases together, scientists tend to talk about all greenhouse gases in terms of the equivalent amount of CO_2. Since 1990, yearly emissions have gone up by about 6 billion metric tones of "carbon dioxide equivalent" worldwide, more than a 20 per cent increase.

According to the IPCC report on the aggregate net economic costs of damages from climate change globally, in 2005, the average social cost of carbon, from 100 peer reviewed estimates, was US$12 per tonne of CO_2, but the range was from \$3 to \$95/tCO_2.

Sir Nicholas Stern, in his report on potential economic impacts suggests that extreme weather might reduce global gross domestic product by up to one per cent and that in a worst-case scenario, global per capita consumption could fall by the equivalent of 20 per cent.

Mitigation of Global Warming

Mitigation of global warming may be accomplished through reductions in the rate of anthropogenic greenhouse gas release. Kyoto Protocol is the world's primary international agreement on reducing greenhouse gas emissions. Kyoto Protocol is an amendment to the United Nations Framework Convention on Climate Change (UNFCCC) negotiated in 1997.

Kyoto Protocol

The Kyoto Protocol set binding targets for 37 industrialized countries and the European community for reducing greenhouse gas (GHG) emissions, amounting to an average of five per cent against 1990 levels, over the five-year period 2008-2012. The Kyoto Protocol was adopted in Kyoto, Japan, on 11th December 1997 and entered into force on 16th February 2005. 184 Parties of the Convention have ratified its Protocol to date. As of June 2009, only the United States, historically the world's largest emitter of greenhouse gases, is yet to ratify the treaty. The treaty expires in 2012. The Kyoto Protocol offers three market based mechanisms to meet the target. These are:

(*i*) Emission Trading

(*ii*) Clean Development Mechanism (CDM)

(*iii*) Joint Implementation

(*i*) **Emission Trading:** Emissions trading, as set out in Article 17 of the Kyoto Protocol, allows countries to sell their surplus emissions (emissions permitted by them but not "used") to countries that are over their targets. Thus, a new commodity is created in the form of emission reductions or removals. Since carbon dioxide is the principal greenhouse gas, trading in carbon is very popular. Carbon is now tracked and traded like any other commodity, thus creating a "carbon market".

Under the Protocol's emission trading scheme, all surplus emissions (emissions permitted but not "used") can be traded and sold. Under the scheme, the other units which may be transferred, each equal to one tonne of CO_2, may be in the form of:

- A removal unit **(RMU)** on the basis of land use, land use change, and forestry activities such as reforestation.
- An emission reduction unit **(ERU)** generated by a joint implementation project.
- A certified emission reduction **(CER)** generated from a Clean Development Mechanism project activity.

(*ii*) **Clean Development Mechanism:** The Clean Development Mechanism (CDM) allows a country with an emission-reduction or emission-limitation commitment under the Kyoto Protocol (Annexure B Party) to implement an emission reduction project in developing countries. Such projects can earn saleable certified emission reduction (CER) credits, each equivalent to one tonne of CO_2, which can be counted towards meeting Kyoto targets. A CDM project activity might involve, for example, a rural electrification project, using solar panels or the installation of more energy-efficient boilers. The mechanism gives industrialized countries, some flexibility in how they meet their emission reduction or limitation targets. The Protocol stipulates that a CDM project must provide emission reductions that are additional to what would otherwise have occurred. Operational since the beginning of 2006, the CDM has already registered more than 1,650 projects and it is anticipated to produce CERs amounting to more than 2.9 billion tonnes of CO_2 equivalent in the first commitment period of the Kyoto Protocol, 2008–2012.

(*iii*) **Joint Implementation:** JI allows a country with an emission reduction or limitation commitment under the Kyoto Protocol (Annex B Party) to earn emission reduction units (ERUs) from an emission-reduction or emission removal project in another Annex B Party, each equivalent to one tonne of CO_2, which can be counted towards meeting its Kyoto target. Joint implementation offers Parties a flexible and cost-efficient means of fulfilling a part of their Kyoto commitments, while the host Party benefits from foreign investment and technology transfer. The eligibility for approval for JI was that the project must provide a reduction in emissions by sources, or an enhancement of removals by sinks, that is, additional to what would otherwise have occurred.

Copenhagen Accord

International talks began in May 2007 on a future treaty to succeed the Kyoto Protocol. The United Nations Climate Change Conference, popularly known as the Copenhagen Summit, was held in Copenhagen, Denmark, between 7th December and 18th December 2009, to agree on a framework for climate change mitigation. A framework for climate change mitigation beyond 2012 was to be agreed there. No binding agreement was reached.The Copenhagen Accord was drafted by the US, China, India, Brazil and South Africa on December 18th 2009. The Copenhagen Accord asks countries to submit emission targets by the end of January 2010, and paves the way for further discussions to occur at the 2010 UN Climate Change Conference to be held in Mexico and the mid-year session in Bonn.

2.7 AIR POLLUTION INDUSTRIAL ACCIDENTS

Besides these impacts of air pollution, there are also critical air pollution episodes from industrial accidents, such as the leak of methyl isocyanide from the Union Carbide factory at Bhopal, in India (Box 2.6).

Control of Air Pollution

There are four measures to control air pollution:

(*a*) **Containment** is preventing the emission of toxic substances into the atmosphere. This is achieved by the use of equipments, such as electrostatic precipitators (ESP) and scrubbers.

(*b*) **Replacement** is the change in the production process—from a dirty process to a clean process. This may be a change in the raw material/input used, such as a change to lead-free petrol.

(*c*) **Dilution** is achieved by improving the self-cleansing potential of the environment. This is achieved through an increase in forest coverage.

(*d*) **Legislation** refers to the framing of rules and regulations that specify ambient and emission standards for industries to comply with and also specify the penalties for non-compliance. This method is called as command and control measure. Almost all the countries of the world have a good framework of rules and regulations for the control of air pollution.

BOX 2.6

Bhopal Gas Tragedy

The **Bhopal disaster** or **Bhopal gas tragedy** is the largest chemical industrial disaster in the world and took place in the Indian city of Bhopal, Madhya Pradesh. At midnight on 3rd December 1984, the Union Carbide Plant at Bhopal, India, accidentally released methyl isocyanate (MIC) gas, exposing more than 500,000 people to MIC and other chemicals. More than 2,000 died during the first weeks.and more than 100,000 persons suffered permanent injuries.

The Union Carbide India Limited (UCIL) factory was established in 1969 near Bhopal. 51 per cent was owned by Union Carbide Corporation (UCC) and 49 per cent by Indian authorities. It produced the pesticide, carbaryl (trademark Sevin). In 1979 a methyl isocyanate (MIC) production plant was added to the site to replace the more expensive, less hazardous materials in use by MIC, an intermediate in the manufacture of the insecticide, carbaryl.

The accident occured when a tank containing methyl isocyanate (MIC) leaked. MIC is an extremely reactive chemical and the accident took place because water entered the tank where about 40 cubic meters of MIC was stored which started an exothermic chemical reaction producing a lot of heat. This increased the pressure inside the tank leading to the burst of the safely valve of the tank. This burst was so violent that the coating of concrete around the tank also broke. The explosion released between 20 and 30 tonnes of MIC during the hour that the leak took place. The gas leaked from a 30 m high chimney and this height was not sufficient to reduce the effects of the discharge. The high moisture content (aerosol) in the discharge when evaporating, gave rise to a heavy gas which rapidly sank to the ground. The weather accentuated the whole process on the fateful day. The weak wind and the weak vertical turbulence caused a slow dilution of gas and thus allowed the poisonous gas to spread over considerable distances.

Many experts in industrial safety, believe that the tragedy was preventable, arguing that it was due to "...the negligence on the part of the Union Carbide Corporation and its corporate subsidiary, Union Carbide of India Ltd.(UCIL), which had the responsibility for taking care of the day-to-day operations of the facility".

The deficiencies in the Bhopal plant design can be summarized as follows:

- Location close to a densely populated area.
- Choosing a dangerous method of manufacturing pesticides.
- The use of hazardous chemicals (MIC) instead of less dangerous ones.
- Large-scale storage of MIC prior to selling.
- Possible corroding material in pipelines.
- Poor maintenance after the plant ceased production in the early 1980s.
- Failure of several safety systems, due to poor maintenance and regulations.

Eckerman Engrid (2001) Chemical Industry and Public Health—Bhopal as an example, Nordic School of Public Health.

Source: http://www.hu.mtu.edu/hu_dept/tc@mtu/papers/bhopal.htm
http://www.icmrindia.org/casestudies/catalogue/Business%20Ethics/BECG009.htm
http://en.wikipedia.org/wiki/Bhopal_disaster

2.8 WATER POLLUTION

Water pollution is the change in the physical, chemical and biological quality of water, caused by anthropogenic activities that are detrimental to the existing, intended and potential uses of water. It is the contamination of water by undesirable foreign matter that adversely affects the water in the oceans, surface water and underground water.

Water is a basic requirement for mankind. Geographically, 70 per cent of the earth is made up of water and the rest is made up of land. But it is about 0.007 per cent of total available water that is potable water. Yet water is being misused, posing challenges to future availability, in both qualitative and quantitative sense. To refine a ton of sugar, 4,000 litres of really pure water are required. Water required to manufacture a tonne of paper is 300,000 litres, while for generating one kilowatt of electricity in a thermal plant, about 3,500 litres are needed. A ton of steel needs 240,000 litres of water. The water requirement of agriculture far exceeds that of industrial needs. For growing a ton of cotton, 8 million litres of water are needed while a ton of sugar crop consumes nearly a million litres of water. Further, water used in agriculture cannot be reused as is often possible in industry. Thus, the adverse impact on water from anthropogenic use (and abuse) is becoming a very crucial factor to be considered for future policy options in the area of water management.

Any body of water has a self-cleansing potential – a capacity to absorb or break down wastes; these are broken down naturally by microorganisms into forms in which they are useful to aquatic life. But if the wastes discharged into water bodies exceed its self-cleansing capacity to dissolve, disperse or recycle all additional substances, water becomes polluted.

The principal sources of water pollution are sewage, industrial waste, garbage and refuse, and fertilizers, pesticides and herbicides used in agriculture. Water pollution includes substances that accumulate in oceans, lakes, streams, and ground water, that are either directly harmful to life or that have harmful secondary or long term effects.

Water Pollutants

Water pollutants may be classified as organic and inorganic pollutants.

Organic pollutants are easily decomposable pollutants and include:

- Detergents and disinfectants
- Insecticides and herbicides
- Bacteria from livestock operations
- Food processing wastes
- Tree debris from logging operations
- Volatile Organic Compounds, such as solvents and hydrocarbons
- Dense non-aqueous phase liquids (DNAPLs), such as chlorinated solvents
- Detergents and chemical compounds found in cosmetics products.

Inorganic pollutants include:

- Ammonia from food processing wastes
- Heavy metals
- Acidity caused by industrial discharges such as sulphur dioxide by power plants

- Chemical waste
- Fertilizers from agricultural use
- Silt from construction sites, logging, slash and burn operations.

Eutrophication

The enrichment of water with inorganic nutrients, like nitrates and phosphates, is called eutrophication. Pollutants like sewage, organic wastes and fertilizers contain nitrates and phosphates. These inorganic nutrients enrich the water by promoting the growth of algae. Growth of algae increases the presence of decomposers, which along with algal growth and other plants, depletes the oxygen content of the water, resulting in eutrophication.

Measures of Water Pollution

The extent of pollution in a water body is measured commonly in terms of:

(*i*) Dissolved Oxygen (DO), (*ii*) Biochemical Oxygen Demand (BOD), (*iii*) Chemical Oxygen Demand (COD), and (*iv*) Total Suspended Solids (TSS).

(*i*) **Dissolved oxygen (DO)** is measured in milligrams per litre (mg/l) or parts per million (ppm).

(*ii*) **Biochemical Oxygen Demand (BOD)** is a measure of the amount of oxygen that bacteria will consume while decomposing organic matter under aerobic conditions. Biochemical oxygen demand is determined by incubating a sealed sample of water for five days and measuring the loss of oxygen from the beginning to the end of the test.

(*iii*) **Chemical Oxygen Demand (COD)** is a measure of the capacity of water to consume oxygen during the decomposition of organic matter and the oxidation of inorganic chemicals, such as ammonia and nitrite. COD values are always greater than BOD values, but COD measurements can be made in a few hours, while BOD measurements take five days.

(*iv*) **Total Suspended Solids (TSS)** gives a measure of the turbidity of water. TSS are solid materials, both organic and inorganic, that are suspended in the water. These would include silt, plankton and industrial wastes.

Effects of Water Pollution

Notable effects of water pollution include the effects on human health. Nitrates in drinking water affect the red blood cells of infants, which sometimes results in death. Cadmium, in sludge-derived fertilizer, absorbed by crops and ingested in sufficient amounts, causes acute diarrhea and liver and kidney damage.

The hazardous nature of mercury, arsenic, and lead, on human health has been well documented. The Minamata tragedy is an example of the impact of mercury poisoning on human health and on other animals and marine organisms (Box 2.7).

When toxins enter the water, the toxins travel from the water which the animals drink and pass on to humans, when the animals' meat is eaten. Pollutants in the water will alter the overall chemistry of the water, causing changes in acidity, temperature and conductivity. Altered water temperatures (due to human actions) can kill the marine life and affect the delicate ecological balance in water bodies, especially lakes and rivers. These factors affect the marine life. Further, marine food sources are contaminated or eliminated by water pollution. Pollution caused by oil spills and pesticide run-offs from agriculture cause serious havoc on fish and other aquatic organisms in seas and rivers. Oil spill is an ever present threat to surface waters and to marine life. Several major oil spills have occurred resulting in severe damage to marine life and heavy clean up costs to the governments. The grounding and breaking up of the Torry Canyon in 1967 along the English shore and the Amaco Cadiz on March 17, 1978 on the French coastline are examples of extensive marine pollution by oil spills.

Table 2.4 Sources and Effects of Select Water Pollutants

Pollutant	Source/Cause	Effect
Sewage that includes domestic wastes, hospital wastes, excreta, etc.	Sewerage of rural and urban areas	Oxygen depletion, spread of diseases/epidemics
Metals, Mercury	Industrial wastes	(Minamata Tragedy) Numbness of limbs, lips and tongue, blurred vision, deafness and mental derangement.
Lead	Industrial wastes	Absorbed into blood and affects liver, kidney, bone, brain and the peripheral nervous system. Lead poisoning can even lead to coma.
Cadmium	Cadmium industries, fertilizers	Deposited in organs like the kidney, pancreas, liver, intestinal mucosa, etc. Cadmium poisoning causes headache, vomiting, bronchial pneumonia, kidney necrosis, etc.
Arsenic	Fertilizers	Arsenic poisoning causes renal failure and death. It can cause nervous disorder, kidney and liver disorders, muscular atrophy, etc.
Agrochemicals like DDT	Pesticides	Accumulates in the bodies of fishes, birds, mammals, including man. Adversely affects the nervous system, fertility. Causes thinning of egg shells in birds.

Source: http://www.tutorvista.com/content/biology/biology-ii/environment-and-environmental- problems/water-pollution.php

Control of Water Pollution

The policy for controlling water pollution makes a distinction between point sources of pollution and non-point sources of pollution. The common characteristic of **point source discharges** is that they are identifiable and can be monitored. Point sources of pollution occur when harmful substances are emitted directly into a body of water. The Exxon Valdez oil spill best illustrates point source water pollution. Effluents discharged from factories, also belong to this category. The point sources of pollution entering the water environment are controlled using two methods:

End-of-pipe method controls only what is released from a discharge point, with little or no control of the processes which produce the effluents. **Process control**, on the other hand, starts at the beginning of the process and accomplishes minimization of the effluent by promoting the use of Best Available Technology (BAT) in order to minimize the impact on the environment from the process as a whole.

BOX 2.7

Minamata Tragedy

Minamata is a city located in Kumamoto Prefecture, Japan. It is on the west coast of Kyushu. In 1907, the Chisso Corporation built a factory in the small fishing village of Minamata, Japan, along the shore of the Minamata Bay. Fish populations began to decline in 1925. By 1950, fish began to float on the surface; shellfish and other aquatic organisms began to perish. Cats were the first land animals to show signs of distress. In 1952, they began having convulsions, whirling in violent circles, slobbering, becoming disoriented and throwing themselves into the sea. By 1953, dogs, pigs, birds and other animals started exhibiting the same strange behaviour. By 1958, virtually no cat was to be found in Minamata. Mercury affected human beings too. The victims had common symptoms, such as severe convulsions, intermittent loss of consciousness, repeated lapses into crazed mental states, and then finally, permanent coma. Then, after the onset of a very high fever, they would die.

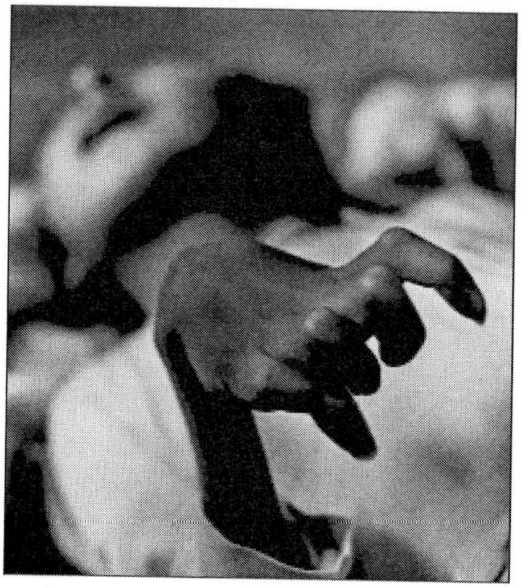

Beginning in the 1930's, the Chisso Corporation began dumping mercury into the waters and continued to dump throughout most of the 1960's. Chisso denied all allegations as long as they possibly could. The poisoning became known as Minamata disease and its victims took the Chisso Corporation to court to sue for damages. It wasn't until March 20, 1973 that the victims triumphed and won their case. As of 1992, the number of people, officially diagnosed as having Minamata disease totalled 2,252 people; 1,043 were dead and another 12,127 people were waiting to be tested.

Efforts were made to restore the bay; in 1974, a three-mile long net was placed around the bay to contain the contaminated fish. After 53 years of being considered as deadly waters, in 1998 the bay was declared safe again. Chisso finally took responsibility and have made their final payments.

However, in recent decades, Minamata is trying to overcome the blemishes of its past and has established itself as an exemplary environmental model city of the world. As part of the program, the local people have promised to adhere to the following instructions:

- To transfer the lessons learned from Minamata disease down to the next generation.
- To provide relief measures for victims of Minamata disease and reconciliation among the victims and local residents.
- Encouraging changes in industrial activities to protect people and all living things in the ecosystem.
- To protect the fundamental elements of life, like the sea, rivers, and mountains, and handing them down in proper condition to the coming generations.
- Reviewing the structure of modern civilization and proposing new social systems based on the thrifty use of our limited natural resources.

Source: http://members.tripod.com/~Sandra_Justus/MercuryPoisoningReport.html
http://www1.american.edu/TED/MINAMATA.HTM
http://www.mapsofworld.com/japan/japanese-cities/minamata.html

Non-point sources deliver pollutants indirectly through environmental changes. An example of this type of water pollution is when fertilizer from a field is carried into a stream by rain, in the form of run-off which in turn affects aquatic life. Even though non-point source of water pollution arises mainly from agriculture, effluents from urban road run-off that contaminate land and effluents from storm sewage overflows are also defined as non-point sources of water pollution.

Control of water pollution involves essentially, the following measures:

(*i*) Efficient effluent treatment plant for industries and sewage treatment plants to treat domestic sewage, based on one of the following suitable methods:

- Reverse osmosis
- Ion exchange
- Electro dialysis
- Chemical coagulation

(*ii*) Recycling waste water for reuse in industries.

(*iii*) More than the technological measures, an effective water pollution policy should be in place which prudently combines regulations and rules for water quality standards and discharge standards with polluter pays principle.

(*iv*) Public awareness.

2.9 POLLUTION OF THE RIVER GANGA AND THE GANGA ACTION PLAN

The Ganga river basin is the largest among the river basins in India and the fourth largest in the world. It has a total length of 2,525 kms, out of which 1,425 kms is in Uttaranchal and UP, 475 kms is in Bihar, and 625 kms is in West Bengal. Around half a billion people live within the river basin, at an average density of over 500 per sq km, and this population is projected to increase to over one billion people by the year 2030. The Ganga drains 9 states of India. Today, the river supports 29 Class I cities, 23 Class II cities and 48 towns, plus thousands of villages. Although valued for her absolute purity, the river has become a site for an environmental catastrophe in the last hundred years. Nearly all the sewage, industrial effluent, runoff from chemical fertilizers and pesticides used in agriculture within the basin, and large quantities of solid waste, including thousands of animals' carcasses and hundreds of human corpses are dumped into the river everyday.

The Ganges has long been known to decompose organic waste at an accelerated rate. Despite the heavy burden of pollutants, the Ganges has been regarded as incorruptible. Several foreigners have recorded the effects of this river's "magical" cleansing properties:

(*i*) Ganges water does not putrefy, even after long periods of storage.

(*ii*) British physician, C.E. Nelson, observed that the Ganga water taken from the Hooghly - one of its dirtiest mouths—by ships returning to England, remained fresh throughout the voyage.

(*iii*) In 1896, the British physician, E. Hanbury Hankin, reported in a French journal, that cholera microbes died within three hours in Ganga water, but continued to thrive in distilled water, even after 48 hours.

(*iv*) A French scientist, Monsieur Herelle, was amazed to find "that only a few feet below the bodies of persons floating in the Ganga, who had died of dysentery and cholera, where one would expect to find millions of germs, there were no germs at all."

(*v*) An Indian environmental engineer, D.S. Bhargava, at the end of an exhaustive three year study of the Ganga, reported that the River Ganga is able to reduce BOD levels much faster than other rivers and is able to clean up suspended wastes, 15 to 20 times faster than other rivers.

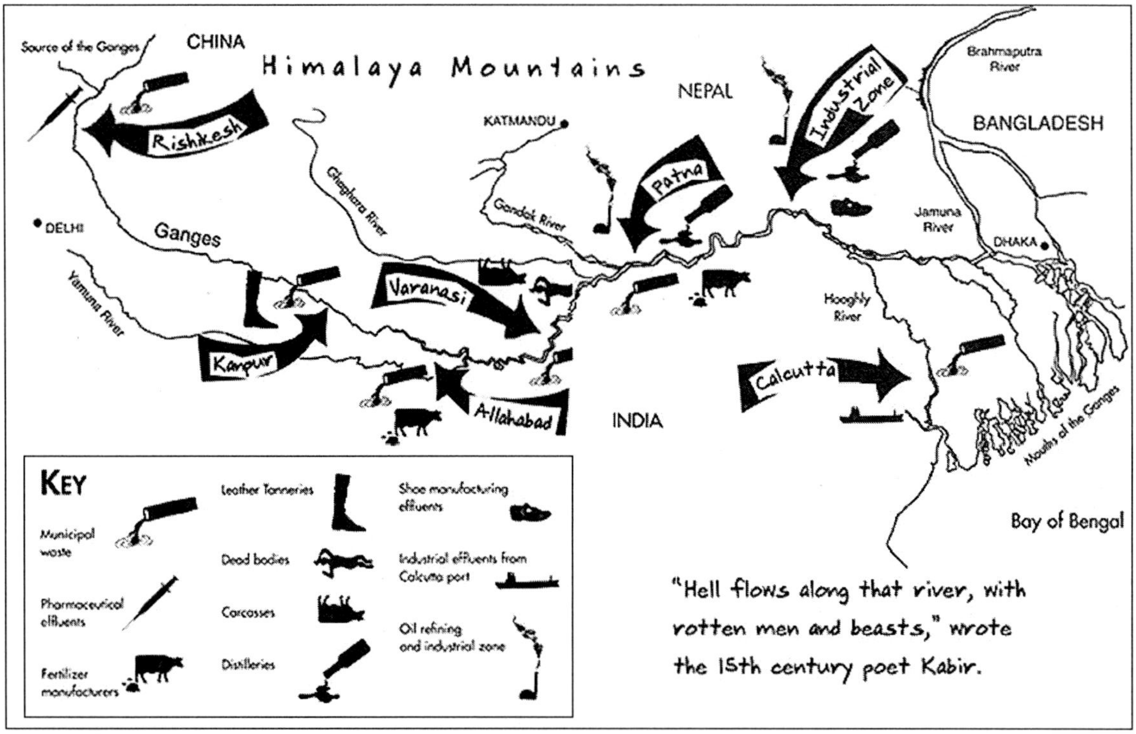

Source: http://reli350.vassar.edu/gosselin/dilemma.html

Fig. 2.3 Contamination of the Ganges

Nearly 80 per cent of the total waste dumped into the Ganges is caused by organic wastes, consisting of municipal sewage, trash, food, and human and animal remains. The inevitable result of this assault on the river's assimilating capacity has been an erosion of river water quality. Large stretches (over 600 km) of the river were virtually dead from an ecological point of view. By the 1990s, indigenous marine life in the Ganga was threatened with extinction. The catch of *hilsa*, a species of Indian salmon, was dramatically reduced. Today, the river poses a considerable public health threat to the people who use the river daily. Most of the fish population that remains contains toxic levels of zinc and lead. In 1996, the WorldWatch Institute reported that, every minute, one person dies of diarrhea in the [Gangetic] region, and that eight of every 10 people suffer from amoebic dysentery each year. Another report in 1998 in 'The New Yorker' claimed that these water-related illnesses account for the death of more than two million Indian children each year. The fast shrinking glaciers, dams, barrages, canals and alarmingly high volume of pollution are posing an increasingly serious threat to the health and life of the river.

The Ganga Action Plan

The Ganga Action Plan (GAP) launched in 1986, by the Government of India has not achieved any success despite an expenditure of approximately 2,000 crore rupees. GAP attempted to solve the problem by installing dozens of sewage treatment facilities along the Ganga, as well as forcing corporations to police themselves with the threat of fines and litigation. Research teams were assigned the task of monitoring coliform counts and BOD levels. The first phase of GAP did not show any evidence of its efficacy in cleaning up the river. In fact, there are reports that the amount of sewage and pollutants has doubled since the institution of GAP policies. GAP I was extended as GAP II, from 1993 onwards, covering 4 major tributaries of the Ganga, namely, Yamuna, Gomti, Damodar and Mahananda. The program was further broadened in 1995, with the inclusion of other rivers and renamed as the National River Conservation Plan (NRCP). Even though the government claims that the schemes under the Ganga Action Plan have been successful, many research articles have reported the failure of the GAP. According to an official report released in 2009, only 39 per cent of the primary target of the Ganga Action Plan has been met so far. One important reason for the failure of the GAP, according to the local population is the failure of the government to involve the immediate community; those who are intimately connected with the Ganga were never included in the planning.

Rakesh K Jaiswal (2007) in his article "Ganga Action Plan – A Critical Analysis" observes, "GAP has been dubbed variously as Ganga Inaction Plan, Pumps and Pipes scheme, a Colossal Failure...Media report that there are GAPING HOLES in GAP and it is a shocking tale of official apathy and corruption . . . All the money has gone down the drain, people are quick to offer their opinion of why GAP has been doomed to failure. Mismanagement, corruption, and incompetence, all rank high on the list of accusations".

In February 2009, it was decided to take up the cleaning of the River Ganga on a mission mode. Mission Clean Ganga ensures that by 2020, no untreated municipal sewage and industrial effluents flow into the Ganga. It is estimated that an investment of Rs 15,000 crores over the next 10 years will be required to create the necessary treatment and sewerage infrastructure. The costs will be borne both by the Centre and the state. The World Bank has offered a loan of $1 billion for the mission. The Centre will bear all the operation and maintenance cost of existing sewage treatment plants for the next five years. A sum of Rs 1,300 crores has been allocated to this end.

The task to clean the river Ganga is Himalayan in nature and requires sustained cooperative work from government, industries and civil society alike. Rakesh K Jaiswal laments: "It took hundreds of years of penance by Sage Bhagirath to bring the celestial river to earth and it would not be an exaggeration to say that today, Ganga requires many Bhagiraths to survive and reclaim its sacred nature".

2.10 LAND POLLUTION – POLLUTION BY SOLID WASTES

Land pollution is the pollution of the earth's natural land surfaces, by industrial, agricultural, domestic and commercial activities of human beings.

Land pollution refers to the deposition of solid wastes on land - *e.g.,* used cans, bottles, plastic containers, paper — that cannot be broken down quickly or, in some instances, cannot be broken down at all by the action of organic or inorganic forces. It is the pollution of the Earth's natural land surface by industrial, commercial, domestic and agricultural activities. Solid wastes may be classified as:

Putrescible or Decomposable Wastes, such as wastes from slaughter houses, market refuse, canning and other food processing industries.

Non-Putrescible or non-decomposable wastes, such as paper, wood, cloth, leather and rubber, which are combustible, and glass, metals and stones which are non-combustible.

Table 2.5 gives the sources of solid wastes and their details.

Causes of Land Pollution

The various causes of land pollution are:

(*i*) Increase in population and increase in urbanization.

(*ii*) The "use and throw" and "not in my backyard" (NIMBY) attitude/lifestyle of people.

(*iii*) Usc of more non-durable products or products without spare parts, which end up as garbage.

(*iv*) The disposal on land, of non-biodegradable wastes, including containers, bottles and cans made of plastic, used cars and electronic goods.

(*v*) Agricultural wastes, including the waste matters produced by crop, animal manure and residues of the farm land are one of the major causes of land pollution. The pesticides and fertilizers used by farmers to increase the crop yield, leaches into the nearby land areas and pollutes them.

(*vi*) The process of mining leads to the formation of piles of coal and slag. When these wastes are not disposed off through the proper channel, they accumulate and contaminate the land.

(*vii*) Dumping of toxic materials such as chemicals and paints without proper precaution by industries.

(*viii*) Improper treatment of sewage leads to the accumulation of solids, such as biomass sludge. These solid wastes overflow through the sewage, making the entire area look dirty.

(*ix*) Burning of solid waste leads to the formation of ashes, which is yet another cause of land pollution.

(*x*) Garbage dumped by people which usually consists of leftover food, fruit and vegetable peels and other non-decomposable solid materials, such as glass, cloth, plastic, wood, paper etc.

Table 2.5 Sources of Solid Wastes

Source	Details
Agriculture	• Accumulation of animal manures. • Excessive input of chemical fertilizers. • Illicit dumping of tainted crops on land.
Mining and Quarrying	• Using of explosives to blow up mines. • Using of machinery which emits toxic byproducts and leaks to the ground.
Sewage sludge Dredged spoils	• Improper sanitation system causes sludge to leak on surrounding soil. • Improper method of dredging on fertile land causes soil infertility, leaving The soil more prone to external pollution.
Household	• Improper waste disposal system causes waste accumulation. • Improper sanitation system.
Demolition and construction	• Non-biodegradable rubble or debris which are not cleared, settle in the Soil and undergo chemical reactions and increase soil toxicity.
Industrial	• Poisonous/Toxic emissions of gases which are not filtered or neutralized.

Source: http://library.thinkquest.org/C0111040/Popups/pop_table_land1.htm

Effects of Land Pollution

(*i*) Damage to wildlife, plants, and humans in a number of ways.

(*ii*) Affects respiratory system.

(*iii*) Skin problems.

(*iv*) Birth defects.

(*v*) Adversely affects the aesthetic beauty of the place.

Methods to Prevent Land Pollution – Solid Waste Management

Solid wastes management is a very complex process, beset with difficulties at each stage. The three stages in solid waste management are:

(*a*) Collection

(*b*) Transporting the wastes

(*c*) Disposal of the wastes

Storing the wastes before transporting, transporting them without spilling them on the way, non-availability of vehicles fitted with extra facilities for loading and unloading the wastes, are some of the challenges faced during the collection and transportation stage. The main methods of disposal in use now are dumping in landfills, dumping in oceans, and incineration.

A relatively recent idea in solid waste management has been to treat the waste material as a resource to be exploited. This is possible by adopting the three **R's—Reduce, Reuse and Recycle. Reduce** refers to the reduction of wastes. This is achieved through source reduction, as well as through extended producer responsibility.

Source reduction involves efforts to reduce hazardous waste and other materials by modifying industrial production. Source reduction methods involve changes in manufacturing technology, raw material inputs, and product formulation.

Extended Producer Responsibility (EPR) is the practice of holding the producer of a product responsible for the management of the wastes associated with that product. The producer is responsible for recovering products that contain toxic and hazardous constituents which may present a threat to the safety of the community. This places a burden on the end-of-life management of the product. Extended responsibility gives incentives to the producer to minimize wastes that would arise from both production and consumption of the product and to reuse the wastes. This concept has arisen in recent years due to the belief that an industry's responsibility for a product should not end with the sale of that product, but should extend to its reuse and/or disposal.

Recycling is reusing a material that would otherwise be considered waste. Recycling is a common practice today in almost all countries. It helps firms to reduce their costs and benefits the society by reducing the generation of wastes.

2.11 POLLUTION BY HAZARDOUS WASTES

Hazardous wastes include all those wastes/substances that pose substantial threat or potential threat to public health or environment; hazardous wastes generally exhibit one or more of the harmful characteristics such as, being corrosive, reactive, explosive, oxidizing, irritant and carcinogenic.

A hazardous waste is a special type of waste because it cannot be disposed off by common means, like other by-products of our everyday lives. Hazardous waste is a waste with properties that make it potentially dangerous or harmful to human health or the environment. Hazardous wastes can be liquids, solids, or in gaseous form. They can be the by-products of manufacturing processes, discarded used materials, or discarded unused commercial products, such as cleaning fluids (solvents) or pesticides.

Hazardous wastes are not peculiar to industries alone. Households contribute to the generation of hazardous wastes. Hazardous wastes from households are:

(*i*) Paints and solvents
(*ii*) Automotive wastes (used motor oil)
(*iii*) Pesticides
(*iv*) Mercury containing wastes (thermometers, fluorescent lighting etc.)
(*v*) Electronics (computers, television, mobile phones)
(*vi*) Aerosols/Propane cylinders
(*vii*) Caustics/Cleaning agents
(*viii*) Refrigerant containing appliances
(*ix*) Some speciality batteries (*e.g.*, lithium, nickel cadmium, or button cell batteries).

Control of Hazardous Wastes

Like non-hazardous wastes, disposal of hazardous wastes are through landfills, incineration and pyrolisis, with extra care to reduce any likely impact that may arise due to the hazardous nature of the wastes. Thanks to technology, controlled recycling of hazardous wastes is also possible. Examples include lead-acid batteries or electronic circuit boards, where the heavy metals can be recovered and used in new products. Similarly, ash generated by coal-fired power plants could be treated and used for pavement filling. Some hazardous wastes can be processed and the hazardous component of the waste can be eliminated, making it a non-hazardous waste. For example, a corrosive acid is neutralized with an alkaline substance and corrosiveness is removed.

Basel Convention

The Basel Convention of 1989 was in response to a series of incidents involving dumping of hazardous wastes in developing countries in Africa and Asia. The increase in the generation of hazardous wastes and the resistance from people in the home country to dump it in their backyards, coupled with the increasingly stringent government laws on generation and disposal of hazardous wastes, made the waste generating industries in the developed and industrialized nations look for cheaper alternatives to dispose off these wastes. Exporting wastes to developing nations, particularly to African and Asian countries, was found to be an easy solution due to the following reasons:

(*a*) Due to poverty and high debt, these nations (particularly, the African countries) saw import of the wastes as a source of foreign exchange. For example, Guinea Bissau, one of the poorest 20 countries in the world, was to be paid $600 million for storing and disposing of imported hazardous waste. At the time of the offer, the amount was twice the country's foreign debt, and about four times its Gross National Product. (Ibitayo, Olurominiyi, 2008).

(*b*) Lack of stringency of environmental regulations for disposal of hazardous wastes in these developing nations and poor nations made them an attractive disposal site for the wastes of the industrialized nations.

(*c*) The high level of corruption in the developing countries made it possible to promote easily, the trade in hazardous wastes.

(*d*) The lack of technical expertise on the part of these destination countries enabled waste exporting countries to disguise the hazardous wastes as useful commodities. Within this context, the wastes are often shipped or labelled as recyclables, liquid fertilizers, road construction or brick-making materials.

However, two incidents of dumping of toxic wastes backfired in 1988. The dumping of more than 15,000 tonnes of incinerator ash from the city of Philadelphia, U.S. on Kassa Island in Guinea by a Norwegian company named Bulkhandling, and the dumping of 8,000 drums of hazardous waste, including the highly toxic PCBs, that were stored on the property of a Nigerian citizen, in Koko (a small delta port) by an Italian businessman, for which the Nigerian was reportedly paid $100 per month. In both the cases, the waste was ordered to be taken back to the source country. Yet another incident which led to the creation of the Basel Convention is the Khian Sea waste disposal incident, in which a ship carrying incinerator ash from the city of Philadelphia in the United States, after having dumped half of its load on a beach in Haiti, was forced away where it sailed for many months, changing its name several times. Unable to unload the cargo in any port, the crew was believed to have dumped much of it at sea.

BOX 2.8

Basel Convention

The Basel Convention on the Control of Transboundary Movements of Hazardous Wastes and their Disposal is the most comprehensive global environmental agreement on hazardous and other wastes. The Convention has 172 Parties and aims to protect human health and the environment against the adverse effects resulting from the generation, management, transboundary movements and disposal of hazardous and other wastes. The Basel Convention was adopted in 1989. The main objectives of the Basel Convention are:

(i) Reduce transboundary movement of hazardous waste to a minimum.

(ii) Ensure that hazardous wastes are treated and disposed off as close as possible to their source of generation.

(iii) Minimize hazardous waste generation at source.

General obligations of the Basel Convention:

- It is prohibited to export or import hazardous wastes or other wastes to or from a non-party State.
- No wastes may be exported if the State of import has not given its consent in writing to the specific import.
- Information about proposed transboundary movements must be communicated to the States concerned, by means of a notification form, so that they may evaluate the effects of the proposed movements on human health and the environment.
- Transboundary movements of wastes must only be authorised where there is no danger attaching to their movement and disposal.
- Wastes which are to be the subject of a transboundary movement must be packaged, labelled and transported in conformity with international rules, and must be accompanied by a movement document from the point at which the movement commences to the point of disposal.
- Any party may impose additional requirements that are consistent with the provisions of the Convention.

Source: http://europa.eu/legislation_summaries/environment/waste_management/l28043_en.htm http://www.basel.int/

2.12 CONCLUSION

The purpose of this chapter has been to highlight the role of ecosystems, their functions and their influence on the way we live our lives. The various types of pollution resulting from anthropogenic activities hamper the functioning of the ecosystem which in turn impacts human beings. The interrelationship between the various components of the environment and the various ecosytems is very complex. Even the smallest change anywhere in any ecosystem has huge impacts on mankind; this dynamic dependence and interrelationship among the various components of the environment is summarized as "a butterfly flapping its wings in China can create a hurricane in Mexico". It is time we realize our responsibility towards nature for "when we heal the earth, we heal ourselves".

QUESTIONS

1. What is an ecosystem? What are its functions?
2. Make a note on any ecosystem and bring out its significance.
3. Explain the effects of pollution on human health
4. Define pollution. List out the sources of various forms of pollution.
5. What is global warming? How is it caused?
6. Write a note on acid rain and give an example.
7. What are the uses of forests?
8. What are the uses of biodiversity?
9. Account for the loss of biodiversity. Enumerate the measures taken to protect the biodiversity.
10. What is happening to the environment and why?
11. Suggest measures to control pollution.
12. What are the problems of waste management?
13. Give an example of illegal dumping of hazardous waste and discuss the role of the Basel Convention in the management of hazardous wastes.

EXERCISES

1. Identify the extinct and endangered species in India.
2. Do a case study of river water pollution in India.
3. Compare the contribution of various countries to global warming.
4. Prepare a note on the state of carbon emission trading in India and compare it with the rest of the world.
5. Study the state of global forests and biodiversity today.
6. How serious is the issue of climate change today? Prepare a note on the outcome of the Copenhagen summit and India's commitment to the same.
7. Prepare a study an the critical nature of the issue of hazardous wastes through an example.

❑❑❑

3

Environmental Movement

> *Only when the last tree is cut, only when the last river is polluted, only when the last fish is caught, will they realize that you can't eat money.*
>
> **Native American Proverb**

Environment can be protected from man only when man realizes his responsibility towards nature. This realization has been responsible for the increase in the number of environmental groups that fight to preserve the environment. Environmental and ecological movements are among the important examples of the collective actions of several social groups. Environmental movements are "expressions of the universal socio-ecological impacts of a narrowly conceived development based on short term commercial criteria."

The environmental movement is a diverse scientific, social and political movement for addressing environmental issues. Gadgil and Guha (1995) define the environmental movement as "organized social activity consciously directed towards promoting sustainable use of natural resources, halting environmental degradation or bringing about environmental restoration". Environmental networks are "broad networks of people and organizations engaged in collective action in the pursuit of environmental benefits" (Rootes, 1997). Environmental movements are diverse and complex organizational forms, ranging from professional, highly organized groups, like Greenpeace, to highly informal networks, like the Spandana Samaja Seva Samudaya, functioning at Sirsi, Mysore, in India. Environmental movements in less developed nations are oriented around issues of human health, shelter, food security, and survival; while those of the developed world focus on post-materialist issues such as wilderness concerns and animal rights. Environmental movements also differ on the issues they fight for. They range from groups raising campaign funds to save the North American Spotted Owl, to "Green Warriors" engaging in guerrilla conflict in the mountains of the Philippines; to small landholders and indigenous peoples in India who refuse to leave their villages, though threatened by the flood waters of the Narmada River as it rises due to its damming. Environmental movements arise out of reaction and response to local issues, which provoked individuals to form local groups which subsequently became national groups. Some of these national movements have become global today.

Essentially, the environmental movements embark upon three distinct initiatives, which are:

- Creating awareness about the need to preserve/conserve our resources in general, and more specifically, about the environmental issues on hand, through the media.
- Preventing environmentally destructive activities.
- Promoting environmental rehabilitation and restoration by promoting sound natural resource management (*e.g.,* afforestation and soil conservation initiatives).

The causes for the rise of the environmental movement of the developed nations differ from that of the developing and underdeveloped nations. While in the developed nations of the North, the movement focuses on the issue of quality of life, the environmental movements in the South are due to conflicts for the controlling of natural resources, initiated by the marginal population – hill peasants, tribal communities, fishermen and other underprivileged people. The Chipko movement in India (Box 3.1) and the movement to save the Brazilian rain forests (Box 3.2) and the Narmada Bachao movement (Box 3.3) are examples of conflicts initiated by local people dependent on and in control of the resources. Environmental movements in developing countries therefore, are not necessarily for greening the earth or for saving the endangered species, as in the West, but for the very survival of the local poor. Hence, the environmentalism of the North is referred to as "full stomach" environmentalism and the environmentalism of the South is called as "empty-belly" environmentalism (Sharma, 2007).

Concern for the impact of environmental problems on human life is not new. Even as early as the Roman times, instances of environmental degradation are cited in historical works. The commentators of Roman history have attributed the fall of the Roman empire to soil erosion and over exploitation of land. The spread of epidemic diseases in Europe between the late 14th century and the mid 16th century was associated with pollution. The fall of the Sumerian civilization, the 400 year old Mesopotamian civilization and the 7th century Mayan civilization have been attributed to mismanagement of natural resources. However, such concerns did not give rise to public activism. The changes in England in the 18th century due to the industrial revolution no doubt made England the foremost economic power in the world, but brought with it, chaos to the natural environment. William Wordsworth, the English poet, describes the darker side of the industrial revolution as the "outrage done to nature". England was described as a "suburb of hell". Sewage and chemical effluent poured into the Thames from the rivers along its banks. In 1858, the Thames became so smelly that it became known as "The Great Stink". In the early 19th century, the Rhine River, one of Europe's great river systems, which flows down from the Swiss Alps and tracks through eastern France into Germany's Ruhr Valley and the Netherlands, was a byword for pollution. As industrialization spread, the Rhine became a vast sink for pollution. In 1828, a visit to the city of Cologne, prompted Samuel Coleridge to write:

The river Rhine, it is well known
Doth wash your city of Cologne
But tell me, Nymphs, what power divine
Shall henceforth wash the river Rhine?

The environmental movement that exists today arose primarily from concerns in the late 19th century about the protection of the countryside in Europe and the wilderness in the United States and the health consequences of pollution during the industrial revolution. The evolution of the environmental movement to its various manifestations today clearly reveals three distinct phases:

- The period before 1962
- The period from 1962 to the 1980s
- The period from 1980s to the present day.

3.1 EVOLUTION OF THE ENVIRONMENTAL MOVEMENT – BEFORE THE PUBLICATION OF *SILENT SPRING* IN 1962

Chronologically, the beginning of the environmental movement is referred to as the "cult of wilderness". The cult of wilderness did not attack economic growth as such but at the same time fought for the need to preserve nature, based on the deeply held values on nature. The deep ecology movement that developed later is an "activist" expression of the cult of wilderness. The main policy proposal emerging from the first current of environmentalism is the preservation of nature through the creation of nature reserves or natural parks. The earth philosophers, who represented the first current of environmentalism, were George Perkins Marsh, Ralph Waldo Emerson, Henry David Thoreau, John Muir, Gifford Pinchot, and Aldo Leopold. The cult of wilderness was marked mainly by literary works highlighting the importance of preserving nature.

George Perkins Marsh (1801–1882) is considered to be America's first environmentalist. In 1864, he published a remarkable book titled *Man and Nature*, one of the first works to document the effects of human action on the environment. The book helped to launch the modern conservation movement. The book is an inventory of our assault on nature. His ideas and book resulted in the first major environmental conference, "Man's Role in Changing the Face of the Earth", held at Princeton University, in 1956. The book was instrumental in the creation of the Adirondack Park in New York and the United Nations National Forest. Gifford Pinchot, the conservationist, called it "epoch making".

Ralph Waldo Emerson (1803–1882) held that nature existed for us as a form of not only physical nourishment, but also spiritual nourishment. Nature was essential for human spiritual development. In 1836, Ralph Waldo Emerson anonymously published an essay entitled *Nature.* In the essay, he set out his belief that all elements in nature are interrelated and interdependent. Emerson advocated a harmonious integration of nature and human culture for the optimal mental, physical and spiritual humankind.

Henry David Thoreau (1817–1862) a friend of Emerson, was an American naturalist, best known for his book *Walden* (1854), a reflection upon simple living in natural surroundings. Henry David Thoreau expressed one of the central axioms of the modern conservation movement when he wrote, "... in wildness is the preservation of the world". In his work *The Maine Woods*, Thoreau called for the establishment of "national preserves" of old-growth forest. Thoreau inspired much later environmental thinking, including specific ideas about national forest preserves and about the destruction caused by dams. Thoreau wrote, "Each town should have a park, or rather a primitive forest, of 500 or a thousand acres, where a stick should never be cut for fuel, a common possession forever, for instruction and recreation." Henry David Thoreau saw farming and the use of trees for fuel and timber as some of the greatest threats to the environment.

John Muir (1838–1914), the founder of the Sierra Club in 1882, wrote about landscapes, forests and individual species. Muir was of the view that wilderness is a necessity and that mountain peaks and (forest) reservations are useful not only for their timber value but also as fountains of life. John Muir was an ecological patriot, who believed that "nature's object in making animals and plants might possibly be first of all, the happiness of each one of them, not the creation of all for the happiness of one . . ." and added that "the universe would be incomplete without man; but it would also be incomplete without the smallest trans-microscopic creatures that dwell beyond our conceitful eyes and knowledge." Muir's greatest achievement was the creation of the Yosemite Park in California in 1890.

Gifford Pinchot (1865–1946), coined the term conservation ethic as applied to natural resources. Pinchot, was called the "apostle of conservation", since he helped to cast conservation as a moral crusade for environmental management. Pinchot's popularization of the term "conservation of natural resources" revealed his utilitarian approach to nature. He said that the aim of conservation was the greatest good, for the greatest number, for the longest time. Conservationists believed that not utilizing the natural resources was a waste, and advocated wise use of natural resources. Pinchot advocated application of scientific principles to the maintenance and use of forests and rivers for the good of humankind. When it was suggested that the hydroelectric development of Niagara would spoil the river's beauty, the conservationists pointed out that not harnessing the available energy would be a waste. On the issue of the construction of the dam on River Tuolumne as a water reservoir for San Francisco, Pinchot supported the dam saying that it was a wise use of nature for the benefit of mankind. Muir opposed the dam, saying that it would spoil the beauty of the valley and destroy nature. The construction of the dam was ultimately a victory for the conservationists.

Aldo Leopold (1887–1948), is considered to be the father of wildlife ecology. An advocate for the preservation of wildlife and wilderness areas, Leopold became a founder of The Wilderness Society in 1935. It is for his book, *A Sand County Almanac (1949),* that Leopold is best known by millions of people around the globe. *The Almanac*, often acclaimed as the century's literary landmark in conservation, melds exceptional poetic prose with keen observations of the natural world. The book was published in 1949, shortly after Leopold's death. In *The Land Ethic*, a chapter in *A Sand County Almanac*, Leopold delves into conservation in "The Ecological Conscience" section. Leopold wrote: "Conservation is a state of harmony between men and land." One of the well-known quotes from the book which clarifies his Land Ethic is "A thing is right when it tends to preserve the integrity, stability, and beauty of the biotic community. It is wrong when it tends otherwise". Figure 3.1 gives the environmental movement in the period before 1962.

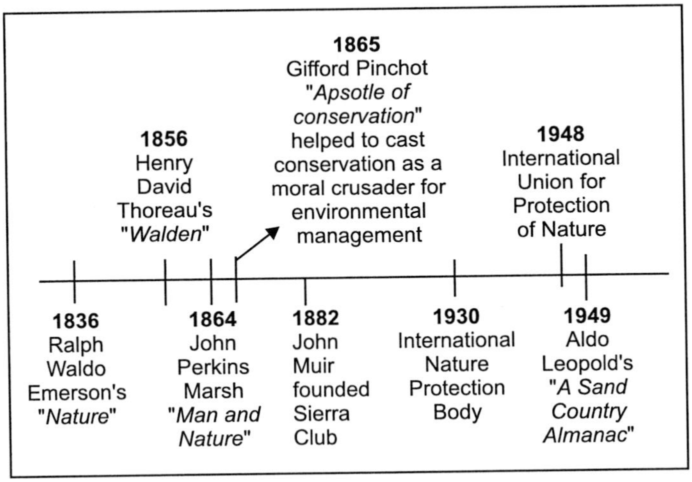

Fig. 3.1 Time Line of the Environmental Movement Before 1962

Thus, the period of the early environmental movement, referred to as the "cult of wilderness", focused on the preservation of nature and protection of flora and fauna, essentially through literary works. This period saw the formation of the Sierra Club (1892), the International Nature Protection Body (1930), and the International Union for the Protection of Nature (1948).

3.2 ENVIRONMENTAL MOVEMENT FROM 1962 TO 1992

After 1962, environmentalism gained ground thanks to the writings of the earlier period, as well as the publication of a few landmark works. This period, (1962-1992), known as the period of "environmental revolution" began with the publication of the *Silent Spring* by Rachel Carson in 1962. *Silent Spring* drew attention to the dangers of the widespread use of pesticides, on both wildlife and humans. Highlighting the adverse consequences of chemical pesticides, such as DDT, Rachel Carson advocated a "biotic" approach—the cheaper, safer, longer acting, natural solutions to pest problems. The primary inspiration for the book was a friend of Carson's who was concerned about dying birds in her hometown, where the authorities had sprayed DDT to control mosquitoes. Carson's attack on the use of chemical pesticides was a challenge to the idea of technological progress. Carson warned that the chemical pesticides contained the prospect of a dying world, in which spring would become silent, due to the absence of the songs of the birds which would become extinct due to the adverse effects of pesticides. *Silent Spring* cautioned the world against the unintended consequences of technology. Rachael Carson's attack against the use of harmful chemicals, which had adverse consequences on nature, transformed environmentalism into a stronger dynamic movement.

Another book, as effective as *Silent Spring* was Stewart Udall's *The Quiet Crisis,* published in 1963. The *Quiet Crisis* was a review of the history of American environmental philosophy. In the book, Udall described the quiet crisis as: "America today stands poised on a pinnacle of wealth and power, yet we live in a land of vanishing beauty, of increasing ugliness, of shrinking open space, and of an overall environment that is diminished daily by pollution and noise and blight".

The two books stimulated environmental activism, and underlined "both the unintended and negative impact that certain human behaviors have on ecological relationships and the philosophy that humans are part of, not apart from, the rest of nature".

During this period, two strands of environmentalism stood distinctively apart: *the shallow ecology and deep ecology movement.* (Discussed in Chapter 1).

Shallow ecology accepts that nature may be harnessed to meet human needs and ends. The phrase "deep ecology", coined by the Norwegian philosopher, Arne Naess, in 1973, completely rejects any belief that human beings are in some way superior to any other species or nature itself.

A few of the several pro-environment books and articles published in the '60s and '70s are:

- Kenneth Boulding's *The Economics of the Coming Spaceship Earth* (1966).
- Paul Ehrlich's *Population Bomb* (1968).
- Hardin's article *Tragedy of Commons* (1968).
- Commoner's *The Closing Circle* (1971).
- The Club of Rome's *Limits to Growth* (1972).
- Edward Goldsmith's article, *Blueprint for Survival* (1972).
- E.F. Schumacher's *Small is Beautiful* (1973).

All these books and articles shared the common philosophy and faith that the present increases in the production and consumption activities of human beings are undermining the very foundations of human survival, by disrupting ecosystems and depleting resources.

In ***The Economics of the Coming Spaceship Earth* (1966),** Boulding refers to the future economy as a "spaceship" with very scarce resources that would always be concerned with stock maintenance. Distinguishing between the cowboy economy and spaceship economy, he says: ". . . I am tempted to call the open economy, the 'cowboy economy', the cowboy being symbolic of the illimitable plains and also associated with reckless, exploitative, romantic, and violent behaviour, which is characteristic of open societies. The closed economy of the future might similarly be called the 'spaceman' economy, in which the earth has become a single spaceship, without unlimited reservoirs of anything, either for extraction or for pollution . . ." Boulding warned that the spaceship economy had arrived already. Boulding expressed concern that the greatest harm will be done to the future generations as they are likely to inherit a highly contaminated earth with less and less natural resources in it and added that a society which loses its responsibility to future generations will soon perish. For Boulding, sustainable development requires the transformation of our increasingly (open) globalized cowboy economy into a (closed) spaceship economy.

In the ***Population Bomb*,** published in 1968, comparing the population explosion of the world to cancer, Ehrlich observes: "A cancer is an uncontrolled multiplication of cells; the population explosion is an uncontrolled multiplication of people. Treating only the symptoms of cancer may make the victim more comfortable at first, but eventually he dies–often horribly. A similar fate awaits the world with population explosion, if only the symptoms are treated. We must shift our efforts from treatment of the symptoms to the cutting out of the cancer. The operation will demand many apparently brutal and heartless decisions. The pain may be intense. But the disease is so far advanced that only with radical surgery does the patient have a chance to survive".

The Tragedy of the Commons, an influential article written by Garret Hardin, was first published in the journal, *Science,* in 1968. The article describes a situation in which several individuals acting independently, motivated solely by self-interest, will ultimately destroy a common (shared) limited resource even though it is not in anyone's long term interest for this to happen. The tragedy of the commons essentially reduces to this: the unrestricted advance of private interest leads to collective ruin. The policy implication is that free access and unrestricted demand for a finite resource, ultimately dooms the resource, through over-exploitation and hence, calls for social arrangements ensuring collective responsibility through collective restraint of private interest.

In ***Closing Circle* (1971),** Commoner blamed capitalist technologies as chiefly responsible for environmental degradation. In his book, Commoner stated four laws of ecology:

(*i*) Everything is connected to everything else. There is one ecosphere for all living organisms and what affects one, affects all.

(*ii*) Everything must go somewhere. There is no "waste" in nature and there is no "away" to which things can be thrown.

(*iii*) Nature knows best. Humankind has fashioned technology to improve upon nature, but such a change in the natural system is likely to be detrimental to that system.

(*iv*) There is no such thing as a free lunch. Everything comes from something. There is no such thing as spontaneous existence.

In 1972, members of the ***Club of Rome*,** led by Donella and Dennis Meadows, prepared a world model known as the Limits to Growth (**LTG**) model. The model identified five factors that are posing a limit to further economic growth on the planet earth. They are:

- Increase in population
- Industrialization
- Increase in food production
- Increase in resource depletion
- Increase in pollution

According to the LTG model:

- If the present growth trends in world population, industrialization, pollution, food production, and resource depletion continue unchanged, the limits to growth on this planet will be reached sometime within the next one hundred years. The most probable result will be a rather sudden and uncontrollable decline in both population and industrial capacity.
- It is possible to alter these growth trends and to establish a condition of ecological and economic stability that is sustainable far into the future.

The LTG model suggested that the collapse of the economic system can be avoided only by an immediate limit on population and pollution, as well as a cessation of economic growth.

In the book, ***The Next 200 Years: A Scenario for America and the World***, published in 1976, Herman Kahn, William Brown and Leon Martel struck an optimistic note as a reply to the LTG model. According to Kahn and his associates, continued growth would provide continued betterment for the people. Khan and his associates argued that technological progress would effectively either remove the limit to economic growth or buy time until a subsequent technology can remove the limit.

Edward Goldsmith's *Blueprint for Survival* was published in January 1972, in *The Ecologist,* Vol. 2 No.1. The Blueprint observed that "the world cannot accommodate this continued increase in ecological demand. Indefinite growth of whatever type cannot be sustained by finite resources." Blueprint suggested that the solution is to create a society which is sustainable—a society that would depend not on expansion but on stability.

The ***Blueprint*** recommends seven operations to meet the conditions of a stable society:

(*a*) A control operation whereby environmental disruption is reduced as much as possible by technical means.

(*b*) A freeze operation, in which present trends are halted.

(*c*) A systemic substitution, by which the most dangerous components of these trends are replaced by technological substitutes.

(*d*) Systemic substitution, by which these technological substitutes are replaced by "natural" or self-regulating ones.

(*e*) The invention, promotion and application of alternative technologies which are energy and material conservative.

(*f*) Decentralization of policy and economy at all levels, and the formation of communities, small enough to be reasonably self-regulating and self-supporting.

(*g*) Education for such communities.

E.F. Schumacher's *Small is Beautiful* (1973) became one of the most popular books among world political leaders in the seventies. In the book, Schumacher suggested that many of the environmental and social problems facing the world were the result of idolatry to giantism. Criticizing the then prevailing and popular ideology, "bigger the better", Schumacher lamented: "We suffer from an almost universal idolatry of giantism", which considers large institutions, multinational corporations, industrial mergers, unlimited economic growth and ever increasing consumption, as symbols of progress. Schumacher was against the Western pursuit of unlimited economic growth on a gigantic scale which according to him is neither desirable nor practicable for the rest of the world. Schumacher argued that the modern economy is unsustainable. Schumacher challenged the appropriateness of using GNP to measure human wellbeing, and advocated that "the aim ought to be to obtain the maximum amount of wellbeing with the minimum amount of consumption". Schumacher advocated the concept of "intermediate technology", known popularly as "appropriate technology", on the grounds that it is "environment-friendly, non-polluting and non-exploitative of people or nature". His concept of appropriate technology is today upheld as a technology for a sustainable future, and as the basis for technologies of renewable energy, of recycling and of ecological restoration.

The various books and articles mentioned above focus on the fact that continued economic growth on a planet with finite resources is not only impossible but also capable of destroying the very basis of growth. Hence, these environmentalists advocated sustainable growth and sustainable development.

Several events that took place during the same period, such as the oil spill from the oil tanker Torrey Canyon that went aground, off the southwest coast of England in 1967, and the culmination in 1971, of a law suit in Japan that drew international attention to the effects of decades of mercury poisoning on the people of Minamata, highlighted the magnitude of environmental damage caused by humans. At the same time, the world witnessed technological accomplishments, such as nuclear proliferation and photos of the Earth from outer space; both these technological accomplishments provided new insights and new reasons for concern over the Earth's unique place in the universe.

Stockholm Conference

Environmentalism since 1972 saw the active participation of many national and international environmental non-governmental organizations (ENGOs). In 1972, the United Nations Conference on the Human Environment was held in Stockholm, which led to the creation of government environmental agencies and the UN Environment Programme. The conference led to global participation and cooperation for solutions to environmental issues. The theme of the Conference, "Only One Earth", was chosen to emphasize that all living and inanimate things among which man dwelt, were part of a single interdependent system, and that man would have no other place to live if he ruined his surroundings through his selfish abuse of the environment. The Stockholm Conference significantly influenced the global environmental movement. It was attended by more than 400 inter-governmental and non-governmental organisations.

The Stockholm Conference produced a Declaration and laid down 26 Principles and Action Plans. McCormic summarizes the 26 principles thus:

(*i*) Natural resources should be safeguarded and conserved. The earth's capacity to produce renewable resources should be maintained and non-renewable resources should be shared.

(*ii*) Development and environmental concerns should go together and less developed countries should be given every assistance and incentive to promote rational environmental management.

(*iii*) Each country should establish its own standards of environmental management and exploit resources as they wish but should not endanger other states. There should be international cooperation aimed at improving the environment.

(*iv*) Pollution should not exceed the capacity of the environment to clean itself and oceanic pollution should be prevented.

(*v*) Science, technology, education and research shall be used to promote environmental protection.

The Conference approved over 100 recommendations to be incorporated in an international Action Plan to combat the earth's environmental ills. The four main impacts of the Stockholm Conference are:

(*i*) The Conference set a new trend in environmental thinking that emphasized the human mismanagement of the environment. The Conference put environmental issues on the international agenda for the first time.

(*ii*) The Conference underlined the significance of the needs of the less developed nations in international environmental policy.

(*iii*) In the post Stockholm era, there was a remarkable growth in the number of ENGOs. By 1982, there were 2,230 NGOs in less developed countries, of which 60 per cent were formed after the Stockholm Conference and 13,000 NGOs in developed countries, of which 30 per cent were formed after the Stockholm Conference.

(*iv*) The most important outcome of the Conference was the creation of the United Nations Environment Programme (UNEP).

In the post Stockholm Conference period, global environmental movement flourished; the environmental movement in developing countries too grew in strength, due to the increasing magnitude of environmental problems in developing countries. The role of women in the environmental movement of the less developed nations since the 1970s cannot be ignored. The Chipko movement in India (Box 3.1) and the Green Belt movement in Kenya (Box 3.2) stand witness to these.

The Chipko Movement, started in the 1970's, was a non-violent movement aimed at protecting, and conserving trees and forests from destruction. The name "Chipko" originated from the word, "embrace", as the villagers used to hug the trees to protect them from wood cutters. The Chipko movement was based on the Gandhian philosophy of peaceful resistance to achieve the goals. It was a strong uprising against those people, who were destroying the natural resources of the forests and disturbing the whole ecological balance.

In early 1973, the Indian forest department refused to allot ash trees to the local cooperative organisation based in the Chamoli district, Dashauli Gram Swarajya Sangha (DGSS), for making agricultural implements. Instead, the ash trees were allotted to a private company known as Symonds Co. This incident provoked the DGSS to fight against this injustice. Thus, Chipko was born under the leadership of Chandi Prasad Bhat, as a protest against cutting trees and depriving the local people of their livelihoods. This form of protest was instrumental in driving away the private company from felling the ash trees.

BOX 3.1

The Chipko Movement

The Chipko movement first started in the Chamoli district in the year 1973, and later spread to other parts of the country. Chipko has strictly adhered to the Gandhian tradition of freedom struggle, *i.e.*, non–violence. The Chipko Movement gained momentum under Sunderlal Bahuguna, an eco-activist, who spent his whole life persuading and educating the villagers, to protest against the destruction of the forests and the Himalayan mountains by the government. It was he, who made an appeal to the Prime Minister of India, Mrs. Indira Gandhi, to ban the cutting of trees. He coined the slogan "ecology is the permanent economy".

One of the major achievements of the Chipko movement was the ban in 1980 on the cutting of trees for 15 years in the forests of Uttar Pradesh. Later on, the ban was imposed in Himachal Pradesh, Karnataka, Rajasthan, Bihar, Western Ghats and Vindhayas. All this was done on the order of the Indian Prime Minister after strong protests by activists throughout the country.

Source: http://www.ecoindia.com/education/chipko-movement.html
http://edugreen.teri.res.in/explore/forestry/chipko.htm

BOX 3.2

The Green Belt Movement

The Green Belt Movement, (GBM) is a grassroot non-governmental organization based in Nairobi, Kenya, that works for environmental conservation, community development and capacity building. Professor Wangari Maathai established the organization in 1977, under the auspices of the National Council of Women of Kenya. Since 1977, over 30 million trees have been planted. Over 30,000 women were trained in forestry, food processing, bee-keeping and other trades that helped them to earn income while preserving their lands and resources. Communities in Kenya (both men and women) have been motivated and organized both to prevent further environmental destruction and to restore that which has been damaged.

Timeline of the Green Belt Movement:

The **1980s**:

- Establishment of over 600 tree nurseries achieved (2,500-3,000 women assisting).
- Establishment of approximately 2,000 public green belts carrying 1,000 tree seedlings on each green belt.
- Network developed (since adopted in Tanzania, Uganda, Lesotho, Malawi, Zimbabwe etc).
- **1988**: Struggle against construction of Africa's tallest skyscraper in Uhuru Park, Nairobi. GBM won the struggle.
- In **1991**, a protest was launched that saved Jeevanjee Gardens from the fate of being turned into a multi-storey parking lot.
- In **1998**, the Movement led a crusade against the illegal allocation of parts of the 2,000 acre (8 km^2) Karura Forest, a vital water catchment area in the outskirts of Nairobi. The struggle was finally won in 2003 when leaders of the newly elected government affirmed their commitment to the forest by planting trees in the area.
- In **2007**, the Green Belt Movement endorsed the *Forests Now Declaration* calling for new market based mechanisms to protect tropical forests.

This activism has come at a high personal cost to both Maathai and the Movement. The Kenyan government closed the Greenbelt offices, and Dr.Maathai was imprisoned twice and in 1992, was subjected to a severe beating by the police, while leading a peaceful protest against the imprisonment of several environmental and political activists. Despite these impediments and hardships, GBM continues as a world-renowned and respected Movement.

The Movement is now vibrant and has succeeded in achieving many of the goals it set out to meet. Environmental protection has been achieved through tree planting, including soil conservation, sustainable management of the local environment and economy and the protection and boosting of local livelihoods. In addition to helping local women to generate their own incomes through such ventures as seed sales, the Movement has succeeded in educating thousands of low-income women about forestry and has created about 3,000 part-time jobs. In 2004, Wangari Maathai received the Nobel Peace Prize, becoming both the first African woman and the first environmentalist to ever win the Nobel Peace Prize for her work with the Green Belt Movement.

Source: http://en.wikipedia.org/wiki/Green_Belt_Movement

The Chipko movement was the "direct inspiration for a series of popular movements in defense of community rights to natural resources. Sometimes these struggles resolved around forests and in other instances, around the control and use of pasture, water, and mineral or fish resources. Most of these conflicts have pitted rich against the poor, logging companies against hill villagers, dam builders against forest tribal communities, multinational corporations deploying trawlers against traditional fisherfolk in small boats" (Sharma, Aviram 2007).

The Green Belt Movement under the leadership of Wangari Maathai in 1977, organized poor rural women in Kenya to plant trees, to fight against deforestation in order to restore their main source of fuel for cooking, to generate income, and to stop soil erosion. (Box 3.2)

The Narmada Bachao Andolan is one of the most powerful mass movements in India, started in 1985, against the construction of a huge dam on India's largest west flowing river, the Narmada, which supports a large number of people with distinguished culture and tradition, ranging from the indigenous (tribal) people inhabiting the jungles, to a large rural population, besides destroying biodiversity by submerging thousands of acres of forests and agricultural land. In all these cases, it was the commercial greed of one group that posed a threat to the livelihood and the control over resources of the local communities. Box 3.3 briefly discusses the Narmada Bachao Movement.

BOX 3.3

Narmada Bachao Andolan

Narmada Bachao Andolan is a powerful mass movement, started in 1985, against the construction of a huge dam on the Narmada River. The Narmada Valley Project, with its two mega projects-Sardar Sarovar Project and Narmada Sagar Project in Madhya Pradesh, is the largest single river valley project with the objective of making the world's largest man-made lake. The state government initiated the project as Gujarat is one of the most water-starved regions in India and the severe droughts in the state between 1985–88 further reinforced this project. The opponents of the dam see it as "the world's worst man-made ecological disaster". The consequences of the project are quite glaring and alarming. The reservoir will submerge 37,000 hectares of land, of which 11,000 hectares are classified as forest. It will displace about one lakh persons of 248 villages—19 of Gujarat, 36 of Maharashtra and 193 of Madhya Pradesh. The Narmada Bachao Andolan, (Save the Narmada Movement) led by Medha Patkar, rose in protest over the resettlement and rehabilitation of the displaced people. In 1988, the NBA formally demanded the stoppage of all work on the Narmada Valley Development Project. In September 1989, more than 50,000 people gathered in the valley from all over India to pledge to fight "destructive development". The achievements of the movement include:

- Exit of the World Bank from Sardar Sarovar in 1993.
- Halt of Sardar Sarovar construction in 1994-99.
- Withdrawal of foreign investors from Maheshwar dam in 1999–2001.

Source: http://www.geocities.com/CapitolHill/6027/Narmada.html
http://www.ecoindia.com/education/narmada-bachao-andolan.html
www.egyankosh.ac.in/bitstream/123456789/33151/1/Unit16.pdf

Table 3.1 Time Line of the Environmental Movement (1962-1980)

Year	Event
1962	***Silent Spring*** by Rachel Carson
1963	***The Quiet Crisis*** by Stewart Udall
1966	***The Economics of the Coming Spaceship Earth*** by *Kenneth Boulding*
1968	***Population Bomb*** by Paul Ehrlich, ***Tragedy of Commons*** by Hardin
1969	International NGO ***Friends of the Earth*** founded.
1971	Publication of Commoner's ***The Closing Circle***
	International NGO ***Greenpeace*** founded
1972	***Limits to Growth*** by Club of Rome, ***Blueprint for Survival*** by Edward Goldsmith
1972	United Nations Conference on the Human Environment held in Stockholm
1973	Naess, Arne's ***The Shallow and the Deep, Long-Range Ecology Movement,***
	E.F. Schumacher's ***Small is Beautiful***
1973	***Chipko Movement***
1977	***Green Belt Movement*** organized by Wangari Maathai in Nairobi, Kenya.

3.3 ENVIRONMENTAL MOVEMENT SINCE THE 1980s TO THE PRESENT DAY

By the 1980s, the "green movement" became a worldwide phenomenon with its presence felt in almost all the countries of the world. Since 1980, the environmental movement addressed many of the previously ignored costs: impact of dams, industrial wastes, energy inefficiencies, etc. The rationale for ecological-economic accounting was pointed out by economists; the impact of agriculture, industries, energy use and transport could no longer be ignored as "external" to the business or account statements. Policies were designed in many countries to internalize the external costs. During the 1980s, environmental awareness and discussions had advanced to include modern focus points, like ozone depletion, global climate change, acid rain, and the potentially harmful, genetically modified organisms (GMOs).

The years 1986–87 are significant dates in the history of the environmental movement. The Chernobyl Disaster in Russia (Box 3.4), the Sandoz Fire in Basel (1986), and the Bhopal Tragedy in India (1984), convinced the world of the importance of greening all aspects of development. The chemical fire in the industrial warehouse, that contained nearly 1300 tonnes of organic chemicals for agricultural use in Schweizerhalle, near Basel, in Switzerland, released on 1 November 1986, highly toxic pollutants and pesticides into the River Rhine, killing aquatic organisms over several hundreds of kilometers of the river, posing a threat of contaminated water supply for neighbouring countries (Germany and France) that depended on the Rhine for their water supply. On the night of 2–3 December, 1984, the Union Carbide plant in Bhopal, India, leaked 27 tonnes of the deadly gas Methyl Isocyanate. Nearly half a million people were exposed to the gas and 20,000 people were reported dead as on date (Box 2.6, Chapter 2). After the environmental disasters at Basel, Bhopal and Chernobyl, the environmental movement accelerated its global and local responsiveness.

BOX 3.4

Chernobyl Disaster

On April 26, 1986, during a test at 1:21 a.m., the No. 4 reactor of the Nuclear Power Plant at Chernobyl, located 128 km northwest of Kiev, that is in the Ukraine part of the Soviet Union, exploded and released thirty to forty times the radioactivity of the atomic bombs dropped on Hiroshima and Nagasaki. The world first learned of history's worst nuclear accident from Sweden, where abnormal radiation levels were registered at one of its nuclear facilities. The cause of the disaster was a malfunction within the plant that caused the radioactive core to become exposed. This caused a particle meltdown that let off large amounts of radioactive material.

Some reports said that the accident was caused because the operators were over confident in their decision making. Others said that there was a flaw in the design of the reactor while others blamed the accident on the poor safety systems. Further investigation revealed that all three factors were involved.

The disaster at Chernobyl affected people all over the world. The effects of the accident were both local and worldwide. Wind carried the huge masses of radioactive particles over a wide area. Europe was greatly affected by the disaster because bans had to be put on many foods which were feared to be contaminated. Belarus, the country to the north of the accident, suffered the most. Thirty-one lives were lost immediately. Hundreds of thousands of Ukrainians, Russians, and Belorussians had to abandon entire cities and settlements within the thirty-kilometer zone of extreme contamination. Billions of roubles have been spent, and billions more will be needed to relocate communities and decontaminate the rich farmland. The accident was by far the most devastating in the history of nuclear power and the people of the region continue to live with its consequences. The estimated recovery time of the disaster is 130 years.

Source: http://nilesema.com/nuclearradio.htm
http://chernobyl486.tripod.com/

By the late 1980s, environmentalism had become a global force with environmental non-governmental organizations like Greenpeace, Friends of the Earth, and the World Wildlife Fund exerting significant international pressure.

These international NGOs have offices throughout the world and a centralized international headquarters to coordinate lobbying campaigns. Transnational coalition building was and remains another important strategy for environmental organizations. Grassroots movements in developing countries also resorted to transnational coalition, primarily because it strengthens lobbying and direct-action campaigns at the international level. One such success story is that of the movement to save the Brazilian rainforests. (Box 3.5)

In the 1980s, environmentalism paved the path for global governance and influenced the agenda of international politics through its international activism. Many multilateral agreements have been signed, covering a variety of environmental issues, such as trade in endangered species, management of hazardous wastes, climate change etc.

BOX 3.5

The Movement to Save Brazilian Rainforests

The Amazon contains one-fifth of the world's fresh water, sustaining the world's largest rainforest—over six million square kilometres and is the home to almost a million indigenous Indians. Thanks to the Amazon, Brazil ranks first in the world for numbers of species of primates, amphibians and plants; third for bird species; and fourth for species of butterflies and reptiles.

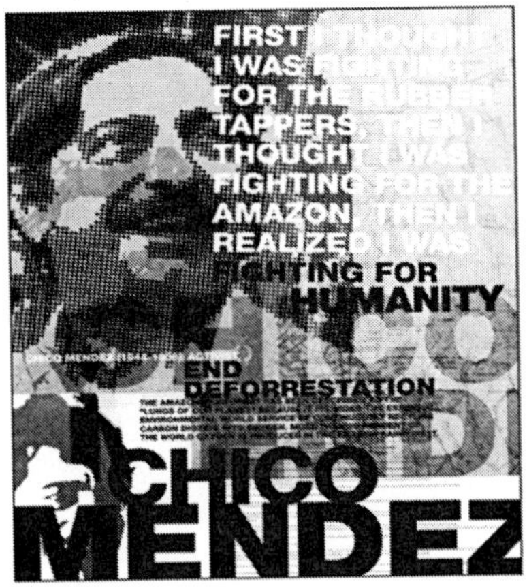

Chico Mendes was the leader of the National Council of Rubber Tappers Union. In his position as leader of the Union, Mendes worked for the interests of the members. Without the rainforest there is no livelihood for the rubber tappers. When the value of rubber declined with the increased use of synthetic substitutes, large landowners turned to more profitable forms of using the Amazon, which mostly meant clear-cutting the forest to make pasture lands for cattle. At the same time, the government of Brazil was undertaking a policy to encourage the settlement and development of these outlying regions of the country through land concessions, loans and tax breaks. Chico Mendes decided to confront the cattle barons who were slashing and burning the forests of the Amazon.

Mendes opposed the destructive practices of such large companies and individuals. He advocated a return to sustainable agricultural systems and led a non-violent protest against the big companies that would rob them of their livelihoods. He fought to prevent the building of a road that would have provided the cattle industry with easy access to the rainforest. He won the United Nations environmental award for the role he played in protecting the forests. Mendes became the international symbol of the effort to save the rainforests, and for this confrontation and for his apparent success he was murdered on December 22nd 1988.

Chico's struggle secured the livelihood of the rubber tappers. In April 1989, the Brazilian government announced the suspension of all subsidies, tax-reliefs, and incentives for cattle ranching. Mendes is famous worldwide as an "environmental crusader" for his campaign against the ranchers and highway development in western Amazonia.

Source: Joseph J. Domask, 1998, Evolution of the Environmental Movement in Brazil's Amazonia, Global Forest Programme, WWF

Trussell Jeff, The Earth Keeper Hero, Chico Mendes, http://www.myhero.com/myhero/hero.asp?hero=c_mendes

The concept of sustainable development was taken further by the UN Conference on Environment and Development (UNCED), which was held in Rio de Janeiro, Brazil, during the summer of 1992. The Rio Conference was an unprecedented historical event with the largest gathering of 114 heads of state, including 10,000 representatives from 178 countries and 1400 non-governmental organizations, represented by additional thousands. The key outcomes of the Conference were: the Rio Declaration, and Agenda 21.

Agenda 21, the key document of the summit, is a 500 page collection of agreed healthy practices and suggestions for countries to achieve sustainable development. The environmental themes with its link to economic development/growth, covered by Agenda 21 are: quality of life, efficient use of natural resources, protection of the global commons, management of human settlements, and sustainable economic growth. The Rio Declaration on the Environment, a key supporting instrument of Agenda 21, made popular, the principles like "Polluter Pays", "Cradle to Grave" and the "Precautionary Principle". The Brundtland Commission succeeded in two breakthrough accomplishments:

(*i*) It linked poverty, equity, and security to environmental issues.

(*ii*) It recognized that the environment was a popular issue around which individuals, NGOs, and governments could rally.

Table 3.2 Time Line of the Environmental Movement after 1980

Year	Event
1984	Bhopal Tragedy in India.
1985	Narmada Bachao Andolan.
1986	Chernobyl Disaster, Russia, and Sandoz Fire in Basel.
1988	Chico Mendes who fought to save the Brazilian rainforests was murdered.
1989	The Montreal Protocol on Substances that Deplete the Ozone layer.
1992	United Nations Conference on Environment and Development.
1994	The Basel Convention on the Control of Transboundary Movement of Hazardous Wastes and their Disposal.
1995	Nigerian government executes journalist and environmental activist, Ken Saro-Wiwa and eight other environmentalists. They had been active in fighting pollution from Shell Oil Co. in the Ogoni homeland.
2000	European Union bans leaded gasoline as a public health hazard.
	Rainforest logging banned in New Zealand following a 30 year campaign by environmental groups.
2002	World Summit on Sustainable Development (also known as Rio + 10) at Johannesburg, South Africa.
2004	Nobel Peace Prize was awarded to the Kenyan environmentalist and human rights campaigner, Wangari Maathai.
	An 8.9 magnitude quake deep under the Indian Ocean triggers massive tsunamis that destroy villages and seaside resorts and kills more than 140,000 people in a dozen countries, including India.
2005	The United Nations Framework Convention on Climate Change (UNFCC)—Kyoto Protocol came into force.
2009	Climate Conference at Copenhagen.

The nature of the environmental movement since the 1980s, has a few distinct features over the movement of the earlier period. Firstly, the fight today is for equity between generations - inter temporal justice - the use of resources to promote development "without compromising the requirements and needs of future generations".

Secondly, the number of local/national environmental non-governmental organizations, (ENGOs) has increased during the 1990s. These include both community based grassroots organizations that fight for protection of livelihoods, such as the Narmada Bachao movement group, as well as advocacy or grassroots support organizations, such as *Friends of the Earth.*

Thirdly, the impact of the movement has been increasingly sensitizing and more procedural; sensitizing implies that the movement has been able to transform public attitude to environment and also bring about changes in the political agenda. Procedural impacts of the movement refer to the achievement of access to the decision making bodies.

Fourthly, the movement's emphasis has shifted from local to global environmental problems. In the past, the environmental movement mainly dealt with local problems which resulted in the enactment of a number of environmental legislations that addressed local problems. From 1990 onwards, the environmental movement shifted its focus to transboundary and global issues, such as the preservation of biodiversity, ozone layer and global warming. While the earlier slogan was: *Think globally, act locally*, now it is: *Think and act locally; think and act globally*. One such significant movement, though local in terms of the issue, yet global in terms of the attention it received, is the fight by the Ogoni tribe in Nigeria, against environmental degradation by the MNC, Shell Oil Co., in the Ogoni homeland. (Box 3.6)

Lastly, the 1990s also saw the establishment of many national ENGOs that made possible indigenous, nation wide response to environmental issues. Examples are: Fundación Nature in Ecuador, the Green Forum, Phillipines, the Kenyan Non Governmental Organisation (KENGO), and WALHI I in Indonesia. Some of these national ENGOs have formed a regional network. For example, 21 African ENGOs together formed the African NGOs Environmental Network (ANEN). Today, more than 500 ENGOs are members in this regional network, ANEN.

Since the late 1980s and the 1990s, the environmental movement has been more oriented towards achieving economic development through efficient use of resources. Eco-efficiency in production and consumption was stressed by environmental thinkers and philosophers. The environmental movement during this period did not reject economic growth but emphasized ecologically efficient growth.

Several concepts, such as sustainable development, industrial ecology, and the environmental Kuznets curve, emerged during this period. The environmental movement focused on measuring the ecological performance of the whole economy in terms of new indicators and indices of (un) sustainability of the economy and developed the application of ecological notions of carrying capacity and resilience to human ecosystems; attempts were made to measure in money terms, the value of the vital functions performed by the environment. (Chapter 5: Section 5.1)

Attempts have been made since the late 1980s to assign money values to the annual flows of some environmental services, and to compare them to GNP in monetary units of account. Physical indicators and indices were developed, in order to judge the overall impact of the human economy. Some of these physical indicators are:

(*a*) Human Appropriation of Net Primary Production (HANPP) proposed by Vitousek et al. (1986). The NPP is the amount of energy made available by the primary producers, the

BOX 3.6

The Oil Industry and Environmental Degradation in Nigeria

Oil production in Nigeria has had severe environmental and human consequences for the indigenous peoples who inhabit the areas surrounding oil extraction. Nigeria earns over 95 per cent of its foreign exchange from the sale of oil on the global market. The social and environmental costs of oil production have been extensive. They include destruction of wildlife and biodiversity, loss of fertile soil, pollution of air and drinking water, degradation of farmland and damage to aquatic ecosystems, all of which have caused serious health problems for the inhabitants of areas surrounding oil production.

Ogoniland is in the eastern part of the Niger Delta. Half a million of the people belonging to the Ogoni tribe live there. Shell-BP, operating under the protection of the ex-colonial power, Great Britain, found oil there in 1956 and has robbed £100 billion of black gold from the region. The money was split between the corrupt Nigerian elite and the corrupt corporate elite. The Ogoni who got nothing but the ruination of their lands and livelihoods, continue to live in abject poverty, with many villages lacking clean water, electricity, schools or basic healthcare.The Ogonis have protested that Shell's oil production has not only devastated the local environment, but has destroyed the economic viability of the region for local farmers and producers. The Ogonis have sought compensation for environmental damage to their land by oil companies since 1990.

Protesters have been jailed, killed and silenced for demonstrating against the multinational company. Ken Saro-Wiwa, the leader of the Movement for the Survival of the Ogoni People, fought to organize the Ogoni ethnic minority to protest against the destruction of their homeland caused by operations of the Multinational Companies, Shell and Chevron, and fought to seek compensation for his peoples' lost farmland and fisheries. But he was jailed on the false charge of inciting members of the group to kill four Ogoni elders. The story of the Ogoni people received world wide attention as a result of the arrest of Saro-Wiwa, which was exposed by the human rights and environmental groups. The campaign of Amnesty International and Greenpeace against his arrest, accused Nigeria's military government of looting and execution of oil protesters. Although Shell earns considerable money from its drilling in the Rivers region, it has done little or nothing to reinvest a portion of its profits back into the local communities, where the drilling takes place.

The Nigerian Federal Government, on the other hand, has been charged with failing to enact and enforce environmental protection against oil damage by Shell and other oil companies. Furthermore, many Ogonis have been harassed and even killed by the Federal government, for organizing protests and threatening sabotage of oil facilities. In November 1995, the **Nigerian government executed the journalist and environmental activist, Ken Saro-Wiwa** and eight other environmentalists. They were framed and executed by the Nigerian military government for campaigning against the devastation of their homeland by oil giant Shell-BP. Many outraged people in the developing world have not forgotten the oil company's role in this tragedy. Saro-Wiwa's last words were: ***"Lord, take my soul, but the struggle continues."***

Source: http://www1.american.edu/TED/ice/ogonioil.htm
http://fading-hope.blog-city.com/shellbp.htm

plants, to the rest of the living species, the heterotrophs. The higher the HANPP, the less biomass is available for "wild" biodiversity. The proportion of NPP appropriated by humans is increasing because of population growth, and also because of increasing demands on land per person for urbanization, for growing foodstuffs, and for growing timber.

(*b*) Ecospace and Ecological Footprint referring to the environmental load of the economy, in terms of space and attempts to measure the quantity of productive land needed (as source and sink) in order to sustain a given population indefinitely, at its current standard of living and with current technologies.

(*c*) EROI, which stands for "energy return on input".

(*d*) MIPS, Material Intensity Input per Unit of Service, which is a measure of the material intensity of production and is measured in tonnes and is compared with the services provided in each and every sector of the whole economy.

(*e*) Direct Material Requirement (DMR) and the Total Material Requirement (TMR) measures developed by the World Resource Institute are improved versions of MIPS and measure the material requirement, both from domestic production, as well as imports.

Some environmental non-governmental organizations, such as Greenpeace, Friends of the Earth, and the World Wildlife Fund established significant international presence, with offices throughout the world and a centralized international headquarters to coordinate activities that includes lobbying and campaigns for preserving and conserving environmental resources and services. These international ENGOs promoted coalitions with national ENGOs to facilitate exchange of information and expertise and for strengthening their campaigns at the local, national and international levels. Table 3.3 gives a list of leading international and national environmental NGOs.

In the 21st Century, the environmental movement has gained strength and momentum. There are a number of environmental groups at the local, national and international level working towards the protection of the environment, by creating awareness and campaigning for specific issues. In the developing countries, environmental movements fight for justice – justice for the poor who are often deprived of their land and livelihood because of the development projects. In the developed nations, the movement fights more often for a cleaner world and protection of the flora and fauna. The NGOs are seen working with the government, in the developed nations, while in the South, environmental groups often have to fight against the government. An example is the confrontation between the local environmental group at Kasargod district in Kerala and the Government, over the spraying of endosulfan, (that resulted in disproportionate incidence of cancer in the district) which needed the support of the Centre for Science and Environment to bring the tragedy to the attention of the world. (Box 3.7) But for the presence of such environmental groups, the voiceless poor in the developing nations would be economically deprived and the developed nations would not have come up with greener production techniques and greener consumption practices. In fact, the making of some of the rules and regulations to protect the environment are also due to the unrelenting efforts of the environmental groups. The Basel Ban is an example.

Table 3.3 Select ENGOs-National & International

S.No	Name of the ENGO	Year of Establish-ment	Nature of the ENGO	Location of Head Quarters	Mission/Objective
1	A Rocha	1983	International/ Independent	United Kingdom	Conservation of nature and environmental education and research.
2	Centre for Environmental Research and Conservation	1994	International/ Independent	Columbia, USA	Building environmental leadershipin order to achieve environmental sustainability and prevent the loss of biological diversity.
3	Centre for International Climate and Environmental Research	1990	International/ Independent	Norway, Oslo	Provide reliable and comprehensive knowledge about all aspects of the climate change problem.
4	Friends of the Earth	1971	International/ Independent	U.K.	Promote campaigns and promote solutions that will help to create environmentally sustainable and socially just societies.
5	Greenpeace	1971	International/ Independent	Amsterdam, Netherlands	Campaigns to change people's attitudes and behaviour, to protect and conserve the environ-ment and to promote peace.
6	Resources for the Future	1952	International	Washington D C, USA	Improves environmental and natural resource policymaking worldwide through objective social science research of the highest calibre on environmental, energy, natural resource and public health issues.
7	Earth Justice	1971	National/ Independent	Oakland, California, USA	Environmental litigation: Protecting the magnificent places, natural resources, and wildlife of this earth, and defending the right of all people to a healthy environment.

S.No	Name of the ENGO	Year of Establishment	Nature of the ENGO	Location of Head Quarters	Mission/Objective
8	Sierra Club	1892	National	San Fransisco, California, USA	To explore, enjoy, and protect the wild places of the earth; to practice and promote the responsible use of the earth's ecosystems and resources; and to use all lawful means to carry out these objectives.
9	World Resource Institute	1982	National/ Independent	USA	Policy research and analysis on global environmental and resource issues and their relationship to population and development.
10	World Watch Institute	1974	National/ Independent	Washington D.C USA	Empower decision makers to create an environmentally sustainable society that meets human needs focuses on the 21st Century challenges of climate change, resource degradation, population growth, and poverty.
12	World Wide Fund for Nature	1961	International	Switzerland	Conserving critical places and critical species that are particularly important for their habitat or for people.Working to reduce humanity's ecological footprint – the amount of land and natural resources needed to supply our food, water, fibre and timber, and to absorb our CO_2 emissions.
13	Bombay Natural History Society	1883	National	Mumbai, India	Disseminate knowledge of flora and fauna by means of lectures, field trips, literature and expeditions and, to study wildlife related problems and recommend management plans to conserve wildlife and its habitat.
14	Centre for Environmental Education	1984	National	Ahemedabad, India	To create environmental awareness in the communities, conduct widespread environmental education and training programmes through a very vast network.

S.No	Name of the ENGO	Year of Establish-ment	Nature of the ENGO	Location of Head Quarters	Mission/Objective
15	Centre for Science and Environment		National	New Delhi, India	Research, investigative and educational work in the field of pollution, forest, wildlife, land and water use.
16	CPR Environmental Education	1989	National	Chennai, India	Promotes environmental awareness, to produce and disseminate basic educational and reference material on environment and to take up environmental projects. It works in the field of environmental education.
17	Development Alternatives	1893	National	New Delhi, India	Design options and promote sustainable development through programmes of economic efficiency, equity and social justice, resource conservation and self reliance, working in the field of pollution monitoring and control; waste recycling management; wasteland development; appropriate technology.
18	Kerala Sastra Sahitiya Parishad	1962	National	Thrissur, Kerala	Action to preserve the environment, to provide alternative models for development and to popularize science among the people.
19	Kalpavriksh	1971	National	New Delhi, India	Inculcates understanding and concern on environmental issues, especially among the youth—also conducts research in environmental problems, and campaigns on environmental issues to evolve a holistic environmental perspective.
20	Madras Naturalist Society	1976	National	Chennai, India	To study environmental problems in and around Chennai; to impart environmental education through seminars and discussions; to imbibe a love for nature through camps and slide shows; to organise visits to sanctuaries in Tamil Nadu.

S.No	Name of the ENGO	Year of Establish-ment	Nature of the ENGO	Location of Head Quarters	Mission/Objective
21	Narmada Bachao Andolan	1986	National	Maharahtra, India	To educate those directly affected by large development projects, such as tribals, on the social and environmental impact of such projects. To protest against the construction of dams in the Narmada Valley in general; struggling towards a right to information and new environmentally sustainable water policy.
22	The Energy and Resource Institute	1974	National	New Delhi, India	Develop and promote technologies, policies and institutions for efficient and sustainable use of natural resources - impart environmenal education.
23	Shristi	1988	National	New Delhi, India	To promote conservation and enrichment of the environment; to carry out research on all aspects of sustainable living; to foster concern for the environment among the people, making its preservation a shared responsibility.

BOX 3.7

The Endosulfan Tragedy

In Kerala, India, endosulfan has been linked to hundreds of deaths and disorders among cashew nut plantation workers and villagers. In the Kasargod province, where aerial spraying of endosulfan occurred for at least fifteen years, alarmingly high levels of endosulfan residues have been detected in the blood and breast milk of the villagers and cancers and disorders of the reproductive and Central Nervous Systems are very common. A survey of only 123 houses found 49 cancer cases, 43 psychiatric cases, 23 epileptics, 9 with congenital abnormalities, and 23 with mental retardation.

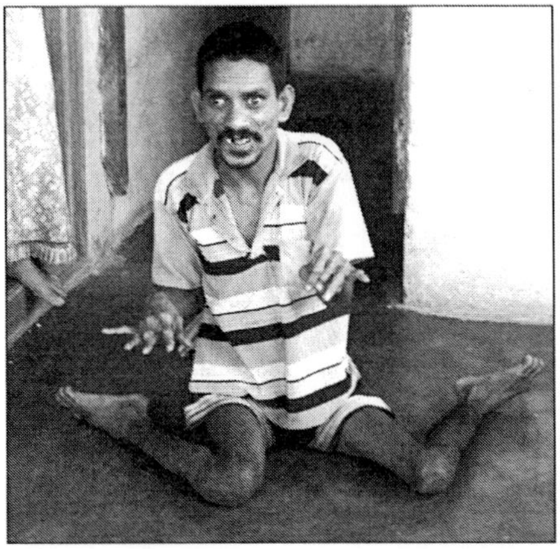

A case controlled study comparing 170 children exposed to endosulfan with 92 unexposed children found, among the former, significantly poorer academic performance, elevated prevalence of congenital abnormalities and learning difficulties, delayed puberty in boys and very high levels of menstrual disorders in girls.

Romeo Quijano, Professor of Pharmacology and Toxicology (University of Phillipines) recently led an investigation of health defects in Kasargod district and stated that, “No other reasonable cause can explain the illnesses experienced by the people, except endosulfan.”

Source: Environmental Justice Foundation, London.

3.4 CONCLUSION

Thus the solution to environmental problems requires an attitudinal/behavioural change that would promote environmental values. It is this change that the environmental groups are constantly trying to bring about and the realization that environmental problems are due to the greed of human beings has strengthened the movement. Thus, the environmental movement has come to stay. They are the trustees for the maintenance and sustenance of the environment.

QUESTIONS

1. Bring out the differences in the nature of the environmental movement in the North and the South.
2. Explain the highlights of the environmental movement prior to the publication of the book, *Silent Spring.*
3. Why is the period 1962 to 1992 referred to as the period of environmental revolution?
4. How is the environmental movement of the present day different from that of the past?

EXERCISES

1. Make a case study of an environmental movement in any developing nation.
2. Prepare a case study of an environmental movement in a developed nation.
3. Study India's environmental movement.
4. Visit the websites given in the reference list and prepare a detailed list of the environmental NGOs, with a case study for each organization.
5. Trace the history of the Narmada Bachao Andolan.
6. Approach a local ENGO and prepare a report of the activities taken up by them.

❑❑❑

4

Business Ethics and Its Relevance Today

> *If you build that foundation,*
> *both the moral and the ethical foundation,*
> *as well as the business foundation,*
> *and the experience foundation, then the building won't crumble.*
>
> **Henry Kravis**

4.1 WHAT IS BUSINESS ETHICS?

Business ethics can be defined as the written and unwritten codes of principles and values that govern decisions and directions within a company.

Business ethics is a form of applied ethics that examines ethical principles and moral or ethical problems that arise in a business environment. In the most basic terms, a definition for business ethics boils down to knowing the difference between right and wrong and choosing to do what is right. The phrase "business ethics" can be used to describe the actions of individuals within an organization, as well as the organization as a whole. In the business world, the organization's culture sets standards for determining the difference between good and bad decision making and behaviour.

In the increasingly conscience-focused marketplaces of the 21st Century, the demand for more ethical business processes and actions (known as ethicism) is increasing. Simultaneously, pressure is applied on industry to improve business ethics through new public initiatives and laws (*e.g.*, the proposed higher road tax for higher-emission vehicles).

Historically, interest in business ethics accelerated dramatically during the 1980s and 1990s, both within major corporations and within academia. For example, today most major corporate websites lay emphasis on commitment to promoting non-economic social values under a variety of headings (*e.g.*, ethics codes, social responsibility charters, to name a few).

4.2 CONFLICTING INTERESTS

Ethical issues can arise when companies must comply with multiple and sometimes conflicting legal or cultural standards, as in the case of multinational companies that operate in countries with varying practices. The question arises, for example, ought a company to obey the laws of its home country, or should it follow the less stringent laws of the developing country in which it does business? To illustrate, United States law forbids companies from paying bribes, either domestically or overseas. However, in other parts of the world, bribery is a customary, accepted way of doing business. Similar problems can occur with regard to child labour, employee safety, work hours, wages, discrimination, and environmental protection laws.

Stakeholder Versus Shareholder

There are two schools of thought regarding how companies should approach a definition for business ethics: the **shareholder perspective** and the **stakeholder perspective**.

Shareholder Perspective

Those who approach ethical decision making from a shareholder perspective focus on making decisions that are in the owners' best interest. Decisions are guided by a need to maximize return on investment for the organization's shareholders. Individuals, who approach ethics from this perspective, feel that ethical business practices are ones that make the most money.

Stakeholder Perspective

The phrase *corporate social responsibility* is often used in discussions of business ethics. The idea behind this concept is the belief that companies should consider the needs and interests of multiple stakeholder groups, not just those with a direct financial stake in the organization's profits and losses. Organizations that approach business ethics from a stakeholder perspective, consider how decisions impact those inside and outside the organization. Stakeholders may include: employees, suppliers, customers, competitors, government agencies, the news media, community residents and others. The idea behind stakeholder based ethical decision making is to make sound business decisions that work for the good of all affected parties. (For more information on stakeholders, refer Chapter 12).

4.3 WHAT IS ETHICAL BEHAVIOUR?

Different people have different beliefs about what constitutes ethical behaviour. The law defines what is and what is not legal, but the distinctions between moral right and wrong are not always so clear. In many situations, the line between right and wrong are blurred. Such situations can lead to ethical dilemmas.

When faced with ethical dilemmas, it is important to consider the outcomes of the decision-making process. One way of dealing with ethical dilemmas is by using the four-way-test to evaluate decisions which involves asking four questions:

(*i*) Is the decision a truthful one?

(*ii*) Is the decision fair to everyone affected?

(*iii*) Will it build goodwill for the organization?

(*iv*) Is the decision beneficial to all parties who have a vested interest in the outcome?

When these four questions can truthfully be answered with a "yes", it is likely that the decision is an ethical one. Another way of making sure that decisions are truly ethical is by using the publicity test. We can ask ourselves how we would feel if our actions were published in our hometown newspaper. If we would be comfortable having other people find out what we have done, the chances are that our decision is an ethical one. However, if we would not want these individuals to learn about our actions, we probably need to rethink our decision.

4.4 MANAGEMENT AND BUSINESS ETHICS

A company's managers play an important role in establishing its ethical tone. If managers behave as if the only thing that matters is profit, employees are likely to act in a similar manner. A company's leaders are responsible for setting standards for what is and is not acceptable employee behaviour. It is, therefore, vital for managers to play an active role in creating a working environment where employees are encouraged and rewarded for acting in an ethical manner.

Managers who want employees to behave ethically must exhibit ethical decision making practices themselves. Managers have to remember that leading by example is the first step in fostering a culture of ethical behaviour in their companies. No matter what the formal policies say or what they are told to do, if employees see managers behaving unethically, they will believe that the company wants them to act in a like manner.

4.5 CORPORATE ETHICS POLICIES

Many companies have formulated internal policies pertaining to the ethical conduct of employees as part of more comprehensive compliance and ethics programmes. These policies can be simple exhortations in broad, highly-generalized language (typically called a corporate ethics statement), or they can be more detailed policies, containing specific behavioural requirements (typically called corporate ethics codes). They are generally meant to identify the company's expectations of workers and to offer guidance on handling some of the more common ethical problems that might arise in the course of doing business. It is hoped that having such a policy will lead to greater ethical awareness, consistency in application, and the avoidance of ethical disasters.

An increasing number of companies also require employees to attend seminars regarding business conduct, which often include discussions of the company's policies, specific case studies, and legal requirements. Some companies even require their employees to sign agreements stating that they will abide by the company's rules of conduct.

Sometimes, there is disconnection between the company's code of ethics and the company's actual practices. Thus, whether or not such conduct is explicitly sanctioned by management, it becomes a mere marketing tool of little actual value.

To be successful, most ethicists would suggest that an ethics policy should be:

(*i*) Given the unequivocal support of top management, by both word and example.

(*ii*) Explained in writing and orally, with periodic reinforcement.

(*iii*) Doable, something employees can both understand and perform.

(*iv*) Monitored by top management, with routine inspections for compliance and improvement.
(*v*) Backed up by clearly stated consequences in the case of disobedience.
(*vi*) Remain neutral and nonsexist.

4.6 OTHER FACTORS IMPACTING ORGANIZATIONAL ETHICS

Many factors impact the decisions (having ethical overtones) that employees and managers make on a daily basis, including:

(*i*) Corporate culture
(*ii*) Existence and application of a written code of ethics
(*iii*) Formal and informal policies and rules
(*iv*) Norms for acceptable behaviour
(*v*) Financial reward system
(*vi*) System for recognizing accomplishment
(*vii*) Company attitude towards employees
(*viii*) Manner of selecting employees for promotions
(*ix*) Hiring practices
(*x*) Applications of legal behaviour
(*xi*) Degree to which professionalism is emphasized
(*xii*) The company's decision making processes
(*xiii*) Behaviour and attitudes of the organization's leaders.

4.7 OVERVIEW OF ISSUES IN BUSINESS ETHICS

Apart from general ethical behaviour, often enshrined in concrete format in the company's Corporate Social Responsibility (CSR) policy and programmes, there are various other facets of professional ethics, namely, the ethics of accounting information, human resource management, sales and marketing, production, intellectual property, knowledge and skills and so on. These issues have been very briefly touched upon as follows:

Ethics of Accounting and Financial Information

Accounting ethics were first introduced by Luca Pacioli, and later expanded by government groups, professional organizations, and independent companies.

Due to the diverse range of accounting services and recent corporate collapses, attention has been drawn to ethical standards accepted within the accounting profession. These collapses have seriously damaged the reputation of the accounting profession. To combat the criticism and prevent fraudulent accounting, various accounting organizations and governments have developed regulations and remedies for improved ethics among the accounting profession.

The nature of the work carried out by accountants and auditors requires a high level of ethics. Shareholders, potential shareholders, and other users of the financial statements rely heavily on the yearly financial statements of a company, as they can use this information to make an informed decision about investment. They rely on the opinion of the accountants who prepared the statements, as well as the auditors who verified it, to present a true and fair view of the company. Knowledge of ethics can help accountants and auditors to overcome ethical dilemmas, allowing for the right choice that, although it may not benefit the company, will benefit the public who rely on the accountant/auditor's reporting.

Accounting ethics has been deemed a difficult balancing act, as the accountants and auditors must consider the interest of the public (which relies on the information gathered in audits) while ensuring that they still remain employed by the company they are auditing. They must consider how to best apply accounting standards, even when faced with issues that could cause a company to face a significant loss or even be discontinued. Due to several accounting scandals within the profession, critics of accountants have stated that when asked by a client "what does two plus two equal?" the accountant is likely to respond "what would you like it to be?" This thought process, along with other criticisms of the profession's issues with conflict of interest, have led to increased standards of professionalism, while stressing ethics in the work environment.

From the 1980s to the present, there have been multiple accounting scandals that have been widely reported by the media and resulted in fraud charges, bankruptcy protection requests, and the closure of companies and accounting firms. The scandals were the result of creative accounting, misleading financial analysis, as well as bribery.

One of the most widely-reported violations of accounting ethics involved Enron, a multinational company that for several years had not shown a true or fair view of their financial statements. Their auditor, Arthur Andersen, an accounting firm considered one of the "Big Five", certified the validity of the accounts despite the inaccuracies in the financial statements. When the unethical activities were reported, not only did Enron dissolve but Arthur Andersen also went out of business. Enron's shareholders lost $25 billion as a result of the company's bankruptcy. Although, only a fraction of Arthur Anderson's employees were involved with the scandal, the closure of the firm resulted in the loss of 85,000 jobs.

A 2007 article in the *Managerial Auditing Journal,* determined the top nine factors that contributed to ethical failures for accountants based on a survey of 66 members of the International Federation of Accountants. The factors include (in order of most significant): "self interest, failure to maintain objectivity and independence, inappropriate professional judgment, lack of ethical sensitivity, improper leadership and ill-culture, failure to withstand advocacy threats, lack of competence, lack of organizational and peer support, and lack of professional body support." The main factor, self interest, is the motivation of an accountant to act in his/her best interest when facing a conflict of interest. For example, if an auditor has an issue with an account he/she is auditing, but is receiving financial incentives to ignore these issues, the auditor may act unethically.

Thus, accounting frauds could take the form of creative accounting, misleading financial analysis, insider trading, manipulation of the financial markets, bribery, kickbacks and facilitation payments, to name just a few. It should be remembered that while in the short term, the shareholders and the company might benefit, in the long run, it may spell ruin to the company.

Ethics of Human Resource Management

The ethics of human resource management (HRM) covers those ethical issues arising around the employer-employee relationship, such as the rights and duties owed between employer and employee. Some of the issues covered under this umbrella would include:

(*a*) Discrimination issues on the bases of age, gender, race, religion, disabilities, and attractiveness.

(*b*) Issues surrounding the representation of employees and the democratization of the workplace: union busting, strike breaking.

(*c*) Issues affecting the privacy of the employee: workplace surveillance, drug testing.

(*d*) Issues affecting the privacy of the employer: whistle-blowing.

(*e*) Issues relating to the fairness of the employment contract and the balance of power between employer and employee: slavery, indentured servitude, employment law.

(*f*) Occupational safety and health.

Apart from the above, an employee or future employee cannot be hired or fired based on race, age, gender, religion, or any other discriminatory act.

Ethics of Sales and Marketing

Marketing, which goes beyond the mere provision of information about (and access to) a product, may seek to manipulate values and behavior. While this is considered to be acceptable to some extent, the question arises as to where the ethical line is to be drawn? Marketing ethics overlaps strongly with media ethics, because marketing makes heavy use of media. Some ethical issues arising out of this area are given below:

(*a*) Pricing: price fixing, price discrimination, price skimming.

(*b*) Anti-competitive Practices: these include but go beyond pricing tactics, to cover issues such as manipulation of loyalty and supply chains.

(*c*) Specific Marketing Strategies: greenwash, bait and switch, planned obsolescence.

(*d*) Content of Advertisements: attack ads, subliminal messages, sex in advertising, products regarded as immoral or harmful.

(*e*) Children and Marketing: marketing in schools.

(*f*) Market: Black markets, grey markets.

Business ethics has been an increasing concern among larger companies, at least since the 1990s. Major corporations increasingly fear the damage to their image associated with press revelations of unethical practices. Marketers have been among the fastest to perceive the market's preference for ethical companies, often moving swiftly to take advantage of this shift in consumer taste. This results in the expropriation of ethics itself as a selling point or a component of a corporate image.

The Body Shop is an example of a company which marketed itself and its entire product range solely on an ethical message, although its products were deceptively characterized and its history was marked by misrepresentations. According to an expose by Jon Entine, an ethics audit of the company, Body Shop, revealed a great gap between its morals and its practices.

Ethics of Production

This area of business ethics, usually deals with the duties of a company to ensure that products and production processes do not cause harm. Some of the more acute dilemmas in this area arise out of the fact that there is usually a degree of danger in any product or production process and it is difficult to define a degree of permissibility.

(*a*) Defective, addictive and inherently dangerous products and services (*e.g.,* tobacco, alcohol, weapons, motor vehicles, chemical manufacturing, bungee jumping).

(*b*) Ethical relations between the company and the environment: pollution, environmental ethics, carbon emissions trading.

(*c*) Ethical problems arising out of new technologies: genetically modified food, mobile phone radiation and health.

(*d*) Product testing ethics: animal rights and animal testing, use of economically disadvantaged groups (such as students) as test objects.

Ethics of Intellectual Property, Knowledge and Skills

Knowledge and skills are valuable but not easily "ownable" as objects. Nor is it clear as to who has the greater rights to an idea: the company who trained the employee, or the employees themselves? The country in which the plant grows or the company which discovered and developed the plant's medicinal potential? As a result, in these areas ethical disputes over ownership arise.

(*a*) Patent infringement, copyright infringement, trademark infringement.

(*b*) Misuse of the intellectual property systems to stifle competition: patent misuse, copyright misuse.

(*c*) Employee raiding: the practice of attracting key employees away from a competitor to take unfair advantage of the knowledge or skills they may possess.

(*d*) The practice of employing all the most talented people in a specific field, regardless of need, in order to prevent any competitors from employing them.

(*e*) Bioprospecting and biopiracy.

(*f*) Business intelligence and industrial espionage.

Ethics and Technology

The computer and the World Wide Web are two of the most significant inventions of the twentieth century. There are many ethical issues that arise from this technology. It is easy to gain access to information. This could lead to data mining, workplace monitoring, and privacy invasion.

International Business Ethics

With the rise of Multinational Corporations, many new practical issues have arisen out of the international context of business. These include bioprospecting, biopiracy, fair trade movement and unethical use of varying global standards (*e.g.,* child labour). The ways in which multinationals take advantage of international differences, such as outsourcing production (*e.g.,* clothes) and services (*e.g.,* call centres) to low-wage countries are not always ethical.

Foreign countries often use dumping as a competitive threat, selling products at prices lower than their normal value. This can lead to problems in domestic markets. It becomes difficult for these markets to compete with the pricing set by foreign markets. In 2009, the International Trade Commission has been researching anti-dumping laws. Dumping is often seen as an ethical issue, as larger companies are taking advantage of other less economically advanced companies.

Companies and business people who wish to thrive in the long-term must adopt sound and ethical decision-making practices. They are then much more likely to enjoy ultimate success than those whose actions are motivated solely by profits. Knowing the difference between right and wrong and choosing what is right is the foundation for ethical decision making. In many cases, doing the right thing often leads to the greatest financial, social, and personal rewards in the long run.

4.8 CERTIFICATION FOR SOCIALLY AND ENVIRONMENTALLY RESPONSIBLE BUSINESS PRACTICES – SOME EXAMPLES

Rising public concern about inhumane working conditions in developing countries led to the creation in 1997, of the Council on Economic Priorities Accreditation Agency. Its purpose was to draw up a universal code of practice for labour conditions in the manufacturing industry, so that consumers in developed countries could be confident that the goods they were buying - in particular, clothes, toys, cosmetics and electronic goods - had been produced in accordance with recognized set of standards.

Other certifications, like the Fair Trade Certification which ensures equity to small growers in international trade and certifications to protect biodiversity are also discussed in the following section.

SA8000 Certification

In 2000, a new entity, Social Accountability International (SAI), was set up whose remit was to develop voluntary standards governing social responsibility, and to certify companies that agreed to meet them. The first such standard is SA8000, which governs employees' working conditions.

The SA8000 programme offers two separate routes for companies that want to demonstrate their commitment to social responsibility. The first, membership, is designed for businesses that are involved in retailing. It involves making a commitment to do business only with socially responsible suppliers. The second route, certification, is intended for manufacturers and suppliers themselves. The process is a rigorous one which begins with the company contacting an accredited auditor. Having demonstrated compliance with existing regulations and assessed how current practice compares with the provisions of SA8000, the company is given the status of "SA8000 applicant". Subsequently, after a formal assessment, if the company is found to be fully compliant, an SA8000 certificate is issued, which is valid for three years.

Requirements of SA8000

The SA8000 code of practice is broken down into nine key areas:

(*a*) Child labour

(*b*) Forced labour

(*c*) Health and safety
(*d*) Freedom of association and collective bargaining
(*e*) Discrimination
(*f*) Disciplinary practices
(*g*) Working hours
(*h*) Compensation
(*i*) Management systems

It has been estimated that upwards of 100 million children worldwide are in full-time labour. The vast majority are in Asia, Africa and South America. Under the terms of SA8000, companies must not support child labour.

Furthermore, they must also provide their staff with a safe and healthy working environment, and respect the right of employees to enroll in trade unions. Discrimination, whether on the grounds of race, nationality, sex, disability or political affiliation, is not allowed, and neither are corporal punishment and verbal abuse. Companies applying for SA8000 certification must ensure that none of their staff, or those working for their suppliers, is required to work more than 48 hours a week, or more than six days a week. Moreover, wages must be at least equal to legal or "industry minimum" levels, and must be sufficient to leave the employee with some discretionary income.

The final category covered by SA8000, governing management systems, sets out the structures and procedures that companies must adopt in order to ensure that compliance with the standard is continuously reviewed.

As well as setting new standards governing workers' rights, SA8000 is designed to embrace existing international agreements, including International Labour Organization Conventions, the Universal Declaration on Human Rights, and the UN Convention on the Rights of the Child. These instruments are explicitly set out in the terms of SA8000.

Fair Trade Certification

Fair trade is a trading partnership, based on dialogue, transparency and respect, which seeks greater equity in international trade. The movement intends to provide market access to otherwise marginalized producers, connecting them to customers and allowing access with fewer middlemen. It aims to provide higher wages than typically paid to producers, as well as helping producers develop knowledge, skills and resources to improve their lives. It focuses in particular, on exports from developing countries to developed countries. Its strategic intent is to deliberately work with marginalized producers and workers to help them move from a position of vulnerability to security and economic self-sufficiency. Coffee and cocoa were among the earliest commodities which were "fair trade certified".

The key fair trade principles are:

(*i*) Creating opportunities for economically disadvantaged producers who have been marginalized by the conventional trading system.
(*ii*) Capacity building, which means to help producers to develop independence
(*iii*) Payment of a fair price to the producers.

(*iv*) To ensure gender equality *i.e.*, the work of men and women to be properly valued and rewarded

(*v*) To provide a safe and healthy working environment for workers.

(*vi*) Fair trade also actively encourages better environmental practices and the application of responsible methods of production.

Fig. 4.1 Some international Fair Trade Certification Marks

Many Fair Trade labelling organizations exist. Some of the largest are:

(*i*) The Fair Trade Labelling Organizations International (FLO), created in 1997, is an association of three producer networks and twenty national labelling initiatives that promote and market the Fair trade Certification Mark in their countries. The FLO labelling system is the largest and most widely recognized standard setting and certification body for labelled Fair trade. It regularly inspects and certifies producer organizations in more than 50 countries in Africa, Asia, and Latin America.

(*ii*) The World Fair Trade Organization (formerly the International Fair Trade Association) is a global association created in 2004. WFTO launched the FTO Mark which identifies registered Fair Trade Organizations (as opposed to the FLO system, which labels products).

Certification for Shade Grown Coffee

In recent years, chains of coffee shops have proliferated in the US and many other western countries. The coffee comes from Central and South America and the growers face a heavy demand. Traditionally, coffee is grown under the shade of the rainforest (without using chemicals) and the ripe berries are handpicked. In order to increase productivity and meet the new demand, the growers have been shifting to unshaded plantations treated with fertilizers and pesticides. Over the past 25 years, about 50 per cent of the shade trees have been replaced with unshaded plantations.

The shade plantations have always provided shelter for large number of birds, vertebrates, and insects. Many migratory songbirds spend the winter in the rainforests. With a decrease in shade trees, there has been an alarming decline in the population of birds, such as warblers and orchard orioles.

Conservation groups like the Rain Forest Alliance and the American Birding Association have initiated programmes to certify coffee as "shade grown" and encourage consumers to ask for such varieties. In fact, one brand already available is called Songbird Coffee!

The Northwest Shade Coffee Campaign is intended to protect the habitat for resident and migratory birds in Latin America and the Caribbean by increasing consumer demand for shade-grown coffee. From Mexico to Colombia, coffee plantation forests often provide the last refuge for birds that have lost their habitat to the vast destruction of tropical forests. The Campaign works with partners like Rainforest Alliance to assure that certification standards prioritize environmental protection.

The Bird Friendly® coffee certification program, administered by the Smithsonian Migratory Bird Center (SMBC), sets the standard for certified shade-grown, organic coffee. SMBC has pioneered much of the leading research exploring the connection between birds, coffee and the farming communities that depend upon healthy, producing forests. The Bird Friendly® certification requires growers to first pursue organic certification; additionally, roasters and retailers participate by paying a fee for use of the certification mark. These funds help to further support the much-needed research to determine the necessary standards for truly sustainable and shade-grown production.

Rainforest Alliance Certified, a certification program administered by the Rainforest Alliance, has developed sustainable product certifications for coffee, cocoa, sugar, produce, flowers and much more. Rainforest Alliance is a non-profit leader in product certification, working with partners around the world to address the needs of farmers and meet the demands of consumers. Rainforest Alliance Certified coffee must meet rigorous criteria, including shade and forest structure, water quality and agrochemical management criteria. Rainforest Alliance Certified farms cover produce coffee in the western hemisphere as well as Africa and Asia. Roaster and retailers selling RA Certified coffee may use the certification seal, free of charge, upon registering with the programme.

4.2 Bird Friendly Certifications

4.9 CONCLUSION

It makes sound business sense for firms to operate in an ethical manner today. While unethical and fraudulent practices may pay off in the short run, it will prove to be disastrous in the long term. Getting ethical certifications like the SA8000, Fair trade and bird friendly labelling, also help in validating the claim of firms about the conduct of business according to ethical principles.

QUESTIONS

1. What is business ethics? Discuss the issue of conflicting interest and its resolution.
2. How does one determine what constitutes ethical behavior?
3. What factors must be present for a company's ethics policy to be successful?
4. Briefly discuss the range of ethical issues confronting a typical business today.

EXERCISE

1. Go to the website and locate the case of Enron where a massive accounting fraud took place. Outline the implications for businesses worldwide. What lessons can be drawn from this case study?

CASE STUDIES

Case A: Coca-Cola India's Corporate Social Responsibility Strategy

This case is about Coca-Cola's corporate social responsibility (CSR) initiatives in India. It details the activities taken up by Coca-Cola India's management and employees to contribute to the society and community in which the company operates.

Coca-Cola India being one of the largest beverage companies in India, realized that CSR had to be an integral part of its corporate agenda. According to the company, it was aware of the environmental, social, and economic impact caused by a business of its scale and therefore it had decided to implement a wide range of initiatives to improve the quality of life of its customers, the workforce, and society at large.

However, the company came in for severe criticism from activists and environmental experts who charged it with depleting groundwater resources in the areas in which its bottling plants were located, thereby affecting the livelihood of poor farmers, dumping toxic and hazardous waste materials near its bottling facilities, and discharging waste water into the agricultural lands of farmers. Moreover, its allegedly unethical business practices in developing countries led to its becoming one of the most boycotted companies in the world.

Notwithstanding the criticisms, the company continued to champion various initiatives such as rainwater harvesting, restoring groundwater resources, and going in for sustainable packaging and recycling, and serving the communities where it operated. Coca-Cola planned to become water neutral in India by 2009 as part of its global strategy of achieving water neutrality. However, criticism against the company refused to die down. Critics felt that Coca-Cola was spending millions of dollars to project a 'green' and 'environment-friendly' image of itself, while failing to make any change in its operations. They said this was an attempt at greenwashing as Coca-Cola's business practices in India had tarnished its brand image not only in India but also globally.

Issues for Analysis and Discussion

(*i*) Analyse the CSR strategy adopted by Coca-Cola India.

(*ii*) Understand the issues and challenges faced by Coca-Cola with regard to its sustainability initiatives in India.

(*iii*) Analyse the underlying reasons for the growing criticism against Coca-Cola in India and explore ways in which the company can address this issue.

(*iv*) Understand the concept of greenwashing and discuss and debate whether Coca-Cola is serious about its water sustainability initiatives.

Case B: The Chinese Tainted Milk Scandal

This case discusses the tainted milk scandal that was unearthed in China in 2008. The milk scandal became public in August 2008, after it was disclosed that the baby formula produced by the Chinese dairy products company, Sanlu Group was contaminated with melamine, which caused kidney failure in many children, resulting in death in some cases. Later, the investigation by the government revealed that the products of 21 other Chinese dairy firms were also contaminated with melamine.

As soon the crisis became public, the Chinese Health Ministry ordered the dairy firms to recall the contaminated products and to destroy the unsold and recalled products. The Chinese Health Ministry started testing dairy products across the country.

Top executives of Sanlu were arrested. Government officials who were found guilty were also sacked. China's dairy industry association announced that the affected children and their families would get compensation from the responsible dairy firms. To support the affected dairy farmers, the government also announced a subsidy.

As a result of this scandal, many countries like Hong Kong, Taiwan, Singapore, South Korea, Australia, and Indonesia banned Chinese dairy products. Several foreign companies which sold China made products or products which used Chinese ingredients recalled their products. The scandal severely affected the reputation of China as a leading food products exporting country.

This case illustrates the serious repercussions of unethical business practices on the fortunes of the Chinese dairy industry. Not only was the reputation of the Chinese industry as a whole, and the dairy industry in particular, badly damaged, it also led to substantial loss of market share worldwide.

Issues for Analysis and Discussion

(*i*) Gain insight into food safety issues in China.

(*ii*) Understand the Chinese milk scandal and its impact on the Chinese dairy industry.

(*iii*) Critically analyse the damage control measures taken by the Chinese government.

(*iv*) Discuss the role of regulation and enforcement to prevent reoccurrence of such incidents.

❑❑❑

5

Economics–Environment Interlinkages

> *Let every individual and institution now think and act as a responsible trustee of the Earth, seeking choices in ecology, economics and ethics that will provide a sustainable future, eliminate pollution, poverty and violence, awaken the wonder of life and foster peaceful progress in the human adventure.*
>
> **John McConnell, Founder of International Earth Day**

Environmental problems are basically economic problems—they are caused by the activities of people (consumers and producers) and end with people as victims. We are therefore, going to make little progress in solving these problems, until we recognize them as economic problems and understand them in the economic sense (Ruff, E.L, 1993). The increase in consumption and production in the past few decades has been accompanied by vast increases in the scale of human impact on the earth. All economic activities either affect or are affected by, natural and environmental resources. Production activities by firms—such as extraction, processing, manufacture, transport, and consumption—and disposal activities by firms and households, introduce wastes into the environment and add stress to the environmental systems. Moreover, economic activities today affect the stock of natural resources available for the future and have inter-temporal welfare effects.

5.1 ECONOMIC FUNCTIONS OF THE ENVIRONMENT

The environment performs three vital functions that have economic implications:

(*i*) Supplier of resources—both renewable and non-renewable—as inputs for production and as final goods for consumption. The natural and environmental resource input function is central to understanding the relationship between economic growth and the environment. Renewable resources like water, air, forest and fisheries and non-renewable resources like deposits of minerals and metals, are vital resources, whose quantity and quality helps to determine the productivity of the economy.

(*ii*) Waste absorption or waste assimilation services, related to the environment's assimilative capacity.

(*iii*) Life sustenance (maintaining biodiversity and genetic diversity) services.

(*iv*) Supply of aesthetic and recreational amenities.

The first function that refers to the environment as a supplier of renewable and non-renewable resources is referred to as the "source function"; the second function that refers to the environment as a waste assimilator is known as the sink function. Protecting the sink function is essential for human health. Protecting the productive or source function is critical to those whose livelihoods depend on these resources. Environmental degradation is likely to be most devastating for the poor, who often depend on natural resources for their survival. Natural resources, as a supplier of aesthetic and recreational services in the form of provision of pristine surroundings, forests, lakes and rivers, contribute to the welfare of the people who enjoy such services.

Environmental problems arise because of the intervention with, and misuse by, humans beings of the vital environmental functions. The failure of the source and sink functions is due to an increase in consumption and production activities, resulting from population explosion and industrialization. Exponentially growing consumption and production activities have depleted the resources beyond the regenerative capacity and produced wastes beyond the assimilative capacity of the environment.

Economic growth results in degradation and overexploitation of resources, which is evident in the decline of fisheries, the growing number of threatened and endangered species, loss of natural habitats and inadvertent introduction of exotics. Box 5.1 providcs an cxample of the impacts of exploitative anthropogenic activities on the environment. The environmental resource base, upon which all economic activity ultimately depends, includes ecological systems that produce a wide variety of services. This resource base is finite. Reckless use of the environmental resource base will irreversibly reduce the capacity for generating material production in the future. All of this implies that there are limits to the carrying capacity of the planet.

The carrying capacity of the environment depends on the technology, the structure of production and consumption and on the ever changing state of interactions between the physical and biotic environment. It is, of course, possible that improvements in the management of resource systems, accompanied by resource-conserving structural changes in the economy, would enable economic growth to take place, despite the finiteness of the environmental resource base, at least for some period of time. However, this depends on signals that effectively reflect increasing scarcities of the resource base (Arrow Kenneth, Bert Bolin and Robert Costanza, et al, 1995).

5.2 LAW OF THERMODYNAMICS AND THE ENVIRONMENT–ECONOMICS INTER-LINKAGES

The Materials Balance Approach, by Kneese and Ayres (1969), traces the physical materials through the economics system. It shows that in a closed economy, the total mass of materials extracted from the natural environment and used in production and consumption activities is equal to the mass of residual discharges back into the environment. The materials balance approach is explained in Fig. 5.1.

BOX 5.1

The Case of Leather Tanneries in Tamil Nadu, India

The leather industry occupies a place of prominence in the Indian economy in view of its massive potential for employment, growth and exports. The tanneries located in the district of Vellore in the State of Tamil Nadu are the source of severe environmental degradation. They are discharging untreated effluents into agricultural fields, road sides, waterways and open lands. The untreated effluent is finally discharged into the river Palar which is the main source of water supply to the residents of the area. The entire surface and subsoil water of the Palar River has been polluted resulting in non-availability of potable water to the residents of the area. A total of 59 villages in the three Divisions of Thirupathur, Vellore and Ranipet are affected by the tanneries. There is acute shortage of drinking water in these 59 villages.

However, the Tanners have come to stay since the industry is the fourth largest foreign exchange earner. Apart from this, the leather industry has tremendous potential for employment generation. Direct and indirect employment of the industry is around 2 million. The skilled and semi-skilled workers constitute nearly 50 per cent of the total work force.

The Loss of Ecology Authority (LEA) was constituted by the Government of India under the direction of the Supreme Court to determine the value of loss to ecology and for fixing the amount of compensation to be paid to the affected parties. The total agricultural damage estimated by the LEA amounted to Rs 34.73 crores out of which, the damage caused by the tanneries in Vellore district alone has been estimated to be Rs 26.82 crore for the period 1991-98. This amount was to be collected from the owners of the 546 tanneries and distributed as 'compensation' to 29,193 families owning 15,164 ha of agricultural lands in 186 villages of the Vellore district in Tamil Nadu.

The Hindu,Business Line, April 15, 2002

Venlatachalam, L, (2005), "Damage Assessment and Compensation to Farmers Lessons from Verdict of Loss of Ecology Authority in Tamil Nadu" Economic and Political Weekly April 9, 2005.

Source: http://www.ielrc.org/content/e9607.pdf
http://www.worstpolluted.org/projects/industries/chem

Fig. 5.1 shows a simple model linking economic activity with environmental resources. Human capital, physical capital and services of labour (L) and environmental services that include the supply of resources and waste assimilation, are the inputs to the production sector. Flows to household sector include manufactured goods (G) and waste assimilation and resource supply services of the environment. The possibility of recycling wastes into resources and the use of such recycled resources in production and consumption however, reduces the negative impacts of economic activity on the environment. Fig. 5.1 highlights the fact that production and consumption activities simply transform resources into wastes. Thus economics–environment linkage explained by the materials balance approach corresponds to the first law of thermodynamics.

Environmental thinkers have used the Laws of Thermodynamics to highlight the environment–economic growth inter-linkages. The laws of thermodynamics are the physical rules which govern the behaviour of matter and energy. The first Law of Thermodynamics, namely the Law of Conservation of Matter and Energy states that matter and energy can neither be created nor destroyed. This implies that consumption and production only transform matter and energy from one form to another. In terms of the functions of the environment, this means that all matter and energy that goes into production and consumption eventually end up as wastes.

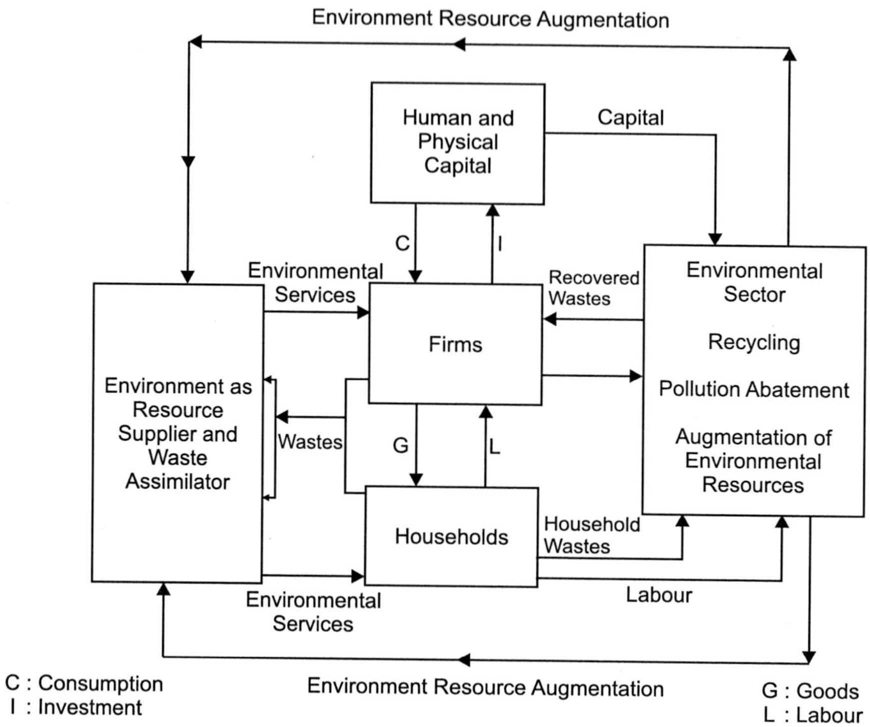

Fig. 5.1 Environment–Economics Interlinkages

The second law is the Law of Entropy which states that in any closed isolated system, available energy and matter are continuously and irrevocably degraded to the unavailable state. *Entropy* is a measure of the disorder in a system. A highly organized system is said to be low-entropy, while a disordered system is said to be high-entropy. Entropy increases as order decreases. Resources have low entropy and wastes have high entropy. Georgescu-Roegen utilized the law of entropy to emphasize the physical limits to the economy. Entropy may be considered to be a measure of the unavailable energy within a closed thermodynamic system. For example, a piece of coal contains available energy and therefore has low entropy. However, once that coal is burnt, the energy is no longer available, but has become dissipated in the form of smoke, heat and ashes. *i.e.,* the coal has now become waste and hence has high entropy.

The two laws together imply that the quantity of resources and wastes are ultimately the same. But they differ in entropic value. As economic growth progresses with increased consumption and production activities, low entropy is constantly being converted into high entropy but the environmental functions—the sink function and the life support function – help in converting high entropy back to low entropy.

The Laws of Thermodynamics are relevant to the economy because economic activity is entropic. The integration between economics and thermodynamics is of crucial importance because economic processes obey thermodynamic laws. This implies that economic development must be consistent with thermodynamics.

5.3 BOULDING'S SPACESHIP EARTH VIEW

In 1966, Kenneth Boulding, in his classic essay, *The Economics of the Coming Spaceship Earth*, described the planet earth as a spaceship and compared the "spaceship economy" to a "cowboy economy". The cowboy economy is characterized by reckless and exploitative behaviour of people who are least worried about the quality of the environment and nature. Conversely, the spaceship economy is characterized by limited material and food supplies and limited capacity to assimilate wastes. The survival strategy in this case is economic use of materials, energy and the environment, and maximization of the recycling of substances, materials and products. A spaceship economy tries to minimize throughput (output) in a closed economy and aims to:

(*i*) Limit extraction and production
(*ii*) Decrease consumption
(*iii*) Continuously reproduce the material form
(*iv*) Increase stock maintenance—goods will be made to last as long as possible.

According to Boulding, "in the cowboy economy, consumption is regarded as a good thing and production likewise; and the success of the economy is measured by the amount of throughput from the factors of production, a part of which, at any rate, is extracted from the reservoirs of raw materials and non-economic objects, and another part of which is output into the reservoirs of pollution. If there are infinite reservoirs from which materials can be obtained, and into which effluvia can be deposited, then the throughput is at least a plausible measure of the success of the economy." Boulding felt that the essential measure of performance of the economy is not production and consumption, but the nature, extent, quality and complexity of the total capital stock. The spaceman economy is concerned about stock maintenance, and any technological change which results in the maintenance of a given total stock with a lessened output (that is, less production and consumption) is clearly a gain (Kenneth Boulding, 1966).

5.4 GREENING OF NATIONAL INCOME

The mechanisms of economic growth may impact the environment in many ways, such as pollution and overexploitation of natural resources that results in the degradation and loss of wildlife habitats. To be precise, economic growth impacts environmental functions both qualitatively and quantitatively. Decline in environmental quality and loss of biological diversity arising from economic expansion are not included in national income estimates. Economic policies do not take into account the value of natural resources in contributing to biological processes such as flood control by wetlands, climate regulation by forests and open spaces through oxygen production and carbon dioxide consumption, and pollination by insects, birds, and mammals.

The greening of national accounts concerns issues related to the environment. For example, production of certain goods contributes to national income, but if the production generates undesirable pollution as a byproduct, the contribution to welfare might be actually negative. Conventional national accounts ignore the reduction in air quality since air quality is not traded on markets and is left out from conventional national accounts. Similarly, oil companies' profits contribute to conventional national income, but the fact that less reserves will be available in future is left unaccounted, even though this may affect the welfare of future generations. If a forest is converted into agricultural land, the cost incurred to do so is part of GNP, but the value of the forest destroyed is ignored. Similarly, the cost incurred towards the reclamation of a wetland to construct buildings is added to the GNP but the value of the ecosystem services lost is ignored. Another example is the cost incurred to remove the oil spill in the ocean caused by an oil tanker accident– in this case the cost incurred to remove the oil is included in the GNP but the value of the lost biodiversity is ignored. Standard accounting measures count revenues from the sale of natural resources as earned income and fail to capture the effects of resource depletion. Environmental accounting refers to adjustments in the conventional measures of economic performance such as the Gross Domestic Product (GDP), Gross National Product (GNP), Net National Product (NNP), Net Domestic Product (NDP), in order to make these measures more sensitive to changes in the natural environment.

Indices of Sustainable Economic Welfare (ISEW) have been calculated for several countries by adjusting the conventional national income accounts (GDP) through the subtraction of social and environmental costs, and the addition of the value of non-market productive activity, such as volunteer work and child rearing. The ISEW was originally developed in 1989 by Herman Daly and John Cobb. The Genuine Progress Indicator, developed by the NGO, *Redefining Progress*, starts with GDP, then adds productive non-market economic activity (*e.g.,* household work) and subtracts other factors (*e.g.,* pollution and crime).

Table 5.1 Environmentally Adjusted NDP (EANDP) as Percentage of NDP in Select Countries

S.No.	Country and Time period	Reduction in NDP (%)	Coverage
1	Japan, 1990	2.4	Depletion of minerals, degradation of land, air, water, including CO_2 and CFCs
2	Korea (1985–1992)	4.1–2.6	Depletion of minerals, degradation of land, air, water
3	Philippines (1988–1996)	NA	Depletion of forests, fish, minerals, degradation of land, air, water
4	Germany	3	Depletion of minerals, degradation of land, air, water
5	Sweden (1993–1997)	0.6	Depletion of minerals, environmental damage due to SO_X, NO_X only, Environmental protection expenditures.

Source: World Bank Paper by Lange Marie Glenn, (2003) Policy Applications of Environmental Accounting, pp. 52.

Due to the inevitable reliance on natural resources to achieve economic growth, national income accounting must incorporate the condition and sustainability of natural resources. The goal of greening national income accounting is to provide policy makers with information on the economy–environment interactions so that environmental goals and consequences can be incorporated into the political processes. Greening national income considers inter-generational impacts of today's production activities. Chapter 8 of Agenda 21 calls for the establishment of integrated environmental and economic accounting as a key tool for integrating environment and development in decision making.

5.5 CONCLUSION

An understanding of the economics-environment inter-linkages is essential if policy and action responses are to contribute to the goals of sustainable development and improved human well-being. The 1987 report of the World Commission on Environment and Development (WCED), *Our Common Future,* rightly observes: "Economics and ecology must be completely integrated in decision making and law making processes not just to protect the environment, but also to protect and promote development".

QUESTION

1. State the economic functions of the environment and bring out the environment-economics interlinkages.

EXERCISES

1. Visit the following website and prepare a note on Indices of Sustainable Economic Welfare.
   http://www.foe.co.uk/community/tools/isew/international.html
2. Read Boulding's "*The Economics of the Coming Spaceship Earth",* in "The. Environmental Quality in a Growing Economy", available at the following site and prepare a comment on the same.
   http://www.eoearth.org/article/The_Economics_of_the_Coming_Spaceship_Earth_(historical)
   or
   http://www.panarchy.org/boulding/spaceship.1966.html

❑❑❑

6

Economic Development and Environmental Degradation

> *Without adequate environmental protection, development is undermined. Without development, resources will be inadequate for needed investments, and environmental protection will fail. In short, promoting development and protecting the environment are complementary.*
>
> **World Development Report, 1992**

Development is about improving the well-being of people. Raising living standards and improving education, health, and equality of opportunity are essential components of development. Environmental conservation and economic development are generally considered as conflicting objectives. It is strongly felt by many economists and environmentalists that economic development is necessarily at the cost of the environment. Some of the books and articles that support this view are: the *Limits to Growth* by the Club of Rome, *Costs of Economic Growth* by Mishan, Barry Commoner's *The Closing Circle, Silent Spring* by Rachel Carson, Goldsmith's *Blueprint for Survival* and Boulding's *The Coming of the Spaceship Earth*. The main contention of these works is that continued and reckless economic growth, that had no concern for the pressure it placed on the environmental functions would result in an environmental catastrophe. They pointed out that the protection of the environment should be an essential part of development.

6.1 ENVIRONMENTAL IMPACT

Past development patterns and processes have had a massive impact on the three vital functions of the environment. The gains in human welfare over the past few decades have been accompanied by a vast increase in thc scalc of human impact on the earth. The impacts of humans on the environment as noted by Paul Ehrlich (Fig. 6.1) is a combination of population, resource use per person (affluence) and environmental damage per unit of resource used (technology). Environmental impact is given as follows:

$$E = P \times A \times T$$

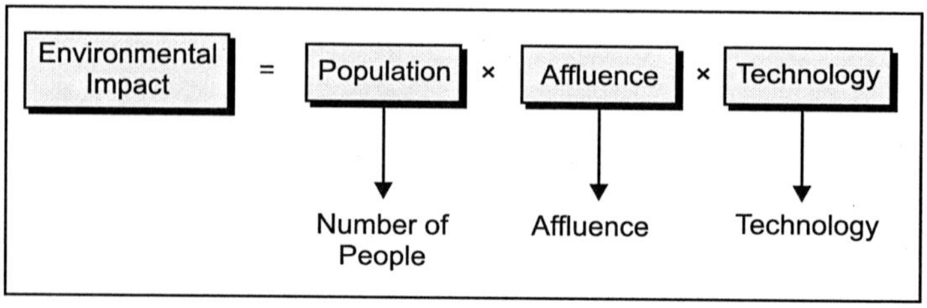

Fig. 6.1 Factors Determining Environmental Impact

This relationship gives an estimate of the three factors which affect the environment: the size of the population, production (or consumption per capita) and the amount of pollution generated per unit of production which reflects the technology in use.

6.2 SOME FACTS ON ENVIRONMENTAL DEGRADATION

Since 1900, the world's population has multiplied more than three times. The world economy has grown twenty-fold. The consumption of fossil fuels has grown by a factor of 30 and industrial production by a factor of 50. Nearly four-fifths of this growth has occurred since the 1950s and is unsustainable. Earth's basic life supporting capital of forest, species and soils are being depleted and its rivers, lakes and oceans are being degraded at an accelerating rate. The global water withdrawals have expanded during the 20th century at rates in excess of population growth. Access to quality water supply has become a great challenge for mankind today.

The 2005 Millennium Ecosystem Assessment reported a substantial and largely irreversible loss in the diversity of life on Earth, along with the deterioration of more than 60 per cent of all ecosystem services assessed. Increasing demands for food and other agricultural products has led to the intensification of agricultural production and the drastic expansion of land under cultivation. Today, farmland covers nearly a quarter of the planet's surface. Entire forest systems have effectively disappeared in at least 25 countries and have declined by 90 per cent in another 29 countries. This destruction continues at staggering rates. Such abrupt and comprehensive changes to ecosystems result in significant stress on the ecological processes and bio-geo-chemical cycles with further adverse implications for both regional and global ecosystem services.

Some evidence of the environmental impacts of human activities is given below:

(*i*) The efforts required to meet the natural resource needs of an additional 3,000 million people in the next 50 years will be immense. A tenfold reduction in resource consumption in the industrialized countries is a necessary, long-term target if adequate resources are to be released for the needs of developing countries.

(*ii*) The human economy now consumes 40 per cent of the mass of plant material produced each year by photosynthesis, using energy from sunlight.

(*iii*) Global emissions of CO_2 reached a new high of nearly 23,900 million tonnes in 1996–nearly four times the 1950 total. Between 1992 and 2002, global emissions of carbon have grown by an additional 400 million tons. Without further policies, by 2030, global emissions of greenhouse gases are projected to grow by a further 37 per cent, and to 52 per cent by

2050. This could result in an increase in global temperature over pre-industrial levels in the range of 1.7–2.4° Celsius by 2050, leading to increased heat waves, droughts, storms and floods, resulting in severe damage to key infrastructure and crops. It is probably too late to prevent global warming as a result of increased greenhouse gas emissions; in addition, many of the targets agreed on in the Kyoto Protocol may not be met.

(*iv*) The earth's ozone layer has suffered severe damage.

(*v*) Tropical forest destruction has gone too far to prevent irreversible damage. It would take many generations to replace the lost forests, and the cultures that have been lost with them can never be replaced.

(*vi*) Many marine fisheries have been grossly overexploited, and their recovery will be slow.

(*vii*) Loss of biodiversity is reflected in the decline of the world's richest species habitats—tropical forests—55 per cent of which has already been destroyed.

(*viii*) Between 1992 and 2002, the proportion of the world's coral reefs that is threatened has grown from 10 per cent to 27 per cent. More than half of the world's coral reefs are potentially threatened by human activities, with up to 80 per cent at risk in the most populated areas. While some may yet be saved, it is too late for many others.

(*ix*) If present consumption patterns continue, two out of every three persons on Earth will live in water stressed conditions by the year 2025.

(*x*) Exposure to hazardous chemicals has been implicated in numerous adverse effects on humans from birth defects to cancer. Global pesticide use results in 3.5 to 5 million acute poisonings a year.

(*xi*) The world water cycle seems unlikely to be able to cope with the demands that will be made on it in the coming decades.

(*xii*) Some 20 per cent of the world's susceptible dry lands are affected by human-induced soil degradation, putting the livelihoods of more than 1000 million people at risk.

(*xiii*) 35 per cent of the land is considered to be degraded, and much of it has been assessed as irreversible within a human time scale. Soil loss currently exceeds soil formation rates by at least tenfold. Land degradation has reduced fertility and agricultural potential. These losses have negated many of the advances made through expanding agricultural areas and increasing productivity.

(*xiv*) Management of solid waste is becoming a serious issue. All production and consumption activities generate wastes in the form of various gases, particulate matter and chemicals, in quantities greater than the assimilative capacity of the environment. This has detrimental effects on the health of human beings and on ecosystems.

(*xv*) Urban air pollution problems are reaching crisis dimensions in many of the mega cities of the developing world, and the health of many urban dwellers has been impaired.

(*xvi*) Average global per capita income has now passed US$5, 000 a year but more than 1,300 million people still live on less than US$1 per day. The number of poor continues to grow throughout the world. Inequality between countries is increasing from 30 to 1 (1960) to 74 to 1 (1997) and over the same period, the richest 20 per cent of the world's population increased its consumption of the world's resources from 70 to over 80 per cent.

6.3 THE ENVIRONMENTAL THREATS TO HEALTH

Economic activities affect the environment and the environmental quality affects the efficient working of the economy. Environmental degradation imposes costs on the economy which results in output and human capital losses. Lost labour productivity resulting from ill health, foregone crop output due to soil degradation and erosion, lost fisheries output and tourism receipts from coastal erosion or lost soil productivity from deforestation can be some of the manifestations of such reduced output. Moreover, many empirical studies suggest that air and water pollution are taking a heavy toll, particularly of people in the developing world, through ill health and premature mortality. China is believed to be losing as much as 10 per cent of its national income to pollution and the corresponding figure for India is 5 - 6 per cent. The direct cost of water and air pollution alone in India is believed to be as high as US$10 billion annually. According to a report by the Asian Development Bank, around 42 per cent of lost disability-adjusted life years (DALY) in Asia are due to water pollution and inadequate sanitation, making it the most important among the major environment-related health risks.

A report on the health and environment world wide, prepared jointly by the World Resources Institute, Washington, DC, the United Nations Environment Programme, the United Nations Development Programme, and the World Bank, reports that around 11 million childhood deaths occur globally (equal to the combined populations of Australia and New Zealand), mostly due to malaria, acute respiratory infections and diarrhea — illnesses that are largely preventable. Further, in an exclusive section on "Environmental Change and Human Health", the report observes how, in spite of vast improvements in human health globally, over the past several decades, preventable illnesses and premature deaths are still occurring in shockingly large numbers in many regions of the world. The report makes the following observations with respect to developing countries:

(*i*) Almost 4 million children die each year of acute respiratory infections, linked with indoor air pollution (especially smoky cooking fuels) and outdoor air pollution (especially from industrialization).

(*ii*) Nearly 1 to 3 million and 2.5 million die each year of Malaria and Diarrhea respectively, both of which are related to the environmental conditions.

(*iii*) In 1991, Cholera claimed some 11,000 lives, causing an economic impact of an estimated $200 million in Peru alone.

(*iv*) Around 3.5 million to 5 million die per year due to acute pesticide poisonings.

In Brazil, Russia, India, Indonesia, China and South Africa (BRIICS), unsafe Water, Sanitation and Hygiene (WSH) was responsible for 2.2 per cent of all deaths and 3.5 per cent of the total burden of disease in 2002—of which 87 per cent occurred in India and China.

6.4 ECOLOGICAL FOOTPRINT

The United Nation's Millennium Ecosystem Assessment published in 2005 found that human beings are already consuming ecosystems at an unsustainable rate and therefore degrading them and that human consumption is likely to increase by 3 to 6 times by 2050. The ecological footprint is a tool for measuring and analyzing human natural resource consumption and waste output within the context of nature's renewable and regenerative capacity.

The "ecological footprint", measures the amount of land that is needed to generate the consumption of a country, including the land needed to assimilate the waste generated and undo climatic change from carbon dioxide emissions by means of carbon sequestration. It is a quantitative assessment of the biologically productive area (amount of nature) required to produce the resources (food, energy and materials) and to absorb the wastes of an individual, city, region, or country. Such analyses highlight the way human populations are dependent on the environment beyond the earth's limits. To be sustainable, our ecological footprint must be within the Earth's limits. If these limits are exceeded, then resources are used faster than they can be renewed, and the environment is degraded and the ability of the Earth to sustain life and economic activity is further reduced. Many recent studies show that humanity's ecological footprint has exceeded the planet's ecological limits and is continuing to rise.

Table 4.1 gives the ecological footprint of ten heaviest nations. Ecological footprint analysis enables the comparison of resource use of different populations and helps in identifying those that are clearly unsustainable. By considering the ecological footprint of each nation, the disparities between nations become evident. USA has the largest footprint of all the nations (9.57 global hectares per person) and various European nations and Australia are in the top ten. Although the United Kingdom is not in the top ten, London's ecological footprint, at 5.8 global hectares per person is amongst the highest and means that an area twice the size of Great Britain is required to support the city. This is the case for all cities.

Table 6.1 Ecological Footprint of Ten Heaviest Nations

Country	Footprint (global hectares per capita)
USA	9.57
United Arab Emirates	8.97
Canada	8.56
Norway	8.17
New Zealand	8.13
Kuwait	7.95
Sweden	7.95
Australia	7.09
Finland	7.00
France	5.74

6.5 LIMITS TO GROWTH

One of the most famous studies published in 1972, written by a group of thinkers from various fields of study, showed that exponential growth rates of population and economic activity could not indefinitely continue on a planet that had only limited natural resources and limited ability to deal with pollution. This famous work was commissioned by the Club of Rome, formed in 1968 by scientists, educators, economists, humanists, industrialists and civil servants under the leadership of an Italian businessman, Aurelio Peccei. The work was published as a book titled *Limits to Growth* by a team of scientists lead by Meadows and others. The study used a computer model of the world economy to show that the existing exponential growth rates of population and economic activity could not continue indefinitely on a planet that had only limited natural resources and limited ability to assimilate wastes. According to this model, the various limits to economic growth are:

(*i*) Increase in population
(*ii*) Increase in resource depletion
(*iii*) Increase in food production
(*iv*) Increase in industrialization
(*v*) Increase in pollution.

The LTG model observed that: "If the present trends in world population, industrialization, food production, pollution and resource depletion continue unchanged, the limits to growth on this planet earth would be reached sometime within the next one hundred years. The most probable result will be a rather sudden uncontrollable decline in both population and industrial capacity." This prediction of the LTG model has been criticized by many. However, the study asserted that "it is possible to alter these growth trends and to establish a condition of ecological and economic stability that is sustainable far into the future". The LTG model started a debate about the limits of the Earth's capacity to support human economic expansion.

6.6 ENVIRONMENTAL KUZNET'S CURVE

The relationship between economic growth and environmental quality is not fixed along a country's economic development path. It may change sign from positive to negative as a country reaches a level of income at which people demand and afford a cleaner environment. The implied inverted 'U' relationship between environmental degradation and economic growth came to be known as the "environmental Kuznet's curve" based on Simon Kuznet's hypothesis about the relationship between income and inequality. At low levels of development, both the quantity and the intensity of environmental degradation are limited; as industrialization and development takes off, resource depletion and waste generation accelerate.

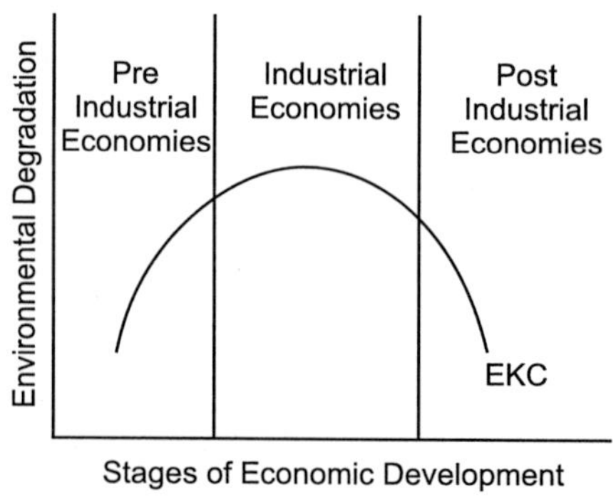

Fig. 6.2 The Environmental Kuznet's Curve – A Development-Environment Relationship

BOX 6.1

The Case of the Aral Sea

The case of the Aral Sea is one of the greatest environmental catastrophes ever recorded. It is the extreme example of how human development has the potential to destroy the environment. The Aral Sea is one of less than twenty ancient lakes in the world, and is estimated to be more than 5 million years old. The Aral sea is situated in the centre of the Central Asian great deserts and hence the whole area experiences high rates of evaporation. The Aral sea basin is shared by seven countries – Afghanistan, Kazakhstan, the Kyrgyz Republic, Tajikistan, Turkmenistan, Uzbekistan and the Islamic Republic of Iran. Two major rivers drain into the Aral Sea - the Amu Darya, flows into the Aral Sea from the south; and the Syr Darya, which reaches the sea at its north end.

Until 1960, the Aral Sea was the fourth largest lake in the world; it has now lost 90 per cent of its source waters and two thirds of its surface area. Salinity has increased fourfold. Until 1960, the lake was brackish, with a salinity averaging near 10g/lir (less than a third of the salinity of the ocean) and was inhabited mostly by fresh water species. The extensive deltas of the rivers Amu Darya and Syr Darya sustained diverse flora and fauna. After the Russian Empire was replaced by the Soviet Union, traditional agricultural practices were destroyed by collectivization; there was a greater push towards agricultural and industrial production in the region. The central planning authority of the Soviet Union devised the "Aral Sea plan" to transform the region into the cotton belt of the USSR and subsequently the Aral region produced 90 per cent of cotton and became a major exporter of cotton.

The intensive cotton monoculture resulted in extreme environmental degradation. Water diversions reduced the Amu Darya and the Syr Darya to relative trickles. Prior to 1960 the annual inflow from the rivers Amu Darya and the Syr Darya was 56 km 3. Following the increase in diversion for agriculture and irrigation, the inflows reduced to 4 km^3 by 1990. The Sea itself lost three-quarters of its volume and half its surface area, and salinity has tripled, all since 1960. The exposed sea beds are thick with salts and agricultural chemical residue, which are carried aloft by the winds as far as the Atlantic and Pacific Oceans.

The Aral Sea acted as a climate regulator for the region: it softened cold Siberian winds in winters and acted as a conditioner, lowering heat in summer months. The sea's shrinkage has resulted in drier and shorter summers, and in longer and colder winters. Regional climate became more continental, shortening the growing season and causing some farmers to switch from cotton to rice, which demanded even more diverted water. From the exposed sea beds, winds picked up an estimated 43 million tons of sediments laced with salts and pesticides, with devastating health consequences for surrounding regions. These contaminated Aral dust storms have been reported as far away as the Arctic and Pakistan. Respiratory illnesses were particularly common, and throat cancers burgeoned. With the dissolution of the Soviet Union at the end of 1991, the five Central Asian nations signed an agreement in 1992 pledging efforts toward Aral rehabilitation. However, the outlook for the remnants of the South Aral Sea still remains bleak.

Source: http://hercules.gcsu.edu/~sdatta/home/teaching/hydro/case_studies/aral_sea.html
http://www1.american.edu/ted/aral.htm
*Newton*http://www.transboundarywaters.orst.edu/research/case_studies/Documents/aral_sea.pdf
http://www.worldlakes.org/lakedetails.asp?lakeid=9219
http://www1.american.edu/ted/aral.htm

At higher levels of development, due to the availability of more efficient technology and increased demand for environmental quality, there is a steady decline in environmental degradation as shown in the above figure. The EKC analysis helps to position a country in terms of the environmental consequences of its development activities and helps in identifying how far it is from the turning point. This helps in policy making towards a greener economy.

Nations are losing more from pollution than they are gaining from industrialization. China is a perfect example. Twenty years of uncontrolled economic development has created serious, chronic air and water pollution. This has increased health problems and resulted in annual losses to farmers of crops worth billions of dollars. Hence, uncontrolled growth is not only bad for the environment, it also makes no economic sense.

Economic development without environmental considerations can thus, cause serious environmental damage, impairing the quality of life of present and future generations. Technology has the potential to diminish or worsen the effects of economic growth, depending on whether the net result has increased or decreased per capita natural resource consumption.

However, some schools of thought believe that there is no limit to economic growth, particularly given that technological progress allows us to use fewer resources for greater returns. However, based on established principles of ecology and physics, there is a limit to economic growth. Moreover, though technological progress can reduce ecological impacts of economic growth, it can also contribute to ecological problems. Uncontrolled economic growth may have negative effects on ecological systems that are essential to wildlife conservation.

6.7 NEED FOR SUSTAINABLE DEVELOPMENT

In 1992, the World Bank observed that the growth of population between 1992 and 2030 at the 1992 growth rate would require the food production to double, industrial output and energy use to increase three times world wide and five times in developing countries. This growth will result in dreadful environmental damages in the absence of appropriate policy choices. We have already wasted and destroyed vast amounts of natural resources, and in doing so have put the planet at risk. The Earth cannot support unrestricted growth.

Herman Daly advocates that the current unrestrained economic growth should be replaced by a steady or stationary state, characterized by "a constant stock of physical capital, and a constant population". For population to remain constant, the birth rate must equal the death rate and for physical capital to remain constant, the level of depreciation must equal the rate of production. Daly stresses that a steady state does not hold constant, knowledge, technology, the distribution of income or the allocation of resources. He therefore claims that a steady state economy will develop qualitatively, rather than quantitatively.

The OECD Environmental Outlook-2030s presents the key environmental challenges for the future according to a "traffic light" system (Table 6.2).

Table 6.2 Key Environmental Challenges for the Future

	Green Light	Yellow Light	Red Light
Climate change		• Declining GHG emissions per unit of GDP	• Global GHG emissions • Increasing evidence of an already changing climate
Biodiversity & renewable natural resources	• Forested area in OECD countries	• Forest management • Protected areas	• Ecosystem quality • Species loss • Invasive alien species • Tropical forests • Illegal logging • Ecosystem fragmentation
Water	• Point-source water pollution in OECD countries (industry, municipalities)	• Surface water quality and wastewater treatment	• Water scarcity • Groundwater quality • Agricultural water use and pollution
Air quality	• OECD country SO_2 and NOx emissions	• PM and ground-level ozone • Road transport emissions	• Urban air quality
Waste and hazardous chemicals	• Waste management in OECD countries • OECD country emissions of CFCs	• Municipal waste generation • Developing country emissions of CFCs	• Hazardous waste management and transportation • Waste management in developing countries • Chemicals in the environment and in products

Source: OECD, (2008) Environmental Outlook to 2030

Key: Green light = environmental issues which are being well managed or for which there have been significant improvements in management in recent years but for which countries should remain vigilant.

Yellow light = environmental issues which remain a challenge, but, for which management is improving or for which current state is uncertain or which have been well managed in the past but are less so now.

Red light = environmental issues which are not well managed, are in a bad or worsening state, and which require urgent attention.

All trends are global, unless otherwise stated.

6.8 CONCLUSION

Economic development without environmental consideration can cause serious ecological damage, impairing the quality of life of present and future generations. It is time to strike a balance between the demands of economic development and the need for protection of the environment. This calls for sustainable development. Sustainable development is the meeting of "the needs of the present generation without compromising the ability of future generations to meet their own needs."

Sustainable development attempts to combine the elements of economic efficiency, intergenerational equity, social concerns and environmental protection. Sustainable development, attempts to accelerate development in an environmentally responsible manner, keeping in mind the inter-generational equity requirements.

Thanks to the Rio Conference, sustainable development has been the development strategy for all the countries since 1992, which has helped in reducing the impacts on the environment. According to UNEP's Global Environment Outlook (GEO), 2000, some of the key successes are:

(*i*) The ozone layer is expected to have largely recovered within half a century as a result of the Montreal Protocol.

(*ii*) The public is now much more concerned about environmental issues. Popular movements in many countries are forcing authorities to make changes.

(*iii*) Voluntary action taken by many of the world's major industries is reducing resource use and eliminating waste. The happy discovery that what is good for the environment can also be good for business may do much to reverse trends for which industry itself was originally largely responsible. This "win-win" situation bodes well for the planet.

(*iv*) Governments in developed regions have been markedly successful in reducing air pollution in many major cities. Innovative legislation has been introduced, and the goal of zero emissions in several important areas is no longer considered utopian.

(*v*) Deforestation has been halted and reversed in parts of both Europe and North America.

(*vi*) Local Agenda 21 initiatives have proved an effective way of developing and implementing sustainable development policies that involve communities and political agencies alike.

This gives us hope that the catastrophe predicted by the "doomsday" models may be at least postponed before the world at large comes up with solutions to avoid the threats faced today by the planet earth.

QUESTIONS

1. Economic development is at the cost of environmental quality. Bring out the arguments for and against this statement.
2. Explain with global data, the impact of environmental degradation on the health of human beings.

EXERCISES

1. Prepare a study of the environmental impact of any development activity - local or national and come out with environmentally friendly alternatives.
2. Calculate your ecological footprint using the information given in the website : http://www.ecologicalfootprint.com/

3. List out the activities in your lifestyle that are against the environment. How do you think they can be changed?
4. Prepare a note on EKC for India with reference to forest clearance and air pollution/water pollution.
5. Compare India with a few developed (like UK, & USA) and developing countries (like China and Sri Lanka) on the basis of ecological footprint, Environmental Sustainability Index, Environmental Performance Index, carbon footprint, water footprint etc., by accessing information from the following websites:
   (*a*) http://www.yale.edu/esi/ESI2005_Main_Report.pdf
   (*b*) http://epi.yale.edu/CountryScores
   (*c*) http://www.photius.com/rankings/

❑❑❑

7

Economics of Pollution

> *Our economic system has a fatal design flaw: it conceals many of the negative consequences of our choices, labelling them 'externalities'.*
>
> **Unknown**

Pollution is "the introduction of contaminants into an environment that causes instability, disorder, harm or discomfort to the physical systems or living organisms they are in". It is the presence in the environment of substances thrown by the production and consumption acts of human beings, in quantities that is in excess of the normal levels, sufficient to cause damage to the properties and to the health of human beings, flora and fauna. Pollution can occur in many forms. Factories discharge waste into the atmosphere in the form of smoke or emissions, depositing particles in the surrounding area. They also discharge waste liquids, referred to as effluents, containing chemicals, into rivers, lakes and the sea.

Pollution is the unintended consequence of economic activities of production and consumption. It is the result of over exploitation of the limited absorptive capacity of the environment, which results in scarcity of pure air, and potable water, besides making many forms of flora and fauna extinct. Pollution can be classified as air pollution, water pollution, soil pollution and marine pollution, depending on the environmental medium into which the wastes are deposited. When the pollutants causing the damage are found in the air, then it is an instance of air pollution. Water pollution occurs when the pollutants causing damage enter water bodies. For example, the discharge of sulphur dioxide (SO_x) or nitrogen dioxide (NO_x) emissions into the air is air pollution and the discharge of effluents into rivers is water pollution. Accidents at sea resulting in oil spillage that contaminates the sea, endangering aquatic and bird life, is marine pollution. Individuals also cause pollution by depositing waste (including litter) in the streets or in rivers and canals. Pollution can also take the form of noise pollution; playing loud music much to the annoyance of the neighbours.

Pollution can also be classified as national and transnational or global pollution. When the effects of pollution are confined to the borders of a nation, it is referred to as national pollution and when the impact of pollutants travels beyond the borders it is transnational or global pollution. Typical examples of global pollution problems are global warming, ozone depletion and acid rain.

7.1 POLLUTION AS AN EXTERNALITY

Environmental pollution is an unintended and non-compensated consequence of an economic activity, on third parties, which economists refer to as externalities. An externality arises if consumers or producers do not take into consideration the full social cost (or benefit) of their activities for accounting purposes.

An externality is defined as an unintended and unaccounted consequence of production and consumption activities of firms and households on the rest of the society towards which no payment or compensation is made. It is external to the decision making of the agent (firm or household). Externalities are also referred to as side-effects, spillover effects, secondary effects and as external economies/diseconomies.

An externality exists when the market price or cost of production of a good excludes its social impact, cost or benefit. Externalities could be positive or negative and may be the result of both consumption and production activities. Thus, there are four types of externalities which are listed in Table 7.1.

Table 7.1 Classification of Externality

Effects	Consumption	Production
Beneficial	Vaccination against an infectious disease (Positive consumption externality)	Pollination of blossoms arising from proximity to an apiary (Positive production externality)
Adverse	Noise pollution from radio playing in the park (Negative consumption externality)	Chemical factory discharging contaminated water into water systems (Negative production externality)

Source: Perman *et al.,* (1996)

Environmental pollution is a negative externality. A crucial characteristic feature of environmental damage is that they are rarely experienced—or at least their full extent is not experienced by the people who cause them. The firm that discharges wastes into the waterways does not take into account the impact of the water pollution it has created on others while deciding its volume of production. They are external costs to the firm that creates pollution. The firm simply equates its marginal revenue (MR) to its marginal private cost (MPC) *i.e.*, MR = MPC. However, due to the externality generated by the production activity of the firm, its marginal private cost (MPC) is less than the marginal social cost (MSC) *i.e.*, MPC < MSC. As a result, at the firm's equilibrium, MSC > MR. Ignoring the external costs, the firm reaches a socially inefficient level of production, causing market failure.

The impact of pollution on market outcome may be explained under both perfectly and imperfectly competitive conditions.

7.2 IMPACT OF POLLUTION UNDER PERFECT COMPETITION

A firm's equilibrium for profit maximization is determined at that level of output at which the following two conditions are satisfied:

(*i*) MC = MR

(*ii*) Marginal cost curve cuts Marginal revenue curve from below.

Marginal cost refers to Marginal Private Cost (MPC) of production, that is, the costs incurred by the firm on labour, raw material, rent, machinery, tax payments etc. To sum up, it includes all the fixed and variable costs of production.

A perfectly competitive market is one in which there are a large number of firms selling homogenous products. The price in such a market is determined by industry's demand and supply for the product. The price is determined by the equality of demand and supply. The firm is a price taker. The firm maximizes its profit at that level of output at which its MPC = MR. This is shown in Figure 7.1a.

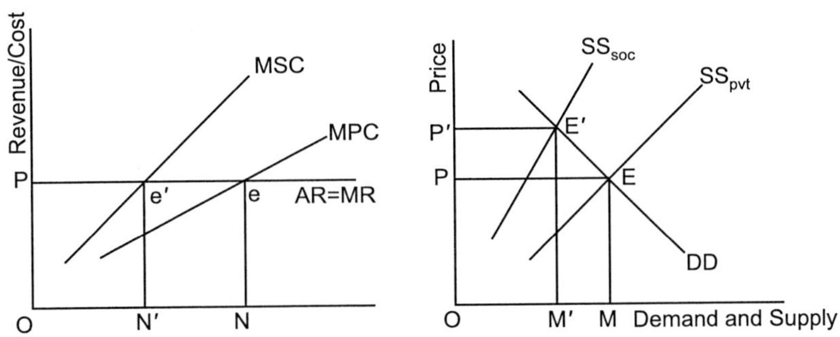

7.1a Impact of Externality on Firm's Output

7.1b Impact of Externality on Market Outcome

Fig. 7.1 Impact of Externality

In Figure 7.1a, the equilibrium price is OP, determined by the supply and demand curve for the product. Since the firm is a price taker, OP is its given price. At this price level, the firm's demand curve (AR curve) is perfectly elastic and hence AR= MR. Firm's MC curve is MPC that includes only its cost of producing the product and does not include any external cost that is likely to occur in the process of production. Hence, the firm's equilibrium is at "e", given by the equality of MPC and MR. The resulting equilibrium output of the firm is ON. In the absence of pollution, ON is an optimal output since at "e", price is equal to marginal cost. However, in the presence of an externality, such as pollution, ON is not an optimum output since optimal output in this case is decided by the equality of MSC to price, and not by the equality of MPC to price. The firm must consider the full costs of its production activities. The presence of externalities results in over production of a good relative to the socially optimal level of output.

Production by the firm creates pollution, which in turn causes adverse effects on the properties, and health of the people living in the area, where the firm is located. These costs are called as external costs. These costs are external to the decision making of the firm and increase with increase in pollution. The society faces such costs only because of the production activities of the firm that cause pollution. Hence, the cost that the firm must actually consider for deciding its profit maximizing output level is Marginal Social Cost (MSC). Marginal Social Cost is the sum of Marginal Private Cost and Marginal External Cost.

$$MSC = MPC + MEC$$

MEC is the additional cost imposed on third parties from the production of an additional unit of output. If MEC per unit of output is constant, MSC would be parallel to MPC. However, in reality it is not so and hence MSC is not parallel to MPC and is drawn in the Figure 7.1a, as diverging from MPC. If the firm takes into consideration both MPC and MEC for deciding its profit maximizing output, then its equilibrium is given by the equality of MSC and MR, *i.e.*, where MSC cuts MR—at e′ in the figure. The output corresponding to the equilibrium at e' is ON′. Clearly, ON′< ON; ON′ is the socially optimal output given by the equality of MSC to MR. Thus, there is a difference of NN′ between the private optimal output and social optimal output. This implies that the society will be better off with ON′ units of output. Non-inclusion of external costs results in ON units of output and clearly NN′ is over production. The resources used in the production NN′ units of output have greater value in other employments and should have been made available to some other industry which is now facing a shortage of resources. Thus, the presence of external costs which are not included by the firm in its decision making, distorts optimum allocation of resources.

Externalities that are not incorporated in cost calculations for decision making by firms affect the entire industry. Figure 7.1b shows this. The supply curve in Figure 7.1b is the summation of marginal cost curves. SS_{pvt} is the summation of MPC curves and SS_{soc} is the summation of MSC curves of all the firms. SS_{soc} lies above SS_{pvt} reflecting the difference between MSC and MPC. The vertical distance between SS_{soc} and SS_{pvt} is the total external costs imposed on the society by all the firms in the industry. DD is the industry demand curve. The market demand curve cuts the SS_{pvt} curve at E and the equilibrium price and output is OP and OM. Since the production of output causes pollution, the relevant supply curve is the summation of MSC curves. In the Figure, SS_{soc} is the relevant supply curve and the market equilibrium is at E′ yielding an output OM′ and price OP′. Comparing this price-output level with the equilibrium outcome at E, it is clear that, when external costs are internalized by all the firms, output is lower and price is higher. OM' is lower than OM. In other words, the industry's output when external costs are ignored by the firms is greater than the output that results when external costs are included by the firms (OM > OM′). There is over production in the industry to the extent of M′M which implies that other industries are producing less than the optimum level. Resources used in producing M′M output in this industry creates scarcity of resources for other industries. Thus, when externalities are present, the market fails to allocate resources efficiently.

The impact of externalities on efficiency and market outcome under imperfect competition is illustrated in Figure 7.2. The Figure illustrates the case of a chemical firm, discharging wastes into a river, downstream of which live a community of fishermen, whose livelihood is affected because of the chemical waste. The chemical plant is imposing an externality on the fishermen by reducing fish stocks in the river.

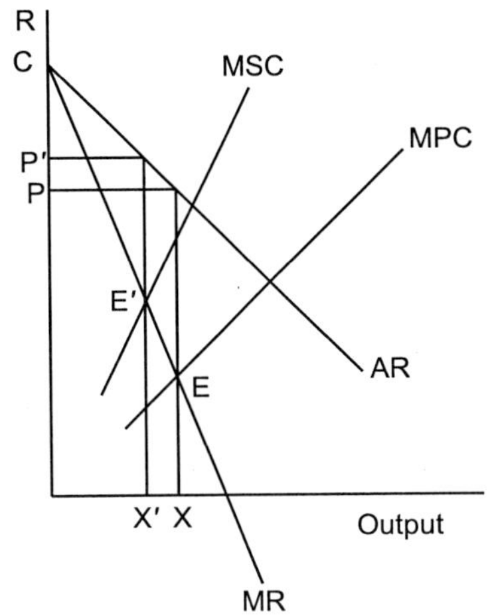

Fig. 7.2 Negative Externality in Production

However, the chemical plant does not take into account the social cost imposed by its activity when deciding its output. AR and MR are the chemical firm's average and marginal revenue curves. Due to imperfect competition, the AR and MR curves decline as its output (X) increases. The firm's marginal (private) cost curve is MPC which rises as output rises. The profit maximizing equilibrium of the firm is at E where MR = MPC. The equilibrium output is OX and price is OP. The presence of externality generates MEC (Marginal External Cost). The firm's MPC is less than MSC. Marginal Social Cost, which is a sum of MPC and MEC, is shown in Figure 7.2 by the MSC curve. It is shown as an upward sloping curve on the assumption that the damage to the fish stock increases as the output of the firm increases. The socially optimum level of output of the firm is the output level given by the equality of MR to MSC equality. In Figure 7.2, MR = MSC at E′. The output, corresponding to E′ is X′, which is lower than the private profit maximizing output, OX. Compliance with the efficiency rule of MPC = MR, results in overproduction of chemicals to the extent of X′X. The firm thus, produces an output that is in excess of the socially optimal output level.

7.3 SOLUTIONS TO THE PROBLEM OF EXTERNALITY

It is clear from the above analysis that there is a welfare loss associated with the externality. This inefficiency, according to many economists, is due to the absence of market for resources. In this case, there is no market for the waste assimilation services of the environment which enables the firm to discharge its wastes into the river at zero cost, while the polluted water affects the society's welfare. Hence, **externality is a case of missing markets**. The market fails to allocate resources efficiently when a firm fails to account for external effects generated by its activity. The solution to this situation of inefficiency requires knowledge of the causes for the externality. Externalities are attributed to:

(*i*) **Market Failure:** It is caused by the absence of market for resources and services provided by the environment. If the use of the atmosphere and rivers and lakes for discharging wastes are priced, then firms will minimize this cost too, by treating the wastes. In other words, if there is a market for the waste assimilation function of the environment, similar to the market for the resources that firms use, then the firms will include the cost incurred for disposing the wastes in their cost calculation and hence, try to minimize this cost also, which would then call for a reduction of wastes discharged.

(*ii*) **Government Failure:** It arises due to implementation of inappropriate policies, ignorance of the effects of policies, incomplete information, etc. Government failure, arises when the government has created inefficiencies. Anderson (1994) refers to Government failure as 'state failure'—attributable to the absence of integrated preventive pollution control strategies and to the subsequent disparity between costs of intervention and the output of environmental regulation. It is the failure of the government to correct the inefficiencies in the market.

Thus, market failure and government failure cause environmental degradation. A number of policy measures are available which may be appropriately employed to arrest environmental degradation. The various instruments work better in combination, rather than as an exclusive instrument.

The various policy measures available to address the issue of pollution have been classified under three categories:

(*a*) Voluntary Measures or Moral Suasion

(*b*) Legal Measures – Command and Control (C & C)

(*c*) Economic Instruments

(*a*) **Moral Suasion** is basically appealing to or persuading the firms and individuals to be more environmentally friendly in their production and consumption activities.

(*b*) **C & C instruments** also referred to as *standards* or *regulations*, consist of a 'command', which sets a standard—the maximum level of permissible pollution, and a 'control', which monitors and enforces the standard (Chapter 18).

(*c*) **Economic instruments** refer to any instrument that provides continuous incentives to encourage responsible parties to reduce their releases of pollutants or make their products less polluting. Economic instruments are more popularly known as Market Based Instruments (MBIs), because of their reliance on market signals to bring about changes in the behaviour of economic agents.

Market mechanism should place a 'proper' price on environmental resources and services or, at the very least, ensure that the social benefits of exploitation exceed the social costs. Accordingly, the solution to environmental problems is through the creation of markets for pollution rights, which includes imposing a tax on pollution or polluting input/product, or granting subsidies for pollution control activities and issuing marketable permits of right to pollute an assigned quantity of a specified pollutant. Such instruments—pollution tax, pollution subsidy and permits—are referred to as economic instruments or market based instruments. Chapters 19–21 of the book deal elaborately with the various pollution control instruments.

7.4 CONCLUSION

Pollution is a cost that polluters do not bear and is hence referred to as an externality by economists. Polluters do not pay all of the costs for producing a good and so they produce too much of it. One way is for victims to sue the polluters for damages, which depends on the presence of stringent legal rules and regulations for pollution control. Some of the other ways include imposing a tax on each unit of pollution on the basis of damage resulting from pollution, imposing a cap on pollution and facilitating trade of the right to pollute (Pollution permits). The various measures have their merits and limitations and a wise mix of various policy options is required to ensure optimum pollution control.

QUESTION

1. Examine the impact of pollution on output and price under perfect and imperfect competition.

EXERCISES

1. Give at least five examples of negative and positive externalities.
2. List all the positive and negative externalities from a programme to cut fertilizer subsidy to farmers.
3. Economists see pollution problems as examples of the class of adverse externality phenomena. An adverse externality is said to occur when the decisions of one agent harms another in an unintended way, and when no compensation occurs. Does this mean that if a pollution source, such as a power station compensates those affected by its emissions, then, there is no pollution problem?
4. Every young couple decides to have at least two children. What are the positive and negative externalities associated with their decision?

❑❑❑

8

Sustainable Development

> *The ultimate test of man's conscience may be his willingness to sacrifice something today for future generations whose words of thanks will not be heard.*
>
> **Gaylord Nelson, Founder of Earth Day**

The facts on the environmental consequences of consumption and production activities of homosapiens reveal that the path of development pursued till date is unsustainable in the long run (Chapter 6). According to the Millennium Ecosystem Assessment, 2005, some 60 per cent of the planet's ecosystems are deteriorating in quality and/or being utilized in an unsustainable way, resulting in depletion of both renewable and non-renewable resources, climate change and causing the extinction of biodiversity. The changes that have been made to ecosystems have resulted in substantial net gains to human well-being and economic development, but these gains have been achieved at increasing costs in the form of the degradation of many ecosystem services, and the exacerbation of poverty for some groups of people. The ecosystem services that have been degraded over the past 50 years include fisheries, water supply, natural hazard protection, regulation of air quality, regulation of regional and local climate, regulation of erosion, spiritual fulfillment, and aesthetic enjoyment (Millennium Ecosystem Assessment, 2005).

Some of the specific findings of the Millennium Ecosystem Assessment Report (2005) are:

(*i*) 60 per cent of the world's ecosystem services have been degraded.

(*ii*) Of 24 evaluated ecosystems, 15 are being damaged.

(*iii*) About a quarter of the Earth's land surface is now cultivated.

(*iv*) People now use between 40 per cent and 50 per cent of all available freshwater running off the land. Water withdrawals have doubled over the past 40 years.

(*v*) Over a quarter of all fish stocks are over-harvested.

(*vi*) Since 1980, about 35 per cent of the mangroves have been lost.

(*vii*) About 20 per cent of corals were lost in just 20 years; 20 per cent degraded.

(*viii*) Nutrient pollution has led to eutrophication of waters and coastal dead zones.

Since 1900, the world economy has grown twenty fold. The 2005 Millennium Ecosystem Assessment reported a substantial and largely irreversible loss in the diversity of life on Earth. By 2030, the number of people living in areas affected by severe water stress is expected to increase by another 1 billion to over 3.9 billion. According to the report, the option for future development is bleak. The economies have already incurred heavy costs of unsustainable development. What is needed is therefore, sustainable development – development that lasts. The term Sustainable development was first coined in the 1980 World Conservation Strategy (IUCN/UNEP/WWF) but gained popularity since the 1987 World Commission on Environment and Development, more commonly known as the Brundtland Report. Sustainable Development is fundamentally about reconciling development and the environmental resources on which society depends. The need to balance environment and development are central to most definitions of sustainable development.

Literally, sustainable development refers to maintaining development over time. The most widely cited definition of sustainable development, is that of the World Commission on Environment and Development (WCED), formed by the United Nations in 1984. According to WCED:

"Sustainable Development is the development that meets the needs of the present generation without compromising the ability of the future generations to meet their own needs."

Defined thus, sustainable development is about the fair treatment of future generations - it is a development which allows all future generations to have a potential average quality of life, at least as high as the average quality of life of the current generation. Early concepts of development focused on desirable economic and social objectives such as:

(*i*) Increases in real income per capita

(*ii*) Improvements in health and nutrition

(*iii*) Educational achievemen

(*iv*) Access to resources

(*v*) More equitable distribution of income

(*vi*) Increases in basic public freedoms.

For development to be sustainable, it must continue to meet these and other objectives defined by society over an indefinite period of time. The World Commission on Environment and Development (WCED) has put forward a number of conditions referred to as eleven strategic imperatives for SD. Some of these conditions which have to be met if development is to be sustainable, include:

(*a*) Growth sufficient to meet human needs and aspirations.

(*b*) More equitable distribution of proceeds of growth within and between nations.

(*c*) Conservation of declining stocks of ecological capital.

(*d*) Reduction of energy and natural resource content of products produced.

(*e*) Integrating environment and economics in all major institutions of decision making – government, industry and home.

8.1 SUSTAINABLE DEVELOPMENT AND ENVIRONMENTAL PROTECTION COMPARED

Similarities

(*i*) By protecting the environment we support sustainable development. A healthy environment means clean air, unpolluted water and healthy soil, which are necessary for the survival of future generations.

(*ii*) The preservation of natural resources supports sustainability. Many environmental concepts like reuse and recycling allow us to save natural resources for future generations.

(*iii*) Environmental training and education support sustainable development. While working to protect the environment, we learn more about the world around us and improve our ability to identify solutions for sustainable development.

Differences

(*i*) Environment is just one of the components embedded in the concept of sustainable development. Society and economy are equally important. Although it is necessary to protect the environment it is not always sufficient, since a healthy environment does not necessarily mean a prosperous society or a healthy economy.

(*ii*) Sustainable development is a goal of the entire society. Thus, a participatory approach is an integral part of sustainability.

(*iii*) Sustainable development explores the relationships between environmental, social and economic benefits. Environmental protection is often limited to the impact on nature.

(*iv*) Environmental protection implies reducing adverse effects, not necessarily allowing future generations to inherit the same amount of natural, social and economic wealth as their predecessors.

(*v*) Whereas environmental protection is often regulated, sustainable development involves going beyond compliance.

8.2 THE COMPONENTS OF SUSTAINABLE DEVELOPMENT

Sustainable development will address three circles of sustainability: economic, social and ecological, each with key issues and objectives (Figure 8.1). Figure 8.1 illustrates that each of the circles of sustainability has independent objectives: yet, there are areas where overlap occurs, implying partial integration between two objectives. Full integration of all three objectives is the ultimate goal.

Economic Sustainability

The economic circle of sustainability is based on the principle of maximizing the flow of income from a stock of assets (or capital) while maintaining the stock yielding this income. Economic sustainability is explained in terms of identifying the types of capital to be maintained - namely, man made capital, human capital and natural capital - and substitutability among various forms of capital. Environmental concerns in economic development focus on valuation of natural resource capital and the degree to which environmental degradation is internalized into economic decisions.

Social Sustainability

The social circle of sustainability addresses issues such as poverty, health, education, local empowerment and maintaining culture and heritage. Sustaining social and cultural systems is more important with more changes in social norms over a time period. The links with the environment focus on the allocation and distribution of natural resources to future generations, as well as local empowerment over natural resource management.

Ecological Sustainability

The ecological circle of sustainability is concerned with maintaining the biophysical environment to preserve resilience and the ability of natural systems to adapt to change. Ecological processes and cycles are fundamental to life on earth and hence, must be protected from degradation. A key linkage with the economy is through the first two functions of the environment, namely, supply of raw material for production and the environment being used as a waste sink. Linkage with social sustainability is through the level of local participation in natural resource management. The concept of carrying capacity is critical, both in terms of human population that can be supported and the ability of the environment to assimilate waste products.

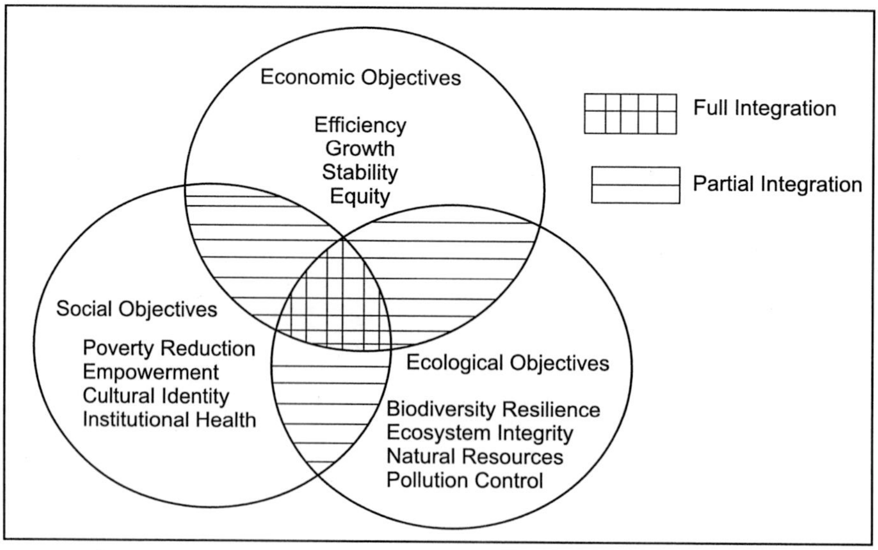

Fig. 8.1 The Three Circles of Weak Sustainable Development

Figure 8.1 is referred to as the weak sustainability model by economists; it assumes that the degradation of one group of assets (environmental, social or economic) can be compensated for by improvement in another. This weak sustainability model assumes substitutability between economic and ecological components and fails to consider the ecological constraints. Weak sustainability aims at achieving a harmony in the interactions of the three systems, which is represented by the shaded area (full integration) in the diagram. Figure 8.1 shows that the area in which the interests of all three systems converge is small relative to the size of each system.

8.3 WEAK AND STRONG SUSTAINABLE DEVELOPMENT

A necessary condition for sustainable development, is that the total stock of resources - human capital (K_H), man made capital (K_M) and natural capital (K_N) consisting of renewable and non-renewable resources, does not decrease over time. Total stock of capital is the sum of human capital, man made capital and natural capital.

$$K = K_H + K_M + K_N$$

Some economists refer to this as the weak sustainability model. Figure 8.1 explains the weak sustainability model which assumes substitutability between various forms of capital. Hence, according to the weak sustainability version, development is sustainable as long as the total stock of capital remains constant. It assumes that the degradation of the stock of any one type of resource can be compensated for by improvement in another and that externalities can be internalized.

The very strong sustainability model assumes that little substitution can occur between K_M and K_N. The weak sustainability model fails to acknowledge the ecological constraints that humans, other species, markets, policies and developments must operate within.

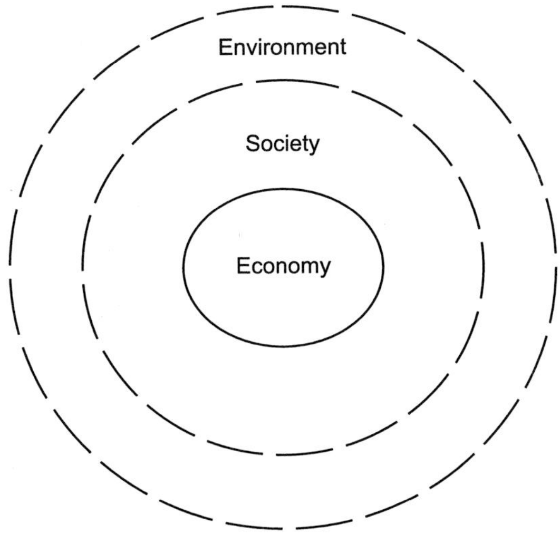

Figure 8.2 The Three Circles of Strong Sustainability Model

The strong sustainability model, on the other hand, recognizes that the economy is a subset of society. The strong sustainability model shows that society and the economy are constrained by the environment. The strong sustainability model is depicted in Figure 8.2:

According to Hunter, sustainable development is not a single absolute standard. He illustrated a wide spectrum of attitudes and levels of commitment to sustainability, ranging from weak and human centered to strong and "life-centered".

Table 8.1 A Simple Description of Sustainability Positions and Characteristics

Position	Defining Characteristics
Very Weak	Growth oriented Natural resources used to satisfy individual needs and desires Substitution between natural and man-made capital Continued human well-being assured through economic growth
Weak	Resource-conservationist Growth is managed and modified Concern for intra- and inter-generational equity Reject infinite substitution between natural and man-made capital Decouple negative environmental impacts from economic growth
Strong	Resource-preservationist Values maintaining ecosystems over human resource utilization Interests of the collective over the interests of the individual Adherence to intra- and inter-generational equity Balanced economic and human population growth
Very Strong	Resource-preservationist to the point where natural resource use is minimized against destructive economic growth; favours reduced human population

Source: Hunter 1997, adapted from Turner et al. 1994 Cox, Linda J and John Cusick (2006)

8.4 COMPONENTS AND GOALS OF SUSTAINABLE DEVELOPMENT

The key components of sustainable development, identified by the World Commission on Environment and Development are listed in Table 8.2

Table 8.2 Components of Sustainable Development

Component	Goal
Ecological limits and equitable standards	Encourage consumption that is ecologically possible for all
Economic activity and equitable resource allocation	Ensure economic growth that allows all people to meet their needs
Population control	Prevent population from exceeding the productive potential of the ecosystem
Resource conservation	Protect all natural systems
Carrying capacity and sustainable yield	Identify the productive potential of the ecosystem
Resource retention	Reduce the rate of depletion for non-renewable resources
Species diversification	Conserve and protect plant and animal species
Adverse impact minimization	Prevent damage to the ecosystem caused by pollution

contd....

Component	Goal
Community control	Prevent the exploitation and degradation of ecosystems
Broad national/international framework	Jointly manage the biosphere
Economic viability	Pursue economic wellbeing, given government policies
Environmental quality	Make environmental quality a corporate goal
Environmental audit	Track the progress of environmental management systems

Source: World Commission on Environment and Development (1987), *Our Common Future*, Oxford University Press, U.K.

8.5 CONDITIONS FOR SUSTAINABLE DEVELOPMENT

A critical condition for SD is the maintenance of a community's or a nation's basic stock of natural capital, that is, the use of the earth's ecological capital is to be brought within the capacity of natural systems to generate it. If nations are to stop depleting their basic stocks of ecological capital, governments will need to reform the present policies that now encourage the infamous 'de's — deforestation, desertification, destruction of habitat and species, and decline of air and water quality.

The twin pillars of SD are respect and concern, for people and ecosystems. Development is likely to be sustainable if:

(*i*) It improves the quality of human life: The purpose of development is to improve the quality of human life. Development is achieved only if it leads to a long and healthy life, education, access to resources needed for a decent standard of living, political freedom, guaranteed human rights, and freedom from violence.

(*ii*) It conserves the earth's vitality and diversity: Development must be conservation based; it must protect the structure, function and diversity of the world's natural systems on which *Homo sapiens* depend. To achieve this, we need to :

(*a*) Conserve life support systems.

(*b*) Conserve biological diversity.

(*c*) Minimize the depletion of non-renewable resources, such as minerals, oil, gas and coal through recycling, and resource substitution.

(*d*) Ensure that all uses of renewable resources like soil, forests, rangelands etc. are sustainable. A use is likely to be sustainable if it is compatible with maintaining the viability of the species and ecosystems affected by the use.

(*e*) Keep within the earth's carrying capacity. Policies, technologies and practices that bring human numbers and lifestyles into balance with the earth's carrying capacity are essential.

8.6 THE IUCN/UNEP STRATEGIES FOR SUSTAINABLE DEVELOPMENT

The 1991 report, *Caring for the Earth* (IUCN/UNEP/WWF) identified nine principles as the basis of a strategy for sustainable development.

(*i*) **Respect and Care for the Community of Life:** This is an ethical principle that reflects the duty of care for other people and other forms of life, now and in the future. It implies that development ought not to be at the expense of other groups or later generations, nor threaten the survival of other species. The benefits and costs of resource use and environmental conservation should be shared fairly among different communities, among people who are poor and those who are affluent and between our generation and those who will come after us. Development should not threaten the survival of other species or eliminate their habitats.

(*ii*) **Improve the Quality of Life:** The aim of development is to improve the quality of human life. It should enable people to realise their potential and lead lives of dignity and fulfilment. The goal of development ought to be the realization of a long and healthy life, education, access to resources needed for a decent standard of living, political freedom, guaranteed human rights and freedom from violence. Development is real only if it makes our lives better in all these respects.

(*iii*) **Conserve the Earth's Vitality and Diversity:** Development must be conservation-based; it must protect the structure, functions and diversity of the world's natural systems, on which our species depend. This calls for the following:

(*a*) Conserving life-support systems, which are the ecological processes that keep the planet fit for life. They shape the climate, cleanse air and water, regulate water flow, recycle essential elements, and create and regenerate the soil and enable the ecosystems to renew themselves;

(*b*) Conserve biodiversity, which includes all species of plants, animals, other organisms; the range of genetic stocks within each species, and the variety of ecosystems;

(*c*) Ensure that the use of renewable resources is sustainable. The use of renewable resources, such as soil, wild and domesticated organisms, forests, rangelands, cultivated land, and the marine and freshwater ecosystems that support fisheries must be within the regenerative capacity of the resources.

(*iv*) **Minimize the Depletion of Non-renewable Resources:** The depletion of non-renewable resources, like minerals, oil, gas and coal must be minimized by recycling, by using less of a resource to make a particular product, or by switching to renewable substitutes, wherever possible. These practices are essential if the earth is to sustain billions of more people in the future and give everyone a life of decent quality.

(*v*) **Keep within the Earth's Carrying Capacity:** The "carrying capacity" of the earth's ecosystems is finite. The limits to the carrying capacity of the ecosystem varies from region to region and depends on the size of the population and on the resource consumption and generation of wastes by the people. It is essential to develop policies that would balance the demand for environmental services with the earth's carrying capacity. Policies to develop technologies that enhance the carrying capacity of the environment by careful management are needed.

(*vi*) **Change Personal Attitudes and Practices:** Society must promote values that support the ethic of sustainable lifestyles and discourage those that are incompatible with a sustainable way of life. Formal and informal education must be used to disseminate information so that polices and actions needed for the survival and well-being of the world's societies are understood.

(*vii*) **Enable Communities to Care for their own Environments:** Communities and citizens' groups (NGOs) who work towards the creation of sustainable communities should be given the required support in terms of information, power and finance to achieve their goals.

(*viii*) **Provide a National Framework for Integrating Development and Conservation:** A national programme for achieving sustainability needs a national framework for integrating conservation and development. It should involve all interests and attempts to identify and prevent problems before they arise. It must be adaptive, continually re-directing its course in response to experience and new needs. Among other things, national measures should also:

(*a*) Relate economic policy to environmental carrying capacity.

(*b*) Increase the benefits obtained from each stock of resources.

(*c*) Promote technologies that use resources more efficiently.

(*d*) Ensure that resource users pay the full social costs of the benefits they enjoy.

(*ix*) **Create a Global Alliance:** Global sustainability depends on a firm alliance among all countries. Global and shared resources, such as the atmosphere, oceans and shared ecosystems, can be managed only on the basis of common purpose and resolve. All nations stand to gain from world-wide sustainability and all are threatened if we fail to attain it.

8.7 POLICY MEASURES FOR ACHIEVING SUSTAINABLE DEVELOPMENT

Transition to a more sustainable form of development requires the integration of the environment and the economy in our decision making. This is crucial for SD. The decision makers - government, industry and households - have to realize that environment and development, are not mutually destructive, but are in fact, reinforcing. Most of the national governments today have committed themselves to the principles of action contained in the Agenda 21 document, a set of 27 principles for promoting SD included in the Rio Declaration on Environment and Development.

There are a host of specific measures which governments can take to help clean up or prevent further environmental destruction. These include:

(*i*) Direct regulation, also known as "command and control measures", that requires the specification of a ceiling (or limits) for effluents and emissions or specifies the equipment to be installed for treating the emission or effluent. The Air Act, Water Act, and the Environment Act in India are expressions of direct regulation.

(*ii*) Market based incentives, like taxes, and tradable permits, based on the principle of making the polluter account for the damages caused by pollution.

Table 8.3 highlights a number of environmental taxes which are now common across many countries, including the developing world. Many countries now tax automobile use, through levies on fuels. In France, recent legislation has enabled the authorities in Paris to restrict the use of cars in the city when pollution levels reach a certain threshold. They effect controls by allowing only cars with even or odd numbered registration plates to be driven into the city when pollution levels merit such action.

In developing countries, SD will also require a commitment to overcoming poverty. Poor people are regularly portrayed as "victims and unwilling agents" of environmental degradation in developing nations. Their environmental concerns are those associated with immediate survival needs, such as fuel, access to clean water and sanitation or securing productive lands. Poverty denies millions of people their basic rights in the short term and the potential to achieve their aspirations in the future. Hence, an important step towards achieving SD in developing countries is that of eradicating poverty.

Table 8.3 Examples of Environmental Taxes

Tax Base	Where Taxed
Solid or hazardous waste generation	Australia, Austria, China, Finland, France, Netherlands, Poland, the United States.
Sale of fertilizers and pesticides	Austria, Finland, Norway, Sweden
Water pollution	Austria, Belgium, Canada, China, France, Germany, Netherlands, Portugal, Spain, most of former Eastern Block Nations.
Air pollution	China, Denmark, France, Japan, Norway, Portugal, Sweden, most of former Eastern Block Nations.
Motor fuel sales and car ownership	Almost all countries.

Besides the legal and tax solutions to protect the environment, voluntary action can be an important course of action. The claim is that nature can be protected from man only when the people realize their moral responsibilities towards nature. Non-governmental Organizations (NGOs) working for environmental protection can play a vital role in promoting sustainable development at the global level. Some of the best known NGOs today are Greenpeace, World Wide Fund for Nature, Amnesty International etc.

8.8 CONCLUSION

The achievement of sustainable development remains the greatest challenge facing the human race. Ensuring SD requires attention to not just economic growth but also to environmental and social issues. Unless the transformation of society and the management of the environment are addressed integrally, along with economic growth, growth itself will be jeopardized over the longer term. The transition to a sustainable development path does not imply returning the planet to a natural state in which human activities have no impact. Life on earth depends on the use of the vital environmental functions. Therefore, people cannot live without altering the environment.

The basic food and energy needs of more than 6 billion people require large scale extraction and use of natural resources. The most basic aspiration for materials consumption, livelihood, and health require even more. The maxim of SD is not limits to growth but it is growth within limits.

Sustainability requires thinking long term, but acting now. There are no blueprints for sustainable development. Sustainable development actions are complex. Yet, it is the obligation of the current generation to exploit and to protect the resources of the world in ways which do not preclude the options for tomorrow.

QUESTIONS

1. Define sustainable development. What are the components of sustainable development?
2. Compare weak and strong sustainability.
3. What are the various strategies and policy measures advocated to achieve sustainable development?

EXERCISES

1. In your opinion to what extent is the Indian Government committed to sustainable development? Explain your stand through examples.
2. What are the steps that individuals can take to achieve sustainable development?

❑❑❑

9

The Rise of Green Consumerism

> *The sun, the moon and the stars would have disappeared long ago . . . had they happened to be within the reach of predatory human hands.*
>
> **Havelock Ellis, *The Dance of Life,* 1923**

A growing trend in recent times is that of consumers emerging as a new force in the global struggle to create an environmentally sustainable world. Aided by labelling programmes, standards, and an expanding group of social and environmental certification organizations, the world's consumers are "voting with their wallets" for products and services that promote sustainable development.

9.1 GREEN CONSUMERISM – DEFINITION

Green consumerism is the intentional purchase of products and services that the consumer considers has to be made, with minimal harm to the natural environment.

Some free market advocates claim that the market automatically gives people all the choices they want and all the information they need, but what consumers are demonstrating is that they want more environmentally acceptable choices than the market has been delivering, and more trustworthy information about the social and environmental impact of the products they might buy.

Underlying green consumerism is the recognition of the fact that all products have an environmental impact, however small. And the idea is to reduce it to the minimum. A consumer has to realize that he does not just buy 'a' product, but everything that went into its production, and everything that will happen in the future as a result of that product.

Long-time environmental activist, Paul Hawken, once described "green consumerism" as an oxymoron. The reason: consumption by its very nature has an impact on the environment—to some degree or other – and therefore, is hard to call truly green. Yet, short of reducing consumption, many consumers, manufacturers and retailers are focusing on greener consumption—a term which implies shifting to products and services that have a lower environmental impact, though in many cases, not specifying by how much.

Today, there are positive signs that demand for greener products is increasing sharply. Vital Signs 2002, produced with the support of the United Nations Environment Programme (UNEP) and the W. Alton Jones Foundation—documents many instances worldwide, where consumers are actively seeking out goods and services that promote sustainable development:

(*i*) The Mexico-based Forest Stewardship Council has certified over 25 million hectares of commercial forest in 54 countries as meeting social and environmental standards for sustainable forestry, more than double the area in 1998.

(*ii*) Worldwide, buyers of energy-saving compact fluorescent lamps (CFLs) have eliminated the need for nearly 40 medium-sized, coal-fired power plants.

(*iii*) At the seafood counter, consumers can now find rock lobster, cockles, hoki, mackerel, herring, and salmon that carry the Marine Stewardship Council's logo as having been harvested under environmentally responsible management.

(*iv*) Thai consumers have used information from an appliance-labelling program to drive the market share of energy efficient, single-door refrigerators from 12 per cent in 1996 to 96 per cent in 1998.

(*v*) In 21 European countries, beachgoers follow the ratings of the European Blue Flag campaign to find some 2,750 beaches and marinas with high environmental standards and sanitary and safe facilities.

(*vi*) Coffee drinkers in the US and Canada can ask for their coffee to be brewed from beans carrying the Bird Friendly seal of approval from the Smithsonian Migratory Bird Centre. This programme certifies that the beans meet standards for shade farming and organic production.

Vital Signs 2002 highlights several sectors where consumer pressure could be pivotal in getting industry and regulatory bodies to address the issue. For example, manufacturing semiconductors is chemical-intensive and the short life-span of these products is creating mountains of electronics waste, poisoning groundwater supplies, and endangering human health. Cell phone and computer users should be demanding that manufacturers take their products back, and design them to be recycled, instead of allowing them to be dumped.

9.2 THE GREEN CONSUMER

Green consumers can be defined as those who care sufficiently about the environment to make a conscious effort to buy products that avoid environmental damage.

Green consumers are those who are very concerned about the environment, and therefore, purchase only eco-friendly products. Products with little or no packaging, products made from natural ingredients and products that are made without causing pollution are all examples of eco-friendly products. Green consumers buy products made with hemp or those made from recycled materials. Criteria for defining "green" products include organic, durable, non-toxic, recyclable and using production methods that do not threaten important ecosystems. They represent a niche market that is undoubtedly growing, despite the premium prices that are charged.

As in defining the "green" company, there are varying degrees of "greenness" as far as the consumer is concerned. At one end of the spectrum are the majority of consumers who pay little attention to environmental issues, despite the concerns expressed by many opinion polls. Their main interest is "value for money", and they would only buy a green product if it were no more expensive. At the other end of the consumer spectrum is the tiny band of committed greens, for whom green credentials are the deciding factor when choosing a product. Since "green" products tend to be more expensive, price "resistance" is a major constraint on market demand.

BOX 9.1

Brent Spar Platform Controversy

In April 1995, Greenpeace boarded a Shell oil platform named Brent Spar in the North Sea to protest its scheduled disposal in the Atlantic Ocean. This action took the operator, Shell Expro (a joint venture between Shell and Esso) totally by surprise, as this was the first protest of any kind that the Shell management had encountered.

The Greenpeace activists occupied the Brent Spar oil storage facility with the objective of stopping plans to scuttle the 14,500 tonne installation. The action was a part of an ongoing campaign to stop ocean dumping, and pitted Greenpeace against the combined forces of the UK government and Shell, the world's then-largest oil company.

Dramatic visual footage of activists being attacked with water cannons and relief teams being flown in by helicopter, brought the stand-off to a massive audience. Spontaneous protests in support of Greenpeace and against Shell broke out across Europe. Some Shell stations in Germany reported a 50 per cent loss of sales. Chancellor Kohl raised the issue with the UK government at a G7 meeting. But despite the UK government's refusal to back down on plans to allow the Spar to simply be dumped into the ocean, public pressure proved too much to bear for Shell, and in a dramatic win for Greenpeace and the ocean environment, the company reversed its decision and agreed to dismantle and recycle the Spar on land. The Spar was eventually brought ashore in 1998 and recycled, being used as the base for a new quay in Norway. All the evidence has since shown that, as Shell itself later concluded, recycling the Brent Spar was the most environmentally sound option.

The decision also led to a ban on the ocean disposal of such rigs by the international body which regulates ocean dumping. Although the Brent Spar campaign is remembered as one of the most significant Greenpeace successes of the 1990s, it was actually just one part of a much larger campaign in which Greenpeace continues to confront industry and governments, challenging them to take action to protect the oceans. The Spar set a precedent for a more open and responsible approach from the offshore oil and gas industry to the decommissioning of obsolete platforms.

Without doubt, if the Spar had been dumped, many more platforms would have followed. There would have been little, if any, international scrutiny of decommissioning operations - and there would have been a cumulative environmental impact way beyond that of the Spar alone. *The Times* summed it up in January 1997, when it identified the dumping of the Spar as "all too clearly a precedent for dumping everything else into the North Sea and turning it into a giant underwater scrap heap."

Source: http://www.greenpeace.org/international/about/history/the-brent-spar

Either the consumer must be persuaded by better product information or encouraged by more competitive prices. The former might be achieved by a comprehensive system of eco-labelling; the latter, by a comprehensive system of environmental taxation. Regulations and market incentives, can thus work together to expand the market for "green" products.

Some companies develop "green" products as a way of diversifying their interests and moving "up market". Green products now come from a wide spectrum of industry, including recycled paper products, energy-saving appliances and organic food. The latter is a good example of how the demand for green products is growing fast.

In the marketplace, the rise of green consumerism translates into an insistence that all products satisfy minimum environmental standards. If the green consumer eventually becomes the green agitator, then the buying power of consumers can have a negative as well as a positive impact on companies. When a majority of consumers will only buy green products and actively boycott products which fail to meet high environmental standards, then the consumer becomes a potent force influencing commercial decisions. Evidence of this occurred sometime ago, in Germany, when motorists were asked to boycott Shell petrol stations, in the wake of adverse media publicity over the intended sinking of the Brent Spar oil platform in the North Sea (Box 9.1).

Thus, consumer boycotts must be the ultimate nightmare for companies and it is likely that environmental consumer groups will increasingly resort to such action to promote their objectives. Avoiding bad publicity and promoting a favourable green image will become increasingly important for companies. Thus, the green consumer represents both a threat and an opportunity to business.

9.3 CAN GREEN CONSUMERISM STOP THE ECOLOGICAL CRISIS?

With the surge in environmental awareness of the general public, companies are fast coming to the realization that being green or environmentally responsible has rewards. Environmentally friendly products are in greater demand, consumers are choosing healthy goods and companies are being punished by clients, consumers and the stock market for ecologically unsound, unsustainable or polluting practices. This demand for clean and green means that there is also a corresponding increase in the unscrupulous practice of claiming green credentials, when in fact there are none, or very little. This practice has come to be known as "greenwashing", a term that is derived from "whitewashing" and "green" the colloquial name adopted for all things associated with a healthy environment. (Chapter 27).

Green consumerism may not really help in solving the ecological crisis. In fact, it could make it worse by creating new markets and thus increasing growth. Though without doubt, using recycled or renewable raw materials, reducing consumption and buying *ecologically friendly* products and technologies are very important, such measures are of very limited use as solutions to the ecological problems we face today. At best, they can only delay, not prevent capitalism's ultimate destruction of the planet's ecological base.

This means that apparently "green" companies and products may not actually be what they claim to be. Many firms hire expensive Public Relations firms and produce advertisements to paint a false image of themselves as being ecologically friendly. This indicates a weakness of market economies - they hinder (even distort) the flow of information required for consumers to make informed decisions. The market does not provide enough information for consumers to determine whether a product **is** actually green or not - it just gives them a price and advertising. Consumers have to rely on other sources, many of which are minority journals and organizations and difficult to locate, to provide them with the accurate information required to countermand the power and persuasion of advertising and the work of PR experts.

Even apparently ecologically friendly firms, like "The Body Shop", can present a false image of what they do. See Box 9.2 below:

BOX 9.2

The Body Shop Debacle

Journalist Jon Entine investigated The Body Shop company in 1994 and discovered that only a minuscule fraction of its ingredients came from **Trade Not Aid** (a program claimed to aid developing countries). Entine also discovered that the company used many outdated, off-the-shelf product formulas filled with non-renewable petrochemicals, as well as animal tested ingredients. When he contacted the company he received libel threats and it hired a PR company to combat Entine's story. This highlights the dangers of looking to consumerism to solve ecological problems. As Entine argues:

"The Body Shop is a corporation with the privileges and power in society as all others. Like other corporations it makes products that are unsustainable, encourages consumerism, uses non-renewable materials, hires giant PR and law firms, and exaggerates its environment policies. If we are to become a sustainable society, it is crucial that we have institutions...that are truly sustainable. The Body Shop has deceived the public by trying to make us think that they are a lot further down the road to sustainability than they really are. We should...no longer...lionize the Body Shop and others who claim to be something they are not."

Source: http://www.jonentine.com/the-body-shop.html

Thus, green consumerism is hindered by the nature of the market - how the market reduces everything to price and so hides the information required to make truly informed decisions on what to consume. Moreover, it is capable of being used to further ecological damage by the use of PR to paint a false picture of the companies and their environmental activities. Even assuming companies are honest and do minimize their environmental damage, they cannot face the fundamental cause of the ecological crisis in the "grow-or-die" principle of capitalism ("green" firms need to make profits, accumulate capital and grow bigger), nor do they address the pernicious role of advertising or the lack of public control over production and investment under capitalism. Hence, it is a totally inadequate solution.

9.4 CONCLUSION

Andrew Watson (*From Red to Green*) sums up green consumerism very eloquently as follows:

"Green consumerism, which is largely a cynical attempt to maintain profit margins, does not challenge capital's eco-cidal accumulation, but actually facilitates it, by opening a new market. All products, no matter how "green", cause some pollution, use some resources and energy, and cause some ecological disturbance. This would not matter in a society in which production was rationally planned, but in an exponentially expanding economy, production, however "green", would eventually destroy the Earth's environment. Ozone-friendly aerosols, for example, still use other harmful chemicals; create pollution in their manufacture, use and disposal; and use large amounts of resources and energy. Of course, up to now, the green pretensions of most companies have been exposed largely as presenting an acceptably green image, with little or no substance. The market is presented as the saviour of the environment. Environmental concern is commodified and transformed into ideological support for capitalism. Instead of raising awareness of the causes of the ecological crisis, green consumerism mystifies them. The solution is presented as an individual act rather than as the collective action of individuals struggling for social change. The corporations laugh all the way to the bank."

Thus, market forces will never meaningfully reduce consumption. The myth that they can or will is an attempt to protect the ideology of growth against the threat posed by its increasingly evident consequences. Achieving a sustainable future is not a task that can be left to the markets; it requires a renewal of non-material values, and political action by people as citizens, not simply as consumers. Ultimately this political action, if it is to be effective, must result not only in local resistance but in the election of governments which are prepared, and mandated, to govern in the interests of citizens as full human beings in the real living world, and not simply as economic units of production and consumption. Such governments will have to explicitly question the desirability of further economic growth and be prepared, when and where necessary, to resist the powerful influence of globalized capitalism.

QUESTIONS

1. What is green consumerism?
2. 'Green consumerism is an oxymoron' – Do you agree? Justify your stand. Can green consumerism stop the ecological crisis?
3. Does green consumerism pose a threat to capitalism? Explain.
4. Who is a green consumer? How can he promote sustainable development?

EXERCISES

1. Do a survey in your neighbourhood to assess the extent of environmentally friendly consumption in your area. Also assess the knowledge among your neighbours on green consumption practices.
2. Look up the website and calculate your ecological footprint based on your consumption pattern and lifestyle.

❑❑❑

10

The Greening of Company Managements

> *We believe it's in business's interest to become more sustainable . . . this will become a must-have rather than a nice-to-have issue, going forward.*
>
> **John Duggan, CEO, Gazeley**

In the past, it was customary for businesses to ignore environmental costs in order to reduce production costs and at the same time to stay competitive. However, in recent times, "green" consumerism is on the rise (Refer Chapter 9 on *Green Consumerism*) reflecting the increasing number of consumers who prefer to buy products that satisfy high standards of environmental protection. Consequently, it is becoming profitable to sell "green" products both in the domestic and international markets. The "pull" of the market is reinforced by the "push" resulting from increasingly stringent environmental legislation which sets higher standards of environmental quality. Many recent surveys of business opinion confirm that environmental issues are of growing importance to companies and a high percentage go beyond the requirements of the law. This suggests that companies are becoming proactive in their management of environmental problems and are beginning to exploit the commercial opportunities that arise from rising environmental standards.

10.1 DEFECTS OF THE MARKET ECONOMY

Under the dictates of free market economics, companies seek to minimize costs in order to maximize profits regardless of any environmental damage that might be caused. Unless compelled by law, companies have a strong incentive to externalize some costs by exploiting the "free" services of the natural environment. Market failure of this kind is very common and results from the need to stay commercially competitive in the short term. A company's impact on the environment can vary enormously according to corporate size and market power, the nature of the product or technology used, the organization of the business and the philosophy of the management.

It is extremely clear that until business is forced to pay for environmental costs, market forces will continue to cause environmental degradation in different ways, some deliberate and others accidental. Equally, however, market forces can be harnessed by the government, both to reduce environmental impact (*e.g.*, pollution control) and restore environmental damage (*e.g.*, soil conservation).

The following points (Roarty, 1997) bring out the inherent defects of the market economy that allow commercial interests to take precedence over environmental considerations:

(*i*) Competitive markets compel companies to cut costs to stay in business even when this damages the environment, *e.g.*, pollution. In fact, there is an incentive to pollute because it is cheaper to discharge waste materials in the local environment than to invest in pollution abatement. Externalization of costs helps to boost company profits.

(*ii*) As market prices reflect private costs (and benefits), business decisions are based on faulty and inadequate assessments. As Hawken has noted: "Markets are superb at setting prices, but incapable of recognizing costs." By ignoring environmental costs, market prices provide the wrong signals for resource management, leading to an overuse of the environment. This is the "market failure" argument.

(*iii*) Short-term profitability, rather than long term sustainability, is the motivating force behind most of the private enterprises. The pressure of shareholders and financial institutions for rising dividends reinforces this philosophy of "short-termism".

(*iv*) The ethos of economic growth has created a materialistic culture and a society preoccupied with "economic progress". Business has a vested interest in promoting this "culture", thus commercializing more and more of our everyday life. Moreover, this "growth ethic" dictates the path of research and technology, tending to focus on productivity and ignoring the question of sustainability.

Thus, the fundamental criticism leveled against the market economy is that it creates a dynamism of ever increasing production and thus ignores any limits to economic growth. The main dilemma facing policy makers today is how to reconcile the profit motive with conservation, so that companies and their customers take full responsibility for environmental costs.

A "stick and carrot" approach consisting of stricter environmental legislation and financial incentives (*e.g.*, tax concessions) could persuade more companies to go green, and there is already evidence of companies anticipating such changes. Without a fundamental change in corporate culture which forges a new, ecological approach to business management, progress in conserving the environment will be tentative and contradictory.

Ultimately, only the government can provide the impetus to create a new framework for business decision making. Ironically, the traditional role of government in the economy has been to remove the obstacles and offset the risks to private investors, thereby encouraging production and stimulating economic growth. Government intervention to remedy the deficiencies of the private sector has been preoccupied with economic objectives, irrespective of their environmental impact.

10.2 CORPORATE RESPONSIBILITY FOR ENVIRONMENTAL PROBLEMS

Decisions taken by businesses about production methods, investment and the type of products to be sold have direct implications for the environment. Nevertheless, such commercial decisions are guided by market forces and the profit motive. The continuous pressure to cut costs in a competitive market encourages companies to externalize costs as much as possible. Thus pollution is an inevitable by-product of an economic system in which companies seek to maximize profits.

Although corporate behaviour is directly implicated in damaging the environment, market signals must be changed to encourage conservation, instead of exploitation. There is a fundamental choice to be made: either business can continue to exploit the environment or be made to play a positive role and take responsibility for environmental damage.

Ultimately, the responsibility for protecting the environment rests with the society as a whole and this implies setting new ground rules (environmental legislation) and creating financial incentives (taxes and subsidies) to conserve rather than destroy the environment. As market "values" reflect society's preferences, the general public will have to campaign, both in their role as consumers and citizens, for a "greener" economy.

If society prefers a more conserving and sustainable economy, then business will have an incentive to develop "green" technologies and products. If consumers are "green", then it will be profitable for business to become "green". If society cares little about conservation, and is blind to the environmental costs of economic growth, then business cannot be entirely blamed for a materialistic culture whose commercial values reflect popular demands. Thus, conservation requires a fundamental shift in economic thinking that takes full account of environmental costs and integrates environmental values into economic decision making.

10.3 PRESSURE FOR A GREENER BUSINESS ENVIRONMENT

An increasing number of "green" companies reflect both a change in traditional corporate behaviour and the emergence of new "green" sectors, like energy conservation and the recycling of waste. This represents a slow evolution in response to environmental legislation and shifts in consumer demand that can be traced back at least 20 years in most industrialized countries. The initial impetus came from the government which now acknowledges that business must take responsibility for damage caused to the environment. Official recognition of the "polluter pays principle" is a good example of this. Moreover, the "push" of the Government has in some cases been overtaken by the "pull" of the market, as more and more consumers seek to purchase green products.

There are also pressures exerted on businesses by a number of groups who have an interest and concern in the environmental performance and track record of the company. Figure 10.1 lists the environmental stakeholders who have had a great impact on the greening of company practices.

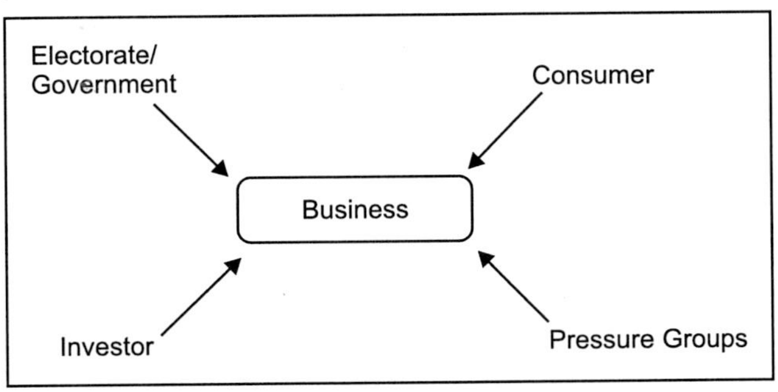

Fig. 10.1 Environmental Stakeholders

Although each group has a particular interest in environmental protection, membership of these groups overlap considerably and coalesce into what is called the "green movement". The influence of the "green movement" is evident in both politics and business. In politics, environmental issues are increasingly important and are now firmly on the political agenda. In business, market forces on the one hand, and concern for corporate image on the other, are making companies more sensitive to environmental issues. Thus, despite the relatively small number of "green" activists, the "green" movement exerts a disproportionate influence on corporate behaviour, especially in environmentally sensitive industries, like chemicals and power generation.

Voters and consumers have a direct impact on government and business respectively. While the "green" voter may be insignificant in number, environmental issues are important to the electorate as a whole and have a growing influence on all the main political parties. In reflecting public opinion, voters influence government, which in turn, can alter the legal framework that governs business. Consumers, on the other hand, "vote" with their money and environmental protection is becoming a potent force in the marketplace. Investors and pressure groups have a more indirect influence on business. The financial institutions, providing the bulk of business finance, are essentially concerned with evaluating risk and reward and how a range of different factors influence the balance between the two.

From the investors' point of view, it is becoming more profitable to invest in companies that are meeting a growing demand for "green" products. On the negative side, the increasing risk to profits associated with the liability of some companies to compensate individuals adversely affected by environmental damage (*e.g.*, contamination of land or water by pollution) makes financing such companies less attractive. Thus the "green" investor is indirectly influencing business through access to finance.

The growing membership of environmental pressure groups like *Greenpeace*, reflects a more fundamental concern with environmental issues and a willingness to campaign for changes in the law. Well organized and articulate pressure groups help to educate the public and raise the political profile of environmental issues. Together and separately, these four groups exert a growing influence and have forced business to become more conscious of environmental issues and the role it can play in protecting the environment. The "greening" of business is set to continue as more and more companies begin to realize that preventing environmental damage by developing "green" products and technologies is a strategy for reducing risk and achieving profitable growth in the long term.

10.4 WHY DO BUSINESSES GO GREEN?

(*i*) Some business owners and executives actually have a conscience.

(*ii*) Probably one of the biggest reasons could be a Public Relations opportunity to be seen as "environmentally conscious". Companies who go green can play up to the emotions of their customers, and say "Hey, buy from us. We're green, we care about our environment, and our non-green competitor apparently does not."

(*iii*) Makes sense in reducing the company's energy consumption expenses.

(*iv*) Some companies have even found ways to sell "green products", adding even more to their bottom line.

The rise of the "green" consumer marks a shift in the pattern of consumer purchasing, away from products that are considered to be damaging to the environment and towards products that are sustainable. Thus, market forces, in the form of a growing demand for "green" products and technologies provide new commercial opportunities and represents a powerful incentive to create a greener business climate. Looking beyond the domestic market, there are growing export opportunities for companies making products that can satisfy high environmental standards. Sweden's decision to eliminate chlorine bleaching in paper production helped paper exports to important markets like Germany. Although some countries are more environmentally conscious than others, environmental legislation is getting tougher in nearly all the countries, especially those with the most lucrative markets. Markets for "green" products and services are growing throughout the world and especially in the affluent markets of Western Europe, Japan and North America. Products include: energy-efficient "white" goods such as fridges and washing machines; organic food which is natural and additive-free; products made from recycled materials (*e.g.,* paper) or using reusable containers (*e.g.,* washing liquid); low emission and fuel efficient cars.

Unless all companies are obliged to meet higher standards, there is an incentive to damage the environment by externalizing some costs. Companies that voluntarily reduce their impact on the environment will incur higher costs that undermine their competitiveness, as their products become more expensive. While there are undoubtedly consumers who are prepared to pay more for "green" products, price resistance among low-income consumers limits demand. Higher environmental standards reduce the risk of investing in new technology and thus enable companies to develop "green" products. Going "green" can then become profitable as all companies compete on a "level playing field". Thus the impetus for change resides with the government which has the ultimate responsibility for guiding market forces to promote conservation. For example, the international agreement to eliminate CFCs (the Montreal Protocol) to protect the ozone layer has stimulated research and the development of alternatives such as hydrocarbon refrigerators.

Thus legislation and market forces play complementary roles in the "greening" of business. Further progress in this direction, however, must concentrate on developing "green" markets by giving consumers a greater incentive to switch to "green"' products. Tax concessions and environmental subsidies are needed to overcome the traditional "price resistance" of consumers who are unwilling or unable to pay more for new products that help to conserve the environment.

Corporate inertia, however, still remains a major obstacle as many companies are reluctant to change production methods or marketing strategy. Nevertheless, the push from the government in the form of higher environmental standards is forcing more companies to invest in new products and technologies to satisfy stricter environmental regulations. Better pollution control, waste management and new product design are good examples of this. While legislation forces companies to change, few companies go beyond satisfying the minimum requirements because of the costs involved. This is when the pull of the market can become a decisive factor and help to reinforce new laws on environmental protection.

10.5 DEFINING "GREENNESS" IN COMPANIES

A large (and growing) number of companies would claim to be "green", although defining a "green" company is difficult and depends on the criteria adopted. While few companies are "green" in all aspects of their operations, a precondition of "greenness" is a corporate philosophy which explicitly incorporates environmental criteria in management decision making. The corporate strategy will include environmental, as well as financial objectives, and indicate how these objectives will be monitored and achieved. Apart from developing "green" products and positioning itself directly in emerging "green" markets, a "green" audit should become a regular and indispensable part of corporate life. Ultimately, a "green" company must be sustainable in every respect and thus, environmental protection becomes a guiding principle, even if this is at the expense of profit.

The following criteria can be used to determine how "green" a company has become:

(*i*) **Product Criterion:** A company making products which are environmentally friendly. *e.g.,* durable, non-polluting, made from recycled materials.

(*ii*) **Technology Criterion:** A company using production/assembly methods that minimize environmental damage, *e.g.,* minimizing waste and pollution, conserving energy.

(*iii*) **Business Ethics Criterion:** A corporate philosophy that embraces environmental values, made effective by an environmental policy with specific objectives. E.g. procurement policy to buy components/services from other "green" companies.

Although all three criteria are important, the essential characteristic of a "green" company is the last one. Corporate values must change so that environmental protection becomes an integral part of the corporate strategy. Green products and technology will tend to follow, if companies adopt environmental criteria when taking decisions. Selling "green" products or using "green" technologies is not sufficient by itself, as it may simply reflect commercial expediency or legal requirements. The truly "green" company goes beyond the dictates of the market or the law and embraces environmental values.

10.6 FIVE STAGE MODEL OF CORPORATE ENVIRONMENTAL RESPONSIBILITY

Environmental considerations touch all aspects of a business's operations and environmental issues are forcing all businesses to manage in new ways. Not all companies are equally "green" or proactive in their response to environmental issues. Researchers have identified five stages of environmental responsibility.

According to this model, companies pass through five distinct stages in the development of green management practices. At the beginner level, managers ignore potential liability and dismiss the need for specialized environmental programmes. Beginners might include older firms established before the modern environmental era, small firms that feel they cannot afford specialized programmes, or simply companies in industries where regulatory oversight is perceived to be minimal.

Firefighters are companies in the next developmental stage, which address environmental issues only when they pose an immediate threat, such as when an unexpected accident or spill occurs. Environmental management is viewed as an exception to "business as usual".

At the third stage in environmental consciousness, are companies as concerned citizens, who feel that environmental protection is worthwhile and may even have specialized staff but devote only very limited resources and top management attention to green issues.

Table 10.1 A Five Stage Model of Corporate Social/Environmental Responsibility

Commitment of Organization			
Developmental Stage	**General Mindset of Corporate Managers**	**Resource Commitment**	**Support and Involvement of Top Management**
Beginner	Environmental management is unnecessary	Minimal resource commitment	No involvement
Fire Fighter	Environmental issues should be addressed only as necessary	Budget for problems as they occur	Piecemeal involvement
Concerned Citizen	Environmental management is a worthwhile function	Consistent, yet minimal budget	Commitment in theory
Pragmatist	Environmental management is an important business function	Generally sufficient funding	Aware and moderately involved
Proactivist	Environmental management is a priority item	Open ended funding	Actively involved

Source: Hunt and Auster (1990)

Pragmatists actively manage environmental issues, have well funded programmes, and evaluate risk as well as immediate problems. Proactivists are companies in the final stage of development. They have senior executives who champion environmental responsibility, extensive training and strong links between environmental staff and the other parts of the organization.

10.7 FINANCIAL REASONS FOR GOING GREEN

Kit Sadgrove suggests that there are good financial reasons for going green. This is presented in Table 10.2. According to him, there are four possible positions for a company to adopt in this regard:

(*i*) The **Laggard** does nothing. It spends no money on environmental protection and has a grey or dirty image. But as new laws come out, the Laggard can easily find itself in the Punished category.

(*ii*) The **Punished** Company has failed to adapt to changing circumstances. It is punished by customers who start buying competitors products, or by legislators who require pollution controls to be retrofitted. Substantial costs often follow, but the company retains its grey image. The expenditure has come too late.

(*iii*) The **Conformer** aims to stay within the law by spending as little as possible. It concentrates on a no-cost or low-cost solution. Many companies like to adopt this strategy; and it is quite feasible to have a green image for minimum outlay.

(*iv*) The **Leader** takes a high cost route, and gains a high profile. It may achieve superiority in technology and innovation, and may become the standard by which other companies are judged.

These different positions have been expressed diagrammatically in Table 10.2. The matrix has an anti-clockwise movement. Leaders who rest on their laurels, become Conformers; Conformers who stop running, become Laggards; and Laggards become Punished.

Table 10.2 Strategic Options

A Company can Choose which Segment it Wants to Occupy

	GREEN	GREY
HIGH COST	LEADER High profile, high investment policy	PUNISHED Retro-fitting required; loss of market share
LOW COST	CONFORMER No cost, low-cost measures	LAGGARD Do nothing

Thus, we see that companies can be either "reactive" or "proactive" in their management of environmental problems. The reactive or defensive company is still wedded to the old system, only changing production techniques or processes if obliged to do so by law. Such compliance with environmental legislation is regarded as a burden, an additional cost which will reduce profits unless the cost can be recouped from the customer.

By contrast, the proactive company treats environmental issues in a positive way, regarding new environmental obligations as an opportunity to increase sales of "green" products where markets are beginning to grow. To become a market leader is potentially very profitable and new investment, while initially adding to costs, will eventually generate more sales revenue. Moreover, such companies position themselves in "green" sectors of the economy where demand is growing fast. Biotechnology, energy conservation, pollution control and recycling are good examples.

The truly "green" company is not just exploiting opportunities to cater for growing numbers of "green" consumers; it is also anticipating changes in environmental legislation that will ultimately force companies to introduce cleaner technologies. The truly "green" company will be in the vanguard of change, taking the initiative in redesigning products and technologies. This might involve "clean" technologies, where waste is automatically recycled or the use of renewable energy sources. Such far-sightedness can also pay dividends as companies become market leaders and gain an international advantage in these new technologies.

Once commercial expediency has led to a reappraisal of corporate objectives, many companies will begin to realize that higher environmental standards are not a threat but an opportunity, and begin to incorporate environmental objectives into their corporate strategies. At this stage, profitability in the long term will depend on environmental excellence achieved by investing in new technologies and developing new products. According to Elkington *et al.* (1989a; 1989b), "excellent" companies have already made this transition, as environmental quality objectives are now considered as core values in their corporate strategy. Consequently, environmental assessment is now included as an integral part of their activities. At this stage in their development, companies are proactive rather than reactive, anticipating changes both in the marketplace and in government regulations.

BOX 10.1

3M's Cost Savings from Green Management Practices

3M, the legendary American company has recorded astounding success in cost savings over the years since the implementation of green management practices – most notably by espousing the principle that Pollution Prevention Pays. Given below are some examples of cost savings achieved in various 3M plants through green practices aimed at pollution prevention:

New Electrode Design Reduces Inherent Waste.

A 3P project team from 3M's Valley, Nebraska facility, reduced the waste inherent to the product design and process from Red Dot Resting (RDR) Electrodes, adhesive electrodes used in electrocardiogram or EKG applications, by redesigning the electrode. The team changed the configuration of the electrodes on the card which reduced silver coating weight, adhesive coating weight, and the overall size of the electrode. The project prevented nearly 11 tons of waste and saved nearly $1,000,000 in its first year of implementation.

3M Brazil Reduces Solvent Emissions from Tape Production.

In 2005, a 3P team from 3M Brazil's Itapetininga facility replaced the solvent-based paper treatment process. The plant used to manufacture packaging, medical and masking tapes with a new, water-based process. As a result of this change, the facility reduced solvent emissions by over 45 tons per year. By preventing solvent emissions at the source, the plant also eliminated the need for pollution control equipment, reducing the plant's energy use and eliminating over 125 metric tons of CO_2 emissions annually. The project is expected to save the facility over $850,000 in its first year of implementation.

3M's Valley, Nebraska Facility Reduces Packaging Waste

3M's Valley, Nebraska facility was recognized under the 3P criteria for working with its vendor to switch to reusable packaging for some of the components it purchases to make respirators. Before this project, Valley received the components on spools packaged in a box. The components vendor did not want the original boxes back, so the empty spools had to be returned to the vendor in new, different boxes. The facility worked with the vendor to change the component packaging to a system where both the empty spools and their containers can be returned, reducing shipping waste by approximately 8 tons in the first year of the project and saving 3M Valley over $1,500 in packaging and disposal costs.

Source: http://solutions.3m.com/wps/portal/3M/en_US/global/sustainability/management/pollution-prevention-pays/3p-examples/

10.8 CONCLUSION

Under pressure from the consumer, investor, environmental groups and politicians, businesses are beginning to accept their responsibility for protecting the environment by developing more sustainable products and technologies. Market forces and environmental regulations have played an important role in the "greening" of business and will continue to do so. Companies, especially smaller ones, require more technical advice on how to achieve higher environmental standards and build sustainable businesses. As the markets for green products begin to develop, financial incentives in the form of tax concessions or even subsidies can help to compensate for the price disadvantage facing many green products. This can help to switch demand from products that damage the environment to those that conserve the environment. This does not remove the need for better environmental legislation as "...to be effectively green, shoppers or investors need guidance" (Cairncross, 1993). New controls, however, should work in tandem with financial incentives, thereby reinforcing the message to business that conservation is commercially expedient.

QUESTIONS

1. Why are companies reluctant to adopt green production processes?
2. "Higher environmental standards are not a threat but an opportunity". Explain your answer through examples.
3. An environmentally proactive company has a sound long term perspective. Discuss.

EXERCISES

1. Make a case study of a firm that practices green production technologies and check if there are cost advantages to the firm.
2. Make a survey of at least 10 firms and find out if firms are willing to voluntarily practice green production methods. Find out the reasons for and against the case.
3. Make a list of the ways by which consumers can influence corporate green practices.
4. Go to the 3M website and make a detailed study of the PPP programme implemented by them.

❑❑❑

11

Environmental Management Systems in Industry

> *Turning every business into an environmental industry will involve applying new principles . . . first, we need to make more with less . . . second, we need to design out waste . . . third, we must begin to decarbonize our energy supply.*
>
> **David Miliband**

For decades, policymakers in different countries have required firms to either install specific pollution-control technologies or to ensure that emissions from their smokestacks or drain pipes stay within specific limits. This two-pronged approach of environmental technology requirements and emission limits has succeeded in reducing certain types of environmental problems. Yet this approach, which forms the backbone of the nation's environmental protection system, has for the most part ignored what goes on inside the firms that actually generate pollution. As long as companies deployed the appropriate technologies or met the specified emissions targets, how they managed their facilities and what systems they used to monitor their environmental performance mattered to no one other than the company managers themselves, and perhaps their corporate boards and shareholders.

The tendency to ignore what goes on inside the firm is beginning to change. As environmental problems persist, even after decades of conventional regulation, policymakers, trade associations, and non-governmental organizations are searching for alternative solutions. Among the most innovative alternatives are strategies that focus directly on how companies manage their internal operations. And this is now being exposed as a direct and explicit target of government regulators and others who seek to induce firms to improve their environmental performance.

11.1 WHAT IS EMS?

Environmental Management System (EMS) refers to the management of an organization's environmental programmes in a comprehensive, systematic, planned, and documented manner. It includes the organizational structure, planning and resources for developing, implementing and maintaining policy for environmental protection.

An EMS is a system of management processes that enables organizations to continually reduce their impact on the natural environment (Deming, 1986). An EMS sets out the company's goals for environmental performance and a plan for achieving those goals. Ideally, company managers will set goals in areas such as compliance with environmental laws, minimization of risks to human health and the environment, use of natural resources, and prevention and reduction of pollution. EMS consists of an environmental policy, as well as a set of evaluation processes that require organizations to assess their environmental impacts, establish goals, implement environmental goals, monitor goal attainment, and undergo management review (Lamprecht, 1997).

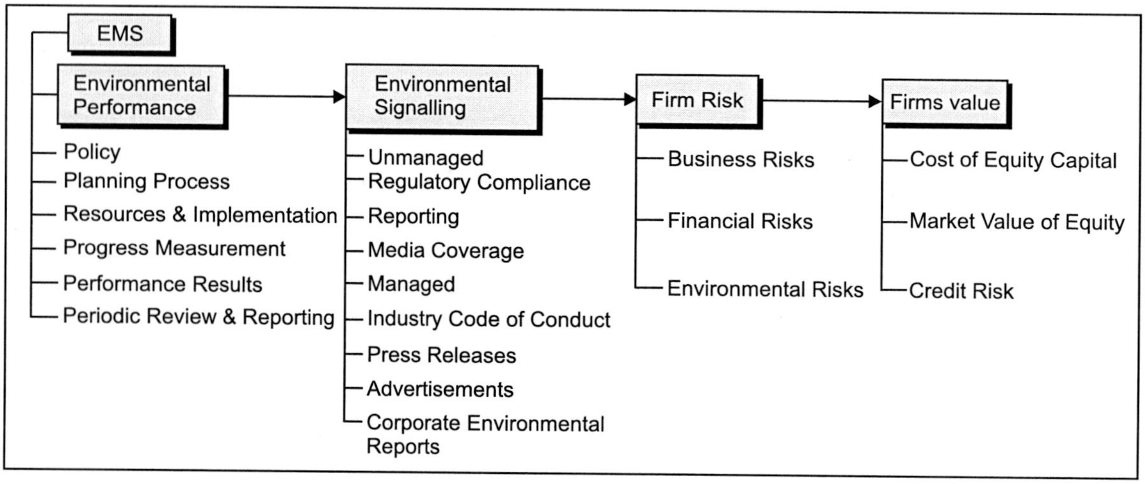

Fig. 11.1 Linking Corporate Environmental Management & Performance with Firm's Value

Investments in environmental management lead to better short-term environmental performance and offer scope for further improvements in the future. Also, crucially, they reduce the firm's risk which is the key factor that investors consider when deciding upon the return that they will require for making a particular investment. In order to obtain the benefits of greater shareholder gains, the firm must improve its environmental management performance. The various components of corporate environmental management and performance are interrelated as shown in Figure 11.1 above.

11.2 EMS MODELS

Today, EMSs can range in complexity from simple reminders of regulatory deadlines at a single facility, to an elaborate, internet-based, enterprise-wide performance management system that tracks regulatory requirements, assigns tasks, controls documentation and records, provides training, and shares information across multiple operations and facilities around the world. EMSs are most effective when they are part of normal business activities, rather than when treated as separate initiatives.

Although businesses typically have many elements of an EMS already in place, the EMS provides a systematic way to integrate those efforts and direct them towards company-established goals. The significant range and variations of EMSs can be attributed to the differences among organizations in size, activities, impacts, regulatory requirements, corporate culture and policy commitments.

11.3 TOTAL QUALITY MANAGEMENT

Most systematic approaches to addressing performance issues derive from the work of W. Edward Deming, the US statistician who is credited with dramatically improving the performance of the Japanese industry after World War II, with a system that has come to be known as Total Quality Management (TQM). Deming also popularized the "plan-do-check-act" cycle that is at the root of all such systems: identify and analyze the problem (plan), develop and implement solutions (do), evaluate and measure the results (check), and fix the problems identified and incorporate the lessons learned into a feedback loop that begins the process anew (act). The feedback loop involves all personnel and elements of an organization and runs counter to traditional top-down "management by objectives" approaches. Environmental management systems turn the TQM process to a specific concern for reducing environmental impacts.

11.4 WHY DO FIRMS CERTIFY THEIR EMS?

In recent years, researchers of business strategy and public policy have become increasingly interested in why facilities certify their environmental management systems (EMS) to International Organization for Standardization (ISO) 14001. Decisions to certify are interesting for several reasons. First, regulators do not require ISO 14001 certification, and prior to the year 2001, buyers in the US were not requiring certification as a condition of doing business. As such, early adopters of ISO 14001 were certifying their EMSs voluntarily and in the absence of coercive market pressures. Second, achieving ISO 14001 certification requires a significant commitment of resources, and whereas the organization incurs the cost of certification, the potential environmental benefits associated with reducing pollution can be enjoyed by society at large. Third, organizations that certify to ISO 14001 may be able to enhance their environmental image and confer external legitimacy. They may also be able to use ISO 14001 to increase their internal efficiencies and create competitive advantage opportunities and economic benefits.

Together, the voluntary nature, commitment of resources, and potential societal and economic benefits of certification create at least the appearance that ISO 14001-certified facilities are trying to be socially responsible. Prior research drawing on institutional theory has shown that a firm's motivation to undertake a voluntary environmental action is affected by pressures from regulators and markets. However, other studies have concluded that organizations with stronger complementary capabilities might undertake proactive environmental strategies. Finally, ISO 14001 has the potential to be utilized by a significant number of corporations, because it does not preclude any industry or company from obtaining certification as long as the company fulfills the environmental standard's goals and receives third-party certification. In addition, ISO 14001 is the only EMS standard established globally, and the most widely recognized voluntary environmental standard. For these reasons, ISO 14001 has the potential to affect more firms globally and affect more facility operations than any other environmental certification program. Understanding why firms see value in the international standard, therefore, provides essential insights about the global adoption of this important standard and its diffusion worldwide.

A firm can implement an EMS that is in line with one of the EMS standards (BS 7750, EMAS, or ISO) without external certification. Some situations in which external certification could become important include the following:

(*i*) A customer requires EMS certification as a condition to sign a contract.

(*ii*) The organization supplies to a customer who strongly suggests that it should become registered.

(*iii*) The government provides benefits to registered organizations.

(*iv*) The company may have a site in the European Union, where market pressure or the regulatory environment forces it to obtain registration or certification.

(*v*) A single international environmental standard can reduce the number of environmental audits conducted by customers, regulators, or registrars.

(*vi*) The business exports to markets where EMS registration is a de facto requirement for entering the market.

(*vii*) The business expects to gain a competitive advantage through EMS registration.

(*viii*) The major stakeholders (local community, shareholders, unions, etc.) expect environmental excellence, and an EMS registration is the way to demonstrate it.

If one of the above situations applies, a firm should decide whether to become certified for the organization as a whole or just for parts of it.

11.5 TEN ELEMENTS OF AN ENVIRONMENTAL MANAGEMENT SYSTEM

In June 2000, the Commission for Environmental Cooperation published the "10 Elements of Effective Environmental Management Systems" (CEC, 2000). The "10 elements" were negotiated by Canada, Mexico and the United States just after the ISO 14001 standards were published and served as the first general policy statement by the three governments on what they believed were important features of an EMS. The "10 elements" are generic in nature and place greater emphasis on compliance with environmental regulations than the ISO 14001 standard. Like the ISO standard, the "10 elements" state that a company's environmental policy should include a provision for compliance with environmental requirements. But the "10 elements" go beyond the ISO in stating that an EMS should establish objectives and targets for achieving and maintaining compliance with environmental requirements and a commitment to continuous improvement in environmental performance.

These ten elements are:

(*i*) Document and clearly communicate an environmental policy.

(*ii*) Clearly communicate all environmental requirements and voluntary undertakings.

(*iii*) Establish specific objectives and targets and establish appropriate time frames to meet those objectives and targets.

(*iv*) Establish the structure, responsibility and resources to ensure that the organization is equipped with sufficient personnel and other resources to meet the objectives and targets of its EMS.

(*v*) Identify and provide for the planning and management of all the organization's operations and activities with a view towards achieving the objectives and targets.

(*vi*) Establish and maintain corrective and preventive action and emergency procedures.

(*vii*) Ensure adequate training and competence of employees.

(*viii*) Describe how the "10 Elements" will be integrated into the organization's overall decision-making and planning.

(*ix*) Establish and maintain document control.

(*x*) Require continuous evaluation and improvement.

11.6 CAN EMS BRING ABOUT POSITIVE CHANGE?

The main reason for expecting that EMS can bring about positive change is that systematic management leads to better environmental outcomes than haphazard management. EMS adoption may change the culture of firms by creating a new awareness of the relationship between business activity and the environment. EMS provides managers with a structure for identifying changes that improve both environmental and business performance.

However, the EMS tool by itself is not necessarily sufficient for firms to create superior environmental improvement. Improvements may depend much more on how effectively and ambitiously an EMS is implemented, how well the organization is managed overall, and how committed the managers are to seeing that the firm achieves real and continuous environmental improvement. One of the key motivators for developing an EMS and using it well may be the fear of regulatory action.

11.7 CAN EMS BE PROPOSED AS A TOTAL SUBSTITUTE FOR ENVIRONMENTAL REGULATION?

EMS standards are flexible, allowing firms to adapt their EMS to their own organizational capacities and needs. This flexibility contrasts sharply with the rigidity usually associated with government regulation. Existing regulations typically require firms to adopt specific technologies or methods designed to protect environmental quality, even if alternative technologies or methods might be cheaper.

Managers of firms with strong environmental performance might respond to such a mandate by formalizing and standardizing their existing practices. Managers of firms with poor environmental performance might use the EMS to think about their environmental impacts for the first time, take responsibility for setting and achieving environmental goals, involve employees in establishing new routines that protect the environment, and institute new systems for reporting and record-keeping. Thus, for lower-performing firms, the process of instituting an EMS might jumpstart their progress towards better environmental performance.

However, it is also possible that managers who are told to adopt EMS may choose trivial goals for their systems, or provide ambitious goals but fail to provide the resources necessary to achieve them. The costs to firms associated with complying with such a mandate would also need to be taken into account.

Hence, it is felt that until reliable and consistent measures of environmental performance can be developed, EMS should be treated as a complement and not as a general substitute for traditional forms of regulation.

11.8 ADVANTAGES OF EMS OVER GOVERNMENT IMPOSED STANDARDS

When people inside an organization take responsibility for managing environmental improvement, the internal regulatory strategies they adopt will presumably turn out to be more effective and efficient than they would be under government-imposed standards. Moreover, when firms have the flexibility to create their own internal regulatory approaches, they are more likely to innovate and will potentially find solutions that government standard-setters would never have considered. Finally, individuals within organizations may be more likely to see their organization's own standards as more reasonable and legitimate, which may in turn enhance compliance with socially desirable norms.

11.9 BENEFITS OF EMS

Designing and implementing an EMS can have tangible benefits for business enterprises. A system can help a company to enhance efficiency and minimize resource use and waste, thereby reducing costs, help to ensure compliance with regulatory requirements, encourage employee involvement and improve relations with customers (Darnall and Edwards, 2006). Despite variation in the sophistication, scope and achievements of environmental management systems, successful EMSs share common characteristics that are directly related to the benefits of an EMS. These benefits can be broadly categorized into five main areas:

Cost Savings

Case studies point most frequently to the financial benefits of implementing an environmental management system. Cost savings are often linked with consuming fewer resources and producing less waste, but savings can also accrue from operational efficiencies, a higher level of management efficiency, and reduced liabilities because of better relations with regulators and communities. Operational efficiency usually involves replacing or renovating equipment and facilities, as well as improving the production process design and paying closer attention to all inputs and outputs. Such changes can reduce inputs (energy, water, etc.) or make operations more efficient, so that production is higher, faster or cheaper than before. Costs are compared pre and post-EMS implementation. Even small changes in operational efficiency can often produce significant results. During its EMS identification process, an American company noticed that one of its large machines had a serious oil leak. The leak was quickly repaired with a $5 gasket. This easy, inexpensive action cut the amount of oil consumed by the company by half, resulting in significant cost savings. In addition, the local municipal authority reclassified the plant as no longer generating hazardous waste (IFC, 2004).

Reduced Liability

This is another financial criterion that can be used to measure the success of an EMS. A court or the government may view a company with an EMS in place more favorably when determining sanctions. For example, in Nova Scotia, a judge dismissed a case against a pulp and paper mill for a small oil spill because the company had an EMS in place that addressed spill issues. The judge cited the company's due diligence, stating "the supervisor who found the leak...knew the equipment, what to do to stop the leak and did so immediately.... He had been instructed on what to do in the event of any oil spill and he did that."

Reductions in Resource Use, Waste and Emissions

Many concerns rate the success of their EMSs by monitoring the resources used and the waste minimized, both of which are closely related to cost savings. Implementing an EMS allows a company to identify opportunities for improvement and to plan expenses. Key performance indicators include: the volume of raw materials, water and energy consumption, recycling rate, hazardous and non-hazardous waste generation and the number and volume of releases. Organizations use self-generated records, bills or data from various utilities to measure consumption and waste, pre- and post-EMS implementation. Both large corporations and small and medium-size enterprises use EMSs to reduce resource and energy consumption, as well as the volume and toxicity of waste generation.

Regulatory Compliance

Another frequent indicator of a successful EMS is achieving the goal of regulatory compliance. The criteria an organization selects to measure improvement can vary widely and depends on the company's compliance history and regulatory burden. Management can use an EMS to monitor the legal requirements and thereby plan expenses associated with obtaining permits, reporting and monitoring, to ensure compliance with the law—ideally, reducing the frequency and severity of violations and the associated costs. An EMS can also help a company to prepare for a more stringent application of environmental regulations by the government.

Employee Involvement

Many companies recognize that the success of an EMS depends on the participation of the full spectrum of employees. Indeed, employee engagement is at the heart of the Total Quality Management (TQM) process on which EMS principles depend. Different types of employees have different insights into environmental performance and suggestions for improvements. Proper implementation of an EMS requires employee involvement and, if successful, creates as a benefit, a sense of responsibility and accomplishment among the employees.

Improved Relations with Customers

An EMS can improve relations with customers. For small and medium enterprises, improved relations usually means larger purchasers in a dominant market position, such as Ford and GM, which require their suppliers to be ISO 14001-certified. Smaller companies, however, may also find that an EMS means wider appeal in a more local market, especially in the context of green consumerism which is on the rise.

11.10 IMPACT OF EMS ON TECHNOLOGICAL INNOVATION

Since the publication of *Changing the Course*, the introductory book on eco-efficiency by Steven Schmidheiny (1992) of the World Business Council for Sustainable Development, companies have increasingly sought win–win solutions that combine simultaneous improvement in corporate competitiveness and environmental performance. Theoretical work supports this approach and argues that pollution is a sign of both environmental and economic inefficiency, and that many cost-effective environmental measures are inadequately exploited by managers. The general corporate response to these challenges has been to improve management controls through the implementation of formalistic and procedural environmental management systems. A variety of European and international environmental management standards have been introduced throughout the1990s and now over 70, 000 companies hold some type of EMS certification world wide (ISO, 2003). Beyond these official registrations, many more companies—and other organizations, including universities and public agencies—have implemented uncertified systems. Thus, EMS has seemingly become the pre-eminent approach to environmental management globally.

The impact of EMS on technological innovation, however, has often gone unevaluated. Technological change theories (Schumpeter, 1984; Nelson and Winter, 1982; Dosi *et al.*, 1988) distinguish between two types of innovation: *continuity* (incremental) and *discontinuity* (radical) type changes. In general, continuity change improves the performance of existing technologies, while discontinuity leads to the replacement of existing technologies by superior alternatives. Distinguishing between the two can be complicated, however, by the fact that what is discontinuous at one level of analysis, may appear continuous at a higher level of analysis. The shift from hard disk drives to flash memory, for example, can be discontinuous for disk drive manufacturers, but continuous for the larger personal computer value network in which memory is an embedded component.

From an environmental perspective, continuity solutions address pollution through adjustments to the input mix, incremental process changes or through end-of-pipe treatment methods. Estimates are that continuity approaches account for 70–90 per cent of environmental technology expenditures, and have focused principally on waste management, energy use and water consumption (Kuisma *et al.*, 2001; Hertin *et al.*, 2003).

Discontinuity type changes, in contrast, are competence enhancing, radical changes that seek the replacement of existing components—or entire systems—and the creation of new value networks. In the environmental case, these approaches generally require returning to the initial design phase to eliminate environmental flaws from the business model at the earliest stages possible (Hawken *et al.*, 1999; McDonough and Braungart, 2002). Such alterations may also require corporate transformation and restructuring of production systems, services, products and markets. It is becoming apparent that some environmental problems, such as global climate change, resource depletion, biodiversity loss, accumulation of persistent pollutants or impacts on the nitrogen cycle, cannot be effectively solved through continuity approaches. Dealing with global climate change, for example, will require nearly 90 per cent reduction in carbon dioxide emissions by industrialized countries, something that currently seems beyond the scope of continuity approaches (Unruh, 2002).

Fostering discontinuous innovations, therefore, appears to be an attractive strategy that could generate large sustainability gains. However, examples of discontinuity innovations are far less abundant than ones of the continuity type and understanding the barriers to discontinuity changes is an important area of research.

A useful starting point for understanding such barriers is the *technological lock-in theory* (Arthur, 1989), which has identified numerous causal factors that can help explain inertia to technological change. The theory, however, has focused dominantly on market coordination and technological interdependencies as the primary sources of inertia in corporate managements.

Technological Lock-In

Technological change theorists, such as David (1989, 1997) and Arthur (1994) have developed the concept of *technological lock-in*, which argues that technological change is not the frictionless adoption of superior innovations by rational agents, but is instead, subject to barriers and irreversibility that can limit the diffusion of superior technologies.

Technological lock-in arises because in the presence of increasing returns, apparently inferior designs can become locked into the production system through a historic process in which circumstantial events in the techno-institutional context can determine the winning alternative (David, 1997). Because technology adoption decisions are made with incomplete information about their impacts, apparent early superiority of a design is no guarantee of long-term suitability. In the realm of sustainability, authors have argued that many environmentally damaging systems have become locked in, hindering environmental improvement efforts by businesses and governments.

11.11 EMS AND GREEN SUPPLY CHAIN MANAGEMENT (GSCM)

EMS adopters are less likely to use GSCM practices, since their EMS allows them to market their environmental proactiveness without burdening their supply chain. This issue may be of particular relevance since some scholars argue that GSCM practices have relatively little reputation consequences that affect the end customers' purchasing decisions. Even for the most widely recognized EMSs, which undergo external certification (such as ISO 14001), organizations are not required to engage their suppliers.

The supply chain consists of all parties who are involved in fulfilling a customer request, including the suppliers, transporters, warehouses, retailers and customers themselves. The most common GSCM practices involve organizations assessing the environmental performance of their suppliers, requiring suppliers to undertake measures that ensure environmental quality of their products, and evaluating the cost of waste in their operating systems. However, GSCM practices also extend to the entire value chain (from supplier to consumer) when organizations inform buyers of ways to reduce their impacts on the natural environment. Each of these actions has the potential to reduce the *direct* and *indirect* environmental impacts of an organization's final product.

An organization's *direct* environmental impacts stem from inputs that increase waste during product storage, transportation, processing, use or disposal. These impacts originate from an organization's first tier suppliers. *Indirect* environmental impacts relate to an organization's second tier suppliers' products. These inputs have an indirect impact on the final producer's products, production, waste and disposal. These distinctions are important because organizations that adopt

GSCM practices generally evaluate the environmental impacts of their first tier suppliers, but often do not control the impact of the waste streams beyond the first tier, since they lack the internal process to do so.

In recent years, some organizations have begun relying on their supply chains to improve their business performance and create value for their end customers. Manufacturers are also calling on their suppliers more frequently to create innovative ideas that exploit new emerging technologies, and reduce costs during the design and development of their products. In some instances, organizations are even relying on their suppliers to deliver state-of-the-art process technology that they cannot deliver internally. Consequently, enterprises wishing to minimize their environmental impacts during product design are learning that their ability to do so is often dependent on their ability to manage their increasingly complex supplier relationships.

For instance, to avoid environmental risks from its suppliers, Dow Chemical, one of the largest global producers of chlorine, partnered with its transportation supplier, to design rail cars that were two times thicker than what was required by US regulations and by the chemical industry association. The company's decision was based on a discovery that, in the event of derailment, the rail car had a significant probability of puncturing upon impact and placing neighbouring communities and ecological systems at risk. However, Dow lacked the internal expertise to address the problem on its own. By collaborating with its transportation supplier to design an innovative car that would not rupture, the new rail car soon became the industry standard. Consequently, Dow Chemical established a leadership position and increased its credibility with regulators and industry peers. Similarly, in the automotive industry, some manufacturers have formed partnerships with their paint and related chemical suppliers, in an effort to develop innovative environmentally benign inputs that car makers could not develop on their own.

In other instances, organizations are focusing more tightly on their core competencies and relying on their suppliers to a greater degree for non-core activities such as new product development through early design and concurrent engineering. These organizations are choosing to green their supply chain to avoid inheriting risk of loss from less environmentally conscious suppliers. The global automotive industry is an example of one sector that is collectively considering the environmental attributes of its suppliers to avoid environmental risks. For instance, by evaluating the plastic and steel components in its product design cycle, the automotive industry has reduced the risk of inheriting environmental problems from its suppliers

Thus the relationship between EMSs and GSCM practices has potentially complementary and significant implications for an organization's environmental sustainability, because together they offer a more comprehensive means of defining and establishing sustainability among networks of business organizations. Moreover, when EMSs are established in the absence of GSCM, environmental benefits are likely to diminish because the organizations supply chain does not share its environmental goals and true environmental sustainability does not result.

11.12 MANAGEMENT-BASED STRATEGIES AND ENVIRONMENTAL MANAGEMENT SYSTEMS

Management-based strategies are broader than and in important ways, different from EMSs. EMSs are the internal rules and organizational structures that managers use to routinize behaviour in order to satisfy their organization's environmental goals and are effectively, "regulatory" structures that arise from within organizations.

Management-based *strategies*, in contrast, are used by those who are *outside* an organization to change the management practices and behaviour of those on the *inside*. A major distinction between management-based strategies and EMSs therefore, lies in who is requiring or encouraging the improved environmental management. When managers within individual companies devise EMSs for use in their own facilities, they are changing their own behaviour or seeking to change the behaviour of those individuals whom they oversee within their organization. When government agencies, major customers, or trade associations encourage or require companies to develop EMSs, they are outsiders deploying a management-based strategy.

While management-based strategies differ from EMSs with respect to who initiates the effort to change environmentally detrimental behaviour, they do share a common focus on management activities. They are both premised on the belief that improvement in environmental management will lead to improvements in environmental outcomes. If the adoption of EMSs leads to an improvement in firms' environmental performance, then perhaps management-based strategies could be an effective means of improving environmental performance too.

Management-based strategies are appealing because they can give firms the flexibility to develop their own solutions and plans, a considerable advantage given the complex, heterogeneous causes of various environmental problems. They can leverage the informational advantage of managers within business organizations, enlisting them to identify ways to solve the specific problems created by their facilities' operations.

Policymakers and business leaders increasingly recognize that what goes on inside the black box of the organization is of critical importance for overall environmental quality. The size of a regulated entity's environmental footprint is neither necessarily nor completely determined by the raw materials it uses or the products or services it produces. An organization's impact on the environment is also based on the actions of its managers: the information they collect and share, the goals they develop and articulate, the types of issues to which they give attention, the reporting structures they establish, the kind of professionals they include in key meetings, the aspects of performance they monitor, and the way they factor environmental performance into employee rewards and penalties.

A growing body of case study evidence suggests that in many instances EMSs have had positive effects on environmental outcomes. The websites of many firms testify to having improved their environmental performance by implementing an EMS. The achievements firms have realized, include, among other things, increased recycling, improved water conservation, reduced releases of toxic chemicals, and reduced consumption of material inputs. In USA, for example, an Alcoa subsidiary in South Carolina cut waste generation in half after implementing an EMS (Rondinelli and Vastag, 2000). EMS adoption helped a Louisiana Pacific wood products plant find a way to recycle wood chips, reducing waste and saving money (Coglianese and Nash, 2001).

Although case studies can show that EMSs might improve environmental performance in some firms, they tell us little about how EMSs will work in general. Generalizing from individual case studies is difficult because these studies do not distinguish between the role of the EMS and the role of other factors that might also contribute to improvements in environmental performance.

Louisiana Pacific, for example, introduced its EMS, after EPA filed a suit against the company for unlawful air releases (Coglianese and Nash, 2001). Was the EMS the causal factor leading the company to improve environmental outcomes? Or was the government's criminal enforcement action the key cause of both the decision to adopt an EMS and to improve environmental outcomes? In the wake of such an enforcement action, Louisiana Pacific's overall heightened commitment to making environmental improvements, rather than EMS, may have been the critical factor in instituting new, environmentally beneficial practices.

11.13 BARRIERS TO EMS ADOPTION

Barriers are factors that hamper and can even bring to an end, the design, implementation and operation of an environmental management system. Even when driving forces exist, many businesses, especially small and medium sized ones, may face formidable barriers when designing and implementing an EMS that larger companies are less likely to face. The National Environmental Education and Training Foundation (NEETF) identified some of the barriers to EMS adoption in its report *Standardizing Excellence: Working with Smaller Businesses to Implement Environmental Management Systems* (NEETF, 2001). These barriers fall into three categories: motivation, resource and implementation issues.

Motivation Barriers

(*i*) Lack of customer requirements or demand to have an environmental management system.

(*ii*) Misconception that environmental issues are a low organizational priority or are believed to be under control.

(*iii*) Belief that an EMS is not important or relevant to the business or capable of adding to the bottom line.

(*iv*) Lack of public or non-governmental organization pressure to implement an EMS.

(*v*) Belief that an EMS is the current management gimmick.

(*vi*) Belief that an EMS is not widely accepted or used in an industrial sector or geographic area.

Resource Concerns

(*i*) Concern about the cost and time needed to establish an EMS.

(*ii*) Concern about the operational management costs after implementation.

(*iii*) Perception that an EMS is complicated and unattainable.

Implementation Concerns

(*i*) Fear of discovering non-compliance with regulations or permits.

(*ii*) Fear of discovering or uncovering internal problems within the organization (staff issues, process issues, company policies, etc.).

A special problem encountered by small firms in EMS implementation is "the lack of sector specific guidance and material tailored to different sizes of the firms" (Hillary, 1999). Another issue is the cost of certification. Because small firms generally do not have in-house expertise, they usually need to hire consultants to help them design, implement and verify the EMS and auditors to certify the EMS, costs which larger firms can more easily handle.

11.14 CONDITIONS ESSENTIAL FOR THE SUCCESSFUL IMPLEMENTATION OF EMS

The success of an organization's EMS can be evaluated by monitoring the organization's progress towards meeting its environment-related objectives and targets. Understanding the common characteristics of a successful EMS will help to ensure that the conditions needed to support successful EMS design and implementation are present.

Designed with a Strong Business Case in Mind

A successful EMS is developed with a strong business case in mind. Its purpose is to improve the value of the company through risk reduction, revenue enhancement and cost reduction.

Supported by Management and Commitment of Resources

Unless the owner and top management are committed to and supportive of the EMS, it is extremely difficult to obtain the resources and cooperation needed to successfully develop and implement an effective system. The environmental policy, as endorsed and supported by management, defines the strategy of the organization and specifies the scope and commitment of the EMS to employees, customers and those outside the company, such as local agencies, investors and community groups.

Engaged Employees

When employees at all levels of an organization are engaged in an EMS, it is more likely to succeed. Under a well-designed EMS, supported by management, individual employees understand their roles and responsibilities, receive adequate training and information, and are aware of the potential environmental impacts of their jobs. Typically, when employees are engaged in such a programme, they enjoy a sense of ownership and possess the motivation to make a positive contribution to the success of the programme.

Integrated into Business

The most successful EMSs are not stand-alone projects or initiatives; they are part of the standard decision-making process of a business. They are also integrated into all aspects of a company's activities, products and services. In many case studies, companies that had adopted EMSs asserted that they saw a business value in improving their environmental performance.

Clearly Defined Objectives and Targets

Successful EMSs tend to set both abstract/overarching and specific/measurable goals. An abstract/overarching goal may be "transparency", whereas a specific/measurable goal may be "Have X document the EMS design and implementation process" or "Reduce air emissions by 35 per cent by 2006". Abstract/overarching goals allow for creativity and problem solving, because managers and employees are not bound to follow certain codes. Specific and measurable goals ensure that the abstract is translated into the feasible and achievable. This duality also places smaller objectives in the context of larger goals.

Continual Monitoring and Measurement

Monitoring and measurement are always cited in EMS success stories, but companies go to widely different lengths to monitor and measure their progress. After setting objectives and targets, a company should devise a means of monitoring and measurement, preferably in quantifiable terms. Are changes being implemented? Are the correct policies being pursued? Is the amount of waste being reduced, and, if so, by how much? How much money is being saved through waste reduction? Are targets being met? Are more effective means of reducing waste available? Should objectives and targets be revised? Questions like these should be asked daily by any company and not limited to the start-up period of the EMS. A key element of any management system is the opportunity it provides for learning from experience. Given the size, resources, and variety of structures, as well as the obstacles faced by small and medium-size enterprises in implementing environmental management systems, it is important that those systems be flexible. Whenever possible, the goals and complexity of an EMS should be set by the company itself. Those goals will necessarily be limited by financial and economic considerations, including the profitability requirements of the organization.

11.15 CONCLUSION

Thus, there has been a tremendous increase in awareness about environmental issues on the part of companies over the last ten years or so, and there is a felt need to develop business models which are sustainable and non-destructive of the environment. Although businesses typically have many elements of an Environmental Management System (EMS) already in place, the EMS provides a systematic way to integrate those efforts and direct them towards company-established goals. The significance, range and variations of EMSs can be attributed to the differences among organizations in size, activities, impacts, regulatory requirements, corporate culture and policy commitments.

QUESTIONS

1. What benefits accrue to a company in installing EMS?
2. What are the reasons for companies getting their EMS certified?
3. Discuss the relationship between TQM and EQM.
4. 'EMS could result in a technological lock in.' Discuss.
5. Throw light on the conditions essential for the successful implementation of EMS.

EXERCISE (CASE STUDY)

IKEA Systems

IKEA Systems BV (IKEA) is a Sweden-based furniture retail giant. The present case examines IKEA's journey in becoming an environmentally responsible company by highlighting initiatives taken by the company to ensure that its operations did not have an adverse effect on the environment. IKEA was primarily involved in furniture retailing; initially most of its furniture was made of wood, which required the felling of trees. To process the wood, many chemicals were used, which were harmful to the environment and to the consumers. IKEA realized that better environmental practices within the company and among its suppliers would have long-term benefits, not only economically but also in presenting a positive corporate image to customers.

Environment Friendly Products: In order to minimize the use of wood in its furniture, IKEA concentrated on bringing out products made of recycled and reusable material. The team ensured that the products were free from substances that caused allergies or products that were harmful to the health and the environment.

Environmental Training: IKEA started off with a "train the trainers" approach to spread environmental awareness across the organization. Trainers from each department, employees involved in product design and those in direct contact with the customers, attended a weeklong training course. The training modules included the imparting of basic environmental knowledge.

Eco-Friendly Practice: Apart from developing a wide range of eco-friendly products, IKEA also adopted several eco-friendly practices, right from choosing the location of its new stores, to using alternative sources of energy, waste management, and transportation. For constructing new stores, IKEA followed policies and procedures that ensured that the buildings were durable and sustainable.

Making Suppliers Environmentally Responsible and Following Sound Forestry Practices: IKEA's main activity was furniture retailing, which required huge quantities of wood. The company relied on its suppliers to obtain wood and realized that if the wood was obtained from illegal sources and protected forests, it could considerably damage its reputation. Hence, an audit of suppliers was put in place to ensure that sustainable forestry practices were employed in sourcing the wood. IKEA obtained timber from 44 countries and took care not to use the timber obtained from intact natural forests. The long-term goal of the company was to source all the wood from well-managed forests.

Issues for Discussion and Analysis

(*i*) Analyse how environmentally friendly practices can help a company minimize its costs.

(*ii*) Examine how environmentally friendly practices can enhance an organization's image.

(*iii*) Study how IKEA went about implementing its environmental policies across its global operations.

(*iv*) Study how IKEA extended its environmental responsibility initiatives to its employees and consumers.

(*v*) Identify a case study of a business, similar to IKEA that has benefited from EMS practices.

❑❑❑

12

Stakeholders and Their Relevance Today

> *Business social responsibility should not be coerced; it is a voluntary decision that the entrepreneurial leadership of every company must make on its own.*
>
> **John Mackey**

Stakeholders are all the groups affected by, or that can affect, an organization's decisions, policies, and operations and include shareholders, employees, customers, suppliers and the community. Most are likely to be concerned about the company's attitude towards the environment (James E. Post et al, 1996). When there is a close and continuous interaction between business and society, a shared interest and interdependence develops between a company and other social groups. When this occurs, corporate stakeholders are created.

12.1 WHAT IS A STAKE?

The concept of stakeholders can be better understood when we understand the idea of a stake. A ***stake*** is an interest or a share in an undertaking. The idea of a stake, therefore, can range from simply an interest in an undertaking at one extreme to a legal claim of ownership at the other extreme. In between these two extremes is a right to something. This right might be a *legal* right to certain treatment rather than a legal claim of ownership, such as that of a shareholder.

Legal rights might include the right of due process (to get an impartial hearing) or the right to privacy (not to have one's privacy invaded or abridged). The right might be thought of as a *moral* right, such as that expressed by an employee: "I've got a right to a healthy, safe and toxic-free working environment." Or a consumer might say, "I've got a right to a safe product after all I've paid for this." Table.12.1 summarizes the various categories or types of stakes:

Table 12.1 Types of Stakes

An Interest	A Right	Ownership
When a person or group will be affected by a decision, it has an interest in that decision. *Examples:* Closure of plant will affect the community. This TV commercial demeans women, and I am a woman.	*Legal Right*: When a person or group has a legal claim to be treated in a certain way or to have a particular right protected. *Examples:* Employees expect due process, privacy; customers or creditors have certain legal rights. *Moral Right*: When a person or group thinks it has a moral right to be treated in a certain way or to have a particular right protected. *Examples:* Fairness, justice, equity.	When a person or group has a legal title to an asset or a property. *Examples:* "This company is mine, I founded it, and I own it, or I own 1,000 shares of this corporation".

Source: Archie B. Carroll and Ann B. Buchholtz (2001)

12.2 WHO IS A STAKEHOLDER?

A stakeholder is a person, group, organization or system who affects or can be affected by an organization's actions.

A *stakeholder*, then, is an individual or a group that has one or more of the various kinds of stakes in a business. Just as stakeholders *may be affected* by the actions, decisions, policies, or practices of the business firm, these stakeholders may in turn, also *affect* the organization's actions, decisions, policies, or practices.

The number of stakeholders and the variety of interests that a company's management must consider can make decisions quite complex. Over the years, there have been far reaching changes in stakeholders and stakeholder relationships. Managers have the challenge of weighing and balancing the interests of the corporate stakeholders. The key point about corporate stakeholders is that they may, and sometimes do, share decision-making power with a company's managers. Their justification in seeking a voice is that they are affected by the company's operations. The interest created between a company and its stakeholders can be a powerful aid to business, or it can be turned against a company. When stakeholders demand a voice in decision-making and policy-making, the company's managers need to respond with great skill if their primary business mission—producing goods and services—is to be achieved. This today, involves balancing a multi-legged stool in contrast with the three-legged stool of the fifties (that of merely balancing the interests of employees, customers and shareholders).

There are many examples of companies disregarding their stakeholders' wishes, either out of the belief that the stakeholder is wrong or out of arrogance and the attitude that "one unhappy customer, employee or regulator doesn't matter." Such attitudes are foolish and often prove costly to the company involved. For example, builders know that it is not possible to locate a power plant in a community that strongly objects. The only way to build a nuclear power plant or locate a landfill in an area, for example, is to work with the community, to respond to concerns, and to invest in creating and maintaining a relationship of trust. Today, many stakeholders have the ability to stick quills into the business. Companies need comprehensive approaches that take into account the needs of a larger and more diverse group of stakeholders. Business cannot be done in a social and political vacuum, and good management planning must take into account this web of considerations.

12.3 PRIMARY AND SECONDARY STAKEHOLDERS

Primary stakeholders are those who are most vital to the organization - a group without whose continuing participation the company cannot survive as a going concern, *e.g.,* customers, suppliers.

Secondary stakeholders are those without whose continuing participation the company can still exist, *e.g.,* community.

Business interacts with society in a variety of different ways and a company's relations differ with different stakeholders. Fig. 12.1 shows business interacting with groups that affect its ability to carry out its primary purpose of providing society with goods and services.

Stockholders and creditors provide financial capital to the company; employees contribute their work skills and knowledge; suppliers provide raw materials, energy and other supplies; and wholesalers, distributors and retailers help move the product from the plant to sales offices to customers. All businesses need customers who are willing to pay for the products and services being produced, and most companies compete against others, offering similar products and services in the marketplace. These are the fundamental interactions every business has with society, and they help us to define the primary economic mission of the company.

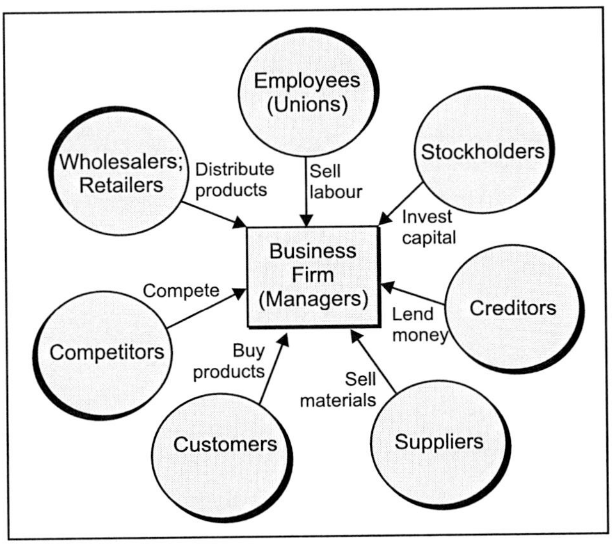

Source: James E. Post et al, 1996

Fig. 12.1 Relationship between a Business Firm and its Primary Stakeholders

A business's primary involvement with society, thus, includes all the direct relationships necessary for it to perform its major mission of producing goods and services for customers. These interactions normally occur in the marketplace and involve processes of buying and selling and shape a company's strategy and the policy decisions of its managers. It also reveals the importance of the stakeholders who are crucial to its existence and activities. These market-driven customers, suppliers, employees, and investors are its **primary stakeholders**.

However, a business's relationships go beyond those primary involvements to others in society. Another level of interaction occurs when other groups express an interest or concern in the organization's activities.

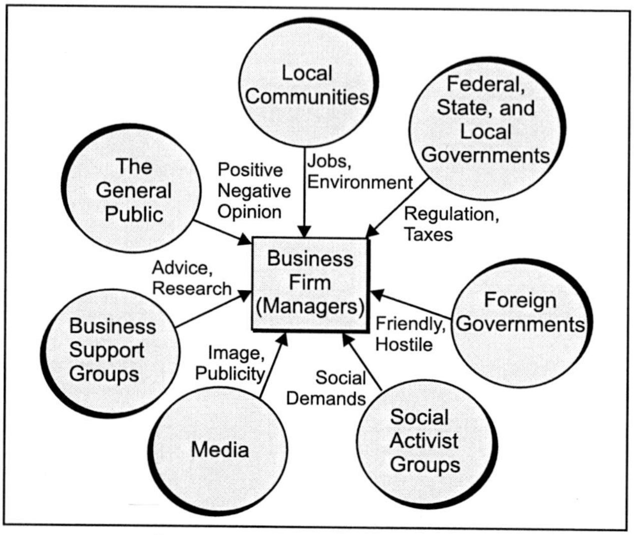

Source: James E. Post et al, 1996

Fig. 12.2 Relations between a Business Firm and its Secondary Stakeholders

Secondary stakeholders are in no way less important than primary stakeholders. Secondary stakeholders occur as a result of the normal consequences of the normal activities of conducting business. Primary and secondary areas of involvement are mutually inclusive. For example, while the safety of a product or the environmental effect of a product (*e.g.,* an automobile) is a primary concern to a consumer, the cumulative effect from the use of the product may represent a secondary effect or environmental concern for the entire community (*e.g.,* smog from automobile emission).

Table 12.2 Primary and Secondary Stakeholders–Nature of Interest and Power

Stakeholder	Nature of Interest – Stakeholder Wishes to:	Nature of Power – Stakeholder Influences Company By:
PRIMARY STAKEHOLDERS		
Employees	• Maintain stable employment in firm • Receive fair pay for work • Work in safe, comfortable environment	• Union bargaining power • Work activities or strikes • Publicity
Owners	Receive a satisfactory return on investments (dividends)	Exercising voting rights based on share ownership
Stockholders	Realize appreciation in stock value over time	Exercising rights to inspect company books and records

contd....

Stakeholder	Nature of Interest – Stakeholder Wishes to:	Nature of Power – Stakeholder Influences Company By:
Customers	• Receive fair exchange: value and quality for money spent • Receive safe, reliable products	• Purchasing goods from competitors • Boycotting companies whose products are unsatisfactory or whose policies are unacceptable
Suppliers	• Receive regular orders for goods • Be paid promptly for supplies delivered	• Refusing to meet orders if conditions are breached • Supplying to competitors
Competitors	• Be profitable • Gain a large share of the market	• Technological innovation, forcing competitors to "keep up" • Charging lower prices
SECONDARY STAKEHOLDERS		
Local Communities	• Employ local residents in the company • Ensure that the local environment is protected • Ensure that the local area is developed	• Refusing to extend additional credit • Issuing or restricting licenses and permits • Lobbying government for regulation of the company's policies or methods of land use and waste disposal
Social Activists	• Monitor company actions and policies to ensure that they conform to legal and ethical standards, and that they protect the public's safety	• Gaining broad public support through publicizing the issue • Lobbying government for regulation of the company
Media	• Keep the public informed on all issues relevant to their health, well-being, and economic status • Monitor company actions	Publicizing events that affect the public, especially those which have negative effects
Foreign Government	• Promote economic development • Encourage social improvements	• Granting permits to do business • Adopting regulations
Federal, State and Local Governments	• Raise revenues through taxes • Promote economic development	• Issuing regulations, licenses and permits • Allowing or disallowing industrial activity
The General Public	• Protect social values • Minimize risks • Achieve prosperity for society	• Supporting activists • Pressing government to act • Condemning or praising individual companies

Source: James E. Post et al, 1996

12.4 INTERACTIVE MODEL OF BUSINESS-SOCIETY RELATIONS

Combining primary and secondary interactions of a business gives an interactive model of business and society as shown below. In Fig. 12.3 below, primary interactions conducted through the market are shown on the left. The secondary interactions, which are carried out without the involvement of market processes are on the right. The main lessons from this interactive model are:

(*i*) In making decisions, a business is influenced by its primary and secondary stakeholders.

(*ii*) The managers of business firms need to become skilled in responding to social and political factors, as well as economic factors involved in their stakeholder relationships.

(*iii*) The acceptance of a business firm by society depends upon its performance in both the economic and socio-political sphere. For example, an auto manufacturer may produce reasonably priced cars that make a profit but encounter public disapproval because they are unsafe or environmentally harmful.

The interactive model of business and society highlights an important dimension to managerial decision-making, namely, that managers must make decisions and take actions for the greater common good, while simultaneously working for the improvement of the company's economic interests. The fundamental objective should be to enhance the quality of life (as defined by the society) in the broadest possible way.

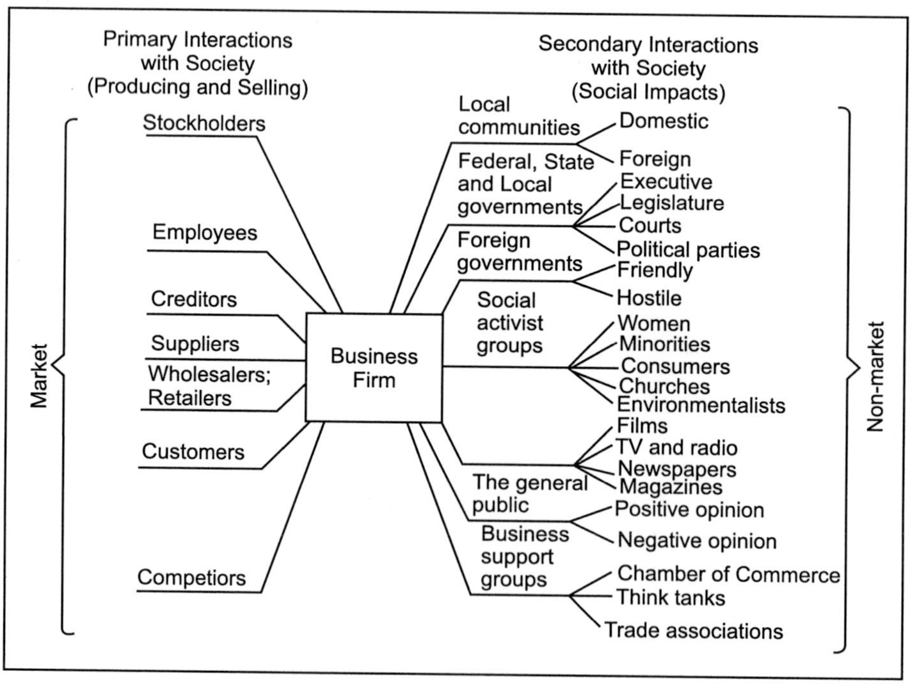

Fig. 12.3 Interactive Model of Business and Society Relations

It should be kept in mind that primary and secondary stakeholders cannot be divided into water-tight compartments and can quickly switch categories. This often occurs with the media or special-interest groups when the urgency of a claim (as in a boycott or demonstration) takes precedence over the legitimacy of that claim. In today's business environment, the media have the power to instantaneously transform a stakeholder's status with coverage on the evening news. Thus, while it is useful to think of primary and secondary classes of stakeholders for discussion purposes, it important to understand how easily and quickly those categories can shift.

12.5 STAKEHOLDER INTERESTS AND POWER WIELDED BY THEM

Stakeholder groups exist in many forms, some being well organized, while others are much less so. This variety makes it more difficult for a company's managers to understand and respond to stakeholder concerns. Each stakeholder has a unique connection with the organization and managers must understand these involvements and respond accordingly. For example, owners are most interested in realizing a return on their investment, while customers and suppliers are most interested in gaining fair value in the exchange for goods and money. Neither has a great interest in the other's stake.

Governments, public interest groups and local communities have another sort of relationship with the company. In general, their stake is broader than the financial stake of owners or persons who produce and sell services to the company. They may wish to protect the environment, assure human rights and advance other broad social interests. Managers can ignore these stakeholder interests only at their peril.

Thus, different stakeholders have different types and degrees of power. Stakeholder power, in this instance, means the ability to use resources to make an event happen or secure a desired outcome.

There are three types of stakeholder power: voting power, economic power and political power.

Voting power means that the stakeholder has a legitimate right to cast a vote. For example, each stockholder has a voting power proportionate to the percentage of the company's stock that he or she owns. Stockholders typically have an opportunity to vote on such major decisions as mergers, acquisitions, and other extraordinary issues. Thus, through their voting power, they may influence the company policy so that their investment is protected and produces a healthy return.

Customers, suppliers and retailers have a direct economic influence on the company. Their power is economic in nature. Suppliers can withhold supplies or refuse to fill orders if a company fails to meet its contractual obligations. Customers can choose to boycott products or an entire company if they believe the goods to be too expensive, poorly made, unsafe or inappropriate for consumption (*e.g.,* the ban on US beef in Europe due to the use of growth hormones in the raising of cattle, popularly viewed as harmful by the European consumers). Other customers may refuse to buy a company's products if the company enacts an improper policy (*e.g.,* the boycott of Nestle's products over its questionable practices in marketing infant formula in LDC countries).

Government exercises political power through legislation, regulation, or lawsuits. Other stakeholders also exercise political power, using their resources to pressure government to adopt new laws or regulations or to take legal action against a company. (Box 12.1 for the Tirupur Hosiery case).

BOX 12.1

Tirupur Hosiery Case

In a landmark case, a group of citizens in Tirupur, near Coimbatore, (Tamil Nadu, India) sued the hosiery mills in the town for allegedly dumping untreated wastes into the river Noyyal, a tributary of the river Bhavani, as a result of which some of the main polluting firms were ordered to be closed by the court. For almost a decade, owners of the dyeing units in and around Tirupur had imagined that they could "manage" the problem of industrial pollution caused by the discharge of toxic effluents into the Noyyal, a non-perennial river that ends in the Cauvery, near Karur. Farmers near the Orathupalayam dam, which is located 30 km downstream on the Noyyal, had been engaging in a bitter legal battle with the dyeing units and the State authorities. They had been complaining for more than a decade that the discharge of effluents had rendered their lands unfit for human use, let alone cultivation. The units paid a heavy price for believing that a business-as-usual attitude would fend off the challenge from those demanding a better way of doing business.

The Pollution Control Board stipulates that the total dissolved solids (TDS) in the water discharged into the river should not be more than 2,100 parts per million (ppm). It is well known—even the dyeing industry admits it—that the TDS levels in and around Tirupur are way above this norm. In fact, a leading dyer who had established an RO plant some years ago admitted that the TDS level in the water in the Orathupalayam dam area is above 9,000 ppm; in summer, when water evaporation is higher, the level of TDS is even higher. The court had, in the course of arguments over the last 10 years, determined that only a zero discharge norm for effluents would save the river.

The Madras High Court ordered the closure of more than 600 dyeing and bleaching units, which are a key element in the production chain in the hosiery garment business. The court took a stern view of the dyeing units' failure to comply with its earlier direction that they furnish proof of steps taken to install RO units. It observed that it was "agonized" by the repeated flouting of its orders and directed that units that had not paid 25 per cent of the cost of RO plants to equipment suppliers as advance be closed down immediately. It added teeth to its order by asking the Tamil Nadu Pollution Control Board (TNPCB) to ensure that the erring units are shut down.

Source: http://www.hinduonnet.com/fline/fl1513/15130660.htm

12.6 STAKEHOLDER COALITIONS

Stakeholder coalitions are the temporary unions of stakeholder groups that come together and share a common point of view on a particular issue or problem.

Stakeholder coalitions (combination) are not static. Stakeholders who are highly involved with a company today may be less involved tomorrow. Issues that are most salient at one point in time may be replaced by other issues at another time; stakeholders who are most dependent on one organization at one point of time, may be less dependent at another point of time. Stakeholders involved with one part of a large company often have little or no involvement with other parts of the organization. Movements such as the environmental movement or the human rights movement involve hundreds of state, national and international organizations and may operate with little or no policy making. The use of fax machines, telephones and computers have enabled like minded people to communicate quickly and are powerful tools in the hands of activist groups trying to monitor how multinational businesses are operating in different locations around the world. The combination of improved skills, national and international networks of experienced activists and media interest in a wide range of local, national and international issues have made the role of stakeholders, an increasingly powerful factor in business.

12.7 STAKEHOLDER MANAGEMENT

The managers of a business firm have the responsibilities of establishing the firm's overall direction (its goals, policies, and strategies) and seeing to it that these plans are carried out. Before the social environment became transient or rapidly changing as is the case today, the managerial task was relatively straightforward and the external environment was stable. In today's turbulent times, however, stakeholder management has become important as managers have discovered that many groups have to be relatively satisfied for the firm to meet its objectives. Without question, the primacy and necessity of profits as a return on the stockholders' investments continues to be recognized, but it is also possible to see the growing claims of other stakeholder groups and the success they have had in getting what they want.

The challenge of stakeholder management, therefore, is to see to it that the firm's primary stakeholders achieve their objectives and that other stakeholders are dealt with ethically and are also satisfied. This is the classic "win-win" situation which may not always occur, but is a legitimate goal for the management to pursue to protect its long-term self-interests. Five major questions must be considered by company managers to capture the essential information needed for stakeholder management:

(*i*) Who are our stakeholders?

(*ii*) What are our stakeholders' stakes?

(*iii*) What opportunities and challenges do our stakeholders present to our firm?

(*iv*) What responsibilities (economic, legal, ethical, and philanthropic) does our firm have to its stakeholders?

(*v*) What strategies or actions should our firm take to best manage stakeholder challenges and opportunities?

To consider the question "who are our stakeholders?" management must identify not only generic stakeholder groups, but also the specific groups. A ***generic stakeholder group*** is simply a broad grouping, such as employees, shareholders, environmental groups, or consumers. Within each of these generic categories, there may be a few or many specific groups. The controversial case of Nestle in the marketing of infant formula in less developed countries (LDCs) illustrates the process of stakeholder identification (Box 12.2).

BOX 12.2

Nestle Infant Formula Controversy

Nestlé, S. A., is the Swiss conglomerate that at one time dominated the marketing of infant formula in the Third World, or less-developed countries (LDCs). Other companies also marketed infant formula in LDCs, but Nestlé was the major company. In the 1970s, Nestlé became involved in a controversy over the morality of selling infant formula in the Third World and of using specific promotional and marketing techniques considered immoral by some. The basic allegation against Nestlé and the others was that in these Third World countries, infant formula was likely to be misused and therefore, might lead to malnutrition, diarrhea, and death. Also, it was claimed that Nestlé's aggressive marketing tactics encouraged women to choose bottle feeding, thus resulting in a decline in breast feeding, which is safer and healthier, particularly in the Third World. Poor sanitation, impure water, inadequacy of water supplies, and inability to read, comprehend, and follow directions resulted in disease and malnutrition. Mothers, who were poor, tried to save money and thus over-diluted the infant formula to make it go further. One of the worst marketing practices entailed the use of "milk nurses"—women dressed in nurses' uniforms who walked the halls of maternity wards urging mothers to get their babies started on formula. In reality, these women were sales representatives employed by the companies on a commission basis.

Although several companies were engaging in these questionable marketing practices, the Swiss conglomerate Nestlé was singled out by a Swiss social activist group in an article published in 1974 entitled "Nestlé Kills Babies". At about the same time, an article appeared in Great Britain entitled "The Baby Killers". From this point on, a protracted controversy developed with Nestlé and other infant formula manufacturers on one side and a host of organizations on the other side filing shareholder resolutions and lawsuits against the company. Among the groups that were actively involved in the controversy were church groups such as the National Council of Churches and its Interfaith Center on Corporate Responsibility (ICCR), UNICEF, the World Health Organization (WHO), and the Infant Formula Action Coalition (INFACT). Nestlé was singled out because it had the largest share of the world market and because it aggressively pushed sales of its infant formula in developing countries, even after the WHO developed a sales code to the contrary. In 1977, INFACT and ICCR organized and led a national boycott against Nestlé that continued for almost 7 years. More than 70 American organizations, representing churches, doctors, nurses, teachers, and other professionals participated in the boycott. These groups mounted an international campaign aimed at changing these objectionable marketing practices in the LDCs. In 1984, after spending millions of dollars resisting the boycott, Nestlé finally reached an accord with the protesters.

Source: http://en.wikipedia.org/wiki/Nestl%C3%A9_boycott

Once stakeholders have been identified, the next step is to determine the stakes of the various groups. Even groups in the same generic category frequently have different specific interests, concerns, perceptions of rights, and expectations. Management's challenge here is to identify the *nature/legitimacy* of a group's stake(s), the group's *power* to affect the organization. *Urgency* is another critical factor.

Once threats and opportunities of stakeholders have been identified and understood, the next logical question is, "What responsibilities does the firm have in its relationships with all stakeholders?" The most pressing threats present themselves as legal and ethical questions. Table 12.3 illustrates the stakeholder /responsibility matrix that management faces when assessing the firm's responsibilities to stakeholders.

Table 12.3 Stakeholder/Responsibility Matrix

	Types of Responsibilities			
Stakeholders	**Economic**	**Legal**	**Ethical**	**Philanthropic**
Owners Customers Employees Community Public at large Others				

Once responsibilities have been assessed, a business must contemplate strategies and actions for dealing with its stakeholders. In every decision situation, a multitude of alternative courses of action are available, and management must choose one or several that seem best. Important questions or decision choices include:

(*a*) Do we deal *directly* or *indirectly* with stakeholders?

(*b*) Do we take the *offense* or the *defense* in dealing with stakeholders?

(*c*) Do we *accommodate, negotiate, manipulate,* or *resist* stakeholder overtures?

(*d*) Do we employ a *combination* of the above strategies or pursue a *singular* course of action?

Savage et al. (1991) argue that development of specific strategies may be based on a classification of stakeholders according to the concepts of the potentials for cooperation and threat. If we use these two dimensions, four stakeholder types and resultant strategies emerge. These stakeholder types and corresponding strategies are shown in Fig. 12.4.

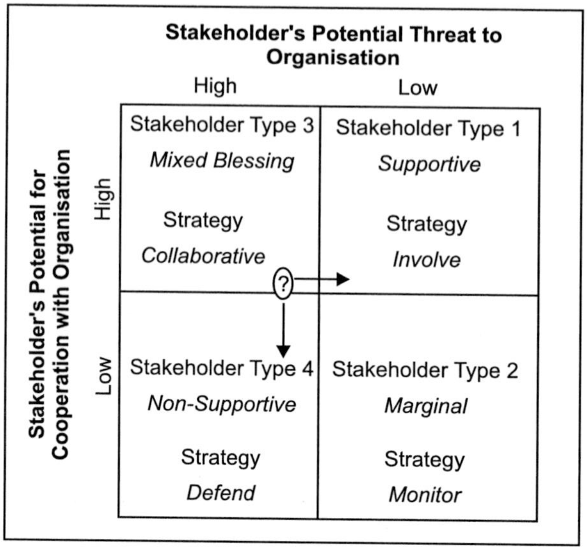

Source: Savage, Nix, Whitehead, and Blair (1991)

Fig. 12.4 Diagnostic Typology of Organizational Stakeholders

Stakeholder Type 1 (The Supportive Stakeholder): It is high on potential for cooperation and low on potential for threat. This is the ideal stakeholder. To a well managed organization, supportive stakeholders might include its board, managers, employees, and customers. Others might be suppliers and service providers. The strategy here is one of involvement. An example of this might be the strategy of involving employee stakeholders through participative management or decentralization of authority.

Stakeholder Type 2 (The Marginal Stakeholder): It is low on both potential for threat and potential for cooperation. For large organizations, these stakeholders might include professional associations of employees, consumer interest groups, or stockholders - especially those who are not organized. The strategy here is for the organization to monitor the marginal stakeholder. Monitoring is especially called for to make sure circumstances do not change. Careful monitoring could avert later problems.

Stakeholder Type 3 (The Non-supportive Stakeholder): It is high on potential for threat but low on potential for cooperation. Examples of this group could include competing organizations, unions, federal or other levels of government, and the media. The authors' recommended strategy here is to defend against the non-supportive stakeholder.

Stakeholder Type 4 (The Mixed Blessing Stakeholder): It is high on both potential for threat and potential for cooperation. Examples of this group, in a well-managed organization, might include employees who are in short supply, clients, or customers. A mixed blessing stakeholder could become a supportive or a non-supportive stakeholder. The recommended strategy here is to collaborate with the mixed blessing stakeholder. By maximizing collaboration, the likelihood is enhanced that this stakeholder will remain supportive.

12.8 CONCLUSION

To deal successfully with those who assert claims on the organization, managers must necessarily learn to balance conflicting interests. Business today cannot turn back the clock to a simpler period. Business will be subjected to sustained and careful scrutiny of all its actions, practices, policies, and ethics. This is the reality and management must accept it and deal with it. Despite the complexity of identifying, assessing, and responding to stakeholder claims, which constitute an extremely difficult and time-consuming process, management cannot neglect this area. Also, the ranking of stakeholder claims is no easy task. Some managers continue to think in *stockholder* terms because this is easier. To think in stakeholder terms increases the complexity of decision making. Despite its complexity, however, the stakeholder management view is most consistent with the environment that business faces today.

It would require some degree of care to identify the nature, legitimacy, power, and urgency of each of these specific groups. However, it could and should be done if the firm wants to get a handle on its environmental stakeholders. Furthermore, it should be stressed that companies have an ethical responsibility to be sensitive to legitimate stakeholder claims, even if the stakeholders have no power or leverage with the management.

QUESTIONS

1. Explain the concepts of *stake* and *stakeholder* from your perspective as an individual.
2. Differentiate between primary and secondary social and non-social stakeholders in a corporate situation.
3. Define the terms *core stakeholders, strategic stakeholders,* and *environmental stakeholders.* What factors affect into which of these groups stakeholders are categorized?
4. Explain in your own words the differences among the production, managerial, and stakeholder views of the firm.
5. Is the stakeholder corporation a realistic model for business firms? Will stakeholder corporations become more prevalent in the twenty-first century? Why or why not?

EXERCISE (CASE STUDY)

The Case of Hooker Chemical Company

Love Canal was a partially dug canal in the southeast corner of the city of Niagara Falls, New York, in the late 1800s. Originally, the canal was to be used for generating and transmitting hydroelectric power from the Falls to the businesses in the city, but the project was abandoned. Hooker Chemical Company, later a subsidiary of Occidental Petroleum Company, built its first plant in the area in 1905. In the 1940s, the abandoned section of Love Canal became a toxic waste dump for several chemical companies. In 1942, Hooker received permission to use the site for chemical dumping. In 1947, Hooker purchased the Love Canal site from Niagara Power and Development Company. In 1953, the canal, filled with years of toxic waste accumulation, was closed and sealed with an impermeable clay top. Subsequently, the land encompassing and surrounding Love Canal was purchased by the Niagara Falls School Board, even though Hooker Chemical advised against it. The board built a school adjacent to the dump site and sold some of the property to developers, who then built a tract of homes. During the construction of the homes, thousands of cubic yards of soil were removed from the surface of the sealed canal. Apparently, the construction work damaged the seal on the Love Canal dump. This, combined with water from heavy rains and snow, resulted in seepage of water into the clay-lined basin, which eventually overflowed, causing seepage of toxic waste into the homes and basements of nearby residents. By 1978, evidence of toxic chemicals was found in the living areas of many homes. After lengthy investigations, a variety of health problems, such as liver damage, miscarriages, birth defects, and other ills, began showing up. Without question, Hooker Chemical was not exclusively responsible for what happened at Love Canal. Others, such as the school board, the developers, and the health department, must shoulder part of the blame. As is so often the case, however, the business firm bore the brunt of the responsibility, especially in the media.

Issues for Analysis and Discussion

(*i*) Who are the stakeholders in this case?

(*ii*) Who are primary and who are secondary stakeholders?

(*iii*) What influence do they have and how are they related to each other?

(*iv*) Identify the key terms and concepts in this chapter that apply to this discussion case.

❑❑❑

13

The Precautionary Principle

> *The problem very often is that long before the science does come in, the harm has already been done.*
>
> **Michael Pollan**

Modern environmental regulations are anticipatory and preventive, but are not necessarily precautionary. They generally aim to prevent known risks rather than anticipate and prevent uncertain potential harm. This is where the precautionary principle comes in as it seeks to provide guidance for protecting public health and the environment in the face of uncertain risks, stating that the absence of full scientific certainty shall not be used as a reason to postpone measures where there is a risk of serious or irreversible harm to public health or the environment.

Risk is usually defined as the amalgam of the probability of an event occurring and the seriousness of the consequences should it occur (Cameron, 1999). For example, the risk of a major nuclear power accident is the combination of a low probability of such an accident, which engineers claim can be calculated, multiplied by the serious damage that would occur as a result of the spread of nuclear radiation, including thousands of deaths, cancers, and birth defects. If the risk of an accident is considered too high then a nuclear power plant will not be granted approval and thus, the risk is prevented. An important point to be noted here is that if the risk of a nuclear accident occurring can be calculated with some degree of accuracy, the precautionary principle does not apply. If, however, one believes that engineers are unable to calculate the probability of a major nuclear accident with any reasonable certainty or accuracy, then the precautionary principle will apply.

13.1 PRECAUTIONARY PRINCIPLE – DEFINITION

The "precautionary principle" or "precautionary approach" is a response to uncertainty, in the face of risks to health or the environment. In general, it involves acting to avoid serious or irreversible potential harm, despite lack of scientific certainty as to the likelihood, magnitude or causation of that harm.

There are many definitions of the precautionary principle. Precaution is caution in advance, or "caution practiced in the context of uncertainty". The 1998 Wingspread Statement (declared in Wisconsin, USA) on the Precautionary Principle summarizes the principle as follows: "When an activity raises threats of harm to human health or the environment, precautionary measures should be taken even if some cause and effect relationships are not fully established scientifically." The February 2, 2000 European Commission communication on the Precautionary Principle notes: "The precautionary principle applies where scientific evidence is insufficient, inconclusive or uncertain and preliminary scientific evaluation indicates that there are reasonable grounds for concern that the potentially dangerous effects on the environment, human, animal or plant health may be inconsistent with the high level of protection chosen by the EU".

The precautionary principle can be found in international treaties that protect human health and the environment from a variety of pollutants and its resulting consequences. One of the earliest forms of the precautionary principle was used in the 1980s in Europe to protect the North Sea. In 1992, the Rio Declaration specifically included the precautionary principle in calling on nations to protect the environment. The key element here is the matter of acting in the face of uncertainty.

BOX 13.1

Definition of the Precautionary Principle

When human activities may lead to morally unacceptable harm that is scientifically plausible but uncertain, action shall be taken to avoid or diminish that harm.

Morally unacceptable harm refers to harm to humans or the environment that is:

- Threatening to human life or health, or
- Serious and effectively irreversible, or
- Inequitable to present or future generations, or
- Imposed without adequate consideration of the human rights of those affected.

The judgment of *plausibility* should be grounded in scientific analysis. Analysis should be ongoing so that chosen actions are subject to review.

Uncertainty may apply to, but need not be limited to, causality or the bounds of the possible harm.

Actions are interventions that are undertaken before harm occurs that seek to avoid or diminish the harm. Actions should be chosen that are proportional to the seriousness of the potential harm, with consideration of their positive and negative consequences, and with an assessment of the moral implications of both action and inaction. The choice of action should be the result of a participatory process.

Source: (COMFEST 2005)

All the definitions have two key elements.

(*i*) An expression of a need by decision-makers to anticipate harm before it occurs. Under the precautionary principle, it is the responsibility of an activity proponent to establish that the proposed activity will not (or is very unlikely to) result in significant harm.

(*ii*) The establishment of an obligation, if the level of harm may be high, for action to prevent or minimize such harm, even if it is difficult to predict the likelihood of harm occurring, or the level of harm, if it occurs.

Principle 15 of the Rio Declaration, 1992, states that: "in order to protect the environment, the precautionary approach shall be widely applied by States according to their capabilities. Where there are threats of serious or irreversible damage, lack of full scientific certainty shall not be used as a reason for postponing cost-effective measures to prevent environmental degradation".

The precautionary principle is most often applied in the context of the impact of human actions on the environment and human health, as both involve complex systems where the consequences of actions may be unpredictable.

Applied to environmental policy, the precautionary principle stipulates that for practices such as the release of radiation or toxins or massive deforestation, the burden of proof lies with the advocates. Examples of cases concerning the potential risks to public health, in which the precautionary principle has been advocated are: the commercialization of genetically modified foods, the use of growth hormones in cattle and poultry rearing, measures to prevent the "mad cow" disease, health claims linked to phthalates in PVC toys, among many others.

An important element of the precautionary principle is that it's most meaningful applications pertain to those that are potentially irreversible, for example, where biodiversity may be significantly reduced. With respect to bans on substances like mercury in thermometers, freon in refrigeration, or even carbon dioxide exhaust from automobile engines and power plants, it implies: "a willingness to take action in advance of scientific proof or evidence of the need for the proposed action on the grounds that further delay will prove ultimately most costly to society and nature, and, in the longer term, selfish and unfair to future generations."

The concept includes an implicit ethical responsibility towards maintaining the integrity of natural systems, and acknowledges the fallibility of human understanding. Some environmental commentators take a more stringent interpretation of the precautionary principle, stating that proponents of a new potentially harmful technology must show that the new technology is without major harm before the new technology is used.

13.2 APPLICATION OF THE PRINCIPLE

The application of the precautionary principle is hampered by both lack of political will, as well as the wide range of interpretations placed on it. As many as 14 different formulations of the principle in treaties and non-treaty declarations have been identified. R.B. Stewart (2002) reduced the precautionary principle to four basic versions:

(i) **Non-Preclusion PP:** Scientific uncertainty should not automatically preclude regulation of activities that pose a potential risk of significant harm.

(ii) **Margin of Safety PP:** Regulatory controls should incorporate a margin of safety; activities should be limited below the level at which no adverse effect has been observed or predicted.

(iii) **Best Available Technology PP:** Activities that present an uncertain potential for significant harm should be subject to best technology available requirements to minimize the risk of harm, unless the proponent of the activity shows that they present no appreciable risk of harm.

(*iv*) **Prohibitory PP:** Activities that present an uncertain potential for irreversible harm should be prohibited, unless the proponent of the activity shows that it presents no appreciable risk of harm.

13.3 SCIENTIFIC UNCERTAINTY

In the area of environmental policy, decisions often have to be made before scientific experts are able to "present unambiguous and scientifically well-founded recommendations". Scientists are usually unable tell policy makers exactly where and how far a pollutant will spread, how it will interact with other pollutants, and how it will affect the health of the people and the functioning of ecosystems. "The more uncertain the threat, the greater the degree of precaution required" (Deville and Harding, 1997).

Types of Uncertainties

Steven Yearly (1991), a British social scientist, identifies four different reasons why scientists face uncertainties when dealing with environmental problems.

(*i*) **Pragmatic Uncertainty:** Scientists are often asked to make recommendations when they do not have enough time or funds to investigate the answers fully. The available research may be of poor quality or not immediately applicable to the situation at hand. Pragmatic uncertainty arises from:

(*a*) Lack of data

(*b*) Doubts on accuracy of data

(*c*) Doubts on relevance of data

(*ii*) **Theoretical Uncertainty:** Ecological science is less developed than other sciences; consequently, there is less agreement than in other scientific disciplines, and more variety of interpretations of data and findings. Theoretical uncertainty arises from:

(*a*) Disagreements over interpretation of data

(*b*) Disagreements over scientific methodology

(*c*) Lack of knowledge about causal connections

(*d*) Doubts over knowledge framework – epistemological uncertainty.

(*iii*) **Complexity in Open Systems:** Uncertainty arises from "the sheer complexity of large-scale phenomena taking place in open systems". Nature is less knowable and less predictable than complex systems, such as nuclear power plants, that are created and controlled by humans. Complexity arises from:

(*a*) Variability of ecological processes

(*b*) Indeterminacy

(*iv*) **Intangible Damage:** Environmental damage may not be easily observable and therefore, maybe difficult to monitor and understand. For example, depletion of the ozone layer can only be measured by high-technology equipment and would previously have been extremely difficult to predict. Thousands of chemicals used commercially have not been tested for their ability to bio-accumulate in the food chain or for their toxicity to a whole variety of organisms, because their cost seems to be prohibitive. Scientists try to fill in gaps in knowledge by extrapolating from what they do know and estimating probabilities based on past experiences and observations and by using computer modelling techniques.

However, where processes are not known or understood, computer modelling may not be of much use because the relationships between various parameters, such as what happens to plankton when surface temperatures change, is unknown and may not change in a linear or predictable fashion. Further, even if the impact of individual chemicals are known, their synergistic impact, that is, the effect of two or more chemicals interacting in the environment, would be difficult to predict.

Even when harm is beginning to occur it may not be self-evident because:

(*a*) The first signs of damage are not outside the bounds of normal variation in individuals or populations.

(*b*) The first effects are not recognized to be harmful.

(*c*) Changes may be followed by a long time period before the consequences become evident.

(*d*) The harm that is caused may be attributed to a number of causes.

13.4 IGNORANCE AND INDETERMINACY

In a situation where change happens chaotically, or where relationships are unstable and subject to sudden dramatic change, the situation is indeterminate and traditional scientific methods have little to offer in terms of assessment of environmental damage. Also, the idea that more scientific research will resolve uncertainties is not necessarily true. Further research may only serve to increase the uncertainties by raising more issues and questions. The ultimate uncertainty is "ignorance" where we are completely unaware of possible threats. The relationship between uncertainty, indeterminacy and ignorance is shown in Figure 13.1

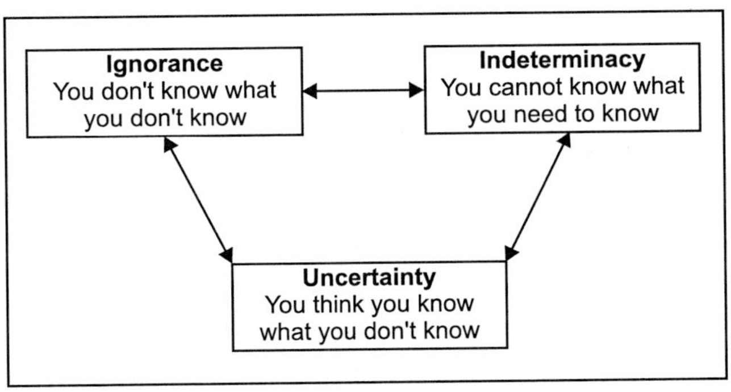

Source: Deville and Harding, 1997

Fig. 13.1 Levels of Uncertainty

Scientific uncertainty is used by both sides in any environmental controversy as an opportunity to "win". Scientific uncertainties seem to increase with the increasing relevance of the science to the policy decision, because those with vested interests in the outcomes of the decision-making frequently seek an advantage by highlighting those uncertainties.

13.5 THE BURDEN OF PROOF

In the past, many products and processes have been marketed without prior approval or any requirement that the manufacturer show evidence that they will not harm human health or the environment. Similarly, many activities and developments have been undertaken without the developers having to show that they will not have an adverse environmental impact. Traditionally, the thinking was that regulations constrained economic activity and would only be justified if there was undisputed scientific evidence that such activity would cause harm. This is basically a "wait and see" approach where the burden of proof is on those asserting that damage is being or will be done.

In the 1970s, the US Environmental Protection Agency (EPA) imposed limits on the content of lead in petrol, based on scientific evidence that it was causing health problems but without absolute proof of the same. The oil industry opposed the regulations in the courts but the EPA won. This case is considered a landmark in US environmental law because it established that EPA could act in a precautionary fashion rather than wait for scientific certainty about the harmfulness of a substance before acting (Ackerman and Heinzerling, 2004).

Today, certain types of activities require the developers to prepare environmental impact assessments/statements and there is also the need to gain approval before they are marketed *e.g.*, products like pharmaceutical drugs, pesticides and food additives. In these cases, it is initially assumed that the activity in question or the product may be hazardous or environmentally damaging, and the developer needs to present a convincing case—supported by scientific evidence—that the activity or product is safe.

Table 13.1 Shifting Burden of Proof

Before Precautionary Principle	After Precautionary Principle
People exposed to risky actions must bear the risks of such actions until it can be demonstrated that they cause harm to health or the environment.	People exposed to risk can ask for precautionary actions to be taken before risky actions can be proven to cause harm.
People exposed to the risk bear the responsibility for demonstrating that actions caused harm.	Once some preliminary basis for taking precautionary action exists, risk creators bear the responsibility of showing that actions are safe, or at least acceptably risky.

Source: Adapted from CPR 2005b

The shifting of the burden of proof from one party to another, for example from the regulatory authority to the polluter, is only one element of the precautionary principle. The fact that those proposing an activity have to show it is safe before it is approved—rather than the government needing to show it is unsafe before it can be restricted—is an important aspect of the precautionary principle.

In practice, the burden of proof has been shifted for new products and activities, only where there is a long history of harm arising from like products and activities. Existing products are generally presumed to be safe. This bias is based partly on the assumption that it is cheaper and more politically acceptable to prevent new products being manufactured, than it is to ban existing products.

What the precautionary principle does is to ease the standard of proof so that scientific evidence of possible harm is sufficient to prompt regulatory action. The assumption that an activity or product is safe until proven harmful shifts, so that it can be considered harmful even before that proof is available. In this way, the balance between environment and economic development is shifted a little more towards environmental protection: previously the polluter benefited from scientific doubt; henceforth doubt will work to the benefit of the environment (de Sadeleer 2002).

In deciding how to apply the principle, analysts may use a cost-benefit analysis that factors in both the opportunity cost of not acting, and the option value of waiting for further information before acting. One of the difficulties of the application of the principle in modern policy-making is that there is often an irreducible conflict between different interests, so that the debate necessarily involves politics.

13.6 CRITICISMS

The Precautionary Principle remains largely controversial mainly because of the confusion spread by vested corporate interests. Opponents argue that the Precautionary Principle is unscientific; that it can be triggered by irrational concerns; that it aims at an unrealistic goal of zero risk; and that it will result in the banning of useful chemicals and the prevention of technological innovation. Excessive caution, it is argued, could lead to paralysis and stagnation. Other criticisms have been elaborated below:

Threshold of Plausibility

One of the versions of the PP takes the following form: "When an activity raises threats of harm to human health or the environment, precautionary measures should be taken even if some cause and effect relationships are not fully established scientifically". Does mankind need a minimal threshold of scientific certainty or plausibility before undertaking preventative action? Normally, even the slightest indication that a particular product or activity might possibly produce some harm to human health or the environment is sufficient to invoke the principle and often an outright ban on the incriminated product or activity is the recommended action.

Negative Consequences of Poor Application

In some applications, the Precautionary Principle may cause more harm than it alleviates. This is because people are more acutely aware of negative changes than they are of positive changes. Because of this effect, a technology which brings great advantages may be ruled out by the Precautionary Principle because of its potential for severe negative impacts, leaving the overriding positive benefits unrealized.

Critics of the principle argue that it is impractical, since every implementation of a technology carries some risk of negative consequences. Proponents counter that the principle is not an absolute rule; it is a conceptual tool to clarify arguments, and clarify the issue of where the burden of proof lies.

Critics also claim that proponents are sometimes selective in their use of the precautionary principle—applying it for political reasons, rather than scientific reasons. They note that the selective application of principles by the government is considered a fundamental form of injustice, which is why selective enforcement is considered an abuse of power. Proponents respond to this criticism by arguing that acting with insufficient knowledge of risk (*e.g.*, spreading new life forms into the biosphere) can also be socially unfair, costly, and detrimental when applied to complex environmental choices. They note that the reckless application of technology is a worse abuse of power.

13.7 CONCLUSION

In conclusion, it could be said that the precautionary principle does not conflict with technological innovation, but requires a new approach–an approach that "encourages the exploration of alternative modes of development that are compatible with a good quality of life, for present or future generations". It calls for greater effort in the development of safer and cleaner technologies. What the precautionary principle does, is to redirect innovation into more humane and environmentally sound directions.

QUESTIONS

1. What is the precautionary principle? Examine its applications and the hurdles to its application.
2. Discuss the controversial issue of 'scientific uncertainty' in the context of the Precautionary Principle.

EXERCISES

1. Give an example to prove that the precautionary principle does not conflict with technological innovation and that it promotes development of cleaner technologies.
2. Give a case study where precautionary principle had averted serious environmental consequences.
3. List out the probable environmental repercussions that could be averted by following the precautionary method.

❑❑❑

14

The Polluter Pays Principle

> *Pollution should never be the price of prosperity.*
>
> **Al Gore**

In the decades since the advent of the industrial revolution, companies which have polluted have not paid the cost of that pollution. They have been allowed to discharge pollutants into the air and water, while others bear the consequences. "When companies are allowed to pollute, or to use natural resources without paying their full price, they are in effect appropriating natural capital—land, air, and water—without compensation to society at large" (Templet, 2001). The resulting resource depletion or pollution is called an "externality" by economists because it is a cost that is external to the company's accounts, and external to the market transactions the company is involved with (Chapter 7).

The Polluter Pays Principle (PPP) seeks to alter this, so that the company has either to pay to prevent the pollution or pay for the damage (or its remediation) that it causes. Governments can ensure that the polluter pays by:

(*i*) Regulating what polluters are able to discharge into the environment, so that they have to install their own pollution control equipment.

(*ii*) Charging polluters taxes and levies to cover government's costs of protecting the environment, including the cost of sewage treatment facilities.

(*iii*) Making polluters liable for the damage they cause.

14.1 DEFINITION OF PPP

The Polluter Pays Principle (PPP) is an environmental policy approach which requires that the costs of pollution be borne by those who cause it. In its original emergence, the PPP aimed at determining how the costs of pollution prevention and control must be allocated: the polluter must pay.

The immediate goal of PPP can be taken to be that of internalizing the environmental externalities of economic activities, so that the prices of goods and services fully reflect the costs of production. Bugge (1996) has identified three versions of the PPP: economically, it promotes efficiency; legally, it promotes justice; and globally, it promotes harmonization of international environmental policies.

14.2 HISTORY OF THE PPP

The first major reference to the PPP appeared in 1972 in the OECD Guiding Principles Concerning International Economic Aspects of Environmental Policies (henceforth, the OECD Guiding Principles), where it stated that: "The principle to be used for allocating costs of pollution prevention and control measures to encourage rational use of scarce environmental resources and to avoid distortions in international trade and investment is the so-called Polluter-Pays Principle." It then went on to elaborate: "This principle means that the polluter should bear the expenses of carrying out the above-mentioned measures decided by public authorities to ensure that the environment is in an acceptable state."

The OECD emphasizes the necessity for removal of subsidies which would prevent polluters from bearing the costs of pollution which they have caused, urging that those costs be internalized into the prices of goods and services. However, the PPP evolved into what is called extended or strong PPP. In 1989, OECD included in the PPP, costs related to accidental pollution; the recommendation of the council concerning the application of the Polluter-Pays Principle to accidental pollution states that: "In matters of accidental pollution risks, the Polluter-Pays Principle implies that the operator of a hazardous installation should bear the cost of reasonable measures to prevent and control accidental pollution from that installation".

Only one year later, the European Community followed the example of the OECD Principles of 1972 by adopting the first Environment Action Programme (EAP). From 1987, the PPP has been part of European Law. It is included in Article 174 of the European Union Treaty (1997). Since 1990, when the International Convention on Oil Pollution Preparedness, Response and Cooperation was agreed upon by the International Maritime Organization (IMO), the PPP has been acknowledged as "...a general principle of international environmental law."

The PPP has also been reaffirmed in the 1992 Rio Declaration in Principle 16: "National authorities should endeavor to promote the internalization of environmental costs and the use of economic instruments, taking into account the approach that the polluter should, in principle, bear the cost of pollution, with due regard to the public interest and without distorting international trade and investment."

The PPP is widely acknowledged as a general principle of International Environmental Law, and is explicitly mentioned or implicitly referred to in a number of Multilateral Environmental Agreements.

14.3 DEFINING POLLUTION IN THE CONTEXT OF PPP

There has been a change in the perception of what constitutes pollution in the context of PPP, from the 1970s, when pollution referred to waste products that were put into the air and water, to the expanded definition given by the OECD in 2002: "The introduction by man, directly or indirectly, of substances or energy into the environment resulting in deleterious effects of such a nature as to endanger human health, harm living resources and ecosystems, and impair or interfere with amenities and other legitimate uses of the environment." (JWPTE, 2002).

The definition of pollution was later broadened to cover many types of environmental damage, not just caused by discharge of contaminants. The EC (2004) defines environmental damage as:

(*a*) Damage caused to protected species and natural habitats, which is any damage that has significant adverse effects on reaching or maintaining the favourable conservation status of such habitats or species . . .

(*b*) Water damage, which is any damage that significantly and adversely affects the ecological, chemical and/or qualitative status and/or ecological potential of waters concerned . . .

(*c*) Land damage, which is any land contamination that creates a significant risk of human health being adversely affected as a result of the direct or indirect introduction, in, on or under and, of substances, preparations, organisms or microorganisms.

The EC and the OECD define pollution by its impact on the environment and human health, rather than in terms of compliance with government regulations. This raises the question of whether a company that complies with environmental regulations and standards set by the government authorities should bear the costs of its pollution.

Nicolas de Sadeleer (2002) argues that the definition of pollution should be independent of what may or may not be legal. He argues that this is a fair approach because polluters are responsible for their discharges, even if a government body authorizes them, otherwise the public would have to bear the costs of clean-up when government regulations are inadequate. Given that companies have a direct influence on the limits and standards which governments set or don't set, when government regulation allows too much pollution, it is often because of industry pressure.

Defining pollution by impact, rather than by government-set standards is also appropriate, according to de Sadeleer, because it provides polluters with an incentive to do better than government-set standards. Thus, being allowed to pollute by the government should not absolve a polluter from liability.

In 1972, the Organisation for Economic Cooperation and Development (OECD) Council recommended the following:

The principle to be used for allocating costs of pollution prevention and control measures to encourage rational use of scarce environmental resources and to avoid distortions in international trade and investment is the so-called "Polluter Pays Principle". This principle means that the polluter should bear the expenses of carrying out the above-mentioned measures decided by public authorities to ensure that the environment is in an acceptable state. In other words, the cost of these measures should be reflected in the cost of goods and services which cause pollution in production and/or consumption. Such measures should not be accompanied by subsidies that would create significant distortions in international trade and investment.

The intention of the PPP was not to provide a way for polluters to pay to be allowed to pollute; the OECD intended that it be a way to get the polluter to both "limit their pollution and bear the cost of measures taken to that end".

Thus, the PPP was introduced with the objective of integrating the use of the environment into the economic sphere through the use of price signals and use of economic instruments such as pollution charges and permits (OECD, 1992). The PPP was endorsed by the European Commission in 1975 and is now strengthened by the following:

(*i*) The PPP to force those creating pollution to pay the costs of meeting socially acceptable environmental quality standards.

(*ii*) The prevention or precaution principle, which explicitly recognizes the existence of uncertainty and seeks to avoid irreversible damages via the imposition of a safety margin into policy; it also seeks to prevent waste generation at source, as well as retaining some "end of the pipe" measures.

(*iii*) Economic efficiency/cost effectiveness principle, applying both to the setting of standards and design of the policy instruments for attaining them.

(*iv*) The subsidiarity principle to assign environmental decision and enforcement to the lowest level of government, capable of handling it, without significant residual externalities.

Today, the PPP is a generally recognized principle of International Environmental Law, and it is a fundamental principle of environmental policy of both the Organisation for Economic Co-operation and Development (OECD) and the European Community. It favours a curative approach which is concerned with repairing ecological damage, and is not as bothered with the idea of fault. It started as a principle in international environmental law where the polluting party pays for the damage done to the natural environment. The PPP as a guiding principle across countries became necessary because some countries faced complaints by national firms about rising costs and a loss of international competitiveness following a national implementation of the PPP within their borders.

14.4 APPLICATION OF PPP

The PPP is normally implemented through two different policy approaches: command-and-control (C & C) and market-based. C & C approaches include performance and technology standards. Market-based instruments include pollution taxes, tradable pollution permits and product labelling.

At the international level, the Kyoto Protocol is an example of the application of the PPP: parties that have obligations to reduce their greenhouse gas emissions must bear the costs of reducing (prevention and control) such polluting emissions.

14.5 PERSISTENT QUESTIONS

Most developing countries are yet to completely subscribe to the PPP as a major environmental policy guideline. This is largely due to adverse economic conditions. Vagueness still exists in determining "who is a polluter". In legal terminology, a "polluter" is someone who directly or indirectly damages the environment or who creates conditions relating to such damage. Clearly, this definition is so broad as to be unsupportive in many situations. Secondly, a large number of poor households, informal sector firms, and subsistence farmers cannot bear any additional charges for energy or for waste disposal. Thirdly, small and medium-size firms from the informal sector, which mainly serve the home market, find it difficult to pass on higher costs to the domestic end-users of their products. Fourth, exporters in developing countries usually cannot shift the burden of cost internalization to foreign customers due to elastic demand. Lastly, many environmental problems in developing countries are caused by an overexploitation of common pool resources.

All of these problems make it difficult to implement the PPP as a guideline for business activity.

14.6 APPROACH OF THE INDIAN JUDICIARY

India is fortunate in having an apex court which has been able to respond effectively to situations demanding urgent redressal—like, for example, the threat to India's environment from industrial pollution, among others.

The judiciary in India recognized the Polluter Pays Principle in the judgment delivered by the Supreme Court of India in the Indian Council for Enviro-Legal Action. In its order dated 4 Feb 2005, The Supreme Court held that "The Polluter Pays Principle means that absolute liability for harm to the environment extends not only to compensate the victims of pollution, but also to the cost of restoring environmental degradation. Remediation of damaged environment is part of the process of sustainable development".

In this case, a number of private companies operating as chemical companies, were creating hazardous wastes in the soil, polluting the village area situated nearby, and all without the required licenses. The Court ruled on the PIL that "Once the activity carried on is hazardous or inherently dangerous, the person carrying on such activity is liable to make good the loss caused to any other person by his activity, irrespective of the fact whether he took reasonable care while carrying on his activity. The rule is premised upon the very nature of the activity carried on". The "Polluter Pays" principle, as interpreted by the Court, means that the absolute liability for harm to the environment extends not only to compensate the victims of pollution but also the cost of restoring the environmental degradation. Remediation of the damaged environment is part of the process of "Sustainable Development" and as such polluter is liable to pay the cost to the individual sufferers as well as the cost of reversing the damaged ecology.

Loss of Ecology Authority

The Supreme Court of India in a landmark judgment in the Vellore Citizens Forum case, ordered the creation of a new agency, the Loss of Ecology (Prevention and Payment of Compensation) Authority for the State of Tamil Nadu to provide compensation to those affected by pollution from tanneries.

The Loss of Ecology Authority was set up in 1996 to assess the damage caused by industrial pollution in the districts of Vellore, Dindigul, Kancheepuram, Tiruvallur, Erode and Tiruchi. This authority was constituted by the Central Government under Notification No. 671 (E), Ministry of Environment and Forests dated 30/9/1996. Formation of this authority has been made possible by a litigation filed in the Supreme Court by a "consumer welfare forum" based in Vellore, against the tannery units causing pollution in Vellore and the surrounding regions in Tamil Nadu. The major tasks of the LEA were determining the value of loss to ecology; identifying the affected people; fixing the amount of compensation to be paid to the losers which should be collected from the polluters; and suggesting alternative measures of repairing damage inflicted on ecology in the affected regions—all within the framework of the "polluter-pays-principle" and the "precautionary principle".

The LEA undertook assessment of lost ecology in Vellore, Dindigul, Kancheepuram, Thiruvallur, Erode and Trichy districts in Tamil Nadu. According to the assessment by the LEA, the total agricultural damage estimated amounted to Rs. 34.73 crore. Further, the LEA assessed that tannery pollution affected 17,170 hectares of farmland in Vellore and Dindigul districts (but not in the other districts) impacting 36,056 farmers; 621 tanners in the two districts were required to pay a compensation of Rs. 30.75 crores to the affected farmers. In Vellore, Dindigul, Kancheepuram and Tiruvallur districts, 731 tanners were to pay Rs. 3.98 crores to reverse the damage caused to the ecology. The damage caused by the tanneries in Vellore district alone was estimated to be Rs. 26.82 crore for the period 1991–98. This Rs. 26.82 was to be collected from the owners of the 546 tanneries and be distributed as 'compensation' to 29,193 families owning 15,164 ha of agricultural lands in 186 villages of Vellore district in Tamil Nadu.

In the case of the Noyyal River Basin, the LEA awarded compensation of Rs. 248 million for the period 2002–2004 to a total of 28,596 farmers located in 68 villages in seven taluks in the Noyyal River Basin. The industries were asked by the Court to reverse the damaged ecology, namely the restoration of the Orathapalayam Dam. The Tiruppur Dyers Association have offered to pay for the desilting of the dam. The Public Works Department has estimated that the cleaning of the dam would cost Rs.100 million. The LEA did not require any additional compensation from the industries for reversing the damaged ecology, since the industries have made a commitment to the Court and have begun to make the payments for cleaning the dam.

14.7 SOME LANDMARK CASES

Some famous landmark cases have been discussed here:

The Taj Trapezium Case: Taj Mahal, one of the wonders of the world and the pride of India was facing serious threat from pollution caused by the Mathura Refinery, iron foundries, glass and other chemical industries. (Chapter 2).

Ganges Pollution Case: Three landmark judgments and a number of orders against polluting industries numbering more than fifty thousand in the Ganga basin were passed from time to time. In this case, apart from industries, more than 250 towns and cities have been ordered to put up sewage treatment plants. Six hundred tanneries operating in highly congested residential areas of Kolkata have been shifted out of the City and relocated in a planned Leather Complex in the State of West Bengal. Refer Chapter 2 for more details.

Vehicular Pollution Case: Against vehicular pollution in India, the Supreme Court delivered a landmark judgment in 1992. A retired Judge of the Supreme Court was appointed, along with three members to recommend measures for the nationwide control of vehicular pollution. Orders for providing Lead free petrol in the country and for the use of natural gas and other types of fuels for use in vehicles in India have been passed and carried out. Lead-free petrol has been introduced in the four metropolitan cities from April 1995; all new cars registered from April 1995 onwards have been fitted with catalytic convertors; COG outlets have been set up to provide CNG as a clean fuel in Delhi and other cities in India, apart from adopting Euro 2 norms. As a result of this case, Delhi has become the first city in the world to have the entire public transportation system running on CNG.

Aquaculture Case: Big industrial houses and multinationals had started commercial prawn farming in a big way in the coastal states of Orissa, Andhra Pradesh and Tamil Nadu in a totally unplanned, unscientific and unscrupulous manner, and in the process, destroyed large areas of rich fertile lands, caused salinity in the ground water, uprooted small farmers and destroyed the livelihood of lakhs of fishermen. A writ petition was filed in the Supreme Court consequent to which it banned intensive prawn culture within 500 mtrs of High Tide Line and within 1000 mtrs of Chilka lake and Pullicat lake. An Authority under the Chairmanship of a retired Supreme Court Judge was ordered to to be constituted by the Central Govt. under the Environment Protection Act 1986, to implement the "Precautionary Principle" and the "Polluter Pays Principle", to assess the loss of ecology and recover the cost of eco-restoration and amount of compensation from the polluters.

Ground Water Depletion Case: Unsystematic and unscientific tapping of groundwater all over the country had led to an alarming fall in the level of groundwater and data provided by the Ground Water Board showed a near crisis situation developing in many areas of the country. Further, the contamination of ground water due to indiscriminate discharge of toxic effluents on the ground and surface water bodies was going on in an unchecked and uncontrolled manner and the Pollution Control Boards were not in a position to either assess the extent of ground water contamination or identify the sources of contamination. The Ground Water Board had no teeth or legal authority to take action against offending parties. This matter was taken up in the Supreme Court and by a historic judgment, the Ground Water Board was made into an Authority vested with legal powers under the Environment Protection Act 1986 to issue licenses and take action against polluters, even to the extent of closing down the offending industries.

14.8 CONCLUSION

The ideal of polluters paying the full cost of their pollution and environmental impact so that external costs of economic activities are internalized into the company's decision making is not only politically difficult, because companies argue that they cannot afford such costs, but also practically difficult, because the value of environmental damage is very hard to quantify, particularly in the case of irreversible or irreparable damage. One way of dealing with the problem is to ensure that polluters are truly liable for the cost of repairing or cleaning up the environmental damage they cause.

The recognition and implementation of the Polluter Pays Principle by the Supreme Court has acted as a check on the unbridled pollution and environmental degradation by businesses. Though all development comes at a cost, the polluters cannot be allowed to get away with irredeemable environmental damage. The plethora of cases, some of which have been mentioned in this chapter, indicate clearly that the days of irresponsible business practices are over.

QUESTIONS

1. What is the polluter pays principle? Explain its relevance.
2. Discuss the role of the judiciary in India in upholding the Polluter Pays Principle. Mention briefly some landmark cases in this regard.

EXERCISE

1. From the policy mix of any country give details of a pollution control instrument such as a pollution tax or permit or liability rules that is based on polluter pays principle.

❑❑❑

15

Sustainable Industrialization

> *There is something fundamentally wrong in treating the Earth as if it were a business in liquidation.*
>
> **Herman E Daly**

During the period of environmental awakening in the late 1960s and early 1970s, most of the problems appeared to be local—the problems of individual pipes and smokestacks. Solutions were sought through regulation of these pollution points. But when environment re-emerged on the political agenda in the 1980s, the main concerns had become international, namely, acid rain, depletion of the ozone layer and global warming. Analysts sought causes, not in pipes and stacks, but in the nature of human activities. Many research findings stressed the fact that "the so-called progress" being made was simply unsustainable.

All development involves some degradation of the environment. Even substances which might be environmentally benign in their final form may have been unfriendly in their manufacture. They might have been produced using non-renewable resources and may also pose problems after they have been used and are disposed off, *e.g.,* batteries. If we take what is known as the cradle-to-grave view of products, there would be very few products that are completely unconnected to environmental damage. But the question is, how can we reduce the damage over time and achieve a state of balance so that the quantum of environmental damage is minimized.

15.1 EVOLUTION OF PRODUCTION PARADIGMS

Various production paradigms have evolved over time, ending with the latest paradigm, namely, sustainable production. These stages have been briefly dealt with below:

Craft Production

Craft production is the process of manufacturing by hand with or without the aid of tools. It refers to a manufacturing technique applied in the hobbies of handicraft but was also the common method of manufacture in the pre-industrialized world. For example, the production of pottery uses methods of craft production. Most of the early automobiles were craft produced. Because each vehicle was unique, replacement parts had to be manufactured from scratch or at least customized to fit a specific vehicle.

A side effect of the craft manufacturing process is that the final product is unique. While the product may be of extremely high quality, the uniqueness can be detrimental as seen in the case of early automobiles.

Mass Production

Mass production (also called flow production, repetitive flow production, or series production) is the production of large amounts of standardized products on production lines. It was popularized by Henry Ford in the early 20th Century, notably in his Ford Model T. The idea was first developed in Venice several hundred years earlier, where ships were mass-produced using pre-manufactured parts, and assembly lines. The Venice Arsenal, apparently produced nearly one ship every day, in what was effectively the world's first factory which, at its height, employed 16,000 people. Mass production in the publishing industry has been commonplace since Johannes Gutenberg's Bible was published, using a printing press in the mid-1400s.

Mass production typically uses moving tracks or conveyor belts to move partially complete products to workers, who perform simple repetitive tasks to permit very high rates of production per worker, allowing the high-volume manufacture of inexpensive finished goods. Mass production is capital intensive, as it uses a high proportion of machinery in relation to workers. With fewer labour costs and a faster rate of production, revenue is increased while expenditure is decreased. However, the machinery that is needed to set up a mass production line is so expensive that there must be some assurance that the product is to be successful so the company can get a return on its investment.

Advantages and Disadvantages

The economies of mass production come from several sources. The primary cause is a reduction of non-productive effort of all types. In craft production, the craftsman must locate and use many tools, many times, for varying tasks. In mass production, each worker repeats one or a few related tasks that use the same tool to perform identical or near-identical operations on a stream of products. The exact tool and parts are always at hand, having been moved down the assembly line consecutively. The worker spends little or no time retrieving and/or preparing materials and tools, and so the time taken to manufacture a product using mass production is shorter, than when using traditional methods.

The probability of human error and variation is also reduced, as tasks are predominantly carried out by machinery. A reduction in labour costs, as well as an increased rate of production, enables a company to produce a larger quantity of one product at a lower cost than by using traditional, non-linear methods.

However, mass production is inflexible because it is difficult to alter a design or production process after a production line is implemented. Also, all products produced on one production line will be identical or very similar, and introducing variety to satisfy individual tastes is not easy.

However, some variety can be achieved by applying different finishes and decorations at the end of the production line, if necessary.

Lean Production

Lean production is so known because it utilizes small quantities of everything in comparison to mass production. It utilizes half the number of industrial workers, half of the space for manufacturing, half of the investment in tools, half of the hours of planning to develop new goods in half of the time.

The central idea of lean production is to reduce costs by flexibility. It means the possibility of frequent changes of the moulds, to adapt in a simple way, the mechanisms that permit profitable production and the simultaneous accomplishment of customer demands, observing the individual satisfaction of their wishes. In other words, "lean production combines the best features of mass production (speed, less cost per product) with those of craft production (flexibility, quality) to form a new production concept".

It involves:

(*i*) The decentralization of some decisions at the entrepreneurial level which makes the hierarchy more flexible.

(*ii*) The reduction of hierarchical levels (in Toyota, for example, there are just three organisational levels: group manager, section manager and firm manager).

(*iii*) The consensual way of management.

(*iv*) Working in groups.

(*v*) Organizational process innovations by using total quality control, quality circles and other managerial tools.

Lean production is the alliance of several Japanese techniques of work organization. It has in its view—teamwork; *kaizen*—Continuous Improvement Process; the Zero-Defect Principle; the JIT–Just in Time or Zero Buffer Time Principle; customer orientation; efficient research and development; an enterprise culture and integration of suppliers; prime cost reduction; and no stockpile—*kanban*.

It believes that perfection cannot be attained, but the incessant search for it can bring surprising results. It values work in groups, participation, inter-firm industrial organization, intensification of work and the suppression of everything that is superfluous.

The features of the various production paradigms may be summed up as follows:

Craft Production—Pre-1800s

- Highly skilled workers
- Simple tools
- Custom products
- Low volume
- High cost
- Maximum job satisfaction

Mass Production—1900s

- Work force specialization into professional, skilled and unskilled labour
- Inter-changeability of parts
- Standardized products
- High volume
- Low cost
- Minimum job satisfaction
- Introduction to flow
- Economies of scale

Lean Production—1950s

- Multi-Skilled, knowledgeable workforce
- Team orientation
- Flexible processes
- High volumes, greater variety
- Low cost
- Higher job satisfaction
- Organization-wide view of production

Table 15.1 Craft, Mass and Lean Production Systems - A Comparison

Phase	Focus	Characteristic	Results
Craft	Skill	Labour Intensive	Low Volume
Mass	Volume	Capital Intensive	Market Saturation
Lean	Waste Reduction	People Involvement	Limited Change

15.2 TRADE, CONSUMPTION PATTERNS, AND THE ENVIRONMENT

World trade has promoted patterns of consumption that not only harm local ecology, but also lead to levels of consumption that cannot be sustained by the earth's resources. Trade changes what we consume and consumption today has become environmentally destructive. One example is the trade in frogs' legs. By 1988, more than 50 million frogs were being exported every year by Bangladesh, mostly to the US. Frog exports peaked at \$10.5 million but research showed that the real price of export was phenomenally high. Frogs are insectivorous and each frog can eat up to its body weight (200 gms) every day. An acre of paddy field can be kept insect-free with just 50 frogs. Frogs protect crops; they are natural biological pest control agents. Also frog waste is organic fertilizer.

It was during the period of flourishing frog trade that the use of pesticides in Bangladesh increased. Government figures revealed that they were spending \$90 million to earn \$10 million!

The trade was stopped only when *Friends of the Earth* helped the Bangladeshi government to realize that export of frogs' legs was economic and environmental suicide.

Likewise, a lot of the so-called development that has taken place in India has had a devastating impact on the ecosystem. To take an example, the river Noyyal in South India, originates from the Western Ghats and empties into the Kaveri in Tamil Nadu. Its basin is polluted by the 800 odd dyeing and bleaching units of Tirupur and is the scene of confrontation between the agriculturists and the textile processing industry (Chapter 12).

15.3 THE CONCEPT OF SUSTAINABLE INDUSTRIALIZATION

Sustainable industrialization is a process of development that strives to promote economic growth through increased capacity to produce goods and provide for future generations.

Sustainable industrialization is an offshoot of sustainable development and plays a vital role in promoting the sustainable use of the earth's finite resources. Sustainability implies the characteristics of a process or activity which can go on forever, without hampering or imperiling the functioning of the environment and without causing ecological imbalance or environmental crisis.

15.4 SUSTAINABLE DEVELOPMENT: A BUSINESS DEFINITION

If sustainable development is to achieve its potential, it must be integrated into the planning and measurement systems of business enterprises. And for that to happen, the concept must be articulated in terms that are familiar to business leaders.

For the business enterprise, sustainable development means adopting business strategies and activities that meet the needs of the enterprise and its stakeholders today while protecting, sustaining and enhancing the human and natural resources that will be needed in the future.

This definition captures the spirit of the concept as originally proposed by the World Commission on Environment and Development, and recognizes that economic development must meet the needs of a business enterprise and its stakeholders. The latter include shareholders, lenders, customers, employees, suppliers and communities who are affected by the organization's activities. It also highlights business's dependence on human and natural resources, in addition to physical and financial capital. It emphasizes that economic activity must not irreparably degrade or destroy these natural and human resources.

The most broadly accepted criterion for corporate sustainability constitutes a firm's efficient use of natural capital. This eco-efficiency is usually calculated as the economic value added by a firm in relation to its aggregated ecological impact. This idea has been popularized by the World Business Council for Sustainable Development (WBCSD) under the following definition: "Eco-efficiency is achieved by the delivery of competitively-priced goods and services that satisfy human needs and bring quality of life, while progressively reducing ecological impacts and resource intensity throughout the life-cycle to a level at least in line with the earth's carrying capacity."

Similar to the eco-efficiency concept, is the second criterion for corporate sustainability, namely, socio-efficiency, which describes the relation between the value added by a firm and its social impact. Whereas, it can be assumed that most corporate impacts on the environment are negative (apart from rare exceptions, such as the planting of trees) this is not true for social impacts. These can be either positive (*e.g.,* creation of employment) or negative (*e.g.,* work accidents, human rights abuses).

Both eco-efficiency and socio-efficiency are concerned primarily with increasing economic sustainability. In this process, they instrumentalize both natural and social capital aiming to benefit from win-win situations.

15.5 PRINCIPLES OF SUSTAINABLE INDUSTRIALIZATION

Sustainable industrialization requires more than pollution prevention and tinkering with environmental regulations. The larger challenge of sustainable industrialization is the necessity for bringing about clean, equitable economic growth, using strategies that maximize added value while minimizing resource and energy use. Given the significant role played by businesses in the exploitation of natural resources, any attempt to bring about sustainable industrialization would be ineffective without their active participation and leadership.

A vision of sustainable industrialization calls for:

(i) **A Rethinking of Time Scales:** Most businesses consider a 2-year time horizon a luxury, focusing instead on quarter-by-quarter results. Environmentalists, on the other hand, are concerned about the future and the world that future generations will inherit, their central message being "we do not inherit the planet from our parents and grandparents, we borrow it from our children." Thus, businessmen and environmentalists work to different time clocks.

(ii) **A Realization that Pollution = Inefficiency:** All pollution is a form of economic waste. When scrap, harmful substances or energy are discharged into the environment as pollution, it is a sign that the resources have been used incompletely, inefficiently or ineffectively. Moreover, companies have to incur additional costs on storing, handling and disposal of the discharges

(iii) **Awareness that Pollution Prevention Pays:** A natural follow up of the above is the realization that greening is in fact rewarding. A number of case studies attest to the substantial cost savings that accrue from pollution prevention. The famous case of the American company 3M, which reduced air pollutants by 1,22,000 tons, water pollution by 1.6 billion gallons and in three years, saved $482 million is well known. (Refer Chapter 10)

(iv) **Acceptance of Polluter Pays Principle:** This recognizes the irrevocable responsibility on the part of the polluter to bear all costs in connection with the cleaning up of the pollution caused and restoring the environment, as nearly as possible, to its old unpolluted state.

(v) **Adoption of the Precautionary Principle:** This was agreed upon at the World Industry Conference on Environmental Management in 1989 held in Paris and implies that the conclusive absence of scientific proof of the link between certain developmental activities and the degradation of the environment should not stand in the way of safeguards and precautions being taken in the interests of conservation of the environment.

BOX 15.1

The Case of the Dutch Flower Industry

The example of the Dutch flower industry is relevant to illustrate how it has responded to its environmental problems. Intensive cultivation of flowers in small areas was contaminating the soil and groundwater with pesticides, herbicides and fertilizers. Facing increasingly strict regulations on the release of chemicals, the Dutch understood that the only effective way to address the problem would be to develop a closed loop system. In advanced Dutch greenhouses today, flowers now grow in water and rock wool, not in soil. This lowers the risk of infestation, reducing the need for fertilizers and pesticides, which are delivered in the water that circulates and is reused.

The tightly monitored closed-loop system also reduces variation in growing conditions, thus improving product quality. Handling costs have gone down because the flowers are cultivated on specially designed platforms. In addressing the environmental problem, the Dutch have innovated in ways that have raised the productivity with which they use many of the resources involved in growing flowers. The net result is not only dramatically lower environmental impact but also lower costs, better product quality, and enhanced global competitiveness.

Source: http://www.questia.com/googleScholar.qst;jsessionid=LGnRqFyGNhk17k23gsCR10KJqpPCBJGjBN3v6J LQNz35Lt69Fb1H!-1089623074!532237999?docId=5001899829

(*vi*) **Adoption of Full Cost Pricing:** Including environmental costs in the accounts of business is full cost pricing. For agricultural and industrial production, the full cost is the cost of production plus the cost of any environmental degradation associated with it. For example, clearing a forest might degrade the environmental services provided by that forest, such as protecting a watershed, preventing soil erosion and so on.

(*vii*) **Shift from Anthropocentrism to Ecocentrism:** Anthropocentrism, a value which underlies virtually all human activities, is in conflict with the environmentalist value which accepts the absolute right of nature to exist and prosper independent of its benefits to humans. (Refer to Chapter 1for more details).

15.6 THE SUSTAINABLE DEVELOPMENT JOURNEY

According to the International Institute for Sustainable Development, for the business firms, the journey to sustainable development is marked by three distinct phases, given below:

(*i*) Environmental compliance

(*ii*) Environmental risk management

(*iii*) Long-term sustainable development strategies

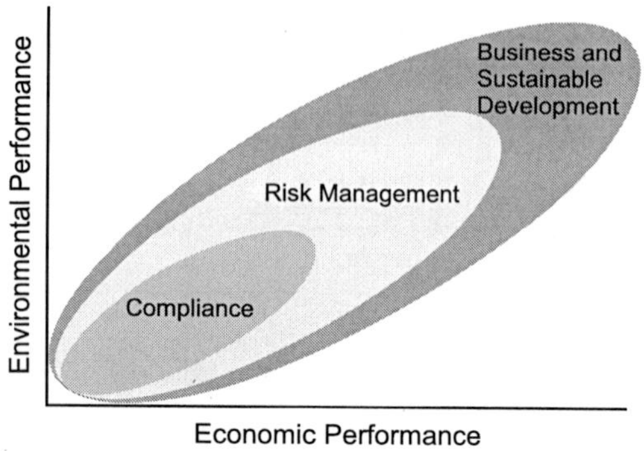

Fig. 15.1 Sustainable Development Journey by Firms

In the initial phase of the journey, the need to comply with environmental regulations drives improvements in environmental performance. Businesses adopt a more proactive approach in the next phase. Environmental risk management is introduced, to reduce environmental liabilities and to minimize the costs of regulatory compliance. A substantial number of companies recognize that the implementation of sustainable business strategies can lead to new opportunities and improved results - the business and sustainable development phase. These stages are discussed in some detail below:

Environmental Compliance Stage

The first step on the journey is compliance with regulatory measures. The introduction of new environmental regulations, both national and international, forces businesses to improve their environmental performance. But compliance often creates unexpected costs that threaten profitability. The most significant financial liabilities for companies are those associated with remediation, clean-ups and penalties for breaches of legislation. Businesses can face difficulties if they fail to anticipate their environmental liabilities. To comply with legislation and to avoid liabilities, businesses put in place remediation and abatement measures. However, this reactive approach often prevents them from establishing efficient cost control systems and growth strategies.

Operating in "compliance" mode, businesses commonly regard environmental protection as an unnecessary burden, a costly undertaking that decreases a company's competitiveness and adversely affects market performance and business results. Faced with the increasing burden of regulation, some businesses choose to go beyond compliance, towards comprehensive environmental programmes and sustainable development.

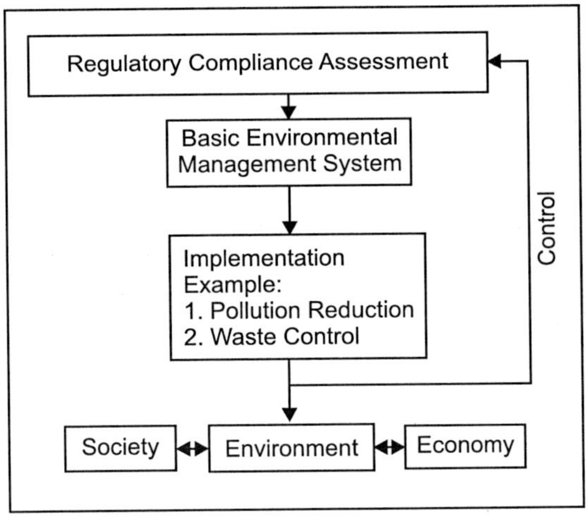

Fig. 15.2 Step 1: Regulatory Compliance

Environmental Risk Management Stage

Environmental risk management is the next stage on the journey towards sustainable development. Liability—both corporate and personal—for the cost of environmental clean-ups and claims, prompts business executives to adopt more proactive strategies in dealing with environmental issues. Driven by the need to minimize risk, some businesses adopt a precautionary approach which involves anticipating potential risks and preventing environmental hazards. This approach offers a greater flexibility of response than is available through regulatory compliance.

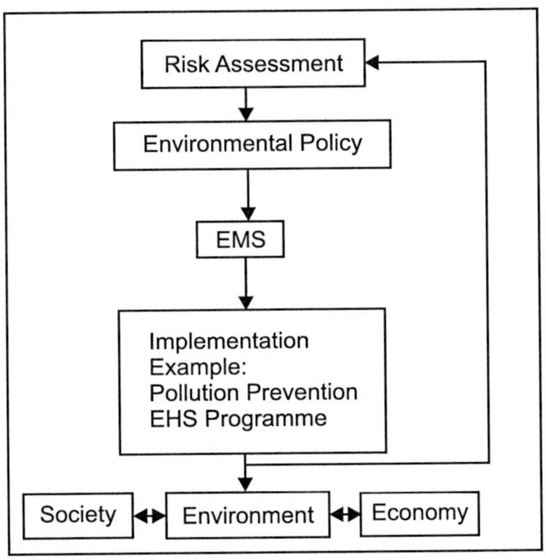

Fig. 15.3 Step 2: Environmental Risk Management

To improve their control of environmental performance, some companies conduct environment, health and safety (EHS) assessments, develop environmental policies, and implement environmental management systems (EMSs). Techniques such as pollution prevention or recycling are used to translate policy objectives into practice.

The risk management approach allows companies to save money by anticipating and avoiding expenditures arising from environmental damage, and by minimizing the cost of complying with future legislation. In addition, operating costs can be reduced through waste minimization, pollution prevention and the elimination of health and safety hazards.

Sustainable Business Strategies Stage

Business strategies for sustainable development mark the final phase in the journey. The aim is to seek win-win situations which can achieve environmental quality, increase wealth, and enhance competitive advantage. Companies integrate sustainable development into their business strategies. Sustainable development is a natural extension of many corporate environmental policies. In the pursuit of economic, environmental and community benefits, management considers the long-term interests and needs of the stakeholders.

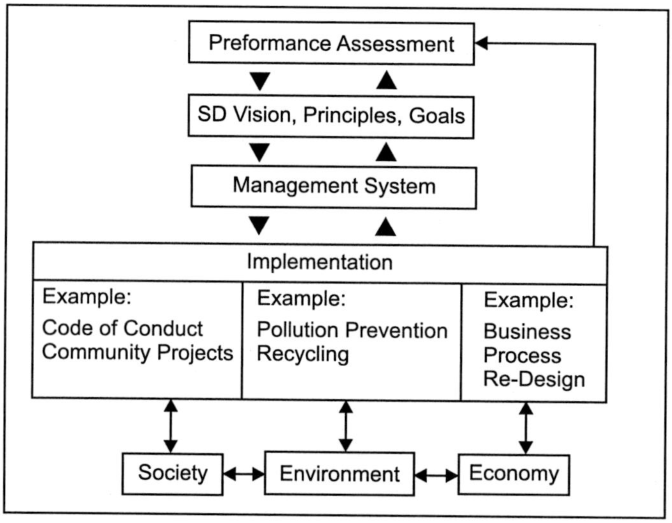

Fig. 15.4 Step 3: Sustainable Business Strategies

Thus, sustainable development strategies uncover business opportunities in issues which, in earlier stages of the journey, might be regarded as costs to be borne or risks to be mitigated. Results include new business processes with reduced external impacts, improved financial performance, and an enhanced reputation among communities and stakeholders.

15.7 STEPS REQUIRED FOR MANAGING AN ENTERPRISE ACCORDING TO SUSTAINABLE DEVELOPMENT PRINCIPLES

These are set out below:

(*i*) **Perform a Stakeholder Analysis:** A stakeholder analysis is required in order to identify all the parties who are directly or indirectly affected by the enterprise's operations. It must also include people who are affected, or who consider themselves affected, by the enterprise's effect on the biosphere and on social capital. It sets out the issues, concerns and information needs of the stakeholders with respect to the organization's sustainable development activities.

After the stakeholders have been identified, management should prepare a description of the needs and expectations of these groups. The stakeholder analysis may reveal conflicting expectations. For example, customers may demand new, environmentally safe products, while employees might be concerned that such a policy could threaten their jobs. Shareholders, meanwhile, may be wary about the return on their investment. A stakeholder analysis can be a useful way to identify areas of potential conflict among stakeholder groups before they materialize.

(ii) **Set Sustainable Development Policies and Objectives:** The next objective is to articulate the basic values that the enterprise expects its employees to follow with respect to sustainable development, and to set targets for operating performance.

Senior management is responsible for formulating a sustainable development policy for the organization, and for establishing specific objectives. They are also expected to take into account, economic considerations that may be absent from a strictly "environmental" viewpoint. In particular, emphasis must be placed on maintaining or enhancing the earth's capital endowment, and highlighting the limits to society's ability to substitute manmade capital for natural capital. A policy on environmental responsibility is a good first step towards the broader concerns of sustainable development.

There are many benefits in actively involving the board of directors in the development of a sustainable development policy. It is the board of directors that determines overall priorities and sets the tone for management and employees.

It is important that sustainable development objectives be clear, concise and, wherever possible, expressed in measurable terms. Establishing measurable objectives is essential if management and others are to be able to assess whether their business activities have met the established objectives.

A successful implementation plan depends on "rethinking the corporation" if it is to respond to the paradigm shift associated with sustainable development. It is important to address not only the positive forces for change but also the barriers and sources of resistance.

While the basic management framework may remain intact, substantial changes will probably be needed in the culture, the organization and its systems. The plan must have full "buy-in" if it is to be effective. This in turn, requires broad consultations and cultural change.

(iii) **Develop a Supportive Corporate Culture:** In order to ensure that the organization and its people give their backing to the sustainable development policies, an appropriate corporate culture is essential. Increased participation of employees not only generates practical ideas, but also increases enthusiasm for the programme itself. Most customers and employees enjoy being part of an organization that is committed to operating in a socially responsible manner.

Implementing sustainable development objectives will probably require managers to change their attitudes. This may be accomplished only after retraining. For example, some executives may feel that their sole responsibility is to maximize the wealth of the enterprise's owners. As a result, they may have difficulty in understanding the sustainable development concept and in accepting it as a legitimate business objective.

The concept of sustainable development requires organizations to develop a culture that emphasizes employee participation, continuous learning and improvement. The International Chamber of Commerce explains the process of continual improvement thus:

"...To continue to improve corporate policies, programmes and environmental performance, taking into account technical developments, scientific understanding, consumer needs and community expectations, with legal regulations as a starting point and to apply the same environmental criteria internationally."

Internal reporting systems can have a significant effect on corporate culture. They must be designed to reinforce positive behaviour with respect to sustainable development. They also need to be linked to the enterprise's recognition and promotion systems. The active and visible involvement of senior executives and directors can be a powerful force in forming attitudes, and in creating a supportive culture in which sustainable business practices can flourish.

Equally, it is important that the board provides an oversight in the allocation of responsibilities for sustainable development objectives. This umbrella role should include ensuring that responsibilities are assigned in a manner that holds key executives accountable. It also means ensuring that reward and promotion systems recognize those people who achieve, or help to achieve, sustainable development objectives.

(iv) **Develop Measures and Standards of Performance:** The implementation of sustainable development objectives, and the preparation of meaningful reports on performance, require appropriate means of measuring performance.

The measures used to assess and report on performance will be influenced by the company's sustainable development objectives, and by standards that have been established by government and other public agencies. For example, performance targets may be set in terms of emission levels and energy usage per tonne of output, or perhaps working hours lost due to accident or illness. The information generated must be in the right units if actual performance is to be compared with the set targets. This might require new measuring procedures to be introduced.

In many cases, companies are ahead of governments in establishing sustainable development performance criteria. There is a significant opportunity for the business sector to work with governments in establishing performance measures and standards, and to help develop reporting and monitoring systems that are cost-effective and which meet the needs of both the public and business.

(v) **Preparation of Reports:** The next step in the process is to develop meaningful reports for internal management and stakeholders, outlining the enterprise's sustainable development objectives and comparing performance against them.

Directors and senior executives use internal reports to measure performance, make decisions and monitor the implementation of their policies and strategies. Stakeholders use external corporate reports to evaluate the performance of a corporation, and to hold the directors and senior executives accountable for achieving financial, social and environmental objectives.

Regulators and government officials add to the task by requiring an ever-expanding degree of disclosure, in order to ensure compliance with their regulations.

Internally, several companies now ask their line managers to include in their regular reporting procedures, a statement on whether they have achieved the environmental and sustainable development targets. Similarly, the board of directors should receive periodic reports from senior management on whether these objectives have been achieved. External reporting on sustainable development issues can take a number of different formats. Some organizations are experimenting with special reports for particular stakeholder groups, such as employees. Others provide a general-purpose report on environmental activities. Still others include the subject of environmental and social issues in a separate section of their annual reports.

A system that provides a meaningful picture of a company's sustainability achievements is essential for strengthening accountability. This is necessary if an effective relationship is to be maintained with stakeholder groups.

(vi) **Enhance Internal Monitoring Processes:** On an ongoing basis it will be important to develop mechanisms to help directors and senior managers ensure that the sustainable development policies are being implemented. The key to any system's effectiveness is whether the management monitors operations and outputs on an ongoing basis.

Monitoring can take many forms, such as:

(*a*) Reviewing reports submitted by middle managers;

(*b*) Touring operating sites and observing employees performing their duties;

(*c*) Holding regular meetings with subordinates to review reports and to seek input on how the procedures and reporting systems might be improved;

(*d*) Implementing an environmental auditing programme.

Organizing internal environmental audits is a practical way to monitor the implementation of management policies. For example, many organizations now perform internal audits to monitor compliance with environmental policies and legislation. These normally require multidisciplinary teams of experts (for example engineers, auditors and scientists) who possess the necessary knowledge and experience, both in auditing and in the areas being audited.

(vii) **Management Leadership:** Establishing sustainable development objectives, systems and monitoring mechanisms requires leadership on the part of senior management, and a commitment to continuous improvement.

(viii) **The Role of the Board:** Without the active involvement of the Board of Directors, it will be difficult for an organization to implement sustainable business practices. Corporations are encouraged to establish a "social responsibility committee", responsible for setting corporate policies on sustainable development and for dealing with issues such as health and safety, personnel policies, environmental protection, and codes of business conduct.

It is important that corporate sustainable development policies be implemented consistently throughout an organization. The Board of Directors must ensure that variable levels of corporate ethics and integrity, depending on the country in which they are operating, does not prevail. The board also has a role in monitoring the implementation of its policies. It should receive regular reports on how the policies are implemented, and should be accountable to its stakeholders on the company's performance against these policies.

(*ix*) **Self-Assessment:** The first step for businesses in adopting sustainable development principles is to assess their current position. Management should know the degree to which the company's activities line up with sustainable development principles. This requires evaluating the company's overall strategy, the performance of specific operations, and the effect of particular activities.

This process should compare the company's current performance with the expectations of the stakeholders. Management philosophies and systems should be reviewed; the scope of public disclosures on sustainability topics should be analyzed; and the ability of current information systems to produce the required data should be evaluated.

(*x*) **Deciding on a Strategy:** Once managers have gained an understanding of how its own operations shape up, they should gauge the performance of other, comparable organizations. Comparisons against the standards set by other industries and environmental groups can be instructive.

Management should then consider ways to narrow the gap between the current state of the corporation's performance and its objectives for the future. A strategy will need to be developed, outlining where the company hopes to position itself relative to its competitors and its stakeholders' expectations.

A general plan is needed to describe how and when management expects to achieve that goal, together with the various milestones it will reach along the way. Senior management should review and approve the strategy and the plan before submitting them to the Board of Directors for final approval. Because of the pervasiveness of sustainable development, it is essential that members of the senior management team (representing all facets of the company's activities) "buy in" to the project. Anything less than full commitment may doom the plan to failure.

(*xi*) **Strategy Implementation:** Once the strategy and the general plan have been approved, detailed plans should be prepared indicating how the new strategy will affect operations, management systems, information systems and reporting. These should set out measurable goals to be achieved in each area, and explain how progress will be monitored. They should also specify spending and training requirements.

These plans should be developed through consultation with employees throughout the organization, possibly with the assistance of outside specialists. It will be a time consuming and dynamic process, which will entail frequent modifications as input is obtained from several sources. Once finalized, the plans should be approved by senior management and ideally, by the Board of Directors as well.

15.8 BUSINESS CHARTER FOR SUSTAINABLE DEVELOPMENT

The International Chamber of Commerce (ICC), a non-governmental organization serving world business for more than 80 years, with a membership extending to more than 130 countries, works to promote world trade and investment based on free and fair competition, and to harmonize trade practices and formulate guidelines and terminology for importers and exporters. In response to the World Commission on Environment and Development report, ICC developed a "Business Charter for Sustainable Development" which sets out 16 principles for environmental management. The Charter covers environmentally relevant aspects of health, safety and product stewardship. The principles laid down are:

(*i*) **Corporate Priority:** To recognize environmental management as among the highest corporate priorities and as a key determinant to sustainable development; to establish policies, programmes and practices for conducting operations in an environmentally sound manner.

(*ii*) **Integrated Management:** To integrate these policies, programmes and practices fully into each business as an essential element of management in all its functions.

(*iii*) **Process of Improvement:** To continue to improve corporate policies, programmes and environmental performance, taking into account technical developments, scientific understanding, consumer needs and community expectations, with legal regulations as a starting point, and to apply the same environmental criteria internationally.

(*iv*) **Employee Education:** To educate, train and motivate employees to conduct their activities in an environmentally responsible manner.

(*v*) **Prior Assessment:** To assess environmental impacts before starting a new activity or project and before decommissioning a facility or leaving a site.

(*vi*) **Products and Services:** To develop and provide products or services that have no undue environmental impact and are safe in their intended use, that are efficient in their consumption of energy and natural resources, and that can be recycled, reused, or disposed off safely.

(*vii*) **Customer Advice:** To advise and, where relevant, educate customers, distributors and the public in the safe use, transportation, storage and disposal of products provided, and to apply similar considerations to the provision of services.

(*viii*) **Facilities and Operations:** To develop, design and operate facilities and conduct activities taking into consideration the efficient use of energy and materials, the sustainable use of renewable resources, the minimization of adverse environmental impacts of waste generation, and the safe and responsible disposal of residual wastes.

(*ix*) **Research:** To conduct or support research on the environmental impacts of raw materials, products, processes, emissions and wastes associated with the enterprise and on the means of minimizing such adverse impacts.

(*x*) **Precautionary Approach:** To modify the manufacture, marketing or use of products or services or the conduct of activities, consistent with scientific and technical understanding, to prevent serious or irreversible environmental degradation.

(*xi*) **Contractors and Suppliers:** To promote the adoption of these principles by contractors acting on behalf of the enterprise, encouraging and where appropriate, requiring improvements in their practices to make them consistent with those of the enterprise; and to encourage the wider adoption of these principles by suppliers.

(*xii*) **Emergency Preparedness:** To develop and maintain, where significant hazards exist, emergency preparedness plans in conjunction with emergency services, relevant authorities and the local community, recognizing potential transboundary impacts.

(*xiii*) **Transfer of Technology:** To contribute to the transfer of environmentally sound technology and management methods throughout the industrial and public sectors.

(*xiv*) **Contributing to the Common Effort:** To contribute to the development of public policy and to business, governmental and inter-governmental programmes and educational initiatives that will enhance environmental awareness and protection.

(*xv*) **Openness to Concerns:** To foster openness and dialogue with employees and the public, anticipating and responding to their concerns about the potential hazards and impact of operations, products, wastes or services, including those of transboundary or global significance.

(*xvi*) **Compliance and Reporting:** To measure environmental performance; to conduct regular environmental audits and assessment of compliance with company requirements, legal requirements and these principles; and periodically to provide appropriate information to the board of directors, shareholders, employees, the authorities and the public.

The primary objective of the Charter is "that the widest range of enterprises, commit themselves to improving their environmental performance in accordance with the principles, to having in place management practices to effect such improvement, to measuring their progress, and to reporting this progress as appropriate, internally and externally".

To date, more than 2,300 companies have signed up for it, and the list includes corporations such as Norsk Hydro, Deloitte and Touche, Akzo Nobel, and Xerox. In addition, several industry associations use it as the basis for their sustainability programmes. Endorsement of the ICC Charter is voluntary. By signing it, companies commit themselves to respecting its 16 principles for environmental management. The ICC is currently assessing how companies that have endorsed the Charter are applying the principles, and what their experiences were with implementation.

15.9 CONCLUSION

Speaking at a global level, or at least in the developed countries, it may be said, that rethinking of business strategies on the lines of sustainability is here to stay. Businesses have moved a long way from their original profit maximizing goal, to recognizing their responsibility and symbiotic relationship to the social fabric of which they are such an important part. Stringent regulations and command-and-control approaches to environmental protection are giving way to market based instruments such as green taxes and tradable pollution permits. The latest trend is self-regulation, wherein the firms consciously and voluntarily choose to tread the path of least ecological damage as a result of their operations. Waste elimination, recycling, dematerialization, and clean technology, to name only a few, are being increasingly perceived as bringing in substantial cost savings to firms. All said and done, it has to be recognized that profit motive is one of the main driving forces behind business operations, and not philanthropy. So when economic benefits in the form of substantial cost savings and improved product quality are widely publicized and understood, businesses will be willing to adopt the same.

QUESTIONS

1. Sustainable Industrialization is a utopian dream. Do you agree?
2. Briefly discuss the main principles underlying sustainable industrialization.
3. Enumerate the principles given in the Business Charter for Sustainable Development.

EXERCISES

1. Make a case study of any industry that follows sustainable business strategies.
2. Give real world examples of sustainable business strategies.

❑❑❑

16

Industrial Ecology

> *We believe it's in business's interest*
> *to become more sustainable . . . this will become*
> *a must-have rather than a nice-to-have issue, going forward.*
>
> **John Duggan, CEO, Gazeley**

Industrial ecology is a new approach to the industrial design of products and processes and the implementation of sustainable manufacturing strategies. It is a concept in which an industrial system is viewed not in isolation from its surrounding systems but in concert with them. Industrial ecology seeks to optimize the total materials cycle, from virgin material to finished material, to component, to product, to waste product, and to ultimate disposal.

16.1 INDUSTRIAL ECOLOGY—MEANING AND DEFINITION

Paul Hawken in his book, *The Ecology of Commerce,* defines industrial ecology as follows: "Industrial ecology provides for the first time, a large-scale, integrated management tool that designs industrial infrastructure as if they were a series of interlocking artificial ecosystems interfacing with the natural global ecosystem."

Industrial ecology refers to the exchange of materials between different industrial sectors where the wastes of an industry become the resource for another industry. It is the shifting of industrial processes from linear open loop systems in which resource and capital investments move through the systems to become wastes—to a closed loop system where wastes become inputs for new processes. For example, the excess steam from an electricity generating facility can be used as a heat source for a nearby chemical manufacturer. The flyash from a coal fired power generating station can be used as an input for the cement industry. "Industrial ecosystems" refer to situations in which a number of different companies, usually in close proximity to each other, exchange a variety of "waste" outputs. Implementing industrial ecology involves such things as life cycle analysis, closed loop processing, reusing and recycling, design for environment and waste exchange.

Industrial ecology refers to:

(*i*) A systems view of the interactions between industrial and ecological systems.

(*ii*) The study of material and energy flows and transformations.

(*iii*) A multidisciplinary approach.

(*iv*) An orientation towards the future.

(*v*) A change from linear (open) processes to cyclical (closed) processes, so that the waste from one industry is used as an input for another, in an effort to reduce the industrial systems' environmental impacts on ecological systems.

(*vi*) An emphasis on harmoniously integrating industrial activity into ecological systems with the idea of making industrial systems emulate more efficient and sustainable natural systems.

16.2 ORIGIN OF THE CONCEPT

The development of industrial ecology is an attempt to provide a new conceptual framework for understanding the impact of industrial systems on the environment. The concept aims to identify and then implement strategies to reduce the environmental impacts of products and processes associated with industrial systems, with an ultimate goal of sustainable development.

Frosch and Gallopoulos (1989) first introduced the term "Industrial Ecology" together with the concept of "Industrial Ecosystems", referring to the design of production sites in analogy to natural ecosystems in a *Scientific American* article. Their vision was "that our industrial system ought to behave like an ecosystem, where the wastes of a species may be resource to another species. The outputs of an industry should become the inputs of another, thus reducing use of raw materials, pollution, and saving on waste treatment."

The relationship between natural ecosystems and that of industrial activities has been discussed by Frosch and Gallopoulos as follows:

"In a biological ecosystem, some of the organisms use sunlight, water, and minerals to grow, while others consume the first, alive or dead, along with minerals and gases, and produce wastes of their own. These wastes are in turn food for other organisms, some of which may convert the wastes into the minerals used by the primary producers, and some of which consume each other in a complex network of processes in which everything produced is used by some organism for its own metabolism. Similarly, in the industrial ecosystem, each process and network of processes must be viewed as a dependent and interrelated part of a larger whole. The analogy between the industrial ecosystem concept and the biological ecosystem is not perfect, but much could be gained if the industrial system were to mimic the best features of the biological analogue."

Recognizing that industrial processes that harm and waste are, by definition, less economic and therefore, more costly in the long run, companies and industries are trying to dovetail their material and waste flows, attempting to eliminate pollution by tailoring manufacturing by-products so that they become the raw materials of subsequent processes. This philosophy goes well beyond the concept of curtailing waste; it entails using waste so that it is no longer waste at all. Not only does this prevent material from entering the wastestream, it garners sales and therefore, income for what was once an expense.

Industrial ecology provides a positive means for corporations to address environmental needs while also working within their own natural predilections. The proponents of industrial ecology argue that this nascent but increasingly popular idea offers the most realistic means for corporations to change.

It is important to note that there are assumptions within industrial ecology that run counter to what some economists and biologists believe. For example, industrial ecology implies that resource shortages may have technological fixes, such as biotechnology, or that degraded ecosystems—soil, oceans, and forests—can be restored through market mechanisms to former levels of activity, while the world economy continues to grow. Ecologists conversant with the level of degradation worldwide would call that optimistic. Yet, industrial ecology for the first time provides a large-scale integrated management tool that designs industrial infrastructures as if "they were a series of interlocking, artificial ecosystems interfacing with the natural global ecosystem." For the first time, industry is going beyond life-cycle analysis methodology and applying the concept of an ecosystem to the whole of an industrial operation, linking the metabolism of one company with that of others.

A prototype of industrial ecology and cooperation is in place right now in Kalundborg, Denmark, where several linkages of byproducts and waste heat can be found between numerous entities such as a large power plant, an oil refinery, a pharmaceutical plant, a plasterboard factory, an enzyme manufacturer, a waste company and the city itself.

16.3 GOALS OF INDUSTRIAL ECOLOGY

The primary goal of industrial ecology is to promote sustainable development at the global, regional, and local levels. Industrial ecology aims to promote the sustainable use of renewable resources and minimal use of non-renewable ones. Industrial activity is dependent on a steady supply of resources and thus, should operate as efficiently as possible. Depletion of non-renewables and degradation of renewables must be minimized in order that industrial activity is sustainable in the long term. It is important that industrial activities do not cause catastrophic disruptions to ecosystems or slowly degrade their structure and function, thus jeopardizing the planet's life support system.

16.4 KEY CONCEPTS OF INDUSTRIAL ECOLOGY

(*i*) **Systems Analysis:** Critical to industrial ecology is the systems view of the relationship between human activities and environmental problems. A systems view enables manufacturers to develop products in a sustainable fashion. Central to the systems approach is an inherent recognition of the interrelationships between industrial and natural systems.

(*ii*) **Material and Energy Flows and Transformations:** A primary concept of industrial ecology is the study of material and energy flows and their transformation into products, byproducts, and wastes throughout industrial systems. One strategy of industrial ecology is to lessen the amount of waste material and waste energy that is produced and that leaves the industrial system, subsequently impacting ecological systems adversely. Recycling efforts could be intensified or other uses found for the scrap to decrease this waste. Efforts to utilize waste as a material input or energy source for some other entity within the industrial system can potentially improve the overall efficiency of the industrial system and reduce negative environmental impacts. The challenge of industrial ecology is to reduce the overall environmental burden of an industrial system that provides some service to society.

(*iii*) **Multi-disciplinary Approach:** Since industrial ecology is based on a holistic, systems view, it needs inputs and participation from many different disciplines. Furthermore, the complexity of most environmental problems requires expertise from a variety of fields— law, economics, business, public health, natural resources, ecology, engineering — to contribute to the development of industrial ecology and the resolution of environmental problems caused by industry. Along with the design and implementation of appropriate technologies, changes in public policy and law, as well as in individual behavior, will be necessary in order to rectify environmental impacts.

16.5 EVOLUTION OF INDUSTRIAL SYSTEM

The evolution of the industrial system from a linear system (Type 1 System), where resources are consumed and damaging wastes are dissipated into the environment, to a more closed system, like that of natural ecological systems, is a central concept to industrial ecology. Figs. 16.1, 16.2 and 16.3 illustrate the evolution from a Type 1 Linear System, to more evolved Type II and Type III systems.

Type I System

A Type I system is depicted as a linear process in which materials and energy enter one part of the system and then leave either as products or by-products / wastes. Because wastes and by-products are not recycled or reused, this system relies on a large, constant supply of raw materials. Unless the supply of materials and energy is infinite, this system is unsustainable; further, the ability of natural systems to assimilate wastes (known as "sinks") is also finite.

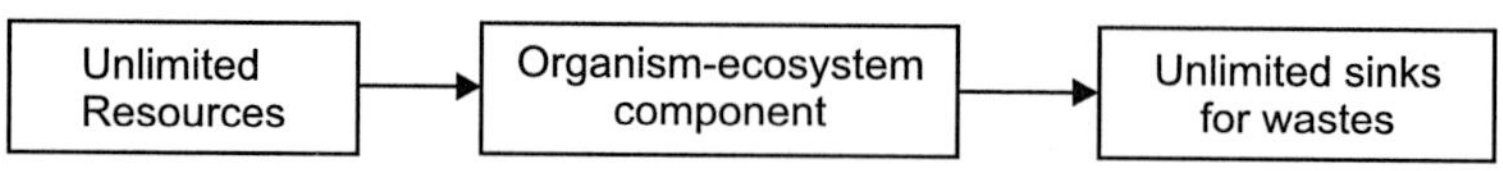

Fig. 16.1: Type I System – The Linear System

Type II System

In Type II System which characterizes much of our present-day industrial systems, some wastes are recycled or reused within the system, while others are discharged into the environment.

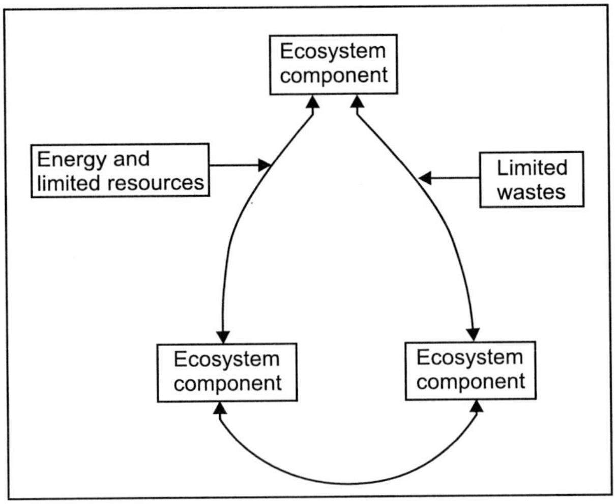

Fig. 16.2 Type II System

Type III System

A Type III system represents the dynamic equilibrium of ecological systems, where energy and wastes are constantly recycled and reused by other organisms and processes within the system. This is a highly integrated, closed system. In a totally closed industrial system, only solar energy would come from outside, while all byproducts would be constantly reused and recycled within. A Type III system represents a sustainable state and is an ideal goal of industrial ecology.

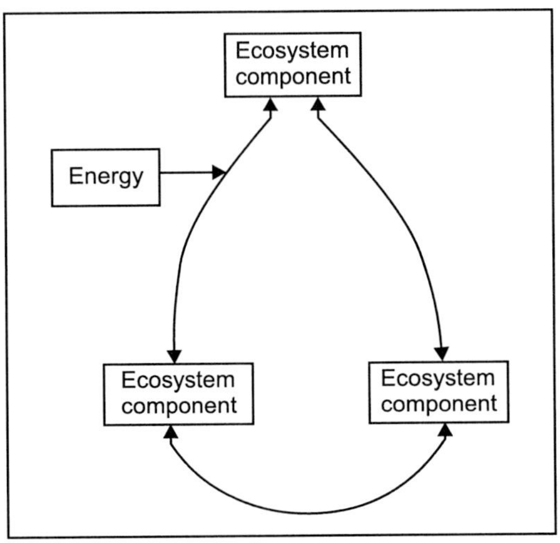

Fig. 16.3 Type III System

16.6 INDUSTRIAL ECOLOGY AS A POTENTIAL UMBRELLA FOR SUSTAINABLE DEVELOPMENT STRATEGIES

Strategies related to industrial ecology are given below:

(*i*) Pollution prevention

(*ii*) Waste minimization

(*iii*) Source reduction

(*iv*) Total Quality Environmental Management (TQEM), it integrates environmental considerations into all aspects of a firm's decision-making processes, operations, and products.

The above strategies represent approaches that individual firms can take to reduce the environmental impacts of their activities. A famous example is that of the American company 3M who pioneered a programme called Pollution Prevention Pays (3P), the first integrated, intracompany approach to designing out pollution from manufacturing processes. The plan created incentives for the technical staff to modify manufacturing methods so as to prevent hazardous and toxic waste, and to reduce costs. By reformulating products, changing processes, redesigning equipment, and recovering waste for reuse or recycling, 3M has been able to save $537 million. During the fifteen-year period, it reduced its air pollution by 1,20,000 tonnes, its wastewater by 1 billion gallons, its solid waste by 410,000 tonnes. Over 3,000 separate initiatives have contributed to the cause, and the key to the whole enterprise was a strong mandate from the top management of the corporation linked with on-going support and assistance to line employees. In 1986, 3M expanded the scope of the programme with a goal to eliminate 90 per cent of all emissions by the end of the decade, and to achieve zero emissions sometime after. Now known as 3P Plus, the plan requires the incorporation of environmental issues at all levels of business planning and is used as a factor in employee performance reviews. The 3M programme is an example of making money from preventing waste, which for most companies is the first step to becoming socially and environmentally responsible.

As a corollary to what companies can achieve individually, what industrial ecology potentially offers is an organizing umbrella that can relate these individual activities to the industrial system as a whole. Whereas strategies such as pollution prevention, TQEM, and cleaner production concentrate on firms' individual actions to reduce individual environmental impacts, industrial ecology is concerned about the activities of all entities within the industrial system. The goal of industrial ecology is to reduce the overall, collective environmental impacts caused by the totality of elements within the industrial system.

16.7 THE INDUSTRIAL SYMBIOSIS AT KALUNDBORG, DENMARK

One of the favourite cases presented by industrial ecologists is the story of the spontaneous but slow evolution of the "industrial symbiosis" at Kalundborg, Denmark. This web of materials and energy exchanges among companies (and with the community) has developed over the last 20 years in a small industrial zone on the coast, 75 miles west of Copenhagen. Originally, the motivation behind most of the exchanges was to reduce costs by seeking income-producing uses for "waste" products. Gradually, the managers and town residents realized they were generating environmental benefits as well, through their transactions.

The Kalundborg system comprises five core partners:

(*i*) Asnaes, Denmark's largest thermal (coal-fired) power station, 1,500 megawatts capacity.

(*ii*) Statoil Refinery, Denmark's largest, with a capacity of 3.2 million tonnes/year (increasing to 4.8 million tonnes/year).

(*iii*) Gyproc, a plasterboard factory, making 14 million square meters of gypsum wallboard annually (roughly enough to build all the houses in 6 towns, the size of Kalundborg).

(*iv*) Novo Nordisk, an international biotechnological company, with annual sales of over $2 billion. The plant at Kalundborg is their largest, and produces pharmaceuticals (including 40 per cent of the world's supply of insulin) and industrial enzymes.

(*v*) The City of Kalundborg which supplies heating to the 20,000 residents, as well as water to the homes and industries.

Over the last two decades, these partners spontaneously developed a series of *bilateral exchanges* which also include a number of other companies. There was no initial planning of the overall network; it just evolved as a collection of one-to-one deals that made economic sense for the pairs of participants in each.

The symbiosis started when Gyproc located its facility in Kalundborg to take advantage of the fuel gas available from Statoil. Today, Gyproc is still the only company to have located there to take advantage of an available supply.

The Kalundborg Network, 1995

Fig. 16.4 illustrates the network of companies in the symbiosis, showing the extent of the material and energy exchanges, currently about 3 million tonnes per year.

Energy Flows

The power station is coal-fired and operates at about 40 per cent thermal efficiency. Like all other fossil-fuel power stations, the majority of energy generated goes up the stack. At the same time, another large energy user, the Statoil refinery flared off most of its gas by-product.

Then, starting in the early 1970s, a series of deals were struck:

(*a*) The refinery agreed to provide excess gas to Gyproc, which had seen Statoil's flares and recognized that this burning gas was a potential low-cost fuel source.

(*b*) The power station began to supply the city with steam for its new district heating system in 1981 and then added Novo Nordisk and Statoil as customers for steam.

(*c*) The district heating, encouraged by the city and Danish government, replaced about 3,500 oil furnaces (a significant non-point source of air pollution).

(*d*) The power plant uses salt water, from the fjord, for some of its cooling needs. By doing so, it reduces the withdrawals of fresh water from Lake Tissø.

(*e*) The resulting by-product is hot salt water, a small portion of which is supplied to the fish farms' 57 ponds.

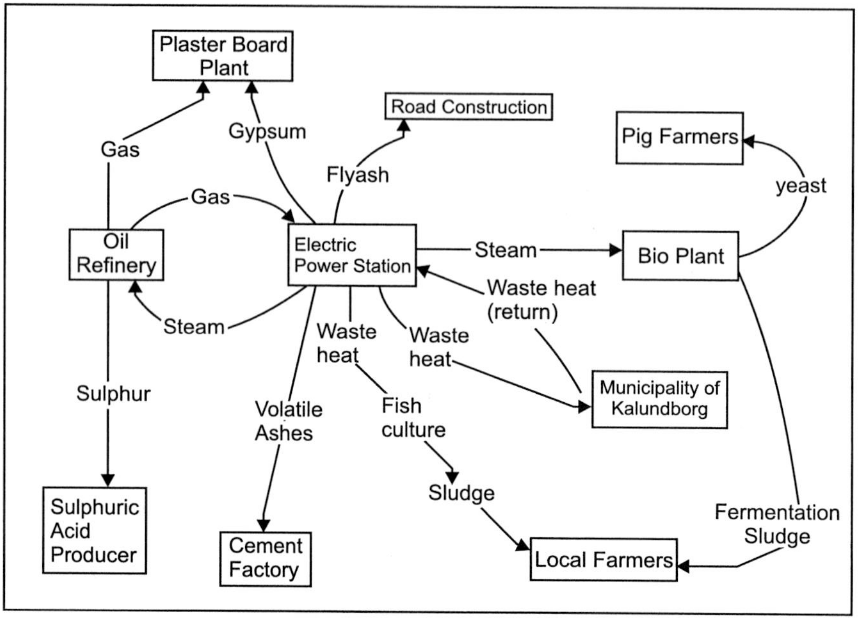

Fig. 16.4 Industrial Ecosystem at Kalundborg

(*f*) In 1992, the power plant began substituting fuels, using surplus refinery gas in place of some coal. This only became possible after Statoil built a sulphur recovery unit to comply with regulations on sulphur emission; the gas was then clean enough to permit use at the power plant.

Material Flows

In 1976, the Novo-Nordisk plant started the pattern of materials flows, matching the evolving energy flows at Kalundborg:

(*a*) Sludge from Novo Nordisk's processes and from the fish farm's water treatment plant is used as fertilizer on nearby farms. This is a large portion of the entire Kalundborg exchange network, totalling over 1 million tonnes per year.

(*b*) A cement company uses the power plant's desulphurized flyash. The Asnaes Power Plant reacts the SO_2 in its stack gas with calcium carbonate, thereby making calcium sulphate (gypsum), which it sells to Gyproc, supplying 2/3 of the latter's needs.

(*c*) The refinery's desulphurization operation produces pure liquid sulphur, which is trucked to Kemira, a sulphuric acid producer.

(*d*) Surplus yeast from insulin production at Novo Nordisk goes to farmers as pig food.

This web of recycling and reuse has generated new revenues and cost savings for the companies involved and reduced pollution to air, water, and land in the region. In ecological terms, Kalundborg exhibits the characteristics of a simple food web: organisms consume each other's waste materials and energy, thereby becoming interdependent on each other.

This pattern of inter-company reuse and recycling has reduced air, water, and ground pollution, conserved water and other resources, and generated new revenue streams from the byproducts exchanged. Through 1993, the $60 million investment in infrastructure (to transport energy and materials) has produced $120 million in revenues and cost-savings.

16.8 LESSONS FROM THE EXPERIENCE OF KALUNDBORG

Firstly, such an approach can lead to a significant reduction in the environmental impact, as is shown in Table 16.1.

Table 16.1 Environmental Aspects of the Symbiosis at Kalundborg

Environmental Aspect	Quantity
Reduction in Consumption of Resources	
Oil	45,000 tonnes per year
Coal	15,000 tonnes per year
Water	600,000 m^3 per year
Reduction in Waste Emission	
Carbon dioxide	175,000 tonnes per year
Sulphur dioxide	10,200 tonnes per year
Value from Wastes	
Sulphur	4500 tonnes per year
Calcium sulphate (gypsum)	90,000 tonnes per year
Flyash (for cement)	130,000 tonnes per year

A second lesson is that a more rational utilization of resources can save money.

A third point is that the symbiosis in Kalundborg essentially "organized itself" over a relatively long period of time, using sound financial criteria to decide which projects would be put in place.

A fourth lesson is that the close proximity of the partner companies has undoubtedly helped in terms of reducing the cost of infrastructure to facilitate material exchanges, such as pipelines.

While the success of 3M in preventing waste speaks to what a company can accomplish "in-house" and with no great sacrifice, the Kalundborg success speaks for the wealth of exchanges that are possible between industries, without design or preplanning. It defies imagination to think of what a team of designers could come up with if they were to start from scratch, locating and specifying industries and factories that had potentially synergistic and symbiotic relationships.

16.9 CONCLUSION

Two hundred years ago, industry changed from a small, labour-intensive activity to one that has become large and potentially destructive to the resources that support it. Industry now has the opportunity to take a step as great as what was taken in the industrial revolution of the 18th Century:

to move from unconstrained use and disposal of materials to manufacturing approaches that take products and impacts into account—towards sustainable industrialization.

QUESTIONS

1. Discuss the business implications of the principle—Pollution Prevention Pays.
2. Industrial ecology is an attempt to make industry mimic natural ecosystems. Explain.
3. Explain the concept of industrial ecology with the help of the Kalundborg example.

EXERCISE

1. Identify a group of facilities that could create synergies among their by-products; examine material and energy flows for these facilities and propose a specific collection of facilities that would be suitable for a more detailed design.

❑❑❑

17

Economic Theory of Pollution Control – I: Optimum Pollution and Pollution Control Policy Measures

> *It is simply economically impossible*
> *to require controls that even approach zero emissions.*
> **Barry Commoner**

It was seen in Chapter 7 that pollution problems are cases of negative externality – costs imposed on the society and on third parties without compensation. The solution that economic theory prescribes for this is internalizing the externality, using economic instruments, such as an emission charge or an effluent charge or pollution permits. Besides, regulation of pollution using the legal powers of the state through setting of standards is a common policy measure adopted by almost all countries in the world. While the use of economic instruments see pollution as a normal consequence of economic activities of production and consumption, direct regulation (command and control) considers pollution as a crime and polluters are punished with fines and imprisonment.

Pollution occurs due to two forms of failure:

(*i*) Market failure

(*ii*) Government failure

Market failure implies that in the presence of pollution, firms fail to account for full cost (MSC) and ignore marginal external cost (MEC), which results in over production by all firms in the industry. Hence, the market fails to allocate resources efficiently and sends wrong signals in the form of lower price and higher output. This occurs because there is no market for the assimilative capacity of the environment.

Government failure occurs when the government does not correct a market failure efficiently. It refers to the failure of the government to take appropriate action, both to prevent pollution and also to reduce the impact of pollution that occurs in the absence of prevention of pollution. Government failure arises when the government is responsible for creating inefficiencies.

17.1 OPTIMUM POLLUTION OR ZERO POLLUTION

The inefficiencies created by firms and the government need to be addressed through a set of well designed policies that will restore market efficiency. Any attempt to address the problem of pollution immediately raises the question "how much of pollution is to be reduced?" In an ecological sense, it can be argued that pollution should be reduced to a level that is within the assimilative capacity of the environment; this may be specified in terms of the normal concentration of the particular pollutant in air or water.

There is a limit to the capability of ecological systems in accepting the residuals without discernable changes in the quality of recipient bodies. The assimilative capacity of the environment is the maximum amount of pollution load that can be discharged without violating the best-designated use of the resource (air or water) in the region. The principal factor governing the assimilative capacity of a water source is its self-purification capacity. But achieving a reduction of pollution to this level involves cost and hence, the policymaker has to consider the costs and benefits of pollution reduction and arrive at an efficient or optimal level of pollution.

Optimum pollution is not zero pollution, since zero pollution implies zero production. Zero production is impossible. Therefore, reducing pollution to zero level is not the objective of a pollution control policy. A prudent pollution control policy aims to reduce pollution to an efficient or optimal level given by the equality of marginal damage cost and marginal abatement cost. The only exception where zero pollution by any pollutant may be justified is where even the smallest dose of the pollutant causes irreversible damage. This warrants a total ban on the use of the polluting substance. A ban on the use of DDT, is an example. An examination of the concept of optimal pollution requires knowledge of the basic concepts of the cost of pollution.

17.2 COSTS OF POLLUTION

Any pollution control policy that sets out to reduce pollution to an optimum level involves a trade off. On the one hand, the damages that people suffer due to pollution and the cost associated with it should be minimized. On the other hand, the cost of controlling pollution that firms have to incur, is an additional cost to the firm which it prefers to avoid/minimize. Reducing emissions reduces the damage to the people involved and also reduces the resources which the firm would have used in production related activities. For the firm, such costs involve opportunity costs in terms of foregone output. Hence, a pollution control policy has to balance this trade off.

From a purely economic perspective, the total cost has to be minimized. Total cost of pollution control (TCPC) is expressed as:

TCPC = TPAC + TPDC where TPAC is the Total Pollution Abatement Cost and TPDC is the Total Pollution Damage Cost.

17.3 TOTAL DAMAGE COSTS AND TOTAL ABATEMENT COSTS

Pollution damages refer to all the negative impacts of pollution from consumption and production activities. These damages include damages to the health of human beings, damages to properties and damages to ecosystems and flora and fauna. Greater the pollution, greater the damages it produces. The relationship between pollution and damage can be expressed using the damage function. A damage function shows the relationship between the quantity of a pollutant and the resulting pollution.

Pollution Damage Cost is the total monetary value of all the various damages resulting from the discharge of untreated waste into the environment. In general, pollution damage costs are measured in terms of the losses of or damage to plants and animals and their habitats; aesthetic impairment; rapid deterioration of physical infrastructure and assets; and various harmful effects on human health and mortality. The total pollution abatement cost (TPAC) and total pollution damage cost (TPDAC) are illustrated in Fig. 17.1.

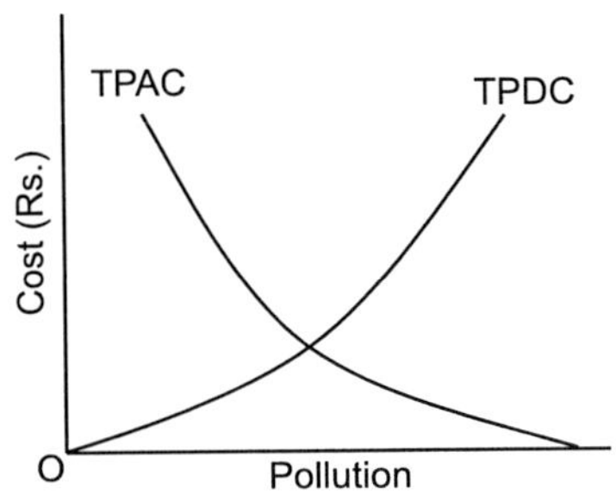

Fig. 17.1 Total Cost of Pollution Control

The damage cost curve measures the cost of the damage to the environment in monetary terms, resulting from each additional unit of waste emission. Damage cost is considered to be an increasing function of pollution. In other words, the damage caused by a unit of pollution increases progressively as the amount of pollution (untreated waste) emitted increases. The total cost of controlling pollution increases with increase in pollution controlled.

17.4 MARGINAL POLLUTION ABATEMENT COST AND MARGINAL DAMAGE COST

Marginal Pollution Abatement Cost is the cost incurred to prevent and reduce an additional unit of pollution. It is the rate of change in TPAC. In general, the marginal pollution control cost increases with increase in pollution reduced/prevented. This is because incrementally higher levels of environmental quality require investments in technologies that are increasingly costly.

The MPAC curve is the slope of the TPAC curve. The position of the marginal control cost is determined by the technology of pollution control, input switching, residue recycling and production technology. A more efficient technology of production and pollution control, recycling the wastes for reuse that reduces the use of the polluting input and switching to a less polluting input will shift MPAC downwards. A downward shift of MPAC implies that the given level of pollution can be reduced at a lower cost on a lower curve.

In Fig. 17.2, reduction of pollution by MP* costs Rs OC with the cost curve MPAC, while it costs only OC′ with the cost curve MPAC′, to reduce pollution by the same extent. Similarly, an upward shift of the MPAC will increase the cost of abating any given level of pollution. With MPAC", the cost of reducing pollution by MP* level is OC″.

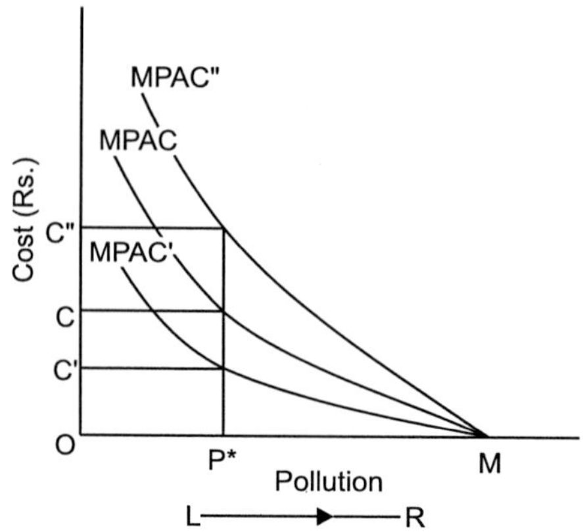

Fig. 17.2 Marginal Pollution Abatement Cost

Marginal Pollution Damage Cost refers to the damages to the society from an additional unit of pollutant. Each type of pollution impacts the society in several ways. MPDC is the rate of change in TPDC. It is assumed that the marginal damage cost is an increasing function of pollution emissions. In other words, the damage caused by a unit of pollution increases progressively as the amount of pollution (untreated waste) emitted increases. The damage cost curve measures the social cost of the damage to the environment in monetary terms, resulting from each additional unit of waste. The MPDC curve is the slope of the TPDC curve. Fig. 17.3 illustrates marginal damage cost.

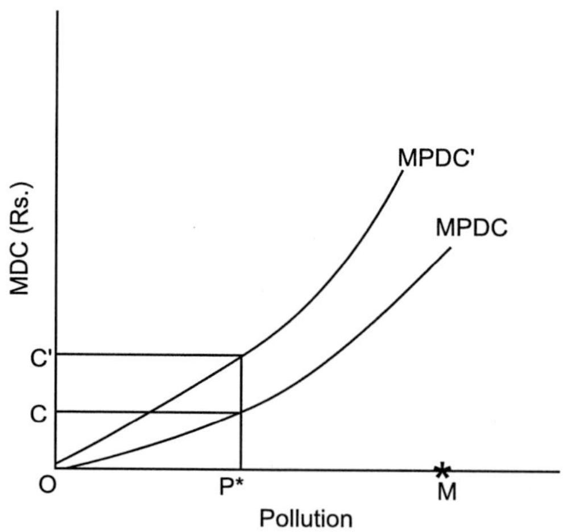

Fig. 17.3 Marginal Damage Functions

Two points deserve to be mentioned:

(*i*) The marginal pollution damage cost curve actually represents what people are willing to pay, to avoid damage or the demand function of environmental quality.

(*ii*) Damage costs are externalities—costs incurred by members of the society after the pollution damages have occurred.

Exogenous factors which affect the marginal damage cost and cause a shift of the MPDC are:

(*i*) Change in people's preference for environmental quality.

(*ii*) Changes in population exposed to the pollutant.

(*iii*) Discovery of new treatment(s) to alleviate the damage caused by environmental pollution.

(*iv*) A change in the nature of the assimilative capacity of the environment.

The upward shift of the MPDC could also be due to a change in climate conditions, such as a sudden temperature inversion which increases damage from an additional unit of pollutant, or a change in location. In Fig. 17.3, MPDC could be for a rural area and MPDC′ could be for a congested town or urban area, where the impact is severe. In Fig. 17.3, the damage cost from OP* of pollution is OC with the damage function MPDC, and it is OC′, if the damage function is MPDC′. Clearly OC′ is greater than OC.

17.5 OPTIMUM POLLUTION

The objective of the pollution control policy is to control pollution at the least cost and arrive at an efficient level of pollution. The economic rationale of minimizing the total waste disposal cost is: a rupee worth of expenditure on pollution control will make sense if, and only if, the benefits from pollution control to the society is worth more than a rupee.

As pointed out already in Section 17.1, the objective of the pollution control policy is not to achieve zero pollution, since that would mean zero production as well. The aim is to contain pollution within the assimilative capacity of the environment, taking into consideration the costs to the firm and society in achieving this.

An optimum pollution level is defined in terms of marginal damage cost from pollution to the society (MPDC) and the marginal pollution abatement cost of the firm (MPAC). Optimum level of pollution is at point E, at which MPDC = MPAC. Fig. 17.4 illustrates the optimum level of pollution. The Marginal Pollution Abatement Cost Curve in Fig. 17.4 can be interpreted as the Marginal Benefit Curve (MBC). MBC shows the benefit from the marginal unit of pollution reduced.

Optimum level of pollution is that level of pollution, at which the benefit from the marginal (last or additional) unit of pollution controlled, is equal to the marginal damage cost of pollution. It is the level of pollution at which MPAC = MPDC.

The optimal level of pollution, P* can also be analyzed in terms of total cost. Since marginal cost function is the slope of total cost function, the area under the marginal abatement cost curve and marginal damage cost curve depicts total abatement cost and total damage cost, respectively. In Fig. 17.4, the area marked 'a' is the total damage cost (TPDC) caused by a pollution level of P*, while the area marked 'b' is the total abatement cost (TPAC) of reducing pollution to P* level. The sum of these, a + b is the total cost from P* level of pollution. At P* level of pollution, the sum of total abatement cost and total damage cost are minimized. However, at P* level of pollution, TPAC and TPDC are not necessarily equal to each other. In Fig. 17.4, the area marked 'a' is not equal to the area marked 'b'. At E, MPAC = MPDC, which implies that the total cost of pollution, (*i.e.*, a + b) is minimum. Equilibrium requires the equality of MPAC and MPDC and not the equality of TPAC and TPDC.

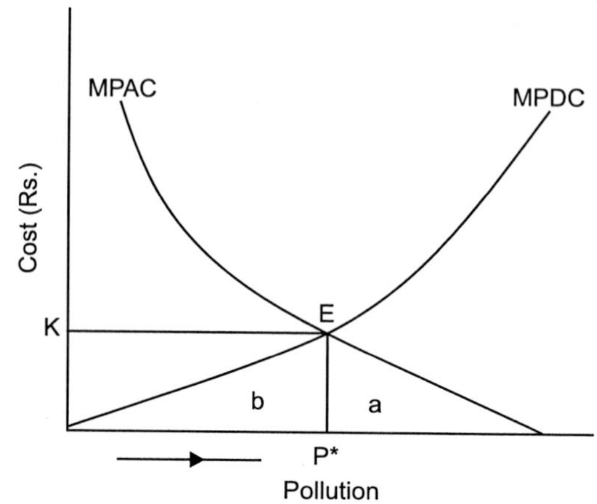

Fig. 17.4 Optimum Pollution

The various policy measures available to address the issue of pollution have been classified under four categories:

(*i*) Voluntary Measures or Moral Suasion.

(*ii*) Legal Measures—Command and Control (C & C).

(*iii*) Market Based Instruments or Economic Instruments.

- Charges/Taxes, Subsidies, Refundable Deposits
- Marketable Permits.

(*iv*) Government Production or Expenditure.

Table 17.1 Policy Instruments to Reduce Pollution

Policies	Direct Instruments	Indirect Instruments
Moral Suasion/ voluntary compliance	Publicity	Social pressure
Command and Control measures	Regulation of emission/effluent source specific, non-transferable quotas	Regulation of equipments, process, inputs and outputs
Market Based Incentives	Effluent charges, emission charges, tradable permits, deposit refund system	Input/output taxes, and subsidies
Government production or expenditure	Regulatory agency-expenditure for purification, cleanup, waste disposal and enforcement.	Development of clean technologies

Source: Eskeland and Jimenez (1991); Baumol and Oates (1975, 1979) Tietenberg (1990).

The various policy instruments mentioned in Table 17.1 have their own strengths and weaknesses. Many economists suggest that the various instruments work better in combination rather than as an exclusive instrument. Chapters 18, 19, 20 and 21 discuss the merits and limitations of the various measures in detail, with appropriate examples for each measure.

17.6 CONCLUSION

The concept of optimum pollution is very useful in designing the appropriate policy for pollution reduction, such as in the fixation of tax rates and standards. However, the difficulties in the determination of marginal damage cost, poses problems in fixing the efficient level of pollution accurately. Information on marginal pollution abatement cost is also not available. Hence, in practice, it is more appropriate to think of an effective pollution control method which achieves pollution reduction of a given amount at the least cost. Further, the optimum level of pollution explained above is the desired level of pollution. If the actual level of pollution is the same as this, then no pollution control policy is required. But this is not so in the real world. Hence, an appropriate pollution control policy is required.

QUESTIONS

1. Can optimum level of pollution be equal to zero? Justify your answer.
2. In the case of pollutants that are highly toxic, what is the optimum level of pollution?

EXERCISES

1. Draw MPDC curve for toxic pollutants.
2. Illustrate the impact of technological innovation on MPAC.
3. Illustrate cases when efficient level of pollution is zero.
4. Show that at the point of optimum pollution total damage costs need not be equal to total abatement costs.
5. Examine the change in optimum pollution level following shifts in MPDC and MPAC.

❑❑❑

18

Pollution Control Policy – II: Command and Control

> *We cannot command Nature except by obeying her.*
>
> **Francis Bacon**

The nature of environmental problems is a classic example of externality which necessitates government intervention. Individuals, producers or consumers, are seldom motivated to internalize the external cost they impose on third parties through their production and consumption activities. Hence, the need for government to design policy measures that would alter the behaviour of individuals and internalize the external costs imposed on the society. Traditionally, a set of regulations to penalize the polluter was considered as the most appropriate measure. Hence, in most of the countries, the first step towards control of pollution took the form of command and control, through enforcement of environmental legislation.

18.1 A GENERAL DEFINITION OF COMMAND AND CONTROL

Command and control refers to specific guidelines prescribed by a government or its agency, to the affected parties on how to comply with its mandatory requirements, *e.g.,* traffic rules.

Command and Control (C & C) instruments, also known as *standards* or *regulations*, are the most common forms of policies, in both the developed and developing countries.

18.2 COMMAND AND CONTROL AS AN ENVIRONMENTAL POLICY MEASURE

In matters relating to environmental protection, C & C refers to any regulation or standard set by the government to deter enterprises and individuals from undertaking environmentally unsound activities or actions.

Command and Control measures for environmental protection consist of a "command" which sets a standard—the maximum level of permissible pollution - and a "control" which monitors and enforces the standard.

Regulations are enforced at the national level or firm level or on an individual. Command and control measures take the form of environmental legislation, license requirements, or the reservation of certain areas or activities for a special class of industries. The failure to comply with the regulations generally sanctions legal punishment, such as fines or imprisonment. Since they are legally binding and have penalties attached for non-compliance, they can act as a sufficient deterrent to prevent unsound practices. These measures provide a strong incentive for compliance when the costs of non-compliance to individuals or industries are higher than those of undertaking the environmentally sound action.

18.3 COMMAND AND CONTROL AND STANDARDS FIXATION

Command and control regulations involve the setting of standards:

(*i*) A standard is a mandated level of performance that is enforced by law.

(*ii*) A standard simply makes excessive amounts of pollution illegal.

In principle, the government can set the standard to yield an efficient level of pollution control.

Standards may be broadly classified into two types—performance based and technology based. Performance standards set an overall target for each firm, or plant, and give firms some discretion on how to meet the standard. Performance based standards could be an ambient standard or an emission standard. Ambient standards set the minimum desired level of air or water quality, or the maximum level of a pollutant that must be maintained. It is a never exceed limit for any pollutant. Examples:

- Parts per million (ppm) of dissolved oxygen in a river
- Sulphur dioxide (SO_2) in an air shed
- Ground ozone levels (ppm).

Measures are often an average (*e.g.,* over a 24 hour period, or per year). This is important, as concentrations vary with the time of day and by season (*e.g.,* due to changes in weather).The level itself cannot be directly enforced. Rather, the sources of the pollution must be found and regulated to ensure that the ambient standard is met.

An "emission standard" is a performance based standard that specifies the maximum level of permitted emissions. An emission standard sets an overall target for each firm or plant and gives firms some discretion on how to meet the standard.

- Emission rates (pounds of SO_2 per hour)
- Concentration [parts per million of biochemical oxygen demand (BOD) in wastewater]
- Total quantity of a pollutant
- Residuals per unit of output (SO_2 per K Wt of electricity)
- Residual content per unit of input (sulphur content of coal)
- Percentage removal of pollutant (90 per cent of SO_2 scrubbed).

A technology-based standard specifies the "best" technology that must be used. A technology standard simply prescribes the technology or practice that a polluter must adopt. An example is the use of catalytic converters in autos, effluent treatment plants and the specification of stack height, etc. Standards could also be product standards specifying the characteristics that the product must have. Standards could also be input standards.

18.4 SETTING THE STANDARD

C & C approach requires setting the standard—ambient standard or emission standard. Economic theory holds that the criterion for a standard should be efficiency which requires that the standard is set at the level at which MPAC = MPDC (e* in Fig. 18.1).

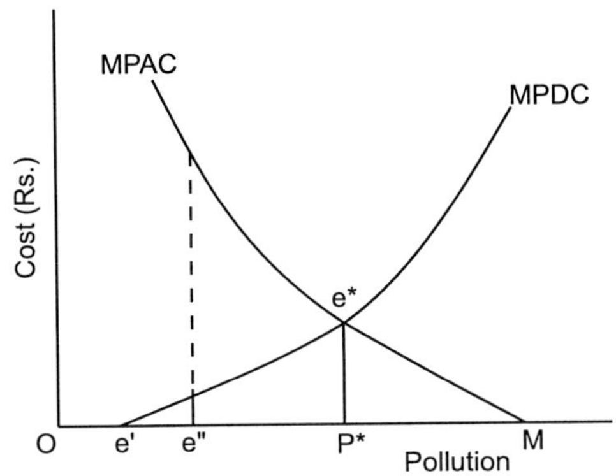

Fig. 18.1 Emission Standard

However, calculation of MPDC is very difficult. Hence, it is suggested that the standard may be set at zero risk level, that is, the level at which every one will be protected from environmental damages. This requires setting a threshold level. Fig. 18.1 shows such a threshold level. But defining threshold level poses problems.

For many pollutants, there may not be any threshold level *i.e.*, the marginal damage function is positive from the first unit of pollutant released into the environment. However, setting a standard at zero risk level is most appropriate in the case of highly toxic pollutants, such as lead and mercury.

Setting standards at a very low level, such as at e″, fails to include abatement cost and hence, may not be acceptable to the firms. The standard which balances both damage cost and abatement cost will lead to an efficient emission level. Such a standard for emissions is at P* in Fig. 18.1.

18.5 UNIFORM Vs VARIABLE STANDARDS

The next issue in setting the standard is whether standards should be uniform across firms. Uniform standards violate the conditions of both equity and efficiency, since the MAC of the firms differs. Equity here refers to the distribution of financial burden among firms. For example, if all firms are required to reduce pollution by 50 per cent and the cost of controlling pollution differs among firms, then the firm with a lower cost will be able to control pollution without strain but the firm with a higher cost may not be able to afford it. In such situations, allowing the firm with a lower cost to control more pollution is more equitable than imposing uniform standards. When costs of controlling pollution differ across firms, setting standards at levels that would equate marginal abatement cost of all the polluters will yield efficient and fair reduction in pollution.

Similarly, setting uniform standards overlooking local variations will result in inefficient control of emissions. For example, consider the task of setting standards to control mercury emissions in two areas, one, densely populated urban area and the other, a sparsely populated rural area. If it is assumed that the cost of abatement is the same in both the areas but the damages are severe in the urban area than in the rural area, then uniform standards will produce inefficient results in the urban area.

Uniform standards are preferred by the administrators due to simplicity in implementation. Uniform standards give the impression of being fair, treating all polluters alike. But in reality, uniform standards are neither fair not efficient.

18.6 MERITS AND LIMITATIONS OF COMMAND AND CONTROL

Command and control regulations were initially based on "end of pipe" solutions and ignored possibilities of reducing pollution through changes in the production process or changes in product design. C & C or the regulatory approach is most suitable when the economic activity is likely to result in irreversible damage to the environment or when the social cost of damages from the activity is very high. In such cases, the application of C & C is justified on the grounds of the precautionary principle. It is useful when there is uncertainty about the effects of pollution on the environment. Further, the political costs of standards are lower compared to economic instruments.

However, the C & C approach has several limitations:

(*i*) Difficulty in defining an optimal standard.

(*ii*) The requirement of detailed knowledge about industrial processes and polluting activities and the information and data required to design and develop effective standards, makes C & C a complex approach. The enormity of the statutes and associated regulations of C & C, pose problems of compliance with all the legal obligations applicable to firms

(*iii*) C & C is very expensive and defies the criterion of economy. It takes little account of the differences of pollution control costs between sources. Since the pollution abatement costs vary between firms, a regulation that requires all firms to comply with uniform standards is very costly and sometimes even counter productive.

(*iv*) There is no incentive for the firm to reduce pollution beyond the standard. C & C offers neither flexibility nor any financial incentive to firms in reaching the standards prescribed.

(*v*) It has been observed that command-and-control regulations force firms to shoulder identical shares of the pollution control burden, regardless of the differences in costs. Controlling pollution using technology based standards and performance standards set uniform standards for firms. Technology-based standards specify the method or the actual equipment that firms must use to comply with a particular regulation. For example, all cement factories may be required to install an electrostatic precipitator. This will make pollution control expensive (Stavins, 1997).

(*vi*) It is often said that command and control does not offer any incentive to firms to invent new and more efficient pollution control technologies. A business experimenting with a new technology may be able to achieve a higher standard of performance than before, but the firm does not gain financially from its investment, except that it will be able to reach the standard more efficiently than its competitors.

(*vii*) To be effective, command and control measures must carry with them, significant penalties for non-compliance with standards prescribed. Often, this is not the case, which renders the measures ineffective. C & C will work only if the penalties for violating standards are sufficiently high.

Strict enforcement is a must for the effectiveness of command and control. Command and control measures require elaborate structures for proper enforcement, which result in high administration costs. Many developing countries may lack the financial resources to administer the measures effectively. In Philippines, for example, penalties for non-compliance with rules are rarely levied, partly owing to bribe seeking behaviour on the part of the bureaucrats responsible for monitoring compliance with standards or giving out licenses.

BOX 18.1

Malaysia's Control of Palm Oil Mill Effluent

Palm Oil Industry (POI) is a significant contributor to the economic growth of Malaysia. Malaysia currently accounts for 51 per cent of world palm oil production and 62 per cent of world exports. The industry provides employment to more than half a million people and livelihood to an estimated one million people. The exponential growth of the palm oil industry not only brought with it export earnings for the Malaysian economy but it also caused a serious deterioration in the quality of water in Malaysian rivers into which the palm oil refineries discharge the untreated effluents. The pollution severely reduced the income of the rural poor in Malaysia and posed a threat to the poverty reduction programme of the government, enacted under the New Economic Policy.

There has been remarkable progress in the response of the Malaysian palm oil industry to regulations. Between 1978 and 1989, in spite of an increase in the number of palm oil mills from 130 to 254, and increase in crude palm oil (CPO) production from 1.8 million tonnes to 6.1 million tonnes, the reduction in BOD load increased from 76 per cent to 99.7 per cent; that is, the daily biological oxygen demand load released to public water bodies fell steadily from 563 tonnes a day in 1978 to just 5 tonnes in 1989. This reduction in BOD concentration was due to the introduction of a two tier effluent charge to complement the direct regulation rules. By 1991, 75 per cent of the mills reduced BOD concentrations to below 100 ppm and organic pollution was less than 1 per cent of its level when regulation began, even though palm oil production was at an all-time high. This was achieved through more stringent regulations that threatened mills with either suspension of license or closure of the mill for non-compliance with the regulation. The motivation to comply with the standards was the risk of being shut down for violating the mandatory standards.

Source : Vincent (1997), Khalid A.R, (1994), Kathuria and Khan (2002), Kathuria.V (2005)

Even though C & C appeals because of greater certainty of achieving a given effluent or emission standard, it is, in general, found to be deficient in a number of ways, due to higher cost of compliance and high information requirement. There is substantial evidence on the limitations of poorly designed and administered C & C regulations.

However, in certain specific instances of pollution, such as those mentioned below, there are no alternatives to C & C:

(*i*) Activities that involve highly hazardous pollutants which seriously affect life and health.

(*ii*) Situations involving adverse environmental conditions that call for immediate solution.

(*iii*) Situations in which non attainment of environmental targets would result in large risks (*e.g.*, storage of nuclear wastes).

Industries oppose the financial costs of meeting the standards imposed on them by C & C; they also resist the interference by the administrative agency that dictates the choice of their technology. Regulators are also not happy with the command and control measures. They complain that they have to constantly keep abreast of technological developments in many different industries. Moreover, the process of increasing standards over time, often results in conflicts between industries and administrators.

18.7 CONCLUSION

In spite of the objections, command and control continues to remain an important component of the policy mix. The various other measures, such as a pollution charge or permit, have not been able to replace command and control measures. World over, economic instruments have been introduced only as a complement to the command and control measures. The experience of many countries, such as the Republic of Korea and Malaysia (Box 18.2) has shown that the various market based instruments work better when used in combination with command and control measures.

QUESTIONS

1. Bring out the merits and limitations of the command and control approach in controlling pollution.
2. Is a uniform standard a viable solution for controlling pollution?
3. Comment on the desirability of : (*a*) High standards and weak enforcement (*b*) Relatively lower standards and strict enforcement.

EXERCISE

1. Visit the pollution control authority office in your city (or visit their website) and collect information on standards prescribed for various pollutants and check how far they are comparable with standards in developed nations.

❑❑❑

19

Pollution Control Policy – III: Taxes and Subsidies

> *If anyone intentionally spoils the water of another . . . let him not only pay damages, but purify the stream or cistern which contains the water . . .*
>
> **Plato**

Economists see environmental degradation as a result of the failure of the market system to assign any value to the functions of the environment and hence, they consider that the most effective means of dealing with environmental problems is to create a market for the various environmental resources and services, so that they are available only for a price; such a price will restrict the use of scarce resources. When environmental waste assimilative services are priced, the producer has the incentive to restrict pollution to a socially efficient level. For example, a tax on wastes (emissions/ effluents) will compel the firms to reduce the quantity of waste generated. The rationale behind economic incentives is to price the use of environmental services, providing incentives to the firms to adopt cost effective solutions to pollution control.

Environmental problems generally involve either overuse of a natural resource or emissions of pollutants. The general objectives of an environmental policy are:

- To modify, slow, or stop resource extraction
- To reduce or eliminate emissions of concern
- To shift consumption and production patterns towards greater sustainability.

The appropriate policy response to achieve these general objectives is to internalize the cost of environmental degradation. Regulatory approaches (C & C) are popular and have been adopted by almost all the countries in the world and have been relatively successful in controlling pollution. But the limitation of C & C is that they ignore market mechanisms, besides being inflexible and lacking in dynamic efficiency. The use of economic instruments, on the other hand, is observed to increase the overall efficiency of environmental policies.

19.1 MARKET-BASED INSTRUMENTS

Market-based instruments are policy instruments that use price and other economic variables to provide incentives for polluters to reduce harmful emissions. They address the issue of market failure caused by negative environmental externalities, such as pollution, by making the polluter internalize the external costs of production through taxes or charges on processes or products or by creating a proxy market for environmental services. MBIs are also known as pricing or fiscal instruments.

Market-based instruments (MBIs), such as taxes, charges, subsidies and tradable permits help to take account of the ***hidden costs*** of production and consumption on peoples' health and the environment, in a cost-effective way. These hidden costs include damage from air and water pollution, waste disposal, soil and species losses, climate change and floods, heat waves and the storms that it brings, and health costs. MBIs are known as market based instruments because of their reliance on market signals to bring about changes in the behaviour of economic agents through price signals. They are also known as **economic instruments** since they provide incentives to firms and consumers to integrate environmental concerns in their decision making. Supporting market based instruments, the OECD observes: "prices need to reflect the cost of preserving environmental quality, as well as other resources".

MBIs internalize the negative environmental externalities, either through taxes on processes or products, or by creating property rights and facilitating the establishment of a proxy market for the use of environmental services. MBIs offer the potential to achieve efficiency gains over more traditional regulatory instruments. MBIs include charges, subsidies, marketable (or tradable) permits, deposit/refund systems, and licenses. Economists recommend market based instruments, not as a replacement but as a complement to command and control measures and as a cost effective alternative to direct regulation. If properly designed and implemented, MBIs help to realize pollution reduction to any desired level, at the lowest overall cost to society. This is achieved by providing incentives to firms that can achieve these reductions most cheaply. MBIs achieve the targeted reduction in pollution efficiently by equalizing the incremental (marginal) cost of pollution abatement among firms, in contrast to C & C that prescribes uniform emission standards.

19.2 EVOLUTION OF MARKET BASED SOLUTIONS

The use of MBIs or economic instruments, to control pollution was strongly recommended by the Brundtland report, which emphasized the need for integrating environment and economics. Agenda 21 of the UN Conference on Environment and Development (UNCED) held at Rio de Janeiro, in 1992, defined the objectives of environmental policy as:

(*i*) To incorporate environmental costs in the decisions of producers and consumers.

(*ii*) To move more fully towards the integration of social and environmental costs into economic activities so that prices will appropriately reflect the relative scarcity and total value of resources.

(*iii*) To include, wherever appropriate, the use of market principles in the framing of economic instruments and policies to pursue sustainable development (Agenda 21, Chapter 8).

Principle 16 of the Rio Declaration stated that individual countries should endeavor to internalize their environmental costs through the use of economic instruments, emphasizing the polluter pays principle (Chapters 13 and 14).

19.3 TYPES OF ECONOMIC INSTRUMENTS / MARKET BASED INSTRUMENTS

Market based instruments can be broadly classified into three categories:

(*i*) Pricing environmental resources—green taxes that include emission or effluent tax or charges and subsidies.

(*ii*) Quantity rationing, like marketable permits.

(*iii*) Liability rules, like deposit refund systems and performance bonds.

Table 19.1 Economic Instruments for Pollution Control

Category	Instruments
Quantity rationing or market creation	Tradable permits.
Pricing or Fiscal Instruments	Pollution taxes, input taxes, subsidies, effluent charge, user charge, product charge, access fees etc.
Liability Rules	Deposit refund schemes to encourage recycling, environmental performance bonds.

Pollution Charges/Taxes

Pollution tax as a measure to combat pollution and to preserve the environment was suggested by the British economist, A.C.Pigou. Pigou's discussion on externality, referred to the sparks from a railway steam engine that set fire to surrounding woods, resulting in economic damages that included the cost of extra laundry cleaning, costs of artificial lighting necessitated by the darkened air and the costs of repair to corroded buildings; the total cost was estimated at £290,000 per year—about $10 million at today's prices (Roodman, D.M., 1997).

Pigou's prescription for the problem of externality is to tax the polluter—to make the people who create environmental problems, absorb the costs of the harm that they do. Pigou suggested that the revenue raised by the taxation of externalities, should be spent on generation of positive externalities *i.e.*, revenue from effluent tax could be used to maintain common effluent treatment plants in the industrial area. Pigou recommended a pollution tax equal to the marginal damage caused by the pollution. Pollution tax is often in the form of a charge—an emission or effluent charge. Even though the terms, taxes and charges are used interchangeably, they are different; the revenue from taxes goes to the treasury, rather than being earmarked for local or sectoral use. The revenue from a charge, on the other hand, is typically earmarked for specific purposes.

A charge is a price paid by the polluter for the use of the environment in general, and for polluting the environment, in particular. There are various types of charges—such as effluent charges, user charges and product charges (Box 19.1).

Effluent/Emission Charges, used mainly to control water pollution, are based on the toxicity and quantity of a firm's effluent. They are levied commonly on emissions and on the Biochemical Oxygen Demand (BOD) or on Chemical Oxygen Demand (COD) of the effluents discharged by the firm. The experience of various countries shows that the charges are deliberately kept low due to political pressure and pressure from industries, which resist higher charges and due to the concern that higher charges might encourage illegal dumping and evasion of the charges.

BOX 19.1

Defining Environmental Taxes and Charges

Environmental **taxes** are **any compulsory, unrequited payments to general government, levied on tax-bases deemed to be of particular environmental relevance.** Taxes are unrequited in the sense that benefits provided by the government to taxpayers are not normally in proportion to their payments. Requited payments to the government, such as **fees and charges** are levied more or less in proportion to services provided (*e.g.,* the level of wastes collected and treated).

Emission taxes involve tax payments that are directly related to the measurement (or estimation) of the pollution caused, whether emitted into air, water, or soil, or due to the generation of noise. Emission taxes generally deal with one type of pollution at a time. They are directed to those actually emitting a certain substance into the environment, and are usually only suitable for stationary sources because of their high monitoring and administrative costs.

Product charges or taxes can be a substitute for emission taxes when direct measurement of emissions is not possible. More generally, product taxes may be levied to price environmental effects correctly, and could be used to correct externalities other than pollution. A product tax may be levied on the units of harmful substance contained in products. For example, a carbon tax is based on the carbon content of each particular fossil fuel. The product tax may also be levied per unit of the product, if the objective is to reduce usage of the product generally. Product charges may be applied to raw material, intermediate product or final (consumer) product. When applied to consumer products, they are often called consumption taxes or final-product taxes. Consumption taxes may be used when pollution is closely linked to consumer demand, such as disposable products that compete with reusable alternatives, or non-fuel efficient cars. In this case, the taxation may be linked to the product itself or parts of its contents that are detrimental to the environment. When applied to raw material (*e.g.,* coal to produce electricity) or intermediate products (*e.g.,* polyvinylchloride to produce plastic), product taxes are referred to as input taxes. Emission taxes on production activities and input taxes are referred to as production taxes.

Source: OECD (1996)

Norregarrd and Hill (1999)

User charges are fees charged for using a resource or for being provided with a service. They are direct payments on treatment and collection of effluents, such as sewage and solid wastes.

Product/Input charges are charges on the products, the production of which causes pollution. A carbon tax and sulphur tax are examples of input tax, while the tax on fertilizer and pesticides are product charges. These taxes increase the price of these products (inputs), thereby discouraging their use.

Administrative charges are payments for administrative services, such as licensing, registering etc.

The logic behind an emission or effluent charge is explained in Fig. 19.1. In the Figure, MPAC is the marginal pollution abatement curve. In the absence of any emission charge, OM is the total emission. However, with an emission charge of OT, the firm will reduce pollution to OP* level, that is, emissions are reduced by MP* level. The total abatement cost to the firm is the area marked 'b' in the Figure. Along with this, the firm has to pay a tax equal to the area 'a' for the unabated pollution of OP* level (OP* × T). If the firm fails to control pollution, then it would pay tax on the total pollution of OM which is equal to OTRM. By controlling pollution to OP* level, the firm saves the area equal to 'c'. If pollution is controlled through regulation, which sets a standard of OP* level of emission as permissible level, then the firm would incur an abatement cost of SP*M or the area marked 'b' in Fig. 19.1 Hence, the polluting firms may prefer a standard to a tax, but society at large will be better off with a tax.

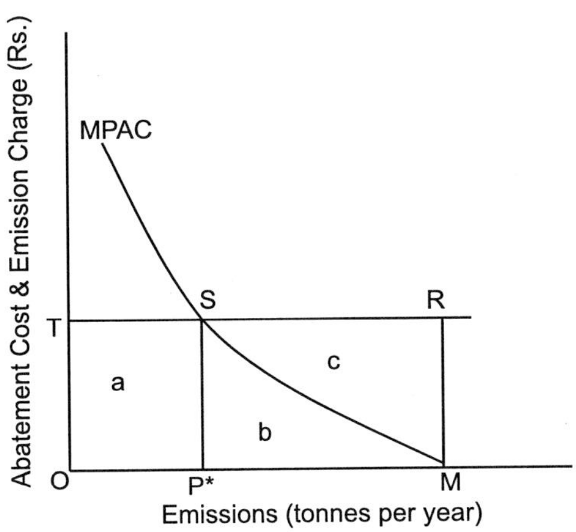

Fig. 19.1 An Emission Charge

19.4 LEVEL OF CHARGE

Efficient level of emissions is defined as the level of emissions at which the marginal damage cost of pollution is equal to marginal abatement cost of pollution, at OP* level of pollution as shown in Fig. 19.2. With an emission tax of T, emissions are OP*and the marginal damages are equal to marginal abatement cost (P*e). A better alternative to a flat tax is a two tier tax. A two part emission charge allows some initial quantity of emission to go untaxed, applying the charge on emissions in excess of this threshold.

In terms of Fig.19.2, if OP′ level of emissions is the threshold level, then emissions exceeding this are subject to a tax rate of T and emissions below OP' level are tax free.

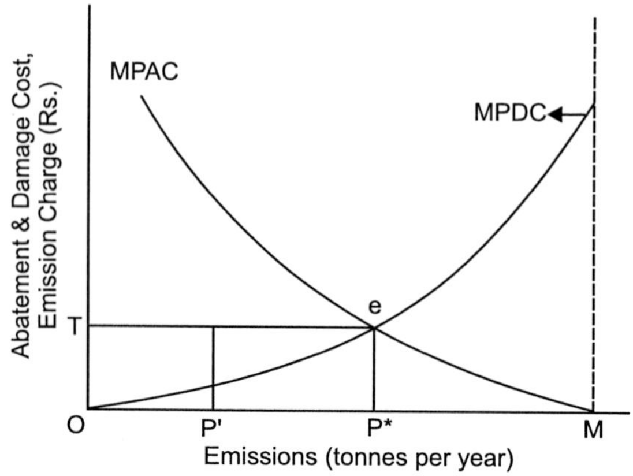

Fig. 19.2 An Efficient Emission Charge

19.5 EMISSION CHARGES AND INCENTIVES TO INNOVATE

One of the main advantages of a pollution tax is the incentive for dynamic efficiency, that is, an ongoing incentive to reduce pollution abatement costs. A pollution tax provides an incentive to the firm to innovate more efficient pollution control techniques. A tax requires the polluters to pay for residual emissions on top of abatement costs. It is this feature that provides the dynamic efficiency. In its constant drive for minimizing cost and thus maximizing profit, the firm searches for newer and more efficient technology of pollution control. Fig. 19.3 explains the impact of this incentive to innovate arising from a pollution tax.

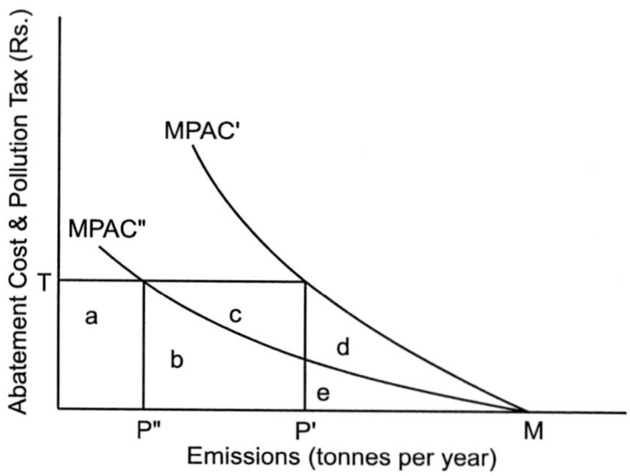

Fig. 19.3 Pollution Tax and Incentive to Innovate

In Fig. 19.3, MPAC′ is the initial pollution abatement cost the firm would have to incur with the current technology and MPAC″ is the cost curve after the firm invests in R and D to innovate more efficient technology/ method to control pollution. If the firm is subject to a pollution charge of T per tonne of pollutant, the firm will initially reduce pollution to MP′ level and pay tax on remaining pollution (OP′) that is not controlled. The total cost to the firm is d + e of pollution abatement cost and a + b + c of pollution tax bill. It is the tax on the remaining uncontrolled pollution that creates a dynamic incentive for further reduction in pollution abatement and innovation to reduce costs. If the firm is able to innovate new technology that will shift the pollution abatement cost curve downwards to MPAC″, and if the tax remains at the same level, then the firm will reduce pollution to OP″. In the post innovation period, with the new MPAC curve MPAC″, the total cost to the firm to control pollution to OP″ level is b + e of control cost and area 'a' of tax bill. Cost saving arising out of innovation is c + d. Thus, a pollution tax will encourage firms to invest in R & D to reduce its pollution abatement costs.

19.6 DISTRIBUTIONAL IMPACT OF POLLUTION TAX

The most important distributional impact of a pollution tax is on the price and output of the goods affected by the charge. A pollution tax is an addition to the production cost of the firm and hence, the firm will pass on at least a part of the tax to the consumer, depending on the demand and competitive conditions. If the tax is on just one or few firms in a competitive industry, then the firm will have to entirely bear the cost and may find itself in a disadvantageous position. In such an event, the labourers working for such a firm will be hard hit if the firm reduces its output, following the tax. If the charge or tax is applicable to the entire industry, then the tax will result in a price rise. By how much the price will rise depends on the demand and cost conditions.

Double Dividend Effect and Tax Shifting

Besides, the environmental aspect of the tax, currently, another attribute of a green tax, is the theme of a number of seminars and articles, namely, its revenue potential, which along with its environmental attribute, provides a double dividend potential to the pollution tax. A tax on pollution will not only make the firms account for environmental costs, but will also reduce the need for other taxes. It is observed, that in addition to reducing pollution, the revenue raised by a green tax can be used to bring about revenue-neutral reduction of other distortionary taxes, thus increasing the efficiency of the tax system. The environmental "dividend" of the green tax is complemented by an economic "dividend" due to reduced tax burden. This is the double dividend effect of green taxes. The green tax is therefore, supported on the grounds of lowering of some of the distortionary taxes (such as tax on labour) and the resulting reduction in the overall tax burden. This is referred to as environmental tax shifting (ETS). The double dividend effect, thus, provides incentive for shifting from taxes on wages and profits to eco taxes. Sweden became the first country to take up the idea in 1991. The government earned \$2.4 bln from new taxes on carbon and sulphur dioxide emissions equal to 1.9 per cent of all tax revenues and used it to cut income taxes. In mid 1990s, Denmark, Finland, Netherlands, Spain and UK, focused more on cutting wage taxes. Earmarking the revenue from a green tax for tax shifting is also questioned on the grounds that the environment is already in a critical state and hence, the revenue from a tax on environmental resources and services should be used only to clean up the environment.

19.7 ADVANTAGES OF A POLLUTION TAX

A pollution tax views pollution as a consequence of normal economic activity—consumption or production. This is in contrast to the C & C approach which sees pollution as a crime and polluters as criminals. Hence, for C & C to be effective, polluters have to be caught in action and their guilt proved in a court of law. Besides, the fine for non-compliance with rules, regulations and standards should be set sufficiently high to deter the polluters from polluting. If any of these steps is weak or overlooked, the measure becomes ineffective. It is not so with a tax.

Pollution taxes or charges are preferred over C & C on the grounds of both efficiency and equity. But it is the revenue raising potential that makes it popular among politicians. Thus, environmental taxes are a useful alternative and if properly designed and effectively implemented, have a lot of advantages over regulation, such as:

(*i*) A pollution tax achieves pollution control at the least cost, by equating the marginal abatement cost across firms. This is referred to as static efficiency of a pollution tax

(*ii*) Pollution tax promotes equity also. Firms for which abatement is not very costly, will abate more pollution than firms for which abatement is more expensive.

(*iii*) They give market agents (firms, consumers) freedom of choice over the method to control pollution, thus promoting cost effective pollution abatement.

(*iv*) A pollution tax also provides dynamic efficiency—"an ongoing incentive to reduce pollution abatement costs". Through innovation of cleaner production techniques and better abatement technologies, taxes provide firms with a continuous incentive to reduce pollution further.

(*v*) They provide revenue which can be used to reinforce the incentive effect or reduce other distortions in the economic system.

19.8 LIMITATIONS OF POLLUTION TAX

It is feared that green taxes may harm international competitiveness. Some eco tax leaders have therefore, granted tax exemptions to some heavy emitters of greenhouse gases, although such exemptions will impair the double dividend effect of the tax. For example, Finland has exempted the electricity sector from the carbon tax. Denmark "recycles" the yield from emissions taxes to industry and, in some cases, has replaced taxation with voluntary agreements. Norway has been considering scaling back its carbon tax, in response to falling investment in the oil sector. So, policy trade off between environmental goals and industries' competitiveness considerations have played a major role in the way green taxes are actually designed and used (Norregaard and Hill, 2000).

While environmentalists fear that a tax on pollution may become a license to pollute, the consumers of the product, (production which pollutes and is hence subject to a pollution tax) feel that the tax is inevitably passed on to them in the form of a price rise. The firms object to a pollution tax on the ground that it is a double burden on them since they have to pay tax, as well as incur control costs. This is not true, since tax is paid only on pollution that is not controlled and the firm can always reduce the tax bill by innovating better techniques of reducing pollution. Thus, in fact, a pollution tax promotes efficiency.

A serious limitation of a pollution tax is the measurement and monitoring of pollution. In the absence of required technology to monitor pollution it may not be possible to arrive at the appropriate tax rate. Data on pollution from various sources must be available to design an appropriate charge/tax. It is due to the absence of technology to monitor and measure pollution that developing and less developed nations have not yet introduced tax on pollution.

19.9 EXPERIENCES WITH POLLUTION TAX / CHARGE

Pollution taxes are becoming an increasingly popular instrument of environmental policy. Its spread has been gradual, yet there has been a substantial contribution from such taxes to both environmental protection and raising revenue. Box 19.2 briefly gives the experience of China and Columbia with pollution charges and taxes.

Pollution taxes are widely employed in Europe and are currently gaining popularity in many transition economies and developing nations too. Denmark, Finland, Italy, the Netherlands, Norway, and Sweden have carbon taxes. Norway, Sweden, France, Denmark, Italy, and the Spanish autonomous region of Galicia, tax sulfur emissions or the sulfur content of fuels. France, Italy, Sweden, and Galicia, tax nitrogen oxide emissions, but only the Swedish tax has reduced emissions. Germany, France and Netherlands have water pollution charges. In Czechoslovakia, Bulgaria, Hungary, and Poland, effluent charge systems were introduced much before the beginning of the economic transitions in the late 1980s. Malaysia was one of the first countries to have introduced effluent charges (in 1978) to control pollution from the palm oil industry. The Philippines has imposed environmental fees on wastewater discharge from industrial sources in 1997. South Korea imposes charges on ten air pollutants.

The experience of various countries suggests that the success of a pollution tax/charge depends on:

(*i*) A powerful institutional capacity to design and enforce the tax/charges.

(*ii*) Political backing.

(*iii*) Inclusion of all stakeholders in the design of the taxes/charges.

(*iv*) Low transaction costs of implementation.

(*v*) Earmarking the revenue from tax/charge for the development of clean technologies, installation of effluent treatment plants and pollution control devices, environmental awareness campaigns, capacity building and most important, to compensate the victims of environmental pollution.

(*vi*) Introducing the tax/charge after a pilot survey and giving sufficient time to the firms to prepare for the charge/tax.

BOX 19.2

Case Studies of MBIs

China's Pollution Levy

China's pollution levy is one of the few economic instruments with a long, documented history of application in a developing country. Article 18 of China's Environmental Protection Law specifies that "in cases where the discharge of pollutants exceeds the limit set by the state, a compensation fee shall be charged according to the quantities and concentration of the pollutants released". China imposes levies on 29 pollutants in wastewater, 13 industrial waste gases, and various forms of industrial solid and radioactive waste. Of the fees collected, 80 per cent is used for grants and low-interest loans for pollution control projects, and the remaining 20 per cent is dedicated to local administration and monitoring activities. The effluent charges have brought down both water and air pollution intensity during the period of rapid industrial growth in China since 1979. Each 1 per cent increase in the water pollution levy has reduced the intensity of organic water pollution by 0.8 per cent; each 1 per cent rise in the air pollution levy has reduced the pollution intensity of industrial air emissions by 0.4 per cent. The effluent fees are also a major source of revenue for environmental projects. In 1995, pollution levies were applied to 368,200 Chinese enterprises and raised about $460 million, or 0.6 per cent of national income.

Source: Robert N. Stavins, (2001) Experience with Market-Based Environmental Policy Instruments. http://ksghome.harvard.edu/~rstavins/papers/Handbook_Chapter_on_MBI.pdf

Columbia's Pollution Charge System

Columbia's charge on water pollution has been successful in generating funds for environmental activities, in addition to providing incentives for reducing water pollution. Each region sets its own pollution reduction goals, imposes national base charges, and tracks discharges for six months. The charge is applied progressively over five years, with six-monthly increases by pre-established amounts, until the regional environmental quality is achieved. The collaboration between the Agencies and local businesses and communities has contributed immensely to the success of the programme. The pollution tax has generated substantial revenues for the cash impoverished environmental authorities. Between 1997 and 2000, the environmental authorities collected 17.9 billion pesos (US$15 million). However, the revenue raised by the tax is less than half a per cent of total government tax revenues.

Source: World Bank, (2005).

19.10 SUBSIDIES

Subsidies are in many ways similar to taxes, yet they differ from taxes in crucial ways. In fact, many refer to subsidies as negative taxes. Subsidies have traditionally been used for economic or social reasons, for example, to support small industries, or to help develop vital infrastructure or to help marginal/small farmers etc.

The OECD (1998) broadly defines a subsidy as:

A subsidy is any measure that keeps prices for consumers below market levels or for producers above market levels or reduces costs for consumers and producers.

The WTO (1004) definition of subsidies contains three basic elements:

(*i*) A financial contribution, including direct transfer of funds (*e.g.,* grants, loans, and equity infusion) and potential direct transfer of funds or liabilities (*e.g.,* loan guarantees). A financial contribution also exists where government revenue that is otherwise due, is forgone or not collected (*e.g.,* fiscal incentives, such as tax credits); where a government provides goods or services, other than general infrastructure, or purchases goods; or where a government entrusts or directs a private body to carry out these functions;

(*ii*) The financial contribution must be made by a government or any public body, including sub-national governments and public bodies, such as State-owned companies;

(*iii*) It must confer a benefit.

Subsidies are used to modify market outcomes. A subsidy, through its effect on consumer and producer behaviour, leads to changes in demand/supply decisions. Subsidies are often aimed at:

(*a*) Inducing higher or lower consumption/production

(*b*) Offsetting market imperfections, including internalization of externalities;

(*c*) The achievement of social policy objectives, including redistribution of income, population control, etc.

Subsidies are the mirror image of emission fees or taxes. Rather than imposing charges on firms for their emissions, the subsidy approach offers incentives (in the form of cash payments) to firms for reducing emissions. Polluters who release emissions, forgo the cash payment. Environmental subsidies are financial incentives given to firms to discourage environmentally destructive activities and to encourage firms to behave in environmentally friendly ways. Subsidies can be used to encourage pollution abatement activities by helping firms to meet abatement costs. The main objectives of these subsidies are:

(*i*) To assist in the implementation of direct regulation

(*ii*) To support research and development in cleaner technologies

(*iii*) To assist firms, especially small firms, that face financial difficulties in installing pollution control equipment.

19.11 TYPES OF SUBSIDIES

A subsidy can be either a direct partial payment of pollution abatement cost or a fixed payment per unit of pollution reduction. When it is in the form of a reward for pollution reduction, it is seen as a negative tax. Subsidies could take the form of tax incentives (investment tax credits, tax exemptions/deferrals), grants and low interest loans designed to induce polluters to reduce the quantity of their discharges by investing in various types of pollution control measures. Often a subsidy is in the form of repayment of the cost of a pollution abatement equipment or activity such as the cost of an electrostatic precipitator or a catalytic converter or a scrubber or bag house. For example, the Government of India provides a subsidy of 25 per cent of the project cost subject to a maximum of Rs 5 million to firms to set up common effluent treatment plants.

Often subsidies offered to private firms are in the form of tax incentives rather than partial coverage of cost of pollution abatement equipment. For example, the Water (Prevention and Control of Pollution) Cess Act (1977), in India, offers a rebate of 25 per cent on the water cess payable to those industries that consume water within the quantity prescribed for that category of industries and also comply with effluent standards prescribed under the Water Act, 1974 and the Environment Protection Act, 1986.

Subsidies can be categorized under four heads:

(*i*) Resource-related subsidies—*e.g.,* Subsidy for fish cultivation, research about environment and eco-cycles, ecological farming, landscape conservation measures.

(*ii*) Energy-related subsidies—*e.g.,* energy efficiency measures, energy technology support, introduction of new renewable energy technologies, energy research, bio-energy research, grants for energy-saving technologies, nuclear energy, renewable energy or coal mining.

(*iii*) Transport-related subsidies—infrastructure subsidies, fuel tax exemptions and rebates.

(*iv*) Pollution-reducing subsidies—subsidies to set up effluent treatment plants and to install pollution control equipment.

Subsidies aimed at pollution reduction take many forms, such as grants, low-interest loans, favourable tax treatment, and preferential procurement policies for products believed to pose relatively low environmental risks. Subsidies are used to support private-sector pollution prevention and control activities, the cleanup of contaminated industrial sites, farming and land preservation, consumer product waste management, alternative automobile fuels, clean-running cars, and municipal wastewater treatment (NCEE, Washington, 2004).

19.12 ADVANTAGES AND LIMITATIONS OF SUBSIDIES

Pollution subsidies (carrot) are preferred by policy makers over pollution taxes (stick) because they ease the transition to a more stringent regulatory environment. Subsidies are mostly given to small and medium enterprises which find pollution abatement expensive relative to large firms, and hence, are at a financially disadvantageous position. In such cases, subsidies are justified on equity grounds. However, there are disadvantages in the use of subsidies as a pollution control instrument. Subsidies are likely to aggravate inefficiencies, by an increase in the polluting activity. Moreover, subsidies are a drain on government resources.

The main difference between a tax and a subsidy is that, with the tax, the government "punishes" the firm (polluter) by imposing a charge and with the subsidy they "encourage" the firm to improve its behaviour. However, a tax is considered to be more efficient than a subsidy. This is because, in the long run, a subsidy reduces the average cost of production, while the tax increases the average cost of production. A firm with costs above the market price may still be able to operate if they receive a subsidy, which is not the case with a tax. While subsidies are supported on equity grounds, taxes are supported on efficiency grounds. The effect of taxes and subsidies on output and price is illustrated in Fig. 19.4. While a tax decreases the output of the polluting output, a subsidy tends to increase it.

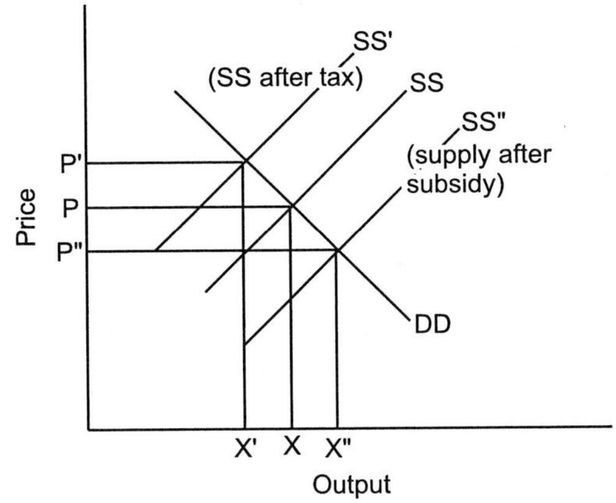

Fig. 19.4 Pollution Tax Vs Pollution Subsidy

A tax on polluting output, increases the cost and hence, the supply curve shifts upward, resulting in higher price (OP′) and lower output (OX′). A subsidy per unit of pollution reduction shifts the supply curve downward, resulting in lower price (OP″) and higher output (OX″).

Environmental subsidies are criticized for helping firms financially to bear the costs that should be the responsibility of the polluter. Moreover, subsidies give wrong signals to consumers and producers. Subsidies may encourage consumption of scarce resources and cause harm to the environment. For example, water subsidies in Egypt, encourage the cultivation of rice and sugarcane and discourage individuals from repairing leaking pipelines. By the time it reaches the Mediterranean, the Nile is heavily polluted and its flow is reduced to a trickle.

The WTO (World Trade Organization) also recognizes that some subsidies are desirable, and has provided an exception in the Agreement on Subsidies and Countervailing Measures to allow for certain subsidies to be paid to enterprises to meet new environmental regulations (up to 20 per cent of the costs of a one-time expenditure). In addition, there are also provisions in WTO rules that allow subsidies to encourage the spread of environmentally sound technologies.

Table 19.2 Environmental Subsidies in Select Countries

Country	Type	Description of the Subsidy
Indonesia	Tariff reduction	Tariffs are reduced on imported waste water treatment equipment
Korea	Direct incentives for pollution control and soft loans	Direct investment tax credit of 3 per cent (or 10 per cent for equipment made in Korea) of the value of the investment which is restricted to facilities for increasing productivity, energy-saving facilities, anti-pollution facilities, facilities for preventing industrial hazards and other specified facilities. Under the Energy Utilization Act of 1979, low interest loans are provided for a variety of energy-efficiency investments.
China	Tariff reduction	Reduced tariffs for pollution control equipment and advanced technology goods

contd....

Country	Type	Description of the Subsidy
Philippines	Tax exemption and tariff reduction	Exemptions of up to 100 per cent of import duties and local taxes are given on anti-pollution devices for industries covered by the Investment Priorities Plan. The Environmental Code enacted in 1977 allowed half of the tariff and compensating tax on imported pollution control equipment to be waived for a period of years from the date of enactment. The code also made available rebates for domestically produced equipment and a deduction for certain pollution control research.
Thailand	(*a*) Import and income tax exemptions for pollution control activities (*b*) Soft loans and grants from environmental fund.	(*a*) Pollution control equipment not produced in Thailand is exempt from import duties, and foreign specialists working on pollution control activities are exempt from income taxes. (*b*) Partial grants and low interest loans are made available from the Environment Fund to local administrations and private businesses required to set up treatment facilities. Other subsidies include the reduction of import duties to no greater than 10 per cent for equipment used for any treatment facilities.
Taiwan	(*a*) Corporate income tax deduction on pollution control equipment (b) Government offers and subsidies	(*a*) In 1981, the Taiwan government approved income tax deductions for corporations purchasing pollution control equipment or clean technology. A real estate tax concession is also offered for the relocation of a polluting facility and a number of other tax concessions are offered for pollution control investments, including duty free importation of pollution control equipment, corporate income tax reduction for purchasing such equipment, two year accelerated depreciation for pollution control facilities, and a 20 per cent profit tax reduction for R & D on pollution control. (*b*) The government offers a range of subsidies. Among activities eligible for subsidy are acquisition of land for waste treatment facilities and the installation of pollution control equipment
Indonesia, Korea, Taiwan and Thailand	Soft loans	With assistance from international donor organizations, firms in Indonesia, South Korea, Taiwan and Thailand can borrow for pollution control equipment and clean technology at favourable interest rates and other loan terms.
Turkey	Soft loans and tax concessions	Subsidised credit for relocating polluting industries to alternative industrial zones. For example, leather tanneries relocating to the Maltepe Industrial Zone were entitled to subsidised interest rates of 35 per cent for general loans and 22 per cent for construction and infrastructure investment. The Government has also offered a 40 per cent tax deduction on investment for tanneries relocating to another industrial zone during the first two years of estate construction and a 7 per cent reimbursement on investment for small and medium-scale tanneries.

Many countries have subsidies in the form of soft loans, tax concessions and income tax concessions for firms installing pollution control equipment. Besides, countries like Belgium, U.K., Portugal, Finland, Spain, Turkey, Japan and Finland, give subsidies for reforestation/ afforestation activities. Subsidies have been used extensively in the promotion of resource conservation. Most of the countries offer subsidies for renewable energy source power generation and energy-saving measures. Table 19.2 provides information on subsidies in different countries.

19.13 ENVIRONMENTAL SUBSIDIES IN INDIA

The Water Cess Act of 1977 provides for a 25 per cent rebate on the cess payable if the person or local authority concerned, installs a plant for treatment of sewage or trade effluent. It is an instrument for pollution abatement.

Customs or Excise Duties and Sales Tax Rebate

The customs duty on some specified pollution control equipment has been reduced to a concessional rate of 35 per cent. The countervailing duty has also been eliminated for such items and auxiliary duty has been reduced to 5 per cent. Since March 1992, a rebate of over 5 per cent has been allowed on excise duty of over 5 per cent. In addition to the rebate on customs and excise duties levied by the Central Government, certain states too have offered concessions on Sales Tax for specified pollution control equipment.

Depreciation allowance

In 1983, for the first time, a higher rate of depreciation was introduced for pollution control equipment as compared to 25 per cent applicable for the general plant and machinery. This 30 per cent was gradually increased to 100 per cent in 1993–94 budget.

Investment Allowance

A provision is available in the Income Tax Act under which a company can deduct up to 35 per cent of the actual cost of pollution control equipment for computation of taxable profit.

Exemption of Capital Gains

The Income Tax Act also provides for exemption of capital gains arising from transfer of building, land, machinery etc., for establishing business in a new place to reduce industrial congestion.

Subsidies are interesting policy tools in the environmental arena. They are popular with administrators because they can be a practical instrument in cases when other instruments are not feasible, *i.e.,* when it is difficult to identify the polluters. Subsidies are beneficial when they encourage producers to take action that is environmentally beneficial to the community as a whole and not simply to the producers themselves.

19.14 CONCLUSION

The use of market based instruments, such as a pollution tax and a subsidy help to internalize the externality by bringing about changes in the behaviour of polluters. This policy option is considered by many economists, as a more efficient and economical policy option, that promotes a fairer distribution of the costs of pollution control among polluters.

QUESTIONS

1. Examine a case of a pollution tax/charge on (*i*) air pollution (*ii*) effluent (*iii*) polluting input/output.
2. Compare a pollution tax with a subsidy.
3. Prepare a note on carbon tax and examine its scope as a global instrument to control climate change.

EXERCISES

1. Visit the web sites of UNEP, OECD and World Bank and prepare a chart of the various taxes, charges and subsidies currently prevailing in the different countries of the world.
2. Is it true that a tax on leaded petrol provides a larger incentive to reduce air emissions from motor vehicles than an annual tax on owning a vehicle?
3. Highlight the incentive that has encouraged you to adopt an environmentally friendly lifestyle.
4. Make a brief note on the adverse pollution subsidies in India. Do you think they should be eliminated?

❑❑❑

20

Pollution Control Policy – IV: Transferable Discharge Permits and Refundable Deposits

> *Economy and environment are the same thing. That is the rule of nature.*
>
> **Mollie Beattie**

A major cause of environmental degradation is the open access to many environmental resources, which are regarded as common property by economic agents. As a result, the users of these "free access resources" lack incentives to take into account the full costs of environmental degradation. Over time, this leads to degradation and depletion of more and more resources.

Economists see environmental problems as a consequence of absence of property rights to environmental resources, which gives the user the right to misuse the resources and this in turn leads to what Hardin referred to as "tragedy of commons" situation (Box 20.1). Economist and Nobel laureate, Ronald Coase, suggested that efficient use of resources may be achieved through definition of property rights for common resources. Permits are based on this principle.

The instrument of tradable discharge permits is one of several market-based instruments used in the management of environmental protection. While a tax on a pollutant, such as an effluent charge or emission charge, controls pollution by altering the relative prices of goods, the marketable permits scheme, on the other hand, gives producers/polluters, the right to consume environmental resources; further, it facilitates trading of surplus rights. The use of transferable permits has evolved as a key ingredient in the UN programme to control global warming.

Advocates of transferable permits argue that people tend to overexploit and degrade common property resources. Common property resources are those that belong to everyone and for which no private rights exists. In the absence of a market for the services of the environment (for resources and assimilative capacity), they tend to be overused. Tradable permit is a measure to protect such common resources from being exploited by restricting access to their use.

BOX 20.1

Tragedy of Commons

The concept of the Tragedy of Commons is extremely important for understanding the degradation of our environment. The concept was first explained by Garret Hardin in 1968. Hardin used the expression "Tragedy of Commons" as a metaphor to explain the problems of overuse and degradation of natural resources, including the destruction of fisheries, the over harvesting of timber, and the degradation of water resources. The basic philosophy of the concept of Tragedy of Commons is:

If a resource is held in common, for use by all, then ultimately, that resource will be destroyed. Hardin's analysis focuses on a pasture that herders use in common for grazing their cattle. Overgrazing of the pasture beyond its carrying capacity ultimately causes its destruction. In the words of Hardin, "each man is locked into a system that compels him to increase his herd without limit in a world that is limited. Ruin is the destination towards which all men rush, each pursuing his own best interest in a society that believes in the freedom of commons. Freedom in a common brings ruin to all."

Examples of Tragedy of Commons

- Harvesting timber on public land: each tree cutter knows that a tree not harvested this year, will be bigger, and hence, more valuable, next year. But he also knows that if he doesn't cut the tree down this year, someone else will.
- Harvesting whales in international waters: each individual whaler knows that harvesting an extra whale reduces the breeding population of whales and hence, the size of future whale populations, but he also knows that any whale he fails to harvest today, will just be taken by some other whaler.
- Environmental pollution: each individual polluter has no incentive to take into account the cost his pollution imposes on others.

Source: http://dieoff.org/page95.htm
http://oceanworld.tamu.edu/resources/oceanography-book/tragedyofthecommons.htm
http://www.coastalwiki.org/coastalwiki/The_Tragedy_of_the_Commons_-_The_Tuna_Example
http://people.oregonstate.edu/~emersonp/201/notes/22.pdf

20.1 PERMITS – DEFINITION

Transferable discharge permit is a quantity based or rights based economic instrument to protect the environment .They are a free market solution to the problems caused by negative externalities. They allow the government to define the overall level of pollution that is socially acceptable and then issue tradable permits corresponding to that amount. Companies who wish to pollute must hold permits equal to their emissions; companies can buy, sell and trade these permits on the market.

In simple terms, a tradable permit may be defined as a transferable right to a common pool resource. Tradable permits address the commons problem by restricting access to the resource and "privatizing the resulting access rights". For example, in the case of fisheries, such a restriction of user access implies a limit on the total allowable catch. Similarly, for water supply, a limit will be placed on the amount of water that can be extracted. For pollution control, the aggregate amount of emissions allowed in the relevant control region for the particular period would be specified (Tietenberg, 2002). The limit defines the access rights referred to as permits which are allocated to potential users according to some criteria (described later in this chapter). Polluters can bid for a permit that allows them to create a fixed amount of pollution. These permits are tradable and bankable for future uses. A tradable or marketable discharge permit gives its holder the right to emit at any location, provided the pollution by the permit holder does not exceed the prescribed limit. It creates a new type of property right—that of a right to discharge emissions or effluents. The total emission level is controlled by gradual reduction in the number of permits issued by the government. There are penalties for exceeding the limit prescribed in the permit.

The idea of establishing markets in pollution rights was first advocated by J.H. Dales in 1960 and the instrument gained popularity gradually. The basic idea underlying tradable permits was stated by Ronald Coase (1960). Coase suggested that regulation of pollution might be accomplished as effectively and efficiently by a market as by the more conventional forms of regulation. The Coasean solution to externality was to create a market for pollution rights through permits. The market for pollution rights acts as a proxy for the missing market (for clean air or clean water). In 1985, Bruce Ackerman and Richard Stewart strongly advocated pollution permits as an alternative to command and control. In recent years, the instrument has been more widely applied at local, regional and national levels to combat air and water pollution.

20.2 TYPES OF PERMITS

Denny Ellerman, classifies tradable permits into three forms:

(*i*) Credit trading

(*ii*) Averaging

(*iii*) Allowance trading

Credit Trading

Under credit trading, a polluting firm that controls pollution beyond the stipulated level earns credit for extra effort which can be transferred to another polluting firm. Credit trading awards exemplary behaviour and allows compensating regulatory relaxations of a common requirement. A distinctive feature of credit trading is that the regulator determines the credit worthiness of the activity and certifies that the credit-worthy activity has occurred and that the credit can be transferred. However, extra credit will not be given to a firm for what it would have done "anyway", since granting credit in this case, would lead to higher emissions by the firm to whom the credit is transferred.

Averaging

Averaging refers to automatic credit trading in which firms that do better than required in their permits, automatically receive credits that can be transferred to others without any question from the regulator.

Allowance Trading

Allowance Trading is also known as cap-and-trade, so called because of the absolute cap on emissions and the ability to trade emissions under the cap. Under this arrangement, firms are required to surrender a permit for every unit of emission discharged. No firm is expected to meet any specific standard. All that the firm has to do is to buy and surrender allowance for every unit of discharge. The regulator's task is not to specify an emissions standard, but a cap. This requires initial decisions concerning (*i*) An acceptable or optimal quantity of emissions and (*ii*) The limits to trading, both spatially and temporally. The rights to discharge are now explicit and must be allocated according to some pre determined criterion.

Emission trading in the U.S. has four programmes, designed with the common objective of increasing flexibility and reducing the costs of achieving the national ambient air quality. These are:

(*a*) **Netting:** This allows large new sources to be exempt from certain burdensome review procedures, if existing emissions elsewhere in the same facility were reduced, so that the net addition from the new source was below the level requiring new source review.

(*b*) **Offsets:** These allow a major new source to settle in an area that has not attained the national air quality standard, if the emissions from an existing source are reduced by at least what the new source is likely to add.

(*c*) **Bubbles:** The "bubble" policy allows firms to combine standards for several different sources into one overall emission level.

(*d*) **Banking:** This allows firms to reduce emissions below the standard and then "bank" the credits for future use or sale.

20.3 WORKING OF PERMITS – A SIMPLE EXAMPLE

Permits work by creating a market, where rights to pollute may be traded among the firms. If rights to use resources (pollute) are defined and offered for sale or traded in the form of permits to emit pollutants, then a market for pollution rights is created and the resulting price of pollution rights in such a market is expected to provide incentives to polluters for efficient pollution abatement. Each permit gives its holder the right to emit one unit of a specified pollutant (say a tonne) during the specified period. The pollution permits can be traded between the polluters. Basically, a firm that finds pollution abatement to be cheaper than buying permits will find it profitable to sell its permits to a polluter, who finds pollution abatement to be more expensive than buying a permit. The high cost polluter, on the other hand, will find it profitable to buy permits if the price of permits is less than its pollution abatement cost. Therefore, permit buyers tend to pollute, while permit sellers will control pollution and the overall environmental standards will be maintained because just enough permits are issued to achieve the prescribed aggregate standard. Trading permits between polluters thus minimizes the cost of complying with the standard. Marketable permits are referred to as quantity instruments because they permit a fixed supply of pollution.

The use of permits may be explained through an example. Consider two firms, A and B. Firm A has a lower abatement cost than Firm B. Let us assume that initially, in the absence of permits or any other form of regulation, the emission levels from the two firms, A and B, are 25 tonnes of SO_2 each, and hence there is a total pollution level of 50 tonnes of pollution. The government decides that only 20 tonnes of SO_2 may be allowed for each firm and hence, gives each firm 20 permits, each permit authorizing the permit holder to emit one tonne of pollution.

The firms have three choices:

(*i*) Reduce emissions to the level awarded by permits, namely, 20 tonnes.

(*ii*) Buy additional permits to emit more than 20 tonnes. Firms can probably buy four more permits and add it to their initial quota of 20 tonnes so that they can now emit a total of 24 tonnes.

(*iii*) Reduce emissions to a level lower than that allotted to it initially, and sell the surplus permits—that is, the firms can reduce their emissions to 16 units and sell the permit for 4 units. This option is exercised by the firm if its marginal pollution abatement cost (MPAC) is lower than the price of the permission.

In our example, Firm A, with a lower marginal cost of abatement reduces more pollution and emits only 16 units of SO_2 and earns 4 credits, which it sells to Firm B. Firm B now has 24 permits and hence, can emit 24 tonnes of SO_2, abating less pollution than Firm A. Total pollution emission falls to for 40 tonnes of SO_2 (two firms combined). Thanks to the policy of tradable permits, there has been efficient pollution control, since the firm with lower abatement cost has abated more pollution.

The supply and demand curves for the permits are illustrated in Fig. 20.1. The supply curve of permits is perfectly inelastic since the total number of permits at any time is fixed. The intersection of the demand and supply curve of permits gives the equilibrium price (P*) of permits as shown in Fig. 20.1.

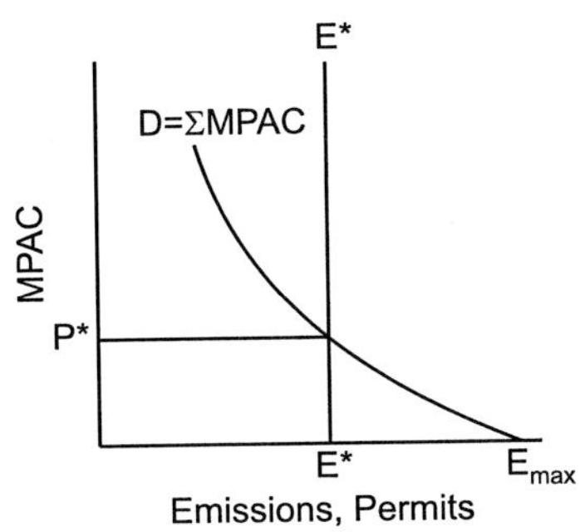

Fig. 20.1 Equilibrium in the Permit Market

20.4 DESIGN AND IMPLEMENTATION OF POLLUTION PERMITS

According to Revesz and others, (2000), the design and implementation of a tradable emission permit regime involves several steps:

The first step is the identification of the pollutant to be regulated, and the region over which the regulation will extend.

The second step is the determination of the aggregate level of emissions in a given year (or any other time period) that will be acceptable. Having determined the aggregate level of acceptable pollution, the policy maker then subdivides this amount into a number of discrete emission permits, each of which authorize the holder to emit a fixed amount of the regulated pollutant.

The third step is the definition of the bundle of rights that accompanies each permit, including their longevity, whether the government can eliminate the permits before their expiry, and whether the unused permits can be retained for future use.

Fourth step is the adoption of a mechanism by the policy maker for allocating these permits among prospective polluters. For example, it can distribute the permits to existing polluters according to their prior emission history—**the grandfathering option**. Alternatively, it can distribute all or part of the permits, through an auction.

The policymaker must devise rules for the subsequent trading of the permits in an open market. For example, the policy maker should make it clear whether emission permits may be purchased and held by non-polluters, either for investment purposes or to make them unavailable to polluters, as a means of improving environmental quality.

20.5 REQUIREMENTS OF AN EFFECTIVE PERMIT SYSTEM

The successful implementation of pollution permits depends on:

(*i*) Ability to measure, monitor and control accurately the total emissions for clearly defined pollutants in order to determine compliance.

(*ii*) Allocation of emission rights - who is entitled to receive how much of emission rights - is of great consequence. Allocation involves a two-level decision, first, whether to auction the permits or grant them gratis to various polluters.

(*iii*) The amount constituting pollution, the spatial and temporal relation of discharges to the harmful effects, and the potentially polluting discharge must be separately identified.

(*iv*) Adequate competition in the permit market to sustain a functioning price mechanism.

(*v*) Ability to set geographical limits on the market.

If the above mentioned conditions are fully satisfied, then in the presence of marked differences in pollution abatement costs and expected increase in pollution volume, tradable permits will be useful as an additional tool to combat pollution.

20.6 ADVANTAGES OF TRADABLE PERMITS

The major advantage of a tradable permits system is that it creates an opportunity for efficient exchange - one potential polluter can buy permits from another, leaving the total amount of pollution constant.

Efficiency

A permit system will reduce the total costs of meeting a predetermined environmental standard relative to C & C based regulation, since under the permit system, polluters with low costs of abatement will find it relatively easier to abate pollution, rather than buy permits.

Eliminates Uncertainty

There is no uncertainty regarding the achievement of environmental objectives, since the total number of permits in the market is fixed *a priori* and is equal to the target for total pollution. If a new pollution source enters the region, then the increased demand for permits will push up the price of permits and thus, the quantity of pollution will remain constant. This is a distinct advantage of permits in a dynamic economy. New plants can buy permits from existing plants and thus, permits make economic growth and environmental protection non-competing goals.

Adjustment for Inflation

Since price of permits respond to supply and demand of permits, inflation is already taken into account. This is a clear advantage over command and control, as well as over other market based instruments. In the case of taxes, for example, adjustments must be made to account for inflation, failing which the tax becomes ineffective.

Opportunities for Third Parties to Purchase Permits

A unique advantage of permits is that it facilitates purchase of permits by third parties, such as an environmental group which is more concerned with lowering pollution than an average individual. Environmental groups can buy permits and then not use them, as a way of protecting the environment. In this case, the purchase of the permits creates a major positive externality on the rest of society, since the environmental group expends its own resources to reduce the pollution created by others.

Equity

Permits allow fairer distribution of control costs among firms, in the sense that the firm with a lower cost of pollution control will abate more pollution, as long as the permits are not cheaper than controlling pollution.

20.7 PROBLEMS AND PROPOSED SOLUTIONS

Tradable permit systems work best where (OECD, 1991):

(*i*) The number of pollution sources is large enough to establish a well functioning market

(*ii*) The sources of pollution are well defined.

(*iii*) The amount of pollution generated by each source is easily computed.

(*iv*) There are differences in the marginal costs of pollution control among the various sources.

(*v*) There is potential for technical innovation.

(*vi*) The environmental impact is not dependent on location of the source and time of the year.

The determination of the overall permissible level of environmental standard, which is a prerequisite for the effective functioning of permits, is a problem. The determination of such standards is mostly based on some method of valuation of the environmental aspect under consideration. Most of these valuation techniques are beset with a lot of limitations, such as subjectivity of individual preferences, choice of discount rate etc. To that extent, the determination of the overall permissible level of environmental standard may lack precision. The number of competing agents is an important condition for the smooth functioning of the permit market. Too many or too few permit holders might create problems. While too large a number would increase the administrative costs, too few firms will act as an entry deterrent for new firms. Even though it does not matter to whom the rights are assigned, the initial allocation of permits creates problems. If allocated on an ad hoc basis, it creates distributional problems.

If permits are allocated by auctioning, it is feared that manipulations will create equity problems. Only the rich will be able to bid for natural resources - aggravating the wealth distribution problem, since a monopoly situation will be created in the market. Equity issues also arise under allocation by the method of "grandfathering".

20.8 EXPERIENCES WITH PERMITS

Marketable permits have not been tried in many countries. A few European nations and the USA have successful tradable permits schemes for pollution control. In Singapore, an auction mechanism has been introduced for the trading of ozone-depleting substances. Box 20.2 gives a note on some of the permit programmes in the USA.

BOX 20.2

Tradable Permits Programmes in the US

1. Acid Rain Programme (ARP)

The Acid Rain Program (ARP) was created under Title IV of the 1990 Clean Air Act (CAA) Amendments to reduce the adverse effects of acid deposition through reductions in annual emissions of SO_2 and NO_X. The Act calls for SO_2 reductions from all sources of 10 million tonnes from 1980 emission levels, largely achieved through a market-based cap and trade programme. The cap and trade programme imposes a permanent emission cap on SO_2 emissions from Electric Generating Units (EGUs) at power plants. NO_X reductions under the ARP are achieved through a programme that applies to a subset of coal-fired EGUs and is closer to a more traditional, rate-based regulatory system. The goal of the NO_X program is to limit NO_X emission levels from the affected coal-fired boilers by at least 2 million tonnes from the projected level, for the year 2000.

Findings:

- In 2007, for the first time, SO_2 emissions were below the ARP's long term annual emission cap of 8.95 million tonnes—three years before the 2010 statutory deadline. Total SO_2 emissions were 8.9 million tonnes in 2007.
- NOx emissions declined by about 3.5 per cent from 2006 levels.
- Acid deposition decreased significantly from levels measured before the implementation of the ARP in 1995. Surface water quality improvements in lakes and streams and related indicators from long term monitoring, show signs of ecosystem recovery.

Source: http://www.epa.gov/airmarkt/progress/docs/2007ARPReport.pdf

2. The US Lead Trading Programme

The U.S. Lead Trading Program was developed in the 1980s, to allow gasoline refiners greater flexibility in meeting emission standards. In 1982, EPA authorized inter-refinery trading of lead credits, in order to lessen the financial burden on smaller refineries, which had significantly higher compliance costs. Refineries that produced gasoline with a lower lead content earned lead credits. The permits were distributed on the basis of historical levels of gasoline production. In 1985, EPA initiated a program allowing refineries to bank lead credits. Firms made extensive use of this option. In each year of the program, more than 60 per cent of the lead added to gasoline was associated with traded lead credits. The program was terminated at the end of 1987, with the completion of the lead phasedown.

Source: Stavin (2001)

3. The US RECLAIM Programme

RECLAIM is a revolutionary new approach to air quality regulation, started in January 1, 1994, to reduce nitrogen oxide and sulfur dioxide emissions in the Los Angeles area. The programme was designed to achieve a regional 75 per cent reduction in nitrogen oxide emissions, and a 60 per cent reduction in sulfur oxide emissions, by 2003. RECLAIM encloses the facility in an imaginary "bubble". Rather than regulating each source, the total pollution in the bubble is regulated. Data from the first three years of the RECLAIM program revealed a "robust" trading market. Through December 31, 1997, there had been 1,200 trades, with a total value of $42 million. These trades represent the transfer of 244,000 tonnes of nitrogen and sulfur oxides.

Source:http://www.aqmd.gov/RECLAIM/reclaim.html

Evidence from USA and other countries which have a permit system in practice, shows that in most cases, the type of permit programme deployed has been cap and trade, and the initial allocation has been "grandfathered". Table 20.1 gives information on permit programmes in some of the countries.

Table 20.1 Permit Programmes in Select Countries

Country	Programme	Traded Commodity	Period of Operation	Environmental and Economic Effects
Canada	ODS[1] Allowance Trading	CFCs and Methyl Chloroform	1993–1996	Low trading volume except among large methyl bromide allowance holders
		HCFCs	1996 – present	
		Methyl Bromide	1995 – present	
	PERT[2]	NO_x, VOCs, CO, SO_2,	1996 – present	Pilot Programme
	GERT[3]	CO_2	1997 – present	Pilot Programme
Chile	Santiago Air Emission Trading	Total suspended particulate emission rights among stationary source	1995 – present	Low trading volume; decrease in emissions since 1997 not definitely tied to tradable permit system
European Union	ODS Quota Trading	ODS production quota under Montreal Protocol	1991–1994	More rapid phase-out of ODS
Singapore	ODS Permit Trading	Permits for use distribution of ODS	1991 – present	Increase in permit prices; environmental benefits unknown
USA	Emission trading under CAA	Criteria pollutants	1974 – present	Performance unaffected: savings $5 - 12 billion
	Lead Gasoline Phasedown	Rights for lead in gasoline among refineries	1982–1987	More rapid phase-out of leaded gasoline; $250m annual savings
	Water Quality Trading	Point/Non-point sources of nitrogen and phosphorous	1984–1986	No trading occurred because ambient standards not binding
	CFC Trading for Ozone Protection	Production rights for some CFCs based on depletion potential	1987 – present	Environmental targets achieved ahead of schedule; effect of TP system unclear.
	Heavy Duty Engine Trading	Averaging, banking, and trading of credits for NO_x and particulate emissions	1992 – present	Standards achieved; cost savings unknown

contd....

Country	Programme	Traded Commodity	Period of Operation	Environmental and Economic Effects
	Acid Rain Reduction	SO_2 emission reduction credits; Mainly among electric utilities	1995 – present	SO_2 reductions achieved ahead of schedule. Savings of $1 billion per year.
	RECLAIM Programme	SO_2, NO_2 emission among stationary sources	1994 – present	Unknown

Note: **ODS[1]:** Ozone Depleting Substances **PERT[2]:** Pilot Emission Reduction Trading **GERT[3]:** Greenhouse Gas Emission Reduction Trading

Source: Stavins (2002)

20.9 TAX Vs PERMITS

A permit is similar to a tax on many grounds, such as efficiency, economy and equity criteria. If that is true, there is no reason why many countries should prefer a tax over a permit.

Table 20.2 Tax Vs Permit

Criteria	Tax Vs Permit
Efficiency	Efficiency due to asymmetric information. Both require information on MPAC and MPDC and hence, both the instruments yield inefficient results. However, efficiency losses are the same under both and hence, both are equally preferred. Under tax and permit, there is efficiency loss due to non-competitive conditions in the output market. But the inefficiency is smaller under permits.
Ease of monitoring/ enforcement	A tax requires the monitoring of emissions only, while a permit requires monitoring of emissions, as well as monitoring of trade of permits.
Flexibility when there are changes	In the case of permits, once the target is fixed, then the trade automatically adjusts for economic growth and inflation. But a tax has to be adjusted for inflation and growth in the face of changes in the economy to ensure that the ambient quality is maintained at the desired level.
Dynamic incentives	Both tax and permits provide adequate incentives to innovate more efficient technologies to abate pollution. But under permits, the market has to be sufficiently strong. If the market is thin, incentive to adopt more efficient technologies are weak and tax scores over permits.
Revenue raising potential	If permits are auctioned, both tax and permits are the same in terms of revenue raising potentiality. If permits are distributed freely, then tax scores over permits in terms of this criterion.

contd...

Criteria	Tax Vs Permit
Equity	If permits are auctioned, the distributional impacts of a tax and permit are the same. If permits are distributed freely, then new firms may suffer and hence, taxes may be more equitable.
Impact on Competitiveness	Impact on competitiveness is less visible under a permit than under a tax.

However, empirical evidence suggests that a pollution tax is preferred over a permit. The experience of the developed nations, which have both tax and permits, offer valuable lessons to be learnt regarding the design and implementation of both the instruments. However, at present there is increasing attempt by countries to use pollution permits, particularly after the inclusion of carbon emission trading as one of the instruments to control global warming under the Kyoto Protocol. Table 20.2 compares a pollution tax with a pollution permit on select criteria.

20.10 CARBON EMISSION TRADING

Thanks to the Kyoto Summit on Climate Change, in the last few years, there has been a greater use of internationally traded pollution permits, with respect to greenhouse gases, particularly, CO_2. The Kyoto Protocol (1997) sets binding targets for 37 industrialized countries (called "Annex I countries") and the European Union for a reduction of six greenhouse gases (carbon dioxide, methane, nitrous oxide, sulphur hexafluoride, hydro fluorocarbons and per fluorocarbons) produced by them, to an average of 5.2 per cent from the 1990 level, over the five-year period 2008–2012. The Kyoto Protocol offers several flexible mechanisms to the Annex I countries to meet their targets. The Kyoto mechanisms are:

(*i*) Emissions Trading
(*ii*) Clean Development Mechanism
(*iii*) Joint Implementation

The Kyoto Protocol permits the transfer or exchange of emissions reduction among the signatory countries through the use of the flexible mechanisms. Accordingly, industrialized countries may transfer or acquire from each other, emissions reductions on a project basis through Joint Implementation (JI). The Clean Development Mechanism (CDM) allows emissions credits to be obtained from projects undertaken in developing countries. Finally, the Kyoto Protocol marks the creation of an international emissions trading (IET) system among the signatory states. The Kyoto Protocol also allows a group of countries to have an aggregate target by setting up a bubble.

Kyoto provides for a "cap and trade" system which imposes national caps on the emissions of Annex I countries. On an average, this cap requires countries to reduce their emissions by 5.2 per cent below their 1990 baseline over the 2008–2012 period. Although these caps are national-level commitments, in practice, most countries have developed their emissions targets to individual industrial entities, such as a power plant or paper factory.

International Emission Trading Mechanism

This facilitates trade between countries in the international carbon credit market. The concept of Carbon Credit trading seeks to encourage countries to reduce their GHG emissions, as it rewards those countries which meet their targets and provides financial incentives to others to do so as quickly as possible. Countries with surplus credits can sell the same to countries with quantified emission reduction commitments under the Kyoto Protocol. Each nation gets a limited amount of carbon credits, which are then made available to individual companies; the companies are then able to sell or buy credits from each other. In countries like India, GHG emission is much below the target fixed by Kyoto Protocol and hence, they are excluded from reduction of GHG emission. On the contrary, they are entitled to sell surplus credits to developed countries. Developed countries have to spend nearly \$300–500 for every tonne of reduction in CO_2, against \$10–\$25 to be spent by developing countries.

A country that produces more CO_2 than it can absorb, must purchase, "absorption ability" from another nation, thus creating a carbon credit in favour of the nation that sells the "absorption ability". Foreign companies who cannot fulfill the protocol norms can buy the surplus credit from companies in other countries through trading. Thus, the stage is set for Credit Emission Reduction (CER) trade to flourish. One Carbon Credit is equal to one tonne of CO_2 and is called a **CO_2e (CO_2 equivalent)**. Costs are between US \$10–40 per credit. The money gained from selling carbon credits will ultimately be used to give grants to further carbon saving schemes. The trading takes place on two stock exchanges, the Chicago Climate Exchange and the European Climate Exchange. CC trading can also take place in the open market. European countries and Japan are the major buyers of carbon credit

There are four stages in the earning of credits. The first stage is at the domestic level, where the project gets approved by the National CDM Authority (NCDMA). After the NCM's approval, the project is sent to the United Nations Framework Convention on Climate Changes. Subsequently, the project is reviewed by the executive board of UNFCCC. The project gets evaluated on every front and is then registered under UNFCCC only if it meets all the norms. Thereafter, certification is done for the reduction in emissions and credits are issued. Det Norske Veritas (DNV) of Oslo, Norway, well known in the field of ISO certification, was accredited by the UN to act as a validating body. The first organisation to get the accreditation, DNV has already won a few projects around the world. In India, DNV is in the process of validating 9–10 projects.

World over, a total of 64 million metric tonnes of CO_2 were exchanged through CDM projects, from January to May 2004. The value of the global carbon market went up by 80 per cent in 2007, as nearly 2.7 billion tonnes of carbon credits, worth •40.4 billion were traded during the year. According to the figures, Asia is the largest supplier of emission reduction projects, followed by Latin America, Eastern Europe, Brazil, Indonesia, Chile, and Romania. India is considered as the largest beneficiary of carbon trading, claiming about 31 per cent of the total world carbon trade through the Clean Development Mechanism (CDM), which is expected to rake in at least \$5-\$10 billion over a period of time. A recent analysis shows that India will stand to gain \$5 billion from carbon credit in seven years.

The demand for carbon credits is expected to grow for the following reasons:

(*i*) Because of the higher relative carbon abatement costs, it is predicted that OECD countries will fail to meet their Kyoto target by 2012. The relatively higher emissions abatement costs in these countries will make the purchase of carbon credits attractive.

(*ii*) Private companies in industrialized countries will increasingly be subject to "cap and trade" mechanism, such as the EU Emissions Trading Scheme which was started on 1st January 2005.

(*iii*) The Government will also have to buy Carbon Credits because they are responsible under the Kyoto Protocol for meeting their country's targets. It is said that OECD Governments and European Companies subject to the EU Emission Trading Scheme will be the main buyers of Carbon Credits.

Evidence from the application of tradable permits suggests that emission trading has several potential advantages compared to traditional regulatory approaches. Besides, permits also adapt to changes, a clear advantage over tax. However, the success of tradable permits depends on the availability of a well-developed administrative system for recording changes in possession of permits, monitoring emissions and enforcement. If these requirements are not met, the scheme will fail to be environmentally effective. Given that the common property attribute of natural resources is mainly responsible for the environmental problems we face, the problem is best solved through the use of well designed tradable permits that confer tradable property rights for the use of resources.

20.11 REFUNDABLE DEPOSITS

Deposit-refund systems or "refundable deposit systems" combine a front end product charge (the deposit) and a subsidy for recycling or proper disposal. The front-end charge (deposit) is combined with a refund payable when quantities of the substance in question are turned in for recycling or proper disposal. Deposit-refund systems require a monetary deposit (charge/fee) at the time of sale of a product. The deposit is returned when the item is returned at the end of its useful life. The fees are partly used to subsidize the administrative costs associated with the return, recycling and reuse of the products. Deposit-refund systems are most likely to be appropriate when the incidence and the consequences of improper disposal are high.

Worldwide, deposit systems are applied to help control the disposal of lead-acid batteries, to products such as beverage containers, pesticide containers, tyres, and automobile bodies and to other consumer products.

The two important objectives of a deposit refund scheme are to:

(*i*) Discourage illegal or improper disposal.

(*ii*) Divert recyclable items from the waste stream.

Deposit refund systems do not always require government mandates. When used products are valuable, as is the case for lead-acid batteries, the private sector manages a disposal system. Whether the refundable deposit system is managed by the Government or by the private sector, fees are charged as deposit, which helps to subsidize the return of valuable and recyclable products. Deposit refund system is the best policy option to address the hazardous wastes disposal problem. Deposit systems are commonly applied to beverage containers, pesticide containers, lead-acid batteries, and tyres.

One factor that limits the widespread use of deposit-refund systems is the additional cost incurred in collecting and refunding deposits on the sale of individual products, such as beverage containers and the additional costs involved in collecting and returning used products for disposal. But these costs are at least partially offset by the interest earned on deposits, unclaimed deposits, and sales of collected used products. The share of the deposit fee in the total product cost is an important consideration in deposit-refund schemes. If the deposit rate is relatively low, in relation to the product cost, then return rates are correspondingly low, while for a high deposit rate, the return rates are high. For example, in the case of refundable deposits for car hulks in Norway and Sweden, the system worked well in Norway and poorly in Sweden, because in Norway, the deposit in 1988 was ECU 130 per vehicle, while in Sweden, it was only ECU 42. While in both countries, a larger amount was refunded when the hulk was delivered, in Sweden the deposit and the refund were lower than the cost of scrapping. Hence, while more than 90 per cent of the disused cars were returned in Norway, in Sweden, a much smaller per centage of disused cars were returned.

20.12 MERITS AND LIMITATIONS OF REFUNDABLE DEPOSITS

Merits

(*i*) Achieves intended environmental goals – reducing littering problems and diverting solid wastes from disposal at landfills.

(*ii*) Achieves higher return rates than curb-side recycling programs and programs involving only collecting product user fees and charges.

(*iii*) Provides for the introduction of new technologies to improve collection and sorting as in the case of beverage containers pursued by the beverage industry.

Limitations

Administrative and transaction costs on the sale of individual products, and additional costs to consumers tend to be high.

Deposit refund schemes are cost effective schemes since they don't involve any monitoring costs and collection costs. They are also compatible with the polluter pays principle.

Deposit-refund systems on beverage containers, combined with product charges on non-reusable containers have been operating successfully in Finland, Norway, Sweden and the US. Evidence suggests that consumers are responsive to the level of the deposit. For example, in 1983 Sweden introduced a deposit of ECU 0.04 on aluminum beverage cans, which resulted in the return of 60 per cent to 70 per cent of the cans. A doubling of the deposit in 1987 increased the response—nearly 80 per cent of the cans were returned. Following the success of the instrument, several European countries have extended the system to other products, such as batteries, car hulks, and pesticide residues. Denmark and the Netherlands introduced refundable deposits for batteries with a high content of cadmium and mercury, to control soil contamination. Several countries are considering a deposit-refund system for car batteries.

Table 20.3 gives the various forms of refundable deposits in use in various countries.

Table 20.3 Deposit Refund Systems

Product Subject to Refundable Deposits	Country
Specified Beverage container – PET bottles and Glass Bottles	Australia, Austria, Barbados, Belgium, Bolivia, Brazil, Chile, Canada, Colombia, Czechoslovakla, Denmark, Ecuador, Finland, Iceland, Jamaica, Japan, Mexico, Netherlands, Norway, Sri Lanka, Sweden , Switzerland, Taiwan, United States, Venezuela
Auto Batteries	US (some states), Mexico
Scrap autos, car hulks	Norway, Sweden
Small chemical containers	Denmark
Tyres	South Korea
Plastic shopping bottles	Italy
Packaging Wastes	France, Germany
Refrigerators, Flourescent light bulbs	Austria
Air conditioners, Washing machines, Television and lubricants	South Korea

20.13 PERFORMANCE BONDS

A performance bond is similar to a deposit refund system. Performance bonds are fees levied upon companies that extract certain natural resources, such as timber, coal, oil and gas. Amount deposited in performance bonds is refunded when the payer fulfills certain obligations. According to Theodore Panayotou (1994) performance bonds ensure that:

(*i*) Resource extracting companies and potential polluters take adequate measures to minimize the environmental damage caused by their activities.

(*ii*) Clean up and restoration of residual damage takes place in the most cost efficient manner.

(*iii*) Adequate funds are available for the cleanup of waste and restoration of damaged environments by anyone who fails to comply. Since environmental bonds can be invested in interest-bearing accounts or replaced by bank guarantees, they are not a constraint on economic activity.

20.14 CONCLUSION

Creating a market for pollution rights to control pollution is a highly sophisticated instrument, mostly used by developed nations. This solution to the problem of degradation of the common property resources, through the use of permits, is based on Coasean property resource approach. It is only recently that some of the developing countries have also introduced the use of permits. The deposit refund approach is a very popular instrument which is in use in almost all countries. The various instruments discussed yield best results when used in combination with command and control approach to pollution control.

QUESTION

1. Explain the basics of pollution permits. Discuss its advantages and limitations.
2. What makes the refundable deposit scheme a market based instrument?
3. Compare a pollution permit with a pollution tax.

EXERCISES

1. Study the fast growing carbon trading market—both global market and Indian market.
2. Prepare a case study of a well functioning permits policy in a developed country and a developing country.
3. List out the various refundable deposit and other similar schemes in India operating both formally and informally.
4. Give examples of performance bonds.
5. Allowing any individual organisation such as an ENGO or any individual trade in transferable discharge permits in addition to the pollution sources themselves—Is this an advantage or limitation?

❑❑❑

21

Comparison of Pollution Control Policy Instruments

> *The earth lies polluted under its inhabitants; For, they have transgressed laws, violated the statutes, broken the everlasting covenant.*
>
> **Prophet Isaiah**

Environmental problems relate to the supply of natural resources when they manifest as over harvesting or over extraction of renewable and non-renewable resources. With high levels of pollution, they lead to deterioration in the quality of the environment. The objective of the environmental policy is to restrict resource extraction; reduce or eliminate emissions of concern; and to change consumption and production patterns to more environmentally friendly patterns. Irrespective of the policy chosen, the objectives are the same.

Careful analysis of the recent environmental policies in various countries raises issues that are important when making a choice among the policy options available for environmental protection. Although numerous policy instruments are available today, most of the countries still rely on command and control measures. In a theoretical perspective, environmental problems are the result of both market failure and government failure (Chapter 17). Hence, much of the discussion on policy instruments is conducted as if there were only two policy options for pollution control, namely, Command and Control (C & C) and market-based economic instruments (MBIs). The various policy instruments have been dealt with in detail in Chapters 18, 19 and 20.

The World Bank (1997) classifies the various policy approaches for pollution control into four categories: "Using markets", "Creating markets", "Environmental regulations", and "Engaging the public". Table 21.1 gives the World Bank classification.

Globally, there is a reliance on one or few of the instruments in the four categories as discussed in Table 21.2.

Table 21.1 World Bank Classification of Policy Instruments

Policy Instruments			
Using Markets	**Creating Markets**	**Environmental Regulations**	**Engaging the Public**
Subsidy reduction	Property rights/ decentralization	Standards	Public participation
Environmental charges	Tradable permits and rights	Bans	Information disclosure
User charges	International offset system	Permits/Quotas	Auditing
Deposit refund		Zoning	Labelling
Targeted subsidies		Voluntary agreements	Certification

Source: World Bank (1997)

Instruments such as subsidy reduction, targeted subsidies, charges and deposit refunds are easy to administer and implement and offer important fiscal incentives to the government. The fiscal incentives take the form of reduced costs for the exchequer arising from reduced subsidies; besides, fiscal incentives also include increased revenue to the treasury from charges. Creation of markets for natural resources where there is no market, by defining property rights, decentralizing and establishing tradable permits and rights and creating international offsets, promotes better resource management and encourages efficient use of scarce resources. Using regulations in the form of standards, bans and quotas are the most popular instruments with policy makers because of its certainty of outcome. However, empirical evidence shows that C & C is neither efficient nor fair and works well only when penalties for non-compliance are considerably higher than the firm's pollution abatement costs. The last category that includes policies such as information provision, labelling and community participation are now gaining prominence and play a crucial role in bringing about political commitment towards environmental protection.

Table 21.2 Use of Various Policy Instruments in Select Countries

Policy Approach	**Specific Approach**	**Country**	**Sector**
Using Markets	Subsidy reduction	Bangladesh	Agriculture—fertilizers
		China	Coal
		France	Undeveloped land
		Hungary	Irrigation and public water supply
		Indonesia	Agriculture, Agriculture—pesticides

contd...

Policy Approach	Specific Approach	Country	Sector
	Environmental taxes	China	Industrial pollutants and wastes
		Denmark	Agriculture, industry
		Netherlands	Industrial waste
		Philippines	Industrial wastewater
		United States	Ozone-depleting chemicals
	Taxes and Subsidies	Many Countries: China, Germany, Japan, Russia, United States	Energy
	User Fees	Costa Rica	Eco Tourism
		Brazil, Costa Rica, Indonesia, Malaysia, Philippines	Forestry stumpage fees, taxes, removal of subsidies
	Deposit Refund Fees	Many countries—See Table 20.3 in Chapter 20	
Creating Markets	Property Rights or decentralization	Cote d'Ivoire United States	Concession to private Water supply, Solid wastes
	Tradable Permits	United States Singapore	NO_x, SO_x emissions Ozone depleting substances
	International Offset Systems	Joint Implementation (Kyoto Protocol) US with Belize, Bolivia, Costa Rica, Honduras, Mexico, Nicaragua, Panama	Mainly in land use and energy
Using Environmental Regulations	Standards and Charges	Malaysia	Palm Oil Industry
	Quotas and Charges	Israel	Irrigation and public water supply
	Standards and charges with penalties for non-compliance	Malaysia Many Countries: China, India.	Palm oil industry Industrial Wastes
Engaging the Public	Information Disclosure	Australia, Indonesia Philippines	Industry energy efficiency labelling Industry Eco labelling
	Public Participation	Kenya, Philippines	Water Supply, Protected Areas

Source: World Bank, 1997 (Modified version)

21.1 COMPARISON OF ENVIRONMENTAL POLICY INSTRUMENTS

The various policy instruments may be compared on the basis of the following broad criteria:

(*i*) Economic considerations

(*ii*) Administrative considerations

(*iii*) Political considerations

Economic Considerations

While comparing environmental policy instruments on the basis of economic criterion, the basis for comparison are effectiveness, economy, efficiency, equity and incentive to innovate.

Environmental effectiveness refers to the certainty that the target for aggregate pollution reduction of the firms participating in the scheme is realized. It implies dependability on the instrument for achieving the prescribed target. Legal standards ensure that firms meet particular targets, but do not provide any incentive to go beyond the prescribed standards, once the standards have been met. The market based instruments, on the other hand, constantly motivate businesses to "improve their financial performance by developing technologies that allow them to reduce their output of pollutants". (Stavins and Whitehead, 1992).

Efficiency

Economic instruments allow and stimulate emission control to be concentrated where control cost is lowest. Direct regulation often prevents this. Uniform standards imposed for heterogeneous sources result in allocative inefficiencies. Regulation places a high cost on industry and impedes economic growth. Empirical studies show that control cost in the case of regulation can be twenty to fifty per cent higher than they are when economic instruments are applied.

Economy

Economy questions the relative cost of administering the various policy tools to achieve the objective of the environmental policy. Theoretically, market based instruments are said to be more economical than direct regulation. Direct regulation requires detailed laws to be framed, implemented effectively; further, monitoring of compliance with laws is required. Non-compliance has to be proved in the court of law before imposing suitable punishment/penalty on the firm for non-compliance. All these consume more time and resources than market based instruments, particularly a charge or tax on pollution, which requires just the definition of the tax rate. Hence, direct regulation is said to be more expensive than a tax or charge.

Equity

Equity refers to distribution of the financial burden of controlling pollution among firms. Direct regulation which sets a uniform standard for all firms is said to be more equitable than market based instruments. But this merit of direct regulation is only apparent, since by imposing a uniform rule, it requires the high cost firms and low cost firms to control pollution to the same extent. Market based instruments, on the other hand, will provide incentives for greater reduction of pollution by firms with lower control cost.

Incentive to Innovate

Incentive to innovate refers to the incentives available to the firm from the use of the various policy instruments for innovating pollution control technologies. Incentive to innovate is higher under market based instruments, since greater the emission reduction, lesser will be the tax / charge. Hence, firms constantly strive to reduce pollution control costs by inventing newer and more efficient technologies (refer to Section 19.5 and Fig. 19.3 in Chapter 19). Under direct regulation, firms have no incentive to innovate, since there is economic advantage to firms in reducing pollution by a greater extent than stipulated by law.

Administrative Considerations

This criterion refers to the feasibility of introduction, implementation and enforcement of compliance with the instrument. This depends on whether the instrument is compatible with the existing administrative framework and environmental legislation, without radical changes and without any additional bureaucratic costs. Bureaucratic costs include the amount and reliability of information that is necessary to design and introduce the instrument, time needed to inform and negotiate with the polluting industry, costs of implementing the instrument, such as costs of monitoring emissions, costs of inspection and the costs of enforcing compliance (Le, Thi Thuy Phuong, 2009). Bureaucrats and firms are familiar with the working of the direct regulation (C & C) since it is the traditional instrument. They are often found to have inertia towards introducing a new instrument which is not as direct as C & C. Direct regulation is particularly easy if it is in the form of a technology standard. The administrator has to just prescribe the appropriate instrument and check that the instrument has been installed and that it is in operation. Market based instruments, particularly a tax, poses issues of designing the instrument, which requires a lot of information on the damage and abatement costs of the firms, adjustment time for the firms to the proposed tax, and precise measurement of emissions. Permits require a well developed administrative system, capable of fixing the emission ceilings for a group of polluters and collection of information on sources of pollution and their potential emissions. Besides, the authority must keep track of the permit trades, so that it can compare a firm's emissions to its permit holding. Therefore, the authority needs to supervise the registration of permit trade as well. For these reasons, the bureaucracy tends to prefer direct regulation, over market based instruments.

Flexibility in Decision Making

It is held that MBIs require less bureaucracy and governmental intrusion into business decisions and provide flexibility to firms to determine the best way to reduce pollution. Under a system of MBIs, individual firms take the decision about the amount of pollution to be controlled and the tax to be paid, but in the case of direct regulation, the regulator decides the amount of pollution to be controlled.

Political Acceptability

The revenue potential of the market based instrument is one strong reason why politicians prefer MBIs over direct regulation. Further, politicians are cautious about the impact of their policy decisions on their vote bank and are generally reluctant to impose stringent regulations on firms.

21.2 PERFORMANCE OF THE POLLUTION CONTROL POLICY TOOLS

The performance of the different tools on the basis of various criteria have been summarized as in Table 21.3

Table 21.3 Comparison of Instruments of Environmental Policy

Criteria	Policy Tool		
	C & C (DR)	**Taxes/ Charges**	**Permits**
Effectiveness/Dependability	×	✓	✓
Static Efficiency	×	✓	✓
Dynamic efficiency—Incentive to Innovate	×	✓	✓
Economy	×	✓	✓
Equity	×	✓	✓
Incentive for maximum effort	×	✓	✓
Adaptability to economic growth/inflation	×	×	✓
Flexibility in decision making	×	✓	✓
Administrative feasibility/ease	✓	×	×
Political attractiveness	×	✓	✓

Due to internal constraints, different countries have adopted different measures for dealing with the same environmental issue. Many countries have complemented existing C & C with market based instruments, such as an effluent/emission charge and a few countries have introduced tradable permits. Reliance on any one policy instrument—whether market-based or conventional—is not appropriate for all environmental problems. Suitability of any instrument or a mix of instruments depends upon a variety of characteristics of the environmental problem, and the social, political, and economic conditions of the specific situation. Experience of various countries suggests that a combination of various measures works better than exclusive reliance on a single measure.

Performance of the policy tools depends on three important situation characteristics. These situation characteristics are:

(i) **Character of Pollution:** This includes severity/irreversibility of pollution and relationship between discharge and damage.

(ii) **Character of Pollution Control Process:** This includes availability of clean substitutes or the options to develop such substitutes, differences in pollution abatement cost among various polluting sources, complexity of the process and feasibility of monitoring pollution discharges.

(iii) **Character of the Target Group and the Market:** Includes size and level of organization of the target group, market form, presence of market imperfection, dynamics of the market form.

Table 21.4 Non-Suitability of Pollution Control Instruments to Various Situations

Instrument	Severity of pollution	Non linearity of pollution	Few substitutes/	Market imperfection	Innovations likely	Large variation in control cost	Complex process	Poor measurability of emissions	Poor accessibility of target group	Little competition	Dynamic sector
C & C: Emission standard						×		×	×		×
C & C: Design standard	×	×			×	×	×				×
Emission charge	×	×	×	×				×		×	
Product / input charge	×	×	×	×						×	
Tradable Permits (free distribution of initial permits)				×				×		×	
Tradable Permits (auction sale of initial permits)			×	×				×		×	
Deposit refund		×		×						×	
R & D Subsidies	×						×		×		×

Source: Adapted from Bovenberg *et al.,* (1991) in Kuik O.J *et al.,* 1997

Non-suitability of the various instruments to the various situation characteristics are given in Table 21.4. In this table, the rows represent various instruments and columns represent the various situation characteristics. A situation that is not suitable for a particular instrument is marked with an '×'. For example, we can infer from Table 21.4 that when environmental damages are severe, charges, subsidies and design standards are less suitable.

21.3 ENVIRONMENTAL REGULATION IN DEVELOPING COUNTRIES

Environmental regulation in developing countries is far more problematic than in developed nations, due to political, institutional and financial constraints and due to the priority given for further development and growth vis-à-vis environmental quality. The only advantage for the developing countries is the fact that they can learn from the vast experience of the developed nations. Any form of environmental regulation requires an institution capable of establishing rules of conduct for polluters, monitoring and enforcing compliance, which is lacking in most developing economies.

Five key constraints have been identified for the effective implementation of environmental regulations in developing countries:

(*i*) Priority for development over environmental protection.
(*ii*) Lack of political will.
(*iii*) Weak institutions (judiciary, legislative) for environmental regulation. Judicial systems in developing countries operate with long lags.
(*iv*) Shortage of fiscal and technical resources for environmental protection.
(*v*) Presence of large number of small scale units which have neither the technology nor the financial resources to abate pollution.

21.4 CONCLUSION

Almost all the countries in the world, developing and developed – first attempted pollution control with the use of direct regulation. The developed nations have complemented direct regulation with market based instruments as early as 1980. Since 1990s, there has been a shift towards increased use of market-based incentives to achieve environmental objectives. According to Theodore Panayotou (1994), the shift was prompted by four factors:

(*i*) The lacklustre performance of regulations in achieving the objectives of environmental management.
(*ii*) The high costs of administration, monitoring and enforcement of regulations, as well as the high cost of compliance with regulations.
(*iii*) The need to raise revenue to pay for these costs, as well as the costs of residual clean up, which have been substantial.
(*iv*) Increasing evidence that market-based incentives might accomplish the same benefits at lower costs.

The experience of developed nations is a good guide for developing nations. Ultimately, the experience of developed countries and an accommodation of local conditions and realities indicate which instrument and in what form might be appropriate. In the case of developing nations, the stage of development and associated constraints and opportunities, the country's cultural traditions and social organization, are critical factors influencing the choice of an appropriate policy mix.

The experience of various countries shows that the evolution of environmental policy follows a fixed pattern. Most of the countries start with an "easy to administer" instrument, such as the prescription of a technology standard. Economic instruments such as taxes, charges and permits are introduced when the nations are convinced of the superior qualities of the instrument and they have developed the necessary infrastructure for the use of new instruments. The gap before the introduction of more sophisticated instruments differs from nation to nation, depending on their level of economic development. There are conflicts arising from the use of various instruments – an effective and efficient instrument may not be politically attractive and may not appeal to industries who may try to prevent the use of such instruments by heavy lobbying with the bureaucrats. Nations have to take all these into consideration while designing their policy mix to control pollution.

QUESTIONS

1. Compare the various policy instruments to control pollution on grounds of efficiency, economy, effectiveness and equity.
2. What are the factors that determine the performance and suitability of the various pollution control policy instruments?
3. Outline with adequate examples, an appropriate pollution control policy mix for developing nations. What lessons do developed nations offer to the developing nations?

EXERCISE

1. Using the information on the use of the various policy instruments in various countries, give examples of the merits and limitations of the various instruments.

❑❑❑

22

Life Cycle Analysis and Cradle to Cradle Concept of Industrial Design

> *How can we support and perpetuate the rights of all living things to share in a world of abundance? How can we love the children of all species - not just our own - for all time? Imagine what a world of prosperity and health in the future would look like, and begin designing for it right now.*
>
> **McDonough and Braungart**

Life Cycle Analysis (LCA), also known as "ecobalance", and "cradle-to-grave analysis" is the investigation and valuation of the environmental impacts of a given product or service caused or necessitated by its existence.

22.1 DEFINITION OF LCA

LCA is a tool to evaluate the environmental consequences of a project or activity holistically across its entire life. The development of this tool emerged from the recognition of the fact that the products and services which a company provides will also have their own environmental impacts. It covers every stage and every significant environmental impact of a product from the extraction and use of raw materials through to the eventual disposal of the components of the product and its decomposition back to the elements. Life cycle assessment allows us to track the environmental impact of these products and services throughout their life (from cradle to grave) and identify areas of environmental damage. In doing so, it is possible to redesign products and production and distribution methods which will reduce environmental damage. This methodology, therefore, represents a very powerful tool in the strategies available to businesses to improve their environmental performance.

The immediate precursors of life cycle analysis and assessment (LCAs) were the global modelling studies and energy audits of the late 1960s and early 1970s. These attempted to assess the resource cost and environmental implications of different patterns of human behaviour. LCAs were an obvious extension, and became vital to support the development of eco-labelling schemes which are operating or planned in a number of countries around the world. In order for eco-labels to be granted to chosen products, the awarding authority needs to be able to evaluate the manufacturing processes involved, the energy consumption in manufacture and use, and the amount and type of waste generated.

LCA is sometimes seen as a controversial field of study. A detailed LCA research study may, for example, include mining, forestry techniques, energy and water use, air and water pollution, solid and hazardous waste production, damage occurring during use of the product (including an assessment of possible misuse) and the repair, re-use, recyclability and disposal of a product. For example, it might be used to assess the environmental impact of a polystyrene cup versus a paper cup versus a conventional pottery cup. Starting from the acquisition of raw material and the effects of the manufacturing process, and working throughout the product life cycle, from manufacture to disposal (including an evaluation of the energy and water used in washing the pottery alternative), the sum of net effects can be evaluated, compared and a decision taken about the option which causes the least damage (Welford, 1996).

Yet another example to illustrate the use of LCA in decision making is the ongoing debate over disposable diapers versus washable diapers which centres around the assertion that the disposable product is less desirable from an environmental perspective. It uses more natural resources to manufacture, and it takes up more room in landfills when discarded. On the other hand, the reusable diaper consumes energy, water and detergents every time it is cleaned for reuse. So what is the answer?

This is where life-cycle assessment (LCA) comes in. The life-cycle method considers the air, water and solid waste pollution that is generated when raw materials are extracted. It examines the energy used in the extraction of raw materials, and the pollution that results from manufacturing the product. It also accounts for environmental harm that might occur during the distribution and use of the product. Finally, LCA considers the solid and liquid wastes that enter the environment following the final use of the product.

The LCA process by its very nature is quite complex and detailed. It requires the active cooperation of suppliers and collaboration is a prerequisite for progress. However, since LCA has been taken seriously by businesses, there is increasing concern that it may become a non-ecological activity. For example, it is clearly in the interest of the suppliers of bulk commodities to draw the boundaries of LCA quite tightly in order to focus attention on those factors which are most easily controlled: wastes, polluting emissions and energy consumption. However, a full ecological consideration of product life cycles also has to take into account the impact of raw material procurement on biodiversity, endangered habitats, human and animal rights and non-renewable resources. Ignoring these issues may be convenient (especially to the agrochemical, petrochemical, chemical and mining industries), but it is not acceptable from an ecological perspective.

22.2 GOALS AND PURPOSE OF LCA

The goal of LCA is to compare the full range of environmental and social damages assignable to products and services, to be able to choose the least burdensome one. The term "life cycle" refers to the notion that a fair, holistic assessment requires an evaluation of raw material production, manufacture, distribution, use and disposal, including all intervening transportation steps necessary or caused by the product's existence. The sum of all those steps—or phases—is the life cycle of the product. The concept can also be used to optimize the environmental performance of a single product (ecodesign) or to optimize the environmental performance of a company.

Common categories of assessed damages are global warming (greenhouse gases), acidification, smog, ozone layer depletion, eutrophication, eco-toxicological and human-toxicological pollutants, habitat destruction, desertification, land use, as well as depletion of minerals and fossil fuels. The procedures of life cycle assessment (LCA) are part of the ISO 14000 environmental management standards.

22.3 APPLICATIONS OF LCA

The uses of LCA as set out by the Canadian Standards Association include:

Evaluation and Policy-making

(*i*) Supply information for evaluating policies that affect resource use and releases.

(*ii*) Develop regulations on materials use and environmental releases where a comprehensive inventory and impact analysis have been conducted.

(*iii*) Identify gaps in information and knowledge, and help establish research priorities and monitoring requirements.

(*iv*) Evaluate product statements of quantifiable reductions in energy, raw materials, and environmental releases.

Public Education

(*i*) Develop materials to help the public understand resource use and release characteristics associated with products, processes, and activities.

(*ii*) Design curricula for training those involved in product, process, and activity design.

Internal Decision-making

(*i*) Compare alternative materials, products, processes, or activities within an organization.

(*ii*) Compare resource use and pollution information with those of other manufacturers.

(*iii*) Train staff responsible for reducing the environmental burdens associated with products, processes, and activities, including product designers and engineers.

Public Disclosure of Information

(*i*) Provide information to policy makers, professional organizations and the general public on resource use and pollution.

(*ii*) Help substantiate product-related statements relating to energy, raw materials, and environmental releases.

(*iii*) Life-cycle assessment helps companies to look at all aspects of their operations and integrate them into the overall decision-making process.

22.4 ADVANTAGES OF LCA

Life Cycle Assessment brings with it a number of advantages often overlooked by traditional environmental auditing methodologies. The concentration on the product, rather than on the system, facilitates direct measurement of the environmental impact. Being directly linked to products also means that environmental strategy can be linked into the marketing system and therefore, marketing and environmental strategy become connected. LCA also widens the environmental analysis beyond management systems and site-specific production attributes which can so easily hide environmental damage up or down the supply chain. The product specific approach also aids environmental communication because of the clear link between LCA and eco-labelling.

A concentration on the product also helps to track the inputs going into the production process, track the source of those inputs and therefore, to help determine the possible impacts on developing countries and the concepts of equity and futurity. It is therefore, a tool which can more clearly measure progress towards sustainable development. Moreover, tracking the life cycle of a product forward enables us to say much more about environmental damage than can be done under a traditional assessment of production processes.

22.5 FOUR MAIN PHASES

There are four generally accepted stages in the LCA methodology:

Inventory

The definition of the inventory involves gathering quantifiable data relating to the material and energy inputs into a product across its whole life cycle and any associated emissions, discharges and wastes. This should relate to all stages of the product life cycle, from packaging, to distribution, use, disposal and decomposition. Resources used and emissions generated should be measured per unit of output produced. Although this stage may demand extensive research, particularly for companies which use a large number of inputs or who operate along lengthy supply chains, it is relatively straightforward.

Impact Analysis

Impact analysis considers how the information gathered on the working of the company, may affect the environment and it is therefore, much less straightforward than the definition of the inventory. It involves establishing the environmental impact of each of the areas documented under the inventory. This could be extremely complicated because, in many cases, the impact of an emission will depend upon the nature of the emission, the environment into which it is emitted and the interaction of a number of characteristics. The analysis should ideally cover ecological damage, human and animal health, habitat modification and lifestyle changes, as a minimum. The boundaries of this stage of LCA, will therefore be defined by the depth of analysis which is deemed appropriate, necessary and possible.

Impact Assessment

Once the scope of the environmental impact has been established, some measurement of this impact is needed. Impact assessment can be broken down into three distinct phases:

(*i*) **Classification:** This involves grouping the data in an inventory table into a number of impact categories (*e.g.*, human health, natural resources, ecological impact etc.).

(*ii*) **Characterization:** This phase involves the quantification, aggregation and analysis of impact data within the agreed impact categories. This leads to a number of impact profiles consisting of impact descriptions and associated measures.

(*iii*) **Valuation:** This phase involves the weighting of the different impact categories so that they can be compared. Impacts can be established both quantitatively and qualitatively. Quantitative impact assessment develops a list of the amounts of emissions and some measurement of their impact. In many cases, this is as much factual assessment as is possible in the absence of an element of subjectivity. An LCA at this point can provide an internal benchmark against which to compare future performance and is therefore of considerable use.

Improvement

The final stage of LCA represents feedback for improving the environmental profile of the product. In effect, the improvement stage demonstrates where the environmental profile of the product ought to be altered through redesign of the product and its manufacturing process. A formal and systematic appraisal of the product's environmental impact will often reveal areas where relatively simple fine tuning will reduce environmental impact.

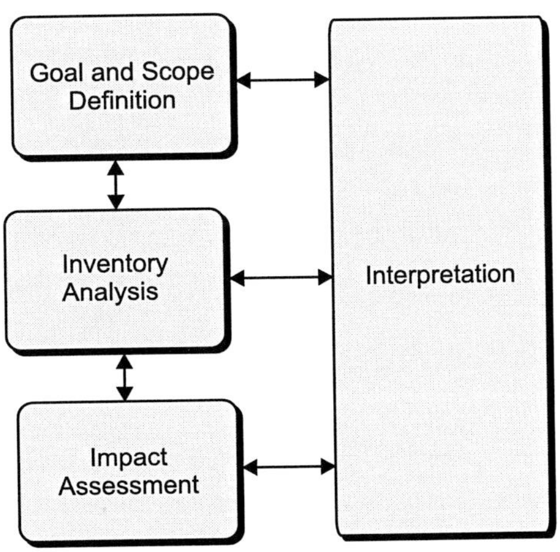

Fig. 22.1 Illustration of LCA Phases

These are often interdependent in that the results of one phase will determine how other phases are completed.

22.6 PROBLEMS WITH LCA

Conducting an LCA can be difficult and the outcomes depend on the scope and depth of analysis to be applied to the situation. This tool also creates other problems because of the judgment and subjectivity which is introduced into an otherwise objective exercise.

Problem 1: Parameters

A fundamental problem that occurs at the outset is deciding how far reaching the assessment should be. If we consider paper production, for example, should we consider the type of saw used for tree felling? An even deeper assessment might consider where the petrol comes from to drive the chain saw, who is the most efficient petrol producer, where the nuts and bolts came from for making the saw and what emissions are generated during its use. It becomes necessary to define appropriate levels of investigation and this can be defined in terms of primary, secondary and tertiary levels of analysis. These boundaries set the cut off points for analysis and must be agreed before any inventory is finally completed.

In the paper production example, we can consider the sources of wood used in paper production to be at the primary level, along with issues of distribution, processing, use and disposal. The environmental impact of the chain saw might be considered at the secondary level and the production of the chain saw itself as a tertiary level issue. The decision then relates to how much of the impact at the secondary and tertiary levels is to be considered in the life cycle assessment.

Problem 2: Comparison of Data

Data for energy can be expressed in joules, mass of physical waste can be measured in kilograms and air pollution in terms of parts per million. A problem arises when the environmental impact of these different measures are to be compared in terms of their impact on the environment. For example, is one extra part per million of an air pollutant more or less damaging than an extra kg of a waterborne waste, given the same toxic level? Any such comparison would seem to depend on a significant degree of subjectivity because it is impossible to combine all the inventory data into a single number that gives a weighting to all the possible unknowns.

The same sort of questions arise when comparing end products. For example, to what extent is it possible to compare two different technologies which perform the same task? Like the electric kettle versus the gas kettle. Where would we begin to make the sort of comparisons necessary to begin to form some sort of judgment?

Problem 3: Combination of Issues

How do we decide that disposal to the ground may or may not be more damaging than disposal to air or sea—we cannot really tell without a thorough investigation of the impacts on ecosystems in the short and long term. Moreover, one kg of waste may not cause much damage alone but when combined with other wastes and discharges, may react to cause a significant problem in the future. Thus, any comparison of wastes must consider timescales, the combined impact of other polluters' activities and must in turn, value different kinds of ecosystems in different ways. Therefore, any comparison of different effects must consider the direct and indirect impacts of a pollutant and might involve some scenario planning and analysis.

Problem 4: Disposal and Decomposition

A major problem in today's consumerist society is that when some products have been used up, it is economically and environmentally more efficient to throw them away rather than to use up the energy and other resources that might be needed in recycling them. However, what is rarely considered in this sort of analysis is the damage done to the environment in the longer term. If products are sent to the landfill sites, then we evaluate the disposal in terms of the cost of landfill and the loss of resources. It is seldom that there is estimation of the impact of decomposition, of landfill leakage which will in part be caused by our product and the effect of land use change. Extending the analysis beyond disposal to include decomposition effects has its own difficulties.

Problem 5: Assignable Cause

The LCA process and the quantification of environmental damage assumes that impact occurring as a result of the product belongs to that product and should be assessed and costed accordingly. However, where pollution is caused by a combination of impacts from two or more different products, which should be assigned that damage? It might be that one product's impact is negligible until mixed up with the other. Both owners of the product are likely to want to assign the damage to the other in those cases.

These five problems need to be gone into thoroughly and addressed at the planning stage of any LCA. They are very often difficult to reconcile but that does not make the LCA process ineffective or useless. In many cases, a change in the attitude or business practices towards ecological management holds the answer to the problem. In terms of the problem over assignable cause, the acceptance of strict liability would seem to provide an answer here. In terms of disposability, if we imposed the true cost of disposal and decomposition into the price of the goods, less may be bought. Moreover, if we put more emphasis on designing products which were worth repairing and reusing, then the issue of disposal is reduced. This in turn will result in the production of goods which are of high quality.

22.7 VARIANTS OF LCA APPROACH

Cradle-to-Gate

Cradle-to-Gate is an assessment of a *partial* product life cycle from manufacture ('cradle') to the factory gate (*i.e.*, before it is transported to the consumer). The use phase and disposal phase of the product are usually omitted. Cradle-to-gate assessments are sometimes the basis for environmental product declarations (EPD).

Cradle-to-Cradle

Cradle-to-Cradle is a specific kind of cradle-to-grave assessment, where the end-of-life disposal step for the product is a recycling process. From the recycling process originate new, identical products (*e.g.*, glass bottles from collected glass bottles), or different products (*e.g.*, glass wool insulation from collected glass bottles). This concept is discussed in more detail later on in this chapter.

Gate-to-Gate

Gate-to-Gate is a partial LCA looking at only one value-added process in the entire production chain.

Well-to-Wheel

Well-to-Wheel is the specific LCA of the efficiency of fuels used for road transportation. The analysis is often broken down into stages such as "well-to-station" and "station-to-wheel, or "well-to-tank" and "tank-to-wheel".

Life Cycle Energy Analysis

Life Cycle Energy Analysis (LCEA) is an approach in which all energy inputs to a product are accounted for, not only direct energy inputs during manufacture, but also all energy inputs needed to produce components, materials and services needed for the manufacturing process. An earlier term for the approach was energy analysis. With LCEA, the total life cycle energy input is established.

The LCA is an underused, under-researched and underrated tool of analysis. By forcing us to track a particular product (or service) from cradle to grave it compels us to widen our environmental dimensions. Central to the outcome of LCA, is the improvement analysis which enables us to redesign products to improve their environmental characteristics at all stages of the life cycle. As with most management tools, if LCA must be used effectively, there must be commitment to correcting the deficiencies which the analysis turns up and there must be a continuous process of improvement. Such an approach will need to be ethical and take an even wider view of the definition of the environment and sustainability.

22.8 CRADLE-TO-CRADLE ANALYSIS (C2C)

Cradle-to-Cradle design is a biomimetic approach to the design of systems. It models human industry on nature's processes in which materials are viewed as nutrients circulating in healthy, safe metabolisms. It is a holistic, economic, industrial and social framework that seeks to create systems that are not just efficient, but essentially waste free.

Human progress since the Industrial Revolution has been one big design error. In *Cradle to Cradle: Remaking the Way We Make Things* (2002), a book by the American architect, William McDonough and German chemist, Michael Braungart, there is a compelling explanation for why humans need a completely new framework for how we interact with the world around us.

According to McDonough and Braungart, current human technology is a product of "cradle to grave" design. We pull resources from the Earth, shape them into a product, use it, and throw it away". The problem, as humans have spread all over the planet, is that there really isn't any "away". Consider the typical "recycling" programme. What is presented to the public as a way to endlessly reuse raw materials, is in fact a downward spiral of degradation in material quality until, just as before, it becomes unusable. Sometimes, the recycling process itself produces additional toxic waste. These are measures that only aim to slow the destructive cycle. In the end, the result (ending up in a landfill) is the same.

Convinced that "Less Bad is No Good" McDonough and Braungart propound an entirely different strategy called Cradle to Cradle (C2C) Design that offers a compelling alternative. C2C design rejects the assumption that the natural world is inevitably destroyed by human industry, or that excessive demand for goods and services is the ultimate and inevitable cause of environmental ills. C2C Design takes its inspiration from Nature, in which there is no place for the concept of waste, but in which waste = food.

According to the authors, we can be "wasteful" only if the products we produce go completely back into Nature or are completely reborn as new products. Using a cherry tree as an example, they note how "wasteful" it is. Each year it dumps a great pile of fruit and leaves on the ground to rot. But all of this waste goes back into Nature to be reborn as new trees, bacteria, birds and other parts of the natural ecosystem. According to the authors, we should try to emulate this natural system, instead of trying to do more with less.

From an industrial design perspective, this means developing materials, products, supply chains, and manufacturing processes, modelled on nature's cradle-to-cradle cycles, in which one organism's waste becomes food for another. When designers apply this principle—waste equals food—to product conception and material flows management, they can begin to create goods and services that flow effectively within closed-loop systems, providing after each useful life, either nourishment for Nature or high quality materials for new products. Ultimately, the authors feel that C2C design can lay the foundation for a transition from products designed for a one-way trip to the landfill, to industrial systems that restore Nature, eliminate the concept of waste, and create enduring wealth and social value.

22.9 THE FOUNDATIONS OF CRADLE-TO-CRADLE DESIGN

The C2C Framework is based on natural systems which largely operate on the free energy of the sun, which interacts with the geochemistry of the earth's surface to sustain productive, regenerative biological systems. Human systems designed to operate by the same rules that govern the natural world can approach the effectiveness of the earth's diverse living systems, in which there is no waste at all.

Cradle-to-Cradle identifies three key design principles in the intelligence of natural systems, which can influence human design:

(*i*) Waste Equals Food
(*ii*) Use Current Solar Income
(*iii*) Celebrate Diversity

(*i*) **Waste Equals Food:** Waste does not exist in nature because the processes of each organism contributes to the health of the whole ecosystem. A fruit tree's blossoms fall to the ground and decompose into food for other living things. Bacteria and fungi feed on the organic waste of both the trees and the animals that eat its fruit, depositing nutrients in the soil in a form ready for the tree to use for growth. One organism's waste is food for another and nutrients flow indefinitely in cradle-to-cradle cycles of birth, decay and rebirth. In other words, waste equals food.

Understanding these regenerative systems allows engineers and designers to recognize that all materials can be designed as nutrients that flow through natural or designed metabolisms. While nature's nutrient cycles comprise the biological metabolism, the technical metabolism is designed to mirror them; it is a closed-loop system in which valuable, high-tech synthetics and mineral resources circulate in cycles of production, use, recovery and re-manufacture.

Within this cradle-to-cradle framework, designers and engineers can use scientific assessments to select safe materials and optimize products and services, creating closed-loop material flows that are inherently benign and sustaining. Materials designed as biological nutrients, such as textiles and packaging made from natural fibers, can biodegrade safely and restore soil after use. Materials designed as technical nutrients, such as carpet yarns made from synthetics that can be repeatedly depolymerized and repolymerized, providing high quality, high-tech ingredients for generation after generation of synthetic products.

(ii) **Use Current Solar Income:** Living things thrive on the energy of the sun. Trees and plants manufacture food from sunlight, an elegant, effective system that uses the earth's unrivalled and continuous source of energy income. With a little innovation and creativity, human energy systems can be nearly as effective. Cradle-to-Cradle systems—from buildings to manufacturing processes—tap into current solar income, using direct solar energy collection or passive solar processes, such as daylighting, which makes effective use of natural light. Wind power—thermal flows fueled by sunlight—can also be tapped.

(iii) **Celebrate Diversity:** Nature's diversity provides many models for human designs. When designers celebrate diversity, they tailor designs to maximize their positive effects on the particular niche in which they will be implemented. Engineers might profit from this principle by considering the C2C maxim, "All sustainability is local". In other words, optimal sustainable design solutions draw information from and ultimately "fit" within local natural systems. They express an understanding of ecological relationships and enhance the local landscape where possible. They draw on local energy and material flows. They take into account, both the distant effects of local actions and the local effects of distant actions. The point is this: rather than offering the one-size-fits-all solutions of conventional engineering, designs that celebrate and support diversity and locality grow ever more effective and sustaining as they engage natural systems.

Another simple example is that of a disposable cup, drink bottle, packaging or wrapper, made entirely out of biological materials; when the user has finished with the item it can be disposed off and returned to the natural environment. The cost of disposal of waste - such as landfill charges and recycling costs—is eliminated. The user could also potentially return the item for a refund so that it can be used again.

22.10 C2C CERTIFICATION

The C2C certification mark is the brainchild of McDonough and Braungart to help bring about a new Industrial Revolution: the reinvention of industrial processes to produce clean solutions and create an industry where "everything is reused—either returned to the soil as nontoxic 'biological nutrients,' or returned to industry as 'technical nutrients' that can be infinitely recycled."

CM

CERTIFIED

Cradletocradle

GOLD

The C2C certification trademark (silver, gold or platinum level) distinguishes products, the entire life cycles of which are based on sustainable design.
(Courtesy: W. McDonough and M. Braungart)

Fig. 22.2 C2C certification Trademark

22.11 SOME EXAMPLES OF C2C DESIGN

There are many examples of industry switching to C2C Design and profiting by it as well.

(*i*) Moved by environmental concerns, Pendleton Wollen Mills (USA) conceived an ecologically intelligent baby wool blanket. Most wool products are dyed with chemicals that are harmful to human health, which makes recycling of any kind problematic. But working with McDonough Braungart Design Chemistry, Pendleton assessed every ingredient in the dyeing and fixing processes and created a completely safe, perfectly biodegradable product—infants can literally eat the blanket—and when it wears out, it can be tossed into the garden to become food for the soil. The blanket is also a model of thrift and social value, a profitable product that requires no regulations and carries no hidden costs for waste management or health care. It turns on its head, the notion that ecologically intelligent design is expensive.

(*ii*) In 2002, the Swiss textile manufacturer, Rohner Textil, made headlines, cut costs and won new business when they used C2C design principles to produce a biodegradable upholstery fabric that they describe as "safe enough to eat".

While Rohner's textile mills already complied with Swiss environmental regulations, its fabric trimmings had been declared hazardous waste. To produce the new fabric, a fundamental re-design took place in every aspect of production, from the factory work space, to the elimination of all toxic dyes and chemicals, to the sourcing of raw materials. It is woven from the wool of free-range New Zealand sheep and from *ramie*, an organically grown fibre from the Philippines. The manufacturing process generates no pollutants. Extensive testing identified just 16 out of 1,600 colour dyes that met the C2C's sustainability criteria. As a result, Rohner claims that its factory waste water now tests cleaner than the water coming into the plant. The fabric trimmings are recycled with a consortium of strawberry farms, which use the biodegradable scrap as mulch for ground cover and plant insulation. Moreover, the elimination of regulatory paperwork, reduced production overheads by 20 per cent.

William McDonough notes: "Not only did our new design process bypass the traditional responses to environmental problems (reduce, reuse, recycle), it also eliminated the need for regulation, something that any businessperson will appreciate as extremely valuable."

(*iii*) A hypothetical example of C2C design is that of a shoe which is designed and mass produced. The sole might be made of "technical nutrients" (synthetic material) while the upper parts might be made of "biological nutrients" (organic material). The shoe is mass produced at a manufacturing plant which utilizes its waste material by putting it back into the cycle, such as using off-cuts from the rubber soles to make more soles, rather than merely dispose of them (this is dependent on the technical materials not losing their quality as they are reused). Once the shoes have been manufactured, they are distributed to retail outlets, where the customer buys the shoe at a fraction of the price they would normally pay for a shoe of comparable quality; the customer is only paying for the use of the materials in the shoe for the period of time that he will be using the shoe. When he outgrows the shoe, or it breaks or is damaged, he returns it to the manufacturer. The manufacturer separates the sole from the upper parts (separating the technical and biological nutrients); the biological nutrients are returned to the natural environment, while the technical nutrients are used to create the sole of another shoe.

By 2012, McDonough and Braungart are hopeful of seeing millions of designs such as these, celebrating life in diverse and wonderful ways and creating a world in which all children are nourished with fresh healthy food, affordable health care, and a generous prosperity that honours the laws of Nature. Instead of a world of laments, a world full of hope for the future and respect for the Earth's abundant gifts.

22.12 THE TRIPLE BOTTOM LINE – TO TRIPLE TOP LINE

The triple bottom line, a concept developed by John Elkington, has been, and remains, a useful tool for integrating sustainability into the business agenda. Balancing traditional economic goals with social and environmental concerns, it has created a new measure of corporate performance. Unfortunately, in ways Elkington did not intend, the triple bottom line often becomes a measure of the degree to which a company has minimized its liability.

McDonough and Braungart have modified Elkington's concept of the triple bottom line, to come up with a new concept which they call the triple top line, which moves accountability to the beginning of the design process, assigning value to a multiplicity of economic, ecological and social questions that enhance product value. When asked upfront, these questions can drive intelligent product development and lead to design decisions that yield positive effects, rather than limited liabilities.

A business strategy focused solely on the bottom line, however, can obscure opportunities to pursue innovation and create value in the design process. The new design perspective embodied in the Triple Top Line, creates products that enhance the well being of nature and culture while generating economic value. Design for the triple top line follows the laws of nature, to give industry the tools to develop systems that safely generate prosperity. In these new human systems, materials become food for the soil or flow back to industry forever. Value and quality are embodied in products, processes and facilities so intelligently designed, that they leave footprints to delight in, rather than lament. When the principles of ecologically intelligent design are widely applied, both nature and commerce can thrive and grow.

Braungart and McDonough feel that rather than trying to limit economic growth or reduce the impact of industry, they are creating the foundation of a system in which products and industrial processes are so intelligently designed, they don't need to be regulated. Instead, they create wholly positive effects, a large and beneficial ecological footprint. This could be called the new world of commerce, sustaining rather than sustainable, which suggests a more fulfilling agenda than the maintenance of a damaging system.

When good design drives the business agenda, the path toward sustainability turns from trying to be "less bad", to identifying new opportunities to generate a wide spectrum of value. This change of perspective could be called a shift from the triple bottom line to the triple top line. When designing a new textile line, for example, Braungart and McDonough were asked how an upholstery fabric could replenish nature, totally eliminate waste, and provide a safe working environment for the employees of a textile mill. The result was a beautiful fabric created with ingredients so safe, it filtered the water running through the mill during production, making regulations and health concerns obsolete. After its useful commercial life as an upholstery fabric, the material can be composted and used to restore the soil - the trimmings from the mill, in fact, become mulch for the local garden club. Distributed by an international textile design firm, the fabric has been a splendid success. No waste. No liabilities. Lower costs. Higher margins. In short, only assets and positive effects.

The triple top line doesn't obviate the need for triple bottom line accounting. Keeping close track of the bottom line is indispensable: You won't achieve sustainability unless you stay in business. In practice, however, triple bottom line accounting tends to focus on economic concerns, with ecological or social benefits sometimes considered as an afterthought. Lost in this scenario, are rich opportunities to transform the triple bottom line analysis into a strategic design tool, generating new business opportunities and triple top line growth.

Braungart and McDonough feel that designers can also apply triple top line thinking to the design of a single product—or even product packaging. To quote them: "Imagine that you are the CEO of an ice cream company. You sell an all-natural product you are very proud of. It brings pleasure to your customers, while supporting the dairy farmers of your region, and it generates great profits, too. But you have a problem: after a recent outdoor event downtown, hundreds of wrappers from your popular ice cream sandwich littered the city parks. You did the right thing when you sent out a crew to clean up the mess, but clearly, that's not something you want to do for the long-term. You also realize, when forced to face this problem, that your packaging is also dyed with chemicals you'd never put in your ice cream. What to do?"

BOX 22.1

C2C Design: Ford Motor Company's Rouge River Plant, Michigan

The Ford Motor Company's Rouge River plant in Dearborn, Michigan, built between 1917 and 1925, is one of the world's largest industrial sites. Once, an enormously productive complex of blast furnaces, stamping mills, warehouses and assembly buildings, capable of producing automobiles from raw materials, the plant fell into disrepair late in the 20th Century. The aging facilities were rusting and out of date and decades of manufacturing had taken a toll on the soil and water.

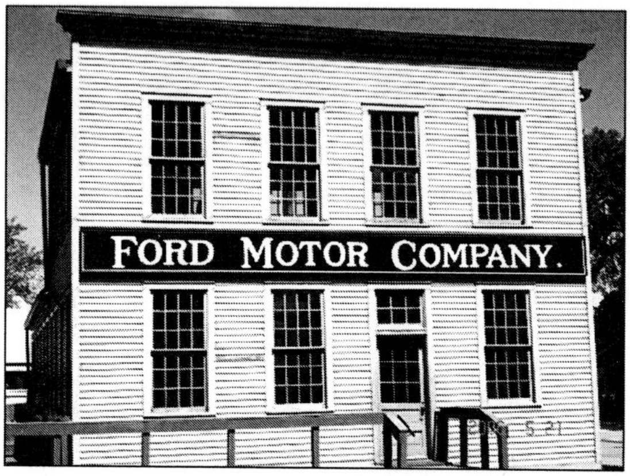

In May 1999, Ford decided to invest $2 billion over 20 years, to transform the Rouge into an icon of 21st Century industry. Led by the then chairman, William Clay Ford, Jr., the company committed to not only rebuilding the complex but to restoring it to a healthy, life-supporting place.

Using C2C as a design tool, Michael Braungart and William McDonough worked with Ford's executives, engineers, and designers and began to explore innovative ways of creating shareholder value. Rather than using economic metrics to try to reconcile apparent conflicts between environmental concerns and the bottom line, the company began to ask triple top line questions, and to explore how profits could be maximized by design decisions that also maximized social and ecological value.

Triple top line thinking energized the company's decision-making process. Ford began to ask revolutionary questions: How can we make the Rouge a place where we would allow our children to play? How do we design a manufacturing facility that creates prosperity and health for employees? What innovations will create habitat for native species? How do we create healthy soil? These are all positive, pro-active questions. They ask not how to "clean up" but how to create life-support systems.

The systems for storm water management on the site illustrate how designs that support life can create tremendous economic value. Expensive technical controls are a typical response to storm water regulations. Ford estimated that new pipes and treatment plants would cost up to $48 million. If Braungart and McDonough had approached the flow of water on the Rouge site from a triple bottom line perspective, they might have tried to cut costs by using pipes made with less material, or by finding ways to treat water with fewer harmful chemicals. By following this path, they would be trying to meet an environmental responsibility as efficiently as possible.

Instead, they tried to design a manufacturing facility that would create habitat, make oxygen, connect employees to their surroundings and invite the return of native species. The result is a day-lit factory with 450,000 square-feet of roof, covered with healthy topsoil and growing plants—a living roof. In concert with porous paving and a series of constructed wetlands and swales, the living roof will slow and filter stormwater run-off, obviating the need for expensive technical controls, and even regulations. All this with first cost savings of up to $35 million, with the landscape thrown in for free. This is the power of intelligent design.

Source : W. McDonough and M. Braungart (2002)

"If we were advising you, we'd suggest some triple top line thinking to try to generate an innovative solution. We would not ask how to reduce the chemicals in your packaging or how to work with the city on litter control. Instead, we'd wonder what kind of positive effects you hoped to create. Maybe, you're interested in continuing to provide the pleasure of a delicious sweet while offering a healthful package that creates new value for your community...we might begin to see that ice cream packaging could be designed for biodegradability with new bio-polymers and safe dyes. This light, healthful packaging could be economically produced. You might decide to provide added value by embedding the seeds of a native wildflower into the packaging designed to dissolve in a day after use—when children toss it on the ground, they'd be planting seeds rather than discarding trash. Suddenly, your problem starts to become an asset: You're supporting the population of native plants; your customers are excited to be young 'Johnny Appleseeds'; the city parks are blooming with colourful flowers; and your sales are through the roof. Not bad for packaging."

22.13 CONCLUSION

These examples begin to suggest some of the ways in which triple top line thinking can create business opportunities. Applied throughout the design process, they introduce a new standard of quality, adding ecological intelligence, social justice, and the celebration of creativity to the typical design criteria of cost, performance, and aesthetics. Design driven by these positive aspirations could lay the foundation for a truly inspiring era in which we transform industry by remaking the way we make things. At every level of industry, productivity and profits will no longer be at odds with the concerns of the commons. Instead, we will be living in a world of sustaining prosperity, a world in which both nature and commerce can thrive and grow.

QUESTIONS

1. What are the various stages of a LCA approach?
2. Explain the advantages and problems of LCA approach.
3. Highlight the features of Cradle-to-Cradle design approach. How is it different from LCA approach?
4. 'Being less bad is not enough'. Explain in the context of C2C design.
5. Examine the role of Triple Top Line to Triple Bottom Line approach to measure corporate environmental performance.

EXERCISES

1. Make a case study of an application of life cycle analysis.
2. Search the websites and come up with real industry examples of C2C design and the benefits to the company from its adoption.

❑❑❑

23

Environmental Management Accounting

> *Socialism collapsed because it did not allow prices to tell the economic truth. Capitalism may collapse because it does not allow prices to tell the ecological truth.*
>
> **Oystein Dahle**

Over the years, accounting for the environment has moved from the fringes—of being considered marginal or irrelevant—to its present position of being seen as an essential element in any organization's environmental response.

23.1 ENVIRONMENTAL MANAGEMENT ACCOUNTING – DEFINITION AND CONTEXT

Environmental Management Accounting refers to the identification, collection, estimation, analysis, internal reporting and use of physical flow information (*i.e.*, materials, water and energy flow), environmental cost information, and other monetary information for both conventional and environmental decision making within an organization.

Environmental Management Accounting (EMA) has no single, universally accepted definition.

According to the International Federation of Accountants (IFAC) based in New York, EMA is "the management of environmental and economic performance through the development and implementation of appropriate environment-related accounting systems and practices. While this may include reporting and auditing in some companies, environmental management accounting, typically involves life-cycle costing, full-cost accounting, benefits assessment, and strategic planning for environmental management."

EMA is broadly defined by the United Nations Expert Working Group to be "the identification, collection, analysis and use of two types of information for internal decision making:

(*i*) Physical information on the use, flows and destinies of energy, water and materials (including wastes);

(*ii*) Monetary information, on environment-related costs, earnings and savings."

These two definitions highlight the broad types of information that organizations typically consider under EMA, as well as some common EMA data analysis techniques and uses.

At the *organization level*, EMA takes place in the context of both management accounting (assessment of an organization's expenditures on pollution control equipment; revenues from recycled materials; annual monetary savings from new energy-efficient equipment) and financial accounting (evaluation and reporting of the organization's current environment-related liabilities).

There are other types of EMA that go beyond the issues typically considered by an organization's financial and management accounting functions. For example, some EMA efforts also include estimates of the magnitude and associated costs/benefits of environmental externalities, that is, the environmental impacts of organizational operations that are allowed by law, but that the responsible organizations are not required to manage or pay for. For example, most environmental regulations allow some legal level of pollutant emissions, which can have an impact on the health of both ecosystems and humans. Because the emissions are legal, however, the emitting organizations do not have to manage those impacts or pay any associated costs. Regardless of the level of pollution permitted by law, however, emissions have detrimental external effects. As most organizations are not the sole contributors to such impacts, such as the water quality of a river or the quality of air in a city, most organizations do not estimate their contribution in monetary terms.

While numerous organizations account for and report physical information on their external environmental impacts (for example, the quantities of different types of pollutant emissions per year), accounting for and reporting the external economic impacts is much less common. An EMA initiative that attempts to take such external costs into account is often referred to as Full Cost Accounting (FCA). FCA has been developed mainly as a means of ensuring that business decisions take full account of an organization's wider environmental impacts.

23.2 ROLE OF ACCOUNTANTS IN ENVIRONMENTAL MANAGEMENT

Broadly speaking, there are four principal reasons for accountants to become involved in environmental management issues:

Environmental Issues are Business Issues

All environmental issues, mainly concerning legislation and market forces, have implications for business in those areas that directly concern accountants. From straight forward profit and loss issues, to competitive advantage issues related to market opportunity and cost efficiency, to the more complex issues of asset values, contingent liabilities and environmental risk, and to investment appraisal decisions that are growing in complexity—most accountants have some role to play.

Environmental Management is Inextricably Linked with Business Management

There is increasing recognition that environmental issues need to be managed holistically within the business, and this has led to the development of standards for environmental management systems, such as the ISO 14000, and EMAS (the European Union Eco-Management and Audit Scheme). And these standards, in turn, have stimulated and reinforced the need for much more specific and quantified performance information, through systematic gathering and reporting of environmental data.

Environmental Issues have Considerable Implications for Financial Advisors

This is particularly important in the more polluting and hence, more regulated industries. Financial auditors may be taken to task if they fail to recognize the profit and loss account and Balance Sheet implications of environmental problems. Also, any major financial transaction (such as an investment, corporate re-structuring or financing) will need to take into account how current and projected environmental performance and role may affect the business's prospects and therefore, its value. The increasing trend towards policies imposing environmental taxes, granting pollution permits etc., also have accounting implications.

Internal and External Stakeholder Pressures

An example of internal stakeholders might be employees affected by pollution in the work environment. External stakeholders include communities affected by local pollution, environmental activist groups, government regulators, shareholders, investors, customers, suppliers and others. The types and intensities of environmental pressures can vary widely from country to country and among different business sectors. It is safe to say, however, that environmental pressure is forcing many organizations to look for new, creative and cost-efficient ways to manage and minimize environmental impacts.

Other examples of environmental pressure relevant at the international level include:

(*i*) Supply chain pressures, such as large companies requiring their suppliers to comply with the Environmental Management System (EMS) standard of the International Standards Organization.

(*ii*) Disclosure pressures from various stakeholders for companies to publicly report their environmental performance in annual financial accounts and reports or in voluntary corporate environmental performance reports, for example, via the guidelines of the Global Reporting Initiative.

(*iii*) Financing pressures via the worldwide growth of socially responsible investment (SRI) funds, investment rating systems such as the Dow Jones Sustainability Index and investment policy disclosure requirements.

(*iv*) Regulatory control pressures, for example, the RoHS Directive, a European Union (EU) regulation that restricts the use of certain hazardous substances in electrical and electronic equipment sold in the EU.

(*v*) Environmental tax pressures, for example, various government-imposed environment related taxes such as carbon taxes, energy use taxes, landfill fees and other emissions fees.

(*vi*) Cap and trade pressures, such as the emissions cap and trading aspects of the Kyoto Protocol.

BOX 23.1

Functions of Accountants in Environmental Management

Accountants perform the following functions towards Environmental management:

- Modify existing accounting systems to include environmental performance within internal management reporting.
- Eliminate conflicting elements of the accounting systems (as in investment appraisal).
- Plan for financial implications of the environmental agenda (as in capital expenditure projections).
- Introduce environmental performance to external reporting (as in annual reports).
- Develop new accounting and information systems (as in eco-balance sheets).

Source: Rob Gray and Jan Bebbington (2001)

According to Ray and Bebbington (2001), research findings indicate that accountants are still not yet as involved as they should be, especially when one considers the financial implications of:

(*i*) Liabilities for cleaning up contaminated land.

(*ii*) Liabilities for being in breach of environmental legislation and regulations.

(*iii*) Opportunities for gaining market share over competitors who have been slower in grasping the need to change (in response, for example, to the implications of the packaging standards in the German market).

(*iv*) The shift in public opinion and the growth of stakeholder interests leading to possible public relations risks or opportunities.

(*v*) Developments in national government policy towards sustainable development. Environmental regulations are beginning to incorporate environmental management requirements, which in turn call for environmental accounting.

In the past, internal costs associated with environmental performance were relatively low as there were few environmental regulations and other pressures to force organizations to better manage and minimize their environmental impacts. Today, however, the scenario has changed and environment-related costs are increasing in many countries in response to growing pressures of various kinds. For example, in countries with strong environmental regulatory regimes, new regulations have led to the internalization of a wide variety of additional environment-related costs. Organizations have seen costs of environmental compliance rise, including costs for required pollution control equipment, pollution monitoring and emission fees and regulatory paperwork and reporting. Pollution clean-up regulations have resulted in increasing liability costs for site remediation and liability-related insurance costs. Pressure from stakeholders, such as local communities, environmental activist groups and business partners (customers, investors and finance providers), has also added to environment-related costs, as organizations need to initiate voluntary programs to respond to the interests of these groups.

Organizations have, however, also come to recognize the potential monetary rewards of improved environmental performance. They have discovered that enhancing efficiency in the use of energy, water and other raw materials brings not only environmental improvements (reduced resource use and reduced waste and emissions), but also potentially significant monetary savings as the costs of materials purchase and waste treatment decrease accordingly. The more strategic benefits of improved environmental performance have also been recognized, such as the ability to design environmentally sensitive products and services for increasingly "green" business and consumer markets, the ability to respond more quickly and cost-effectively to an ever-changing environmental regulatory framework, and better relationships with key stakeholders, such as finance providers and local communities.

For an organization to effectively manage the environmental pressures, costs and benefits mentioned above, it needs various types of expertise, including environmental, technical, accounting and finance, marketing and public relations, and general management. Accountants have a special role to play because of their access to an organization's monetary information, their ability to improve or verify the quality of such information and their skills in using that information to help make sound business decisions in areas such as investment appraisal, budgeting and strategi planning.

23.3 ACCOUNTING FOR SUSTAINABILITY

Gray (2001) points out that businesses need some guidance or performance indicators on their achievements in environmental activity and such an information system needs to run parallel with or be incorporated with the present accounting system. He distinguishes between three types of capital—critical natural capital that is essential for life and must remain inviolate; other (sustainable, substitutable or renewable) natural capital; and artificial capital (buildings, machinery and so on). For sustainability to be achieved, the critical capital must not be touched and all dimunitions in other natural capital must be replaced, renewed or substituted for.

Three approaches have been described by Gray which could be adopted in accounting for sustainability, The first, an inventory approach, is concerned with identifying, recording, monitoring and then reporting, probably in non-financial quantities, the different categories of natural capital and their depletion and/or enhancement. The likely impact of any changes on the various categories of capital, as well as the steps taken to mitigate those effects is also to be reported.

The second approach, the sustainable cost approach, is based on the concept that a sustainable organization is one which leaves the biosphere no worse off at the end of the accounting period than it was at the beginning. This would involve theoretically calculating what the organization would have to spend at the end of the accounting period to place the biosphere in the position it was at the start. The resultant notional amount could be shown as a notional reduction of profit or notional increase of operating expenditure.

The third approach is the resource flow/input-output approach, which is based on a systems conception of the organization and attempts to report its resource flows. While this method does not directly report on sustainability, it ensures greater transparency with respect to the organization's resource use.

23.4 TYPES OF INFORMATION INCLUDED UNDER EMA

Physical Information under EMA

To assess costs correctly, an organization must collect not only monetary data but also non-monetary data on materials use, personnel hours and other cost drivers. EMA places a particular emphasis on materials and materials-driven costs because: (*a*) use of energy, water and materials, as well as the generation of waste and emissions, are directly related to many of the impacts organizations have on their environments and (*b*) materials purchase costs are a major cost driver in many organizations.

Most organizations purchase energy, water and other materials to support their activities. In a manufacturing setting, some of the purchased material is converted into a final product that is delivered to customers. Most manufacturing operations also produce waste—materials that were intended to go into the final product but became waste instead, because of product design issues, operating inefficiencies, quality issues, etc. Manufacturing operations also use energy, water and materials that are never intended to go into the final product but are necessary to manufacture the product (such as water to rinse out chemical tanks between product batches or fuel use for transport operations). Many of these materials eventually become waste streams that must be managed. Non-manufacturing operations (for example, agriculture and livestock, resource extraction sector, service sector, transport, the public sector) can also use a significant amount of energy, water and other materials to help run their operations, which, depending on how those materials are managed, can lead to a significant generation of waste and emissions.

Thus, the most obvious example of materials-related environmental impacts is the generation of waste and emissions, which can affect the health of both humans and natural ecosystems, including plants and animals. Air, water or land can end up polluted or even contaminated.

The second broad area of materials-related environmental impact is the potential impact of the physical products (including by-products and packaging) produced by a manufacturer. These final products have environmental impacts when they leave the company, for example, when a product ends up in a landfill at the end of its useful life.

Some of the potential environmental impacts of products can be reduced by changes in product design, such as decreasing the volume of paper used in packaging or replacing a physical product with an equivalent service, etc. In many manufacturing plants, most of the materials used, become part of a final product, rather than part of waste or emissions. As a result, the potential environmental impact of products is high, and the potential environmental benefit of product improvements is correspondingly high.

Tracking and reducing the amount of energy, water and materials used by manufacturing, service and other companies can also have indirect environmental benefits upstream, because the extraction of almost all raw materials has environmental impacts. For example, activities such as forestry and the extraction of materials such as coal, oil, natural gas, as well as gold and other minerals, can have extreme impacts on the environment surrounding extraction sites. These impacts include not only the pollution and waste generated during extraction operations, but also the erosion or outright removal of topsoil and vegetation, sedimentation of nearby water bodies and the disruption of wildlife feeding, reproduction and migration habitat. In addition, there could be adverse impacts on the local human populations, that depend on the affected ecosystem, for food and clean water. The depletion of non-renewable or slowly renewable natural resources is also a cause for concern.

To effectively manage and reduce the potential environmental impacts of waste and emissions, as well as of any physical products, an organization must have accurate data on all the energy, water and materials used to support its activities. It needs to know which and how much energy, water and materials are brought in, which become physical products and which become waste and emissions. This physical accounting information does not provide all of the data needed for effectively managing all potential environmental impacts, but nontheless, is essential information that the accounting function can provide.

Monetary Information under EMA

Some organizations may prefer to focus their EMA activities on the narrower range of costs encompassed under environmental protection expenditures (EPEs). Others will take a broader and more strategic view of both environmental management and environment-related costs and thus, may be comfortable with attributing a broader range of costs to the environment, even if some of those costs are viewed as quality or efficiency related at the same time.

The majority of EMA initiatives today, typically do not include "external" costs, the environment-related costs incurred by individuals, business partners, society or the planet for which organizations are not legally responsible. Some organizations do consider such external costs, however, and the boundary between internal and external environmental costs is becoming increasingly fluid, both because of changing environmental regulations and a growing emphasis on corporate social responsibility.

23.5 USES AND BENEFITS OF EMA

EMA is particularly valuable for internal management initiatives with a specific environmental focus, such as cleaner production, supply chain management, "green" product or service design, environmentally preferable purchasing and environmental management systems. Also, EMA type information is increasingly being used for external reporting purposes. Thus, EMA is a broad set of principles and approaches that provides the data essential for the success of many other environmental management activities. And, since the range of decisions affected by environmental issues is increasing, EMA is becoming more important, not only for environmental management decisions, but for all types of management activities.

The specific uses and benefits of EMA are numerous, but can be organized into three broad categories, as illustrated in Fig. 23.1.

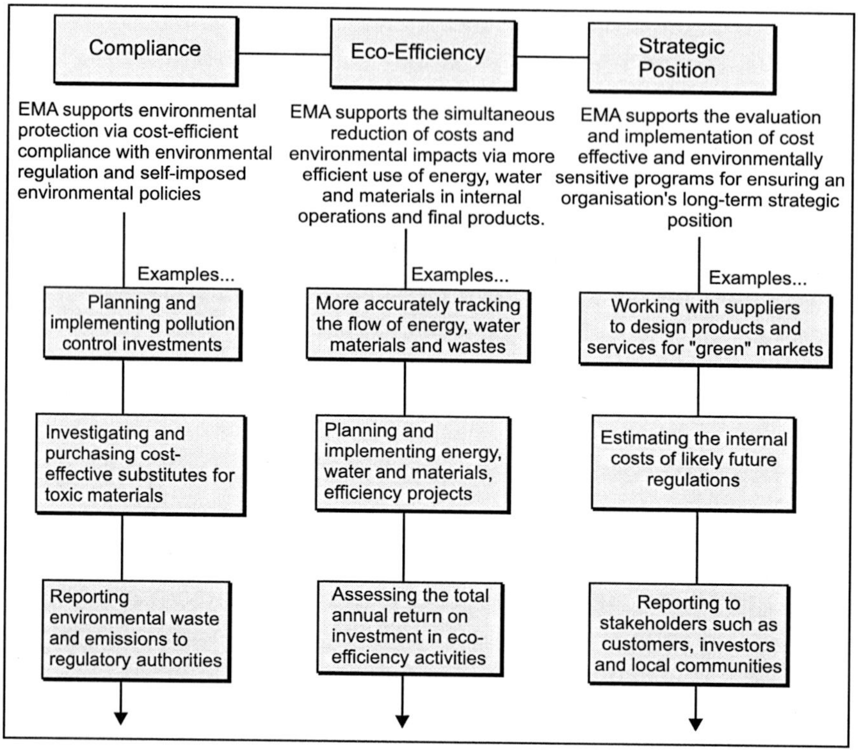

Source: Adapted from the *Guide to Corporate Environmental Cost Management* (2003) Berlin: German Environment Ministry.

Fig. 23.1 Uses and Benefits of EMA

23.6 LIMITATIONS OF EMA

Several limitations of conventional management accounting systems and practices can make it difficult to effectively collect and evaluate environment-related data. These limitations can lead to management decision making being based on missing, inaccurate or misinterpreted information. As a result, managers may well misunderstand the negative financial consequences of poor environmental performance and the potential costs and benefits of improved environmental performance.

(*i*) **Communication/Links between Accounting and other Departments Often not well Developed:** An organization's environmental personnel often have a great deal of knowledge about environmental issues. Similarly, technical staff may have considerable experience with the flow of energy, water and other materials throughout an organization. Environmental and technical personnel, however, often have little knowledge of how those issues are reflected in the accounting records. In contrast, the accountant or controller has much of the accounting information at hand, but often little knowledge of the environmental issues the organization faces, or of the flow of physical resources. Thus, accounting personnel are often not providing the types of accounting information that environmental and technical personnel might find most useful.

(*ii*) **Different Departments may also have Different Goals and Perspectives with Respect to EMA-Type Activities:** For example, they may not have the same perspectives on the issue of who is responsible for managing different types of environment-related costs. Production centres, which may produce waste but may not have data on the costs of waste disposal. The design department, which selects the materials, equipment and processes used may not be knowledgeable about the environmental impact of the same. The environmental manager, though he does not produce waste, must dispose of it in the best possible manner. The accounting department, may inadvertently "hide" environment-related costs by placing them in general overhead accounts without realizing the implications.

In addition, accounting, environmental and technical personnel often use different information systems that are not checked for consistency. In many cases, a consistency check would be quite difficult, if not impossible, because the various information systems use different boundaries for materials tracking. These differences in knowledge, information access and structure can be made worse by language differences in the cultures of accounting, environmental and technical personnel.

Clearly, there is a need to improve communication between accounting and other professionals involved in environmental management. Until there is real dialogue between accountants and the technical and environmental professionals in charge of physical data, development of environmental performance indicators that combine monetary and physical measures, and development of environmental management strategies in general, will remain a challenging task.

(*iii*) **Environment-Related Cost Information is Often "Hidden" in Overhead Accounts:** There are numerous examples of potentially important environment-related costs being inadvertently hidden in the accounting records, where a manager who would benefit from that information cannot find it easily. One particularly common way to inadvertently hide environment-related costs is to assign them to overhead accounts, rather than directly to the processes or products that created the costs. While overhead accounts are a convenient way to collect costs that may be difficult to assign directly to processes or products, this practice can create problems later if a manager does not know where to look for the needed cost information.

(*iv*) **Materials use, Flow and Cost Information is Often not Tracked Adequately:** Although larger companies annually generate millions of data records concerning material movements from Enterprise Resource Planning (ERP) and other software systems, the available information is often not sufficiently accurate or detailed for ensuring environmental efficiency and other decision-making purposes.

For example, sometimes the posting of materials purchase information does not allow clear identification of the amount and value of different categories of purchased materials. In some accounting systems, all materials purchase information is posted into one account, while the detailed material numbers and amounts are recorded only in the stock management records. So, there is no easy way to aggregate the data from stock management by materials group or trace the actual annual consumption of the different categories of materials. Thus, no one knows the amount and value of materials consumed by materials groups. Even if a production manager had an estimate of materials loss percentages during the production process, the total value of lost materials cannot be calculated because of missing data on the value of materials purchased by materials groups.

In addition, conventional cost accounting systems often do not record data on material inputs to and from each cost centre in production, but rely on general calculations provided by the production planning system, which may or may not reflect an organization's real-world use and flow of materials. Many production-planning systems calculate materials loss by using inaccurate average loss percentages. They may have little to do with the actual losses that occur during production. The employees on-site often have more precise estimates than the accounting system does.

(v) **Many Types of Environment-Related Cost Information are not Found in the Accounting Records:** Accounting records typically do not contain much information on future environment-related costs, even though they may be quite significant, because accounting systems have traditionally looked towards the past. Accounting records also lack many other less tangible environment related costs. Examples include the costs incurred when poor environmental performance translates into lost sales to customers who care about environmental issues, lost access to markets with environment-related product restrictions and lost access to financing and insurance when business partners decline to take on the potential environmental risk associated with a business partnership. These types of costs may be difficult to estimate, but they can be both real and significant to an organization's financial health.

(vi) **Investment Decisions are Often made on the Basis of Incomplete Information:** Management decisions on investment projects, materials choices, product pricing and product mix suffer when comprehensive, consistent environment-related information is not available in a timely fashion. Investment decisions pose particular challenges because they involve the uncertainty of questions such as: What will I have to pay in the future if I do not act now? What will I earn in the future if I do act now? A lack of accurate estimates of environment-related costs and benefits adds to the inherent uncertainty of all investment decisions. The ratification of environmental agreements, such as the Kyoto Protocol, is likely to complicate investment decisions further as they expand the options available to companies. For example, under Kyoto, a company involved in emissions trading may choose not to invest in measures that will reduce its emissions but instead purchase sufficient permits to meet any emissions targets imposed. Companies will need to rely on the knowledge and skills of management accountants to help them make the difficult choice between investment and trading.

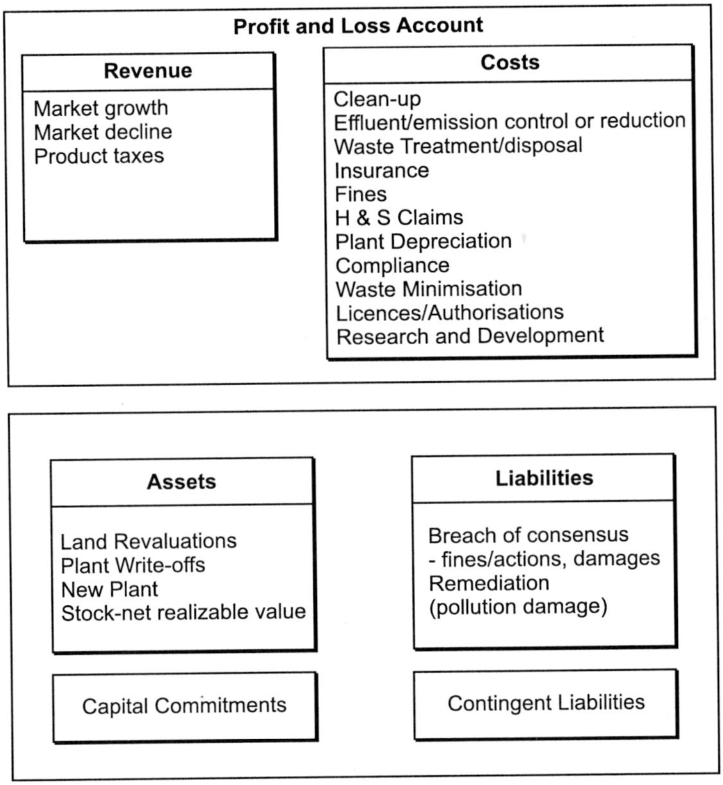

Source: KPMG Sustainability Advisory Services

Fig. 23.2: The Impact of the Environment on the Conventional Financial Statements

23.7 LEGAL FRAMEWORK FOR ENVIRONMENTAL ACCOUNTING IN INDIA

Accounting Requirements

(*i*) A Gazette Notification on Environmental Audit issued by the Ministry of Environment and Forests in 1992 (amended vide notification GSR 386 (E),dt.22-04-1993), under the Environmental (Protection) Act 1986, has made it mandatory for all the industrial units to submit an environmental statement to the concerned State Pollution Control Boards while seeking consent to operate under the relevant environmental norms. The Environmental Statements enable the units to take a comprehensive look at the industrial operations, facilitate the understanding of material flows and help them to focus on areas where waste reduction and consequently, saving in material cost, is possible.

(*ii*) Indian Companies Act, 1956 requires the inclusion in the Director's report, of environment related policies/problems and annexures showing details of energy consumption/energy conservation.

(*iii*) Cost Accounting Record Rules for various industries made by the Central Government also require disclosing monetary and quantitative values in Cost Accounting.

23.8 PRACTICE OF ENVIRONMENTAL ACCOUNTING IN INDIA

Despite the regulatory requirements, very few corporations give adequate information regarding environmental issues. If as per requirement of applicable law they have to prepare and submit any information relevant to the environment, they do so. The Environment Ministry has issued instructions in this regard for every industrial unit to prepare and submit an environment statement. It can be observed through their accounts that mainly the following types of information are given:

(*i*) The type of devices installed for pollution control.

(*ii*) Steps taken for energy conservation.

(*iii*) Steps taken for raw material conservation.

(*iv*) Steps taken for waste water and production process waste.

(*v*) Steps taken for improvement of quality of products and services, production process, etc.

A study conducted by Dr. B.B. Padhan and Dr.R.K. Bal (reported in *The Chartered Accountant*, November 2005) among 80 executives of different industries revealed that while the corporate world is fully aware of the requirements of environmental reporting, the actual environmental reporting by industries is extremely inadequate with very little information revealed in the annual report. It was also reported that most of the companies disclose the environment information in a descriptive manner, rather than in financial terms *i.e.*, no account is taken of the degradation of natural capital when calculating corporate profits.

23.9 CONCLUSION

Environmental accounting is in an extremely preliminary stage in India and whatever is shown in the accounts in this regard is more or less a mere compliance of relevant rules and regulations under the Act. In the past and even today, many companies have simply not considered the full range of environment-related costs needed for sound investment decision making. Organizations need to consider all potentially significant environment-related costs that may influence the return on investment, such as materials flow costs, site recovery costs and any costs associated with certain or likely future regulations. Organizations also need to ensure that environmental managers, technical experts and accountants work together to provide the full picture of environmental issues and the related costs and benefits that are relevant for making an investment decision. It is also important to distinguish between fixed and variable environment-related costs in investment decision making. Businesses with a majority of fixed costs may find it more difficult to reduce these in comparison to variable costs, some of which can be reduced more easily with no or short payback periods.

QUESTIONS

1. What is meant by full cost environmental management accounting?
2. What kind of information is provided by a full fledged environmental management accounting exercise?
3. Briefly discuss the status of environmental accounting and reporting by companies in India.

EXERCISE

1. Search the internet for examples of environmental reporting done by Indian companies and compare it with the reporting done by companies in Europe and the USA.

❑❑❑

24

Environmental Auditing

> *In nature's economy the currency is not money, it is life.*
> **Vandana Shiva**

Environmental auditing is a series of activities initiated by the management to evaluate environmental performance to check compliance with environmental legislation and to assess whether the system in use is effective in managing environmental improvement. Audits are undertaken at regular intervals to assess environmental performance of the company in relation to the company's stated objectives and environmental policies. Environmental auditing is a management tool comprising a systematic, documented, periodic and objective evaluation of the company's organization, management system and processes designed to protect the environment (Welford, 1999).

An environmental audit is central to a company committed to the implementation of an environmental management system. It is an important component of a comprehensive approach to environmental management and is recognized by standards such as BS 7750 and ISO 14000. As with much of environmental management, the role of senior management in the audit process is crucial. Without top management support, an internal environmental audit programme will not succeed. Moreover, management should be fully committed to environmental compliance and to correcting any deficiencies uncovered by the audit programme.

24.1 DEFINITION

Environmental auditing is an examination of a facility's environmental records and practices while checking for both accuracy and conformance to the organization's environmental policies and regulatory responsibilities.

The International Chamber of Commerce (ICC, 1989) has given the following definition:

"A management tool comprising a systematic, documented, periodic and objective evaluation of how well environmental organization, management and equipment are performing with the aim of helping to safeguard the environment by:

(*i*) Facilitating management and control of environmental practices; and

(*ii*) Assessing compliance with company policies, which include meeting regulatory requirements."

The words, *systematic, documented, periodic* and *objective,* indicate that the audit must be an ongoing and thorough assessment of environmental performance which is documented and at the very least, verified by an objective third party.

The Confederation of British Industry defines an environmental audit as:

"The systematic examination of the interactions between any business operation and its surroundings. This includes all emissions to air, land and water; legal constraints; the effects on the neighbouring community, landscape and ecology; and the public's perception of the operating company in the local area...Environmental auditing does not stop at compliance with legislation. Nor is it a 'green-washing' public relations exercise. Rather, it is a total strategic approach to the organization's activities."

The definition of environmental audit given within the Eco-management and Audit Scheme, which is again based on the ICC definition is:

"A management tool comprising a systematic, documented, periodic and objective evaluation of the performance of the organization, management system and processes designed to protect the environment with the aim of:

(*i*) Facilitating management control of practices which may have impact on the environment;

(*ii*) assessing compliance with company's environmental policies."

24.2 AIMS AND OBJECTIVES OF ENVIRONMENTAL AUDIT

The overall aim of environmental auditing is to provide an on-going status check which will enable environmental improvement within the organization to continue, and by doing so will help to safeguard the environment and minimize the risks to human health. Although auditing alone cannot achieve environmental improvement, it is a powerful managerial tool. The key objectives of the environmental audit are:

(*i*) **Verifying Compliance:** One of the primary purposes of an audit is to verify compliance with local, national and international standards or best available techniques, as well as the company's own internal standards as stated in its environmental policy.

(*ii*) **Identifying Problems:** The aim of an audit is to detect any leakage, spills or other such problems with the operations and processes at an early stage, thus reducing the risk of a future problem.

(*iii*) **Formulating Environmental Policy:** Normally the formulation of an environmental policy should precede the audit. However, if such a policy does not exist already, then an environmental audit can be used for formulating the organization's environmental policy. Similarly, the results of an audit can also be used for modifying and updating an existing policy.

(*iv*) **Measuring Environmental Impact:** An environmental audit should measure the environmental impact of each and every process and operation on air, water, soil, worker's health and safety and the society at large.

(*v*) **Measuring Performance:** An environmental audit gives one a measure of the organization's environmental performance, which can then be compared with the best practices in EA, thus enabling the management to know where their organization stands with regard to its environmental performance.

(*vi*) **Confirming the Effectiveness of the Environmental Management System:** An EA, which is the core of an EMS, gives an indication of the effectiveness of the system and how it can be improved.

(*vii*) **Providing a Database for Corrective Action and Future Plans:** An EA identifies areas where steps have to be taken or can be taken to reduce wastes, raw materials, and energy consumption, and adverse impacts on the environment, and help to improve the environmental performance of the company.

(*viii*) **Developing the Company's Environmental Strategy:** The results of an audit should enable the management to develop its environmental strategy, for moving towards a greener culture.

(*ix*) **Communication:** By reporting the results of its environmental audit, a company can effectively communicate its environmental performance to its stakeholders, which goes a long way in enhancing the image of the company.

24.3 ADVANTAGES OF ENVIRONMENTAL AUDIT

There are a number of benefits to firms in having an EA undertaken. These include:

(*i*) Assurance that legislation is being adhered to.

(*ii*) Prevention of fines and litigation.

(*iii*) An improved public image which can be built into a public relations campaign.

(*iv*) A reduction in costs—particularly in the area of energy usage and waste minimization.

(*v*) Improvement in environmental awareness at all levels of the firm, and

(*vi*) An improvement in overall quality.

The primary benefits of environmental auditing are to indicate in good time, whether environmental measures are satisfactory and to assist with the subsequent compliance with legislation, company's policy and the public's demands. Empirical evidence from several companies having an environmental audit has highlighted a range of less tangible benefits. These include:

(*i*) Increasing awareness of environmental policies and responsibilities among the whole work force.

(*ii*) Providing an opportunity for management to give credit for good environmental performance.

(*iii*) Identifying new working practices which can significantly aid waste minimization and energy usage.

(*iv*) Providing an up-to-date environmental database which can be drawn on when making decisions on plant modifications or for use in emergencies.

(*v*) Evaluating training programmes and providing information for training of the staff.

There are a few potential problems associated with the audit. These include the initial costs of the audit and the cost of compliance with it and the temporary disruptions of plant operations.

The environmental audit has to be systematic and comprehensive. However, some firms have carried out specific, narrower assessments of part of their activities for particular purposes. A partial environmental audit will be specific to a particular task or process or issue. Some such partial audits are compliance audit, process audit, occupational health audit, product audit, product quality audit, issues audit, and pre-acquisition audit.

24.4 AUDIT PRINCIPLES

Ten key elements necessary for the conduct of effective and reliable environmental audits are given below. Unless these principles are adhered to by the auditors, companies cannot be assured of the quality and objectivity of the auditing procedure adopted:

(*i*) Formulation of clear and explicit objectives, before the actual commencement of the environmental audit. In addition, there needs to be a clearly defined benchmark in terms of environmental legislation, standards and the best practice of other companies, in order that the audit results can be assessed.

(*ii*) The audit team needs to be proficient and expert with appropriate knowledge of the issues under consideration and an appropriate environmental understanding with respect to scientific, technical, legislative and management issues. Each audit member needs to be able to demonstrate his particular expertise.

(*iii*) Auditors need to have the independence to work in a confidential manner and due professional care should be exercised at all times.

(*iv*) Firms specializing in environmental auditing and individual consultants should be able to demonstrate their own adherence to general principles of environmental improvement.

(*v*) The on-site audit should be planned, managed and supervised so as to ensure minimum disadvantage to the company and appropriate safety and security to the individual auditor.

(*vi*) Environmental audits should include the proper study of management systems in operation and an assessment of the reliability of internal environmental controls.

(*vii*) Sufficient, reliable evidence should be gathered through enquiry, observation and tests to ensure that the audit findings are objective.

(*viii*) Audit reports should be clear, concise and confidential. They should ensure full and formal communication of audit findings and recommendations.

(*ix*) Auditors should ensure that strategies for the implementation of the recommendations of the audit are practicable and possible and should contribute to the implementation of corrections.

(*x*) Auditors should clearly indicate to the companies, the consequences of not correcting shortcomings pointed out by them, particularly when they are likely to result in litigation being taken against the firm. If this is not done, then the auditors should accept their own negligence.

24.5 INCENTIVES TO UNDERTAKE THE AUDIT

Over the last couple of decades, there has been increasing pressure on companies by the public in view of the worsening environmental degradation. Also, insurance companies have become more aware of the potential risks associated with pollution and as more national and international legislation is being enacted for environmental protection, the incentive to undertake an environmental audit has increased. Some particular reasons for undertaking a regular environmental audit are given below:

(*i*) **Insurance:** Cost of remediation following pollution incidents, have been increasing dramatically and consequently, insurance premiums have increased and the number of exclusions from policies have been extended. While it is still possible to find insurance cover for pollution which is sudden, accidental and unforeseen, there are very few insurance companies which will cover general pollution risks, unless regular environmental audits are carried out.

(*ii*) **Market Forces and Competition:** One of the consequences of public interest is that consumers are increasingly willing to switch to products which are more environmentally friendly than their usual purchase. Companies need therefore, to demonstrate that their products and processes cause minimum harm to the environment. In the past, the marketing of the so-called green products has often been misleading, if not downright dishonest. With the growing public awareness and increasing clout exercised by pressure groups, dishonest claims on the part of companies are likely to be exposed and it is therefore, necessary for companies to tell their consumers about the results of the environmental audit of their processes. With the introduction of an eco-label for some products across Europe, which will assess not only the product, but the production process, before an award is made, the role of audit becomes crucial.

(*iii*) **Acquisitions:** Major organizations are becoming increasingly aware of the massive potential risks involved in acquiring land which has already been contaminated or acquiring a business which has a poor environmental performance record. Costs associated with ground remediation, the capital cost associated with introducing or upgrading a pollution control plant and the cost of potential compensation claims for past mistakes can easily outweigh any financial advantage of an acquisition. It is now increasingly standard practice, for purchasers to commission a pre-acquisition environmental assessment to know what they are letting themselves in for, when they acquire a company.

(*iv*) **Legislation:** The number and comprehensiveness of pollution control legislation covering every aspect of a company's activities is increasing day by day. And to ensure compliance with all the rules and regulations relating to emissions, effluents etc., companies need to be aware of the environmental status of the company at any given point in time.

24.6 IMPLEMENTING THE AUDIT

All environmental audits involve gathering information, analyzing that information, making objective judgments based on evidence and knowledge of the industry and of relevant environmental legislation and standards. There is also the need to report the results of the audit to senior management, with recommendations and possible strategies for the implementation of the findings.

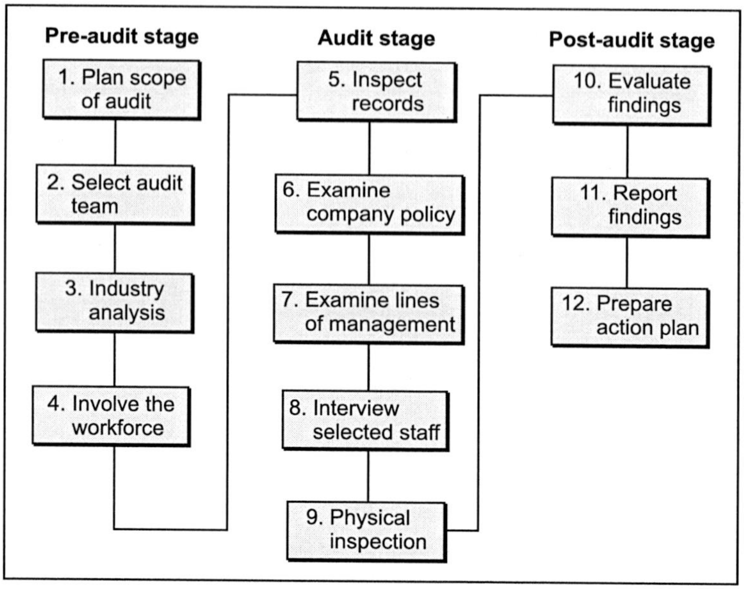

Fig. 24.1 Stages of an Environmental Audit

First Stage (Pre-Audit Activities): Will aim to minimize the time spent at the site and to maximize the audit team's productivity, and will involve the following:

(*i*) Planning the nature and scope of the audit and providing a framework for setting goals and objectives, developing strategies for their achievement and specifying accountability for accomplishing the work and scheduling the audit process.

(*ii*) Selecting members of the audit team and allocating resources to the strategies and policies determined already. The audit team will consist of people chosen for their expertise, not only in environmental matters, but also having knowledge of the industry in which a company operates.

(*iii*) Getting to know the industry and company to be audited. A useful strategy here is to use pre-survey questionnaires submitted to the management, in order that the audit team familiarize themselves with the production process.

(*iv*) Questionnaires may also be sent to a representative sample of the workforce (to be filled in confidence) asking about key issues such as communications, planning, health and safety and working conditions.

Second Stage will include:

(*v*) An inspection of records kept by the company, certificates of compliance, discharge consents, waste licenses etc.

(*vi*) The examination of inspection and maintenance programmes and the company's own policy on what to do in the event of spills and other accidents.

(*vii*) Examining lines of management and responsibility, competence of personnel and systems of authorization.

(*viii*) A confidential interview of selected staff at all levels of operation with a view to collecting information, particularly in the area of the effectiveness of systems and waste management.

(*ix*) A physical information of the plant, working practices, office management systems and surrounding areas, including a check on safety equipment, verifying the company's own sampling and monitoring procedures, investigating energy management systems and wherever necessary, taking samples of waste, liquids, soil, air and noise.

Final Stage involves:

(*x*) Confirming that there is sufficient evidence on which to base and justify a set of findings and evaluating the audit information and observations. Such evaluation will involve a meeting of the audit team, to discuss all facets of the EA.

(*xi*) Reporting the audit findings in written form. This includes a formal review of the audit findings to avoid misinterpretation and discussion about how to improve the environmental performance of the firm based on the audit report.

(*xii*) This will often result in the development of an action plan to address deficiencies. This will include assigning responsibilities for corrective action, determining potential solutions and establishing timetables. Recommendations for the next audit may also be made.

24.7 SUCCESS FACTORS

An effective environmental audit is one that is conducted within a structured management system, is integrated with the overall management activity and considers all aspects that are essential for good environmental performance. The EA is more likely to be successful if the general ethos of the firm is supportive to the success of the programme and the welfare of the company (Welford 1999). Some factors which help to ensure the success of an environmental audit are listed below:

(*i*) **Top Management Commitment:** The most crucial factor contributing to the success of environmental auditing is top management support for the whole exercise. Lukewarm or superficial commitment on the part of the top brass of the company could be the biggest hindrance encountered in the implementation. To gain top management support, the management must be made to realize that environmental management is no longer a passing fad but is here to stay. Standards are becoming higher, regulations stricter and penalties harsher.

(*ii*) **Involvement and Participation:** Staff involvement and participation is extremely important for the success of an audit because the cause of any problem or deficiency in a particular facility or operation can be best understood by the persons working there. Worker participation becomes especially important since a small mistake by a single worker can result in a fatal accident, which could have catastrophic results for the entire company. A single accident is sufficient to wipe out a company's goodwill and whatever good it may have done in the past, as was witnessed in the case of the Union Carbide Plant at Bhopal, India in 2001 (Welford, 1994). It is however important that the auditors take a positive approach in order to prevent the staff from being defensive, thus obstructing rather than helping with the audit.

(*iii*) **Recognition of an Integrated Approach to Environmental Auditing:** An environmental audit must not be considered in isolation, but as an integral part of an environmental management system, which in turn should be integrated with the other systems in the organization.

(*iv*) **Third Party Verification:** An external auditor, not only provides the necessary skill and expertise required for conducting an audit, which might otherwise be missing, but also provides an impartial third party verification of the audit results. This becomes especially important when the results of the audit are communicated to the stakeholders as it gives them additional authenticity.

(*v*) **Well Qualified Audit Team:** Ideally, an audit team comprises 3–5 persons, each of whom has expertise in a different area, contributing to a well balanced expertise and knowledge base. While smaller companies may be audited by just one person, it is usually more beneficial to have more than one person on the audit team. Two minds are always better than one as anything which is overlooked by one person may be spotted by the other. Using the same team for different sites also proves to be useful as it becomes easier to understand and find solutions to similar problems at different sites.

(*vi*) **Audit Frequency:** Environmental audits should be conducted at regular intervals. While an audit should not take place infrequently, it should also not be so frequent that no time is available for the action plan developed during the previous audit to be implemented. Having the same audit frequency for all operations and sites may not always work. Sites/operations that are more risky should be audited more often than others.

24.8 CONCLUSION

Businesses are beginning to realize that it is the environmental management system which should be at the centre of the organization, thanks to standards such as BS7750 and ISO14000. Enterprises have also realized that environmental auditing is an integral part of EMS which not only checks compliance and measures environmental improvements but also checks the effectiveness of the system itself. Environmental audit, like EMS, has to be an on going process, which never ends. The key role of audit must be to check and assess all the other activities of the firm in relation to environmental improvement. But EA is still in its infancy and there is much scope for experimentation. The environmental auditing process should be standardized and auditing reports should be published. In the broader interests of the environment and the society at large, environmental auditing should be made mandatory.

QUESTIONS

1. What are the objectives of an environmental audit?
2. Explain the various stages of an environmental audit.
3. What are the factors that determine the success of an environmental audit?

EXERCISE

1. Make a study of an environmental audit of any company that has been certified ISO 14000.

❑❑❑

25

Environmental Impact Assessment

> *Only when the last tree has been cut down,*
> *Only when the last river has been poisoned,*
> *Only when the last fish has been caught,*
> *Only then will you find that money cannot be eaten.*
>
> **Cree Indian Prophecy**

All developmental activities use natural resources as raw material and the wastes generated are disposed off into different environmental media, resulting in environmental degradation.

An environmental impact assessment (EIA) is a systematic investigation of both positive and negative impacts on the physical, biological and socio-economic environment, which would be caused or induced due to a proposed development project.

EIA is thus a formal process used to predict the environmental consequences of any development project. It can be broadly defined as the systematic identification and evaluation of the potential impacts (effects) of proposed projects, plans, programmes or legislative actions relative to the physical, chemical, biological, cultural and socio-economic components of the total environment (Canter, 1996).

25.1 OBJECTIVES OF AN EIA

The primary objective of an EIA is to encourage the inclusion of environmental considerations in planning and decision making and to ultimately arrive at actions that are more environmentally compatible. EIA systematically examines both beneficial and adverse consequences of the project and ensures that these effects are taken into account during the project design stage. It also ensures that the potential problems are foreseen and addressed at an early stage in the project planning and design. EIA is basically a planning tool. Its main purpose is: "to give the environment its due place in the decision making process by clearly evaluating the environmental consequences of a proposed activity before action is taken" (Gilpian, 1995). The objectives of the environmental assessment process are:

(*i*) Promote development that is sustainable and optimize resource use and management opportunities.

(*ii*) Ensure that environmental considerations are explicitly addressed and incorporated into the decision making process at every stage of planning an activity.

(*iii*) Predict environmental, social, economic, and cultural consequences of a proposed activity.

(*iv*) Assess plans to mitigate any adverse impacts resulting from the proposed activity.

(*v*) Provide for the involvement of the public, Departments of the Government and Government agencies in the review of the proposed activities.

25.2 EVOLUTION OF EIA

Origin of the term Environmental Impact Assessment (EIA) is traced to the formulation of the National Environmental Policy Act (NEPA) in the United States of America (USA) in 1969. The success of EIA in the USA, paved the way for its adoption in other countries, such as Singapore (1972), Japan (1972), Canada (1973), Australia (1974), West Germany (1975), France (1976), China (1979), Indonesia (1982), Spain (1986), New Zealand (1991) etc. In many countries, EIA came into vogue with the introduction of the concept of sustainable development after the World Commission on Environment in 1987 and after the Rio Summit in 1992. Principle 17 of the declaration, states: "Environmental Impact Assessment, as a national instrument, shall be undertaken for proposed activities that are likely to have a significant adverse impact on the environment and are subject to a decision of a competent national authority." In India, EIA came into existence around 1978–79 and was made mandatory in 1994.

25.3 THE EIA PROCESS

The EIA process is characterized by 8 distinct steps. These are:

(*i*) Screening	(*ii*) Scoping
(*iii*) Impact analysis	(*iv*) Mitigation
(*v*) Reporting	(*vi*) Review of EIA
(*vii*) Decision making	(*viii*) Post monitoring

(*i*) Screening: Screening is the first step in any EIA process, undertaken to decide whether EIA should be applied for the project or not. It helps to clear projects that are not likely to cause serious environmental problems and also to identify projects that are likely to do so. The screening process divides the project proposals into the following three categories:

(*a*) Project clearly requiring an EIA.

(*b*) Project not requiring an EIA.

(*c*) Project for which application of an EIA is not clear.

If the project clearly requires EIA, the next stage of scoping is initiated. If the project does not require EIA, environmental clearance is given without EIA. When there is no clarity of judgment, the proponents/assessors are asked to carry out a Rapid Assessment. Rapid Assessment is a process that uses available data and collects data for one season alone and judgment is based on this data. If the results of the rapid assessment show that there are no significant impacts (known as FONSI—Finding of No Significant Impact), then the environmental clearance is granted. If some significant impacts are found, then the proponents are advised to move to the second stage, scoping.

***(ii)* Scoping:** The term scoping is used to describe the process of deciding what should be included in an EIA. This stage identifies the key issues and impacts that should be further investigated and preparation of Terms of Reference (TOR). Sometimes, scoping and screening are merged. This stage also defines the boundary and time limit of the study. It involves assembling baseline information, identifying major issues of concern, and establishing environment assessment priorities, based on public participation. Public participation is highly important in the case of scoping and the issues can only be identified, based on the views from the public, special interest groups and decision makers.

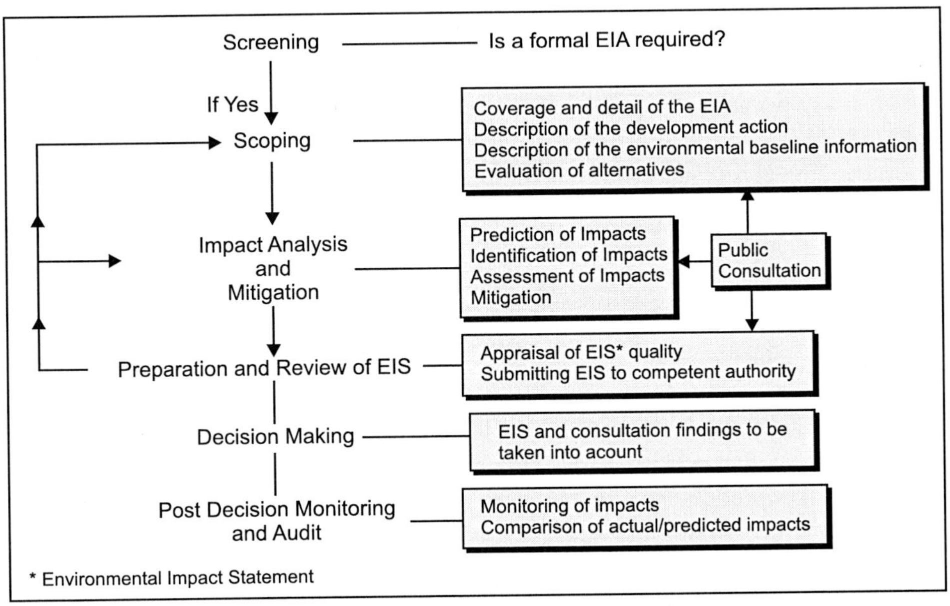

Fig. 25.1 Main Steps in the EIA Process

At the end of scoping, the Terms of Reference (TOR) are prepared. The TOR is a document containing written requirements governing EIA implementation, consultations to be held, data to be procured, methodology to be used etc. After the approval of TOR by the decision makers, the assessor moves to the third and most important step of Impact Analysis.

***(iii)* Impact Analysis:** This stage of EIA identifies and predicts likely environmental and social impacts of the proposed project and evaluates the significance. This step is the heart of EIA and is done to predict the impacts of the proposal, evaluate their significance, and establish measures to prevent, reduce or compensate for the impacts.

The impact analysis process is done through five steps:

(*a*) **Identification of Potential Impacts:** Helps in forecasting the main impacts based on baseline data, using several methods, such as the checklist method, ad hoc method and matrix method.

(*b*) **Description of Existing Environment:** Involves the collection of all pertinent environmental data relating to the project site for all seasons.

(*c*) **Procurement of Relevant Bylaws:** Involves assemblage of relevant standards, regulations and bylaws to know the permissible level and quantity of impact.

(*d*) **Prediction of Impacts:** Refers to a scientific characterization of impacts, causes and effects and their secondary, synergetic consequences for the environment and local community. Prediction is done by the matrix methods, network method, checklist method, literature review and expert judgments.

(*e*) **Assessment of Significant Impacts:** This step evaluates the predicted adverse impacts to determine whether they are significant enough to warrant mitigation. This is done by a combination of methodologies, like expert consultation, mathematical modelling, comparison with bylaws etc.

(*iv*) Mitigation: This step in EIA recommends the actions to reduce and avoid the potential adverse environmental consequences of development activities. If the impacts are significant, then mitigation measures to avoid the impact are necessary. Mitigation measures are generally based on a mixture of legally-mandated criteria, technical/scientific criteria, and social acceptability criteria. Alternate sites and design process should be critically examined to maximize the positive environmental impacts, socio-economic benefits, and profitability, and minimize the temporary adverse impacts. The methodology used in this step includes cost benefit analysis, consultation with stakeholders and decision makers etc. At this juncture, an action plan for impacts and mitigation, called Environmental Management Plan (EMP) is prepared. EMP may include technical control measures, integrated monitoring scheme, monitoring emergency and contingency schedules etc.

(*v*) Reporting: This stage presents the result of EIA in the form of a report to the decision-making body and other interested parties. This report submitted after carrying out environmental impact assessment is called Environmental Impact Statement (EIS).The aim of this step is to provide the decision makers with necessary and correct information to aid their work. The assessor should produce an EIA report (draft EIS) which should be made available to the public for providing inputs and later revised thoroughly to frame the final EIS.

An EIA report typically contains (*a*) an executive summary of EIA findings (*b*) a description of the project and 'no project' scenario (*c*) the impacts of the project on the environment and data pertaining to how they were identified and predicted (*d*) a discussion of various mitigation options and rationale behind choosing a particular option (*e*) an overview of gaps and uncertainties, and finally (*f*) summary of EIA for the general public. To impart clarity and precision to the information presented in the report, visual aids are often used.

(*vi*) Review of EIA: This involves examining the adequacy and effectiveness of the EIA report and provides information necessary for decision-making. This is done to check the adequacy and relevance of the impact assessment report. In reviewing, the reviewer sets a scale of reviewing and gives the project a final rating between A to F, with A representing "well performed" and F representing "unsatisfactory". The reviewer's report consists of the following: (*a*) a brief summary of the strengths and weaknesses of the report (*b*) any need for further study (*c*) any terms/conditions that should apply if proposal is granted.

(vii) **Decision Making:** This is the penultimate step in the EIA process and the most critical. It decides whether the project is rejected, approved or needs further change. The decision makers go through the EIA report, review of the EIA report, consider the practical realities, put in their experience and knowledge and decide on the course of action. Though well rated reviews get the nod of the decision makers, it is not mandatory for the decision maker to give clearance based on the reviews. At the end of this stage, the project either gets the environmental clearance or is asked to be retouched in some areas or asked to forfeit, based on the level, nature and magnitude of impacts. In the absence of immediate clearance and requirement of corrections, the proponent follows the EMP prepared during the identification of mitigation measures. Once the proponent gets environmental clearance, he can start the project.

(viii) **Post Monitoring:** This stage comes into play, once the project is commissioned. It checks whether the impacts of the project do not exceed the legal standards and the implementation of the mitigation measures are in the manner described in the EIA report. Monitoring to manage and audit the impacts of project implementation is done to (*a*) ensure that impacts do not exceed legal standards (*b*) check the implementation of measures provided, and (*c*) to provide early warning of potential damages. After the completion and operation of the project, a post project audit is done to determine the closeness of the predictions to the actual impact. The post project audit forms a valuable record for the future EIAs.

25.4 GUIDING PRINCIPLES OF EIA

There are nine guiding principles of good EIA practice applicable to all types of proposals and all EIA systems. Refer Table 25.1.

Table 25.1 Guiding Principles of Good EIA Practice

Principles	Practical Application
Purposive	EIA should meet its aims of informing decision makers and ensuring an appropriate level of environmental protection and human health.
Focused	EIA should concentrate on significant environmental effects, taking into account the issues that matter.
Adaptive	EIA should be adjusted to the realities, issues and circumstances of the proposals under review.
Participative	EIA should provide appropriate opportunities to inform and involve the interested and affected public, and their inputs and concerns should be addressed explicitly.
Transparent	EIA should be a clear, easily understood and open process, with early notification procedure, access to documentation, and a public record of decisions taken and reasons for them.

contd...

Principles	Practical Application
Rigorous	EIA should apply the best practicable methodologies to address the impacts and issues being investigated.
Practical	EIA should identify the measures for impact mitigation that work and can be implemented.
Credible	EIA should be carried out with professionalism, rigour, fairness, objectivity, impartiality and balance.

Source: http://eia.unu.edu/course/?page_id=100

25.5 EIA METHODOLOGY

Some of the important methodologies available for the various processes of EIA are:

(*i*) Ad hoc Approach	(*ii*) Checklist Method
(*iii*) Interaction Matrix Method	(*iv*) Networks
(*v*) Modelling	(*vi*) Simulation Modelling Workshops
(*vii*) Overlay Mapping	(*viii*) Geographical Information System (GIS).

(*i*) Ad hoc Approach: Ad hoc Approach is the oldest to EIA. This crude method provides qualitative assessment of the total impact and suggests the broad areas of the possible impacts. It is done by considering each area and predicting the impact. This method lacks precision.

(*ii*) Checklist Method: Checklists are the lists of environmental attributes. The evaluator needs to tick against each environmental parameter for adverse, beneficial, or no effects due to proposed project activities. There are four types of checklists. It may be a ***simple checklist,*** involving potentially affected factors or could be a ***descriptive checklist,*** describing the measurement and predictive technique for each factor. It could also be a ***scaling checklist*** that indicates the relative significance of each impact along with details on critical values which represent a threshold of concern for each factor. ***Scaling Weighting Checklist,*** similar to a scaling checklist, provides additional information for the subjective evaluation of each parameter with respect to all the other parameters.

(*iii*) Interaction Matrix Method: Matrix methods identify interactions between various project actions and environmental parameters and components. They incorporate a list of project activities with a checklist of environmental components that might be affected by these activities. A matrix of potential interactions is produced by combining these two lists. Matrix method was developed by Leopold and is also called the Leopold Method. The method uses a matrix format to relate project actions and environmental components. The column of the matrix consists of project actions (normally about 100) against rows of the matrix of environmental components. If a project action is likely to make an impact on environmental components, the appropriate cell is scored for magnitude and importance of the impact. A negative sign is provided for the harmful nature of the impact and a positive sign for the positive impact. Row totals of the matrix reflect the total impact of all project actions on one environmental component, while the column totals reflect the impact of one project action on all components of the environment. The matrix total gives the total environmental impact. Table 25.2 illustrates a simple Leopold Matrix.

Table 25.2 A Simple Leopold Matrix for an Industry

Environmental Components	Plant construction	Transport of raw material	Water intake	Solid waste	Effluent discharged	Emission
Surface water quality					XXX	
Air quality		XX				XXXX
Fisheries			XX		XXX	
Wildlife	XXX					XXX
Forests	XXX					XXX
Agriculture	XXX		XX		XXX	XX
Health				X	XXXX	XXXX

Each action and its potential for impacting each environmental item is considered. The magnitude of the interaction (scale) is described by assigning a value ranging from 1 (for small magnitudes) to 10 (for large magnitudes). The assignment of numerical values is based on an evaluation of available facts and data. Similarly, the scale of importance also ranges from 1 (very low interaction) to 10 (very important interaction). Assignment of numerical values for importance is based on the subjective judgement of the interdisciplinary team working on the EIA study.

The matrix approach is reasonably flexible. The total number of specified actions and environmental items may increase or decrease depending on the nature and scope of the study and the specific TOR for which the environmental impact study is undertaken. This is one of the attractive features of the Leopold Matrix. The matrix can also be employed to identify impacts during the various parts of the entire project cycle — construction, operation, and even dismantling phases. The matrix serves both as a check list and as a summary of impact assessment and is hence considered as the ideal tool for rapid assessment.

***(iv)* Networks:** The Networks Approach links the project and its impacts in an easily understandable format. Networks are used to show interrelationships among the different aspects of the environment of the area and also indicate the flow of energy or impact throughout the environment, such as in the case of upland ecosystem or a drainage basin. Networks are directional diagrams that link primary impact to secondary and tertiary impacts. The network method primarily addresses the need by defining a set of possible networks and allowing the user to identify impacts by selecting and tracing appropriate project actions. The network method aims at working from a list of project activities and establishes cause, condition, and effect relationships. Since the environmental system is dynamic and action-impacting, certain environmental parameters can lead to a series of impacts on other environmental parameters and this is taken care of by the network method. There are different types of networks, such as sequence diagrams, directed diagrams or impact trees. The networks can be used to show both temporal and spatial flows of impacts.

Network diagrams are one of the best ways of representing these causal chains. Network diagrams (Fig. 25.2) provide a means for displaying first, secondary, tertiary, and higher order impacts. In developing a network diagram, the first step is to identify the first order changes in environmental components. The secondary changes in other environmental components that will result from the first order changes are then identified. In turn, third order changes resulting from secondary changes are identified. This process is continued until the network diagram is completed to the practitioner's satisfaction. The network helps in exploring and understanding the underlying relationships between environmental components that produce higher order changes that are often overlooked by simpler approaches.

***(v)* Modelling:** Modelling the most popular of all impact assessment methods, consists of a set of structurally interrelated variables which fit into a set of mathematical equations; the mathematical equations are processed with the help of computers to quantify the desired impacts. Modelling techniques are very useful in the quantification of impacts in a highly precise manner.

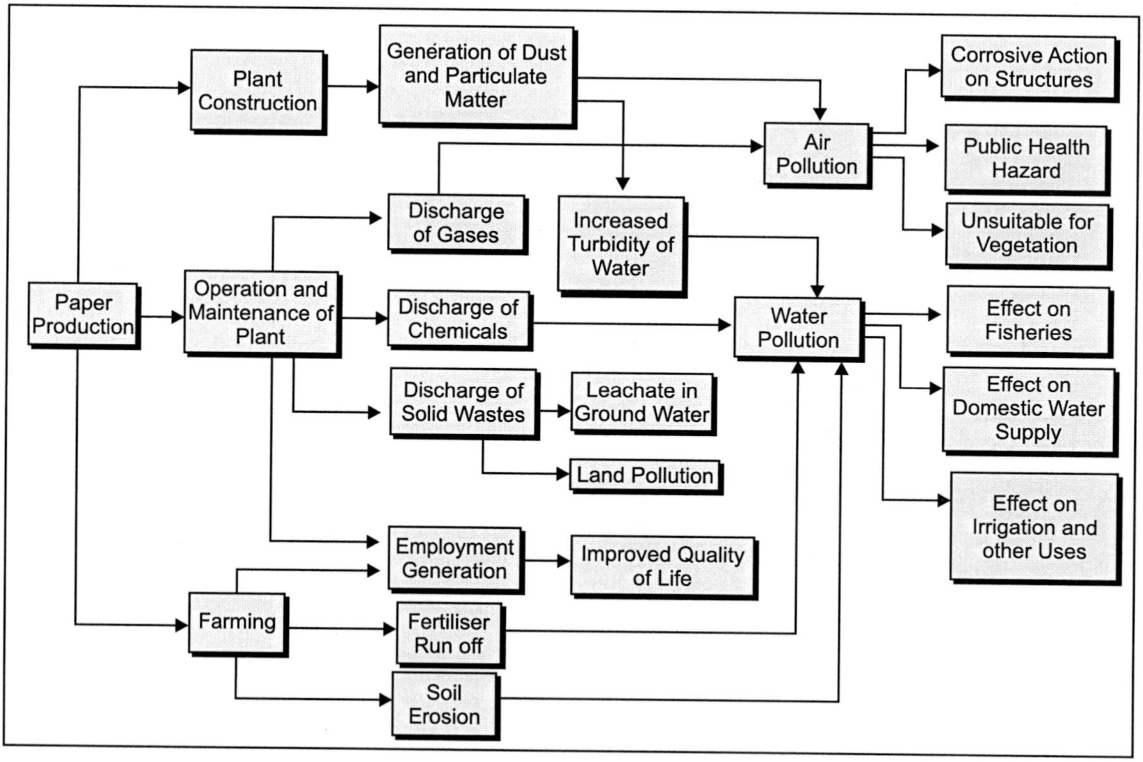

Source: http://www.adb.org/Documents/Books/Environment_Impact/chap3.pdf

Fig. 25.2 Conceptual Model of Impact Network

***(vi)* Simulation Modelling Workshops:** Simulation Modelling System ecologists have developed an approach to EIA and management, commonly referred to as *Adaptive Environmental Assessment and Management* (AEAM). AEAM uses interdisciplinary workshops, composed of scientists and environmental managers, to construct simulation models to predict impacts.

In this approach, short-term interdisciplinary teams interact with experts through modelling workshops, predict impacts and evaluate alternatives. These intensive workshops help in the integration of the information provided by people from different fields of expertise and management. The development of simulation models forces specialists to view their area of interest in the context of the whole system. It leads to clear-cut problem definition and existing data evaluation, and allows the formulation of some initial predictive assessment schemes and sequences in analysis.

There are ten steps in constructing the simulation models. The first five steps are usually constructed by all the participants in the workshop, to be sure that each discipline and interest is represented in the model. These are:

(*a*) Determining actions, including those development activities that have the potential to adversely affect the environment, as well as management and regulatory actions that restrict or control human activity.

(*b*) Determining indicators — those measures of the environmental and social systems that are indicative of the degree of change or impact of actions.

(*c*) Determining the spatial extent and resolution of the study area.

(*d*) Determining the planning horizon and time step.

(*e*) Selection of the sub-model.

(*f*) The sixth step, constructing the "looking outward matrix" is also conducted in a plenary session of the workshop. The "looking outward" process is designed to develop an interaction matrix between the various sub-models.

With the completion of the looking outward matrix, development of the conceptual sub-models begins. The remaining steps are:

(*g*) Programming the sub-models.

(*h*) Integrating the sub-models.

(*i*) Scenario development.

(*j*) Gaming with the model to examine scenario results.

The goals and responsibilities of each group are stated, and each group is required to explicitly identify the information required to make predictions on the nature, scale, and magnitude of change, the respective sub-systems will undergo over time. Workshops often conclude with a discussion of needed model refinements and the information required to be collected.

Subsequent workshops are held at a later date, after model refinement. Available new data are used to refine and develop the model, to enhance its predictive capabilities. The workshops also form the backbone of long term, in-depth analyses in which alternative predictions are made, tested, and alternative management and development schemes are evaluated.

But the limiting factor is that the models will only be as accurate and comprehensive as the data available. The development of an application-specific computer simulation model is not particularly recommended for developing countries because of high costs and the high level of expertise required. The development of an application-specific computer simulation model should be used only in cases where existing predictive computer models are not well suited to the EIA.

***(vii)* Overlay Mapping:** Overlay mapping was first applied by McHarg for studying the environmental impact of highways. An overlay is based on a set of transparent maps, each of which represents the spatial distribution of an environmental characteristic (for example, susceptibility to erosion). Individual impacts such as the effects on soil, water, settlements and noise, are individually summarized and clearly highlighted by mapping the area, using shaded zones to indicate the relative intensity of the impact. With this technique, information for an array of variables is collected for standard geographical units within the study area, and recorded on a series of maps, typically one for each variable. These maps are overlaid to produce a composite map or the individual maps transferred on to transparencies are then laid over one another to produce a composite effect. The resulting composite map, characterizes the area's physical, social, ecological, land use and other relevant characteristics, relative to the location of the proposed development. Thus, the individual effects are summed up to show the total impact of the project. Of course, only a limited number of impacts can be shown by this method. However, it is possible to summarize a large amount of information on each map (or transparency). The physical constraint on this method has been eased with the advent of new computer technology and the Geographic Information System (GIS). It is now easy to carry out temporal changes or projected environmental modifications by revising the raw data directly in the files and perform the repeated overlays.

***(viii)* Geographic Information Systems (GIS):** Geographical Information Systems (GIS) are computer systems that can store, integrate, analyze and display spatial data. The first systems evolved in the late sixties, and by mid seventies they were used for EIA. One of the main methods of analysis in GIS is the overlay mapping, explained above. Most of the development projects generate environmental impacts which are spatial by nature. GIS offers a special environment for dealing with the spatial properties of a project.

GIS shows how a natural resource will be affected by a decision. Based on satellite data, areas that suffer most from deforestation may be identified and analyzed on the basis of overlaying data on soil types, the species required, the likely growth and yield, and the impact of regulatory measures applicable to the area. At the simplest level, GIS can be used for basic mapping of the environment or the project or particular impacts from it to provide visual aids to planners, consultants and managers. GIS can be a powerful tool for displaying and visualizing trends and patterns in spatial data sets. However, the use of GIS in the EIA process in general, and for scoping in particular, has been limited, due in part to their cost in terms of time and money relative to the time and budgets allocated for EIA preparation, especially for scoping.

25.6 BENEFITS OF EIA

The EIA process results in greater environmental awareness among the stakeholders. The benefits from EIA are:

(i) Better environmental planning and design of a proposal. Consideration of environmental effects while planning, helps in reducing the tradeoff between development and environment, and promotes sustainable development.

(ii) EIA helps in minimizing the wastes and impacts on environment, thus reducing the associated costs of treatment or compensation for damage.

(iii) An EIA assures compliance with environmental standards.

(iv) EIA helps in avoiding the cost of unanticipated impacts. These costs can escalate if environmental impacts are not considered in the beginning and the project needs rectification at a later stage to account for environmental impacts.

(*v*) EIA helps to safeguard our natural resources of air, water, land, flora and fauna from haphazard development activities.

(*vi*) EIA helps in reducing the delays in the approval of a project on the grounds of environmental impacts of the project. By considering all environmental impacts from the beginning, time costs are reduced to a minimum.

(*vii*) EIA promotes improved public participation and co-operation and makes decision making more transparent.

(*viii*) EIA promotes increased project acceptance by the public. The transparent and open EIA process, with provision for public involvement, facilitates easy public acceptance of the project.

25.7 LIMITATIONS OF EIA

(*i*) EIA is only an aid to the decision-making process, making it more transparent and informed, but it is **not a decision making tool in itself**. The outcome of the EIA process will benefit the environment only if the required environmental policy and criteria are being applied in other contexts also. EIA does not provide a final decision. By itself, the EIA procedures cannot be expected to stop a proposal. The limited power of EIA may greatly reduce its value.

(*ii*) The transparency and public openness enabled by EIA, **makes decision-making more political**.

(*iii*) EIA is considered by many project proponents and even governments as a **costly exercise**. However, this is not true. Costs of EIA are commonly around 0.6 percent to 0.10 percent of project costs, which is relatively a very small price, considering the cost in terms of the environmental impacts of the project. In contrast, EIA often results in cost saving through reduced changes to the project at later stages, or through identification of easier and more efficient ways to meet project goals.

(*iv*) EIA is a **time consuming** complex process and hence, project proponents are not in favour of it. This criticism is not true. Only if the environmental impacts are complex, EIA becomes complex. A full EIA takes between 3 months to 2 years depending on the complexities of the issues involved. This should not discourage project proponents from doing an EIA, considering the magnitude of the negative effects eliminated through EIA.

(*v*) Many fear that an EIA may cause unnecessary delays in the project. However, experience shows that delay is not due to EIA process but due to poor administration of the process. Essentially, delays occur when:

(*a*) The commencement of EIA is too late in the project cycle.

(*b*) When EIA is not managed to a schedule.

(*c*) When the terms of reference are poorly drafted.

(*d*) When the technical components of EIA are incomplete.

(*e*) When the EIA report which is the basis for decision making is incomplete or deficient.

Besides these limitations, EIA is unpopular because it is:

(*a*) A commitment dependent tool.

(*b*) Susceptible to bias and personal interests (developer, as well as pressure groups).

(*c*) Based on insufficient data or outdated information.

(*d*) Difficult to emphasize interdisciplinary character, even though it is essential.

(*e*) Based on detailed information and data that is not always available or is not compatible with the study requirements data. For example, an EIA may require data on the fragility and quality analysis of the affected land, for which no baseline data is available. Moreover, some environmental components are difficult to address, such as quality analysis, fragility of the land, and landscape value, among others.

(*f*) Based on abstract concepts which cannot always compete with sciences that incorporate quantifiable data.

25.8 REQUIREMENTS FOR THE INTRODUCTION OF AN EIA

According to the basic text prepared by Guillermo Espinoza and Barbara Richards in 2002, for the trainers' course on environmental management and assessment for investment projects, the experience of several countries reveal the following general requirements for the introduction of an EIA system:

(*i*) Definition of the kinds of activities subject to an environmental impact assessment system.

(*ii*) Generation of environmental criteria to distinguish the need for the assessment and the degree of detail required for the proposed project.

(*iii*) Development of the administration of the procedure by means of guidelines acknowledged by all concerned (timeframes, review teams, reception and follow-up of studies, identification of institutions with legal jurisdiction, etc.).

(*iv*) Definition of the contents of the environmental impact study.

(*v*) Drafting of methodological guides for presentation of the environmental impact studies according to project category.

(*vi*) Preparation of terms of reference for different activities and projects.

(*vii*) Definition of a program for the adoption of environmental quality regulations and standards adapted to conditions in the country.

(*viii*) Production of manuals to guide the project or activity manager on how the review should be performed.

(*ix*) Improvement of the reviewing capacity, availability of basic information, and of assessment methodologies applicable to specific situations.

(*x*) Establishment of at least the following eight steps in the system design:

(*a*) Consideration of assessment alternatives.

(*b*) Design of the best alternative.

(*c*) Determination of the need for the study.

(*d*) Definition of the study contents.

(*e*) Preparation of the study report.

(*f*) Report review.

(*g*) Decision on the action proposed.

(*h*) Impact control during execution.

Table 25.3 Comparative Review of EIA Procedures and Practices

Developed countries	EIA in developing countries	EIA in India
Well-framed EIA legislation in place. For instance, in Canada, Canadian Environmental Assessment Act regulates EIA while EU countries are guided by Directive on EIA – (1985).	Lack of formal EIA legislation in many developing countries. For instance, EIA is not mandatory in many African countries	Formal legislation for EIA. It has been enacted by making an amendment in the Environment Protection Act, 1986.
In developed countries, active involvement of all participants including competent authority, government agencies and affected people, at early stages of the EIA.	Limited involvement of public and government agencies in the initial phases.	Limited involvement of public and government agencies in the initial phases.
Integrated approach to EIA followed. All aspects including social and health taken into account.	Mainly environmental aspects considered. Poor on social or health aspects.	No provision in place to cover landscape and visual impacts in the Indian EIA regulations.
Proper consideration of alternatives in EIA	The consideration of alternatives in developing countries is more or less absent.	Same as developing countries.
The process of screening is well defined. For instance, in EU countries, competent authorities decide whether EIA is required after seeking advice from developer, NGOs and statutory consultees. In Japan, screening decision is made by the authorizing agency with respect to certain criteria. In Canada, federal authority determines whether an environmental assessment is required or not.	In developing countries, screening practice in EIA is weak. In most cases, there is a list of activities that require EIA but without any threshold values.	Screening done on the basis of a defined list. Threshold values on the size of the project have been used to decide whether the project will be cleared by the state government or the central government.
Scoping process is comprehensive and involves consultation with all the stakeholders. In many countries, like US, Netherlands, Canada and Europe, the involvement of the public and their concern are addressed in the scoping exercise. Besides this, funding organisations such as World Bank, ADB and ERDB have provision for consultation with the affected people and NGOs during identification of issues in scoping exercise.	Scoping process in most developing countries is very poorly defined. In many countries, including China, Pakistan, etc. there is no provision for scoping. In some countries like Nigeria and Indonesia, a term of reference is followed for scoping while in some countries, like Ghana, Taiwan and Chile, a general checklist is followed. In countries where it is under-taken, there is no public consultation during scoping.	The new notification has put the onus of scoping on the expert committee based on the information provided by the proponent. Consultation with public is optional and depends on the discretion of the expert committee.
Most reports in local language.	Most reports are in English and not in the local language.	Most reports in English and not in the local language. In some cases, executive summary is translated into local language.
A multi-disciplinary approach. Involve-ment of experts with expertise in different areas.	Lack of trained EIA professionals often leads to the preparation of inadequate and irrelevant EIA reports in developing countries	Same in India. Preparation of EIA is done by consultants. Therefore, the selection criterion for the organisation is fees/cost rather than the expertise of EIA team.
Two tier of EIA review. One conducted after the completion of EIA to check the adequacy and effectiveness of EIA and the second done before decision-making.	Poor review or monitoring.	In India too, EIA review is not up to the mark. The review agency called Impact Assessment Agency (IAA) lacks inter-disciplinary capacity. No representation of NGO in IAA, which is a violation of the EIA notification.

Source: Industry & Environment Unit, Centre for Science & Environment, 2006.
http://www.cseindia.org/programme/industry/eia/introduction_eia.htm#hist

25.9 EIA IN INDIA

The Indian experience with Environmental Impact Assessment dates back to 1976-77, when the Planning Commission asked the Department of Science and Technology to examine the river-valley projects from an environmental angle. This was subsequently extended to cover those projects, which required the approval of the Public Investment Board.

Table 25.4 EIAs Cleared by MoEF in Different Sectors in India since 1994 to Mid 2006

Projects/ Year	River Valley Projects	Industrial Projects	Thermal Power Projects	Mininig Projects#	Other Sectors*	Total
1994	8	20	15	13 +24	24	104
1995	13	55	13	19 + 51	29	180
1996	6	54	26	39 + 15	30	170
1997	4	98	39	7 + 17	21	186
1998	9	34	17	9	11	80
1999	5	45	17	25	12	104
2000	5	52	15	17	36	125
2001	12	63	14	9	23	121
2002	12	83	7	31	25	158
2003	16	220	5	19	55	315
2004	8	165	27	62	14	286
2004–2006	30	559	42	302	89	1022
						2851

Note: # Environmental Clearance + Site Clearance
* Includes transport, ports, harbours, airports, highways and communication projects.

Source: MoEF Annual Reports (1994–2006)

On 27 January 1994, Environmental Clearance (EC) was made mandatory by the Union Ministry of Environment and Forests (MoEF), Government of India, under the Environmental (Protection) Act 1986, for the expansion or modernization of any activity or for setting up new projects. Since then, 12 amendments have been made in the EIA notification of 1994. The EIA process is well established in India, and till 2006, more than 2800 projects were given environmental clearance (Table 25.4).

In September 2006, new EIA legilslation was notified by the MoEF. The notification makes it mandatory for various projects, such as mining, thermal power plants, river valleys, infrastructure (road, highway, ports, harbours and airports) and industries, including very small electroplating or foundry units, to get environment clearance. The new legislation has put the onus of clearing projects on the state government, depending on the size/capacity of the project. The EIA experience in India indicates that the lack of timely availability of reliable and authentic environmental data has been a major bottleneck in achieving the full benefits of EIA.

BOX 25.1

Environmental Appraisal of Bodhghat Hydro Electric Project

The case study of the Bodhghat hydro electric project on River Indravati in Madhya Pradesh presents an account of how public pressure, legislative framework and EIA procedures and practices have been effective in arresting a major ecological disaster. The project involved the construction of the following:

- A composite dam of a total length of 1720 m at the dam top level, consisting of a 855 m long and 90 m high concrete gravity dam and fill dams of 500 m and 365 m lengths on the left and right flanks, respectively.
- A 3 km long (with 12.5 m diameter) head race tunnel.
- A 5 km long tail race canal.
- A surface powerhouse to support 4 generating units, each of 125 MW.

This project was designed as a peaking station, with an installed capacity of 500 MW (4 units of 125 MW) to provide a large peaking potential to the power station of M.P. State. The total land requirement for the project was 13,783,147 ha of which 5,704,332 ha comprised forest land. The project involved the displacement of nearly 10,000 tribal people from 42 villages. The Bodhghat Dam was particularly regarded as environmentally damaging because its functional effectiveness was directly linked to the projects proposed downstream. Together, these projects could impose a great stress on the ecology of the Indravati Tiger Reserve, Bhairamgarh Wild Buffalo Sanctuary and other surrounding habitats of Indian wild buffalo (Bubalis bubalis).

- The dam would result in the forced displacement of some 10,000 tribal people whose sustainable way of life based on a mixed economy of agriculture, herding, fishing and forest use would be entirely destroyed.
- The project would also lead to the inundation of a large area of forest, a resource fundamental to the tribal people, whose dependency on the resources from the forest is almost total and complete. The consequential movement of people into the forest interiors that are currently free from biotic disturbance would pose a major threat to the relatively undisturbed tracts of the forest and the wildlife habitat.
- The project would result in a total loss of 20,000 hectares of wildlife habitat.
- The non-availability of cultivable land and wood lots for meeting the resource needs of the people for fuel wood, timber, food and fodder would have adverse effects on people driven from the project area. The entire project area, which provides an ideal setting for designation as a 'Biosphere Reserve', owing to its biological richness and its pristine nature, would become open to ecological destruction.
- The Bodhghat project would inevitably lead to the justification and the imposition of Bhopalpatnam project, Inchampalli project and other projects located downstream.

The project was delayed due to various reasons, such as paucity of funds and concern for environmental impacts raised by NGOs. Under instruction from DoE, Government of India, an EIA was done with a view to provide an independent assessment of the impacts on the wildlife and forests. The study was initiated in October 1989 and was completed in April 1990. The field studies primarily focused on:

- Assessment of the impacts of the project on biophysical environment.
- Assessment of the status of wildlife habitats with special reference to wild buffalo habitat.
- Assessment of the human dependencies on natural resources of the project area.

contd...

- Review of the impacts of the project on wildlife, and the socio-economic status of the resource dependent community.
- Review of the rehabilitation policy for project-affected people.

From the EIA studies conducted by the Wildlife Institute of India, it could be concluded that the ecological and social impacts of the Bodhghat project far outweigh its economic benefits. In view of the findings of the ecological and socio-economic assessment undertaken by the WII team and the independent observations of the Special Committee of the Government of India that visited the project site in 1987, the project could not be granted clearance under the Forest Conservation Act (1980). As a result, even the environmental clearance that was granted on the condition that the project would have to first obtain clearance under the FCA (1980) was revoked in 1994.

Source: http://eia.unu.edu/wiki/index.php Assessed_impacts_of_the_proposed_Bodhghat_ Hydroelectric_project
Dr. Asha Rajvanshi, Environmental Impact Assessment Cell, Wildlife Institute of India.

25.10 CONCLUSION

A study on the practice of EIA in India since 1996, concluded that EIAs helped in realizing a range of direct and indirect benefits such as: early withdrawal of environmentally unsound proposals, 'greening' project design and planning, catalyzing policy and institutional reforms and serving as an educational and awareness raising mechanism. The inclusion of public participation and scrutiny in the EIA process and the well documented reports ensured that EIA reports were taken into account in political decision-making. With experience, the EIA systems have been perfected with the gradual incorporation of additional elements. In the last 30 years, environmental impact assessments have increasingly been carried out in response to the concern of investors or international organizations and to legal requirements that some countries have established. Although there is a growing awareness of the advantages of incorporating EIAs, there is still scope for improvement in the application of EIA systems.

QUESTIONS

1. Examine the various steps in making an EIA. Which method do you think is the best to carry out an EIA?
2. Discuss the costs and benefits of using an EIA process.
3. Provide local examples that highlight the gains that can be obtained from a well managed EIA.

EXERCISE

1. Prepare a write up on the environmental impact assessment for any project in India.

❑❑❑

26

Environmental Certifications

> *The role of modern business: To provide ever better goods and services in a way that is profitable, ethical and respects the environment, individuals and the communities in which it operates.*
>
> **Tomorrow's Company (2007)**

Being environmentally responsible is increasingly viewed as a requirement of doing business. For manufacturing managers, this has meant re-examining their products and processes, with an eye towards the reduction or elimination (if possible) of any resulting waste streams. For the purchasing profession, the corresponding challenge has been to identify suppliers who can provide environmentally responsible goods and services without sacrificing cost, quality, flexibility, or lead time. It has also meant identifying and evaluating any initiative consistent with these new expanded objectives. One such initiative is the ISO 14000 series developed by the International Standards Organization.

The International Organization for Standardization (ISO), based in Geneva, is one of the key international voluntary standards bodies. Standards developed by ISO are available to the 140 or so member countries to adopt as they see fit. Although ISO standards are voluntary, many are eventually cited in legislation.

ISO has a rigorous process for standards development. When a new standard is proposed, it must be approved either by a technical committee or by the Technical Management Board of ISO. Once a technical committee is established, it may establish subcommittees and working groups to carry out the work.

There are currently around 2,850 active technical committees, sub-committees and working groups, made up of qualified representatives from around the world. To date, more than 12,000 ISO standards have been published. ISO has a general rule that all standards are to be reviewed at least once in every five years.

26.1 THE ISO 14000 FAMILY

The ISO 14000 is a standard for environmental management systems that is applicable to any business, regardless of size, location or income. The aim of the standard is to reduce the environmental footprint of a business and to decrease the pollution and waste a business produces.

The ISO 14000 series of standards has been designed to help enterprises meet their environmental management system needs. They have been under development by the International Organization for Standardisation (ISO) since 1991. They consist of a set of documents that define the key elements of a management system that will help an organization address the environmental issues it faces. The management system includes the setting of goals and priorities, assignment of responsibility for accomplishing them, measuring and reporting on results, and external verification of claims. The ISO 14000 series comprises the following parts:

(*i*) **Environmental Management System (EMS):** Specification document of requirements for certification (14001), general guidelines (14004).

(*ii*) **Environmental Auditing (EA):** guidelines and general principles (14010), guidelines and auditing procedures (14011), qualification criteria for environmental auditors (14012).

(*iii*) **Environmental Labelling (EL):** Environmental labelling standards (14020–14024).

(*iv*) **Environmental Performance Evaluation (EPE):** Evaluation guidelines for environmental performance (14031).

(*v*) **Life Cycle Assessment (LCA):** Tools for environmental evaluation (14040–14043).

(*vi*) **ISO 14050:** Terms and definitions.

(*vii*) **ISO 14062:** discusses making improvements to environmental impact goals.

(*viii*) **ISO 14063:** Environmental communication—Guidelines and examples.

(*ix*) **ISO19011:** This specifies one audit protocol, for both 14000 and 9000 series of standards. It replaces ISO 14011 meta-evaluation—how to tell if your intended regulatory tools worked. 19011 is now the only recommended way to determine this.

ISO 14000 shares many common traits with ISO 9000. It is backed by the ISO; as such, it is hoped that it will pave the way for firms to use one standard of practices rather than dealing with conflicting environmental regulations across national borders. Like its predecessor, ISO 14000 does not focus on outcomes, such as pollution output, but focuses on processes. Finally, like ISO 9000, ISO 14000 involves an audit by a third party.

It is a fundamental principle of ISO 14001, which governs environmental management systems that organizations set their own goals, based on whatever considerations they wish to include, such as the demands of customers, regulators, communities, lenders or environmental groups. The ISO 14000 standards do not themselves specify environmental performance goals. These must be set by the company itself, taking into account the effects it has on the environment, and the views of its stakeholders. The ISO 14001 standard provides a framework within which to develop plans to meet those targets, and to produce information about whether or not the targets are met. They are concerned with establishing "how to" achieve a goal, not "what" the goal should be.

By the end of 2001, nearly 32,000 organizations worldwide had received ISO 14001 accreditation. An important benefit of adopting ISO 14001 is to give stakeholders the reassurance they need that the organization's environmental claims are valid. The ISO 14001 standard is intended to be flexible, and to be of value in a wide variety of situations. However, it is applicable most readily to large companies that already have a formal management system in place, and which have the expertise and resources to incorporate environmental issues into that system. However, the principles have been designed to apply also to smaller businesses, and to non-business organizations.

In general, conformance with one of the international standards can lead to the implementation of other standards. For example, once an organization has implemented ISO 14001, it is easier for it to satisfy the requirements of EMAS (the European Eco-Management and Audit Scheme).

26.2 COMPONENTS OF ISO 14000

Firms that wish to adopt ISO 14000 must consider their environmental impacts systematically and include five broad components (Fig. 26.1): an environmental policy, an environmental plan, an implementation strategy, monitoring and corrective-action procedures, and management review.

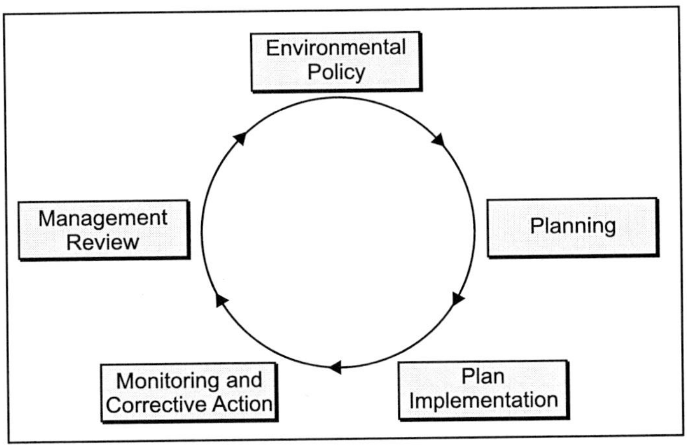

Fig. 26.1 ISO 14001 Environmental Management System Loop

(*i*) **An environmental policy** that commits the organization to prevention of pollution, continual improvement and compliance with relevant environmental legislation and regulations.

(*ii*) **Planning** to implement the environmental policy, which entails identifying all of an organization's interactions with the environment and designating the significant aspects and setting quantifiable objectives and targets for addressing those significant aspects.

(*iii*) **Implementation and operation**, which requires an organization to ensure the availability of resources, defines roles and responsibilities, develops documented procedures, emergency preparedness plans and ensures employee competency, training and awareness.

(*iv*) **Checking and corrective action** to measure and track the performance of the system against its own goals and to evaluate compliance with the relevant laws and regulations. The organization must also identify, investigate and correct any non-conformity. The organization must ensure that internal audits are conducted.

(*v*) **Review** of the EMS by top management to ensure its continuing suitability, adequacy, and effectiveness.

26.3 GLOBAL ISO CERTIFICATIONS

Since 1996, when the environmental management system standard, ISO 14000 was developed, it has gained global popularity. Fig. 26.2 shows the exponential trend in global ISO 14000 certifications. While the ISO standard focuses on conformity with established policies, plans and procedures, it does not specify requirements for environmental performance beyond compliance with the relevant legislation. Organizations are however, free to set goals that exceed compliance requirements. Companies implementing ISO 14000 may choose to have their EMS certified. They can seek third party certification from either accredited certificate bodies (those recognized by a national accreditation body) or non accredited bodies. However, most firms seeking certification employ accredited bodies.

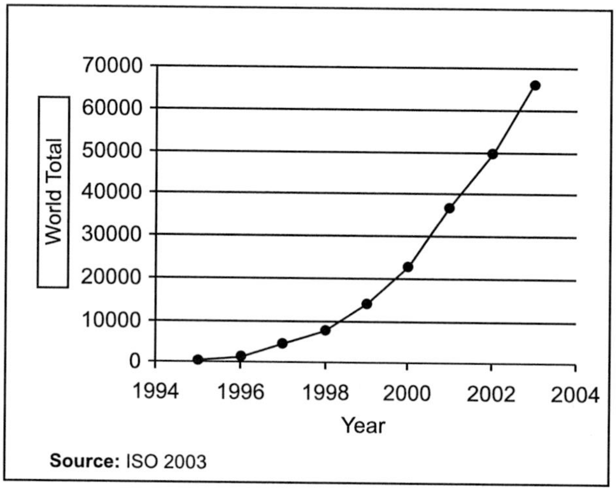

Fig. 26.2 Global ISO 14001 Certifications

26.4 RELEVANCE OF ISO 14000 TO BUSINESSES

In broad terms, ISO 14000 can fill two requirements in an organization. The first is the internal need for a system that will help the organization address all of the legal, commercial and other challenges related to the environment that face it today. The second is the need to be able to assure those outside the company that the company is meeting its stated environmental policies.

Internal Benefits

Reduce Accidents and Liability: A systematic approach to managing environmental issues can help to ensure that environmental accidents and liability are reduced.

Efficiency: A systematic approach can help to identify opportunities to conserve material and energy inputs, to reduce wastes and to improve process efficiency.

Performance: A systematic approach to management leads indirectly to improved environmental performance and improved cost control.

Improved Corporate Culture: Top management commitment to improved environmental performance, clearly defined goals, responsibilities and accountabilities, creates a greater awareness and understanding of environmental issues and an improved corporate culture.

External Benefits

Third Party Assurance and Recognition: Companies often have to demonstrate that their products and services meet certain conditions. This is exactly what standards do efficiently, especially when combined with third party conformity assessment programmes. They reduce or eliminate the need of companies to individually inspect each supplier's products and services with its own auditors. International standards, such as the ISO 14000 series, provide the widest possible recognition of this assurance.

Market Access: ISO 14000 may become a pre-requisite of doing business. Companies have turned to agreed-upon international standards as a way of meeting certain expectations. Customers may demand that their suppliers meet specific environmental goals and have ISO 14000 certification to ensure that the goals are being met.

Regulatory Relief: Regulators may begin to recognize the assurance provided by ISO 14000 and offer some sort of regulatory relief such as easier grant of permits, fewer inspections and streamlined reporting requirements, to those who implement EMS.

Expression of Due Diligence: By using ISO 14000 to systematically identify and manage environmental risk and liability, the courts, investors and lenders, and regulators may all use it as a sign of due diligence and commitment to good environmental management.

Public Image and Community Relations: The presence of an EMS, the information it produces and the attention it demands will help an organization communicate with its stakeholders.

Financial Markets: Having an internationally recognized EMS in place will improve investor confidence and access to capital, and potentially provide access to preferential insurance rates.

26.5 WHY SHOULD ENVIRONMENTALISTS BE INTERESTED?

Most outside stakeholders are more interested in how an organization actually performs than in the tools it may use to achieve that performance. Stakeholder interest goes beyond simply knowing that an EMS is in place. ISO 14000 does not set environmental performance standards. It leaves these to the organization, saying only that its policies must include a commitment to comply with all the relevant laws and regulations.

How then can those interested in improving environmental performance make use of the system? First, ISO 14000 provides a useful tool with which to hold companies accountable. When a company does establish a positive environmental policy, the ISO 14000 system can be used to check that it is actually accomplishing its goals, and reporting appropriately on them.

Furthermore, companies can be encouraged to insist that all of their suppliers meet the environmental policy goals.

Finally, just the existence of an EMS in a company will usually lead to environmental performance improvements. It is in the nature of organizations that when an issue is brought into their management structure they try to deal with it systematically and positively. If encouraged by substantive inputs from customers, environmental groups and other stakeholders, the chances of improvement become greater.

26.6 RELATED INITIATIVES

Three other initiatives have played a significant role in helping to shape the ISO 14000 series: the British Standard (BS 7750) Specification for Environmental Management Systems, the European Union's Eco-Management and Audit Scheme (EMAS), and the Canadian Standards Association (CSA) Environmental Management Program.

BS 7750: Specification for Environmental Management Systems

The British Standards Institute (BSI) published a draft, BS 7750 Specification for Environmental Management Systems, in March 1992. A second edition was published in 1994. It is a specification for an EMS rather than a guidance document. It provides details about how an organization can ensure compliance with its chosen environmental policies and objectives. It also provides guidance on how to implement an EMS.

The BS 7750 EMS specification is designed to improve the environmental performance of all types and sizes of organizations and is underpinned by a systematic and integrated managerial approach, the creation of corporate environmental policy and objectives, and by the key concept of environmental auditing. (BS 7750 shares common management system principles with the BS 5750 specification for quality management systems; though the latter is not an operational prerequisite).

The specification provides details on the following requirements: the environmental management system; environmental policy; organization and personnel; environmental effects; environmental objectives and targets; environmental management programme; operational control; environmental management records; environmental management audits; environmental management reviews. It was designed to be compatible with the EU Eco-Management and Audit Scheme (EMAS), a voluntary regulation which came into effect in April, 1995.

The requirement for an environmental effects register, that is, a list of the significant environmental effects, direct and indirect, of the activities, products, and services of the organization is a major objective of the specification. These effects include registering the significant effects of emissions to the atmosphere, discharges to water, solid and other wastes, land contamination, and resource use.

The BS 7750 does not define or set specific environmental performance criteria, objectives, indicators, targets, or timetables for a business or organization. The single level of performance specified is to meet the requirements of the standard.

British Standards 7750 was a major influence on the development of the ISO 14001 specification document. However, according to the terms of the Vienna Agreement (an agreement between the European Union and the ISO), if an ISO document is ratified by the Union, then all competing

National Standards must be withdrawn. The EU having accepted ISO 14001, it superseded BS 7750 in March 1997.

The Eco-Management and Audit Scheme (EMAS)

The European Union's Eco-Management and Audit Scheme (EMAS), which became effective in 1995, is a voluntary programme which enables organizations within the EU and the European Economic Area to seek certification for their environmental management systems. Each member state was required to designate an independent national authority to oversee the regulation.

Many European countries require large manufacturing facilities to implement the Eco-Management and Audit Scheme (EMAS). The components of EMAS are similar to those of ISO 14001. However, EMAS has two significant additions: a baseline environmental assessment and a public environmental performance report. Many companies outside Europe have also chosen to implement the EMAS system or variations.

Registration under EMAS is on a site-by-site basis, rather than covering entire organizations. Originally, EMAS was confined to industrial operations, but as part of a wide-ranging revision of the regulation, adopted in March 2001 (EMAS II), all sectors of economic activity are now included.

Other amendments embraced by 'EMAS II' include:

(*i*) The integration of ISO 14001 as the environmental management system required by EMAS, to make it easier for companies to make the transition from ISO to EMAS (in general, EMAS is more stringent than ISO 14001).

(*ii*) The creation of an EMAS logo.

(*iii*) Greater participation of employees in the implementation of EMAS.

(*iv*) A greater emphasis given to environmental reporting.

(*v*) More consideration of 'indirect' environmental impacts—for example those associated with investment policies, procurement and planning.

The new regulation, 761/2001, was officially adopted by the Council of the European Union and by the European Parliament on 19 March 2001 and came into effect the following month, replacing Regulation 1836/93. All member states are obliged to implement it, and to establish an accreditation system within 12 months of its coming into force. To date, more than 3,100 sites have been awarded EMAS certification, two-thirds of them in Germany.

The Canadian Standards Association Environmental Programme

The Canadian Standards Association (CSA) has developed consensus based information for a range of environmental initiatives, including EMS and auditing systems. By way of a Voluntary Environmental Management Programme, they are assisting businesses and organizations in improving their environmental performance.

The CAN/CSA Z750-94 information product entitled *A Voluntary Environmental Management System* is based on the premise of prevention, rather than end-of-pipe control. The EMS design should emphasize prevention by identifying the organization's significant environmental effects, applicable laws and regulations, and priorities, and by facilitating corrective actions, systems auditing, and operation processes and procedures.

The framework is based on four general principles for management systems: purpose, commitment, capability, and learning.

(*i*) Purpose concerns the organization's environmental policy; the risks associated with its activities, processes, products, and services; and its environmental objectives and targets.

(*ii*) Commitment refers to motivation according to environmental values; organizational alignment and integration; and accountability and responsibility.

(*iii*) Capability refers to human, physical and financial resources; knowledge, skills, and training; and information management.

(*iv*) Learning is about measuring and monitoring, communication and reporting, system audits and management review; and continuous improvement.

The CSA has also developed guidelines for environmental auditing (CSA Z751-93). This is a process of objectively obtaining and evaluating evidence regarding an environmental matter. The results must be documented by factual data before the findings are communicated to the client. Each process of the audit is performed and documented by an auditing team which is responsible for developing a plan to determine what evidence is to be collected and why. It is the responsibility of the auditee to assist the team by providing them with the relevant information. Evidence is collected from personnel, third-parties, physical measurements, data and reports and other techniques. After the results are evaluated, the findings are released.

Environment, Health and Safety (EHS) Programmes

Historically, the control of safety and health has been driven by occupational health and safety regulations. Health and safety programmes arose from the need to protect workers from occupational hazards and to ensure a productive workforce. It was restricted to those issues which arose within the workplace.

The growing number of regulations concerning impacts that take place beyond the factory gate meant that environmental issues needed to be incorporated into operational practice. Many companies expanded their existing health and safety policies and procedures to include the outside environment. In some cases, "environment" includes the workplace itself.

The emphasis placed on environment, relative to health and safety, varies from company to company. Some companies have developed comprehensive environment, health and safety (EHS) programmes, while others preferred to establish a separate programme to address environmental issues.

Growing public concern over environmental degradation, coupled with increasing regulation, has encouraged businesses to take their EHS responsibilities seriously.

An essential part of managing EHS issues in the workplace is reporting. Many companies issue annual EHS reports, to communicate commitments and targets to external stakeholders. Some choose to report on their environmental issues separately from those for health and safety. Others may not produce stand-alone reports at all, but simply include the information in their annual report.

26.7 CONCLUSION

The ISO 14000 standards series has been one of the most significant international initiatives for sustainable development. Used in conjunction with appropriate goals, and with management commitment, the standards will help improve corporate performance. They will provide an objective basis for verifying a company's claims about its performance. This is particularly important in relation to international trade, where at present, almost anyone can make assertions about environmental performance—and there are only limited means to verify or validate the same.

Consumers, governments, and companies up and down the supply chain, are all seeking ways to reduce their environmental impact and increase their long-run sustainability. For companies, the key goals are to become more efficient—to get more output per unit of input—while earning profits and maintaining the trust of their stakeholders. Implementation of a management system based approach will help companies focus attention on environmental issues, and bring them into the mainstream of corporate decision-making. ISO 14000 is designed to provide customers with a reasonable assurance that the performance claims of a company are accurate. In fact, ISO 14000 will help to integrate the environmental management systems of companies that trade with each other in all corners of the world.

QUESTIONS

1. Why should a company pursue ISO 14000?
2. Explain the salient features of ISO 14000.

EXERCISE

1. Compare the performance of an ISO 14000 certified company before and after certification.

❑❑❑

27

Environmental Marketing

> *Smart companies seize competitive advantage through strategic management of environmental challenges.*
>
> **Andrew Winston and Daniel Esty, *Green to Gold***

The marketing of green products is called environmental or green marketing. Green marketing is becoming more important to businesses because of the consumer's genuine concerns about our limited resources on the earth. By implementing green marketing measures to save the earth's resources in production, packaging, and operations, businesses are showing consumers that they too share the same concerns, thus boosting their credibility.

Green products balance environmental compatibility with performance, affordability, and convenience. They are typically durable, non-toxic, recyclable, and are often made from recycled materials. Green products have minimal packaging, and should carry low environmental impact. Green marketing thrives on the underlying philosophy, *reduce, reuse and recycle*.

Divergent aspects of green marketing include ecologically safer products, recyclable and biodegradable packaging, energy-efficient operations, and better pollution controls. Advances in green marketing include, packaging made from recycled paper, phosphate-free detergents, refillable containers for cleaning products, and bottles using less plastic.

27.1 DEFINITIONS

Green marketing is the marketing of products that are presumed to be environmentally safe. Thus, green marketing incorporates a broad range of activities, including product modification, changes to the production process, packaging changes, as well as modifying advertising.

Pride and Ferrell (1993) define it as "Green marketing, also alternatively known as environmental marketing and sustainable marketing, refers to an organization's efforts at designing, promoting, pricing and distributing products that will not harm the environment."

Polonsky (1994) defines green marketing as all activities designed to generate and facilitate any exchanges intended to satisfy human needs or wants, such that the satisfaction of these needs and wants occurs, with minimal detrimental impact on the natural environment.

Elkington (1994) defines the green consumer as one who avoids products that are likely to:

(*i*) endanger the health of the consumer or others.

(*ii*) cause significant damage to the environment during manufacture, use or disposal.

(*iii*) consume a disproportionate amount of energy.

(*iv*) cause unnecessary waste.

(*v*) use materials derived from threatened species or environments.

(*vi*) involve unnecessary use of, or cruelty to animals.

(*vii*) adversely affect other countries.

27.2 REASONS FOR THE ADOPTION OF GREEN MARKETING BY FIRMS

Green marketing has been widely adopted by firms worldwide and the following are the possible reasons cited for the same:

(*i*) Opportunities: As demands change, many firms see these changes as opportunities to be exploited and have a competitive advantage over firms marketing non-environmentally responsible alternatives. Some examples of firms who have striven to become more environmentally responsible, in an attempt to better satisfy their consumer needs are:

(*a*) McDonald's replaced its clam shell packaging with waxed paper because of increased consumer concern relating to polystyrene production and ozone depletion.

(*b*) Tuna manufacturers modified their fishing techniques because of the increased concern over driftnet fishing, and the resulting death of dolphins.

(*c*) Xerox introduced a "high quality" recycled photocopier paper in an attempt to satisfy the demands of firms for less environmentally harmful products.

(*ii*) Social Responsibility: Many firms are beginning to realize that they are members of the wider community and therefore, must behave in an environmentally responsible fashion, thus resulting in environmental issues being integrated into the firm's corporate culture.

(*iii*) Governmental Pressure: Governmental regulations relating to environmental marketing are designed to protect consumers through regulations designed to control the amount of hazardous wastes produced by firms by issuing of various environmental licenses, thus modifying organizational behaviour. In some cases, governments try to "induce" final consumers to become more responsible by taxing individuals who act in an irresponsible fashion. For example, in Australia, there is a higher gas tax associated with leaded petrol.

(*iv*) Competitive Pressure: Another major force in the environmental marketing area has been the firms' desire to maintain their competitive position. In many cases, firms observe competitors promoting their environmental behaviour and attempt to emulate this behaviour. In some instances this competitive pressure has caused an entire industry to modify and thus reduce its detrimental environmental behaviour. For example, it could be argued that Xerox's "Revive 100% Recycled paper" was introduced a few years ago in an attempt to address the introduction of recycled photocopier paper by other manufacturers. In another example, when one tuna manufacturer stopped using driftnets, the others followed suit.

(*v*) Cost or Profit Issues: Disposing of environmentally harmful by-products, such as polychlorinated biphenyl (PCB) contaminated oil are becoming increasingly costly and in some cases, difficult. In minimizing wastes, firms often develop more effective production processes that reduce the need for some raw materials, thus serving as a double cost savings. In other cases, firms attempt to find end-of-pipe solutions, instead of minimizing waste by trying to find markets or uses for their waste materials, where one firm's waste becomes another firm's input of production.

27.3 PROBLEMS WITH GREEN MARKETING

(*i*) Often, consumers' perceptions on what is environmentally benign behaviour may not be correct.

(*ii*) When firms attempt to become socially responsible, they may face the risk that the environmentally responsible action of today, will be found to be harmful in the future. This may explain why some firms, like Coca-Cola and Walt Disney World, are becoming socially responsible without publicizing the point. They may be protecting themselves from potential future negative backlash, if it is determined that they made the wrong decisions in the past.

(*iii*) Reacting to competitive pressures can cause all to make the same mistake as the leader. A costly example of this was the Mobil Corporation in the USA, who followed the competition and introduced "biodegradable" plastic garbage bags. While technically, these bags were biodegradable, the conditions under which they were disposed did not allow biodegradation to occur. Mobil was sued by several US states for using misleading advertising claims. Thus, blindly following the competition can have costly ramifications.

(*iv*) End-of-pipe solutions may not actually reduce the waste but rather shift it around, though it may minimize its short term affects. Ultimately, most of the waste produced will enter the waste stream; therefore, to be environmentally responsible, organizations should attempt to minimize their waste, rather than find "appropriate" uses for it.

(*v*) Very often, green marketing boils down to nothing more than slick advertising campaigns by big corporate polluters to hype band-aid measures, such as using a few recycled materials or contributing money to a wildlife fund, which are showcased as *concern for the environment* while off camera, the pollution and devouring of non-renewable resources goes on. They also engage in *greenwashing*, in which companies lavishly fund PR campaigns to paint themselves "green" without altering their current polluting practices.

27.4 GREENWASHING DEFINED

Greenwashing can be defined as the misleading act of companies, governments, organizations, and individuals trying to promote unjustified environmentally friendly practices, products and services through branding, mislabelling, packaging, or public relations.

History of Greenwashing

The term greenwashing is believed to have been coined in 1986 when environmentalist, Jay Westerveld, observed the practice of hotels encouraging guests to reuse bath towels as an effort to help the environment. It gave the impression that the hotels were pursuing efforts to be more ecologically sound. The reality was that they had no other environmentally positive policies and simply saved massive amounts of money on laundry costs.

BOX 27.1

Seven Sins of Greenwashing

In December 2007, the environmental marketing firm, Terra Choice, gained national press coverage for releasing a study called "The Six Sins of Greenwashing" which found that more than 99 per cent of 1,018 common consumer products, randomly surveyed for the study, were guilty of greenwashing. According to the study, the six sins of greenwashing are:

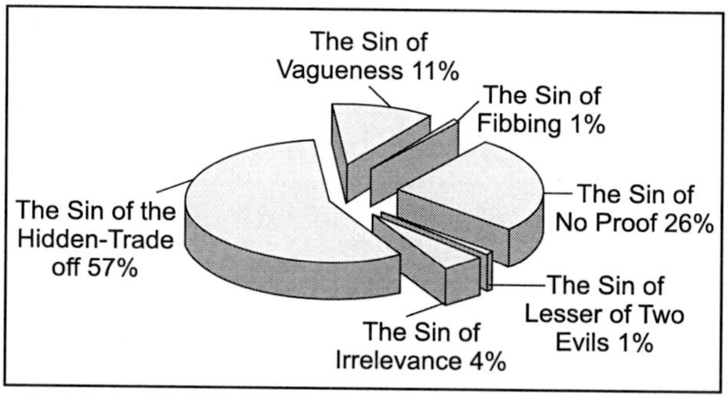

- Sin of the Hidden Trade-Off: *e.g.,* "Energy-efficient" electronics that contain hazardous materials.
- Sin of No Proof: *e.g.,* Shampoos claiming to be "certified organic," but with no verifiable certification.
- Sin of Vagueness: *e.g.,* Products claiming to be 100 per cent natural when many naturally-occurring substances are hazardous, like arsenic and formaldehyde.
- Sin of Irrelevance: *e.g.,* Products claiming to be CFC-free, even though CFCs were banned 20 years ago.
- Sin of Fibbing: *e.g.,* Products falsely claiming to be certified by an internationally recognized environmental standard.
- Sin of Lesser of Two Evils: *e.g.,* Organic cigarettes or "environmentally friendly" pesticides.

In April 2009, Terra Choice published a second report on the subject. This report noted the emergence of a Seventh Sin:

- The Sin of Worshipping False Labels is committed by a product that, through either words or images, gives the impression of third-party endorsement, where no such endorsement actually exists; fake labels, in other words.

Source: http://sinsofgreenwashing.org/findings/

27.5 ECO-LABELLING: A MARK FOR THE FUTURE

To assist consumers to judge the validity of companies' environmental claims, eco-labelling programmes run by governments and non-profit groups have sprung up in several countries.

Eco-labelling is l*abelling of products and materials to indicate their environmental quality - including how they have been produced and their impact on the environment.*

"Eco-labelling" is a voluntary approach to environmental performance certification that is practiced around the world. An "eco-label" identifies a product that meets specified performance criteria or standards. In contrast to "green" symbols or claim statements made by manufacturers and service providers, an eco-label is awarded by a third-party organization for products or services that are determined to meet specific environmental criteria.

Eco-labelling schemes thus, help consumers make decisions about the products they buy and whether they are environmentally friendly. There are several existing eco-label schemes around the world, including the German Green Spot, the Nordic Swan and the US Green Seal. Most current eco-label programmes are "cradle to grave", that is, they involve some form of analysis based on the environmental consequences of their product's manufacture, use and disposal.

Eco-labels can cover a range of environmental attributes, which may include health issues, atmospheric impacts or other environmental impacts, packaging and other industrial issues, to name a few. Labels allow consumers to make comparisons among products/services in the category and essentially, vote for their preferences in the market when making purchasing decisions.

An eco-label could be a graphic symbol and/or a short descriptive text applied on a product, package, or inserted in a brochure or in another informative document that accompanies the product and gives details about the environmental impacts generated by the respective product.

Different types of organizations, including governments, non-profit and for-profit organizations have developed eco-label programs. The breadth of, and issues addressed by, eco-label programmes vary. For example: ENERGY STAR (US certification) is focused on energy use during equipment operation, while other eco-labels address life cycle environmental concerns and still others, cover ergonomic and worker health and safety issues. Purchasers deciding to utilize eco-labels to assist purchasing decisions should carefully review the criteria to be sure that the programme reflects their specific concerns.

Based on overseas experience, appropriate eco-labelling, with associated verification and certification procedures, is a driver for the increased uptake of recycled content and / or sustainable products. Eco-labels belong to the class of "new environmental policy instruments" (NEPls), together with voluntary agreements, eco-taxes and tradable permits. Eco-labels are complementary policy instruments, not only to traditional regulation, but also to other market based instruments. They mainly rely on moral persuasion by influencing the customer's attitude towards protecting the environment and choosing eco-products and/or products with a reduced impact upon the environment.

Environmental performance labels and declarations vary greatly. The International Organization for Standardization (ISO) has identified three broad types of voluntary environmental labels (Table 27.1).

Table 27.1 Types of Voluntary Environmental Labels

Type I	Voluntary, multiple-criteria based, third party programme that awards a license that authorizes the use of environmental labels on products indicating overall environmental preferability of a product within a particular product category, based on life cycle.
Type II	Informative environmental self-declaration claims.
Type III	Voluntary programme that provide quantified environmental data of a product, under pre-set categories of parameters, set by a qualified third party and based on life cycle assessment, and verified by that or another qualified third party.

Source: ISO, Geneva

27.6 ECO LABELS SCHEMES IN VARIOUS COUNTRIES

Internationally, environmental labelling programmes are becoming popular. A number of countries, including India, have launched ecolabelling schemes.

Table 27.2 Eco Labels in Various Countries

Country	Name of Programme	Year Started
Germany	Blue Angel	1977
Canada	Environmental Choice	1988
Japan	Ecomark	1989
Nordic Countries	White Swan	1989
New Zealand	Environmental Choice	1990
Sweden	Good Environmental Choice	1990
United States	Green Seal	1990
Austria	Austrian Eco-label	1991
India	Ecomark	1991
European Union	European Flower	1992
France	NF-Environment	1992
South Korea	Ecomark	1992
Singapore	Green Label	1992
The Netherlands	Stichting Milieukeur	1992
Croatia	Environmentally Friendly	1993

27.7 SOME POPULAR INTERNATIONAL ECO-LABELS

(*i*) **Canada's EcoLogo Programme** certifies products and services based on compliance with environmental criteria focused on the life-cycle impacts of a product or service. The EcoLogo Programme requires third-party verification of compliance with the certification criteria.

(*ii*) **European Union's Eco Flower** is a Europe-wide programme that awards eco-labels to products that have been found to have less of an environmental impact than other similar competing products, based on life cycle considerations.

(*iii*) **Germany's Blue Angel** programme is a voluntary labelling programme. For three decades, the Blue Angel label has been awarded to 3,700 products in 80 product and service categories. The Blue Angel is awarded to products and services which are particularly beneficial for the environment, on consideration of the life cycle, and which also fulfill high standards of occupational health, safety, and fitness for use.

(*iv*) **Sweden's TCO Development** provides certification and environmental labelling of office equipment, designed to improve both the work and external environment. Products must undergo independent testing and documentation.

Fig. 27.1 Some Popular International Eco-labels

(*v*) **Nordic Swan** is the official Nordic eco-label and is the collective effort of 5 countries: Norway, Sweden, Denmark, Finland and Iceland. Products that satisfy strict environmental standards are allowed to display the environmental product label. Companies applying for a license to use the Swan label must provide results from independent testing to prove that the criteria are met.

(*vi*) **Japan's Eco Mark** certification criteria consider environmental impacts throughout the life cycle of each product.

(*vii*) **The U.S. EPA's Comprehensive Procurement Guideline (CPG)** programme promotes the use of materials recovered from solid waste by designating products that are or can be made with recovered materials and by recommending practices (minimum recycled content) for buying these products.

(*viii*) **India's Earthern Pot** prescribes criteria for 14 categories of products which cause substantially less pollution than other comparable products; and which comply with laws and regulations pertaining to the environment.

27.8 INDIAN ECO MARK

The Ministry of Environment and Forests launched the scheme of labelling of environment friendly products in 1991. The label is awarded to consumer goods which meet the specified environmental criteria and the quality requirements of Indian standards.

The earthen pot, chosen as the logo for the Ecomark scheme, uses a renewable resource like the earth, does not produce hazardous waste and consumes little energy in making. Its solid and graceful form represents both strength and fragility, which also characterises the eco-system. As a symbol, it puts across its environmental message. The logo for the Ecomark scheme signifies that the product, which carries it, does least damage to the environment. This scheme is a purely voluntary scheme open for all domestic and foreign manufacturers.

Fig. 27.2 India's Earthern Pot

The scheme identified 16 categories of consumer products for the purpose of development of eco-criteria and labelling. So far, criteria for 14 categories of products have been finally notified by the Government. The manufacturers of these categories of products can apply to the Bureau of Indian Standards, if their products meet the set standards, for the award of the eco-logo. Though the Ministry has launched publicity campaigns for providing necessary awareness among the consumers and manufacturers, it has not become popular because of lack of adequate response from the manufacturers.

Criteria: The following are the environmental criteria that are prescribed for certification:

(*i*) That they cause substantially less pollution than other comparable products in production, usage and disposal.

(*ii*) That they are recycled and/or recyclable where comparable products are not.

(*iii*) That they make a significant contribution to saving non-renewable resources or minimize the use of renewable resources vis-à-vis other comparable products.

(*iv*) That they contribute to a reduction of adverse environmental health consequences.

(*v*) That their price is not extraordinarily higher than comparable products.

(*vi*) That they comply with the laws, standards and regulations pertaining to the environment.

Executing Agency: The Bureau of Indian Standards has been designated as the executing agency for the scheme. On the receipt of an application for the award of the Eco Mark, the Bureau of Indian Standards/Directorate of Marketing and Inspection/Directorate of Plant Protection, Quarantine and Storage organize an inspection of the manufacturer's units to make an appraisal of the control exercised during production and the facilities available for carrying out tests on raw materials and on the final product. Only after the certifying agency is completely satisfied about compliance with the norms, the manufacturer is given a license to affix the Eco Mark on the product. Every license includes a well-defined scheme for testing and inspection (STI), which the licensee has to follow strictly.

27.9 CONCLUSION

Green marketing has not lived up to the hopes and dreams of many managers and activists. Although public opinion polls consistently show that consumers would prefer to choose a green product over one that is less friendly to the environment when all other things are equal, those "other things" are rarely equal in the minds of consumers. And hopes for green products have also been hurt by the perception that such products are of lower quality or don't really deliver on their environmental promises. Yet the news isn't all bad, as the growing number of people willing to pay a premium for green products—from organic foods to energy-efficient appliances—attests.

It is important for companies to keep in mind that consumers are unlikely to compromise on traditional product attributes, such as convenience, availability, price, quality and performance. Since there is no single green-marketing strategy that is right for every company, experts suggest that companies should follow one of four strategies, depending on market and competitive conditions—from the relatively passive and silent "lean green" approach to the more aggressive and visible "extreme green" approach—with "defensive green" and "shaded green" in between. Managers who understand these strategies and the underlying reasoning behind them will be better prepared to help their companies benefit from an environmentally friendly approach to marketing.

QUESTIONS

1. Explain the significance of green marketing to a firm.
2. What is meant by greenwashing? Discuss the seven sins of greenwashing.
3. Discuss the significance of ecolabelling in the context of green marketing.
4. Write a short note on India's eco-mark.

EXERCISE

1. Prepare a list of products that have received the license to affix the ecomark in India.

❑❑❑

28

India's Pollution Control Policy

> *The Earth provides enough to satisfy every man's need, but not every man's greed.*
>
> **Mahatma Gandhi**

Environmental problems in a developing country like India can be classified into two broad categories:

(*i*) Those arising from conditions of poverty and under development.

(*ii*) Those arising as negative effects of the very process of development.

While for developed countries, environmental problems are largely the by-products of affluence marked by resource wasteful lifestyles, the stress on India's environmental resources comes mainly from the pressures of satisfying the basic human needs of a large and growing population, which has crossed the one billion mark.

India is the world's second most populous country, supporting 16.87 per cent of the world's population, on its meagre 2.4 per cent of the world surface area of 135.79 million square kms. Economic reforms have transformed India into one of the fastest growing economies in the world. India is the 12th largest economy in the world, with a GDP of US $ 1,089 trillion in terms of USD exchange rate. According to estimates by the International Monetary Fund (IMF), when measured in terms of purchasing power parity (PPP), India has the world's fourth largest GDP at US $ 4.726 trillion.

This fast economic growth achieved by the economic reforms has had its negative consequences on India's environment. Like other nations, India too bears the scars of damage done to her natural environment, resulting in a wide array of environmental problems affecting the well-being of her citizens. The cost of environmental damage in India would reduce India's GDP by nearly 4 to 4.5 per cent.

28.1 A BRIEF PROFILE OF INDIA'S ENVIRONMENTAL ISSUES

(*i*) India's urban air quality ranks among the world's worst. Of the three million premature deaths in the world that occur each year due to outdoor and indoor air pollution, the highest numbers are assessed to occur in India. According to a World Bank study, Delhi, Mumbai, Kolkata, Ahmedabad and Hyderabad have seen about 13,000 premature deaths from air pollution related diseases.

(*ii*) Air pollution from vehicle exhaust and industry is a worsening problem for India. Exhaust from vehicles has increased eightfold over levels of 20 years ago; industrial pollution has risen four times over the same period. The economy has grown two and a half times over the past two decades but pollution control and civic services have not kept pace. Air quality is at its worst in big cities like Kolkata, Delhi, Mumbai and Chennai, etc.

(*iii*) Industrialization affects environment in many ways. The level of irrespirable suspended particulate matter has gone up in 50 cities across India studied by the All India Institute of Medical Sciences and the Central Pollution Control Board. In these 50 cities, with their population of 110 million, the public health damage costs, due to this was estimated at Rs.15,000 crores in 2004.

(*iv*) India accounts for about five per cent of global carbon dioxide emissions, roughly a quarter of the emissions of China and the United States. India has now overtaken Japan to become the world's number four emitter, in terms of emissions from industrial activities. About 700 million Indians directly face the threat of global warming today, as it affects farming, makes droughts, floods and storms more frequent and more severe, and is raising the sea level. India's emissions are growing at twice the global average rate, increasing 125 per cent between 1990 and 2008. More than 60 per cent of emissions in India come from the energy sector. Forests are estimated to absorb 11 per cent of the emissions. India's per capita emissions are only one twentieth of the United States.

Pollution in Indian Cities

(*i*) **Total vehicle population** of India is more than 85 million (about 1 per cent share of the world), adding to the already existent large amount of vehicular emissions. The number of registered vehicles in Delhi has increased fifty-one times over a thirty year period. Unbelievably, as many as 17 per cent of the cars in India, run in Delhi alone. It has more cars than the total number of cars in the individual states of Maharashtra, Tamil Nadu, Gujarat and West Bengal. The vehicle stock in Delhi is expected to almost quadruple by the year 2020.

Bangalore holds the title of being the asthma capital of the country. Studies estimate that 10 per cent of Bangalore's 60 lakh population and over 50 per cent of its children below 18 years suffer from air pollution-related ailments.

In **Chennai,** exhaust from vehicles, dust from construction debris, industrial waste, burning of municipal and garden waste, are all on the rise in the city. So are respiratory diseases, including asthma. At least six of the 10 top causes of death are related to respiratory disease.

In **Mumbai,** the level of Suspended Particulate Matter has grown at an alarming rate. The levels of Respirable Suspended Particulate Matter (RSPM), or dust, in Mumbai's air, have continued to increase over the past three years. Waste disposal is a serious problem for the Mumbai municipality. In the Deonar landfill site, one of India's largest, the festering pile covers more than 120 hectares and is eight storeys' high. The stench from the site is so strong that the Mumbai authorities have purchased 42,000 litres of perfume to spray on the city's enormous waste dumps at Deonar and Mulund, after the people living nearby complained of the terrible stench.

These cities are on the World Health Organization's list of top most polluted cities. Pollution levels are likely to increase further, with continued economic growth, urbanization, and an increase in the number of vehicles, together with lax enforcement of environmental laws.

(*ii*) **India's water resources** contain 113 river basins, of which 14 are major, 44 are medium and the remaining 55 are minor. The fourteen major river basins account for 83 per cent of the total area of the basins, contribute 85 per cent of the total surface flow, and house 80 per cent of the population served by the basins. The sources of pollution are many and varied. All of India's fourteen major river systems are heavily polluted, mostly from the 50 million cubic metres of untreated sewage discharged into them each year. The domestic sector is responsible for the majority of wastewater generation in India. Combined, the 22 largest cities in the country produce over 7,267 million litres of domestic wastewater per day, of which slightly over 80 per cent is collected for treatment.

(*iii*) **Inadequate treatment of human and animal wastes** also contributes to the high incidence of water-related diseases in the country. Till date, only 19.2 per cent of the rural and 70 per cent of the urban inhabitants have access to adequate sanitation facilities. The level of faecal coliform bacteria in most rivers often exceeds WHO standards and is responsible for causing a number of gastro-intestinal ailments among the population.

(*iv*) **Arsenic contamination** in groundwater has been found in the states of West Bengal, Bihar, Chhattisgarh, Uttar Pradesh and Assam. Arsenic in groundwater has been reported in 15 districts in Bihar, 9 districts in Uttar Pradesh, 8 districts in West Bengal and one district each in Chhattisgarh and Assam.

(*v*) Due to high **concentrations of fluoride** in groundwater, beyond the permissible limits of 1.5 mg/l and 0.05 mg/l, 19 states in India have been identified as 'endemic' areas for fluorosis, with an estimated 44 million people impacted, and another 66 million at risk.

(*vi*) **Wastewater generation from the industrial sector** has been estimated to be 55,000 million m3 per day, of which 68.5 million m3 are dumped directly into local rivers and streams, without prior treatment. Out of the total pollution contributed by industrial sub-sector, 40-45 per cent of the total pollutants can be traced to the processing of industrial chemicals and nearly 40 per cent of the total organic pollution to the food products industry alone. Food products and agro-based industries, together, contribute 65-70 per cent of the total industrial wastewater, in terms of organic load. The share of different industries in water pollution is given in Table 28.1.

Table 28.1 Industrial Distribution of Water Pollution [BOD] (Percent Share)

Industry/Time	1980	1985	1990	1996
Chemical	5.98	7.48	7.29	8.23
Clay and Glass	0.18	0.25	0.22	0.21
Food	53.85	47.52	50.92	51.14
Metal	14.10	16.58	15.32	14.47
Paper and Pulp	7.57	8.76	7.96	7.92
Textiles	14.08	14.44	13.18	12.54
Wood	0.38	0.40	0.32	0.29
Others	3.85	4.57	4.79	5.20

Source: World Development Report, 1999.

The Central Pollution Control Board (CPCB) has identified a total of 1,551 medium and large industrial units in the country, under the seventeen highly polluting industrial sectors. Table 28.2 gives the list of major polluting industries in India. Of these about 77 per cent are predominantly water polluting and 15 per cent are predominantly air polluting, and the remaining 8 per cent are both air and water polluting industries.

The hazardous waste generated in the country is about 4.4 million tonnes, out of which 38.3 per cent is recyclable, 4.3 per cent is incinerable and the remaining 57.4 per cent is disposable in secured landfills. Twelve states of the country (including Maharashtra, Gujarat, Tamil Nadu, West Bengal, Andhra Pradesh and Rajasthan) account for 87 per cent of the total waste generation. The top five waste generating states are Maharashtra, Gujarat, Andhra Pradesh, Rajasthan and West Bengal.

The e-waste inventory based on the obsolescence rate in India for the year 2005 has been estimated to be 146,180 tonnes, and is expected to exceed 800,000 tonnes by 2012.

Table 28.2 Major Polluting Industries in India

Industry	Key Environmental Aspects
Aluminum	Disposal of red mud, bauxite tailings and other hazardous waste, dust emissions and high energy consumption.
Caustic	Water pollution due to disposal of brine mud, mercury and chlorine; chlorine emissions.
Cement	Fugitive dust emissions from material handling and air emissions from stack; energy consumption.
Copper	Sulphur dioxide and dust emissions; water pollution from electrolytic bath and other processes; disposal of slag from smelter.
Distillery	Water pollution due to highly organic effluent from spent wash; soil contamination.

contd...

Industry	Key Environmental Aspects
Dyes and dye intermediates	Water pollution due to toxic azo-dyes, highly organic, coloured and phenolic substances.
Fertilizer	Water pollution due to heavy metal, ammonia and fluoride bearing effluent, ammonia emission, fluoride bearing dust and hazardous material.
Iron and steel	Water pollution from cyanide, fluoride and heavy metal bearing effluent, dust emission from sintering, pelletization, pig iron plants; slag and dust disposal.
Leather	Water pollution, particularly from hexavalent chromium and salt in discharge.
Pesticide	Air pollution due to particulate and volatile organic compounds; effluents containing pesticide residues.
Petrochemicals	Water pollution due to phenol and benzene containing effluent; fugitive emissions of toxic and carcinogenic and volatile organic compounds (VOC); hazardous material disposal.
Pharmaceuticals	Water pollution due to organic residues bearing effluent; VOC and particulate emissions; hazardous waste containing process sludge and spent catalyst.
Pulp and paper	Water pollution from high organic and inorganic substances and chlorinated compounds in black liquor; highly malodorous emissions of reduced sulfur compounds and VOC.
Refinery	Water pollution from effluents containing organic and inorganic material, oil and solvent; air emission of particulate matters, sulfur dioxide, "benzene, toluene, and xylene", VOC.
Sugar	Water pollution due to high biological oxygen demand (BOD) and chemical oxygen demand (COD) effluent and spillage of molasses; air pollution due to combustions of bagasse, coal, etc.
Thermal power plants	Air emission from combustion, coal handling, water pollution due to discharge of boiler blow down, overflow from ash pond; land contamination due to flyash disposal practices.
Zinc	Air pollution due to fugitive zinc dust, water pollution containing residues, disposal of solid and hazardous waste.

To address the various environmental challenges discussed above, the central government, in coordination with the state governments, identified and targeted 17 highly polluting industries and 24 environmental problem areas. The chemical and engineering industries are at the top of the government's list, since they are the major contributors to air, water, and waste pollution. The other industries include integrated iron and steel plants, non-ferrous metallurgical units, pharmaceutical and petrochemical complexes, fertilizers and pesticide plants, thermal power plants, textiles, pulp and paper, tanneries and chloralkali units.

28.2 CONTROL OF INDUSTRIAL POLLUTION IN INDIA

Constitutional Provisions

The UN Conference on Human Environment held at Stockholm in 1972 has been a driving force in the enactment of environmental legislation and policy making in India. To implement the decisions taken at the conference, a number of steps were initiated by the Government of India, such as amendments to the constitution, new legislation relating to environmental protection and creation of institutions for implementing legislation.

India was the first country to insert an amendment in its Constitution, allowing the State to protect and improve the environment for safeguarding public health, forests and wildlife. The 42nd amendment was adopted in 1976 and came into effect from January 3rd 1977. It incorporated environmental protection into the constitution. Specific provisions were inserted into the Directive Principles of State Policy and Fundamental Duties.

The Constitution of India specifies that the State shall endeavor to protect and improve the environment and to safeguard the natural resources of the country. According to the Constitution, it is the fundamental duty of every citizen of India, to protect and improve the natural environment and to have compassion for living creatures. Article 48A of the Directive Principles states, ". . . the State shall endeavor to protect and improve the environment and to safeguard the forests and wildlife of the country". Article 51A (g) in a new chapter entitled, "Fundamental Duties", imposes a similar responsibility on every citizen "to protect and improve natural environment, including forests, rivers, lakes and wildlife, and to have compassion for living creatures." Together, these two provisions lay the foundation for jurisprudence of environmental protection. The protection of environment thus enjoys a constitutional status, rather than a merely legislative one.

Besides provisions in the Constitution, India has a number of national policies governing environmental management, including the National Policy on Pollution Abatement (NPPA, 1992) and the National Conservation Strategy and Policy Statement on Environment and Development (NCS/PSED, 1992). These national policies serve as guiding principles for the central and state governments. The NPPA adopts the following guiding principles to integrate environmental considerations into decision making at all levels.

(*i*) Prevention of pollution at source.

(*ii*) Adoption of best available technology.

(*iii*) The polluter pays principle.

(*iv*) Public participation in decision making.

28.3 INSTITUTIONAL STRUCTURE FOR CONTROL OF POLLUTION IN INDIA

The main institutions responsible for environmental protection in India are the Union Ministry of Environment and Forests (MoEF), Central Pollution Control Board (CPCB), State Departments of Environment and State Pollution Control Boards (SPCBs). The institutional structure of the administrative framework for environmental protection is given in Fig. 28.1.

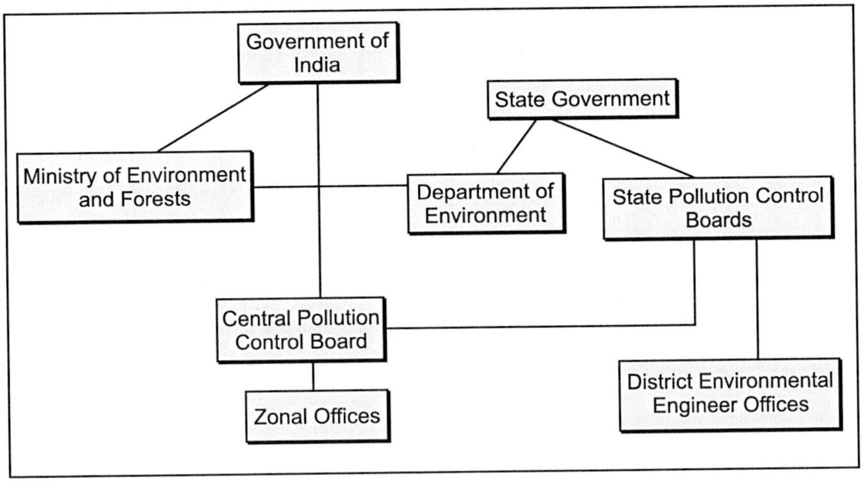

Source: Modified from JICA Country Profile on Environment (2002)

Fig. 28.1 Organizational Structure for Pollution Control in India

Ministry of Environment and Forests (MoEF)

The Ministry of Environment is the nodal agency in the Central Government for policy, planning, and coordination of environmental and forestry programmes. Formulation of environmental policies, enactment of environmental legislation, and dissemination of environmental information, prevention and control of pollution, conservation of biodiversity, afforestation programmes, international cooperation, review of EIAs, and coordination among various Ministries on matters related to the environment are some of the important activities of MoEF.

Further, for the purpose of effective monitoring, the MoEF, has classified all the industries in India, into three categories in accordance with their pollution load. The Green category is of the least polluting, small-scale cottage industries, such as flour mills, tailoring, bakery etc. The Red category includes the most polluting industries, such as distilleries, pulp and paper, smelters etc. The Orange category is of medium polluting industries, such as soft drinks, fish processing, perfumes etc. The CPCB guidance on the frequency of regular inspections is presented in Table 28.3. However, individual states differ in their interpretation of the guidance. For example, red category facilities are supposed to be inspected once a month in Gujarat, once per quarter in Orissa, and once every two years in West Bengal.

Central Pollution Control Board (CPCB)

The Water (Prevention and Control of Pollution) Act, 1974 provided for establishment of the Central Pollution Control Board at the Centre and State Pollution Control Boards in the respective States.

Functions of the Central Board

(*a*) Advise the Central Government on any matter concerning prevention and control of water and air pollution.

(*b*) Co-ordinate the activities of the State Boards and resolve disputes among them.

Table 28.3 Minimum Frequency of Inspections: CPCB Guidelines

Classification	Category	Periodicity of Monitoring
Large and medium-sized	**Red**	Once in three months
	Orange	Once a year
	Green	Once in two years
Small scale (capital investment below 10,000 rupees)	**Red**	Once in a year
	Orange	Once in 3 years
	Green	Once in 5 years

Source: OECD, 2006

(*c*) Provide technical assistance and guidance to the State Boards, carry out and sponsor investigations and research relating to problems of water and air pollution, and for their prevention, control or abatement.

(*d*) Plan and organise training of persons engaged in programmes for prevention, control or abatement of water and air pollution.

(*e*) Organise through mass media, a comprehensive mass awareness programme on prevention, control or abatement of water and air pollution.

(*f*) Collect, compile and publish technical and statistical data relating to water and air pollution and the measures devised for their effective prevention, control or abatement.

(*g*) Prepare manuals, codes and guidelines relating to treatment and disposal of sewage and trade effluents, as well as for stack gas cleaning devices, stacks and ducts.

(*h*) Disseminate information in respect of matters relating to water and air pollution and their prevention and control.

(*i*) Lay down, modify or annul, in consultation with the State Governments concerned, the standards for stream or well, and lay down standards for the quality of air.

(*j*) Perform such other functions as and when prescribed by the Government of India.

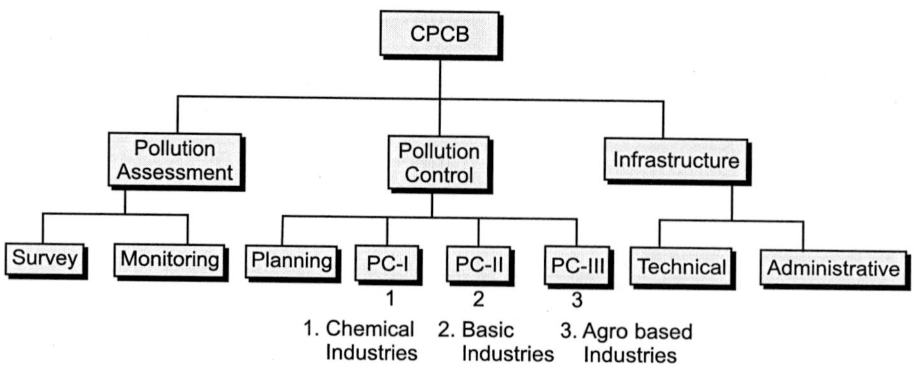

Source: JICA Country Profile on Environment (2002)

Fig. 28.2 Functional Structure of CPCB

The CPCB has three broad wings: pollution assessment, pollution control and infrastructure. The Pollution Assessment Wing has two divisions—Survey Division and Monitoring Division. Pollution Control wing is divided into four wings: Planning, Industrial Pollution Control (Chemicals), PCI – II (Basic Industries), PCI – III (Agro Based Industries), Infrastructure Wing functions with Technical and Administrative divisions.

The Central Pollution Control Board (CPCB) conducts inspections to ensure compliance by industrial units to various pollution control norms. CPCB has identified 17 categories of polluting industries located along the rivers and lakes and in problem areas. The list of categories is given in Table 28.2.

State Pollution Control Boards (SPCB)

State Pollution Control Boards (SPCBs), constituted under the Water (Prevention and Control of Pollution) Act, 1974, are entrusted with the responsibility of monitoring and controlling environmental pollution. Successive enactments and framing of rules have specified the powers and functions of the SPCBs in different areas of their intervention. In a broad sense, SPCBs are responsible for:

(*a*) Inspection of industries and local bodies.

(*b*) Inspection of sites proposed for setting up industries to verify their environmental suitability.

(*c*) Monitoring of Indian National Aquatic Resources System (MINARS) programmes.

(*d*) Ambient Air Quality Monitoring under National Ambient Air Quality Monitoring (NAAQM) programme.

(*e*) Investigations of complaints.

The SPCBs perform three categories of functions. These are:

(*i*) Advisory/policy-related.

(*ii*) Administrative.

(*iii*) Public relations and human resources development (HRD).

(i) Policy-related/Advisory

(*a*) To plan a comprehensive programme for prevention, control and abatement of water and air pollution in the State.

(*b*) To advise the State Government on matters concerning prevention, control or abatement of water and air pollution.

(*c*) To lay down, modify or annul, effluent standards for sewage and trade effluents and for the quality of receiving waters.

(*d*) To develop economical and reliable methods for treatment of sewage and trade effluents, for their utilization in agriculture and for their disposal on land.

(*e*) To advise the State Government in respect of the location of any industry, carrying on of which is likely to cause water and air pollution.

(*f*) To lay down, in consultation with and having regard to the standards set by the CPCB, standards for emission of air pollutants into the atmosphere from different sources, except ships and aircrafts.

(ii) Administrative and Monitoring

(*g*) To inspect sewage or trade effluents, works and plants for the treatment of sewage and trade effluents.

(*h*) To grant, suspend or cancel authorizations for collection, reception, treatment, transport, storage and disposal of hazardous wastes and to allow for import of these wastes for processing and re-use as raw materials.

(*i*) To perform such other functions as may from time to time be entrusted to it by the Central Board or the State Government.

(*j*) The Board may establish or recognize a laboratory or laboratories to enable the Board to perform its functions under the Water Act, 1974 and the Air Act, 1981, efficiently.

(*k*) To lay down standards for treatment of sewage and trade effluents to be discharged into any particular stream.

(*l*) To make, vary or revoke any order for the prevention, control or abatement of discharges of wastes into streams or wells.

(iii) R & D, Training and Awareness

(*m*) To collect and disseminate information relating to water and air pollution and the prevention, control or abatement thereof.

(*n*) To encourage, conduct and participate in investigations and research on water pollution problems.

(*o*) To collaborate with the Central Board in organizing the training of persons engaged or to be engaged in programmes relating to prevention, control and abatement of water and air pollution and to organize mass education programmes thereto.

The SPCBs also have the power to "direct closure, prohibition or regulation of any industry or process or stoppage or regulation of supply of electricity, water or any other service". The SPCBs exercise their powers mainly through three instruments:

- Consent to establish producing units (NOC).
- Consent to operate.
- Standards for air and water pollution.

28.4 LEGISLATION TO PREVENT AND CONTROL INDUSTRIAL WATER POLLUTION

In India, the most important authority in prescribing environmental standards is the legislature. India has a large body of laws and regulations governing the environment. These include laws enacted by the Central and State Governments, as well as an increasing body of judicial decisions affecting industrial activities that generate pollution. Further, there are more than 200 statutes that have a bearing on environmental matters in India. The beginnings of Indian environmental law were sown at the United Nations Conference on the Human Environment, held at Stockholm, in 1972. The Water Act came in the wake of the Stockholm conference; the Air Act, the Environment Protection Act, the National Environment Tribunal Act (NET) and the Public Liability Insurance

Act (PLIA) were enacted in the aftermath of the Bhopal disaster, while most of the rules and notifications implemented in the last decade are to ensure compliance with international obligations.

Legislative Measures

The major legal provisions made in the last twenty years are:

(*i*) The Water (Prevention and Control of Pollution) Act, 1974, amended in 1988.
(*ii*) The Water Cess Act, 1977, amended in 1991.
(*iii*) The Air (Prevention and Control of Pollution) Act, 1981, amended in 1987.
(*iv*) The Environment (Protection) Act, 1986.
(*v*) The Hazardous Waste (Management and Handling) Rules, 1989, amended in 2000.\
(*vi*) The Manufacture, Storage and Import of Hazardous Chemicals Rules, 1989, amended in 2000.
(*vii*) The Manufacture, Use, Import, Export and Storage of Hazardous Micro-organisms or Cells Rules, 1989.
(*viii*) The Public Liability Insurance Act, 1991.
(*ix*) The National Environmental Tribunal Act, 1995.

28.5 THE WATER (PREVENTION AND CONTROL OF POLLUTION) ACT, 1974 (AMENDED IN 1978 AND 1988)

The first major legislation to control industrial water pollution, as well as the first ever major environmental legislation in India is the **Water (Prevention and Control of Pollution) Act** introduced in 1972.

The Water Act is a comprehensive legislation providing for the Prevention and Control of Water Pollution and for maintaining or restoring the wholesomeness of water in streams or wells. Important provisions in the Water (Prevention and Control of Pollution) Act, 1974 (as amended in 1978 and 1988) are:

(*i*) Pollution Control Board (PCB) has the right to:
  (*a*) Obtain any information regarding the construction, installation or operation of an industrial establishment or treatment and disposal system.
  (*b*) Take samples of trade effluents for the purpose of analysis in the prescribed manner.
  (*c*) Enter and inspect any industrial establishment, record, register, document or any other material object.
  (*d*) Prohibit use of stream or sewer or land for disposal system without prior consent of the PCB.
(*ii*) Restriction on establishment and the operation of any industry, process or any treatment and disposal system without prior consent of the PCB.
(*iii*) PCBs to refuse or withdraw consent, for discharge of effluents.
(*iv*) Industries to comply with the conditions stipulated in the consent.
(*v*) PCBs to grant consent within four months after the date of receipt of the application complete in all respects.

(*vi*) Industry to appeal to the Appellate Authority, in case of grievances against the order passed by the PCB regarding grant, refusal or withdrawal of the consent within the specified time in the prescribed manner.

(*vii*) Industry to furnish information to the PCB and other specified agencies in case of discharge of poisonous, noxious or polluting matter into a stream, sewer or land, occurred or likely to occur, resulting in pollution due to an accident or any other unforeseen event.

(*viii*) PCBs to issue orders restraining or prohibiting an industry from discharging any poisonous, noxious or polluting matter in case of emergencies, warranting immediate action.

(*ix*) PCBs to make an application to the court for restraining likely disposal of polluting matter in a stream or on land.

(*x*) Bar of jurisdiction in civil court in respect of any matter under purview of the Appellate Authority constituted under the Act and no grant of injunction in respect of any action taken or proposed in pursuance of the Act.

(*xi*) Bar on filing of any suit or legal proceedings against the Government or Board officials, for action taken in good faith in pursuance of the Act.

(*xii*) PCBs to make inquiries, in the prescribed manner, for grant of consent for discharge of effluents.

(*xiii*) PCBs have the power to issue directions for:

(*a*) The closure, prohibition or regulation of any industry, operation or process or,

(*b*) The stoppage or regulation of supply of electricity, water or any other service to industry in the prescribed manner.

(*xiv*) Industry to comply with the directions of the PCB within the specified time.

(*xv*) PCB's to maintain a consent register containing particulars of the consent issued and to provide access to industry at all reasonable hours.

The Water Act provides both general and industry specific standards for the discharge of various pollutants into water bodies. The Water Act aims to maintain or restore the wholesomeness of water. It seeks to ensure that domestic and industrial effluents are not discharged without adequate treatment into water courses. The Water Act is quite comprehensive in coverage. The act prohibits any discharge of poisonous, noxious, or polluting water in excess of predetermined standards from entering into any water body. The Act specifically prohibits "any poisonous, noxious or polluting matter" into any stream or well. According to the Act, State consent or permit is required for all types of intake and/or discharge of any type of liquid or water either from a running stream or well. The Act prescribed effluent standards to be complied with by persons while "causing discharge of sewage or sullage or both".

Penalties for non-compliance with the standards prescribed or polluting in any way are imprisonment for three months and fine of Rs. 10,000 or fine up to Rs. 5,000 per day of violation or both plus any expenses incurred by the Board for sampling, analysis, inspection etc. These penalties can also be imposed for "obstructing any person acting under the orders or direction of the Board" or for "damages to any work or property of the Board". Water Act requires that any industry likely to discharge waste water into a water body can do so only with the previous consent of the State Pollution Control Boards. In granting consent orders, the Board may lay down conditions for the quality of waste water discharged. The consent granted by the State Boards is conditional, and may be withdrawn in the event of non-compliance with the prescribed standards.

28.6 THE WATER (PREVENTION AND CONTROL OF POLLUTION) CESS ACT, 1977 (AMENDED IN 1991)

The Water Cess Act (1977) was enacted to provide for the levy and collection of a cess on water consumed by industries. Basically, the Act is fiscal in nature. The Cess Act empowers the State Boards to assess the cess, recover it and remit the money to the central government to be credited to the Consolidated Fund of India. The Water Cess Act was amended in 1992 and the Water (Polution Prevention and Control) Cess (Amendement) Act was implemented in 2003. An industry which installs and operates its effluent treatment plant is entitled to a rebate of 25 per cent on the cess payable.

The Water Cess Act grants exemption to all industries consuming water less than ten kilo litres per day from the levy of cess. However, the Act clearly states that no such exemption shall be applicable in case of industries generating "hazardous waste" as defined in Hazardous Wastes (Management and Handling) Rules, 1989.

The cess has been introduced mainly to augment the resources of the Central and the State Pollution Control Boards. Out of the cess collected and credited to the Consolidated Fund of India (CI), 80 per cent of the cess is reimbursed to SPCBs to augment the resources of the Boards. Cess reimbursements to SPCBs are also utilized to execute pollution abatement programmes.

Table 28.4 Water Cess Rates

Purpose for which water is consumed	Maximum rate under sub-section (2) of Section 3	Maximum rate under sub-section (2A) of Section 3
Industrial cooling, spraying in mine pits or boiler feed	5 paise/kilo litre	10 paise/kilo litre
Domestic purpose	2 paise/kilo litre	3 paise/kilo litre
Processing whereby water gets polluted and the pollutants are: (i) easily bio-degradable; or (ii) non-toxic; or (iii) both non-toxic and easily bio-degradable	10 paise/kilo litre	20 paise/kilo litre
Processing whereby water gets polluted and the pollutants are;(i) not easily bio-degradable or (ii) toxic; or (iii) both toxic and not easily bio-degradable	15 paise/kilo litre	30 paise/kilo litre

Source: CPCB (2007)

As per suggestion of the CPCB, cess fund is utilized by the SPCBs for the following activities:

(*i*) Assessment of environmental quality (survey and monitoring).

(*ii*) Strengthening of environmental monitoring facilities and database management (sampling, analysis, including laboratory equipment).

(*iii*) Development of environmental standards (source specific and ambient/recipient system).

(*iv*) Training programmes to SPCBs/PCCs.

(*v*) Organising/Sponsoring mass awareness programmes.

(*vi*) Setting-up of facilities for prevention of pollution from municipal waste disposal sites.

(*vii*) Treatment and disposal and industrial sewage effluents.

(*viii*) Inventorization of polluting sources.

(*ix*) Prevention of pollution from hazardous waste disposal.

(*x*) Prevention of pollution complying siting concept—Zoning Atlas/Industrial Estate Planning

(*xi*) Protection of ecologically sensitive areas etc.

(*xii*) Reclamation/rejuvenation of water resources including conservation strategies.

(*xiii*) Remediation of contaminated ground water sites.

(*xiv*) Prevention and control of direct discharge of sewage and trade effluent into rivers and lakes.

(*xv*) Promotion of rain water harvesting and water conservation activities.

(*xvi*) Any other project/programme regarding prevention and control of water pollution.

28.7 THE AIR (PREVENTION AND CONTROL OF POLLUTION) ACT, 1981 (AMENDED IN 1987)

To counter the problems associated with air pollution, ambient air quality standards were established, under the 1981 Act. The Act provides the means for control and abatement of air pollution. The Act seeks to combat air pollution by prohibiting the use of polluting fuels and substances, as well as by regulating appliances that give rise to air pollution. Under the Act establishing or operating of any industrial plant in the pollution control area requires consent from the State Boards. The Boards are also expected to test the air in air pollution control areas, inspect pollution control equipment, and manufacturing processes. Penalties for non-compliance were:

A minimum of six months imprisonment to a maximum of seven years and fine up to Rs. 5,000 for every day during which contravention continues after conviction for the first such contravention. This law makes it clear that when offenses are committed by a company, its director, manager, secretary or other officers could be held guilty and punished accordingly.

The Air (Prevention and Control of Pollution) Amendment Act was enacted in 1987 to empower the central and state pollution boards to meet grave emergencies. The boards were authorized to take immediate measures to tackle grave emergencies and recover the expenses incurred from the offenders. The power to cancel consent for non-fulfillment of the conditions prescribed was emphasized in the Amended Air Act.

National Ambient Air Quality Standards (NAAQS) for major pollutants were notified by the CPCB in April 1994. These are deemed to be levels of air quality necessary with an adequate margin of safety, to protect public health, vegetation and property. The NAAQS prescribe specific standards for industrial, residential, rural and other sensitive areas. Industry-specific emission standards have also been developed for iron and steel plants, cement plants, fertilizer plants, oil refineries and the aluminum industry.

28.8 THE ENVIRONMENT ACT (1986)

The Environment (Protection) Act, 1986 was introduced as an umbrella legislation that provides a holistic framework for the protection and improvement of the environment. The Act was enacted to "provide for the protection and improvement of environment and for matters connected therewith". The Act empowers the central government to take all measures that are necessary for the purpose of protecting and improving the quality of the environment and preventing, controlling and abating environmental pollution. Thus, the Act empowers the Central Government to:

(*i*) Take all necessary measures for protecting the quality of the environment.

(*ii*) Plan and execute a nationwide programme for the prevention, control and abatement of environmental pollution.

(*iii*) Lay down standards for the emission or discharge of environmental pollutants from various sources.

(*iv*) Lay down standards for the quality of environment.

(*v*) Restriction of areas in which any industries, operations, processes may not be carried out or shall be carried out subject to certain safeguards.

(*vi*) Lay down safeguards for prevention of accidents and take remedial measures in case of such accidents.

(*vii*) Lay down procedures and safeguards for handling hazardous substances.

(*viii*) Constitute an authority or authorities for exercising its powers.

(*ix*) Examination of such manufacturing processes, materials and substances as are likely to cause environmental pollution.

(*x*) Carrying out and sponsoring investigations and research relating to problems of environmental pollution.

(*xi*) Inspection of any premises, plant, equipment, machinery, manufacturing or other processes, materials or substances and giving, by order, of such directions to such authorities, officers or persons as it may consider necessary, to take steps for the prevention, control and abatement of environmental pollution.

(*xii*) Establishment or recognition of environmental laboratories and institutes to carry out the functions entrusted to such environmental laboratories and institutes under this Act.

(*xiii*) Collection and dissemination of information in respect of matters relating to environmental pollution.

(*xiv*) Preparation of manuals, codes or guides relating to the prevention, control and abatement of environmental pollution.

(*xv*) Issue directions to any person, officer or authority including the power to direct closure, prohibition or regulation of any industry, operation or process or stoppage or regulation of supply of electricity, water or any other service.

(*xvi*) The Act confers powers on persons to complain to the courts regarding any violation of the provisions of the Act, after a notice of 60 days to the prescribed authorities.

Rules have been framed and agencies/authorities have been notified under specific sections for carrying out specific functions. The Act and the associated Rules require that environmental clearances are to be obtained for specific types of new/expansion projects and requires the submission of an Environmental Statement to the State Pollution Control Board annually. The rules include:

(*a*) The Hazardous Waste (Management and Handling) Rules, 1989, amended in 2000.

(*b*) The Manufacture, Storage and Import of Hazardous Chemicals Rules, 1989, amended in 2000.

(*c*) The Manufacture, use, import, export and storage of Hazardous Micro-organisms or Cells Rules, 1989.

28.9 HAZARDOUS WASTE (MANAGEMENT AND HANDLING) RULES, (HW RULES) 1989, AMENDED IN 2000

Hazardous waste is a term applied to those wastes that because of their chemical reactivity, toxicity, explosiveness, corrosiveness, radioactivity or other characteristics, constitutes a risk to human health or the environment. Such wastes may be generated as a by-product in the manufacturing processes and hence, should be disposed off safely. The hazardous waste generated in the country per annum currently is estimated to be around 8 million tonnes, out of which 70 per cent is being generated by five states, namely Gujarat, Maharashtra, Tamil Nadu, Karnataka and Andhra Pradesh. Only three States have developed common TSDF (Treatment, Storage, Disposal Facility), which are an essential component of proper hazardous waste management activity.

To address this critical problem, The Hazardous Wastes (Management and Handling) Rules were issued in the year 1989 under the umbrella of Environment Protection Act (EPA).

The Hazardous Wastes (Management and Handling) Rules, 1989, provide for an effective inventory and controlled handling and disposal of hazardous wastes. These rules shall apply to the handling of hazardous wastes as specified in Schedules 1 and 2 and shall not apply to:

(*i*) Waste water and exhaust gases as covered under the provisions of the Water (Prevention and Control of Pollution) Act. 1974 and the Air (Prevention and Control of Pollution) Act, 1981 and rules made thereunder.

(*ii*) Wastes arising out of the operation of ships beyond five kilometres as covered under the provisions of the Merchant Shipping Act, 1958 and the rules made thereunder.

(*iii*) Radio-active wastes as covered under the provisions of the Atomic Energy Act, 1962 and rules made thereunder.

(*iv*) Bio-medical wastes covered under the Bio-Medical Wastes (Management and Handling) Rules, 1998 made under the Act.

(*v*) Wastes covered under the Municipal Solid Wastes (Management and Handling) Rules, 2000 made under the Act; and

(*vi*) The lead acid batteries covered under the Batteries (Management and Handling) Rules, 2001, made under the Act.

The Hazardous Wastes (Management and Handling) Rules classified hazardous wastes into 18 categories based on constituents present in it and quantum of generation. These were listed in two schedules, Schedule 1 and Schedule 2 of the Hazardous Wastes (Management and Handling) Rules (Table 28.5).

According to the Rules

It shall be the duty of the occupier and the operator of a facility to take adequate steps while handling hazardous waste to:

(*a*) Contain contaminants and prevent accidents and limit their consequences on humans and the environment.

(*b*) Provide persons working on the site with information, training and equipment necessary to ensure their safety.

The principal thrust of the HW Rules, 1989, is that occupiers generating hazardous wastes shall take all practical steps to ensure that such wastes are properly handled, *i.e.,* collection, reception, treatment, storage, and disposal, without any adverse effects to human health and the environment. Further, every occupier generating hazardous wastes will do so only with authorization from the State Pollution Control Board (SPCB); the SPCB will grant such authorization only after verifying and satisfying itself that the occupier possesses appropriate facilities, technical capabilities and equipment to handle hazardous wastes safely. State Pollution Control Boards have the power to cancel the authorization or suspend it, if it is found that the occupier is not following the Provisions of Rules. The rules also require that hazardous wastes will be packed and labelled during transport and that they will be deposited in waste disposal sites selected by the State Government after an environment impact study. State government shall maintain the inventory of disposal sites and shall publish the same from time to time. The occupier generating hazardous wastes shall maintain records of all operations and report to the State Boards.

Table 28.5 Categories of Hazardous Wastes in the HW Rules 1989

S. No.	Waste Type	Regulatory Quantities
1	Cyanide wastes	1 kg per year of cyanide
2	Metal finishing wastes	10 kg per year of the sum of the specified substance calculated as pure metal
3	Waste containing water soluble chemical compounds of lead, copper, zinc, chromium, nickel, selenium, barium and antimony	10 kg per year of the sum of the specified substance calculated as pure metal
4	Mercury, arsenic, thallium, and cadmium bearing wastes	5 kg per year the sum of the specified substance calculated as pure metal
5	Non-halogenated hydrocarbons including solvents	200 kg per year calculated as non –halogenated hydrocarbons
6	Halogenated hydrocarbons including solvents	50 kg per year calculated as halogenated hydrocarbons

contd...

S. No.	Waste Type	Regulatory Quantities
7	Wastes from paints, pigments, glue, varnish, and printing ink	250 kg per year calculated as oil or oil emulsions
8	Wastes from dyes and dye intermediates containing inorganic chemical compounds	200 kg per year calculated as inorganic chemicals
9	Wastes from dyes and dye intermediates containing organic chemical compounds	50 kg per year calculated as organic chemicals
10	Waste oil and oil emulsions	1000 kg per year calculated as oil or oil emulsions
11	Tarry wastes from refining and tar residues from distillation or pyrolytic treatment	200 kg per year calculated as tar
12	Sludges arising from treatment of waste water containing heavy metals, toxic organics, oils,emulsions, and spent chemicals, incineration ash	Irrespective of any quantity
13	Phenols	5 kg per year calculated as phenols
14	Asbestos	200 kg per year calculated as asbestos
15	Wastes from manufacturing of pesticides and herbicides and residues from pesticides and herbicide formulation units	5 kg per year calculated as pesticides and their intermediate products
16	Acid/alkali/slurry wastes	200 kg per year calculated as acids/alkalis
17	Off-specification and discarded products	Irrespective of any quantity
18	Discarded containers and container liners of hazardous and toxic wastes	Irrespective of any quantity

Source: B.V Babu and V. Ramakrishna, 2003

The HW Rules 1989 and the Role of SPCBs

The HW Rules, 1989, had been assigned to SPCBs, to ensure safe handling and management of hazardous wastes. The SPCBs were required to:

(*i*) Grant authorization to occupiers/operators to conduct any activity connected with the generation and handling of hazardous wastes. For this, the SPCB had to examine the applications for authorization to deal with hazardous wastes, and to grant authorization for operating facilities for collection, reception, treatment, storage, transport and disposal of hazardous wastes.

(*ii*) Prohibit from granting authorization if it was satisfied that the occupier did not have the necessary facilities, technical capabilities, and equipment for safe handling of hazardous wastes.

(*iii*) Suspend or cancel the authorization or refuse it if conditions imposed in the letter of authorization were not met by the occupier/operator. Further, under the HW Rules, the occupiers/operators were required to maintain proper records and the returns had to be sent annually to the SPCBs. Accidents had to be reported to the SPCB.

The HW (M and H) Rules, 1989, were amended in January 2000. Under the HW (M and H) Amendment Rules, toxic chemicals, flammable chemicals and explosives have been redefined to be termed as "hazardous chemical". As per new criteria, 684 hazardous chemicals have been identified (instead of 4343 chemicals listed in HW Rules, 1989). All the hazardous substances have been kept in 3 categories:

(*a*) Process specific industrial wastes.

(*b*) Waste substances with concentration limits.

(*c*) Waste applicable only for imports and exports.

Authorization application shall be processed by the SPCB within 90 days. It will be valid for 5 years and its renewal will depend on steps taken for reduction in the waste generated, recycled or reused. EIA is to be carried out for selecting the appropriate site. Public hearing for objections and suggestions has to be arranged by the SPCB within 30 days. SPCB will monitor the setting up and operation of a facility regularly. Operation and closure of landfill site is to be carried out by the SPCB in accordance with specified rules. Import and export of hazardous waste for dumping and disposal is strictly prohibited. It is permitted only if raw material is used for recycling or reuse.

28.10 MANUFACTURE, STORAGE AND IMPORT OF HAZARDOUS CHEMICAL RULES 1989, AMENDED IN 2000

The principal objective of the regulation is the prevention of major accidents arising from industrial activity, the limitation of the effects of such accidents, both on humans and the environment and the harmonization of the various control measures and the agencies to prevent and limit major accidents. An important feature of the regulation is that the storage of hazardous chemicals, not associated with the process is treated differently from those coming under process use for which a different list of hazardous chemicals and their manufacture and storage procedures applies. Under these rules, project proponents of any kind of hazardous industry have to identify likely hazards and their danger potential. They also have to take adequate steps to prevent and limit the consequences of any accident at site. Information regarding accidents is to be updated as per Schedule7. Material Safety Data Sheets (MSDS) for all the chemicals handled has to be prepared. Workers on site are required to be provided with information, training and necessary equipment to ensure their safety. On-site Emergency Plan is to be prepared before initiating any activity at the site. Off-site Emergency Plan is to be prepared by the District Collector in close collaboration with the Project proponents for any accident envisaged on site. The public in the vicinity of the plant should be informed of the nature of major accidents that may occur on site and the "do's and don'ts" to be followed in case of such an occurrence. Import of hazardous chemicals is to be reported to the concerned authority within 30 days from the date of import.

In January 2000, Ministry of Environment and Forests made significant amendments in the

1989 MSIHC Rules. The new amendments increased the number of hazardous chemicals in the new Schedule. Renewal of Authorization is to be subject to:

(*i*) Submission of "Annual Returns" for disposal of hazardous waste.

(*ii*) Production of evidence of reduction in the waste generated or recycled or reused; fulfilment of authorization conditions.

(*iii*) Remittance of processing and analysis fee.

Public hearing is also made mandatory and is to be conducted by the State Government before notifying any common hazardous waste disposal site. Central/ State Government will provide guidance for the design, operation and closure of common waste facility/ landfill site. Prior approval from the SPCB is mandatory for design and layout of the proposed hazardous waste disposal facility. Comprehensive procedures have also been laid down in the MSIHC Rules, 2000 for the regulation of export and import of hazardous wastes.

28.11 THE MANUFACTURE, USE, IMPORT, EXPORT AND STORAGE OF HAZARDOUS MICRO-ORGANISMS OR CELLS RULES, 1989

The Ministry of Environment and Forests (MoEF) has notified the Rules for the Manufacture, Use, Import, Export and Storage of Hazardous Micro-organisms/Genetically Engineered Organisms or Cells under the Environment (Protection) Act, 1986. These rules are applicable to the manufacture, import and storage of micro-organisms and Gene-Technological products. The rules and regulations cover the areas of research, as well as large scale applications of Genetically Modified Organisms (GMOs) and products made therefrom, throughout India. The rules also cover the application of hazardous micro-organisms, which may not be genetically modified. Hazardous micro-organisms include those, which are pathogenic to animals, as well as plants. The target substances covered are, besides the hazardous natural microorganisms, all genetically engineered organisms, including micro-organisms, plants and animals. The rules are specifically applicable to:

(*a*) Sale, storage and handling.

(*b*) Exportation and importation of genetically engineered cells or organisms.

(*c*) Production, manufacturing, processing, storage, import, packaging and repackaging of genetically engineered products that make use of genetically engineered micro-organisms in any way.

These rules also define the competent authorities and composition of such authorities for handling of various aspects of the rules. Presently there are six competent authorities, namely:

(*a*) Recombinant DNA Advisory Committee (RDAC)

(*b*) Institutional Bio-safety Committees (IBSC)

(*c*) Review Committee on Genetic Manipulation (RCGM)

(*d*) Genetic Engineering Approval Committee (GEAC)

(*e*) State Biotechnology Coordination Committee (SBCC)

(*f*) District Level Committee (DLC)

The Rules also mandate that every institution engaged in GMO research, establish an IBSC to oversee such research and to interface with the RCGM in regulating it.

Approval and Prohibitions

(*i*) No person shall import, export, transport, manufacture, process, use or sell any hazardous micro-organisms or genetically engineered organisms/substances or cells except with the approval of the Genetic Engineering Approval Committee.

(*ii*) Use of pathogenic microorganism or any genetically engineered organisms or cells for the purpose of research shall only be allowed in laboratories or inside laboratory areas notified by the Ministry of Environment and Forests for this purpose under the Environment (Protection) Act, 1986.

(*iii*) The Genetic Engineering Approval Committee shall give directions to the occupier to determine or take measures concerning the discharge of micro-organisms/genetically engineered organisms or cells mentioned in the schedule from the laboratories, hospitals and other areas including prohibition of such discharges and laying down measures to be taken to prevent such discharges.

(*iv*) Any person operating or using genetically engineered organisms/micro-organisms mentioned in the schedule for scale up or pilot operations will have to obtain licence issued by the Genetic Engineering Approval Committee for any such activity. The possessor will have to apply for licence in prescribed proforma.

(*v*) Certain experiments for the purpose of education within the field of gene technology or microorganisms may be carried out outside the laboratories and laboratory areas specified and will be looked after by the Institutional Bio-safety Committee.

28.12 BT COTTON AND BT BRINJAL CULTIVATION IN INDIA – CASE STUDY ON GMOs IN INDIA

A genetically modified organism (GMO) or genetically engineered organism (GEO) is an organism whose genetic material has been altered using genetic engineering techniques. These techniques, generally known as recombinant DNA technology, use DNA molecules from different sources, which are combined into one molecule to create a new set of genes. This DNA is then transferred into an organism, giving it modified or novel genes.

GMOs have widespread applications. They are used in biological and medical research, production of pharmaceutical drugs, experimental medicine (*e.g.,* gene therapy), and agriculture (*e.g.,* golden rice). The broadest application of GMO technology today is patent-protected food crops which are resistant to commercial herbicides.

The use of GMOs has sparked significant controversy in many areas. The generation and use of GMOs is seen by many as intolerable meddling with biological states or processes that have naturally evolved over long periods of time. Some are concerned about the limitations of modern science to fully comprehend all of the potential negative ramifications of genetic manipulation. It is felt that the GMOs could introduce new allergens into foods, or contribute to the spread of antibiotic resistance. Many environmental activist groups, who protest GM crops, claim that they are unnatural, and therefore unsafe. This has led to the adoption of laws and regulations that require safety testing of any new organism produced for human consumption. The environmentalists gatecrashed into a World Trade Organization conference in Cancun that promoted GM foods, in order to register their protest.

Bt Cotton

The GM technology arrived in India in 1995, when the US biotech giant, Monsanto, teamed up with India's Mahyco, to import Bt cotton seeds, which would be crossed and repeatedly backcrossed with local varieties to ensure they could adapt to local conditions. Much of India's GM debates stems from this point — the technology is seen as an attempt by multinational companies to control India's agriculture and markets. In 2002, India allowed farmers to cultivate Bt cotton — the only GM crop commercially grown in India to date. In 2003, the cotton farmers in the southern state of Andhra Pradesh, whose government had aggressively promoted GM technology, suffered severe agricultural and financial losses and many—including entire families—committed suicide. There was no evidence to firmly link the cotton losses to Bt technology, but in May 2005, the Andhra Pradesh government revoked permission to grow three varieties of Bt cotton. The repeated failures of cotton crops and another spate of farmers' suicides in the central state of Maharashtra this year, once again put Bt cotton in the spotlight. An analysis of Bt adoption data shows that in Maharashtra's Vidarbha district, farmers growing Bt cotton accounted for most of the suicides. It is now admitted in official records, that Bt Cotton is more vulnerable to sucking pests than non-Bt counterparts.

Bt Brinjal

Brinjal is an important ingredient in Ayurvedic medicine and is of special value in the treatment of diabetes and liver problems. Bt Brinjal is a transgenic brinjal created out of inserting a gene [Cry 1Ac] from the soil bacterium Bacillus thuringiensis into Brinjal. This is said to give the Brinjal plant, resistance against insects like the Brinjal Fruit and Shoot Borer (Leucinodes orbonalis) and Fruit Borer (Helicoverpa armigera). It is reported that upon ingestion of the Bt toxin by the insect, there would be disruption of digestive processes, ultimately resulting in the death of the insect.

Bt Brinjal is being developed in India by M/s Mahyco (Maharashtra Hybrid Seeds Company). The importance of this development can be understood from the fact that no GM Brinjal has been released for an advanced stage of field trials, in open conditions, anywhere in the world.

The Ministry of Environment and Forests (MoEF) has a statutory body called the Genetic Engineering Approval Committee (GEAC) which has recommended the environmental release of Bt Brinjal in India, based on the recommendations of the Review Committee on Genetic Manipulation (RCGM), a statutory body and two expert committees constituted by the GEAC between 2006 and 2009.

A raging debate centres around issues of its safety to human health, environment, farmers' seed rights, consumer choice etc. Several studies on bt crops in particular, and GM crops in general, show that there are many potential health hazards in foods bio-engineered in this manner. GM-fed animals in various studies have shown that there are problems with growth, organ development and damage, immune responsiveness and so on. A recent study from Madhya Pradesh in India shows adverse human health impacts on farm and factory workers with allergies caused by Bt Cotton. Itching skin, eruptions on the body, swollen faces etc., were also reported, correlated with levels of exposure to Bt Cotton. A study from Phillippines shows that people living next to Bt Corn crop fields had developed many mysterious symptoms, especially during pollination time. Studies also reveal that genes inserted into GM food survive digestive processes and are transferred into the human body. They are known to have transferred themselves into intestinal bacteria too. Bt toxin is reported to have caused powerful immune responses and abnormal cell growth in mice. Environmental activists say that GM crops fed to rats have severely damaged lungs and kidneys.

According to the French scientist, Professor Gilles-Eric Seralini, of the Committee for Independent Research and Information on Genetic Engineering (CRIIGEN) Bt brinjal "is potentially unsafe for human consumption. The GM brinjal cannot be considered as safe as its non GM counterpart".

On health effects, Seralini found that:

(*i*) Bt brinjal produces a protein in the vegetable cells that induce antibiotic resistance. This is recognized as a major health problem and is inappropriate for commercialized use.

(*ii*) Bt brinjal appears to have 15 per cent less calories and different alkaloid content compared to non-GM brinjal. It contains 16–17 mg/kg Bt insecticide toxin. When fed to animals, effects were observed on blood chemistry with significant differences according to the sex of the animal or period of measurement. Other effects were on blood clotting time (prothrombin), total bilirubin (liver health), and alkaline phosphate in goats and rabbits.

Gilles-Eric Seralini is of the view that Bt Brinjal would be a big threat to India's agriculture with MNCs charging Indian farmers for their seeds. The supply of seeds will be regulated and thus costlier. Indian farmers would have to depend on MNCs for seeds. Bt cotton has already been declared a farce, with crop failures and mass suicides of farmers in India.

In Europe, where there is a strong public opinion against GM food, US agrochemical giants have not been able to make much headway in promoting their genetically engineered food products. For instance, in Switzerland, the moratorium on introducing genetically engineered food was extended on public demand. In Italy and Austria, government-funded studies have shown adverse impact of growing and consuming GM food.

In the words of Jeffrey Smith, Director, Institute for Responsible Technology, Washington, an expert on genetically modified organisms (GMOs), and author of international best-sellers, like "Seeds of Deception" and "Genetic Roulette", "Both Bt cotton and Bt Brinjal have adverse effects on humans and should be banned in India". He adds: "In my experience over the years, I have never come across a country where a particular crop that originated there, goes in for a modified variety of the same." He insisted that the government needs to step in and come up with an alternate policy that bans both Bt cotton as well as Bt Brinjal, "before it is too late".

28.13 PUBLIC LIABILITY INSURANCE ACT, 1991

The Public Liability Insurance Bill was introduced in the Parliament in 1991, to ameliorate the sufferings of members of the public due to accidents which take place in hazardous installations. The Public Liability Insurance Act, 1991 is in consonance with the spirit of Principle 13 of the Rio Declaration, which states that States shall develop national laws regarding liability and compensation for the victims of pollution and other environmental damage. It aims at providing for public liability insurance for the purpose of providing immediate relief to persons affected by accidents occurring while handling any hazardous substance or matters connected therewith or incidental thereto.

The Act covers accidents involving hazardous substances and insurance coverage for these. It imposes on the owner, the liability to provide immediate relief in respect of death or injury to any person or damage to any property resulting from an accident while handling any of the notified hazardous chemicals. This relief has to be provided on "no fault" basis. The owner handling hazardous chemicals has to take an insurance policy to meet this liability of an amount equal to its "paid up capital" or upto Rs. 500 million, whichever is less. The policy has to be renewed every year. New undertakings will have to take this policy before starting their activity. The owner also has to pay an amount equal to its annual premium to the Central Government's Environment Relief Fund (ERF). The reimbursement of relief to the extent of Rs. 25,000/- per person is admissible in case of fatal accidents, in addition to the reimbursement of medical expenses upto Rs. 12,500/-. The liability of the insurance company is limited to Rs. 50 million per accident, upto Rs. 150 million per year or upto the tenure of the policy. Any claims in excess of this liability will be paid from the ERF. In case the award still exceeds, the remaining amount will have to be met by the owner. The payment under the Act covers only the immediate relief and owners will have to provide the final compensation, if any, arising out of legal proceedings. The PLIA was amended in 1992, and the Central Government was authorized to establish the Environmental Relief Fund, for making relief payment.

28.14 THE ENVIRONMENTAL IMPACT ASSESSMENT OF DEVELOPMENT PROJECTS NOTIFICATION (1994 AND AS AMENDED IN 1997)

As per the Environmental Impact Assessment of Development Projects Notification:

(*i*) All projects listed under Schedule I require environmental clearance from the MoEF.

(*ii*) Projects under the delicenced category of the New Industrial Policy also require clearance from the MoEF.

(*iii*) All developmental projects whether or not under the Schedule I, if located in fragile regions must obtain MoEF clearance.

(*iv*) Industrial projects with investments above Rs 500 million must obtain MoEF clearance and are further required to obtain a LOI (Letter of Intent) from the Ministry of Industry, and an NOC (No Objection Certificate) from the SPCB and the State Forest Department, if the location involves forest land. Once the NOC is obtained, the LOI is converted into an industrial licence by the state authority.

(*v*) The notification also stipulates procedural requirements for the establishment and operation of new power plants. As per this notification, a two-stage clearance for site-specific projects such as pithead thermal power plants and valley projects is required. Site clearance is given in the first stage and final environmental clearance in the second. A public hearing has been made mandatory for projects covered by this notification. This is an important step in providing transparency and a greater role to local communities.

28.15 THE NATIONAL ENVIRONMENT TRIBUNAL ACT, 1995

This is an Act to provide for strict liability for damages arising out of any accident occurring while handling any hazardous substance and for the establishment of a National Environment Tribunal for effective and expeditious disposal of cases arising from such accidents. This was enacted with a view to giving relief and compensation for damages to persons, property and the environment and for matters connected therewith or incidental thereto.

28.16 THE NATIONAL ENVIRONMENT APPELLATE AUTHORITY ACT, 1997

The NEAA Act provides for the establishment of a National Environment Appellate Authority to hear appeals with respect to restriction of areas in which any industries, operations or processes or class of industries, operations or processes shall not be carried out or shall be carried out subject to certain safeguards under the Environment (Protection) Act, 1986 and for matters connected therewith or incidental thereto. In accordance with the Act, the National Environment Appellate Authority (NEAA) was formed in March 1997. It deals with the representations, complaints, and appeals made by any person/body/non-governmental organization (NGO) against the decisions of competent authorities (under the Environment (Protection) Act, 1986), granting environmental clearance covered under the Environment Impact Assessment notification

Any person aggrieved by an order granting environmental clearance in the areas in which any industries, operation or class of industries, operations and processes shall not be carried out, may appeal to the authority in the prescribed form. The appeal shall be made within 30 days from the date of such order. The authority may entertain any appeal after expiry of 30 days but not after 90 days from the date of order, if it is satisfied that the appellant was prevented by sufficient cause from filing the appeal in time.

28.17 THE NATIONAL GREEN TRIBUNAL BILL, 2009

The National Green Tribunal Bill, 2009 was introduced by the Ministry of Environment and Forests to create special courts for environmental matters. The Bill has been introduced in response to the Supreme Court and the Law Commission's recommendations pointing out the large number of environment-related cases pending in courts.

The National Green Tribunal Bill, 2009 is to enable the government to establish Green Tribunals at various centres throughout the country, and repeal the National Environment Tribunal Act, 1995 and the National Environment Appellate Authority Act, 1997.

28.18 FISCAL INCENTIVES FOR POLLUTION CONTROL

The C & C approach has proved to be inflexible, and highly expensive, and can succeed only in the presence of effective enforcement, which in turn is dependent on political non-interference and absence of corruption. Alternatively, if C & C is complemented with market based instruments, such as an effluent charge, the pollution reduction targets may be efficiently realised. The Government of India came out with a Policy Statement for Abatement of Pollution in 1992, which declared that market-based approaches would be considered in controlling pollution. It stated that economic instruments will be investigated to encourage the shift from curative to preventive measures, internalize the costs of pollution and conserve resources, particularly water. In 1995, the Ministry of Environment and Forest (MoEF) constituted a task force to evaluate market-based instruments, which strongly advocated their use for the abatement of industrial pollution. Some of the economic incentives that supplement the command-and-control policies in India are depreciation allowances, exemptions from excise or customs duty payment, and arrangement of soft loans for the adoption of clean technologies. Another aspect that is evident is the shift in the focus from end-of-pipe treatment of pollution to treatment at source. The role of remote sensing and geographical information systems in natural resource management and environmental protection has also gained importance over time.

The Indian Pollution control policy does provide a few fiscal incentives for pollution control, though the inclusion of market based instruments, such as an effluent charge is still under consideration. The various fiscal incentives available to business units for pollution control are:

(*i*) The Water Cess Act (1977) provides for a 25 per cent rebate on the cess payable if, the person or local authority concerned, installs a plant for treatment of sewage or trade effluent. It is an incentive for pollution abatement.

(*ii*) The customs duty on some specified pollution control equipment has been reduced to a concessional rate of 35 per cent. The countervailing duty has also been eliminated for such items and auxiliary duty has been reduced to 5 per cent. Since March 1992, a rebate of over 5 per cent has been allowed on excise duty of over 5 per cent. In addition to the rebate on customs and excise duties levied by the Central Government, certain States too have offered concessions on Sales Tax, for specified pollution control equipment.

(*iii*) There is provision for allowing the deduction of a certain percentage of written down actual cost of capital assets, net of any subsidies and concessions, from gross profit, in computing the base for levy of corporate tax. A notification issued in February 1983, introduced for the first time, a higher rate of depreciation for pollution control equipment, as compared to 25 per cent applicable for the general plant and machinery. This was gradually increased to 100 per cent in the 1993-94 budget.

(*iv*) A provision is available in the Income Tax Act, under which a company can deduct upto 25 per cent of the actual cost of some specified new assets for computation of taxable profit. This allowance was raised to 35 per cent for pollution control equipment.

(*v*) A provision has been made in the Income Tax Act which allows deduction of contribution made by tax payers to any institution engaged in the conservation of natural resources, while computing taxable income.

(*vi*) The Income Tax Act also provides for the exemption of capital gains arising from transfer of building, land, and machinery etc., for establishing business in a new place to reduce industrial congestion.

28.19 NATIONAL ENVIRONMENT POLICY, 2006

The National Environment Policy seeks to extend the coverage and filled in the gaps which existed in all the earlier environmental and environment related laws and rules in the light of accumulated experience. The Act is intended to be a guide to action in regulatory reform, programmes and projects for environmental conservation and review and enactment of legislation by agencies of the Central, State, and Local Governments. The policy also seeks to stimulate partnerships of different stakeholders *i.e.,* public agencies, local communities, academic and scientific institutions, the investment community, and international development partners, in harnessing their respective resources and strengths for environmental management. The dominant theme of this policy is that while conservation of environmental resources is necessary to secure livelihoods and well-being of all, the most secure basis for conservation is to ensure that people dependent on particular resources obtain better livelihoods from the fact of conservation, than from degradation of the resource.

The main objectives of the 2006 environmental policy are:

(*i*) Conservation of Critical Environmental Resources
(*ii*) Intra-generational Equity: Livelihood Security for the Poor
(*iii*) Inter-generational Equity
(*iv*) Integration of Environmental Concerns in Economic and Social Development
(*v*) Efficiency in Environmental Resource Use
(*vi*) Environmental Governance
(*vii*) Enhancement of Resources for Environmental Conservation.

The above objectives are to be realized through strategic interventions by the various public authorities at Central, State, and Local Government levels. These strategic interventions, besides legislation and the evolution of legal doctrines for realization of the objectives, may be based on a set of Principles. The National Environmental Policy (2006) has highlighted and recommended the use of the following principles/criterion in matters related to environmental protection:

(*a*) **Precautionary Principle:** According to this "Where there are credible threats of serious or irreversible damage to key environmental resources, lack of full scientific certainty shall not be used as a reason for postponing cost-effective measures to prevent environmental degradation". (Chapter 13)

(*b*) **Principle of Economic Efficiency:** This requires that "the services of environmental resources be given economic value, and such value to count equally with the economic values of other goods and services, in analysis of alternative courses of action". This principle will promote the application of **polluter pays principle** which says that the polluter should, in principle, bear the cost of pollution, with due regard to public interest, and without distorting international trade and investment. This principle of economic efficiency would promote the internalization of external costs through the use of market based instruments.

(*c*) **The Principle of Legal Liability:** This is an embodiment in legal doctrine of the 'polluter pays' approach, itself deriving from the principle of "economic efficiency". The criminal liability approach (fault based liability) of the present policy to be complemented with civil liability approach (strict liability). This may ensure that for any given level of environmental quality desired, the society-wide costs of meeting the standard are minimized.

Accordingly, the legal liability principle has two approaches:

(*a*) **Fault Based Liability:** It holds the party liable if it breaches a pre-existing legal duty, for example, an environmental standard.

(*b*) **Strict Liability:** It imposes an obligation to compensate the victim for harm resulting from actions or failure to take action, which may not necessarily constitute a breach of any law or duty of care.

To administer the incentive based instruments, the policy recommended that the following specific actions will be taken:

(*a*) Set up a permanent machinery comprising experts in all relevant disciplines to review notified ambient and emissions standards, in the light of new scientific and technological information.

(*b*) Strengthen the testing infrastructure and network for monitoring ambient environmental quality.

(*c*) Progressively ensure on-line availability of the monitoring data.

(*d*) Ensure adequate participation by potentially impacted communities, and industry associations and public-private partnerships.

Besides these, the policy also advocated:

(*i*) Decentralization: In order to empower public authorities having jurisdiction at the spatial level at which particular environmental issues are salient, and to address these issues, decentralization involving ceding or transfer of power from a Central Authority to State and Local Authorities is necessary.

(*ii*) Integration: This refers to the inclusion of environmental considerations in sectoral policymaking, the integration of the social and natural sciences in environment related policy research, and the strengthening of relevant linkages among various agencies at the Central, State, and Local Self-Government levels, charged with the implementation of environmental policies.

(*iii*) Environmental Standard Setting: Environmental standards must reflect the economic and social development situation to which they apply. Setting environmental standards would involve several considerations, *i.e.,* risks to human health, risks to other environmental entities, technical feasibility, costs of compliance, and strategic considerations.

(*iv*) Preventive Action: It is preferable to prevent environmental damage from occurring in the first place, rather than attempting to restore degraded environmental resources after the event.

(*v*) Environmental Offsetting: If for exceptional reasons of overriding public interest, it is not possible to protect threatened or endangered species and natural systems that are of special importance to sustaining life, providing livelihoods, or general well-being, cost-effective offsetting measures must be undertaken by the proponents of the activity, to restore as nearly as may be feasible, the lost environmental services to the same public.

In line with the above Principles, the National Environmental Policy (2006) suggested the following measures to achieve the specified objectives:

(*a*) Regulatory Reforms that include revising the policy and legislative framework, process related reforms and substantive reforms related to environment and forests clearances, coastal areas, Living Modified Organisms (LMOs), environmentally sensitive zones, monitoring of compliance, use of economic principles in environmental decision-making.

(*b*) Enhancing and conserving environmental resources that addressed issues of land degradation, desert ecosystem, forest and wild life, biodiversity, traditional knowledge, and natural heritage, fresh water resources, wetlands, mountain ecosystems, coastal resources, pollution abatement, conservation of man-made heritages, and climate change.

(*c*) Environmental standards, management systems, certification, and indicators.

(*d*) Clean technologies and innovation.

(*e*) Promoting environmental awareness, education, and information.

(*f*) Promoting partnerships and stakeholder involvement.

(*g*) Capacity building in all concerned institutions: public, private, voluntary, academic, research, and the media.

(*h*) Research and development related to taxonomies of living natural resources, research leading to better understanding of ecological processes and pathways, research which provides direct inputs to policy making, and R & D in technologies for environmental management and clean production.

(*i*) International cooperation to comply with our commitments to various multi-lateral agreements, and ensure sustained flows of resources for environmental management.

(*j*) Review, updating, and renewal of the National Environment Policy after consultations every three years with groups of diverse stakeholders, *i.e.,* researchers and experts, community based organizations, industry associations, and voluntary organizations.

(*k*) Review of implementation to enhance accountability of the different public agencies responsible for implementation. It would also reveal practical issues in implementation, including absence of political will at concerned levels, or official indifference.

28.20 STATUS OF ENVIRONMENTAL COMPLIANCE BY INDIAN INDUSTRIES

According to the CPCB, as of June 2006, of the 2744 large and medium units under 17 categories of highly polluting industries, 72.3 per cent units were in compliance and have installed required pollution control equipment, while 339 units have closed down. This is a decrease from 84 per cent in 2004. Table 28.6 provides details of non-complying units.

Table 28.6 Defaulting Units

S.No	Category	Number of Defaulting Units	Total Number of Units	Percentage of Non Compliance
1	Aluminium	1	7	14.3
2	Cement	23	236	9.7
3	ChlorAlkali	9	34	26.5
4	Copper	1	4	25
5	Distillery	35	271	12.9
6	Dyes and DI	9	119	7.5
7	Fertiliser	8	139	5.7
8	Iron and Steel	9	40	22.5
9	Oil Refineries	2	21	9.5

contd...

S.No	Category	Number of Defaulting Units	Total Number of Units	Percentage of Non Compliance
10	Pesticides	10	116	8.6
11	Petrochemicals	7	84	8.3
12	Pharmaceuticals	134	571	23.4
13	Pulp and Paper	31	189	16.4
14	Sugar	65	588	11.5
15	Tannery	15	129	11.6
16	Thermal Power	54	190	28.4
17	Zinc	1	6	16.6
	Total	414	2744	100

Source: CPCB 2006 -07

The major non-complying sectors are chloralkali (26.5%), thermal power (28%), copper (25%), iron and steel (22.5%), and pharmaceuticals (23%). According to the MoEF, small and medium enterprises account for 40 per cent of industrial production, but are responsible for an estimated 70 per cent of the total industrial pollution load, nationwide.

28.21 MULTILATERAL AGREEMENTS

India is a signatory to a number of multilateral environment agreements and conventions. Some of the major multilateral environmental agreements and India's obligations under these are discussed below:

Montreal Protocol on Substances that Deplete the Ozone Layer (to the Vienna Convention for the Protection of the Ozone Layer), 1987

The Montreal Protocol to the Vienna Convention on Substances that deplete the Ozone Layer, came into force in 1989. The protocol set targets for reducing the consumption and production of a range of Ozone Depleting Substances (ODS). The agreement sets more stringent standards and accelerated phase-out timetables for countries that have contributed most to ozone depletion.

India acceded to the Montreal Protocol in September 1992. The MoEF has established an Ozone Cell and a steering committee on the Montreal Protocol to facilitate the implementation of the India Country Program, for phasing out ODS production by 2010.

The steps taken by the Government of India to meet India's commitments under the Montreal Protocol include:

(*i*) Goods required to implement ODS phase-out projects funded by the Multilateral Fund are fully exempt from duties. This benefit has also been extended to new investments with non-ODS technologies.

(*ii*) Commercial banks are prohibited from financing or refinancing investments with ODS technologies.

The Gazette of India on 19 July 2000, notified rules for regulation of ODS phase-out called the Ozone Depleting Substances (Regulation and Control) Rules, 2000. They were notified under the Environment (Protection) Act, 1986. These rules were drafted by the MoEF following consultations with industries and related government departments.

BOX 28.1

Clemenceau Waste Disposal Controversy

Alang, the ship breaking yard, at Bhavnagar, Gujarat, became the centre of an international controversy, when the Supreme Court of India temporarily prohibited the French aircraft carrier, *Clemenceau*, from entering the port in January 2006.

In December 2004, before *Clemenceau* had set sail for India, Greenpeace had protested against France's plans to outsource the scrapping of the 27,000 tonne warship—laden with toxins, such as asbestos, PCBs, lead, mercury, and other toxic chemicals to India, in violation of the Basel Convention.

On January 17, 2006, the Supreme Court of India observed: "We do not want the environment to be polluted. When the French Government had not permitted the ship to be broken there, why should we allow the ship to come to India? Whether breaking the ship will result in pollution or not is immaterial. The best thing will be to ask the ship to go back to where it started." The French President, Jacques Chirac, also ordered *Clemenceau* to return to French waters and remain on standby, following a ruling by France's highest administrative court, the Conseil d'État. Finally, the ship headed for Graythorp, Teesside, near Hartlepool, U.K., though India was its original destination.

To environmentalists, the ship highlights the issue of "developed countries dumping waste, which they consider too toxic to deal with at home, onto developing countries". Every year, ships with tonnes of toxic substances that include asbestos, PCBs (polychlorinated biphenyls) and heavy metals, end up in ship breaking yards in Bangladesh, China, India and Pakistan. Here, the vessels are cut up, often in unsafe conditions, seriously affecting the health of the workers and polluting the local environment. Interestingly, the workers at the Alang shipyard, Gujarat (where "Clemenceau" was destined), felt the controversy had robbed them of much needed work, for if India didn't get this ship, other countries would get the work.

In all this, however, is a larger picture—one that involves the Basel Convention. The Convention "aims to minimize the generation of hazardous wastes and to control and reduce their transboundary movements in order to protect human health and the environment, and includes movements of asbestos and PCBs within its jurisdiction." The European Union (including France) has signed and put into law an amendment to the Convention that bans the shipment of hazardous wastes to developing countries.

The relocation of the ship to India thus, violated the Basel Convention, as signatories to the treaty should not ship hazardous waste without assurances that the destination (in this case Alang) observes good environmental policies.

Source: *The Hindu*, Feb 10, 2010.

Basel Convention on Transboundary Movement of Hazardous Wastes, 1989

The Basel Convention, which came into force in 1992, has three key objectives:

(*i*) To reduce transboundary movement of hazardous wastes.

(*ii*) To minimize the creation of such wastes.

(*iii*) To prohibit their shipment to countries lacking the capacity to dispose hazardous wastes in an environmentally sound manner.

India ratified the Basel Convention in 1992, shortly after it came into force. The Indian Hazardous Wastes Management Rules Act, 1989 encompasses some of the Basel provisions related to the notification of import and export of hazardous waste, illegal traffic, and liability. (Box 2.6 in Chapter 2)

As a Party to the Convention, India is obliged to regulate and minimize the import of Hazardous Waste or other wastes for disposal or sham recycling and also to prohibit export of waste to nations, which have prohibited the import of such wastes. Further, hazardous wastes generated in the country are also required to be managed in an environmentally sound manner. India, as a party to the convention, can prevent the import of hazardous waste or other waste if it has reason to believe that the waste in question will not be managed in an environmentally sound manner.

UN Framework Convention on Climate Change (UNFCCC), 1992

The primary goals of the UNFCCC were to stabilize greenhouse gas emissions at levels that would prevent dangerous anthropogenic interference with the global climate. The convention embraced the principle of common but differentiated responsibilities which has guided the adoption of a regulatory structure. (Chapter 2, Section 2.15)

India signed the agreement in June 1992, which was ratified in November 1993. As per the Convention, the reduction/limitation requirements apply only to developed countries. The only reporting obligation for developing countries relates to the construction of a GHG inventory. India has initiated the preparation of its First National Communication (base year 1994) that includes an inventory of GHG sources and sinks, potential vulnerability to climate change, adaptation measures and other steps being taken in the country to address climate change. Further details on UNFCC and the Kyoto Protocol are provided in Chapter 2 and 20.

28.22 CONCLUSION

India's pollution control policy has mostly relied on command and control, based on a set of laws designed to perform a preventive, rather than a proactive role. The presence of well drafted legislations that specify standards for various pollutants and penalties for non-compliance have accomplished pollution reduction to a great extent, but not to the required extent. Adherence to C & C, as the primary and almost only regulatory approach to address the issue of pollution is preferred by the policymakers due to the certainty of outcome and reluctance to adopt economic instruments. Many critics observe that the only strong feature of the Indian pollution control policy is the legal component. Pollution control is far from a satisfactory level because laws exist independent of the policy and fail to incorporate the policy approach. This has impaired the effective enforcement of the legislation. The CPCB and SPCBs need to be given the authority to apply administrative penalty to ensure swifter enforcement of actions. A judicious mix of legal processes and sanctions, duly complemented by administrative procedures is needed. The credibility of enforcement needs to be improved.

QUESTIONS

1. Make a summary of India's main environmental issues.
2. Examine the salient features of the Air and the Water Act.
3. Highlight the significance of the Environment Act.
4. Discuss the main points of the Environment Policy, 2006.
5. What are the fiscal incentives offered by the Indian Government to control industrial pollution?
6. Enumerate the main multilateral agreements signed by India. Give a brief note on each of them.
7. What are the rules and regulations pertaining to GMOs in India?
8. Explain the features of Hazardous Waste Management Rules in India.

EXERCISES

1. Make a case study of pollution with reference to any of the known cases of highly polluting industries in India and discuss the action taken by the government to enforce compliance.
2. Discuss the debate on Bt Cotton and Bt Brinjal.

❑❑❑

Glossary

1. **Abatement Cost:** Abatement costs are the costs of reducing emissions/effluent. The cost incurred when reducing a nuisance like pollution or congestion. The cost per unit of abatement usually increases as the level of nuisance approaches zero.
2. **Acid Rain:** The term "acid rain" is commonly used to mean the deposition of acidic components in rain, snow, fog, dew, or dry particles. The more accurate term is "acid precipitation." Distilled water, which contains no carbon dioxide, has a neutral pH of 7. Liquids with a pH less than 7 are acidic, and those with a pH greater than 7 are alkaline (or basic). "Clean" or unpolluted rain has a slightly acidic pH of 5.6, because carbon dioxide and water in the air react together to form carbonic acid, a weak acid. The extra acidity in rain comes from the reaction of air pollutants, primarily, sulfur oxides and nitrogen oxides, with water in the air to form strong acids (like sulfuric and nitric acid). The main sources of these pollutants are vehicles and industrial and power-generating plants.
3. **Anthropocentrism:** The theory of anthropocentrism says that the world exists for humanity. Believers in this philosophy would say that humans can rightfully try to benefit as much as possible from the environment. It implies:
   - Regarding humans as the central element of the universe.
   - Interpreting reality exclusively in terms of human values and experience.
4. **Aral Sea:** The site of what has been called the greatest environmental disaster of all time. The Aral Sea has been drying up. Massive water diversions to grow cotton in Kazakhstan and Uzbekistan have lead to the Sea drying up. The area which had dried up as of 1996 is bigger than Lake Erie. In the 1960's the Aral Sea's area was 69,000 square km. By the late 1990's it had fallen to about 30,000 km and is likely to shrink much further. The rates of cancer and anemia in the area are extremely high due to the toxic (salt plus fertilizers) dust raised from the dried up basin by the wind. The *Globe and Mail* reported in 1998 that some officials in Uzbekistan fear that the Sea may disappear altogether by 2015.
5. **Basel Convention:** An international agreement on the control of transboundary movements of hazardous wastes and their disposal, drawn up in March 1989 in Basel, Switzerland, with over 100 countries as signatories.
6. **Bhopal Tragedy:** The Bhopal disaster was an industrial catastrophe that took place at a pesticide plant owned and operated by Union Carbide (UCIL) in Bhopal, Madhya Pradesh in India. Around midnight on December 2–3, 1984, the plant released methyl isocyanate (MIC) gas and other toxins,

resulting in the exposure of over 500,000 people. The official immediate death toll was 2,259 and the government of Madhya Pradesh has confirmed a total of 3,787 deaths related to the gas release.

7. **Biochemical Oxygen Demand or BOD:** BOD is a measure of the quantity of oxygen consumed by microorganisms during the decomposition of organic matter. BOD is the most commonly used parameter for determining the oxygen demand on the receiving water of a municipal or industrial discharge. BOD can also be used to evaluate the efficiency of treatment processes, and is an indirect measure of biodegradable organic compounds in water.
8. **Bio-degradable material:** Any organic materials that can be broken down by microorganisms into simpler, more stable compounds. Most organic wastes (e.g., food, paper) are biodegradable.
9. **Biodiversity:** Biodiversity, a contraction of the phrase "biological diversity," is often used to describe all the species living in a particular area. biodiversity can be summarized as "life on earth." At a much broader level biodiversity refers to the variety of life on Earth at all its levels, from genes to ecosystems, and the ecological and evolutionary processes that sustain it.
10. **Bhopal Tragedy:** The site of the worst chemical disaster in the world. In December 1984, 3,000 people were killed immediately and as many as 10,000 have died in total as a result of the accident. About 20,000 more were injured. Methyl isocyanate gas leaked from a Union Carbide plant in Bhopal.
11. **Carbon Sequestration:** It refers to the natural removal of carbon from the atmosphere by the soil and plants as well as to any of the several processes for the removal of excess CO_2 from the atmosphere in an effort to mitigate global warming. It is a geo-engineering technique for the long-term storage of CO_2 or other forms of carbon, for the mitigation of global warming. The most primitive form of carbon sequestration would be to simply plant more trees. Plants naturally take CO_2 from the atmosphere which is integrated into their biomass and release it safely into the soil when trees die.
12. **Carrying Capacity (CC):** CC is the maximum number of individuals of a defined species that a given environment can support over the long term.
13. **Chernobyl Disaster:** On April 26, 1986, during a test at 1:21 a.m. the No. 4 reactor of the Nuclear Power Plant at Chernobyl, located 128 km northwest of Kiev, that is in the Ukraine part of the Soviet Union, exploded and released thirty to forty times the radioactivity of the atomic bombs dropped on Hiroshima and Nagasaki. The cause of the disaster was a malfunction within the plant that caused the radioactive core to become exposed. This caused a particle meltdown that let off large amounts of radioactive material.
14. **Chemical oxygen demand (COD):** COD is a measure of the capacity of water to consume oxygen during the decomposition of organic matter and the oxidation of inorganic chemicals such as ammonia and nitrite. COD measurements are commonly made on samples of waste waters or of natural waters contaminated by domestic or industrial wastes.
15. **Chernobyl Ukraine:** The site of the world's greatest nuclear accident.
16. **Chipko Movement:** The Chipko Movement, started in the 1970's, was a non-violent movement aimed at protecting, and conserving of trees and forests from destruction. It was a strong uprising against those people, who were destroying the natural resources of the forests and disturbing the whole ecological balance. The movement gained momentum under Sunderlal Bahuguna, an eco-activist, who spent his whole life persuading and educating the villagers, to protest against the destruction of the forests and the Himalayan mountains by the government.
17. **Chlorofluorocarbons:** A family of inert, nontoxic, and easily liquefied chemicals used in refrigeration, air conditioning, packaging, and insulation or as solvents and aerosol propellants. Because CFCs are not destroyed in the lower atmosphere, they drift into the upper atmosphere, where their chlorine components destroy ozone.

18. **Clean Development Mechanism:** The CDM of the Kyoto Protocol allows projects in developing countries to generate emission credits if they result in emission levels lower than would otherwise be the case; these credits can be marketed and eventually counted against a developed country's emission obligation.
19. **Command and Control:** This is the policy approach common to many areas of environmental regulation. The essential features of it include:
    - Polluters are given highly specific regulations, that includes standards of emissions/ effluents and ambient standards; it often prescribes specific technologies to adopt
    - Failure to comply with prescribed regulations imposes penalties on the polluter.
20. **Common Property Resources:** Those resources for which property rights are shared.
21. **Composting:** A biological decomposition of solid organic materials by bacteria, fungi, and other organisms into a soil-like product.
22. **Cost of Compliance:** For firms, this is the total cost of complying with environmental regulations. In the case of an effluent fee, this is the abatement costs plus the fees to be paid. In the case of permits, it's the abatement cost plus the cost of additional permits acquired (or less the number of permits sold).
23. **Cradle to Gate approach:** Cradle-to-Gate is an assessment of a *partial* product life cycle from manufacture ('cradle') to the factory gate (i.e., before it is transported to the consumer). The use phase and disposal phase of the product are usually omitted. Cradle-to-gate assessments are sometimes the basis for environmental product declarations (EPD).
24. **Cradle to Grave Management System:** Cradle-to-grave is the full Life Cycle Assessment from manufacture ('cradle') to use phase and disposal phase ('grave').
25. **Damage Function:** Relationship that shows how pollution damage varies with the level of pollution emitted, and what the monetary value of that damage is.
26. **Deep Ecology:** Deep ecology is a holistic approach to the environment that stresses the intrinsic equality of species, including human beings. It claims that, like humanity, the living environment as a whole has the same right to live and flourish.
27. **Deposit Refund System:** A surcharge paid when buying potentially polluting products is refunded when the product or container is returned for recycling or proper disposal. Examples include "Bottle bills" deposits on beverage bottles and cans, containerized hazardous or solid waste, such as motor vehicle batteries, oil, and tires, and deposit-refund systems for car batteries. Recycling and environmentally safe disposal increase because the user is "paid" for doing it right.
28. **Dissolved Oxygen (DO):** DO is one of the best indicators of the health of a water ecosystem. Dissolved oxygen can range from 0–18 parts per million (ppm), but most natural water systems require 5–6 parts per million to support a diverse population.
29. **Entropy:** A measure of qualitative state of energy in a system. It is a measure of how organized or disorganized a system is. Entropy is an important part of the second law of thermodynamics.
30. **Ecocentrism:** Ecocentrism is a philosophy that recognizes that the ecosphere, rather than any individual organism, is the source and support of all life. It focuses on the biotic community as a whole, and strives to maintain ecosystem composition and ecological processes.
31. **Eco-efficiency:** describes a vision for the production of economically valuable goods and services while reducing the ecological impacts of production. In other words eco-efficiency means producing more with less. According to the World Business Council for Sustainable Development, critical aspects of eco-efficiency are:
    - A reduction in the material intensity of goods or services;
    - A reduction in the energy intensity of goods or services;

- Reduced dispersion of toxic materials;
- Improved recyclability;
- Maximum use of renewable resources;
- Greater durability of products;
- Increased service intensity of goods and services.

32. **Ecological Footprint:** The "ecological footprint", measures the amount of land that is needed to generate the consumption of a country, including the land needed to assimilate the waste generated and undo climatic change from carbon dioxide emissions by means of carbon sequestration. It is a quantitative assessment of the biologically productive area (amount of nature) required to produce the resources (food, energy and materials) and to absorb the wastes of an individual, city, region, or country.
33. **Ecosystem:** An ecosystem consists of the biological community that occurs in some locale, and the physical and chemical factors that make up its non-living or abiotic environment. There are many examples of ecosystems — a pond, a forest, an estuary, and a grass land.
34. **Effluent Fee:** An effluent fee is a fixed tax rate per unit (litre or kilogram) of emissions. They are also referred to as emission charges or emission taxes.
35. **Effluent Standards:** Effluent standards refer to the maximum amount of pollutants permitted in effluents.
36. **Emission Trading:** Emissions trading was introduced as a means to lower the global production of greenhouse gases. Emission trading is a way of introducing flexibility into a system where participants have to meet emissions targets. These participants may be countries (as in the case of the Kyoto Protocol), or companies (as in the case of a domestic emissions trading scheme). Participants can buy units to cover any emissions above their targets, or sell units if they reduce their emissions below their targets. The presence of a market for these units creates a value for emissions reductions which stimulates investment in the most cost-effective areas. Emissions trading leads to a reduction in compliance costs compared to meeting the same target through domestic/internal means only.
37. **Environmental Auditing:** "A management tool comprising a systematic, documented, periodic and objective evaluation of how well environmental organization, management and equipment are performing with the aim of helping to safeguard the environment by: (*i*) facilitating management and control of environmental practices; and (*ii*) assessing compliance with company policies, which include meeting regulatory requirements."–The International Chamber of Commerce (ICC, 1989).
38. **Environmental Impact Assessment (EIA):** It is an evaluation designed to identify and predict the impact of an action or a project on the environment and human health. It can include risk assessment as a component, along with economic and land use assessment.
39. **Environmental Kuznet's Curve (EKC):** The EKC hypothesizes that the relationship between per capita income and the use of natural resources and/or the emission of wastes has an inverted U-shape. According to this specification, at relatively low levels of income the use of natural resources and/or the emission of wastes increase with income. Beyond some turning point, the use of the natural resources and/or the emission of wastes decline with income. Reasons for this inverted U-shaped relationship are hypothesized to include income-driven changes in: (*i*) the composition of production and/or consumption; (*ii*) the preference for environmental quality; (*iii*) institutions that are needed to internalize externalities; and/or (*iv*) increasing returns to scale associated with pollution abatement.
40. **Environmental Labelling:** Environmental labelling is the labelling, or 'eco-labelling', of consumer products which have environmental benefits, or at least a lower impact than their alternatives. Environmental labels assist consumers, both organisations and individuals, to make responsible

product choices, by informing them of the environmental impacts of products and providing a standardized means of comparing products.

41. **Environmental Management Accounting:** Environmental Management Accounting refers to the identification, collection, estimation, analysis, internal reporting and use of physical flow information (i. e., materials, water and energy flow), environmental cost information, and other monetary information for both conventional and environmental decision making within an organization.
42. **Environmental Management System:** A systematic and documented verification process to objectively obtain and evaluate evidence to determine whether an organization's environmental management system 'conforms to the environmental management system audit criteria set by the organization, and communication of the results of this process to management.
43. **Environmental Marketing:** Marketing of green products is called as environmental marketing. It is the marketing of products that are presumed to be environmentally safe. Thus, green marketing incorporates a broad range of activities, including product modification, changes to the production process, packaging changes, as well as modifying advertising.
44. **Environmental Policy:** A statement by an organization of its intentions and principles in relation to its overall environmental performance. Environmental policy provides a framework for action and for the setting of its environmental objectives and target.
45. **Environmental Footprint:** A measure of human demand on the ecosystems and natural resources.
46. **Environmental Impact:** Any change to the environment, whether adverse or beneficial, wholly or partially resulting from an organization's environmental aspects (as defined in ISO 14001).
47. **Environmental Sustainability:** Ensuring that the overall productivity of accumulated human and physical capital resulting from development actions more than compensates for the direct or indirect loss or degradation of the environment. Goal 7 of the UN Millennium Development Goals specifically refers to this in part as integrating the principles of sustainable development into country policies and programs and reversing loss of environmental resources.
48. **Eutrophication:** Eutrophication is the enrichment of water with inorganic nutrients, like nitrates and phosphates. Pollutants like sewage, organic wastes and fertilizers contain nitrates and phosphates that enrich the water by promoting the growth of algae which increases the presence of decomposers, which in turn, along with algal growth and other plants, depletes the oxygen content of the water, resulting in eutrophication.
49. **Externality:** Uninternalized costs or benefits resulting from one economic agent's actions that affect the well-being of others. They may be either positive or negative, with pollution and other forms of environmental degradation frequently cited as an example of the latter.
50. **Extended Producer Responsibility (EPR)** is the practice of holding the producer of a product responsible for the management of the wastes associated with that product.
51. **Gaia Hypothesis:** The Gaia hypothesis is an ecological hypothesis proposing that the biosphere and the physical components of the Earth are closely integrated to form a complex interacting system that maintains the climatic and biogeochemical conditions on Earth in a preferred homeostasis. Originally proposed by James Lovelock as the earth feedback hypo thesis, it was named the Gaia Hypothesis after the Greek primordial goddess of the Earth.
52. **Genetically Modified Organism (GMO):** A genetically modified organism (GMO) is an organism whose genetic material has been altered using the genetic engineering techniques.
53. **Global Warming:** An increase in the Earth's temperature caused by human activities, such as burning coal, oil and natural gas. This releases carbon dioxide, methane, and other greenhouse gases into the

atmosphere. Greenhouse gases form a blanket around the Earth, trapping heat and raising temperatures on the ground. This is steadily changing our climate.

54. **Global Warming Potential:** Global warming potential (GWP) is a measure of how much a given mass of greenhouse gas is estimated to contribute to global warming. It is a relative scale which compares the gas in question to that of the same mass of carbon dioxide (whose GWP is by convention equal to 1). GWP is calculated over a specific time interval and the value of this must be stated whenever a GWP is quoted or else the value is meaningless.
55. **Green Belt Movement (GBM):** GBM is a grass roots non-governmental organization based in Nairobi, Kenya, that works for environmental conservation, community development and capacity building. Professor Wangari Maathai established the organization in 1977, under the auspices of the National Council of Women of Kenya. Since 1977, over 30 million trees have been planted.
56. **Green Consumer:** Green consumers those who care sufficiently about the environment to make a conscious effort to buy products that avoid environmental damage. green consumer as one who avoids products that are likely to (*i*) endanger the health of the consumer or others (*ii*) cause significant damage to the environment during manufacture, use or disposal (*iii*) consume a disproportionate amount of energy (*iv*) cause unnecessary waste (*v*) use materials derived from threatened species or environments (*vi*) involve unnecessary use of, or cruelty to animals (*vii*) adversely affect other countries.
57. **Green Consumerism:** Green consumerism is the intentional purchase of products and services that the consumer considers has to be made, with minimal harm to the natural environment.
58. **Greenhouse Effect:** An increase in the earth's temperature resulting from the accumulation of carbon dioxide and water vapor in the atmosphere. Excess amounts of these gases trap heat in the upper atmosphere and reflect it back to earth.
59. **Greenhouse Gas:** Gases in the atmosphere that reduce the loss of heat into space and therefore contribute to global temperatures through the greenhouse effect. Greenhouse gases - water vapor, carbon dioxide, methane, nitrous oxide, ozone and chlorofluorocarbons-affect the temperature of the Earth.
60. **Greenwashing:** This refers to the act of misleading consumers regarding the environmental practices of a company or the environmental benefits of a product or service. It's greenwashing when a company or organization spends more time and money claiming to be "green" through advertising and marketing than actually implementing business practices that minimize environmental impact
61. **Hazardous Waste:** Waste that is reactive, toxic, corrosive, or otherwise dangerous to living things and/or the environment. Many industrial by-products are hazardous.
62. **Incineration:** The process of burning solid waste under controlled conditions to reduce its weight and volume, and often to produce energy.
63. **Industrial Ecology:** Industrial ecology is the shifting of industrial process from linear (open loop) systems, in which resource and capital investments move through the system to become waste, to a closed loop system where wastes become inputs for new processes. Industrial ecology proposes not to see industrial systems as being separate from the biosphere, but to consider it as a particular case of an ecosystem
64. **Inorganic Waste:** Waste composed of material other than plant or animal matter, such as sand, dust, glass, and many synthetics.
65. **Inter-generational Equity:** The principle of equity between people alive today and future generations. The implication is that unsustainable production and consumption by today's society will degrade the ecological, social, and economic basis for tomorrow's society, whereas sustainability involves ensuring that future generations will have the means to achieve a quality of life equal to or better than today's.

66. **Intra-generational equity:** The principle of equity between different groups of people alive today. Similarly to inter-generational equity, intra-generational equity implies that consumption and production in one community should not undermine the ecological, social, and economic basis for other communities to maintain or improve their quality of life.
67. **ISO 14000:** An international standard developed by the International Organization for Standardization (ISO), for setting up and certifying environmental management systems.
68. **Joint Implementation (JI):** JI is one of three flexibility mechanisms set forth in the Kyoto Protocol to help countries with binding greenhouse gas emissions targets (so-called Annex I countries) meet their obligations. JI is set forth in Article 6 of the Kyoto Protocol. JI enables Annex 1 countries (developed countries and economies in transition) to undertake cross-border investments in projects aimed at reducing greenhouse gas emissions. The investor country (or a private actor in that country) provides financial and/or technical assistance to achieve cost-effective greenhouse gas emission reductions in a host country in exchange for emission reduction units (ERUs) or "carbon credits". These credits can then be applied by the investor country toward meeting its obligations under the Protocol.
69. **Kyoto Protocol:** The Kyoto Protocol is a legally binding agreement under which industrialized countries will reduce their collective emissions of greenhouse gases by 5.2% compared to the year 1990. The Kyoto Protocol treaty was negotiated in December 1997 at the city of Kyoto, Japan and came into force on 16 February 2005. The goal is to lower overall emissions from six greenhouse gases – CO_2, methane, nitrous oxide, sulfur hexafluoride, HFCs, and PFCs – calculated as an average over the five-year period of 2008-12.
70. **Landfilling:** The final disposal of solid waste by placing it in a controlled fashion in a place intended to be permanent.
71. **Leachate:** Liquid (which may be partly produced by decomposition of organic matter) that has seeped through a landfill or a compost pile and has accumulated bacteria and other possibly harmful dissolved or suspended materials. If uncontrolled, leachate can contaminate both groundwater and surface water.
72. **Liability Law:** An approach whereby those injured by damages take the parties responsible for the damage to court. If the suit succeeds, the injured parties are awarded damages. Two key drawbacks to using liability law for environmental damages are the difficulties in linking health damages to a single polluter and determining who has been damaged.
73. **Life Cycle Assessment:** A method for assessing the total environmental impact of a product or service "from cradle to grave", including all phases of production, use, and final disposal.
74. **Life Cycle Energy Approach:** Life Cycle Energy Analysis (LCEA) is an approach in which all energy inputs to a product are accounted for, not only direct energy inputs during manufacture, but also all energy inputs needed to produce components, materials and services needed for the manufacturing process. An earlier term for the approach was energy analysis. With LCEA, the total life cycle energy input is established.
75. **Limits to Growth:** One of the most famous studies published in 1972, written by a group of thinkers, known as 'Club of Rome', from various fields of study, showed that exponential growth rates of population and economic activity could not indefinitely continue on a planet that had only limited natural resources and limited ability to deal with pollution.
76. **Marginal External Cost:** It is the cost resulting from the production of one additional unit accruing to a different party than the one producing or consuming the product.
77. **Marginal Social Cost:** The total cost to society as a whole for producing one further unit, or taking one further action, in an economy. This total cost of producing one extra unit of something is not

simply the direct cost borne by the producer, but also must include the costs to the external environment and other stakeholders. Calculated as:

MSC = MPC + MEC

Where,

MSC = Marginal Social Cost

MPC = Marginal Private Cost

MEC = Marginal External Cost

78. **Market Based Instruments:** Market-based instruments are policy instruments that use price and other economic variables to provide incentive for polluters to reduce harmful emissions. They address the issue of market failure caused by negative environmental externalities, such as pollution, by making the polluter internalize the external costs of production through taxes or charges on processes or products or by creating a proxy market for environmental services. MBIs are also known as pricing or fiscal instruments.

79. **Market failure:** It can be viewed as a scenario where individual pursuit of pure self-interest leads to results that are not efficient and that can be improved upon from societal viewpoint. In economics, a market failure occurs when there is an inefficient allocation of goods and services in a market. That is, there exists another outcome where market participants' overall gains from the new outcome outweigh their losses, even though some participants may lose under the new arrangement. Such failures are often associated with non-competitive markets, externalities like pollution or public goods. The existence of a market failure is often used as a justification for government intervention in a particular market.

80. **Minamata Tragedy:** Minamata tragedy refers to mercury poisoning of the Minamata bay by the Chisso Chemical Corporation located on the Japanese island of Kyushu. The Chisso Corporation is believed to have discharged between 70 and 150 tons of methylmercury (an organic form of mercury) into Minamata Bay between 1932 and 1968. Thousands of Minamata Bay residents were exposed to methyl mercury poisoning which caused widespread damage to the central nervous system and this came to be called 'Minamata disease'. In 1973, after a four-year trial, the court of Kumamoto condemned Chisso for its blatant neglect to set forth preventative measures. Chisso was ordered to pay between 16 and 18 billion Yen per plaintiff, for a total of almost a trillion Yen, the largest sum ever ordered by a Japanese court.

81. **Montreal Treaty:** The **Montreal Protocol on Substances that Deplete the Ozone Layer** is an international treaty designed to protect the ozone layer by phasing out the production of a number of substances believed to be responsible for ozone depletion. The treaty was opened for signature on September 16, 1987, and entered into force on January 1, 1989

82. **Narmada Bachao Andolan (NBA):** NBA is a powerful mass movement, started in 1985, against the construction of the huge Sardar Sarovar dam on the Narmada River in Gujarat. It was feared that the dam would deprive thousands of people of their livelihood, besides destroying biodiversity by submerging thousands of acres of forests and agricultural land.

83. **Natural Resource Accounting and Green GDP:** These are alternative systems of national accounting and performance measures, which incorporate ecological and human welfare considerations. They are a way of better understanding the implications of economic activity for environmental integrity and human well-being. However, placing a monetary value on pollution and resource extraction is controversial and presents methodological difficulties.

84. **NIMBY (Not In My Back Yard):** An expression of resident opposition to the siting of a solid waste facility based on the particular location proposed.

85. **Optimal Pollution:** From an economic perspective the socially optimal level of pollution occurs when the marginal benefit of the last unit of pollution exactly equals the marginal cost of pollution. At this level the net benefits to society are maximized. If all of the externalities of pollution are accounted for, the resulting level of pollution will be optimal.

86. **Organic Waste:** Technically, waste containing carbon, including paper, plastics, wood, food wastes, and yard wastes. In practice in MSWM, the term is often used in a more restricted sense to mean material that is more directly derived from plant or animal sources, and which can generally be decomposed by microorganisms.

87. **pH:** A measure of the concentration of hydrogen ions in solution. A solution with a high concentration of hydrogen ions is called an acid and a solution with a low concentration is called a base.

88. **Pollution:** Pollution is the undesirable change in the physical, chemical and biological characteristics of air, water and soil which directly or indirectly affects human life, property, flora and fauna. Environmental pollution is the contamination of physical and biological components of the planet earth to such an extent that normal environmental processes are adversely affected.

89. **Pollution Charges:** A charge is a price paid by the polluter for the use of the environment in general, and for polluting the environment, in particular. There are various types of charges like effluent charges, user charges and product charges.

90. **Polluter Pays Principle (PPP):** The idea that polluters should pay in proportion to their contribution to pollution and resulting damages. Note that some policies which violate the principle (*e.g.*, abatement subsidies) could still be cost-effective.

91. **Pollution Prevention:** Pollution prevention refers to source reduction practices that reduce the amount of any hazardous substance, pollutant, or contaminant entering any waste stream or otherwise released into the environment (including fugitive emissions) prior to recycling, treatment, or disposal. Source reduction practices also reduce the hazards to public health and the environment associated with the release of such substances, pollutants, or contaminants.

92. **Precautionary Principle:** The principle states that if an action or policy has a suspected risk of causing harm to the public or to the environment, in the absence of scientific consensus that the action or policy is not harmful, the burden of proof that it is *not* harmful falls on those who advocate taking the action. This principle allows policy makers to make discretionary decisions in situations where there is evidence of potential harm in the absence of complete scientific proof.

93. **Producer Responsibility:** A system in which a producer of products or services takes responsibility for the waste that results from the products or services marketed, by reducing materials used in production, making repairable or recyclable goods, and/or reducing packaging.

94. **Putrescible:** Subject to decomposition or decay. Usually used in reference to food wastes and other organic wastes that decay quickly.

95. **Pyrolysis:** Chemical decomposition of a substance by heat in the absence of oxygen, resulting in various hydrocarbon gases and carbon-like residue.

96. **RECLAIM:** It is a revolutionary tradable permits approach to air quality regulation, started on 1 January 1994, to reduce nitrogen oxide and sulfur dioxide emissions in the Los Angeles. The programme was designed to achieve a regional 75 per cent reduction in nitrogen oxide emissions, and a 60 per cent reduction in sulfur oxide emissions, by 2003.

97. **Recyclables:** Items that can be reprocessed into feedstock for new products. Common examples are paper, glass, aluminum, corrugated cardboard and plastic containers.

98. **Recycling:** The process of transforming materials into raw materials for manufacturing new products, which may or may not be similar to the original product.

99. **Refundable Deposits:** A deposit refund system requires consumers to pay a deposit which is subsequently refunded when consumers return the reusable part of the commodity. One method of providing an incentive to increase recycling and decrease waste is the deposit-refund system. In this system, people who return certain recyclable items are given a certain amount of money in exchange. When purchasing a product in a container, the consumer pays a deposit which will be returned to the consumer when he returns the container. The scheme encourages the consumer to return the container for recycling, so that it can be reused and not simply thrown into a landfill.

100. **Resource Recovery:** The extraction and utilization of materials and energy from wastes.

101. **Reuse:** The use of a product more than once in its original form, for the same or a new purpose.

102. **Shallow ecology:** Shallow ecology is anthropocentric or human-centered. It views humans as above or outside of nature, as the source of all value, and ascribes only instrumental or "use" value to nature.

103. **Sludge:** Any solid, semi-solid, or liquid waste generated from a municipal, commercial, or industrial wastewater treatment plant or air pollution control facility. Also referred to as bio-solids or processed organic waste.

104. **Stakeholder:** An individual or a group that can affect or is affected by the activities of an organization.

105. **Subsidy:** Direct or indirect payment from government to businesses, citizens, or institutions to encourage a desired activity.

106. **Sustainable Industrialization (SI):** It is a process of development that strives to promote economic growth through increased capacity to produce goods and provide services whilst improving peoples' livelihood without compromising on the needs of future generations.

107. **Tradable Discharge Permit:** A permit that allows a certain source to emit a specified volume of some pollutant.

108. **Tragedy of Commons:** The tragedy of the commons refers to the case of a communal pasture area where all individuals are free to graze their livestock. The "tragedy" arises because these "commons" were typically heavily over grazed. It is a classic example of an open access resource.

109. **Tsunami:** A tsunami (pronounced *su-nah-me*) is a wave train, or series of waves, generated in a body of water by an impulsive disturbance that vertically displaces the water column. Earthquakes, landslides, volcanic eruptions, explosions, and even the impact of cosmic bodies, like meteorites, can generate tsunamis. Tsunamis can savagely attack coastlines, causing devastating property damage and loss of life. Tsunami is a Japanese word with the English translation, "harbour wave".

110. **Waste Minimization:** It is the designing efficient production processes or making consumption choices according to what will result in the least generation of waste. It includes the "4 Rs" of waste minimization – Rethink, Reuse, Recycle and Reduce.

❑❑❑

Bibliography

1. Ackerman, F., & Heinzerling, L., *Priceless: On Knowing the Price of Everything and the Value of Nothing*. New York: The New Press, 2004.
2. Andorno, Roberto, "The Precautionary Principle: A new legal standard for the technological age", *Journal of International Biotechnology Law* (1), (2004); 11-19.
3. Andy, G., and Keolelan, G.A., "Industrial Ecology an Introduction", National Pollution Prevention Centre for Higher Education, University of Michigan, (1995).
4. Annandale D., Saunders, M.A., Bouma G., "The impact of voluntary environmental protection instruments on company environmental performance". *Business Strategy and the Environment* 13, (2004); 1–12.
5. Archie B. Carroll and Ann B. Buchholtz, Business and Society: Ethics and Stakeholder Management, fourth edition, Springer Netherlands Volume 5, Number 1/February, 2001
6. Arora, S., Cason, T.N., "Why do firms volunteer to exceed environmental regulations? Understanding participation in EPA's 33/50 program", *Land Economics* 72, (1995); 413-432.
7. Arrow, K., et al., "Economic Growth, Carrying Capacity, and the Environment", *Ecological Economics* 2, (1995); 15.
8. Austin, Duncan, (1999). Economic instruments for pollution control and prevention – a brief overview, *World Resources Institute*, September.
9. Backman, J., *Social Responsibility and Accountability*. New York: New York University Press, 1975.
10. Bansal, P., Hunter, T., "Strategic explanations for the early adoption of ISO 14001", *Journal of Business Ethics* 46, (2003); 289–299.
11. Barrass, R., and Madhavan, S., *European Economic Integration and Sustainable Development*. Maidenhead: McGraw-Hill, 1996.
12. Baumol, W.J., and Oates, W.E., *Economics, Environmental Policy, and the Quality of Life*. New Jersey: Prentice-Hall, 1979.
13. Baumol, W.J., and Oates, W.E., *The Theory of Environmental Policy*. Cambridge: Cambridge University Press, 1975/1988.
14. Bebbington, J., Gray, R., Hibbitt, C., and Kirk, E., *Full Cost Accounting: An Agenda for Action*. London: The Association of Chartered Certified Accountants, 2001.
15. Beder, S., "Charging the Earth: The Promotion of Price-Based Measures for Pollution Control", *Ecological Economics* 16, (1996); 51–63.

16. Beder, S., *Environmental Principles and Policies: An Interdisciplinary Introduction.* London: Earthscan, 2006.
17. Bergh, J.C., and Van Den, J.M., Themes, "Approaches and Differences with Environmental Economics", Tinbergen Institute Discussion Paper, (2000), TI2000 - 080/3 accessed at http://ftp.tinbergen.nl/discussionpapers/00080.pdf
18. Bezanson, K., "Some Hopes for a New Journal on Environmental Strategies", *International Review for Environmental Strategies* Vol.1, (2000); 3-8.
19. Bhattacharya, N. R., *Environmental Economics - An Indian Perspective.* New Delhi: Oxford University Press, 2001.
20. Boulding, K.E., "The Economics of the Coming Spaceship Earth", in Jarrett, H., (Eds), *Environmental Quality in a Growing Economy.* Baltimore: Johns Hopkins Press, 1966.
21. Braungart, M., and McDonough, W., *Cradle to Cradle: Remaking the Way We Make Things.* New York: North Point Press, 2002.
22. Brenner, S.N., "The Stakeholder Theory of the Firm and Organizational Decision Making", *International Association for Business and Society* (1993); Proceedings 205–210.
23. Brown and Caldwell, "Watershed Protection Plan Development Guidebook". (2001). Prepared for Northeast Georgia Regional Development Center.
24. Bugge, H.C., "The Principles of Polluter Pays in Economics and Law", in Eide E., and Van der Bergh R., (eds), *Law and Economics of the Environment.* Oslo: Juridisk Forlag, 1996.
25. Cairncross, F., *Costing the Earth.* Boston: Harvard Business School Press, 1993.
26. Cairncross, F., *Green Inc: Guide to Business and the Environment.* London: Earthscan Publications Ltd., 1995.
27. Cameron, J., "The Precautionary Principle: Core Meaning, Constitutional Framework and Procedures for Implementation", In R.Harding & E.Fisher (eds), *Perspectives on the Precautionary Principle.* Sydney: Federation Press, 1999.
28. Canadian Institute of Chartered Accountants, "Full Cost Accounting from an Environmental Perspective" (Toronto: 1997).
29. Carroll, A.B., and Buchholtz, A.B., "Business and Society: Ethics and Stakeholder Management", (Fourth edition), *Springer, Netherlands.*
30. CEC (Commission of Environmental Cooperation), *Improving Environmental Performance and Compliance: 10 Elements of Effective Environmental Management Systems.* Montreal: CEC, June 2000.
31. Central Pollution Control Board (CPCB), 2007.
32. Christensen, C. M., *The Innovator's Dilemma.* Boston: HBS Press, 1997.
33. Christmann, P., "Effects of 'best practices' of environmental management on cost competitiveness: the role of complementary assets", Academy *of Management Journal.* 43 (2000); 663–880.
34. Čiegis Remigijus, Raimondas Čiegis, "Laws of Thermodynamics and Sustainability of the Economy", *Engineering Economics* No 2 (57), (2008); ISSN 1392-2785.
35. Clifford, R.S., and William J. Vaughan, "The Choice of Pollution Control Policy Instruments in Developing Countries: Arguments, Evidence and Suggestions" in "International Yearbook of Environmental and Resource Economics", Vol. VII, Ed. Henk Folmer and Tom Tietemberg Cheltenham , U.K: Edward Elgar, 2003.
36. Coglianese, C., and Lazer, D., "Management-Based Regulation: Prescribing Private Management to Achieve Public Goals", Law *and Society Review* 37 (4), (2003); 691–730.

37. Coglianese, C., Nash, J., (eds). *Regulating from the Inside: Can Environmental Management Systems Achieve Policy Goals?* Washington, DC: Resources for the Future, 2001.
38. Cole, M.A., Limits to Growth, Sustainable Development and Environmental Kuznets Curves: An Examination of the Environmental Impact of Economic Development. *Sustainable Development* 7, 2, (1999) pp. 87-97.
39. COMEST, *The Precautionary Principle: World Commission on the Ethics of Scientific Knowledge and Technology*, UNESCO, Paris, March 2005.
40. Cowan, R., "Nuclear Power Reactors: a Study in Technological lock-in", *Journal of Economic History* 50, (1990); 541–569.
41. Cox, A., "Power, Value and Supply Chain Management", *Supply Chain Management* 4, (1999); 167–175.
42. Cox, L. J., and Cusick, J., "What is Sustainable Development*?", Resource Management* RM 14, (April 2006).
43. CPCB, "Assessment of Industrial Pollution: PROBES/92", CPCB Highlights, (2003).
44. CPCB, 2005, Highlights.
45. CPCB, Annual Report, 2006-07. http://www.cpcb.nic.in/Environmentalpercent20Standards/Water_Quality_Criteria.htm.
46. Curmally, A., "Environment and Rehabilitation in India", *Infrastructure Report* 3I, Network, (2002); 96 –165.
47. Daly (Ed.), *Toward a Steady-State Economy*. San Francisco: Freeman, 1973.
48. Daly, H. E., and Cobb, J. B., *For the Common Good: Redirecting the Economy toward Community, the Environment and a Sustainable Future*. Boston: Beacon Press, 1989.
49. Darnall, N., "Motivations for participating in a voluntary environmental initiative: the Multi-state Working Group and EPA's EMS pilot program", *Research in Corporate Sustainability*. Sharma S. & Starik M., (eds.), Boston: Edward Elgar Publishing, 2003.
50. Darnall, N., "Why Firms Mandate ISO 14001 Certification", *Business and Society* 45 (3), (2006); 354–381.
51. Darnall, N., Edwards D., "Predicting the cost of environmental management system adoption: the role of capabilities, resources and ownership structure". *Strategic Management Journal* 27 (2006); 301–320.
52. David, P. A., "Path Dependence and the Quest for Historical Economics: One More Chorus in the Ballad of QWERTY", Discussion Papers in Economic and Social History 20, University of Oxford, (1997).
53. David, P.A., "Path Dependence and Predictability in Dynamic Systems with Local Network Externalities: a Paradigm for Historical Economics". High Technology Impact Program Working Paper, Center for Economic Policy Research, Stanford University, (1989).
54. Davis, *Greening Business*. Oxford: Basil Blackwell, 1991.
55. de Sadeleer, N., *Environmental Principles: From Political Slogans to Legal Rules*. Oxford: Oxford University Press, 2002.
56. Deming, W.E., *Out of the Crisis*. Cambridge: MIT Press, 1986.
57. Department of the Environment, *Indicators of Sustainable Development*. London: HMSO, 1996.
58. Department of the Environment, *Making Markets Work for the Environment*. London: HMSO, 1993.
59. Devall, B., and Sessions, G., *Deep Ecology*. Gibbs M. Smith. 1985.
60. Deville, Adrian & Harding, R., *Applying Precautionary Principle*. Sydney: The Federation Press, 1997.

61. "Does It Pay to Be Ethical?" *Business Ethics* 14, (March/April 1997).
62. Domask, J.J., "Evolution of the Environmental Movement in Brazil's Amazonia, Global Forest Programme", WWF, 1998.
63. Donaldson, T., and Preston, L., "The Stakeholder Theory of the Corporation: Concepts, Evidence, Implications", *Academy of Management Review* Vol. 20, No.1, (1995); 65–91.
64. Dosi, G., Freeman, C., Nelson, R., Silverberg, G., Soete, L., (eds). *Technical Change and Economic Theory*. London: Pinter, 1988.
65. Dupre, K., "The Environmental Movement: A Status Report and Implications for Pricing", *Advanced Management Journal*, (1994) available at the site: http://www.allbusiness.com/sales/453046-1.html
66. EC Directive 2004/35/CE of the European Parliament and of the Council of 21, on "Environmental Liability with regard to the Prevention of Environmental Damage", *Official Journal of the European Union* (April 2004).
67. Eckerman, E., (2001) "Chemical Industry and Public Health. Bhopal as an Example", MPH 24, (2001); Nordic School of Public Health.
68. Elkington, J., "Toward the Sustainable Corporation: Win-Win-Win Business Strategies for Sustainable Development", *California Management Review* Vol. 36, (1994).
69. Elkington, J., and Burke, T., *The Green Capitalists: Industry's Search for Environmental Excellence*. London: Victor Gollancz Ltd., 1987.
70. Elkington, J., and Hailes, J., *The Green Consumer Guide*. London: Victor Gollancz Ltd., 1989.
71. Ellerman, A., Denny, "A Note on Tradable Permits", *Environmental & Resource Economics 31*, (Springer 2005); 123–131.
72. Elliott, E. D., "Toward Ecological Law and Policy". In *Thinking Ecologically: The Next Generation of Environmental Policy*. Marian R. Chertow and Daniel C. Esty (Ed). New Haven: Yale, 1997.
73. Elliott, J., *An Introduction to Sustainable Development*. London and New York: Routledge, 1994.
74. Eskeland, Gunnar, S., and Emmanuel Jimenez (1991), "Choosing Policy Instruments for Pollution Control." Policy Research Working Paper: 624, World Bank, Policy Research Department, Washington, D.C.
75. European Environment Agency (2006), "Using the Market for Cost-Effective Environmental Policy, Market-Based Instruments in Europe", EEA Report, No 1, (2006).
76. Field, B., *Environmental Economics: An Introduction*. New York: McGraw-Hill, 1994.
77. Foreman, D., *Confessions of an Eco-Warrior*. New York: Crown Publishers, 1991.
78. Fox, W., "From Anthropocentrism to Deep Ecology", *Re-vision* Vol. 16, (1993).
79. Fox, Warwick, *Toward a Transpersonal Ecology: Developing New Foundations for Environmentalism*. Boston and London: Shambhala Publications, 1990.
80. Freeman, E.R., *Strategic Management: A Stakeholder Approach*. Boston: Pitman, 1984.
81. Gadgil, M. R., and Guha, R., *Ecology and Equity: The Use and Abuse of Nature in Contemporary India*. Penguin Books India (P) Ltd., 1995.
82. Gangadharan, L., "Transaction Costs in Pollution Markets: An Empirical Study", *Land Economics* 76 (4), (2000); 601-14.
83. Geffen, C.A., and Rothenberg, S., "Suppliers and Environmental Innovation: the Automotive Paint Process", *International Journal of Operations and Production Management* 20, 2000; 166-186.
84. George, Richard T. de (1999). *Business Ethics*. Prentice Hall. ISBN 0-13-079772-3.
85. Global Biodiversity Outlook 2, (2006), Secretariat of the Convention on Biological Diversity.

86. Goodpaster, K.E., "Business Ethics and Stakeholder Analysis", *Business Ethics Quarterly* Vol. 1, No. 1, (January, 1991); 53–73.

87. Grabosky, P., (1993), "Economic Instruments and Regulatory Orderings", Paper presented to "Environmental Economics - Moving to Sustainability" conference, Canberra, November, 1993, cited from Bedar, S., "Charging the Earth: The Promotion of Price-Based Measures for Pollution Control", *Ecological Economics* 16, (1996); 51-63.

88. Grant, T. Savage, Timothy W. Nix, Carlton J. Whitehead, and John D. Blair, "Strategies for Assessing and Managing Organizational Stakeholders," *Academy of Management Executive*, Vol. V, No. 2, (May, 1991), 61–75.

89. Gray, R., and Bebbington, J., *Accounting for the Environment*. London: Sage Publications Ltd., 2001.

90. Grubb, M., Kohler, J., Anderson, D., "Induced technical change in energy and environmental modeling: analytic approaches and policy implications", *Annual Review of Energy and the Environment* 27, (2002); 271–308.

91. Guha, R., *Environmentalism: A Global History*. New Delhi: Oxford University Press, 2000.

92. Guillermo, E., and Richards, B., (2002), Fundamentals of Environmental Impact Assessments–Basic Text prepared for Trainers' Course on Environmental Management and Assessment for Investment Projects, Inter American Development Bank – IDB, Inter-American Association of Sanitary and Environmental Engineering – AIDIS.

93. Gupta, G., "Environment, Ecology and Economy" in Bhattacharya, R.N., *Environmental Economics – An Indian Perspective*. New Delhi: Oxford University Press, 2001.

94. Gupta, M., Piero, T., "Environmental Management is Good Business", *Industrial Management* 45, (2003), 14-19.

95. Gururaj, S., "Towards Greener Tomorrow – Understanding Carbon Credit" in *The Chartered Accountant Student* Vol 11, No2, (July 2007); 8- 11, (Available at http://www.icai.org/resource_file/9569newsletter_july07.pdf).

96. Handfield, R., Nichols, E., *Supply Chain Redesign*. Upper Saddle River, NJ: Prentice Hall, 2002.

97. Handfield, R., Ragatz, G., Monczka, R., Peterson, K., "Involving Suppliers in New Product Development", *California Management Review* 42, (1999); 59-82.

98. Handsfield, R., Sroufe, R., Walton, S., "Integrating Environmental Management and Supply Chain Strategies, *Business Strategy and the Environment* 14, (2004); 1-10.

99. Hanley, N., Jason, F., Shogren and Ben White, *Environmental Economics in Theory and Practice*. Macmillan, 1997.

100. Hants, *Environment in the Third World*. London: Edward Elgar Publishing.

101. Hardin, G., *Living Within Limits*. USA: Oxford University Press, 1995.

102. Harding, S., *Animate Earth: Science, Intuition, and Gaia*. White River Junction, VT: Chelsea Green Publishing Company, 2006.

103. Hart, S.L., "A Natural Resource-based View of the Firm", *Academy of Management Review* 20, (1995); 986-1014.

104. Hartman, L., *Perspectives in Business Ethics*. Burr Ridge, IL: McGraw-Hill, 2004.

105. Harwood, S., *Business as Ethical and Business as Usual*. Belmont, CA: The Thomson Corporation, 1996.

106. Hawken, P., Lovins, A., Lovins, L.H., *Natural Capitalism: Creating the Next Industrial Revolution*. Boston, MA: Little, Brown, 1999.

107. Hawken, P., *The Ecology of Commerce: A Declaration of Sustainability*. Harper Business, 1994.

108. Hay, R. D., Gray, E.R., and Gates, J.E., *Business and Society*. Cincinnati, OH: Southwestern, 1976.

109. Helmer, R., and Ivanildo Hespanhol (1997), "Water Pollution Control - A Guide to the Use of Water Quality Management Principles", WHO /UNEP publication.

http://ksghome.harvard.edu/~rstavins/papers/Handbook_Chapter_on_MBI.pdf

110. Hertin, J., Berkhout, F., Tyteca, D., Wehrmeyer, W., "Are 'soft' policy instruments effective? Establishing the link between environmental management systems and the environmental performance of companies". Berlin Conference on the Human Dimension of Global Environmental Change, (2003).

111. Hillary, R., "Evaluation of study reports on the barriers, opportunities and drivers for small and medium sized enterprises in the adoption of environmental management systems", *Network for Environmental Management and Auditing*, (1999).

112. Howes, R., *Environmental Cost Accounting: An Introduction and Practical Guide*. London: The Chartered Institute of Management Accountants, 2002.

113. Hunt, C.B., and Auster, Ellen R., "Proactive Environmental Management: Avoiding the Toxic Trap", *Sloan Management Review*, (Winter 1990).

114. Hussen, M.A., *Principles of Environmental Economics: Economics, Ecology and Public Policy*. London: Roultledge, 2000.

115. Ibitayo, Olurominiyi (Lead Author), William C.G. Burns (Topic Editor). (2008), "Trans-boundary Dumping of Hazardous Waste" In: *Encyclopedia of Earth*. Eds. Cutler J. Cleveland (Washington, D.C.: Environmental Information Coalition, National Council for Science and the Environment). [First published in the Encyclopedia of Earth October 2, 2006; Last revised August 26, 2008; Retrieved November 5, 2009]. Available at: http://www.eoearth.org/article/ Transboundary_dumping_of_hazardous_waste>

116. International Federation of Accountants, New York, Environmental Management Accounting (Guidance Document). August 2005.

117. International Institute for Sustainable Development, Deloitte & Touche & World Business Council for Sustainable Development (1992) *Business Strategy for Sustainable Development: Leadership and Accountability for the '90s*.

118. International Institute for Sustainable Development, *Global Green Standards: ISO14000 and Sustainable Development*. (1996).

119. Jacob, M., "Economic instruments: objectives or tools?" Paper presented to the 1993 Environmental Economics Conference, Canberra, November, cited from Beder, Sharon, "Charging the Earth: The Promotion of Price-Based Measures for Pollution Control", *Ecological Economics* 16, (1996); 51–63.

120. Jacob, M., *The Green Economy*. London: Pluto Press, 1991.

121. Jeroen, C.J.M., van den Bergh, *Handbook of Environmental and Resource Economics*. Springer Netherlands, 1999.

122. JWPTE: Joint Working Party on Trade and Environment, "The Polluter Pays Principle as it Relates to International Trade", OECD, Paris, (2002).

123. Kalshian, R., "Ganges Has Magical Cleaning Properties," *Geographic* 66, (April 1994); 5.

124. Kanner, Roszak, and Gomes (Ed), *Ecopsychology: Restoring the Earth, Healing the Mind*. New York: Sierra Club Books, 1995.

125. Karpagam.M., *Environmental Economics*. New Delhi: Sterling Publishers Pvt Ltd., 1999, 2000.

126. Kathuria V and Khan.N, Environmental Compliance Vs Growth: Lessons from Malaysia's Regulation of Palm Oil Mills. *Economic and Political Weekly*. September 2002, 3393 –98

127. Kathuria V, Controlling Water Pollution In Developing And Transition Countries—Lessons From Three Successful Case, ***Journal of Environmental Management,*** Volume 78, Issue 4, March 2006, Pages 405-426

128. Kathuria V and G. S. Haripriya, *Industrial Pollution Control in India: Need for flexibility, in the India Development Report 2001*. Oxford Publishers, (2002) New Delhi.

129. Kerry, T.R., Pearce, D., and Bateman, I., *Environmental Economics - An Elementary Introduction*. Johns Hopkins University Press, 1993.

130. Kettl, D.F., *Environmental Governance: A Report on the Next Generation of Environmental Policy*. Washington, DC: Brookings Institution Press, 2002.

131. Khalid, A.R., "Unilateral Environmental Regulations and the Implications for International Commodity-Related Environmental Agreements", paper p*resented at the Nautilus Institute Workshop on Trade and Environment in Asia-Pacific: Prospects for Regional Cooperation, Honolulu,* (1994).

132. Khanna, M., Damon, L.A., "EPA's voluntary 33/50 program: Impact on toxic releases and economic performance of firms", *Journal of Environmental Economics and Management* 37, (1999); 1–25.

133. Kline, D., "Positive Feedback, Lock-in, and Environmental Policy", *Policy Sciences* 34, (2001); 95–107.

134. Krut, R., Gleckman, H., *ISO 14001: a Mixed Opportunity for Sustainable Global Industrial Development*. London: Earthscan, 1998.

135. Kuik, O.J., Nadkarni, M.V., Oosterhuis, F.H., Sastry, G.S., Akkerman, A.E., *Pollution Control in the South and North, A Comparative Assessment of Environmental Policy Approaches in India and the Netherlands*. Sage Publications, 1997.

136. Kuisma, M., Lovio, R., Niskanen, S., *Hypotheses on the Impact of Environmental Management Systems in Industry*. Helsinki:Ministry of the Environment, 2001.

137. Kumar, A., *Industrial Pollution: Problems and Solutions*. New Delhi: Daya Books, 2006.

138. Lamprecht, J.L., ISO 14001: Issues and Implementation Guidelines for Responsible Management. New York: Amacom, 1997.

139. Lange Glenn-Marie, "Policy Applications of Environmental Accounting, Paper No88, Environmental Economics series", World Bank Environment Department, (2003).

140. Le, Thi Thuy Phuong (2009) "The Development of Instruments of Environmental Policy: Can Developing Countries Learn from Developed Countries?"- unpublished thesis.

141. Leopold, A., *A Sand County Almanac*. Oxford: Oxford University Press, 1949.

142. MacNeill, J., Winsemiun, P., and Yakushiji, T., *Beyond Interdependence – The Meshing of the World's Economy and the Earth's Ecology*. Oxford: Oxford University Press, 1991.

143. "Malaysia's Regulation of Palm Oil Mills", *Economic and Political Weekly* 33, (September 2002); 93 -98.

144. Managi, Shunsuke and Jena, P.R., "Productivity and Environment in India", *Economics Bulletin*, Vol. 17, No.1, (2007); 1–14.

145. Mandal, S., and Rao, M.G., "Overlapping Fiscal Domains and Effectiveness of Environmental Policy in India", Working Paper No 25, National Institute of Public Finance and Policy, (2005).

146. Manes, C., *Green Rage: Radical Environmentalism and the Unmaking of Civilization*..USA: Little, Brown and Company (Canada) Ltd., 1990.

147. Manne, H., and Wallich, H., *The Modern Corporation and Social Responsibility*. Washington, DC: American Enterprise Institute, 1972.

148. Martinez-Alier, J., *The Environmentalism of the Poor: A Study of Ecological Conflicts and Valuation.* New Delhi: Oxford University Press, 2004.

149. McCormic, J., *Reclaiming Paradise –The Global Environmental Paradise*. Blackwell Publishing, 1991.

150. McDonough, W., and Braungart, M., *Cradle to Cradle: Remaking the Way We Make Things*. New York: North Point, 2002.

151. Meyer, A.C., "The Greening of National Accounts: The Role of Ideas in a Theory of Institutional Change", Unpublished paper, George Mason University, (1999).

152. Meyer, John M. "Gifford Pinchot, John Muir, and the Boundaries of Politics in American Thought". *Polity* (Palgrave MacMillan) 30 (2): 267–284, 1997.

153. Millennium Ecosystem Assessment (MEA), *Ecosystems and Human Well-Being: Synthesis*. Washington: Island Press, 2005.

154. Ministry of Environment and Forests, Government of India, (2006), National Environmental Policy.

155. Ministry of Environment and Forests, Government of India, (2009) *State of Environment Report–India, Environmental Information System*, 2009.

156. Naess, A., "The Shallow and the Deep, Long-Range Ecology Movement", *Inquiry* 16, (1973); 95–100.

157. Narayanan, K., and Palinivel,T., (2003) "Industrialisation and the Environmental Quality under Economic Reforms: An Indian Case Study," UNU/IAS Working Paper No. 106.

158. National Centre for Environmental Economics (NCEE), (2005) "International Experiences with Economic Incentives for Protecting the Environment".

159. NEETF (National Environmental Education and Training Foundation), "Standardizing Excellence, Working with Smaller Businesses to Implement Environmental Management Systems" (2001).

160. Nelson, R.R., "The Co-evolution of Technology, Industrial Structure, and Supporting Institutions". *Industrial and Corporate Change* 3, (1994); 47-63.

161. Nelson, R.R., Winter, S.G., *An Evolutionary Theory of Economic Change*. Cambridge, MA: Harvard University Press, 1982.

162. Nicolaisen, J., Dean, A., and Hoeller, P., "Economics and the Environment: A Survey of Issues and Policy Options", *OECD Economic Studies* No.16, (Spring 1991); 1-50.

163. Norregaard, J., and Reppelin-Hill, V., "Taxes and Tradable Permits as Instruments for Controlling Pollution Theory and Practice", (January 2000), IMF Working Paper No. 00/13.

164. O'Connor, D., "Applying Economic Instruments in Developing Countries: From Theory to Implementation," *Environment and Development Economics* (4), (1999); 91-110.

165. O'Riordan, T., (Ed), *Eco-taxation.* London: Earthscan, 1997.

166. OECD, (1991), Environmental Policy: How to Apply Economic Instruments.

167. OECD, (2004), *Emission Trading: Taking Stock and Looking Forward.* by Cédric Philibert and Julia Reinaud, OECD Environment Directorate International Energy Agency.

168. OECD, (2006), Environmental Compliance and Enforcement in India – A Rapid Assessment.

169. OECD, (2008), Environmental Outlook to 2030.

170. Opschoor, J.B., and Turner, R.K., (Ed), *Economic Incentives & Environmental Policies*. Dordrecht: Kluver Academic Publisher, 1994.

171. Palmer, C., *Contemporary Ethical Issues*. BC-CLIO, 1997.

172. Pan International Cooperation Agency (JICA), "Country Profile of Environment – India", (2002).

173. Panayatoe, T., (1994), "Economic Instruments for Environmental Management and Sustainable Development", Prepared for the United Nations Environment Programme's Consultative Expert Group Meeting on "The Use and Application of Economic Policy Instruments for Environmental Management and Sustainable Development", Nairobi, February 23–24, 1995, Environmental Economics Series Paper No. 16.

174. Pearce, D., Barbier, E., and Markandya, A., *Sustainable Development: Economics and Environment in the Third World*, Edward Elgar Pub., 1990, 217 p.

175. Pearce, D., *Blueprint 3: Measuring Sustainable Development*. London: Earthscan, 1994.

176. Pearce, D., Markandya, A., and Barbier, E., *Blueprint for a Green Economy*. London: Earthscan.

177. Pearce, D.W., and Turner, R.K., *Economics of Natural Resources and the Environment*. New York: Harvester Wheatsheaf, 1990.

178. Pearce, D.W., *Environmental Economics*. London: Longman, 1972.

179. Pearson, S., Charles, *Economics and the Global Environment*. Cambridge: Cambridge University Press, 2000.

180. Perman, R., Yue Ma, McGilvray, J., *Natural resource and Environmental Economics*. Longman Ltd., 1996.

181. Perrow, C., Normal Accidents: *Living with High-Risk Technologies*. New York: Basic Books, 1984.

182. Phillips, R.A., "Stakeholder Theory and a Principle of Fairness", *Business Ethics Quarterly* Vol. 7, No. 1, (January 1997); 51–66.

183. Porter, M.E., van der Linde, C., "Toward a New Conception of the Environment–Competitiveness Relationship", *Journal of Economic Perspectives* 9, (1995); 97–118.

184. Portney, R.P., Stavins, R.N., (2000) *Public Policies for Environmental Protection*, Resources for Future, Washington D.C.

185. Post, J.E., Frederick, W.C., Lawrence, A.T., and Weber, J., *Business and Society: Corporate Strategy, Public Policy, Ethics*. New York: McGraw-Hill Inc., 1996.

186. Prahalad, C.K, Hamel, G., "Core Competencies of the Corporation", *Harvard Business Review* 68, (1990); 79–91.

187. Preston, L., and Sapienza, H.J., "Stakeholder Management and Corporate Performance", *The Journal of Behavioral Economics* Vol. 19 No. 4, (1990); 361–375.

188. Preuss, I., "Rhetoric and Reality of Corporate Greening: a View from the Supply Chain Management Function", *Business Strategy and the Environment* 14, (2005); 123-139.

189. Reddy, V., Ratna, (1997), "Environmental Movements in India: Some Reflections", Discussion Paper 64, Heidelberg (URL: http://www.rzuser.uni-heidelberg.de/~t08).

190. Revesz, R.L., and Nash, Jonathan Remy, "Markets and Geography: Designing Marketable Permit Schemes to Control Local and Regional Pollutants", *Ecology Law Quarterly Issue* 28, (July 3, 2001). Available at SSRN: http://ssrn.com/abstract=261756 or DOI: 10.2139/ssrn.261756.

191. Roarty, M., "Greening Business in a Market Economy", *European Business Review*, Vol. 97· No. 5 (1997).

192. Rondinelli, D.A., Vastag, G., "Panacea, Common Sense, or Just a Label? The value of ISO 14001 environmental management systems", *European Management Journal* 18, (2000); 499–510.

193. Roodman, M.D., *The Natural Wealth of Nations*. New York, London; W.W. Norton & Company, 1998.

194. Rootes, C., *Environmental Movement – Local, National and Global*. London: Frank Cass Publishers, 1999.

195. Roszak, Theodore, *The Voice of the Earth: An Exploration of Ecopsychology*. USA: Phanes Press, Inc., 1992.
196. Rugman, A.M., Verbeke, A., "Corporate Strategies and Environmental Regulations: Organizing Framework", *Strategic Management Journal* 19, (1998); 363-375.
197. Rus-sell, Bertrand, *History of Western Philosophy*. London: Routledge, 2004.
198. Russo, M.V., and Fouts, P. A., "A resource-based perspective on corporate environmental performance and profitability", *Academy of Management Journal* 40, (1997); 534-559.
199. Sadgrove, Kit, *The Green Managers Handbook*. USA: Gower Publishing Company, 1992.
200. Salzman, James, and Barton H. Thompson, Jr., *Environmental Law and Policy: Concepts and Insights*. Westbury, NY: Foundation Press, 2003.
201. Sayre, D., Inside *ISO 14000: The Competitive Advantage of Environmental Management*. Delray Beach, Florida: St.Lucie Press, 1996.
202. Schmidheiny, S., and Zorraquin, F., *Financing Change*. Cambridge, MA: MIT Press.
203. Schmidheiny, S., *Changing Course: a Global Business Perspective on Development and the Environment*. Cambridge, MA: Massachusetts Institute of Technology Press, 1992.
204. Schumpeter JA. 1934. *The Theory of Economic Development*. Harvard University Press: Cambridge, MA. 1996.
205. *Science Frontiers ONLINE*, No. 94, (Jul-Aug 1994).
206. Seglin, J.L., *The Right Thing: Conscience, Profit and Personal Responsibility in Today's Business*. Spiro Press, 2003.
207. Seneca, J., and Taussig, M., *Environmental Economics*. Prentice-Hall, 1984.
208. Sharma, A., *Emergence of Environmental Movements in India: An Analysis*. Eco Vista, ecovistawordpress.com, 2007.
209. Sharma, S., and Vredenburg, H., "Proactive corporate environmental strategy and the development of competitively valuable organizational capabilities", *Strategic Management Journal* 19, (1998); 729–753.
210. *Social Trends*. (1996), HMSO, London.
211. Solomon, R.C., *Above the Bottom Line: An Introduction to Business Ethics*. Harcourt Trade Publishers, 1983.
212. Sparkes, R., *The Ethical Investor*. London: HarperCollins, 1995.
213. "Stakeholder Capitalism", *The Economist*, (February 10, 1996); 23–25.
214. "Stakeholder Symbiosis", *Fortune*, (March 30, 1998); S2–S4, special advertising section.
215. Starik, M., "Is the Environment an Organizational Stakeholder? Naturally!" *International Association for Business and Society* (IABS) 1993 Proceedings, 466– 471.
216. State of the World Report, (2002), Report on "Progress Towards to a Sustainable Society", The WorldWatch Institute.
217. Stauber, J., and Rampton, S., *Toxic Sludge is Good for You: Lies, Damn Lies and the Public Relations Industry*. Common Courage Press, 2002.
218. *Stavins, N.R., (1997), "Economic Incentives for Environmental Regulation"*, Prepared for *The New Palgrave Dictionary of Economics and the Law*, edited by Peter Newman.
219. Stavins, N.R., (2001), "Experience with Market-Based Environmental Policy Instruments", Resources for the Future, Washington.

220. Stavins, N.R., 2002. "Experience with Market-Based Environmental Policy Instruments" in *The Handbook of Environmental Economics*. Edited by K.G. Ma, J. Vincent, Amsterdam: North-Holland.

221. Stavins, N.R., and Bradley W. Whitehead, 1996, "The Next Generation of Market Based Environmental Politics", Resources for the Future, (Washington D.C).

222. Stavins, N.R., and Whitehead, B., "Dealing with pollution: Market-based incentives for environmental protection", *Environment* 34(7), (September 1992); 7-11, 29–42.

223. Sterner, T., (2003), "Policy Instruments for Environmental and Natural Resource Management", A co-publication of Resources for the Future, the World Bank, and the Swedish International Development Agency (SIDA).

224. Steven, N.B., and Cochran, P., "The Stakeholder Theory of the Firm: Implications for Business and Society Theory and Research", *International Association for Business and Society* (1991); Proceedings 449–467.

225. Templet, P.H., (2001), *Defending the Public Domain: Pollution, Subsidies and Poverty*. Political Economy Research Institute, University of Massachussetts, Amherst, M.A.

226. Thomas, W., *Moving Beyond Environmental Compliance*. Boca Raton, FL: Lewis Publishers, 1998.

227. Tibor, T, and I. Feldman, *ISO 14000: A Guide to the New Environmental Management Standards*. Burr Ridge, IL: Irwin Professional Publishing, 1996.

228. Tietenberg, T., "The Tradable Permits Approach to Protecting the Commons: What Have We Learned?" Fondazione Eni Enrico Mattei, 2002.

229. Tietenberg, T.H., *Environmental and Natural Resource Economics*. (4th Ed), New York: HarperCollins College Publishers, 1996.

230. Turner, R.K. (1993), 'Sustainability: Principles and Practice', in Turner, R.K. (Eds), *Sustainable Environmental Economics and Management. Principles and Practice*, Belhaven Press, London, pp.3–36.

231. Tushman, M.L, O'Reilly, C.A., *Winning Through Innovation*. Boston, MA: Harvard Business School Press, 1997.

232. Ulhoi, J., Welford, R., (2000). "Exploring Corporate Eco-modernism: Challenging Corporate Rhetoric and Scientific Discourses". First International Conference on "Systems Thinking in Management", 613–618.

233. UNEP (2004), *The Use of Economic Instruments in Environmental Policy: Opportunities and Challenges*.

234. UNEP, (1999) *Global Environment Outlook*, 2000.

235. United States Environmental Protection Agency, (2007) "Acid Rain and Related Programmes".

236. Unruh, G.C., "Understanding Carbon Lock-in", *Energy Policy* 28, (2000): 817–830.

237. Venkatachalam, L, (2005), "Damage Assessment and Compensation to Farmers Lessons from Verdict of Loss of Ecology Authority in Tamil Nadu", *Economic and Political Weekly* (April 9, 2005); 1556 -1560

238. Vincent, J., and Farrow, S., (1997) "A Survey of Pollution Charge Systems and Key Issues in Policy Design", in: R. Bluffstone and B.A. Larson, eds., *Controlling Pollution in Transition Economies*. Cheltenham, (UK): Edward Elgar.

239. *Vital Signs 2002*. Worldwatch Institute, May 2, 2002

240. Vitousek, P.M., Lubchenco, J., Mooney, H.A., Melillo, J., "Human domination of Earth's ecosystems", *Science* 277, (1997); 494–499.

241. Von Weizsäcker, E., Lovins, A.B., Lovins, L.H.,. *Factor Four: Doubling Wealth – Halving Resource Use*. London: Earthscan, 1997.

242. Waddock, S.A., and Samuel B. Graves, "Quality of Management and Quality of Stakeholder Relations", *Business and Society* Vol. 36, No. 3, (September 1997); 250–279.

243. Warford, J.M., Munasinghe, and Cruz, W., 1997, "The Greening of Economic Policy Reform", (Vol I) (Principles) World Bank, Washington D.C.

244. Wathern, Peter (Ed). *Environmental Impact Assessment –Theory and Practice*. Unwin Hyman, 1988.

245. Welford, R., and Gouldson, A., *Environmental Management and Business Strategy*. London: Pitman Publishing, 1993.

246. Welford, R., *Cases in Environmental Management and Business Strategy*. London: Pitman Publishing, 1994.

247. Welford, R., *Corporate Environmental Management: Systems and Strategies*. Universities Press (India) Ltd., 1993.

248. Welford, R., *Environmental Strategy and Sustainable Development*: *The Corporate Challenge for the 21st Century*, London: Routledge, 1995.

249. Welford, R., *Hijacking Environmentalism: Corporate Responses to Sustainable Development*. London: Earthscan, 1997.

250. Wheeler, D., and Sillanpää, M., *The Stakeholder Corporation: A Blueprint for Maximizing Stakeholder Value*. London: Pitman Publishing, 1997.

251. Whitten, S., Martin van Bueren and Drew Collins, An Overview of Market-Based Instruments and Environmental Policy in Australia 6th Annual National AARES Symposium, Canberra, (2003)

252. Winter, G., *Blueprint for Green Management*. England: McGraw Hill Book Company, 1995.

253. World Bank (1997), "Five Years after Rio: Innovations in Environmental Policy", Environmentally Sustainable Development Studies and Monograph Series No. 18.

254. World Commission on Environment and Development, *Our Common Future*. Oxford: Oxford University Press, 1987.

255. World Resource Institute (2005), Millennium Ecosystem Assessment, 2005. "Ecosystems and Human Well-being: Biodiversity Synthesis", Washington, DC.

256. World Resources Institute (1998-99): Environmental Change and Human Health, A Joint Publication by the World Resources Institute, the United Nationas Environment Programme, the United Nations Development Programme, and The World Bank

257. Yearley, Stephan, *The Green Case: A Sociology of Environmental Issues, Arguments and Politics*. London: HarperCollins, 1991.

❑❑❑

References Websites

1. http://en.wikipedia.org/wiki/Deep_ecology
2. www.businessethics.ca
3. http://www.gutenberg.org/etext/11238
4. http://www.schumachercollege.org.uk/learning-resources/from-gaia-theory-to-deep-ecology
5. http://www.eoearth.org/article/Ecosystem.
6. http://www.tutorvista.com/content/biology/biology-i/environment/functions-ecosystem.php.
7. http://www.globalchange.umich.edu/globalchange1/current/lectures/kling/ecosystem ecosystem.html.
8. http://www.newworldencyclopedia.org/entry/Ecosystem#Types_of_ecosystems
9. http://www.buzzle.com/articles/pond-ecosystem.html.
10. http://web.ead.anl.gov/ecorisk/fundamentals/html/ch1/1.3.htm.
11. http://www.buzzle.com/articles/pond-ecosystem.html.
12. http://www.millenniumassessment.org/documents/document.300.aspx.pdf
13. http://www.millenniumassessment.org/documents/document.353.aspx.pdf. http://en.wikipedia.org/wiki/Ecosystem_services.
14. http://www.millenniumassessment.org/documents/document.299.aspx.pdf
15. http://www.tropical-rainforest-animals.com/Environmental-Pollution.html. http://www.epa.vic.gov.au/air/aq4kids/main_pollutants.asp.
16. http://www.tropical-rainforest-animals.com/Air-Pollutants-Summary.html.
17. http://environment.about.com/od/environmentalevents/a/waterdayqa.htm.
18. http://wwwbrr.cr.usgs.gov/projects/SW_corrosion/teachers-pupils/.
19. http://www.hu.mtu.edu/hu_dept/tc@mtu/papers/bhopal.htm.
20. http://www.icmrindia.org/casestudies/catalogue/Business%20Ethics/BECG009.htm.
21. http://en.wikipedia.org/wiki/Bhopal_disaster.
22. http://www.ace.mmu.ac.uk/Resources/Fact_Sheets/Key_Stage_3/Global_Warming/pdf/Global_Warming.pdf
23. http://www.learner.org/courses/envsci/unit/text.php?unit=12&secNum=7
24. http://www.learner.org/courses/envsci/unit/text.php?unit=12&secNum=0
25. http://en.wikipedia.org/wiki/Global_warming#cite_note-16

26. http://environment.nationalgeographic.com/environment/global-warming/gw-causes.html
27. http://en.wikipedia.org/wiki/2009_United_Nations_Climate_Change_Conference
28. http://en.wikipedia.org/wiki/2009_United_Nations_Climate_Change_Conference
29. http://cdm.unfccc.int/Statistics/index.html
30. http://cdm.unfccc.int/about/index.html
31. http://unfccc.int/ghg_data/items/3800.php
32. http://scipeeps.com/effects-of-water-pollution/.
33. http://members.tripod.com/~Sandra_Justus/MercuryPoisoningReport.html
34. http://www1.american.edu/TED/MINAMATA.HTM
35. http://www.mapsofworld.com/japan/japanese-cities/minamata.html
36. http://www.who.int/water_sanitation_health/resourcesquality/wpccasestudy1.pdf
37. http://www.tutorvista.com/content/biology/biology-ii/environment-and-environmental-problems/water-pollution.php
38. http://www.gaepd.org/Files_PDF/techguide/wpb/devwtrplan_b.pdf
39. http://www.ndhealth.gov/wq/sw/Z6_WQ_Standards/WQ_TSS.htm
40. http://www.umich.edu/~gs265/society/waterpollution.htm
41. http://lifestyle.iloveindia.com/lounge/causes-and-effects-of-land-pollution-4470.htmlhttp://www.greenstudentu.com/encyclopedia/pollution
42. http://www.britannica.com/EBchecked/topic/468070/pollution/25556/Land-pollution
43. http://www.buzzle.com/articles/land-pollution.html http://library.thinkquest.org/C0111040/Popups/pop_table_land1.htm
44. http://infao5501.ag5.mpi-sb.mpg.de:8080/topx/archive?link=Wikipedia-Lip6-2 210555.xml&style
45. http://en.wikipedia.org/wiki/Hazardous_waste
46. http://en.wikipedia.org/wiki/Hazardous_waste#Characteristic_wastes
47. http://en.wikipedia.org/wiki/Basel_Convention
48. http://www.eoearth.org/article/Transboundary_dumping_of_hazardous_waste
49. file:///C:/Documents%20and%20Settings/KALPA/Desktop/Basel%20Convention.htm
50. http://europa.eu/legislation_summaries/environment/waste_management/l28043_en.htm
51. http://www.gdrc.org/uem/waste/inverted-pyramid.html
52. http://www.basel.int/
53. http://www.globalchange.umich.edu/globalchange2/current/lectures/biodiversity/biodiversity.html
54. http://www.controllingpollution.com/ecosystem/forest-ecosystem/
55. ftp://ftp.fao.org/docrep/fao/008/A0400E/A0400E07.pdf
56. http://www.cbd.int/doc/gbo/gbo2/cbd-gbo2-en.pdf
57. http://www.globalissues.org/article/170/why-is-biodiversity-important-who-cares#Ahealthybiodiversityoffersmanynaturalservices
58. http://en.wikipedia.org/wiki/Biodiversity
59. http://www.panda.org/?2143/Speed-Kills-Rates-of-Climate-Change-are-Threatening-Biodiversity
60. http://reli350.vassar.edu/gosselin/dilemma.html
61. http://www.science-frontiers.com/sf094/sf094g11.htm
62. http://news.oneindia.in/2009/02/16/marathon-in-varanasi-to-save-river-ganga.html

63. http://epaper.timesofindia.com/Default/Scripting ArticleWin.asp?From=Archive&Source= Page&Skin= ET&BaseHref=ETD/2009/10/06&PageLabel=3&EntityId=Ar00301& ViewMode=HTML&GZ=T
64. http://www.ecofriends.org/main/eganga/images/Critical%20analysis%20of%20GAP.pdf
65. http://en.wikipedia.org/wiki/Paul_R._Ehrlich
66. http://en.wikipedia.org/wiki/Barry_Commoner
67. http://www.britannica.com/EBchecked/topic/189205/environmentalism.
68. Ecology, Global network, http://ecology.com/featuresarchive/henrydavidthoreau/
69. http://en.wikipedia.org/wiki/John_Muir accessed on 28.10.09
70. http://en.wikipedia.org/wiki/Aldo_Leopold accessed on 24.08.09
71. http://www.uh.edu/engines/epi595.htm accessed on 24.08.09
72. http://en.wikipedia.org/wiki/Gifford_Pinchot accessed on 24.08.09
73. http://www.edwardgoldsmith.com/
74. http://www.iph.ufrgs.br/posgrad/disciplinas/hidp04/Boulding,
75. %20The%20Economics%20of%20Spaceship%20Earth.PDF
76. http://nilesema.com/nuclearradio.htm
77. http://chernobyl486.tripod.com/
78. http://www.earthmind.net/earthmind/docs/boulding-1965.pdf
79. http://www.earthmind.net/earthmind/docs/boulding-1966.pdf
80. http://www.earthmind.net/sustainability.htm
81. http://www.myhero.com/myhero/hero.asp?hero=c_mendes
82. http://sovereignty.net/p/gov/rise/g_part12.html
83. http://www.mumbaisuburbs.com/articles/ngo-environmental-conservation.html
84. http://edugreen.teri.res.in/explore/ngos.htm
85. http://sovereignty.net/p/gov/rise/g_part06.html
86. http://www.shvoong.com/social-sciences/sociology/1677251-tragedy-commons/
87. http://www.theecologist.info/page34.html
88. http://en.wikipedia.org/wiki/Small_Is_Beautiful
89. http://june2008.unric.org/index2.php?option=com_content&do_pdf=1&id=227
90. http://www.pacificislandtravel.com/south_america/brazil/about_destin/nature.html
91. http://www.cook.rutgers.edu/~humeco/COURSES/GMCLASSES/GLOBAL/TRANSPARE/ WEEK9AND10_FOREST/CHICOMENDEZ_CASESTUDY.DOC
92. http://ecovista.wordpress.com/2007/09/28/emergence-of-environmental-movements-in-indiaan-analysis/.
93. http://en.wikipedia.org/wiki/Kyoto_Protocol
94. http://www.berr.gov.uk/whatwedo/sectors/ccpo/kyotoprotocol/page20655.html
95. http://www1.american.edu/TED/ice/ogonioil.htm
96. http://fading-hope.blog-city.com/shellbp.htm
97. http://en.wikipedia.org/wiki/Genetically_modified_organisms#Controversy
98. http://www.expressindia.com/latest-news/ban-both-bt-cotton-and-bt-brinjal-in-india-gmo-expert/ 417641/
99. http://www.indiaresource.org/issues/agbiotech/2003/btcottonseeds.html

100. http://www.sarkaritel.com/news_and_features/infa/january2009/28introduction_brinjal.htm
101. http://www.scidev.net/en/features/gm-in-india-the-battle-over-bt-cotton.html
102. india.org/downloads/GE/bt_brinjal_briefing_paper.pdf
103. http://en.wikipedia.org/wiki/Business_ethics
104. http://www.jonentine.com/the-body-shop.html
105. http://siteresources.worldbank.org/INTEEI/214574-1115814938538/20486189/Policy Applications of Environmental Accounting 2003.pdf
106. http://www.idebate.org/debatabase/topic_details.php?topicID=648.
107. http://www.precaution.org/lib/06/econ_growth_and_carrying_capacity.pdf
108. http://www.ktu.lt/lt/mokslas/zurnalai/inzeko/57/1392-2758-2008-2-57-15.pdf
109. http://www.ceepa.co.za/docs/PolicyApplicationsofEnvAcct-WB2003.pdf
110. http://ndctws.org/newsletters/2004-2-may.pdf.
111. http://ftp.tinbergen.nl/discussionpapers/00080.pdf
112. www.cleanganga.com
113. http://www.oecd.org/dataoecd/38/18/40396531.pdf
114. http://www.ecologicalfootprint.com/
115. http://www.oecd.org/dataoecd/30/10/40202689.pdf
116. http://www.unep.org/GEO2000/ov-e/0012.htm
117. http://www.econ4env.co.za/training/MODULE2.pdf
118. http://www.iisd.org/sd/principle.asp?pid=57anddisplay=1
119. http://www.greenatworkmag.com/gwsubaccess/03janfeb/special.html
120. http://flag.blackened.net/sai/faq/secE7.html
121. http://wiki.answers.com/Q/What_is_a_'green'_consumer
122. http://www.icmrindia.org/casestudies/catalogue/Business%20Ethics/BECG067.htm
123. http://www.epa.gov/compliance/resources/policies/incentives/ems/cecguidedoc.pdf
124. http://en.wikipedia.org/wiki/Stakeholder_theory
125. http://en.wikipedia.org/wiki/Stakeholder_theory
126. http://www.pprinciple.net/the_precautionary_principle.html
127. http://www.sehn.org/wing.html
128. http://en.wikipedia.org/wiki/Wingspread_Conference_on_the_Precautionary_principle
129. http://www.iisd.org | webmaster@iisd.ca
130. http://en.wikipedia.org/wiki/Industrial_ecology
131. http://doi.eng.cmu.ac.th/Thailca/pdf/INDEintro.pdf
132. http://www.envfor.nic.in/divisions/cltech/ac.htm
133. www.unescap.org/drpad/publication/dp21_1990/dp21_vi.PDF
134. http://classes.maxwell.syr.edu/ppa777/lectures/envlct6.html
135. http://www.ecosystemservicesproject.org/html/publications/docs/MBIs_overview.pdf
136. http://ksghome.harvard.edu/~rstavins/papers/Handbook_Chapter_on_MBI.pdf
137. http://en.wikipedia.org/wiki/Subsidies_in_India
138. http://www.wto.org/english/res_e/booksp_e/analytic_index_e/subsidies_01_e.htm#article1
139. http://unstats.un.org/unsd/envaccounting/londongroup/meeting14/LG14_19a.pdf

140. http://wmc.nic.in/chapter1-Initiatives-prevention.asp#5.1
141. http://www.conservationfinance.org/Documents/CF_related_papers/panyouto_econ_ instru.pdf
142. biodiversityeconomics.org/document.rm?id=713
143. http://economics.lakeheadu.ca/rizzo/2006/links/Tradable%20Permits%20in%20Pollution%20Markets.pdf
144. http://papers.ssrn.com/sol3/papers.cfm?abstract_id=261756
145. http://www.tutor2u.net/economics/content/topics/externalities/pollution_permits.htm
146. http://www.flatworldknowledge.com/pub/1.0/introduction-economic-analysis/29539
147. http://dieoff.org/page95.htm
148. http://oceanworld.tamu.edu/resources/oceanography-book/tragedyofthecommons.htm
149. http://www.coastalwiki.org/coastalwiki/The_Tragedy_of_the_Commons_-_The_Tuna_Example
150. http://people.oregonstate.edu/~emersonp/201/notes/22.pdf
151. http://en.wikipedia.org/wiki/Emissions_trading
152. http://www.epa.gov/airmarkt/progress/docs/2007ARPReport.pdf
153. http://www.aqmd.gov/RECLAIM/reclaim.html
154. http://ssrn.com/abstract=261756 or doi:10.2139/ssrn.261756
155. http://www.dreamgains.com/report-id/upload/134.pdf
156. http://en.wikipedia.org/wiki/Carbon_emission_trading
157. http://en.wikipedia.org/wiki/Emissions_trading
158. http://en.wikipedia.org/wiki/Kyoto_Protocol
159. http://www.icai.org/resource_file/9569newsletter_july07.pdf
160. http://www.icmrindia.org/casestudies/catalogue/Business%20Ethics/Carbon%20Credits-
161. http://www.who.int/water_sanitation_health/resourcesquality/watpolcontrol.pdf
162. http://www.oecd.org/dataoecd/38/18/40396531.pdf
163. www.oecd.org/environment/outlookto2030
164. http://www.conservationfinance.org/Documents/CF_related_papers/panyouto_econ_ instru.pdf
165. http://www-wds.worldbank.org/external/default/WDSContentServer/WDSP/IB/1997/06/01/000009265_3971031092327/Rendered/PDF/multi_page.pdf
166. http://www.uow.edu.au/arts/sts/sbeder/economics.html
167. http://en.wikipedia.org/wiki/Cradle_to_Cradle
168. http://www.emawebsite.org/documents/emaric_110.pdf.
169. http://www.emawebsite.org/library_detail.asp?record=326.
170. http://www.un.org/esa/sustdev/sdissues/technology/estema1.htm.
171. http://www.iaia.org
172. http://www.fao.org/docrep/005/v9933e/v9933e02.htm
173. http://www.adb.org/Documents/Books/Environment_Impact/chap3.pdf
174. http://homepages.ge.ucl.ac.uk/~mhaklay/eia.htm
175. http://ec.europa.eu/regional_policy/sources/docgener/evaluation/evalsed/downloads/sb2_environmental_impact_assessment.doc .
176. http://eia.unu.edu/wiki/index.php/Assessed_impacts_of_the_proposed_Bodhghat_ Hydroelectric_project
177. http://eia.unu.edu/wiki/index.php/Case_Studies
178. http://www.cseindia.org/programme/industry/eia/introduction_eia.htm#hist

179. http://www.iisd.org
180. webmaster@iisd.ca
181. http://www.sa-intl.org
182. http://www.greenatworkmag.com/gwsubaccess/03janfeb/special.html
183. http://isebindia.com/95_99/99-04-1.html
184. http://www.iimm.org/knowledge_bank/8_ecolabeling-scheme.htm
185. http://ec.europa.eu/environment/ecolabel/index_en.htm
186. http://www.ecologo.org/en/
187. http://www.blauer-engel.de/englisch/navigation/body_blauer_engel.htm
188. http://www.tcodevelopment.com/
189. http://www.svanen.nu/Eng/
190. http://www.ecomark.jp/english/
191. http://isebindia.com/95_99/99-04-1.html
192. http://www.federalelectronicschallenge.net/resources/docs/ecolabel.pdf
193. http://www.escholarship.org/uc/item/49n325b7
194. http://www.moef.gov.in, http://envfor.nic.in
195. http://www.indiaenvironmentportal.org.in/reports_and_documents_page
196. http://ibnlive.in.com/news/state-of-indias-environment-sickening-report/99008-3.html
197. http://news.mongabay.com/2009/0812-india.html
198. http://envfor.nic.in/divisions/ic/wssd/doc2/ch2.html
199. http://www.toxicslink.org/art-view.php?id=130
200. http://www.ppcb.gov.in/hazardous_waste.php
201. http://www.worstpolluted.org/projects/regions/south_asia
202. http://www.moefroclko.org/actrules-summary.htm
203. http://dbtbiosafety.nic.in/act/_Annex-4.htm
204. http://www.apcoab.org/bioregulations/India.pdf
205. http://yarnspinning.co.cc/Cotton/Bt_Cotton_Cultivation_in_India_2.html.
206. http://www.prsindia.org/uploads/media/Green%20Tribunal/Final%20Version%20%20National%20Green%20Tribunal%20Bill.pdf
207. http://www.keralaplanningboard.org/html/eco_2008/2008_ch_6.pdf
208. http://web.worldbank.org/WBSITE/EXTERNAL/EXTOED/EXTENVIRONMENT/0,,contentMDK:21813865~menuPK:5189977~pagePK:64829573~piPK:64829550~the SitePK:4681890,00.html
209. http://www.gdrc.org/uem/ait-terms.html
210. http://www.atlascopco.com/us/glossary.asp
211. http://info.wlu.ca/~wwwsbe/faculty/rwigle/ec238/ref/glossary.shtml
212. http://en.wikipedia.org/wiki/Industrial_ecology
213. http://sunrisebridgepartners.com/page1.php
214. From http://www.gdrc.org/uem/waste/swm-glossary.html

❑❑❑